PLACE-NAMES OF NORTHERN IRELAND

Volume Two

COUNTY DOWN II

THE ARDS

Published 1992
The Institute of Irish Studies
The Queen's University of Belfast
Belfast

Research and Publication funded by the
Central Community Relations Unit

ISBN 0 85389 433 7

ISBN 0 85389 450 7

Printed by W. & G. Baird Ltd, Antrim.

Place-Names of Northern Ireland

VOLUME TWO

County Down II
The Ards

A.J. Hughes and R.J. Hannan

The Northern Ireland Place-Name Project
Department of Celtic
The Queen's University of Belfast

General Editor: Gerard Stockman

RESEARCH GROUP

Professor Gerard Stockman

R.J. Hannan MA
Dr A.J. Hughes
Dr Kay Muhr
Mícheál B. Ó Mainnín MA
Dr Gregory Toner
Eilís McDaniel BA, MSc (1987–1990)

LIST OF ILLUSTRATIONS

Cover: The Ards in 1595, from *Ultoniae Orientalis Pars* by Gerard Mercator

The cover logo is the pattern on one face of a standing stone found at Derrykeighan, Co. Antrim. The art style is a local variant of the widespread "Celtic Art" of the European Iron Age and dates to about the 1st century AD. The opposite side of the stone is similarly decorated. (Drawing by Deirdre Crone, copyright Ulster Museum).

Map of the area covered by this book (Maura Pringle, QUB) vi

Map of the baronies of County Down (OSI Barony map, 1938) xviii

Townland maps:
Ardkeen 8
Ardquin 28
Ballyphilip 40
Ballytrustan 54
Ballywalter 66
Castleboy 76
Inishargy 82
St Andrews alias Ballyhalbert 100
Slanes 114
Witter 122
Bangor 142
Donaghadee 178
Grey Abbey 198
Newtownards 214

The townland maps have been prepared from OSNI digitized data by Kay Muhr. Based on the Ordnance Survey map with the sanction of the Controller of HM Stationery Office, Crown Copyright reserved (Permit no. 354)

ACKNOWLEDGEMENTS

In a multi-disciplinary field of study such as place-names, consultation with outside experts is of vital importance. We cannot thank by name all those who have given us of their time and knowledge, but among them we count the following:

Eilís McDaniel, formerly of the Northern Ireland Place-name Project, who initiated the computerization of the scheme.

Jim Blaney who assisted with fieldwork and shared his local knowledge of the barony of Ards Upper.

Dr Cathair Ó Dochartaigh, Dr Leslie Lucas, W.C. Kerr, J.F. Rankin, Canon R.E. Turner, Mrs Maeve Walker.

Dr Kieran Devine, Dr A. Sheehan, Dr M.T. Flanagan, Mary Kelly, Dr Hiram Morgan, of Queen's University, Belfast.

Art Ó Maolfabhail, Dónall Mac Giolla Easpaig, Pádraig Ó Cearbhaill, and Dr Nollaig Ó Muraíle of the Place-Names Branch of the Ordnance Survey of Ireland.

Angélique Day and Patrick McWilliams, Ordnance Survey Memoir Project, Institute of Irish Studies QUB.

Members of the Steering Committee: Michael Brand, Professor Ronnie Buchanan, Dr Maurna Crozier, Dr Alan Gailey, Dr Ann Hamlin, Dr Maurice Hayes, Tony McCusker, Dr Brian Walker.

Claire Foley, Ann Given, Dr Chris Lynn of the Archaeological Survey of Northern Ireland.

Leonard Brown, John Buckley, Chris Davidson, Geoff Mahood, Larry Toolan of the Ordnance Survey of Northern Ireland.

Dr Bill Crawford, Clifford Harkness, of the Ulster Folk and Transport Museum.

Dr Brian Trainor of the Ulster Historical Foundation.

Richard Warner of the Ulster Museum.

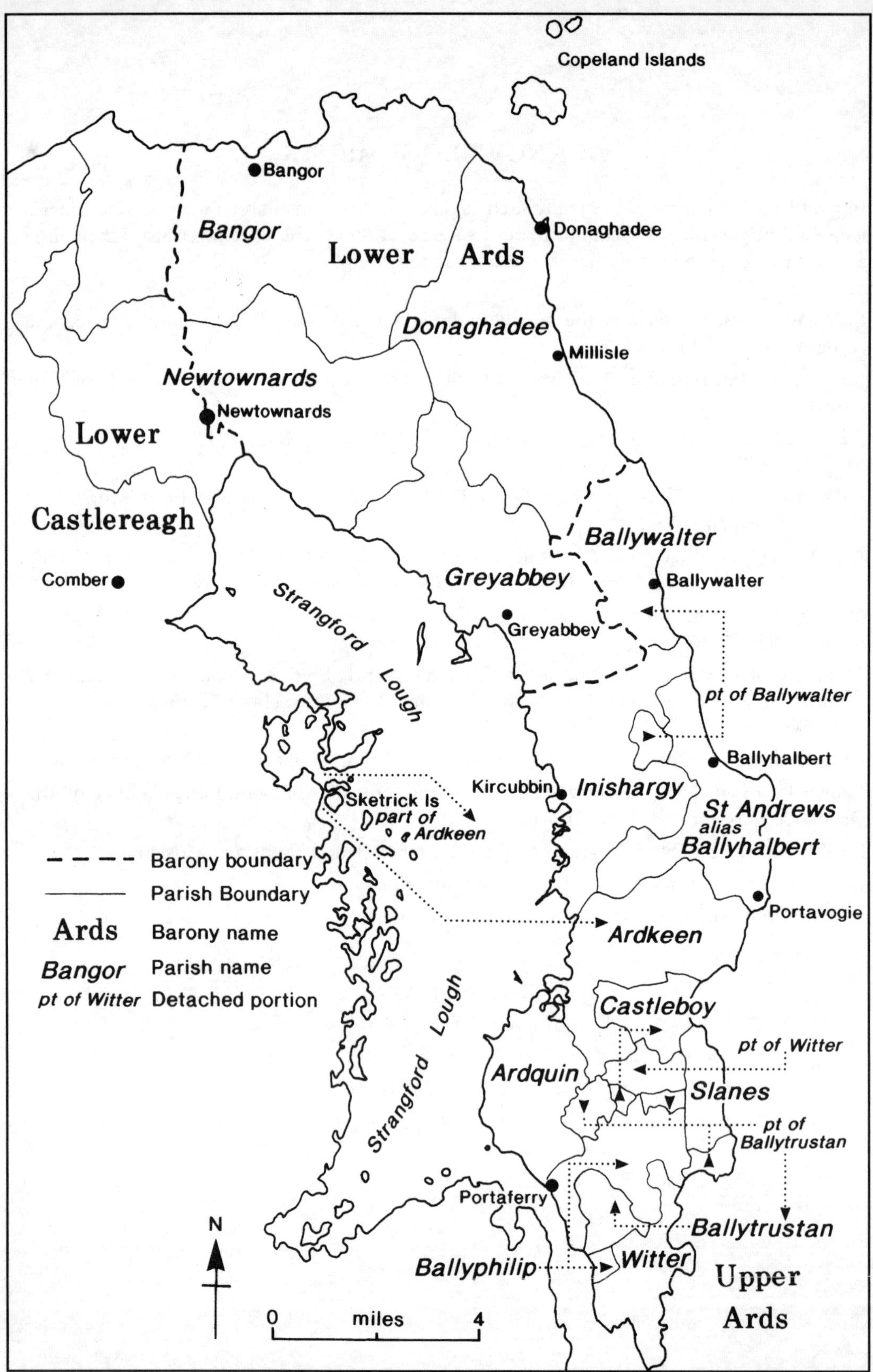

Copeland Islands
Bangor
Bangor
Lower Ards
Donaghadee
Donaghadee
Millisle
Newtownards
Newtownards
Lower
Castlereagh
Comber
Ballywalter
Ballywalter
Greyabbey
Greyabbey
Strangford Lough
pt of Ballywalter
Ballyhalbert
Kircubbin
Inishargy
St Andrews alias Ballyhalbert
Sketrick Is part of Ardkeen
Barony boundary
Parish Boundary
Ards Barony name
Bangor Parish name
pt of Witter Detached portion
Portavogie
Ardkeen
Castleboy
pt of Witter
Ardquin
Slanes
pt of Ballytrustan
Strangford Lough
Portaferry
Ballytrustan
N
Ballyphilip
Witter
Upper Ards
0 miles 4

CONTENTS

Page

General Introduction ix

Introduction to County Down xix

The Barony of The Ards 1

Strangford Lough 5

Barony of Ards, Upper

The Parish of Ardkeen (*A.J. Hughes*) 9

The Parish of Ardquin (*A.J. Hughes*) 27

The Parish of Ballyphilip (*A.J. Hughes*) 41

The Parish of Ballytrustan (*A.J. Hughes*) 55

The Parish of Ballywalter (*A.J. Hughes*) 67

The Parish of Castleboy (*A.J. Hughes*) 75

The Parish of Inishargy (*A.J. Hughes*) 83

The Parish of St. Andrews (*A.J. Hughes*) alias Ballyhalbert 99

The Parish of Slanes (*A.J. Hughes*) 115

The Parish of Witter (*A.J. Hughes*) 121

Barony of Ards, Lower

The Parish of Bangor (*R.J. Hannan*) 141

The Parish of Donaghadee (*R.J. Hannan*) 177

The Parish of Grey Abbey (*R.J. Hannan*) 197

The Parish of Newtownards (*R.J. Hannan*) 213

CONTENTS—*continued*

	Page
Appendix A: Language	239
Appendix B: Land Units	245
Abbreviations	253
Primary Bibliography	255
Secondary Bibliography	273
Glossary of Technical Terms	279
Index to Irish forms of Place-names (with pronunciation guide)	287
Place-name Index (with map references)	293

GENERAL INTRODUCTION

BRIEF HISTORY OF PLACE-NAME STUDY IN IRELAND

Place-name lore or *dindsenchas* was a valued type of knowledge in early Ireland, to be learnt by students of secular learning in their eighth year of study. Stories about the origin of place-names appear regularly in early Irish literature. At the end of the epic "Cattle Raid of Cooley" the triumphal charge of the Brown Bull of Cooley around Ireland is said to have given rise to names such as Athlone (Irish *Áth Luain*), so called from the loin (*luan*) of the White-horned Bull slain by the Brown Bull. In the 10th, 11th and 12th centuries legends about the naming of famous places were gathered together into a number of great collections. Frequently, different explanations of the same name are offered in these legends, usually with no preference being expressed. In an entry on the naming of *Cleitech*, the palace on the Boyne of the early king *Muirchertach mac Erca*, five separate explanations of the name are offered, none of which can be correct in modern scholarly terms. Place-name study was cultivated as a branch of literature.

Knowledge of Irish place-names was of practical importance during the English conquest and exploration of Ireland in the 16th century. Recurring elements in the place-names were noted by surveyors, and a table giving a few English equivalents appears on some maps of this period. There was concern that Irish names were "uncouth and unintelligible". William Petty, the great 17th-century surveyor and map-maker, commented that "it would not be amiss if the significant part of the Irish names were interpreted, where they are not nor cannot be abolished" (Petty 1672, 72–3). However, although the English-speaking settlers created many new names, they did not usually change the names of the lands they were granted, and the names of land units remained as they were, albeit in an anglicized form.

Interest in the meaning of Irish place-names developed further towards the end of the 18th century. The contributors to William Shaw Mason's *Parochial Survey of Ireland* often included a table explaining their local townland names, and this aspect was retained in the Statistical Reports compiled by the officers of the Royal Engineers on the parishes they surveyed for the first six-inch survey of Ireland in the early 1830s. Information on the spelling of place-names for the maps was collected in "name-books", and the Ordnance Survey was concerned to find that a variety of anglicized spellings was in use for many Irish place-names. The assistant director, Thomas Larcom, decided that the maps should use the anglicized spellings that most accurately represented the original Irish (Andrews 1975, 122) and he employed an Irish scholar, John O'Donovan, to comment on the name-books and recommend standard forms of names. O'Donovan was sent to the areas being surveyed to talk to local inhabitants, where possible Irish speakers, to find out the Irish forms. These were entered in the name-books, but were not intended for publication.

In 1855, a reader of *Ulster Journal of Archaeology* calling himself "De Campo" asked "that a list of all the townlands should be given in their Irish and English nomenclature, with an explanation of their Irish names" (*UJA* ser. 1, vol. iii, 251b). Meanwhile William Reeves, the Church of Ireland Bishop of Connor, had decided to compile a "monster Index" of all Irish townlands, which would eventually include the etymology of the names, "where attainable" (Reeves 1861, 486). Reeves' project was cited favourably by William Donnelly, the Registrar General, in his introduction to the first Topographical Index to the Census of Ireland: "It would greatly increase the value of a publication of this nature if it were accompanied by a glossary or explanation of the names, and an account of their origin" (*Census 1851* 1, 11–12).

However, it was left to another scholar, P. W. Joyce, to publish the first major work dealing exclusively with the interpretation of Irish place-names, and in his first chapter he acknowledges his debt to both O'Donovan and Reeves (*Joyce* i 7–8, 10). At this period the progress made by Irish place-name scholarship was envied in England (Taylor 1896, 205). The high standard of Joyce's work has made him an authority to the present day, but it is regrettable that most popular books published since on Irish place-names have drawn almost entirely on the selection and arrangement of names discussed by Joyce, ignoring the advances in place-name scholarship over the last hundred years (Flanagan D. 1979(f); 1981–2(b)).

Seosamh Laoide's *Post-Sheanchas*, published in 1905, provided an Irish-language form for modern post towns, districts and counties, and research on place-names found in early Irish texts resulted in Edmund Hogan's *Onomasticon Goedelicum* (1910). Local studies have been published by Alfred Moore Munn (Co. Derry, 1925), and P. M'Aleer (*Townland Names of County Tyrone*, c. 1920). The idea of a comprehensive official survey was taken up again by Risteard Ó Foghludha in the introduction to his *Log-ainmneacha* (1935). A Place-Names Commission was founded in Dublin in 1946 to advise on the correct forms of Irish place-names for official use and this was followed by the Place-Names Branch of the Ordnance Survey. They have published the Irish names for postal towns (*AGBP* 1969), a gazetteer covering many of the more important names in Ireland (*GÉ* 1989), a townland survey for Co. Limerick (1990), and most recently bilingual lists of the place-names of Cos Louth, Limerick and Waterford (1991).

John O'Donovan became the first professor of Celtic in Queen's University, Belfast, and in the 20th century members of the Celtic Department continued research on the place-names of the North of Ireland. The Ulster Place-Name Society was founded by the then head of department, Seán Mac Airt, in 1952 (Arthurs 1955–6, 80–82). Its primary aims were, (a) to undertake a survey of Ulster place-names; and (b) to issue periodically to members a bulletin devoted to aspects of place-name study, and ultimately to publish a series of volumes embodying the results of the survey. Several members undertook to do research on particular areas, much of which remains unpublished (Deirdre Flanagan on Lecale, and Dean Bernard Mooney on the names of the Diocese of Dromore).

The primary objective of the Ulster Place-Name Society was partly realized in 1987, when the Department of Celtic was commissioned by the Department for the Environment for Northern Ireland to do research into, "the origin of all names of settlements and physical features appearing on the 1:50,000 scale map; to indicate their meaning and to note any historical or other relevant information". In 1990, under the Central Community Relations Unit, the brief of the scheme was extended: to include work on all townlands in Northern Ireland, and to bring the work to publication. Although individual articles have already been published by various scholars, the *Place-Names of Northern Ireland* series is the first attempt in the North at a complete survey based on original research into the historical sources.

METHOD OF PLACE-NAME RESEARCH

The method employed by the Project has been to gather early spellings of each name from a variety of historical records written mainly in Irish, Latin and English, and arrange them in chronological order. These, then, with due weight being given to those which are demonstrably the oldest and most accurate, provide the evidence necessary for deducing the etymology. The same name may be applied to different places, sometimes only a few miles apart, and all forms are checked to ensure that they are entered under the correct modern name. For example, there are a number of references to a place called *Crosgare* in 17th-century sources, none of which refer to the well-known town of Crossgar in Co. Down, but to a townland also called Crossgar a few miles away near Dromara. Identification of forms is most readily facilitated by those sources which list adjoining lands together or give the name of the landholder. Indeed, one of the greatest difficulties in using Irish sources and some early Latin or English documents is the lack of context which would enable firm location of the place-names which occur in them.

Fieldwork is an essential complement of research on earlier written sources and maps. Sometimes unrecorded features in local topography or land use are well-known to local inhabitants. More frequently the pronunciation represented by the early written forms is obscure, and, especially in areas where there has been little movement of people, the traditional local pronunciation provides valuable evidence. The members of the research team visited their respective areas of study, to interview and tape-record informants recommended by local historical societies etc., but many others met in the course of fieldwork kindly offered their assistance and we record here our gratitude. The local pronunciations have been transcribed in phonetic script and these are given at the end of each list of historical forms. The tapes themselves will become archive material for the future. The transcription used is based on the principles of the International Phonetic Alphabet, modified in accordance with the general practice in descriptions of Irish and Scottish Gaelic dialects. The following diagram illustrates the relative position of each of the vowels used:

Front						Central			Back	
i									ʎ u	High
			ɩ							
	e			ï		ö			o	High-mid
					ə					
							o̤			
		ɛ							ɔ	Low-mid
			a						ɑ	Low

Although this research was originally based on the names appearing on the 1:50,000 scale map, it soon became clear that many townland names, important in the past and still known to people today, were not given on the published version. Townlands form the smallest unit in the historical territorial administrative system of provinces, counties, baronies, parishes, and townlands. This system, which is that followed by the first Ordnance Survey of Ireland in its name-books, has been used in the organization of the books in this series. The names of all the relevant units are explained in Appendix B. Maps of the relevant barony and parish divisions within the county are supplied for the area covered in each book, to complement the published 1:50,000 series, and to make the historical context more accessible.

In the process of collecting and interpreting early forms for the *Place-Names of Northern Ireland* each researcher normally works on a group of 4 or 5 parishes. Since some books will contain 10 or more parishes, joint authorship will be the norm, and there may be differences of style and emphasis in the discussions within and between books. It seemed better to retain individuality rather than edit everything into committee prose. The suggested original Irish forms of the place-names were decided after group discussion with the general editor. The members of the group responsible for the text of each book will be distinguished by name on the contents page.

All the information in this book is also preserved in a computer database in Queen's University Belfast. It is hoped that this database will eventually become a permanent resource for scholars searching for examples of a particular type of name or name element. Modern map information, lists of the townlands making up historical parishes and baronies, historical sources and modern Irish forms are all available on separate files which can be searched and interrelated. The database was designed by Eilís McDaniel, and the Project gratefully acknowledges her continuing interest and assistance.

LANGUAGE

Since Ulster was almost wholly Irish-speaking until the 17th century, most names of townlands are of Irish-language origin. Some early names were also given Latin equivalents for use in ecclesiastical and secular documents but few probably ever gained wide currency. Norse influence on northern place-names is surprisingly slight and is largely confined to coastal features such as **Strangford Lough** and **Carlingford Lough**. The arrival of the Anglo-Normans in the 12th century brought with it a new phase of naming and its influence is particularly strong in east Ulster, most notably in the Barony of Ards. Here, the names of many of their settlements were formed from a compound of the owner's name plus the English word *tūn* "settlement" which gives us Modern English "town". Names such as **Hogstown** and **Audleystown** have retained their original form, but a considerable number, such as **Ballyphilip** and **Ballyrolly**, derive from forms that were later gaelicized.

By the time of the Plantation of Ulster in the 17th century the system of townland units and their names already existed and this was adopted more or less wholesale by the English- and Scots-speaking settlers. These settlers have, nevertheless, left their mark on a sizeable body of names, particularly those of market towns, country houses, villages and farms which did not exist before the 17th century. What made the 17th-century Plantation different from the earlier ones was its extent and intensity, and it was the first time that the Irish language itself, rather than the Irish aristocracy, came under threat. The change from Irish to English speaking was a gradual one, and Irish survived into the 20th century in parts of Antrim and Tyrone. However, the language shift, assisted by an official policy that discriminated against Irish, eventually led to the anglicization of all names to the exclusion of Irish versions.

SPELLING AND PRONUNCIATION

Most of the historical sources used in this series were originally handwritten and this inevitably led to a considerable number of errors, both by contemporary copyists and by modern editors. Many of the documents, particularly grants, were copied time and again, while other sources sometimes only survive in late copies or published calendars. Mistakes could occur in any transcription but were particularly likely when the language or names being copied were unfamiliar. There is a long history of confusion in the Roman alphabet between letters of the type *i, u, n, m, w*. *U* and *n* are frequently confused, as are *m* and *w*. Where two or more of these letters occur together, the minims (vertical strokes) may be read in different combinations: the simple pair *ui* may be read as *iu, ni, in, m*, or *w*. Another common error is the confusion of long *s* (ʃ) and *f*. The name **Ballyhaft** (par. Newtownards, Dn) is frequently spelt in 17th-century sources with *s* instead of *f* and the modern form of the name may result from confusion of the written forms. In early sources, horizontal strokes (suspension strokes) could be written over a vowel as shorthand for a following *n* or *m*, but they were easily overlooked by scribes or editors. Spellings such as *Ballemulle* for **Ballymullan** (par. Bangor, Dn) may be explained in this way.

As well as taking account of spelling mistakes, there is sometimes difficulty in interpreting just what the spellings were intended to represent. For example, *gh*, which is usually silent in modern English dialects (e.g. night, fought) often retained its original value in the 17th century and was pronounced like the *ch* in Scots *loch* and *nicht*. Thus, *gh* was the obvious way to represent the Irish sound in words like *mullach* "summit", although both the English and Irish sounds were being weakened to [h] in certain positions at the time.

In Irish the spelling *th* was originally pronounced as in modern English *thick*, but in the 13th century it came to be pronounced [h]. The original Irish sound was anglicized as *th* or as *gh* at different periods but where the older form of the spelling has survived the sound *th* has often been restored by English speakers. In names such as **Rathmullen** and **Rathfriland** where the initial element represents *ráth* "a ringfort", the *th* has almost invariably been re-established.

It is clear that some spellings used in place-names no longer signify what they did when first anglicized. The *-y* in the common elements "bally-" and "derry-" was selected to represent the final vowel in the corresponding Irish words *baile* and *doire* (the same sound as the *a* in "above") but this vowel is now usually pronounced as a short *ee* as in English words such as *happy, sorry*. In modern Ulster English, the vowel in words ending in *-ane*, such as *mane, crane*, is a diphthong, but in the 17th century it was pronounced as a long *a*. Thus, Irish *bán* "white" was usually represented in anglicized forms of names as *bane* as, for example, in the names **Kinbane** (Ant.) and **Carnbane** (Arm.) and this is frequently how the names are still pronounced locally.

SOURCES

The earliest representations of Irish place-names are found in a broad range of native material, written mostly in Irish although occasionally in Latin, beginning in the 7th or 8th centuries. The Irish annals, probably begun about 550 AD (Byrne 1973, 2) but preserved in manuscripts of much later date, contain a large number of place-names, particularly those of tribes, settlements, and topographical features. Tribal names and those of the areas they inhabited frequently appear among genealogical material, a substantial proportion of which is preserved in a 12th-century manuscript, Rawlinson B 502, but is probably much older. Ecclesiastical records include martyrologies or calendars giving saints' names, often with the names and locations of their churches. The Latin and Irish accounts of the life of St Patrick, which depict him travelling around Ireland founding a series of churches, contain the first lists of place-names which refer to places owned by a particular institution. Later Irish saints' lives also may list lands dedicated to the founder of a church. Medieval Irish narrative shows a great interest in places, often giving, for example, long lists of place-names passed through on journeys. Although many of these sources may date back to the 7th or 8th centuries, the copies we have often survive only in manuscripts of the 12th century and later, in which the spelling may have been modernized or later forms of names substituted.

The administrative records of the reformed Church of the 12th century are among the first to provide detailed grants of land. There are also records from the international Church, such as the papal taxation of 1302–06 (*Eccles. Tax.*). These records are more productive for place-name study, since the names are usually of the same type (either parishes or other land units owned by the church) and are usually geographically related, making them easier to identify with their modern counterparts. However, the place-names in these documents are not usually spelled as they would be in Irish.

Paradoxically, perhaps, the 17th-century Plantation provides a massive amount of evidence for the place-names of Ulster. Grants to and holdings by individuals were written down by government officials in fiants, patents and inquisitions (in the latter case, the lands held by an individual at death). A series of detailed surveys, such as the *Escheated Counties* maps of 1609, the *Civil Survey* of 1654–6, and Sir William Petty's Down Survey (*Hib. Del.* and *Hib. Reg.*), together with the records of the confiscation and redistribution of land found in the *Books of Survey and Distribution* (*BSD*) and the *Act of Settlement* (*ASE*), meant that, for the first time, almost all the names of smaller land units such as townlands were recorded. Unfortunately the richness of these resources has been depleted by two serious fires among the Irish public records, one in 1711 and the other in the Four Courts in Dublin in 1922. As a result, some of the original maps, and the Civil Survey covering the north-eastern counties, are lost, and the fiants, patents, inquisitions and Act of Settlement now only exist in abridged form in calendars made by the Irish Record Commission in the early 19th century. These calendars were criticized even at the time of publication for their degree of précis and for inaccurate transcription of names.

After the 17th century, little surveying of an official nature was carried out in Ireland, despite the clearance of woods and bogs and reclamation of waste land. The best sources for the 18th century, therefore, are family papers, leases, wills and sometimes estate maps, most of which remain unpublished. It became clear in the early 19th century that much of the taxation system was based on records that were out of date. The Ordnance Survey came to Ireland in 1824 and began in 1825 to do the first large-scale (six inches to the mile) survey of the country. Most of the variant spellings which they collected in their name-books were of the 18th or early 19th centuries, though in some cases local landowners or churchmen allowed access to earlier records, and these again provide a convenient and invaluable source of place-names. Minor names were also recorded in the descriptive remarks of the name-books, or in the fuller treatment of local names (water features, ancient monuments, church sites and other landmarks) in the associated Ordnance Survey Memoirs (*OSM*).

Early maps are an extremely valuable source, since they show the geographical relationship between names that is often crucial for identification purposes, and in many cases they are precise enough to locate lost townlands or to identify the older name of a townland. In parts of Ulster, maps by 16th-century surveyors may antedate texts recording place-names, thus providing the earliest attestation of the names in those areas.

However, maps have their own problems. Like other written texts they often copy from each other, borrowing names or outline or both. Inaccuracies are frequent, especially in the plotting of inland water features, whether due to seasonal flooding, or the lack of a vantage point for viewing the course of a river. Frequently the surveyor of the ground was not the person who drew or published the surviving map. The great continental and English map and atlas publishers, such as Ortelius, Mercator and Speed, all drew on earlier maps, and this custom undoubtedly led to the initiation and prolongation of errors of form and orthography. Sixteenth-century maps of Lough Neagh, for example, regularly show rivers entering the lake on the south between the Blackwater and the Bann where there are known to be none (Andrews 1978, plate 22). Unsurveyed territory was not always drawn to scale. Modern Co. Donegal, for example, is usually drawn too large on 16th-century maps, while Co. Derry is frequently shown too small. The *Escheated County* maps appear to have been partly drawn from verbal information and, in the map for the barony of Armagh, the draughtsman has produced a mirror image reversing east and west (Andrews 1974, 152).

William Petty's Down Survey provided the standard map of Ireland for the 17th century. In the 18th and early 19th centuries various individuals produced local county maps: Roque (1760) Co. Armagh; Lendrick (1780) Co. Antrim; Sampson (1814) Co. Derry; Sloane, Harris, Kennedy and Williamson (1739–1810) Co. Down; Knox and McCrea (1813) Co. Tyrone. These were consulted for the place-names on their own maps by the Ordnance Survey in the 1830s. Apart from published maps, a number of manuscript maps, some anonymous, others the original work of the 16th-century surveyors Lythe and Jobson, still exist. Richard Bartlett and Thomas Raven left important manuscript maps of Ulster from the early 17th century.

HOW TO USE THIS SERIES

Throughout the series, the editors have tried to adhere to the traditional territorial and administrative divisions used in Ireland, but this has not always proved possible. The convenient unit on which to base both research and publication has been the civil parish and all townland names and minor names are discussed under the relevant parish, regardless of whether they are in the same barony or county. Each book normally deals with the parishes in one or more barony, but where the barony is too large they are split into different books, some of which may contain material from geographically adjacent baronies. Every effort has been made to accommodate the historical system in a series of volumes of regular size. Each parish, barony and county is prefaced by an introduction which sets forth its location and history, and discusses some of the sources from which the older spellings of names have been extracted.

Within each parish, townland and other names are arranged in alphabetical order in separate sections following a discussion of the parish name. The first section deals with townland names. The second section deals with names of towns, villages, hills and water features which appear on the OS 1:50,000 map, but which are not classified as townlands. This section may also include a few names of historical importance which do not appear on the map but which may be of interest to the reader. Lesser names on the 1:50,000 are only treated if relevant material has been forthcoming. An index of all the names discussed in each book is given at the back of the relevant volume.

Each name to be discussed is given in bold print on the left-hand side of the page. Bold print is also used elsewhere in the text to cross-refer the reader to another name discussed in the series. The four-figure grid-reference given under each place-name should enable it to be located on modern Ordnance Survey maps.

Beneath the map name and its grid reference, all the pre-1700 spellings that have been found are listed, together with their source and date, followed by a selection of post-1700 forms. Early Irish-language forms are placed above anglicized or latinized spellings because of their importance in establishing the origin of the name. Irish forms suggested by 19th- and 20th-century scholars are listed below the historical spellings. Irish-language forms collected by O'Donovan in the last century, when Irish was still spoken in many parts of the North, require careful assessment. Some may be traditional, but there are many cases where the suggestion made by the local informant is contradicted by the earlier spellings, and it is clear that sometimes informants merely analysed the current form of the name. The current local pronunciation as collected by the editors appears below these Irish forms in phonetic script.

Spellings of names are cited exactly as they occur in the sources. Manuscript contractions have been expanded within square brackets, e.g. [ar]. Square brackets are also used to indicate other editorial readings: [...] indicates three letters in the name which could not be read, while a question mark in front of one or more letters enclosed in square brackets, e.g. [?agh], denotes obscure letters. A question mark in round brackets before a spelling indicates a form which cannot be safely identified as the name under discussion.

The dates of all historical spellings collected are given in the right-hand column, followed, where necessary, by *c* when the date is approximate. Here, we have departed from the normal practice, employed elsewhere in the books, because the database would otherwise have been unable to sort these dates in numeric order. In Latin and English sources a *circa* date usually indicates an uncertainty of a year or two. Irish language sources, however, rarely have exact dates and *circa* here represents a much longer time-span, perhaps of one or two centuries where the dating is based purely on the language of a text. Where no date has been established for a text, forms from that text are given the date of the earliest MS, in which they appear. Following normal practice, dates in the Irish annals are given as in the source, although this may give certain spellings an appearance of antiquity which they do not deserve. The Annals of the Four Masters, for example, were compiled in the early 17th century using earlier material, and many of the names in the text were modernized by its compilers. Moreover, annals were written later for dates before the mid-6th-century, and the names, let alone the spellings, may not be that old. Another difficulty with dates concerns English administrative sources. The civil year in England and Ireland began on March 25th (Lady Day) until the year 1752, when the calendar was brought into line with changes made in the rest of Europe in 1582. Thus, the date of any document written between 1st of January and 24th of March inclusive has had to be adjusted to reconcile it with the current system by adding a year.

The original or most likely original Irish form of a name, where one is known to have existed, is given in italics on the top line to the right of the current spelling, with an English translation below. This includes Norse, Anglo-Norman and English names for which a Gaelic form once existed, as well as those of purely Irish origin. *Loch Cairlinn*, for example, was used by Irish-speakers for *Carlingford Lough* and this, rather than the original Norse, is printed on the top line. Although the name may have originally been coined at an early period of the language, standard modern Irish orthography is employed throughout, except in rare cases where this may obscure the meaning or origin of the name. The rules of modern Irish grammar are usually followed when not contradicted by the historical evidence. Where some doubt concerning the origin or form of a name may exist, or where alternatives may seem equally likely, plausible suggestions made by previous authorities, particularly the *OSNB* informants, are given preference and are printed at the top of the relevant entry. Nevertheless, where there is firm evidence of an origin other than that proposed by earlier scholars, the form suggested by our own research is given prominence.

Names for which no Irish original is proposed are described according to their appearance, that is, English, Scots etc. The form and meaning is usually obvious, and there is no evidence that they replace or translate an original Irish name. Names which are composed of two elements, one originally Irish and the other English or Scots, are described as hybrid forms. An important exception to this rule is names of townlands which are compounded from a name derived from Irish and an English word such as "upper", "east" etc. In these cases, the original Irish elements are given on the right-hand side but the later English appendage is not translated.

In the discussion of each name, difficulties have not been ignored but the basic consideration has been to give a clear and readable explanation of the probable origin of the name, and its relationship to the place. Other relevant information, on the language of the name, on other similar names, on historical events, on past owners or inhabitants, on physical changes or local place-name legends, may also be included, to set the name more fully in context.

The townland maps which appear at the beginning of each parish show the layout of all the townlands in that parish. They are based on printouts from the Ordnance Survey's digitized version of the 1:50,000 map.

The rules of Irish grammar as they relate to place-names are discussed in Appendix A, and the historical system of land divisions in Ulster is described in Appendix B. The bibliography separates primary sources and secondary works (the latter being referred to by author and date of publication). This is followed by a glossary of technical terms used in this series. The place-name index, as well as providing page references, gives the 1:50,000 sheet numbers for all names on the published map, and sheet numbers for the 1:10,000 series and the earlier 6-inch county series for townland names. The index of Irish forms gives a semi-phonetic pronunciation for all names for which an Irish form has been postulated.

SUGGESTIONS FOR FURTHER INVESTIGATION

A work like this on individual names cannot give a clear picture of any area at a particular time in the past. Any source in the bibliography could be used, in conjunction with townland or other maps, to plot the references to a particular locality at that date, or to lands with a particular owner. Also the Public Record Office of Northern Ireland holds a considerable amount of unpublished material from the eighteenth century and later, which awaits investigation for information on place-names arising at that period.

Although fieldwork forms an integral part of place-name research, it is difficult for a library researcher to acquire the familiarity with an area that the local inhabitants have. Local people can walk the bounds of their townlands, or compare boundary features with those of the early 6-inch maps. Written or tape-recorded collections of local names (especially those of smaller features such as fields, rocks, streams, houses, bridges, etc.), where exactly they are to be found, how written and pronounced, and any stories about them or the people who lived there, would be a valuable resource for the future. The Place-Name Project will be happy to talk to anyone engaged on a venture of this kind.

Kay Muhr
Senior Research Fellow

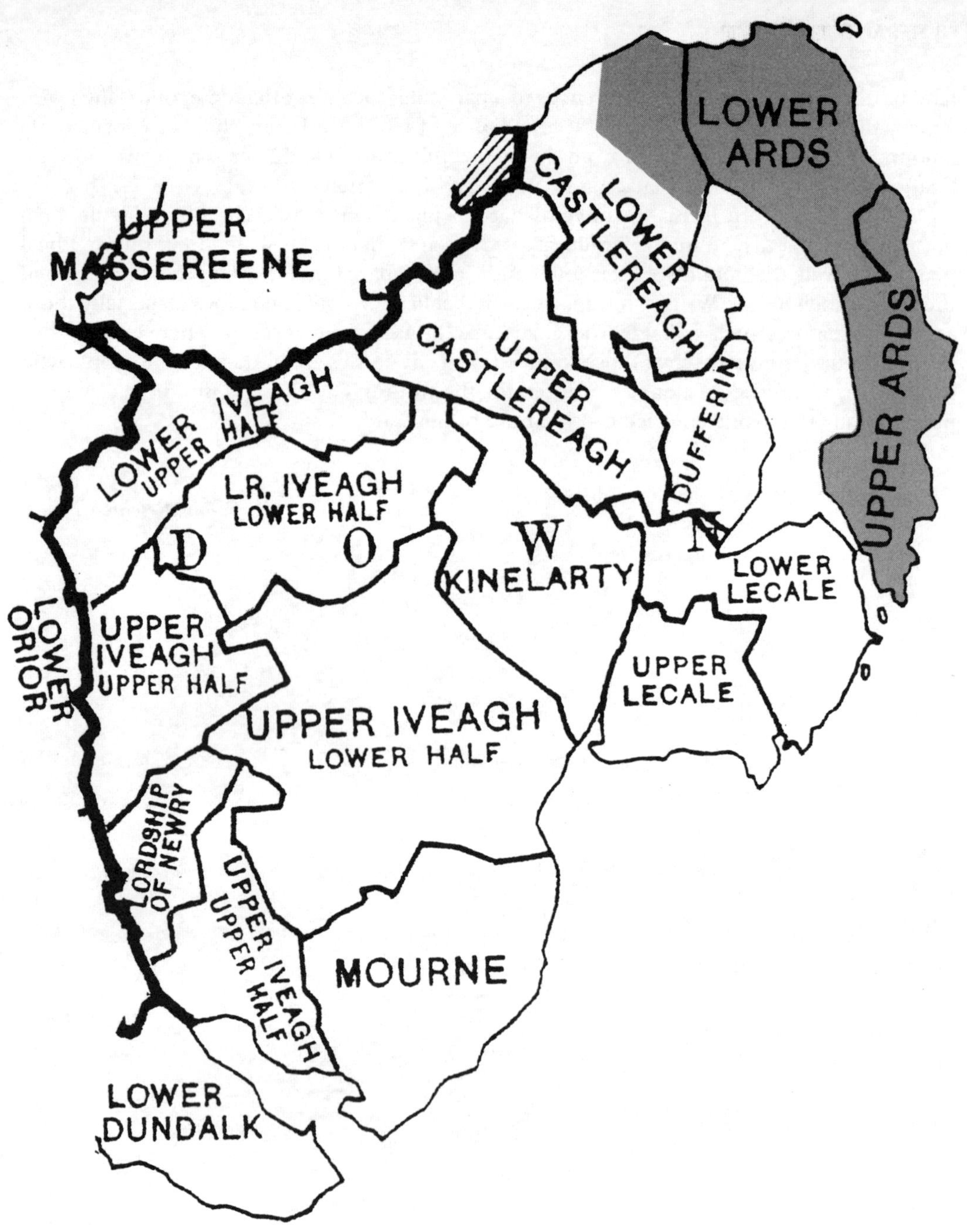

Map of Baronies in Co. Down

Ards Lower
Ards Upper
Castlereagh Lower
Castlereagh Upper
Dufferin
Iveagh Lower, Lower Half
Iveagh Lower, Upper Half
Iveagh Upper, Lower Half
Iveagh Upper, Upper Half
Kinelarty
Lecale Lower
Lecale Upper
Lordship of Newry
Mourne

Districts treated at one time as being in Co. Down are shown around the left-hand margin of the map. The area described in this volume, the baronies of the Ards, Upper and Lower, with part of Lower Castlereagh, has been shaded to highlight its position.

INTRODUCTION TO COUNTY DOWN

The division of Ireland into counties was effected under English rule and is the most recent tier in the territorial administrative system of province, county, barony, parish and townland. The counties of Ulster as they now stand were established in the early 17th century, but were built up out of pre-existing smaller districts, some of which were preserved as baronies within the county. County Down is bounded by the sea to the south, east and north-east, but, although some of its inland boundary markers are notable geographical features, the area they delimit has partly been decided by historical events.

The *Ulaid* were once the most powerful tribal group in the north of Ireland and it is from them that the province of Ulster derives its name (Flanagan D. 1978(d)). However, in the 4th and 5th centuries they were driven eastwards into the modern counties of Antrim and Down under pressure from the *Uí Néill* and the *Airgialla*. In the south the new boundary between the Ulaid and the Airgialla may have been marked by the erection of the Danes' Cast along the marshes between the northern limit of the Newry River and the ford of the Bann at Banbridge. Of the chief Ulaid tribes, *Uí Echach Coba* were located along this borderland and *Dál nAraide* east of Lough Neagh and the lower Bann. A third tribe, *Dál Fiatach*, the "true Ulaid", settled in Lecale and in the vicinity of Strangford Lough. Their capital at *Dún dá Lethglas* (modern Downpatrick) was to become an important ecclesiastical centre. Other less important kingdoms within the reduced Ulster were the *Conaille Muirthemne* in north Louth (the Cooley peninsula) and *Dál Riata* in the Glens of Antrim.

From the 6th to 10th centuries the kingship of the Ulaid was shared by Dál Fiatach, Dál nAraide and Uí Echach Coba, but in the 8th century Dál Fiatach extended their influence northward over the area east of Lough Neagh. After the Anglo-Norman invasion the whole area east of the Upper and Lower Bann became the feudal Earldom of Ulster. However, the influence of the local Dál Fiatach church was increased in 1186 when the Norman knight John de Courcy transferred the relics of three of the greatest Irish saints, Patrick, Brigid and Columcille, to Downpatrick cathedral. The diocese of Down, the boundaries of which were settled in the 12th century, was centred on this famous church and stretched as far north as the contemporary territorial limits of Dál Fiatach, though limited on the west by the Uí Echach diocese of Dromore. Through their ruling family of *Mac Duinnshléibhe* (MacDonlevy) Dál Fiatach retained some power as "king of the Irish of Ulidia" (*rex Hibernicorum Ulidiae*) until the late 13th century, though after their extinction the Gaelic title of *rí Ulad*, or "king of Ulster" (the province of the Ulaid), was claimed by the expanding O'Neills of *Cenél nEógain* to the west (Byrne 1973, 128–9).

Under the feudal Earldom of Ulster, English shire government was established in the territory of the Ulaid. It was divided into various native and other areas: the "bailiwicks of Antrim, Carrickfergus, Art, Blathewyc, Ladcathel" in 1226, the "counties of Cragfergus, Antrim, Blathewyc, Dun and Coulrath" in 1333 (*Inq. Earldom Ulster* i 31, ii 136, 141, iii 60,63, iv 127). In 1549 the area was described as "the county of Ulster, that is to say the baronies of the Grenecastle, Dondalk, Lacayll, Arde, Differens, Gallagh, Bentry, Kroghfergous, Maulyn, Twscard and Glyns" (*Cal. Carew MSS* 1515–74, 223–4). In 1571 a commission was set up "to survey the countries of Lecale, the Duffrens, M'Carton's country, Slaighte M'Oneiles country, Kilvarlyn, Evaghe, M'Ghenes' country, Morne, the lands of the Nury, and O'Handlone's country, and to form them into one county, or to join them to any neighbouring counties or baronies" (*Fiants Eliz.* §1736). This led to the separation from Antrim of the modern county of Down, containing the baronies of Lecale, Dufferin, Kinelarty (McCarton's country), Castlereagh (part of the Clandeboy O'Neill's country), Iveagh

(Kilwarlin and Magennis' country), Mourne and Newry. However *O'Handlone's country* became part of Co. Armagh.

The county name, appearing as *Dun* in 1333, derives like that of the diocese from the Dál Fiatach capital *Dún dá Lethglas*. In the Norman and post-Norman period, Downpatrick usually appears in Latin and English documentation as *Dunum*, *Dun* or *Down(e)*, and in Irish writing of the medieval period the common form is *Dún*, never *Dún Pádraig* (Flanagan D. 1971, 89). In the *Ordnance Survey Memoirs* it is noted that Downpatrick was "more commonly called by the country people Down", and "even today *Down* rather than *Downpatrick* is the local usage" (*ibid.*). Thus, when the modern county was established at the end of the 16th century, Down was still the name of the shire town. The form *Downpatrick*, which had no currency before the early 17th century, became more popular from 1617 onwards, perhaps due to the creation in that year of the Manor of Downpatrick (*ibid.*). However it never influenced the county name.

The county boundaries were not settled all at once. Jobson's set of Ulster maps (c. 1590) and Norden's map of Ireland (1610) show the names and bounds of the three counties of Antrim, Down and Armagh. Both cartographers still include in Down the Cooley peninsula (now in Co. Louth) and also Loughgilly, O'Hanlon's chief seat in the barony of Orior (Co. Armagh). According to Jobson, Armagh extended across the outflow of the Bann into Lough Neagh to include Clanbrasil (later the barony of Oneilland East), and Down included Killultagh on the east bank of Lough Neagh (later the barony of Upper Massareene in Co. Antrim). A document in the state papers of 1603 refers to "Downe county alias Leycaile" (which includes *Cowley* and *Omethe* in modern Co. Louth), but gives *Kilulto* as a separate "country" (*Cal. Carew MSS* 1601–3, 451). In 1605 Killultagh was annexed to Co. Antrim (*CSP Ire.* 1603–6, 321). In the same year an inquisition on Clandeboy stated that the most noted boundary between the parts of it called Killultagh and Upper Clandeboy (later Castlereagh) was the river Lagan (*Inq. Ult.* §2 Jac. I), and the Lagan remains the boundary between Cos Antrim and Down to this day.

The land east of the Upper Bann on the shore of Lough Neagh, known as Clanbrasil, was traditionally Uí Echach Coba or Magennis territory. In 1605 *Clanbrassilagh* "which before lay doubtful between it and the county of Down" was formally annexed to the new county of *Ardmaghe* (*CSP Ire.* 1603–6, 318), becoming eventually the barony of Oneilland East. A dispute arose between John Brownlow and Capt. Edward Trevor in 1612 concerning the ownership of six townlands in Kilmore, a district between Clanbrasil and Killultagh. Brownlow had been granted the area as lying in Co. Armagh while Trevor had been granted exactly the same lands as lying in Co. Down (*Ulst. Plant. Paps.* 266, §60). The plantation commissioners found that the land was in Co. Armagh and awarded it to Brownlow, compensating Trevor with other lands. Sir Arthur Magennis then claimed the area from Brownlow as part of his own property in Co. Down, but the commissioners refused to recompense him unless he could prove title, and the lands remained in Brownlow's possession (*ibid.* 269, §61). Modern Co. Down has retained one townland still called Kilmore, a strip of land connecting it with Lough Neagh, although Kilmore is part of the civil parish of Shankill, all the rest of which is in Co. Armagh. The artificiality of the county boundary in this area continued to cause problems: Sir William Petty in his barony and county maps (*Hib. Reg.* c. 1657; *Hib. Del.* c. 1672) thought that the Bann formed the northern boundary between Cos Down and Armagh, and placed the Armagh parishes of Seagoe and Shankill to the west of the river instead of to the east. The diocese of Dromore, however, reflects the earlier boundary between Uí Echach Coba and Airgialla, in that it includes Seagoe and Shankill and follows the river Bann all the way to Lough Neagh (see **Iveagh**).

The date at which the southern border of Co. Down was settled is difficult to ascertain from the sources. The ancient territory of the Ulaid had stretched as far south as the river Boyne, and even after the Ulaid were driven east by the Uí Néill the Conaille tribe of north Louth remained part of the Ulaid confederation. The feudal Earldom of Ulster covered the same area, so that in 1549 the "county of Ulster" still extended from the north Antrim coast to Dundalk (*Cal. Carew MSS* 1515–74, 223–4, quoted above). In 1552 the royal grant of Newry, Mourne, Carlingford, Omeath and Cooley to Sir Nicholas Bagenal preserved the cohesion of the older territory, but already the first two areas were said to be in the county of Down or in *Ullestere*, and the others in the county of Louth (*CPR Ed. VI iv*, 387–90). The latest documentary reference to Cooley being part of Co. Down is in the Carew MSS for 1603, though it is shown on Jobson's and Norden's maps (all quoted above). However in an earlier document in the Carew collection (1596) the northern limit of Co. Louth in the English Pale is given as "the fues and o'hanlon's country" (i.e. Co. Armagh, as at present) (Falkiner 1904, 141). By the time of the Plantation this is also the border of the re-established province of Ulster.

THE BARONIES OF ARDS UPPER AND LOWER

Ards	*Aird Uladh* "peak or promontory of the Ulstermen"	
1. Arda Ua nEchach, ri	Cáin Adomnáin 205–6	697
2. i nAirdd nepotum nEchdaigh	AU (Mac Airt) 162	703
3. (?)ac Airtiu	AU (Mac Airt) 280	824
4. i nAird Ulad	Mart. Tal. May 29 p. 46	830c
5. Aird Uladh	AFM ii 766	1011
6. An Aird	AFM ii 766	1011
7. Aird Ulad, co rici	AU (Mac Airt) 442	1012
8. in Aird, coro ort	AU (Mac Airt) 442	1012
9. na hArda, tuaristal ríg	Lebor na Cert l.1312	1050c
10. na Harda, do Ríg	Lebor na Cert l.1250	1050c
11. na hArda, co hairther	AFM ii 1036	1130
12. na hArda, co hairther	AU (Mac Airt) 578	1130
13. i nAird Uladh	Mart. Tal. May 29 p. 106n	1170
14. i nAird Uladh	Mart. Tal. June 24 p. 122n	1170
15. i nAird Uladh	Mart. Tal. Sept. 25 p. 184n	1170
16. na hArdda, Húi Echach	CGH 331 a 9	1170c
17. Aird, isin	Descendants Ir 46	1200c
18. Aird Ulad, righ airm-derg	CMR(2) 230	1350c
19. a h-Aird Ulad	Fél. Óeng. May 29 p. 136	1400c
20. Aird Uladh, in	AFM iv 897	1433
21. a n-Aird Ulad	Fél. Óeng. May 29 p. 136	1453c
22. ic Ard Ulad	Fél. Óeng. May 29 p. 136	1453c
23. in Aird	Fél. Óeng. Sept 25 p. 212	1470c
24. a n-Ard Uladh	AU iii 232	1470
25. a n-Aird Uladh	AU iii 232	1470
26. a n-Aird Ulad	AU iii 632	1540
27. go hAird Uladh	LCABuidhe 114 l.87	1600c
28. Ard Uladh	Tribes Ire. 60–1	1600c
29. (?)ardaibh, ar	LCABuidhe 160 l.200	1617c
30. ó Ard Uladh	LCABuidhe 247 l.122	1680c
31. Ard Uladh, Ó mhullach	Mac Cumhaigh (b) 21:124	1760c
32. in Ardo	British Museum MS (EA) 16n	1034
33. altitudo Vltorum	VSSH (Plummer) ii 7 §13	1125c
34. Art	Cartae Dun. 421 §8	1192c
35. de Arce	Pontif. Hib. i 126	1204
36. in Arte	Pontif. Hib. i 126	1204
37. de Art	Pipe Roll John 82	1211c
38. in Arte	CDI i §1264	1225
39. del Art	Close Roll Hen. III (EA) 16n	1226c
40. Arte, in	Cartae Dun. 422 §10	1227c
41. del Ard, Brianus	Onom. Goed. 35	1237c
42. in Ardo	Cartae Dun. 424 §14	1280
43. in Ardis in Ultonia	Chart St Mary's Abbey i 4	1300c

44. Ardo, Decanat' de	Eccles. Tax. 16	1306c
45. in Ards (?)	CPR (de hÓir) 83	1389
46. in Ardo	Reg. Mey §170	1449
47. in Ardo	Rot. Ant. Ecc. Dun. 171	1450c
48. Arde, the barony of the	SP Hen. VIII 24	1515
49. in Ards	Cal. Carew MS 149	1538
50. Ardd, the lordship of	Quinn 1933–4:77	1540c
51. Arde	Cal. Carew MSS 224	1549
52. Arde Savage	Cal. Carew MSS 242	1553
53. Ard	Cal. Carew MSS 333	1562
54. the Arde	JRSAI xi 20	1566
55. Arde	Goghe's Map	1567
56. in Ardee	Fiants Eliz. §1659	1570
57. the Ardes	MacDonnells Antrim 406	1572
58. the Arde	MacDonnells Antrim 407–8	1572
59. the Ardes	Cal. Carew MSS 438	1573
60. the Ardes	Cal. Carew MSS 462	1574
61. the Ardes	Cal. Carew MSS 465	1574
62. in the Ards	CSP Ire. 589	1573
63. Great Ardes	Cal. Carew MSS 436	1586
64. Little Ardes	Cal. Carew MSS 436	1586
65. Ardes	Dartmouth Map 6	1590
66. Great Ardes	Dartmouth Map 5	1590
67. Great Ardes	Jobson's Ulster (TCD)	1590
68. Little ardes	Jobson's Ulster (TCD)	1590
69. Little Ardes, the	Fiants Eliz. §5590	1591
70. Ards	Hondius Map	1591
71. Arde	Boazio's Map (BM)	1599
72. Ardis	CSP Ire. 118	1601
73. Ardes, the	CSP Ire. 506	1602
74. little Ards	Fiants Eliz. §6711	1602
75. Little Ardes	Fiants Eliz. §6712	1602
76. Little Ardes, the	CPR Jas I 35b	1603
77. Great Ardes	Bartlett Maps (Esch. Co. Maps) 1	1603
78. the Ardes	CPR Jas I 39a	1604
79. the two Ardes	CSP Ire. 212	1604
80. the Ardes	CPR Jas I 86b	1605
81. Great Ardes	CPR Jas I 73a	1605
82. le great Ardes	Inq. Ult. (Down) §2 Jac. I	1605
83. lez Ardes magn'	Inq. Ult. (Down) §2 Jac. I	1605
84. lez great Ardes	Inq. Ult. (Down) §2 Jac. I	1605
85. in the Little Ardes	CPR Jas I 84b	1605
86. in little Ardes	Inq. Ult. (Down) §2 Jac. I	1605
87. le little Ardes	Inq. Ult. (Down) §2 Jac. I	1605
88. Arde	Boazio's Map (NG)	1609
89. Greate Ardes	Norden's Map	1610c
90. Little Ards	Norden's Map	1610c
91. Ardes	Speed's Ireland	1610
92. Ardes	Mercator's Ire.	1610

93. the Little Ardes	CPR Jas I 548b	1622
94. Great & Little Ardes	Ham. Copy Inq. xxx	1623
95. Ardes, the	Ham. Copy Inq. xlvi	1623
96. little Ardes, lez	Inq. Ult. (Down) §10 Car. I	1627
97. magna Ardia, le	Inq. Ult. (Down) §75 Car. I	1636
98. little Ards, le	Inq. Ult. (Down) §104 Car. I	1644
99. Ardia, de	Inq. Ult. (Down) §104 Car. I	1644
100. Ardes, ye	Descr. Ards 34	1689
101. d'Ardes, la peninsula	Sav. Ards 126	1690
102. ðə 'ɑ(:)rdz	Local pronunciation	1992

In the 7th and early 8th centuries the Ards peninsula was known as *Aird Ua nEchach* "the point or promontory of the Uí Echach" (forms 1–2). There are several tribes called *Uí Echach* dispersed throughout Ireland, including one in southern Co. Down who later gave their name to the modern Barony of Iveagh, but this particular tribe claimed their descent from Echu Gunnat of the *Dál Fiatach*, the chief tribe of the Ulaid (*CGH* LL 331a). In the early 9th century, however, the Uí Echach succumbed to the Vikings and, following their demise, their name disappeared from the place-name and was replaced by *Ulad* "of the Ulstermen" (4–5, 7, 13, etc.).

The vast majority of the forms listed above indicate that the modern name Ards derives from an Irish word *aird*. Recent authorities have taken this to mean "a promontory" (de hÓir 1965: 83, Flanagan 1981–2(b): 64) and, indeed, this suitably describes the large peninsula which forms the barony. Although, this meaning is not attributed to *aird* in any Irish dictionary, it is so attested in Scottish Gaelic and in Scottish place-names (de hÓir 1965: 79). Moreover, Éamonn de hÓir has collected ten reasonably certain instances of the use of *aird* in this sense in Irish place-names (de hÓir 1965).

However, the author of the medieval Life of St Comgall translates the name into Latin as *altitudo Vltorum* "height(s) of the Ulstermen" (*VSSH (Plummer)* ii 7 §xiii). It might be suggested that the old nom. sing. form *aird* meaning "a promontory" was reinterpreted as the plural form of *ard* meaning "a height" as both forms are identical, but the continued use of the form *aird* after prepositions throughout the next three hundred years weighs heavily against such a view.

According to the Royal Irish Academy's *Dictionary of the Irish Language*, one of the early uses of *aird* was in the sense of "peak, point" (*DIL* s.v. 1 *aird*) and in a Middle Irish poem on the history of Ireland uttered by the legendary figure, Fintán mac Bóchra, *aird* is used almost certainly in the sense of "height, peak" (*Ériu* iv 130 l.8). Clearly, therefore, the latinization of *Aird* as *altitudo* "height(s)" by Comgall's biographer does not require us to suppose some re-analysis of the name. Indeed, it may suggest that "peak" was the original meaning of the name and that it was properly understood as such by this medieval hagiographer whose knowledge of medieval Irish was undoubtedly far superior to our own.

A by-form *Ard* begins to appear in Irish manuscripts as early as the 15th century (22, 24, 28, 30). The earliest of these (22, 24) may be explained as the result of the omission of the *i* from *aird*, either by the scribes of these texts or by their modern editors as both appear alongside the older, more correct, spellings, *aird* (21, 25). However, an earlier gen. sing. *Aird* (18) shows that the name had already been re-analysed as *ard* "a height" as early as the late 14th century and similar forms reappear in some 17th-century texts (28, 31). Nevertheless, the older form *aird* continues to appear in texts up until the dawn of the 17th century (27), although its original meaning had probably become obscure by this time and may well have been understood as a by-form of *ard* "a height".

In late manuscripts a plural form of the name is regularly employed (de hÓir 1965: 83). The very early form *Airtiu* cited above (3) looks like an old accusative plural but is irreconcilable with the grammatical forms of both *aird* and *ard* in the Old Irish period, as well as with the other attested forms of the name, and it can probably be dismissed as a scribal error. De hÓir (*ibid.*) suggests that the use of the plural in our late manuscripts may have been influenced by anglicized plural forms such as *the Ardes*. The origin of a plural form in the anglicized forms, however, is not so obvious.

It is clear from the historical forms that the barony was divided into two portions, *Great Ardes* and *Little Ardes* (63–4 etc.), at least as early as 1586. This division does not correspond exactly to the modern barony division of Lower and Upper Ards, as three parishes formerly belonging to the *Great Ardes* have since been added to the Upper Ards.

It might, therefore, be suggested that the current plural form of the name originated with the division of the territory into two portions (e.g. de hÓir 1965: 83). However, a number of plural forms do occur in our sources some time before the division was realized (43, 45, 49, 57, 59–62) and, if they are genuine, this suggestion is rendered less probable. De hÓir suggests that *aird* was re-analysed in Irish as a plural form of *ard* and this resulted in the appearance of a plural form in English and Latin documents. The transference of a plural from Irish to English is a well-attested phenomenon in Irish place-names and has resulted in many anglicized names, such as Killybegs and Downings in Co. Donegal, bearing the English plural ending, *s*. However, there is no evidence of a plural form among our Irish sources until long after it appears in the anglicized forms of the name so that this suggestion may be rejected. Another possibility is that the English plural is a reflex of the pronunciation of the final *d* in *Aird* as [dʒ] (rhyming with "targe"), but this phenomenon is not repeated in other names in the Ards which end in final palatal *d*.

STRANGFORD LOUGH

Strangford Lough	*Loch Cuan* "lough of the harbours"	
1. Loch Cúan, for	Mart. Tal. Aug. 6 p. 60	830c
2. Loch Cúan, for	Fél. Óeng. Jun. 23 p. 158	830c
3. Loch Cuan, Cath for	AFM i 520	874
4. Locha Cuan, do Ghallaibh	AFM i 522	876
5. Loch Cuan, occ	AU (Mac Airt) 332	877
6. Loch Cuan	AFM ii 610	922
7. Locha Cuan, do Ghallaibh	AFM ii 614	924
8. Locha Cuan, co nGallaibh	AFM ii 628	931
9. Loch Cuan, for	Lebor na Cert l.1311	1050c
10. Loch curchach Cuan	Met. Dind. iv 146	1100c
11. Loch Cuan, co	Met. Dind. iv 262	1100c
12. Loch Cuan, oc	CSH p. 179	1125c
13. Locha Cuan, for innsibh	AFM ii 1088	1149
14. Loch Cúan, for	Mart. Tal. Aug. 5 p. 150	1170c
15. Loch Cuan, ag	Aeidhe ma chroidhe p. 158	1260
16. Loch Cuan, for	AFM v 1417	1534
17. Loch Cuan, ar	ALC ii 283	1534
18. Lacha Cuan, do ghríbh...	LCABuidhe 174 l.67	1680c
19. Loch Cúain	LCABuidhe 178 l.182	1680c
20. um Loch Cuain	LCABuidhe 247 l.123	1680c
21. Loch Cuan	Donnellan MSS 38	1680c
22. Loch Cuan, ó thraighe	Donnellan MSS 38–9	1680c
23. Loch Cuan	LCABuidhe 144 l.166	1687c
24. go Loch Cuan	O'Neill Fun. Oration 265	1744
25. Lochwene (the water called)	Confirm. Lands Nendrum (EA) 193	1203
26. Loughquoon near Strangford	L/P Hen VIII ii 268	1515
27. lough Coine	Fiants Eliz. §1530	1570
28. L. Conne	Nowel's Ire. (1)	1570c
29. Lough Conn	Dartmouth Map 5	1590
30. L. Coney	Jobson's Ulster (TCD)	1590
31. L Coyn	Hondius Map	1591
32. L. Coyn	Mercator's Ire.	1595
33. Lo Cone	Bartlett Map (Esch. Co. Maps) 1	1603
34. Loughdowne	CPR Jas I 14b	1603
35. Lough Coane by the river of Strangford	CSP Ire. 315	1602
36. Loughconn	Inq. Ult. (Down) §1 Jac. I	1605
37. Loughcon	Inq. Ult. (Down) §2 Jac. I	1605
38. Loughcone/Loughcon	CPR Jas I 14a	1605
39. Lough Cone	Boazio's Map (NG)	1609
40. Lo Cone	Speed's Ireland	1610
41. Lough Cone	Speed's Antrim & Down	1610
42. Lough-coyne	CPR Jas I 326b	1617

43. Loughdowne otherwise Loughcoine	CPR Jas I 336b	1617
44. Loughcon otherwise Loughcoyne	CPR Jas I 337a	1617
45. Loughcoine	CPR Jas I 460b	1619
46. Loughcoyne	Inq. Ult. (Down) §12 Jac. I	1620
47. Loughcoyne	CPR Jas I 511a	1621
48. Loughcoyne, the lough called	Ham Copy. Inq. xxx	1623
49. Lough Cone	Raven Map Clandeboye 50	1625
50. Loughdowne al' Loghcone al' Loughcone	Inq. Ult. (Down) §63 Car. I	1633
51. Loughcoyne	Inq. Ult. (Down) §104 Car. I	1644
52. Loghdowne al' Loghcoine	Inq. Ult. (Down) §22 Car. II	1662
53. Loghcoine, l'extremité ...	Inq. Ult. (Down) §23 Car. II	1662
54. du lac de Cone	Sav. Ards 126	1690
55. Strangford L	Lamb Maps Co. Down	1690c
56. Lake Cuan	MacCana's Itinerary 50	1700c
57. Lough Coan	OSM vii 9	1701
58. Lough Cone	Map D'patrick (JRSAI xliv 56)	1729
59. Lough Coyn or the lake of Strangford	Harris Hist. 26, 152	1744
60. the Lake of Strangford	Harris Hist. 36, 42, 74, 76	1744
61. Lough-Coyn	Harris Hist. 36	1744
62. Strangford lake, now more commonly called Strangford Lough	OSM vii 9	1837c
63. Loch Cuan "lough of (the) harbours"	Flanagan (1978c: 24)	1978
64. 'strɛŋfərd 'lɔx	Local pronunciation	1992
65. 'straŋfərd 'lɔx	Local pronunciation	1992

The name *Strangford* is interesting in several respects, not least in that it derives from Old Norse *Strangfjörthr* meaning "strong fiord" (see Reeves *UJA* 2 (1854) 53n; Flanagan 1978(e): 24). It clearly derives from a strong tidal current which converges at the narrow strait between the modern towns of Strangford and Portaferry and it was originally to this part of the lough that the name referred. However, the name soon spread to the port of Strangford which is so called in a chronicle from the Isle of Man as early as 1205 (*in portum qui vocatur Stranfeord, Chron. Mann.* 71 §61).

In the 17th and 18th centuries the name Strangford spread to the lough itself. Prior to this, the lake had been known by its Irish name *Loch Cuan*, anglicized *Lough Cone* etc. (1–54 above). Flanagan (1978(c): 24) states that the name *Loch Cuan* was still used in the 17th century, but one could add that the anglicized form had not totally disappeared from ordinary use until the mid–18th century and, indeed, O'Donovan states that *Loch Cuan* was still the Irish name for Strangford Lough in the middle of the 19th century (*AFM* i 7n).

Flanagan (1978(c): 24) interprets *Loch Cuan* as "lough of the harbours", and this is certainly borne out by the vast majority of the Irish-language forms listed above. Two spellings in late 17th-century poems show a re-analysis of the name as *Loch Cuain* "lough of the harbour" (19–20), but this form did not gain widespread currency. Descriptions of the lough throughout the centuries appear to justify "lough of the harbours" as a suitable appellation. Knox, writing in the last century, speaks highly of the lough's capacity as a haven:

> The Lough of Strangford has been accurately charted by Nimmo and subsequently by Captain Hoskyns, of the Royal Navy, and it appears that few bays afford such safety to wind-bound vessels, as there is abundance of water over the bar at all times. Its capacities are very well known, and Captain Hoskyns, who had charge of the late Admiralty Survey stated that, 'if it were lighted there would not be a better harbour of refuge in the United Kingdom, for all classes of vessels, including men of war'. (*Knox Hist.* 473)

The very fact that there are also quite a few early historical references to the Vikings of Strangford Lough in the Irish Annals would of course suggest that these expert seafarers also saw the advantages of this lough as a sea-base, and the reference to *Loch curchach Cuan* "Loch Cuan of the coracles" in a medieval Irish text dealing with place-name lore (*Met. Dind.* iv 146–7) also suggests that Strangford Lough has long been associated with sailors and vessels.

A form *Loughdowne* occurs in some of our 17th-century documents (34, 43, 50, 52). This might mean something like "the lough of Down (or Downpatrick)", although Flanagan (1978(e): 47) states that it is unlikely to have had any real currency. Indeed, it probably arose from a mistranscription and only acquired some degree of verisimilitude from its association with Downpatrick (*ibid.*).

Edmund Hogan, in his *Onomasticon Goedelicum*, refers to a name *Bréne* which he identifies with Strangford Lough (*Onom. Goed.* 125). Many of the instances of the name which he cites are ambiguous but one occurrence in the Book of Armagh, referring to "the strait called *Brene*", perhaps indicates that it was the name of the stretch of water at the mouth of the lough, while several others, although less certain, clearly suggest that it was the name of a smaller portion of the lough than indicated by Hogan. *Bréne*, is probably related to the common noun *bréine* "stench, rotteness", and may have referred to the stench at low tide.

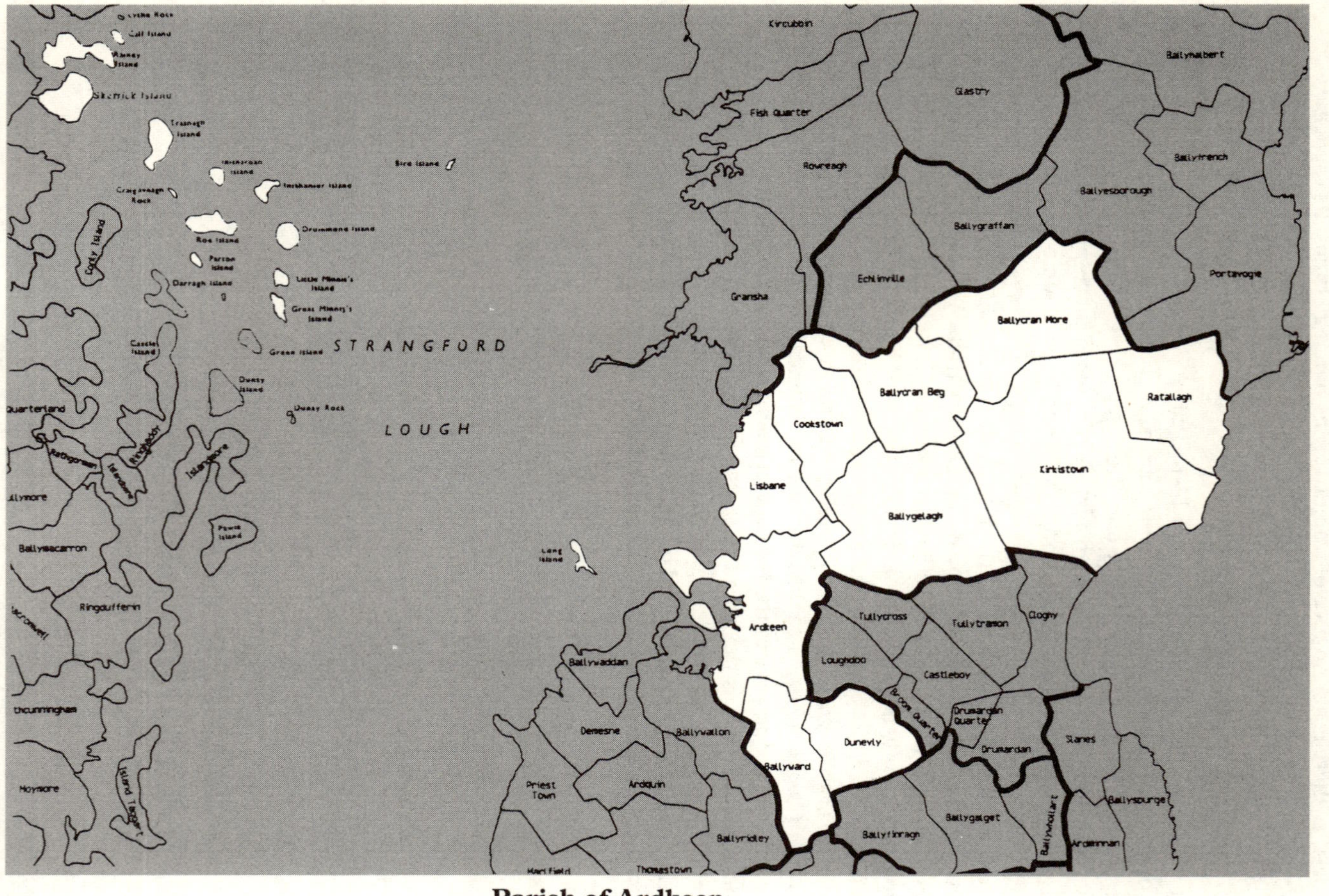

Parish of Ardkeen

Barony of Ards Upper

Townlands		*Islands*
Ardkeen	Dunevly	Bird Island
Ballycran Beg	Kirkistown	Calf Island
Ballycranmore	Lisbane	Craigaveagh Rock
Ballygelagh	Ratallagh	Drummond Island
Ballyward		Great Minnis's Island
Cookstown		Inishanier Island
		Inisharoan Island
		Little Minnis's Island
		Long Island
		Lythe Rock
		Parton Island
		Pherson's Island
		Rainey Island
		Roe Island
		Round Island
		Sketrick Island
		Trasnagh Island

PARISH OF ARDKEEN

There is little documentation concerning this parish before the Anglo-Norman period and apart from the doubtful reference to an *Ard Caoin* in relation to a St. Finntan discussed below (under the parish, and townland, name of **Ardkeen**), it is only in the Anglo-Norman era and the periods following that references to Ardkeen begin to appear:

> The castle, with the church, indicates a manorial centre, established by the Savage family of the Ards in the late 12th or early 13th century. There is a reference to John de Courcy's 'Castle of Archen' in his foundation charter of St. Andrew in Ards
> (*ASCD* 197–8; for Ardkeen church see 297–8).

Reeves provides a variety of information on Ardkeen (*EA* pp. 21, 171, 179 and 361, n. g), including a reference to the castle of "Archen" in John de Courcy's charter to the Black Abbey (*Mon. Ang.* ii, p. 1019). The advowson of the parish descended to William de Burgus (d.1333) in right of his Earldom of Ulster but this was later seized into the king's hands and subsequently presented to Thomas de Bredon in 1347, and to Thomas Cuthbert in 1386. In the charter of James I 1609 it was annexed to the prebend of St. Andrew's. Lewis (*Lewis' Top. Dict.* i 53) records that in 1561 "Shane O'Nial, who had overrun and destroyed the neighbouring country on every side, besieged this castle but was so vigorously repulsed that he retreated with great loss and never penetrated further southward into the Ardes".

There was a saltworks here in the seventeenth century: "'le saltwork', Hen' Savage de Arkine" (*Inq. Ult.* §103 Car. I 1641). Harris (*Harris Hist.* 48) describes Ardkeen in 1744: "*Ardchin*, an antient Seat of the Family of the Savages, now of *Francis Savage Esq.*; pleasantly seated on the Lake". Mention is then made of a *Hugh Savage* demolishing the old house and moving down to a less exposed part. The only parts of the old castle which still remain are the foundations and they are to be traced on an eminence still called Castlehill.

According to *Knox Hist.* 463–4 the population of the parish in 1871 "amounted to 1,507 persons, including the residents in the adjacent islands in Lough Strangford". For a description of the area in 1837 see *OSM* vii 1–3.

PARISH NAME

Ardkeen — *Ard Caoin*
J 6057 — "fair height"

1. (?) Arda caoin, Fionntain	Mart. Don. Sep. 8 238	1630c
2. (?) Archen	Mon. Ang. ii 101	1180c
3. Arkien, ecclesiam de	Pontif. Hib. i §59	1204
4. Arhen	Cartae Dun. §10 422	1227c
5. Ardkene, Ecclesia de – cum capella de Moyndele	Eccles. Tax 20	1306c
6. Ecclesia Sanctae Mariae de Ardkene	Cal. Canc. Hib. (EA) 131 b	1316
7. Arkyen	Inq. Earldom Ulster iii 65	1333
8. Ardkeen	Cal. Canc. Hib. (EA) 48 b	1386
9. Arkyn	Reg. Mey 165, 170	1449
10. Ardkene	Reg. Mey 159	1449
11. Arkyn	Reg. Mey 170	1449
12. Arkyne	Sav. Ards 366	1574
13. Arrochyne	Mercator's Ulst.	1595

14. Ardchin	CPR Jas I 85a	1605
15. Earchin	Jas I to Down Cath., 179	1609
16. Archine	CPR Jas I 183b	1610
17. Arkine	Speed's Ireland	1610
18. Arkine C.	Speed's Antrim & Down	1610
19. Arkine C.	Speed's Ulster	1610
20. Ardkeene	Inq. Ult. (Down) §5 Jac. I	1617
21. Ardkine	Inq. Ult. (Down) §5 Jac. I	1617
22. Ardkeene	CPR Jas I 340b	1617
23. Ardkine	CPR Jas I 340b	1617
24. Ardkyne	CPR Jas I 455b	1620
25. Earchin	Ulster Visit. (Reeves) 31	1622
26. (?) Archyne	Inq. Ult. (Down) §27 Car. I	1631
27. Arkine	Inq. Ult. (Down) §101 Car. I	1641
28. Arkine	Inq. Ult. (Down) §102 Car. I	1641
29. Arckine	Inq. Ult. (Down) §102 Car. I	1641
30. Arkin	Inq. Ult. (Down) §109 Car. I	1650c
31. Ardkine	Will (Sav. Ards) 192	1655
32. Archin	Inq. Down (Reeves 1) 129	1657
33. Arkin	Census 91	1659c
34. Ardkeene	Inq. Ult. (Down) §19 Car. II	1662
35. Ardkin	Sub. Roll Down 282	1663
36. Ardchin	Trien. Visit. (Margetson) 20	1664
37. Arkin	Hib. Del. Ulster	1672c
38. Arkin	Descr. Ards 35/6	1683
39. Arkin	Map, Petty's Sur. (OSNB)	1683
40. Arkin	Lamb Maps Co. Down	1690c
41. Archin	Sav. Ards 198	1701
42. Ardkeen	Wm. Map (OSNB)	1810
43. Ardkeen	Bnd. Sur. (OSNB)	1830c
44. Archin i.e. the head of the Ards	Sav. Ards 198	1701
45. Ard Caoin "beautiful height or hill"	J O'D (OSNB)	1834c
46. ɑrd'ki:n	Local pronunciation	1991

Lewis (*Lewis' Top. Dict.* i 53) suggests that the name goes back to "*Ard-Coyne*, from its situation on the shores of the Lake which was formerly called *Lough Coyne*" but this can be dismissed, as can the suggestion made by Harris (*Harris Hist.* 48) that *Ardkeen* means "High Head", i.e. Irish *Ardcheann*. Orpen (*JRSAI* xlv (1915) 142 n. 2) identifies the form *Arweghun* from the 1333 Inquisition with modern *Ardkeen*, although it is probably modern *Ardquin*, but early forms of these two names can be difficult to distinguish.

Reeves (*EA* 21n) proposes that the name is "probably so-called from *ard caoin* 'the pleasant height'", a view reproduced in *Knox Hist.* 463–4, and it is further suggested (*Sav. Ards* 288) that the entry *Fionntain Arda caoin*, i.e. "Fionntan, of Ard-caoin" which occurs in the 17th-century *Martyrology of Donegal* (at September 8 p. 238), is a reference to a St Fionntan in this area, a view also tentatively endorsed by W. Stokes (p. 295 of his edition of *Mart. Gorm.*). Leaving aside the difficulty of turning up evidence of a St. Fionntain here, *Ard Caoin* "pleasant height" would seem a reasonably safe etymology for Ardkeen were it not for the fact that there is the issue of an earlier name *Oirer Caoin* which would appear to have been located somewhere in the Ards. O'Curry (1861:284–8) discusses an early Irish story *Sluaghid Dathi co Sliabh n-Ealpa* "The expedition of Dathí to the Alps", concerning the adventures of *Dathí* (d.428), nephew and successor of Niall of the Nine Hostages (d.405). O'Curry desribes how Dathí made his way to Scotland by going through Newry and on up to *Maigh Bile* (presumably Movilla, par. Newtownards, Co. Down). He is then reported to have departed for Scotland from a place near to *Maigh Bile* called *Oirear Caoin.* O'Curry (287) suggests that "*Oirear-Caoin* may probably have been the ancient name of the place now called Donaghadee". O'Laverty points out that "*Oirear Caoin* sounds not unlike Ardkeen" (*O'Laverty* ii 33) but he adds that Ardkeen "would not have been so convenient as Donaghadee, for fitting out such a fleet as that of King Dathi". The word *oirer* (listed in *DIL* under its more common form *airer*) means "coast, shore". This word occurs in the Scottish place-name *Argyll,* i.e. Gaelic *Airear Gaedheal* "coastline of the Gaels". The reduction of *Airer* to *Air,* i.e. *Airear Gaedheal* > *Argyll* is due to the linguistic process of haplology and, in the light of this Scottish example, we can envisage how an Irish form *Oirer Caoin* could yield a form *Arkien* in 1204 (no. 3). Thus *Airear Caoin* "fair coast(line)" could be considered as a possible meaning for Ardkeen with a reduced form *Air Caoin.*

We are, then, faced with a dilemma here in that, although we have an Irish-language name *Oirear Caoin* attested for the Ards which could possibly have yielded 13th–14th-century *Arkien, Arkyen,* etc., the stated proximity of this *Oirer Caoin* to Movilla would appear to rule out modern Ardkeen on geographical grounds. However, even if, as seems possible, *Oirear Caoin* were the original form for Ardkeen, it seems quite clear that the name was subsequently reinterpreted as *Ard Caoin* "pleasant height". This reinterpretation may have occurred in the Irish language but, whether or not this is the case, it can be seen (from form no. 5) that *Ardkene* occurs as early as 1306 AD. The element *Ard* "height", whether it occurred in the original name or whether it replaced an earlier **Airear,* would certainly be applicable to Ardkeen judging by the remarks made by Harris (*Harris Hist.* 46):

> The name of the place imports *an high head* [more correctly *fair height*], and with great Propriety, according to the Ancient Situation of this Seat, which was a Castle and dwelling House inclosed within a Ramberd and standing boldly over the lake on a pretty high Hill.

TOWNLAND NAMES

Ballycran Beg — *Baile Crannaí Beag*
J 6159 — "townland of the tree-area, little"

	Form	Source	Date
1.	Ballycrannymore	Inq. Ult. (Down) §5 Jac. I	1617
2.	Ballecranemore	CPR Jas I 340b	1617
3.	Ballycranemore	Ham. Copy Inq. xliv	1623
4.	Ballecranmore	Inq. Ult. (Down) §27 Car. I	1631
5.	Ballycranymore	Inq. Ult. (Down) §102 Car. I	1641
6.	Ballycranymore	Inq. Ult. (Down) §109 Car. I	1650c
7.	Ballycranebeg	Will (Sav. Ards) 192	1655
8.	Ballycranmore	Census 91	1659c
9.	Ballycranemore	BSD 85	1661
10.	Ballycranymore	Inq. Ult. (Down) §16 Car. II	1662
11.	Ballycrannymore	Inq. Ult. (Down) §19 Car. II	1662
12.	Ballycranmore	Map, Petty's Sur. (OSNB)	1683

13. Ballycranmore	Wm. Map (OSNB)	1810
14. Ballycranmore	High Const. Applot. (OSNB)	1830c
15. Ballycranmore	Bnd. Sur. (OSNB)	1830c
16. Baile na gCrann Mór "town of the trees (great)"	J O'D (OSNB)	1834c
17. ˌbaliˈkrɑnˈbɛg	Local pronunciation	1991

Ballycran More — *Baile Crannaí Mór*
J 6259 — "townland of the tree area, great"

1. both Ballycranes	PCR Eliz. I (Sav. Ards) 175	1559
2. Ballycranybegg	Inq. Ult. (Down) §5 Jac. I	1617
3. Ballecranebegg	CPR Jas I 340b	1617
4. Balli-crainbeg	Hib. Reg., Ards	1657c
5. Ballycranbeg	Census 91	1659c
6. Ballycranebeg	BSD 85	1661
7. Ballycranebegg	Inq. Ult. (Down) §19 Car. II	1662
8. Ballycranbeg	Map, Petty's Sur. (OSNB)	1683
9. Ballycranbeg	Wm. Map (OSNB)	1810
10. Ballycranbeg	High Const. Applot. (OSNB)	1830c
11. Ballycranbeg	Bnd. Sur. (OSNB)	1830c
12. Ballycranbeg td. "town of the trees (little)"	J O'D (OSNB)	1834c
13. ˌbaliˈkrɑnˈmo:r	Local pronunciation	1991

These townlands would have initially constituted a single large townland *Ballycrann(y)*, i.e. *Baile Crannaí* "townland of the tree-area". This was then subdivided into two portions (see form 1) by means of the appendages *-beg* and *-more*, reflecting Irish *beag* "small" and *mór* "large". *Ballycran-* seems to be derived from an Irish form *Baile Crannaí*, where *crannaí*, earlier Irish *crannaighe*, is the genitive of a word *crannach* listed, in *DIL* 509, with the meaning "trees, grove, wooded place".

Ballygelagh — *Baile Gaelach*
J 5167 — "Irish townland"

1. Villae Hibernicorum	Compotus Dun. 168	1305
2. Irishtown	PCR Eliz. I (Sav. Ards) 175	1559
3. Irishtowne other Ballygellagh	CPR Jas I 340b	1617
4. Irishtowne al. Balligelagh	Inq. Ult. (Down) §5 Jac. I	1617
5. Irishtowne	Inq. Ult. (Down) §27 Car. I	1631
6. Irishtowne al. Ballygealagh	Inq. Ult. (Down) §102 Car. I	1641
7. Krickestowne al. Evene-Irishtowne al. Ballygealagh	Inq. Ult. (Down) §102 Car. I	1641
8. Irishtown	Will (Sav. Ards) 192	1655
9. Ballygelagh	Census 91	1659
10. Irishtowne	BSD 85	1661
11. Irishtowne al. Ballygealagh	Inq. Ult. (Down) §19 Car. II	1661

12. Irishtown	Sub. Roll Down 16	1663
13. Irishtowne	Hib. Del.	1672c
14. Ballygelagh	Wm. Map (OSNB)	1810
15. Ballygeloch	High Const. Applot. (OSNB)	1830
16. Ballygelagh	Bnd. Sur. (OSNB)	1830
17. Baile Gaedhlach "Irish Town"	J O'D (OSNB)	1834c
18. ˌbɑliˈgeːlɑx	Local pronunciation	1991
19. ˌbaliˈgiːlə	Local pronunciation	1991

This name, like that of **Whitechurch** (par. Ballywalter), is extremely interesting in that we have evidence of its existence in three different languages. In the 19th century it is consistently *Ballygelagh*, which reflects an Irish *Baile Gaelach* "Irish, or Gaelic, town", while in the 17th century we see both the anglicized *Ballygealagh* and an English form *Irishtowne*, as in forms 2–8, 10–13. *Joyce* (i 87) comments: "**Ballygelagh** in Down and Derry; *Baile-Gaodhlach*, Irish town, indicating that the natives kept, or were allowed to keep, possession of these places, where all around were peopled by Scotch settlers". However, the Latin form *Villae Hibernicorum*, "town of the Irishmen", from a document of the year 1305 (*EA* 168 n. p), would suggest that Joyce's view as regards the name originating among "Scotch settlers" is not to be accepted, at least in this particular case, as this name clearly dates back to the earlier Anglo-Norman period. *Census 1871* lists 20 or so *Irishtown*s for the whole of Ireland and a fuller examination of all these names will be necessary before we can comment authoritatively on the Ards name *Ballygelagh*. As the Ards name, however, dates from the Anglo-Norman period, and since we find *Irishtown* in 1559 (form 2), it is probable that the Irish-language form *Baile Gaelach* (suggested by 17th-century spelling resembling *Ballygel(l)agh*) may represent a translation of an original Anglo-Norman *Irishton*. We can, of course, compare other modern Ards place-names of the type **Ballyphilip**, **Ballyhalbert** etc., which we know to be derived from earlier *Feliptone* and *Talbetone* in the Papal Taxation of 1306. Compare also **Cookstown** below.

Ballyward — *Baile Bhaird* (?)
J 6055 — "Ward's townland"

1. Ballyward	PCR Eliz. I (Sav. Ards 175)	1559
2. Balleward	CPR Jas. I 340b	1617
3. Ballyward	Will (Sav. Ards) 192	1655
4. Ballyward	Census 91	1659
5. Ballyward	BSD 85	1661
6. Balliward	Sub. Roll Dn 16	1663
7. Ballyward	Wm. Map (OSNB)	1810
8. Ballyward	Bnd. Sur. (OSNB)	1830c
9. Baile Bháird "Ward's Town"	J O'D (OSNB)	1834c
10. ˌbaliˈward	Local pronunciation	1991

This name is difficult to penetrate with any degree of certainty. If it were to represent an Irish original, we might expect either *Baile an Bhaird* "the townland of the bard, or poet", or *Baile Mhic an Bhaird* "Mac an Bhaird's townland", which contains the Gaelic surname *Mac an Bhaird*, i.e. "the son of the bard", a surname which is variously anglicized MacEward, Ward etc. However none of the anglicized forms shows any sign of an Irish definite article *an* "of the", or *Mac an* of the surname *Mac an Bhaird*. We must also bear in mind that the surname *Ward(e)* also occurs in English surnames from the early Anglo-Norman period, and Reaney (1958:348), who lists many examples of this name in England from 1194 onwards, connects the English surname *Ward(e)* with Old English *weard* "watching, guarding" and suggests that *Ward*, in this latter context, would mean "Watchman".

Ballyward, then, may in fact go back to an earlier Anglo-Norman **Wardeston*. Anderson (1979:21) draws attention to the surname Ward listed in *Survey Estate Rolls 1775–6*, but it is difficult to connect these Wards with original Anglo-Norman settlers. Indeed the origin of *Ballyward*, whether Gaelic or Anglo-Norman, still remains uncertain.

Cookstown
J 6058

Baile Chócaire
"Cook's townland"

1. Cookestown	PCR Eliz. I (Sav. Ards) 175	1559
2. Cokestown al. Ballicokeris	Inq. Ult. (Down) §5 Jac. I	1617
3. Cookeston orse Ballekokere	CPR Jas I 340b	1617
4. Cookstown	Will (Sav. Ards) 192	1655
5. Cookstowne	Hib. Reg., Ards	1657c
6. Cookstowne	Census 91	1659c
7. Cookestowne	BSD 85	1661
8. Cookestowne al. Ballycockery	Inq. Ult. (Down) §19 Car. II	1662
9. Cookstown	Map, Petty's Sur. (OSNB)	1683
10. Cookstown	Wm. Map (OSNB)	1810
11. Cookstown	High Const. Applot. (OSNB)	1830c
12. Cookstown	Bnd. Sur. (OSNB)	1830c
13. 'kukstən	Local pronunciation	1991
14. 'ku:kz 'tɔun	Local pronunciation	1991

This townland appears to reflect an original Anglo-Norman surname *Cook*, and the 17th-century alias forms (2, 3, 8) indicate that the name had a Gaelic version *Baile Chócaire* "townland of Cook". The surname *Cook* was common in Anglo-Norman Britain, judging by Reaney (1958:76). For Anglo-Norman *Cook* in Ireland we may cite mention of a "John Cook" in Co. Louth in a Pipe Roll from 18 Edward II (c. 1325 AD) – *42 Rept DKPRI* (1909) p. 64.

It is interesting to note that, in the 17th century, this townland name and the neighbouring townland of **Ballygealagh** showed variance between original Anglo-Norman **Cookston* and **Irishton*, and the gaelicized *Baile Chócaire* and *Baile Gaedhealach*. However, by the time of the early 19th century we see that *Ballygelagh* had dropped its original Anglo-Norman form and adopted its gaelicized form, whereas *Cookstown* discarded its gaelicized form to retain its Anglo-Norman original.

Dunevly
J 6155

Dún Eichmhílidh
"Eichmhíleadh's fort"

1. (?) Dún Eathlaigh	Descendants Ir 352 4	1200c
2. Ballydonyvill	Fiants Eliz. §5264	1588
3. (?) Downe ¼ of a townland	Inq. Ult. (Down) §5 Jac. I	1617
4. Downeally	Inq. Ult. (Down) §14 Jac. I	1625

5. Donnely	Inq. Ult. (Down) §14 Jac. I	1625
6. (?) Doneruly	Inq. Ult. (Down) §10 Car. I	1627
7. Donevley	Sav. Ards 369	1628
8. Downevely	Inq. Ult. (Down) §78 Car. I	1637
9. Dunnevally	Sav. Ards 373	1637c
10. Donneuilly	Hib. Reg., Ards	1657c
11. Dunevally	Census 91	1659c
12. Dunevilly	BSD 85	1661
13. Dunevelly	Inq. Ult. (Down) §19 Car. II	1662
14. (?) Dunevily al. Rosemount Park	ASE 170b §36	1668
15. Dunevly	Wm. Map (OSNB)	1810
16. Dunavely	High Const. Applot. (OSNB)	1830c
17. Dunevly	Bnd. Sur. (OSNB)	1830c
18. Dún Eichmhilidh "Echvily's dun or fort"	J O'D (OSNB)	1834c
19. do̤'nɛvlı	Local pronunciation	1991
20. do̤'nɑvəlı	Local pronunciation	1991

In her article "The history of the descendants of Ir" (*ZCP* 13), Dobbs discussed material from Irish genealogies among which occurred (pp.350–3) material relating to Eochaidh and Cumasach (two sons of Dunchadh) who were apparently blessed by Fintan of Movilla (d.580) and Bec mac Dé (*c.* d.557). Dobbs was unable to identify the Eochaidh in question but in the text Bec is reported to have made a short prophecy concerning Eochaidh and in these quatrains of prophecy, according to Dobbs' reading, mention is made of a place-name *Dún Eathlaigh*. Dobbs (p. 353, n. 1) identifies this as Dunevly, but she points out that the manuscript readings vary on this. If *Dún Eathlaigh* can be accepted, although other manuscripts have *Eachlaigh*, then it would appear that a personal name *Eathlach* (or even *Eachlach*) was reinterpreted, or attracted at a later point to another Gaelic personal name *Eichmhíleadh*. John O'Donovan states (*OSNB*) that the name "Echvily was common among the Magennis family". O'Brien (*CGH* 161 bc 49, 51, 53) provides a genealogy of the *Uí Echach* tribe, a tribe whose name survives in the modern barony name of *Iveagh*, in the south of Co. Down, and in this latter genealogy we note three members with the name *Echmíled* The personal name *Eichmhíleadh* (which means "horse-warrior" from *each* "horse" + *míleadh* "warrior") seems to satisfy the later anglicized spellings and the local pronunciation of this place-name. However, more research will be required on the manuscript copies of the genealogical material before the supposed original *Dún Eathlaigh*, or *Dún Eachlaidh* can be either confirmed or rejected.

Kirkistown — "Kirk(e)'s townland"

J 6358

1. the lough of Keirgescon	Inq. Ult. (Down) §2 Jac. I	1605
2. stagn' de Keirgescon	Inq. Ult. (Down) §2 Jac. I	1605
3. Keirgeston, the lough of	CPR Jas I 73b	1605
4. Kirchestowne	Inq. Ult. (Down) §5 Jac. I	1617
5. Kirkiston	CPR Jas I 340b	1617
6. Kirgestowne	Ham. Copy Inq. xxx	1623
7. Kirckston	Inq. Ult. (Down) §27 Car. I	1631

8. Kirkston	Inq. Ult. (Down) §27 Car. I	1631
9. Kirkistone	Will (Sav. Ards) 247	1640
10. Kirkestowne	Inq. Ult. (Down) §101 Car. I	1641
11. Krickestowne	Inq. Ult. (Down) §102 Car. I	1641
12. Krickestowne al. Evene-Irishtown al. Ballygealagh	Inq. Ult. (Down) §102 Car. I	1641
13. Kirkestowne	Inq. Ult. (Down) §103 Car. I	1641
14. Kirkystowne	Hib. Reg., Ards	1657c
15. Kirkestown	Census 91	1659c
16. Kirkestowne	BSD 85	1661
17. Kirkestowne	Inq. Ult. (Down) §11 Car. II	1662
18. Kirkiston	Inq. Ult. (Down) §19 Car. II	1662
19. Kirkstowne	Hib. Del. Ulster	1672c
20. Kirkestown	Descr. Ards 35, 36	1683
21. Kirkstown	Descr. Ards 41	1683
22. Kirkstowne	Map, Petty's Sur. (OSNB)	1683
23. Kirkistowne	Lamb Maps Co. Down	1690c
24. Kirkistown alias Eren Castle	Sav. Ards 198	1701
25. Kirkistown alias Erew Castle	Sav. Ards 199	1701
26. Kirkistown	Wm. Map (OSNB)	1810
27. Kirkistown	Bnd. Sur. (OSNB)	1830c
28. ˈkɩrkəstən	Local pronunciation	1991
29. ˈkə(:)rkəsən	Local pronunciation	1991
30. ˈkergəs ˈtɔun	Local pronunciation	1991

It seems likely that the *Kirkis-* element refers to an Anglo-Norman surname. According to Reaney (1958:191) *Kirk, Kirke* etc. is a surname signifying "dweller at the church" and, in England, he cites Reginald *Attekierke* 1209 AD, "at the kirk", and Adam *Ofthekirke* 1308 etc. Although we have not, as yet, uncovered any evidence of an Anglo-Norman surname *Kirk* in the Ards, the townland of *Kirkistown* (parish Ballyrashane, Co. Derry) occurs as *Kyrketon* in 1308 (Orpen *JRSAI* xlv (1915) 139, n. 2) and this, albeit indirect, evidence would suggest that the *Kirk-* element in *Kirkistown* (par. Ardkeen) represents an Anglo-Norman surname. In *AU* 1510 AD there is mention of a "Bearnabhlach Circistóun", i.e. Barnwell of Circistown which MacCarthy (*AU* p. 494, n. 8) identifies as a place in Co. Meath, modern *Creektown* or *Crikstown*, described in *Lewis' Top. Dict.* s.v.

Seemingly, then, we can add *Kirkistown* to **Cookstown** (above) as one of the relatively few place-names in the Upper Ards containing an original Anglo-Norman name + *to(w)n* which has not been replaced by a gaelicized form, along the lines of *Ballyphilip*, *Ballyhalbert*, etc. For an example of an earlier Anglo-Norman name resisting gaelicization in the Lower Ards see **Hogstown** (parish of Donaghadee).

The castle at Kirkistown was erected by Rowland Savage in 1622. A description of this castle in the 17th century is given in *Descr. Ards* 36, and further descriptions are contained in *Harris Hist.* 67, *ASCD* 238–41 and *Sav. Ards* 252, especially 256 which describes its occupation until 1731 and its desertion. By Knox's day, 1875, the castle was in the possession of Mr. Hugh Montgomery, the previous occupant being a Colonel Johnston, and it had evidently undergone some form of renovation: "When recently paying a visit to the place I found the castle in wonderfully good condition, repairs having been effected from time to time by the Montgomery family" (*Knox Hist* 465).

Lisbane — *Lios Bán*
J 6057 — "white fort"

1.	Ballylisbane	PCR Eliz. I (Sav. Ards) 175	1559
2.	Lisbane, Rowland Savadge of	Fiants Eliz. §5590	1591
3.	Ballylissbane	Inq. Ult. (Down) §5 Jac. I	1617
4.	Ballylisbane	CPR Jas I 340b	1617
5.	Lisbane	Will (Sav. Ards) 192	1655
6.	Lisbue	Hib. Reg., Ards	1657c
7.	Lisbane	Census 91	1659c
8.	Lisbur al. Lisbanne	BSD 85	1661
9.	Ballylisbane	Inq. Ult. (Down) §19 Car. II	1662
10.	Lisbane	Wm. Map (OSNB)	1810
11.	Lisban	High Const. Applot. (OSNB)	1830c
12.	Lisbane	Bnd. Sur. (OSNB)	1830c
13.	Lios Bán "white fort"	J O'D (OSNB)	1834c
14.	ˌlɪsˈbɑːn	Local pronunciation	1991

This is a fairly straightforward name and, while there is no earthwork marked on the OS six-inch maps, *ASCD* 171 points out that aerial photography reveals the remains of an earthwork "squarish in plan with rounded corners with a single bank and ditch" in the south of the townland. See also **Lisbane** (parish of Bangor).

Ratallagh — *Ráth tSaileach*
J 6458 — "fort of the willow"

1.	Ratalla	Inq. Ult. (Down) §5 Jac. I	1617
2.	Ratala	CPR Jas I 340b	1617
3.	Rathalla	Inq. Ult. (Down) §27 Car. I	1631
4.	Rathallow	Inq. Ult. (Down) §101 Car. I	1641
5.	Rathallowe	Inq. Ult. (Down) §102 Car. I	1641
6.	Rathalloe	Inq. Ult. (Down) §103 Car. I	1641
7.	Rathalla	Inq. Ult. (Down) §103 Car. I	1641
8.	Ratalla	Will (Sav. Ards) 192	1655
9.	Ratallo	Hib. Reg., Ards	1657c
10.	Rattallo	BSD 85	1661
11.	Rottallagh	Inq. Ult. (Down) §11 Car. II	1662
12.	Rattallagh	Inq. Ult. (Down) §11 Car. II	1662
13.	Ratalla	Inq. Ult. (Down) §19 Car. II	1662
14.	Rattala	Sub. Roll Down 282	1663
15.	Rattall	Map, Petty's Sur. (OSNB)	1683
16.	Rattallagh	Wm. Map (OSNB)	1810
17.	Ratalla	High Const. Applot. (OSNB)	1830c
18.	Ratallagh	Bnd. Sur. (OSNB)	1830c
19.	Rath tSaileach "fort of the willows"	J O'D (OSNB)	1834c
20.	rəˈtɑlə	Local pronunciation	1991

O'Donovan's suggestion of *Ráth tSaileach* "fort of the willows" seems as likely as any other, although we might also consider *Ráth Salach* "dirty fort". Hogan (*Onom. Goed.* 577) lists both a *Ráith Saileach* (Fanad, Co. Donegal) and a *Ráith Salach* (Co. Wicklow). The *-t*-sound in the name is presumably due to the *-th* in *Ráth* being delenited before the following *S-*.

OTHER NAMES

Bird Island J 5661	An English form	
1. Bird Island	Wm. Map (OSNB)	1810
2. ðə 'bɩrd 'ailən	Local pronunciation	1991

Our earliest reference to this island is in the *OSNB*, where it is described as "... rocky pastureland". It would appear to have been named from the birds which frequent it.

Blackstaff River — See parish of Inishargy
J 6159

Calf Island J 5363	An English form	
1. the Calfe island	CPR Jas. I 340b	1617
2. the Calfe island	Inq. Ult. (Down) §19 Car. II	1662
3. Calf Island	Harris Hist.	1744
4. Calf Island	Wm. Map (OSNB)	1810
5. ðə 'kɑf 'ailən	Local pronunciation	1991

This place probably received its name from the practice of grazing calves here, a tradition which dates back to at least 1617 (form 1), and one which continued into the last century, judging by the remarks in *OSNB* (par. Killinchy p. 36): "Pasture land, uninhabited and is about 1100 yards from the mainland, belongs to the parish of Ardkeen in the Ards Barony".

Conly Island J 5360	*Oileán Uí Chonghaile* (?) "Connolly's island"	
1. Island-connolly	Inq. Ult. (Down) §5 Jac. I	1617
2. Island-conly	Inq. Ult. (Down) §19 Car. II	1662
3. Connely-Isle	Harris Hist. 154	1744
4. 'kɔnli 'ailən	Local pronunciation	1991

Forms 1 and 2 strongly suggest an original Irish name *Oileán* "island" + qualifier, possibly a personal name or a descriptive feature. The family name Connolly is popular on the western shore of Strangford Lough but a definite origin is difficult to propose based solely on the present fairly limited evidence.

Craigaveagh Rock J 5361	*Creag na bhFiach* "rock of the ravens".	
1. Craigaveagh Island	Wm. Map (OSNB)	1810
2. Craigavey Rock	Wm. Map (OSNB)	1810
3. Craig na bhFiach "rock of the ravens"	J O'D (OSNB)	1834

4. Craig a Bheithe "rock of the birch"	J O'D (OSNB)	1834
5. kriəgˈva ˈrɔks	Local pronunciation	1991

In the *OSNB* (par. Killinchy p. 38) this island is described as: "A narrow rocky island ... uninhabited and belongs to the parish of Ardkeen".

Of the two suggestions offered by O'Donovan in the *OSNB* the suggestion "rock of the birch" (form 4) is rejected in favour of the seemingly more likely "rock of the ravens" (form 3), where *fiach*, normally "raven", may even be taken as an example of unqualified *fiach mara* "cormorant", literally "sea-raven".

Deer Park
J 5965

An English form

Local pronunciation [di:r ˈpɑrk]. According to Mr John Donaldson, born Thomastown townland and recorded in 1990, this place was so called because "they used to rear deer in it".

The Dorn
J 5965

An Dorn
"the fist"

Local pronunciation [ðə ˈdɔrn]. Harris (*Harris Hist.* 48) describes *The Dorn* as the "Site of a house built by Hugh Savage Esq. who found the dwelling at Ardkeen too exposed" and continues further on that the house was "on the Shore of a little narrow Bog formed here by the Lough called the *Dorn*, perhaps from the Resemblance it bears to the haft of a sword, which the Word signifies in *Irish*". This meaning is repeated in *Sav. Ards* 288, but it is also possible that *The Dorn* is to be understood as "the fist", or "fist(-shaped) area", the primary meaning of *dorn* in Irish.

Drummond Island
J 5560

Oileán an Dromáin
"the island of the little ridge"

1. Dromon	CPR Jas I 340b	1617
2. Iland-dromond	Inq. Ult. (Down) §5 Jac. I	1617
3. Ilandroman	Inq. Ult. (Down) §27 Car. I	1631
4. Illandroman	Inq. Ult. (Down) §102 Car. I	1641
5. Illandromane	Inq. Ult. (Down) §102 Car. I	1641
6. Island-droman	Inq. Ult. (Down) §19 Car. II	1662
7. Drumon-Isle	Harris Hist. 154	1744
8. Drumon	Harris Hist. 2	1744
9. Drummond Island	Wm. Map (OSNB)	1810
10. Drumond	Wm. Map (OSNB)	1810
11. Oileán an Dromainn "the island of the ridge"	J O'D (OSNB)	1834
12. Drumann "a ridge"	J O'D (OSNB)	1834
13. ðə ˈdromən ˈailn̥	Local pronunciation	1991

The early spellings of this name point to Irish *oileán* "island" + either *dromán* or *dromann*, both derivative forms of Irish *droim* "back > back-shaped ridge".

Inishanier Island	*Inis an Fhéir*	
J 5461	"the island of the grass"	
1. the Grass island	CPR Jas I 340b	1617
2. Grass-iland, the iland called	Inq. Ult. (Down) §5 Jac I	1617
3. Grasse-iland	Inq. Ult. (Down) §19 Car. II	1662
4. Inisinair Island	Wm. Map (OSNB)	1810
5. Inisineir	Wm. Map (OSNB)	1810
6. Inishanier Island	OSNB	1830c
7. Inishanear	Post Chaise Comp. (OSNB)	1834c
8. Inishanear	OSNB	1834c
9. Inis a niar "western island"	J O'D (OSNB)	1834c
10. ˌɪnʃənˈiːr	Local pronunciation	1991

Because of the geographical location of this island, and several others in the parish, on the western shore of Strangford Lough, it is hardly surprising that these very westerly islands in the parish of Ardkeen were also treated in the volumes of the *OSNB* dealing with mainland parishes on the western shore, such as Killinchy parish, and as a result one often finds an island referred to both in the name-book for Killinchy parish and that for Ardkeen. In the case of anglicized *Inishanier* John O'Donovan (*OSNB* Ardkeen) recommended the spelling *Inisanier*, but a later hand reminded him: "You made this *Inishanier* in Killinchy [*OSNB*]".

Leaving aside the modern anglicized map form of the name, and turning to O'Donovan's suggestion of "western island" for *Inishanier*, we can safely dismiss this suggestion in the light of the 17th-century forms in *Grass island* (forms 1–3). These latter forms strongly suggest that modern *Inishanier* goes back to an earlier Irish-language form *Inis an Fhéir* "island of the grass". It is difficult to determine whether the early 17th-century form *Grass Island*, or the like, represents the original form of the name or whether it is an English translation of an original Irish-language form *Inis an Fhéir*.

There is no evidence of human settlement here and in the early nineteenth century the island is described as "Pasture land uninhabited it belongs to the Barony of Ards being part of the Parish of Ardkeen" (*OSNB* Killinchy, p. 37).

Inisharoan Island	*Inis an Róin*	
J 5461	"island of the seal"	
1. Inishe-anroyne	Inq. Ult. (Down) §5 Jac. I	1617
2. Inishanrow	CPR Jas I 340b	1617
3. Inishe-auroyne	Inq. Ult. (Down) §19 Car. II	1662
4. Aroan-Isle	Harris Hist. 154	1744
5. Inisharoan Island	Wm. Map (OSNB)	1810
6. Inisharoan	OSNB	1834
7. Inis an Róin "island of the seal"	J O'D (OSNB)	1834c
8. ˌinʃəˈroːn	Local pronunciation	1991

The Irish form of this name appears quite easy to restore. This island is described in the *OSNB* for Killinchy parish (p. 37): "Pastureland, uninhabited and belongs to the Barony of Ards being part of the Parish of Ardkeen".

Islandabreen
J 6360

Oileán Uí Bhraoin (?)
"Breen's island-hill"

There are no earlier spellings available for this name, but the tentative suggestion of a link with the surname *Breen* is made on the basis of Anderson (1981: 3) who lists it as "the twentieth most numerous surname in the Upper Ards".

Islandgorm
J6459

An tOileán Gorm
"the blue island-hill"

This feature refers to a hill on dry land: "the island or hill called Islandgorm in the Great Ards" *CPR Jas I* 73a, c. 1605 AD. For a discussion of the use in place-names of Irish *oileán* and its corresponding English term *island* to describe such a feature, particularly on dry land in what is, or once was, a boggy area, see Ó Mainnín (1989–90).

Knowehead
J 6359

An English/Scots form

Local pronunciation [ˈnɔu ˈhed]. No documentation is available but we can take the first element as *Knowe* "hill", and compare a similar minor name in this parish *Hillhead.*

Long Island
J 5857

An English form

1. Long Island	Wm. Map (OSNB)	1810

This island appears to be named from its shape. There is no evidence of settlement here and it is described thus in 1830s: "Contains 5 acres, 0 roods, 37 perches (of) rocky pasture land". *OSNB.*

Long Sheelah
J 5658

A hybrid form

Local pronunciation [ˈlɔŋ ˈʃi:ləz]. The term *Sheelagh* occurs quite frequently in Strangford Lough (cf. for example **Sheelah's Island** and **South Sheelagh's Island** parish of Inishargy) and it appears to apply to rocks or a reef below the surface of the water. It would be unwise, however, to conjecture on the etymology of this term without some further comparative studies of the island names from other regions which may contain this element.

Lythe Rock
J 5363

A Scots/English form

1. Lythe Rock	Bnd. Sur. (OSNB)	1830c
2. Lythe: popular name	J O'D (OSNB)	1834c
3. ˈlaið ˈrɔk	Local pronunciation	1991

In the *OSNB* "Lythe" is listed as a "popular [family?] name". It seems likely, however, that *lythe* refers to a species of fish, see *Scot. Nat. Dict.* s.v where it is rendered "pollack". It is also noteworthy that "lythes" are mentioned among the fish plentiful off the Ards in William Montgomery's *Descr. Ards* 24.

Minnis's Island Great	*Mion-ais Mhór*	
J 5560	"little ridge(-shaped island), great"	
1. two Mynisses	Inq. Ult. (Down) §5 Jac. I	1617
2. lez 2 Monassies al. Little rocks	Inq. Ult. (Down) §27 Car. I	1631
3. le 2 Monashes	Inq. Ult. (Down) §102 Car. I	1641
4. les 2 Miniss'	Inq. Ult. (Down) §19 Car. II	1662
5. Minnes-South-Isle	Harris Hist. 154	1744
6. Minis Island	Wm. Map (OSNB) No. 44	1810
7. Minnses Little	Bnd. Sur. (OSNB)	1830c
8. Minnis's Island	J O'D (OSNB)	1834c
9. ðə 'litl̥ 'mïnəsəz	Local pronunciation	1991
10. ðə 'griət 'mïnəsəz	Local pronunciation	1991

The 1631 forms "lez 2 Monassies al. Little Rocks" would appear to be a translation of Irish *Mion-ais* "little ridge", or "little ridge(-shaped island)", from *mion* "small" and *ais* "back, ridge". There is not much documentation available for these islands although the following description is found in *OSNB* (Killinchy par. p. 40): "Little Minnis's ... is about 160 yards north of the great Minnes, they are connected by a rocky bank which is fordable at low water".

Minnis's Island Little — *Mion-ais Bheag*
J 5560 — "little ridge(-shaped island), little"

Needoo — *An Nead Dubh* (?)
J 5758 — "the black nest"

Local pronunciation [nə'du]. There is no written evidence available for this name although it may possibly represent an Irish original *An Nead Dubh* "the black nest". It should be stressed, however, that this suggestion is tentative in the extreme.

Old Man's Head — An English form
J 5756

Local pronunciation ['əul 'mɑnz 'hed]. No evidence of earlier written forms, but it would appear to be named from the similarity of its shape to an old man's head.

Parton Island	*Oileán Partán*	
J 5460	"island of the crabs"	
1. the Partan-iland	Inq. Ult. (Down) §5 Jac. I	1617
2. Partan	Inq. Ult. (Down) §5 Jac. I	1617
3. the Partan island	CPR Jas I 340b	1617
4. Ilandpartan	CPR Jas I 587b	1624
5. Portan-iland	Inq. Ult. (Down) §27 Car. I	1631
6. Partane	Inq. Ult. (Down) §102 Car. I	1641
7. le Partan-illand	Inq. Ult. (Down) §102 Car. I	1641
8. the Partan-island	Inq. Ult. (Down) §19 Car. II	1662
9. Parton Island	Wm. Map (OSNB)	1810
10. Parton Island	Bnd. Sur. (OSNB)	1830c
11. Parton Island	J O'D (OSNB)	1834
12. 'pɑrtən 'ailn̥	Local pronunciation	1991

The form *Ilandpartan* from 1624 (no. 4) strongly indicates an Irish form *Oileán Partán* "island of (the) crabs". The anglicized spellings in *Parton* and *Partan* indicate that *partán* was the Co. Down Irish word for "crab" as opposed to modern standardized *portán*, as listed in Ó Dónaill. In actual fact the change of Irish *Oileán Partán*, or anglicized *Ilandpartan*, to modern *Parton Island* may indicate that the Irish element *partán* in this name was understood as "crab" by 17th-century English, or Scots speakers. *Partan* "crab" occurs in Scots and certain English dialects and *DIL* (s.v. *partán*) points out that the Scots and English dialect word *partan* was taken by the *OED* to be a borrowing from Celtic.

In the *OSNB* (Killinchy parish p. 40) the island is desribed as follows: "Pastureland, is uninhabited and belongs to the Parish of Ardkeen"

Peeltown — An English form
J 6157

This appears to be named from a member of the Peel family, although information is difficult to find.

Phersons Island — A Scots/English form
J 5956

Pherson's Island was taken as containing a surname by Anderson (1979:4), whereas in another article Anderson (1981:5) mentions the settlement of Ellisons, now confined to Portaferry and 36th most popular name in Ards, who were a branch of the Clan Mac Pherson, Invernesshire. Further information is needed on the Phersons who gave their name to this island.

Rainey Island — *Ré-inis* (?) "island of the level piece of ground"
J 5362

1. Raynche	EA 193	1178
2. Raynche	Charts Nendrum 193	1180c
3. Rannys	Inq. Ult. (Down) §1 Jac. I	1605
4. the island of Ranish called the Calfe-iland	Inq. Ult. (Down) §5 Jac. I	1617
5. Ranisse-iland	Inq. Ult. (Down) §5 Jac. I	1617
6. Ilandrenish	CPR Jas I 587b	1624
7. insul' de Ranish	Inq. Ult. (Down) §19 Car. II	1662
8. Ranish Island	Wm. Map (OSNB)	1810
9. Rainey Island	Bnd. Sur. (OSNB)	1830c
10. Oileán na Raithnighe i.e. "ferny island"	J O'D (OSNB)	1834c
11. ˈriənɪ	Local pronunciation	1991

It is difficult to propose a meaning for this name with any degree of certainty. The 17th-century forms resembling *Ranis(h)* (nos. 3–8) might suggest *Raithinis* "fern-island", i.e. *raith* "fern" + *inis* "island", which would tie in with O'Donovan's suggestion (no. 10). However, as the early forms *Raynche* (nos. 1 & 2) date from the late 12th century one would expect to find a trace of the *-th* if *raith* "fern" is contained in the name. One possibility might be *Ré-inis* "island of the level piece of ground", based on early Irish *róe* "level piece of ground"

(*DIL*) + *inis* "island". The word *róe* is found in modern dictionaries: as *rae* in *Dinneen*, and *rae* and *ré* in *Ó Dónaill* where it is given the meaning "stretch of ground, level ground". No mention of settlement of this island occurs in *ASCD*, but *OSNB* (Killinchy par. p. 36) records: "Arable with some wood. There are three dwellings on this island. The island belongs to the parish of Ardkeen".

Rig Pladdy — A Scots form?
J 5563

Local pronunciation ['rïg 'pladi]. On the element *pladdy* "a sunken flat rock" see **McCammon's Pladdy** in the parish of Inishargy.

Ringboy — *An Rinn Bhuí*
Ringboy Point — "the yellow promontory"
J 6458, J 6557

Local pronunciation [rɪŋ 'bɔi]. The addition of *Point* to *Ringboy* is obviously a later addition to Irish *Rinn Bhuí*, from *rinn* "promontory, point, headland" + *buí* "yellow".

Roe Island — *An tOileán Rua*
J 5460 — "the red island"

1.	Iland-roee	Inq. Ult. (Down) §5 Jac. I	1617
2.	Roe-iland	Inq. Ult. (Down) §5 Jac. I	1617
3.	Ilandroe	CPR Jas I 587b	1624
4.	Iland-roe	Inq. Ult. (Down) §27 Car. I	1631
5.	Illandroe	Inq. Ult. (Down) §102 Car. I	1641
6.	Illanroe	Inq. Ult. (Down) §102 Car. I	1641
7.	the Iland-roe	Inq. Ult. (Down) §19 Car. I	1662
8.	Roe Isle	Harris Hist. 154	1744
9.	Roe Island	Wm. Map (OSNB)	1810
10.	Roe Island	Bnd. Sur. (OSNB)	1830c
11.	Ruadh-oileán "red island"	J O'D (OSNB)	1834c
12.	'ro: 'ailn̥	Local pronunciation	1991

The earlier forms of this name point to a word order *Oileán Rua*, i.e. "red island" rather than O'Donovan's *Rua-oileán* (no. 11). It may even be that the *-roe(e)* element represents a noun, i.e. *Oileán Ruaidhe* "island of the redness", or the like. In the *OSNB* (Killinchy parish p. 39) Roe Island is described as "Arable land ... uninhabited, it belongs to the parish of Ardkeen".

Round Island — An English form
J 5756

In the *OSNB* there was some hesitation as to whether this was called "Horse", or "Round Island". Round Island is more than likely named from its fairly round shape. However, the lack of early written forms demands caution, *Roundstone*, Co. Galway, for example goes back to an Irish form *Cloch na Rón* "stone of the seals" where Irish *rón* "seal" has been reinterpreted as English *round*. For *rón* on the other side of Strangford Lough cf. **Inisharoan** in this parish.

Saltwalter Bridge A Scots/English form
J 6059

This is officially spelt as *Saltwater Bridge* but it is pronounced both as ['salt wɑ:tər 'brïdʒ] *Saltwater Bridge* and ['salt wɑtər 'brɪg], i.e. *Saltwater Brig*. The *Brig* version of the name represents the Scots version for, according to *Scot. Nat. Dict.*, *brig* is "the general Scottish form of English *bridge*".

Seneschal's Port An English form

This name is not on the 1:50,000 map, but owes its origin to a member of the Savage family who held the office of seneschal. The seneschal was an agent or bailiff in charge of a lord's estate in medieval times.

> A little Bay under the Castle Hill of Ardkeen is still known as 'Seneschal's Port' and is so marked on the Ordnance Map. Whether it took its name from this SIR ROBERT SAVAGE [i.e. the Sir Robert appointed Seneschal of Ulster by Edward III in the mid–14th cent.], the Seneschal, or whether it received it a later period we are unable to say. (*Sav. Ards* 134, n. 2)

Sketrick Island *Oileán Scathdeirge*
J 5265 "red-pointed island" (?)

1.	Caislén Sgath Deircce	AFM iv 1066	1470
2.	Scatra	EA 193	1178
3.	Skaterig	Mercator's Ulst.	1595
4.	Skatterick in le Duffrin	Inq. Ult. (Down) §2 Jac. I	1605
5.	Skatericke in the Dufferin	CPR Jas I 73b	1605
6.	Scatrick, the Castle of	Terrier (Reeves) 55	1615c
7.	the castle and land of Skaterick	Inq. Ult. (Down) §5 Jac. I	1617
8.	Ballygaban al. Scatriek-iland	Inq. Ult. (Down) §5 Jac. I	1617
9.	Iland-skatrick	Inq. Ult. (Down) §5 Jac. I	1617
10.	the castle and island of Scatrick	CPR Jas I 340b	1617
11.	Ballegavan al. Scatterick	Ham. Copy Inq. xlvii	1623
12.	Satterick [sic.]	Ham. Copy Inq. xxx	1623
13.	Ballygaven otherwise Scatrick otherwise Tillyneagh otherwise Tullynoagh	CPR Jas I 587b	1624
14.	Ilandscatrick	CPR Jas I 587b	1624
15.	Scatericks	Raven Map Clandeboye 55	1625c
16.	Skaterick (Mc Savage)	Raven Map Clandeboye 60	1625c
17.	Scetrick, the Castle of	Will (Sav. Ards) 192	1655
18.	castr' & insul' de Skaterick	Inq. Ult. (Down) §19 Car. II	1662
19.	Scatrick, Castle called	Descr. Ards 35	1683
20.	Sketrick	Sav. Ards 198	1701
21.	Scatrick Island	Wm. Map (OSNB)	1810
22.	Sketrick Island	Bnd. Sur. (OSNB)	1830c
23.	Sgáth Dearg "red shadow or shelter"	J O'D (OSNB)	1834c

24. 'skɑtrɪk 'ailənd	Local pronunciation	1991
25. 'skïtrik ailn	Local pronunciation	1991

The form *Caislén Sgath Deircce* in the *Annals of the Four Masters* was referred to by John O'Donovan in the *OSNB* and formed the basis of his translation "red shadow or shelter". However, the pronunciation, with stress on the initial syllable would not tend to support this origin. It also appears that the vowel in *Sketrick*, *Scatrick,* etc. is a short *a* vowel; it is also spelt with a short *a* in *AFM* (no. 1). One possibility might be a compound of *scoth,* which is listed in *DIL* (s.v. 2 *scoth*) as "point edge" + *dearg* "red", thus "red-pointed" or "red-edged island", but this is a tentative suggestion. Indeed, one also wonders, in the light of the earliest attested form *Scatra* (no. 2), if the Gaelic form represents a reinterpretation of an underlying non-Gaelic name. More research is required here.

For fairly full descriptions of the castle, see *ASCD* 250–2 and *Sav. Ulst.* 334-5. For the island itself, cf. "Sketrick Island, arable and inhabited and connected with the mainland by a causeway ... There are the ruins of a castle on the east side of the island which was built to defend the ... of the island as well as for a stronghold. Belongs to the Parish of Ardkeen". *OSNB* (Killinchy par. p. 36).

Trasnagh Island — *Oileán Trasna*
J 5362 — "cross island"

1. Trasne	EA 193	1178
2. the Trashnagh-iland	Inq. Ult. (Down) §5 Jac. I	1617
3. Tranagh	CPR Jas I 340b	1617c
4. Irasnagh [r. Trasnagh ?]	Inq. Ult. (Down) §19 Car. II	1662
5. Transnaugh-Isle	Harris Hist. 154	1744
6. Trasnagh Island	Wm. Map (OSNB)	1810
7. Trasnagh Island	Bnd. Sur. (OSNB)	1830c
8. Oileán Trasna "cross island, transverse island"	J O'D (OSNB)	1834c

This island is described in the *OSNB* (Killinchy parish p. 37): "Arable and pasture land, is inhabited and belongs to ... the Parish of Ardkeen".

Tullybrick — *Tulaigh Bhric* (?)
J 6055 — "speckled hillock"

This is pronounced [tọli 'brik]. There are no early spellings for this name and while the first element is clearly Irish *tulaigh* "a hillock" the suggestion that second element is *bric*, a dative form of the adjective *breac*, is a tentative one.

PARISH OF ARDQUIN

O'Laverty describes the history of the parish from the early Anglo-Norman period onwards and attempts to link the initial founding of the church at Ardquin, for which we appear to have no pre-Norman historic record, with a St *Cú M(h)aighe*:

> The ancient church of Ardquin occupied the site of the Protestant church of Ardquin. In the Taxation of Pope Nicholas [*c.* 1306], it was valued under the name of 'The church of Ardquienne' at six marks. It was a mensal parish having been transmitted by the bishops probably from their predecessor St. Cowey, from whom the place seems to have been named Ardquin – the height of Cu (mhaighe) – and until the Disestablishment the greater part of the parish was held under the Protestant bishop, who was also the rector. (*O'Laverty* i 402).

The existence of a St Cú Mhaighe is to be implied from the local names **Loch Cowey** (this parish) and **Templecowey** and Cooey's Wells (par. Witter), although as O'Laverty remarks the historical record throws little, if any, light on this saint's career – see the discussion under **Ballyquintin** (par. Witter). The connection between St *Cú Mhaighe* and the name *Ardquin* is problematic and is discussed below under the PARISH NAME.

For a discussion of the parish in more recent times see *Lewis Top. Dict.* i 52–3, Ewart 1866: 38–9 and *OSM* vii 4.

PARISH NAME

Ardquin J 5854	*Ard Choinn* (?) "Conn's height"	
1. Arecum, In	Grant Ralph Bp. Down 165/6	1203c
2. Archiwhyn	EA 22 n.p.	1225
3. Ardwhum	Cartae Dun. 422 §10	1227c
4. Arwhum	EA 164	1235c
5. Arwhum	Cartae Dun. 422 §10	1235c
6. Ardwyn	Compotus Dun. 1305 168	1305
7. Ecclesia de Ardquienne	Eccles. Tax. 65	1306c
8. (?) Arkenan	Inq. Earl Ulster (EA) 360 n. g	1333
9. (?) Arkeuan	Inq. Earldom Ulster iii 65 n. 2	1333
10. Arweghun	Inq. Earldom Ulster iv 142	1333
11. Ardgune	Rot. Ant. Ecc. Dun. 171	1450c
12. Airrwgh whin	S-E Ulster Map	1580c
13. Arraugh whin	Mercator's Ire.	1595
14. Arrawghwhin	Mercator's Ulst.	1595
15. Ardquinn	Bartlett Map (Esch. Co. Maps) 1	1603
16. Argum	Norden's Map	1610c
17. Mo[nastery] Argum	Speed's Antrim & Down	1610
18. Ardwhin	Inq. Ult. (Down) §1 Jac.I	1605
19. Arechewen	Terrier (O' Laverty) 328	1615
20. Archewen	Terrier (Reeves) 59	1615
21. Ardquin	Terrier (O' Laverty) 319	1615
22. Ardquin, Maneriae, villae, et terrae	EA 174	1616

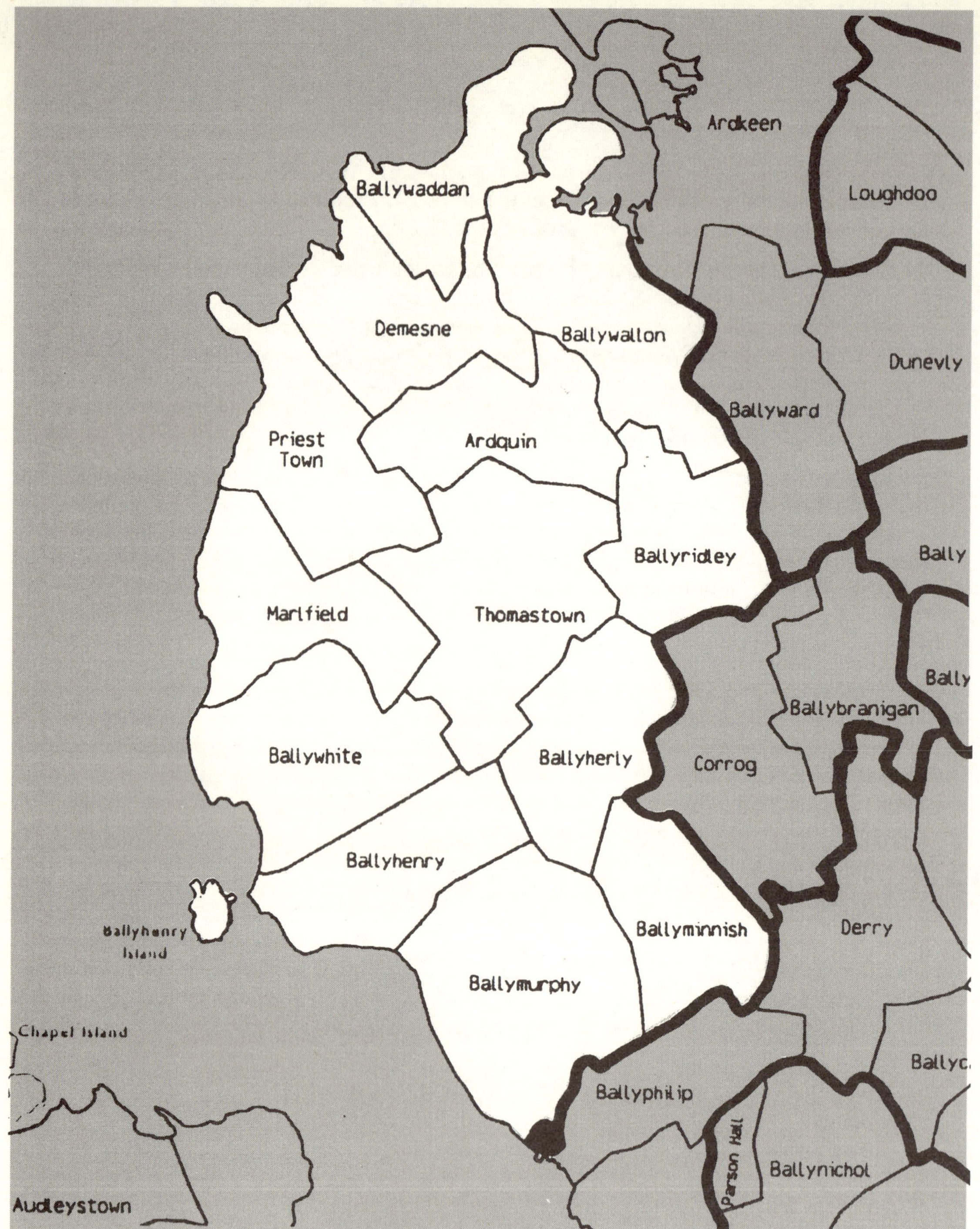

Parish of Ardquin

Barony of Ards Upper

Townlands
Ardquin
Ballyhenry
Ballyherly
Ballyminnish
Ballymurphy
Ballyridley
Ballywaddan
Ballywallon
Ballywhite
Demesne
Marlfield
Priest Town
Thomastown

Islands
Ballyhenry Island
Ballywallon Island

23. Ardwhyne	Inq. Down (Reeves 1) 133	1657
24. Ardvin	Hib. Reg. Ards	1657
25. Ardwhin	Census 91	1659
26. Ardquin	BSD 85	1661
27. Ardwhins	Sub. Roll Down 17	1663
28. Ardquin	Trien. Visit. (Margetson) 20	1664
29. ye old Abby of Arquin	Descr. Ards 35	1683
30. Arquin	Descr. Ards 36	1683
31. Ardvin	Lamb Maps Co. Down	1690c
32. Ardquin	Wm. Map (OSNB)	1810
33. Ardquin	Bnd. Sur. (OSNB)	1830c
34. Ard Cuinn "Altitudo Quinti, "Con' s height or hill"	J O'D (OSNB)	1834c
35. "The ancient name Ardquinne signifies 'Con's height'"	Ewart (1866: 38)	1866
36. Ardquin – the height of St. Cowey	O'Laverty i 402	1878
37. Ard-Chuinn [-cuin], "Conn's height"	Joyce iii 47	1913
38. ˌard'kwïn	Local pronunciation	1990

O'Donovan (*OSNB*), Reeves (*EA* 21–2, n. p), Ewart (1866: 38), Knox (*Knox Hist* 465) and *Joyce* (iii 47) all opt for *Ard Chuinn* "Con's height/hill", a meaning certainly supported by the modern form *Ardquin* although some of the early forms pose problems for such an interpretation. Indeed the early spellings of this name can be difficult to distinguish from Ardkeen, as has been stated in the section dealing with **Ardkeen**. Harris (*Harris Hist.* 47) suggested: "*Ardquin*, the name of this place, is a corrupted Word from Ard-Cuan, signifying a Heighth over the Lough of *Strangford*, formerly called Lough-Cuan, and the situation of the place corresponds herewith". While this latter suggestion is certainly not accurate, it is interesting to note that Deirdre Flanagan (in her personal copy of *EA*) has pencilled in *Ard Cuain*, at form 7, presumably "height of the harbour", or the like, but again this explanation is by no means free from difficulty. O'Laverty suggests a connection between *Ardquin* and St Cú Mhaighe (form no. 36) a form which would presumably have resembled *Ard Con* (from *Ard Con Maighe*), but again the early forms pose difficulty for this imaginative suggestion of O'Laverty's.

All things considered, then, it is difficult to propose a satisfactory etymology for this name.

TOWNLAND NAMES

Ballyhenry — *Baile Héinrí*

J 5851 — "Henry's townland"

1. Ballyhenry	Fiants Eliz. §2090	1571
2. Ballyhenrye	Savage Lands 3	1588
3. Ballyhenrye	Fiants Eliz. §5264	1588
4. Ballehenrie	Inq. Ult. (Down) §9 Jac. I	1620
5. Ballehenry	Inq. Ult. (Down) §10 Car. I	1627
6. Ballyhenry	Sav. Ards 368	1628
7. Ballyhenry	Sav. Ards 373	1637c
8. Ballyhenry	Will (Sav. Ards) 247	1640

9. Ballyhenry	Inq. Ult. (Down) §102 Car. I	1641
10. Ballyhenry	Census 91	1659c
11. Ballyhendry	BSD 86	1661
12. Ballihenry	Sub. Roll Down 282	1663
13. Ballyhendry point	Descr. Ards 34	1683
14. Ballyhindry	Forfeit. Estates 384b §16	1702
15. Ballyhendry	Forfeit. Estates 384b §16	1702
16. Ballyhenry	Wm. Map (OSNB)	1810
17. Ballyhenry	High Const. Applot. (OSNB)	1830c
18. Ballyhenry	Bnd. Sur. (OSNB)	1830c
19. Baile Enri "Henry's town"	J O'D (OSNB)	1834c
20. ˌbɑliˈhenrɩ	Local pronunciation	1990

Sav. Ards 326–7 (citing *O'Laverty*) mentions a surname "M'Henry" of Carrstown in the Ards. However, the *-henry* part of this townland name is more likely a christian name and indicates an original Anglo-Norman **Henry(s)ton* which was subsequently gaelicized *Baile Héinrí*, i.e. with *H-* rather than the common standard Irish *Éinrí*.

Ballyherly — *Baile Shéarla*
J 5963 — "Searlo's townland"

1. Ballyherly	Fiants Eliz. §2090	1571
2. Ballyherlye	Savage Lands 3	1588
3. Ballyherlye	Fiants Eliz. §5264	1588
4. (?)Balleharlyce	Inq. Ult. (Down) §9 Jac. I	1620
5. Balliherlie	Inq. Ult. (Down) §9 Jac. I	1620
6. Ballyhearly	Inq. Ult. (Down) §14 Jac. I	1625
7. Ballyhearly	Inq. Ult. (Down) §10 Car. I	1627
8. Ballyhearly	Sav. Ards 368	1628
9. Ballyhorly	Sav. Ards 373	1637c
10. Ballyherly	Census 91	1659c
11. Ballykearley	BSD 86	1661
12. Balleherly	Sub. Roll Down 282	1663
13. Ballyherley	High Const. Applot. (OSNB)	1830c
14. Ballyhearly	Bnd. Sur. (OSNB)	1830c
15. Baile Shamhairle "Sorley's town"	J O'D (OSNB)	1834c
16. ˌbɑliˈherlɩ	Local pronunciation	1990

O'Donovan's suggestion of "Sorley's town" (form 15) does not seem convincing. Anderson (1979:18) opts for "Ballyherly (i.e. Charles)" and regards the second element as a surname, although the evidence suggests that, if the second element is a name, it is a christian name rather than a surname. In view of the nature of many of the other townland names in this area one would strongly suspect an Anglo-Norman origin for the *-herly* element in this name. Reaney (1958) does not have any name in *Herley*, or the like, but he does have a name *Searl(e)* (p. 287) which, if aspirated, would give *Herle*. *Searl(e)*, occurring in 11th- and 12th-century England as *Serlo* or *Serle*, was apparently introduced into England via Normandy. Thus **Searlo(s)ton* is a distinct possibility for this townland, especially in the light of the Serlo who was the father of one "Robert son of Serlo" who was described in the early Anglo-

Norman period as dwelling in "Arte [i.e. The Ards] near Strangford" – details in O'Laverty (i 403).

The house in this townland is described in the 19th century:

> The principal mansions in the parish are, Ballyherly House, the property of Mr. William Maxwell, and the Rectory, built in 1818, at a cost of £1,090, at present occupied by the Rev. James L.M. Scott, and standing on the site of the ancient grave-yard. In a garden adjoining, there was a crypt, mentioned in Archdall's Monasticon, which in a boyish frolic, was blown up by Robert, second Marquis of Londonderry, and his schoolfellow who were at the time, under the tuition of the rector, the Rev. Dr. Sterrock.
>
> (*Knox Hist.* 468–9)

Ballyminnish — *Baile Mhic Nais* (?)
J 5952 — "townland of the son of Nash"

1.	Ballym'kinyshe	Fiants Eliz. §5264	1588
2.	Nachestowne	Inq. Ult. (Down) §9 Jac.I	1620
3.	Ballynish	Inq. Ult. (Down) §14 Jac.I	1624
4.	Ballevicknish	Inq. Ult. (Down) §10 Car.I	1627
5.	Ballymniske otherwise Ballyvickenishe	Sav. Ards 368	1628
6.	Balvicknishe	Sav. Ards 368	1628
7.	Ballymekinsh otherwise Ballyvikerish	Sav. Ards 373	1637c
8.	Ballyvicknisse	Sav. Ards 373	1637c
9.	Bally McNish	Census 91	1659
10.	Ballymccnish	BSD 86	1661
11.	Ballyminish	Wm. Map (OSNB)	1810
12.	Ballyminish	Tythes Applot. (OSNB)	1830c
13.	Ballyminish	Bnd. Sur. (OSNB)	1830c
14.	Baile Minis .i. Baile Maighe-inis "town of the insular plain"	J O'D (OSNB)	1834c
15.	ˌbɑli'mənɪʃ	Local pronunciation	1990

O'Donovan's suggestion (form no. 14) can safely be disregarded as a "Wil' Macknish" is mentioned in this area in *Inq. Ult.* (Down) §103 Car. I, 1641 AD. Anderson (1979:18) suggests "Ballymanish (formerly Ballyvickinishe, both mean son of Ennis)", but it may also be derived from the surname *Mac Naois*, "son of Naos", provided the name can even be viewed as originating in the Irish language. *Naos* is a variant form of Gaelic *Aonghus* (lit. "one-choice") which is anglicized *Angus* and, according to Woulfe (1923:395), the surname *Mac Naois*, occurring as anglicized M'Niece, MacNish, Minnish etc., was a dialectal form of *Mac Aonghuis*, *Mac Aonghusa*, (=Magennis) which was found in Ulster, Scotland and the Isle of Man.

Although the form *Baile Mhic Naois* appears to be a strong possibility, judging by forms 1 and 4–10, form no. 2 suggests another likely possibility. *Nachestowne* could conceivably represent the survival of an earlier Anglo-Norman **Nasheston* and as Reaney (1958:12) states, *Nash(e)* could be taken as a variant of the surname *Ash(e)* "dweller by the ash-tree", or from a place called *Ash*, or even *Nash*. So the anglicized forms resembling *Bally McNish* may contain a Gaelic surname **Mac Nais*, based on *Mac* "son" and Anglo-Norman *Nash*, or even a translation of an Anglo-Norman **FitzNash*.

Ballymurphy	*Baile Uí Mhurchaidh*	
J 5851	"Murphy's townland"	
1. (?) Balymorky	Inq. Earldom Ulster iii 65	1333
2. Ballyomorghie	Fiants Eliz. §2090	1571
3. Ballymurphy	Ulst. Roll Gaol Deliv. 264	1613
4. Ballieomorghie	Inq. Ult. (Down) §9 Jac. I	1620
5. Ballymurfie	Inq. Ult. (Down) §14 Jac.I	1624
6. Ballymurphye	Sav. Ards 368	1628
7. Ballymurphy, Portferry otherwise	Sav. Ards 373	1637c
8. Ballymurphy	Census 91	1659
9. Ballymurphie	BSD 86	1661
10. Ballymurphy	Bnd. Sur. (OSNB)	1810
11. Ballymurphy	Wm. Map (OSNB)	1830c
12. Baile Uí Mhurchadha "Murphy's town"	J O'D (OSNB)	1834c
13. ˌbɑliˈmọ̤ rfi	Local pronunciation	1990

Orpen (*JRSAI* xliv (1914) 65 n, 8), referring to *Balymorky* 1333 (form 1) wonders: "*Baile Murchadha*? Ballymurphy, a townland in the parish of Greyabbey". Although Orpen may well be correct in his identification, we must also bear in mind Ballymurphy in Ardquin as an alternative possibility.

On the other hand, if *Ballyomorghie* 1571 (form 2) is our earliest definite example, we can view *Ballymurphy* as either "the townland of the descendants of Murchadh (the *Uí Mhurchaidh*)", or as representative of the surname, "the townland of *Ó Murchaidh*, or Murphy". *Murchad* is an Old Irish personal name etymologized "sea-battler" by Ó Corráin/Maguire (1981:142). The historical genitive was *Ó Murchadha* but there was also a later o-stem genitive *Murchaidh* which occurs in the late Old Irish period as a variant of u-stem *Murchadha*. The attested forms suggest that the genitive is o-stem *Murchaidh*.

Ballyridley	*Baile an Riodalaigh*	
J 6054	"Ridel's townland"	
1. Balliriddily	Hib. Reg. Ards	1657c
2. Ballyriddelly	Census 91	1659
3. Ballyriddilly	BSD 85	1661
4. Ballyridley	Wm. Map (OSNB)	1810
6. Ballyridley	Tythes Applot. (OSNB)	1830c
7. Ballyriddley	Bnd. Sur. (OSNB)	1830c
8. Baile Ridley, i.e. Ridley's town	J O'D (OSNB)	1834c
9. ˌbɑliˈrïdlɩ	Local pronunciation	1990

Stevenson (1920:17) mentions Ridels among the Anglo-Norman families: "So came to settle in the East and North of Down the Jordans, Chamberlains, Savages, Copelands, Martels, Ridels, and others". We might also cite Riddells in *Harris Hist.* 4, and the Anglo-Norman form *de Ridal* cited in *Sav. Ards* 120.

Given the fact that the townland of *Ballyrusley*, (parish of Ballyphilip) points to an Irish form *Baile an Ruiséalaigh* "town of *Ruiséalach*, i.e. Russel", we might consider a gaelicized form for *Ballyridley* such as *Baile an Riodalaigh*. Woulfe (1923:274/664) lists Gaelic forms *de*

Riodal and *Riodal* common in Limerick and, in citing *de Riodal* as ultimately Norman *de Ridal*, he suggests "i.e. of Ridal(?) some spot in England". Whatever the etymology of the Anglo-Norman surname *de Ridal* may be, it is quite clear that a gaelicized form of the name is preserved in Ballyridley.

Ballywaddan	*Baile Bhodáin* (?)	
J 5856	"Wodan's townland"(?)	
1. (?) Kiel Bodan	EA 166	1227c
2. Ballywaddan	Census 91	1659
3. Ballywoddan	BSD 85	1661
4. Ballywadan	Wm. Map (OSNB)	1810
5. Ballywoodan	Tythes Applot. (OSNB)	1830c
6. Ballywaddin	Bnd. Sur. (OSNB)	1830c
7. Baile Mhadadhain "Maddan's town"	J O'D (OSNB)	1834c
8. ˌbɑliˈwɔdən	Local pronunciation	1990

Reeves (*EA* 166) cites *Kiel Bodan* in the Ards ("in Ard") from a document *c.* 1227, but in a footnote he tentatively suggests a connection with either "Ballywodan" in Ardquin or the townland *Balibodan*, as it occurred in the taxation of Pope Nicholas IV *c.* 1306, now *Ballywoodan* (parish of Saul, Co. Down). However, as the "Ard" is specified in the document, there seems to be no difficulty in identifying *Kiel Bodan* of *c.* 1227 as belonging to the Ards, but whether or not it refers to *Ballywaddan* is another question.

Considering that there is a narrow strait of water between this townland and **The Dorn** (a minor name in the townland of Ardkeen) *Kiel Bodan* 1227 AD may represent a Gaelic form *Caol Bodáin*, where *Caol* means "strait, a narrow channel or 'kyle'", and *Bodán* may be equated with Dinneen's *badán* "... a rock covered with long sea-weed just above waves ...", a word found in the Gaelic of Co. Antrim. *Caol Bodáin*, then, might mean "strait of the partly submerged rock". The variation *bodán/badán*, may even be suggested by the written forms themselves in that they vary between *Ballywoddan* and *Ballywaddan*. With regard to the meaning "rock" for *bodán*, it should also be noted that we may be dealing with a diminutive of Irish *bod* "penis" (cf. Dwelly *bodan* "Membrum puerile") and that *bodán* may also refer to a particular shape of rock.

On the other hand, both Dinneen and Dwelly give various other meanings for *bodán/badán* which may also be considered. Dinneen also has under *badán* "a tuft as of trees ... a shrub ... name of a plant *badán meascáin* bog violet", while Dwelly has: *badan* "small cluster or tuft. 2 Little grove etc. *b.-coille* a thicket of wood, clump or grove"; in addition to *bodan* "lesser reed-mace or cat's tail".

While a Gaelic form *Baile Bhadáin* may be proposed, an exact indication of what is implied is difficult to ascertain. The issue is, of course, further complicated by the fact that we may be dealing with a gaelicized Anglo-Norman name such as **Wodin(s)ton* or **Bodin(s)ton*. The first name may be connected to the surname *Wooding* ... *Wod(d)in* etc. listed by Reaney (1958:359) who cites examples such as William Woding 1247, and offers an etymology along the lines of "dweller at the place where wood has been cut". The second may be related to Reaney's (1958:37) surname *Bodin* which occurs in England as early as 1066 and which goes back to Old French *Bodin*. However, in favour of an Anglo-Norman **Wodinston* one could cite the evidence from the neighbouring barony of Lecale where references available for the modern townlands of *Ballywodan Big* and *Ballywodan Little* (par.

Saul, Co. Down) seem to suggest a form resembling **Wodinston*, e.g. "the towns of Wodanstown or Ballywodan" *CPR Jas I* 14a (1603 AD).

All things considered, then, an etymology for the Ards *Ballywaddan* is difficult to propose with any degree of certainty.

Ballywallon	*Baile Bhaldúin*	
J 5955	"Baldon's or Baldwin's townland"	
1. Ballywaldin	Hib. Reg. Ards	1657c
2. Ballywallen	Census 91	1659c
3. Ballywaldin	BSD 85	1661
4. Ballywallon	Wm. Map (OSNB)	1810
5. Ballywollen	High Const. Applot. (OSNB)	1830c
6. Ballywallan	Bnd. Sur. (OSNB)	1830c
7. Baile Mhalláin "town of the little brow or brae"	J O'D (OSNB)	1834c
8. ˌbɑliˈwɑl̥n	Local pronunciation	1990

The 17th-century spellings in *-waldin* (forms 1 & 3) seem to rule out O'Donovan's suggestion "town of the little bray" (form 7). One suspects an Anglo-Norman origin. Woulfe (1923:227) lists a surname *Baldún* which he interprets as a Gaelic form of *Baldoon, Ballon, Baldin, Baldwin* and which he interprets as "son of Baldon, a diminutive of Baldwin". He further records:

> Families of that name settled soon after the Anglo-Norman invasion in Dublin, Wexford, Kilkenny, Waterford and Cork. The pronunciation is sometimes *Bállún* or *Ballún*. The town of Cobh stands in the townland of Ballyvalloon, so called from Baldwin Hodnett, a member of the family who once owned the Great Island.

It appears, then, that we can add Co. Down to the list of counties in which Anglo-Normans of this name settled in Ireland.

Ballywhite	*Baile Faoite*	
J 5752	"White's townland"	
1. Balliwhit	Hib. Reg. Ards	1657c
2. Ballywhyte	Census 91	1659c
3. Balliwhite	BSD 86	1661
4. Ballywhite	Wm. Map (OSNB)	1810
5. Ballywhite	High Const. Applot. (OSNB)	1830c
6. Ballywhite	Bnd. Sur. (OSNB)	1830c
7. Ballywhite	Reg. Free. (OSNB)	1832
8. Baile an Fhaoitigh "White's town"	J O'D (OSNB)	1834c
9. ˌbɑliˈwhait	Local pronunciation	1990

Woulfe (1923:257), commenting on a gaelicized form *de Faoit(e)*, mentions the surname "le White, le Whyte, i.e. the white, of fair complexion; the name of an Anglo-Norman family who came to Ireland at the time of the invasion". He then goes on to add "There are several respectable families of the name, which is common in all parts of Ireland". For Whites among early Anglo-Norman knights arriving in Ulster in the late 12th century, see *Sav. Ards*

119. We have Whites across the Lough in the baronies of Lecale and Dufferin, in fact Dufferin was also known as *the Whites Country* in the time of Elizabeth I (Reeves *EA* 186). Quite clearly, then, we are dealing with a gaelicized form of this Anglo-Norman surname in the townland *Ballywhite*. Anderson (1979:18) records six families of that name in latter-day Little Ards.

Knox Hist. 465 describes *Ballywhite House* as "... the residence of Mr. John Warnock ... in highly improved grounds, overlooking Strangford Lough".

Demesne — An English form

J 5855

1.	Demeens	Hib. Reg. Ards	1657c
2.	(?) Poundlands	Wm. Map (OSNB)	1810
3.	Domain	High Const. Applot. (OSNB)	1830c
4.	Domain	Bnd. Sur. (OSNB)	1830c
5.	də'me:n	Local pronunciation	1990

A *demesne* is defined as the land surrounding a manor or large house, which is occupied by the owner rather than held by tenants, although it can often mean merely landed property. Anderson (1978:19) associates the naming of this place with part of the property of the early 17th-century Bishop Robert Echlin, on whom see **Abbacy** below.

Priest Town — An English form

J 5755

1.	Prestowne	Hib. Reg. Ards	1657c
2.	Preston	BSD 85	1661
3.	Priestown	Tombstone (Sav. Ards) 291	1714
4.	Priestown	Sav. Ards 265	1779
5.	Priesttown	Sav. Ards 376	1779
6.	Priesttown	Wm. Map (OSNB)	1810
7.	Priestown	Bnd. Sur. (OSNB)	1830c
8.	'pri:stɔun	Local pronunciation	1990
9.	'pri:stən	Local pronunciation	1990

Anderson (1979:18) takes the "Priest" here as a surname and, although "Priests" was listed as a surname in this county (*Surnames Dn 1858* 83, locality unspecified), more information will be required in order to tie the naming of this place to a particular period, as Reaney (1958:260) shows that *Prest, le Prest,* etc. was a common surname in Anglo-Norman Britain. Therefore modern *Priest Town* may well represent the survival of an original Anglo-Norman **Prest(s)t* which, like **Cookstown** in Ardkeen Parish, resisted the general trend in the Ards to gaelicize older Anglo-Norman names.If the name is to be placed in the Anglo-Norman period one may even have to consider that the *Prest-* part of the name refers to Anglo-Norman *prest,* land lent or advanced, in this case by King John to Thomas Savage (who may even have given his name to the neighbouring townland of **Thomastown**):

> Five years later, July 10th, A.D. 1210, he [Robert Savage of the Ards Knt] is mentioned along with Thomas Savage, who was possibly his younger brother, as one of the knights to whom *prests* (loans or advances) were made by King John at Carrickfergus Castle during the King's sojourn in the great royal fortress of Ulster. (*Sav. Ulst.* 18)

All things considered this seemingly straightforward name poses considerable interpretative difficulties.

Thomastown An English form
J 5853

1.	Thomastowne	Hib. Reg. Ards	1657c
2.	Thomastown	Census 91	1659
3.	Thomastowne als Ballintleyne	BSD 86	1661
4.	Thomastown	Sub Roll Down 17	1663
6.	Thomastown	Wm. Map (OSNB)	1810
7.	Thomastown	Bnd. Sur. (OSNB)	1830c
8.	Thomastown	High Const. Applot. (OSNB)	1830c

Anderson (1979:18) takes this place-name to reflect a surname although it seems more probable that it is an Anglo-Norman christian name. One might suggest a member of the Savage family, as many of these were called Thomas, e.g. Thomas, a younger son of William Baron le Savage *c.* 1200 AD mentioned in *Sav. Ards* 123/125. However, the *Thomas* referred to here may even refer to "Thomas, Bishop of Down who was granted four carucates of land in the Ards by Hugh de Lacy", according to O'Laverty (i 402).

Knox (*Knox Hist.* 465) describes Thomastown as "a well cultivated site" and Atkinson (1821:i 210) describes *Thomastown House* as follows:

> Thomastown, the seat of Mr. Donning, (a worthy sea-faring citizen, formerly connected with other merchants in the West India trade, but now retired from business to spend the remainder of his days in this pleasing retreat,) comprehends a handsome farm lodge and 80 acres of land, devoted to agricultural uses. – In point of prospect it commands several interesting broken views of Strangford lough, and of the elevated country beyond it, between the hills which grace the landscape extending from this farm to the eastern shore of the lough just noticed.

OTHER NAMES

Abbacy An English form
J 5854

Local pronunciation [ðə 'ɑbəsɪ]. This residence was built by Bishop Echlin in the early seventeenth century. "Seven Town Lands (being Bishop's Lands) about *Ardquin*, leased to Mr. *Echlin*, are said to have been given to the Church by *Savage* of *Portaferry*, as an expiratory Devotion, when all *Ireland* was Popish" (*Harris Hist.* 268). An earlier account is given in *Descr. Ards 1683* 35–6 of "ye old Abby of Arquin with seven townes (the Bishopps lands) leased to John Echlin, Esquire who's father was y[e] grandson of one of y[e] same sirname Bishopp of Down at ye beginning of y[e] British plantation vnder King James ...".

Reeves *EA* 22, n. p. comments on how this place was erroneously identified by Harris and Archdale:

> Harris (*Hist.* p. 47), and after him Archdall (*Mon. Hib.* p. 120) conjectured that this 'Abbacy' was the site of the alien priory of 'Eynes in the Ards', of which mention is made in a patent roll, 12 Hen. IV. [*c.* 1411] (see *Cal. Canc. Hib.* p. 197; Harris *MSS.* vol. iv, p. 178); but erroneously; for the priory in question was none other than the

> Black Abbey, which was a cell of St. Mary's of Lonley in Normandy, and was the only alien priory in the diocese. The name 'Eynes' was probably borrowed from the neighbouring church of Inishargy, of which Black Abbey was parson.

Knox (*Knox Hist.* 465) states: "The Abbacy, built by Bishop [i.e. Robert] Echlin, was destroyed by Cromwell, but the ruins are, in part, tolerably well preserved". A fuller account of the ruins is provided in *ASCD* 255–6. For **Rubane House**, also called **Echlinville**, dating to the late 18th century see **Echlinville** (par. St Andrews alias Ballyhalbert).

Bishops Mill — An English form
J 5955

Local pronunciation [biʃəp ˈmı̃lz]. Described thus by John O'Donovan (*OSNB*, c. 1834): "Bishop's Mill Village, a small village of about 12 houses". Anderson (1978:18–9) associates Bishops Mill with bishop Robert Echlin (on whom cf. **Abbacy**, above).

Limestone Pladdies — A Scots form ?
J 5554

For the use of the term *pladdie* "sunken rock" in Strangford Lough, see **McCammon Pladdy** (par. Inishargy).

Lough Cowey — *Loch Chú Mhaighe*
J 5954 — "(St) Cú Mhaighe's lough"

1. (?) Logh Cavan	BSD 85	1661
2. Loch Cumhaighe i.e. "Cooey's lough, Cowey"	J O'D (OSNB)	1834c
3. Lɔx ˈkɔui	Local pronunciation	1990

Reeves (*EA* 25, n. v) connects the Irish name *Cú Mhaighe* (lit. "hound of the plain") with an early saint:

> The Irish name Cooey (*Cu-mhaighe*, see Annals of Ulster A.D. 1102, and Four Masters Æ.C. 1102, 1176) is always anglicized in the Ards and elsewhere by 'Quintin'.

Reeves further cites local names *Templecowey*, *Cruachan Cowey* and *Ballyquintin*. Although we can be fairly certain that the *Cowey* element in names such as **Lough Cowey** and **Templecowey** goes back to an earlier Irish *Cú M(h)aighe*, the case of a connection between *Cú Mhaighe* and the townland of **Ballyquintin** must be treated with caution, as can be seen from the discussion of that name in this volume (parish of Witter). While we have local traditions concerning St Cú Mhaighe, or Cowey, for example water from his well being a cure for poor eyesight, we have no record of him in the early martyrologies.

Marlfield — An English form
J 5754

1. Marlefield	Wm. Map (OSNB)	1810
2. Marlfield	High Const. Applót. (OSNB)	1830c
3. Marlefield	Bnd. Sur. (OSNB)	1830c
4. Marlfield	Reg. Free. (OSNB)	1832

5. Marlefield "field of the marle"	J O'D (OSNB)	1834c
6. 'mɑrlfi:ld	Local pronunciation	1991

Marl(e), composed chiefly of clay and silt and rich in calcium carbonate, was quite commonly employed as a fertilizer in many areas of the country, not least in the Ards:

> This Peninsula produces large Quantities of Barley, and a kind of Oats called Light Foot-Oats, as well from the Help of Marle abounding in the Marshy grounds, as from Ore-Weed, which they have in great plenty, both from the Islands in the Lake, and the Eastern Shore. (*Harris Hist.* 88).

With regard to the success of this method of cultivation we may cite the following:

> Mr Echlin one of the earlier proprietors, received a prize from the Dublin Agricultural Society for sowing 100 acres of barley on reclaimed moss, being the largest quantity produced by any individual throughout the kingdom in a single year.
> (*Knox Hist.* 462).

Mill Park — An English form

Local pronunciation [mïl 'pɑrk]. In the *OSNB* for Ardquin Parish there is listed "Mill Park. A Farm House".

Portaferry House — An English form
J 5951

Described by *Knox Hist.* 465 as: "the residence of Lieutenant Colonel Nugent ... standing in a lofty position in a picturesque demesne commanding extensive views of both sea and land". *ASCD* 316 remarks: "The Greek revival is best seen at Seaforde House (1819), and the 18th century Portaferry House was redecorated internally in Hellenistic taste by William Farrell *c.* 1820". The earliest house on the site was reportedly built by Andrew Savage (obit 1773), see *Harris Hist.* 46, *Sav. Ulst.* 359–60 and *ASCD* 379–81.

On **Portaferry** see parish of Ballytrustan.

The Pound — An English form
J 5855

The *pound* in question here probably refers to an enclosure for livestock.

Ringburr Point — *Rinn Beara* (?) "headland of the skewer-shape"
J 5755

Local pronunciations [rɪŋ 'bo̜r 'pɔint / raŋ'bo̜r 'pɔint]. There are no early written forms available for this name, but anglicized *-burr* might suggest Irish *bior* "spit, skewer, lance, a point, spike" (*Dinneen*) and, as the headland certainly does jut out like a skewer, one can see how *bior* could well apply to its shape. However, we still have a problem of the exact form of the genitive: do we opt for genitive singular *beara* or plural *bior*?

Selk Rock — A Scots/English form
J 5752

Local pronunciation ['sïlk 'rɔk]. This presumably preserves the Scots word *selk* "seal", although the word *selk* was no longer understood by any of the dozen or so older speakers I interviewed in the Ards. There are three **Selk Island**s in Strangford Lough, in this parish and those of Inishargy and Killyleagh. There is also another **Selk Island** off the east coast of the Ards in the Parish of St Andrews alias Ballyhalbert.

Templecraney Of uncertain origin
J 5951

Local pronunciation [ˌtʃemplˈkrɑni]. *Templecraney* is described as "Portaferry Old Church" in *ASCD* 309, see also *Harris Hist.* 46, and *EA* 24, n. t. The first element is evidently *Teampall* "church", but the second element is difficult to interpret.

Thomastown House See **Thomastown**

The Walter Rocks An English form
J 5850

Reeves (*EA* 24/5, n. t) draws attention to the Register of Octavian (1478–1513 AD) which records that "Walter Raynocke *alias* Dany was rector of the church 'S. Nichol de Philipton'". This corresponds to modern Ballyphilip townland and, although *The Walter Rocks* are off Ballyphilip, we cannot be sure of any connection between the naming of these rocks and rector Walter Raynocke alias Dany above. According to G.F. Savage-Armstrong (*Sav. Ulst.* 360) there is *The Walter Meadow*, which is on the mainland opposite The Walter Rocks, and tradition has it that this place was named when a girl from Killinchy with whom a member of the Savage family had fallen in love was landed here by a boatman named "Watty".

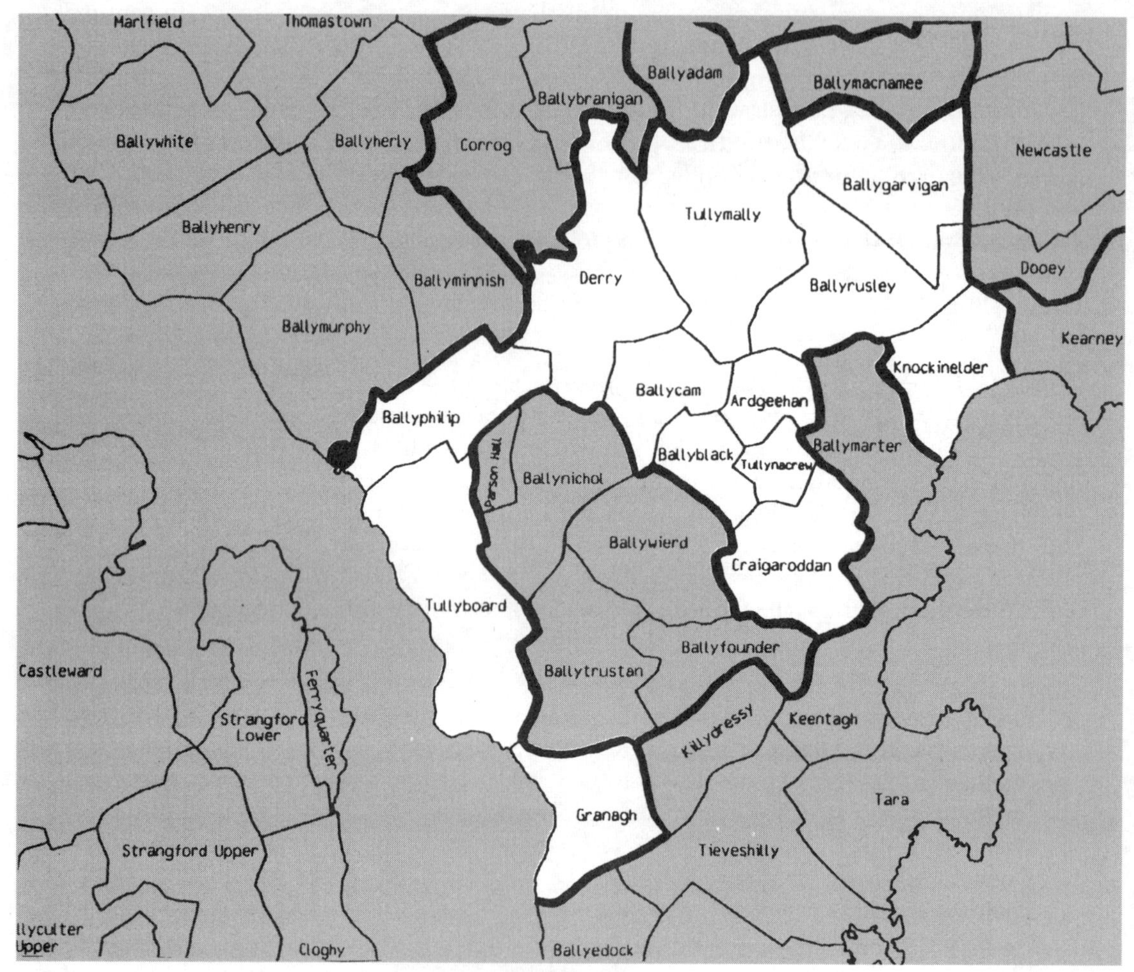

Parish of Ballyphilip

Barony of Ards Upper

Townlands
Ardgeehan
Ballyblack
Ballycam
Ballygarvigan
Ballyphilip
Ballyrusley
Craigaroddan
Derry
Granagh
Knockinelder
Tullyboard
Tullymally
Tullynacrew

Town
Portaferry

PARISH OF BALLYPHILIP

In the *Ordnance Survey Name Books* the civil parishes of Ballyphilip, Ballytrustan and Slanes are listed together as a Union. The date of this Union goes back to the early 17th century and was approved in a charter dating from the 7th year of James I according to Lewis (*Lewis' Top. Dict.* i: 161). The Union initially included Ardglass as a fourth parish. However, in 1831 the Commissioners of Ecclesiastical Inquiry decided that the parish of Ardglass, some seven miles distant in the neighbouring barony of Lecale, should be severed from the Union. See also parish of Witter for the subsequent inclusion of the old parish of Witter townlands in Ballyphilip.

There is very little known of the parish in the pre-Norman period, although Walter Harris in his *History of County Down* (p. 46) describes a ruined church site in the area in 1744, which Reeves, writing a century later, describes as possibly Templecraney (*EA* 24 n. t). Information on this church is at present difficult to find. On the parish of Ballyphilip, see Reeves *EA* 24, *Knox Hist.* 467, Ewart (1866:38–9), O'Laverty (i 390 ff.), Lewis (*Lewis' Top. Dict.* 161) and *OSM* vii 7–14. On the town of **Portaferry**, part of which is in this parish, see the section on *Other Names* in the parish of Ballytrustan.

PARISH NAME

Ballyphilip	*Baile Philib*	
J 6050	"Philip's townland"	
1. Felipton, Ecclesia de	Eccles. Tax 24	1306c
2. Phyllipestoun	Inq. Earl Ulster (EA) 361	1333
3. Phelpeston in le Arde	Reg. Swayne 123	1430
4. Phelpeston, St. Nicholai de	Reg. Swayne (EA) 24 n. t	1430
5. Phelpton	Reg. Swayne 174	1438
6. Phelpton	Reg. Mey 170	1449
7. Donatus Mcgloro rector de Phelpton in Ards	Reg. Mey 170	1449
8. Nicholas Cornwalshe rectore de Phelpton	Reg. Mey 218	1451
9. Philipton, S. Nichol de	Reg. Octavian 24 n. t	1482
10. Tolnecrewe	PCR Eliz. I (Sav. Ards) 175	1559
11. Phillips towne	S-E Ulster Map	1580c
12. Philipstoun	Mercator's Ulst.	1595
13. Phillips Towne	Boazio's Map (BM)	1599
14. Ba:Philip	Bartlett Map (TCD)	1601
15. Phillips Towne	Boazio's Map (NG)	1609
16. Philipston	Jas I to Down Cath. 178	1609
17. B.Phil	Speed's Antrim & Down	1610
18. B:Phillip	Speed's Ulster	1610
19. Philipstowne, Ecclesia de	Terrier (Reeves) 61	1615
20. Phillipstowne	Ulster Visit. (Reeves) 25	1622
21. Ballephillip	Inq. Down (Reeves 1) 117	1657
22. Ballyphillip	Hib. Reg. Ards	1657
23. Ballyphillip	Census 91	1659

24. Rector de Phillipstown als Portferry	Trien. Visit. (Bramhall) 8	1661
25. Ballyphillip	BSD 86	1661
26. Ballyphillip	Sub. Roll Down 16	1663
27. Ballyphillip Rectoria	Trien. Visit. (Margetson) 20	1664
28. Balliphillip	Trien. Visit. (Boyle) 42	1679
29. Bally Phillip	Descr. Ards 36	1683
30. Ballyphillip	Wm. Map (OSNB)	1810
31. Ballyphillip	Bnd. Sur. (OSNB)	1830c
32. Ballyphillip	Reg. Free. (OSNB)	1832
33. Baile Philib "Phillip's town"	J O'D (OSNB)	1834c
34. ˌbɑliˈfiləp	Local pronunciation	1991
35. ˌbaliˈfalɪp	Local pronunciation	1991

As the early written forms clearly show, this name started off as an Anglo-Norman name which was gaelicized in the post-medieval period as *Baile Philib*. We have no certain knowledge who this Philip was but the personal name was popular among the early Anglo-Norman settlers, as can be seen from "Philippo et Hugone de Cestria", "Philippo de Hastig" (*Cartae Dun.* 420 §4, 421 §7 c. 1183 AD). The personal name *Philip*, borrowed into English from French, goes back to Latin *Philippus*, a borrowing from Greek *Philippos* meaning "fond of horses" (Klein 1967:1173).

Ardgeehan — *Ard Caocháin*
J 6151 — "*Caochán*'s height"

1. Ardkighan	Inq. Ult. (Down) §9 Jac.I	1620
2. Ardkieghan	Inq. Ult. (Down) §14 Jac.I	1624
3. (?) Ardkehime	Inq. Ult. (Down) §14 Jac.I	1624
4. Ardkeaghan	Inq. Ult. (Down) §10 Car.I	1627
5. Ardkeaghan	Sav. Ards 368	1628
6. (?) Ardkeaghan	Sav. Ards 373	1637c
7. Ardkighan	Census 91	1659
8. Ardkeeghane	BSD 86	1661
9. Ardgeehan	Wm. Map (OSNB)	1810
10. Ardgehan	High Const. Applot. (OSNB)	1830c
11. Ardgeehan	Bnd. Sur. (OSNB)	1830c
12. Ard Gaoithene "Gahan's height or hill"	J O'D (OSNB)	1834c
13. ˌɑrdˈgiːxˈən	Local pronunciation	1991

In the grant of Bishop Malachy to St Patrick's Abbey in Downpatrick in 1183 there occurs the place-name *Arthgothin*. This was transcribed as *Arthgothin* by Reeves (*EA* 163), and *Athgothin* by Mac Niocaill (*Cartae Dun.* 419 §3) although in his index Mac Niocaill (p. 428) spells this as *Arthgothin* and tentatively suggests that this 12th-century place-name *Arthgothin* may represent modern *Ardgeehan*. This identification is, however, far from certain as (a) *A(r)thgothin* occurs in the manuscript among names that occur in Ballee parish in the barony of Lecale, Co. Down – see *EA* 163 for details – and (b) we can see that the *-g-* in the modern anglicized form of the name *Ardgeehan* is only detectable from the early

19th century, while the eight 17th-century sources all show *Ardk-*. The anglicized forms 1–8 suggest that we are dealing with Irish *Ard* "height" plus a second qualifying word beginning in *C-*. The forms might suggest *Ard Cíocháin* "pap-shaped height or hill", or perhaps a personal name *Ard Caocháin* "Caochán's height". The Gaelic personal name *Caochán* (meaning "blind or one-eyed one") was a fairly common name in the early Irish period as can be seen from the genealogies (e.g. *CGH* Index p.528).

Ballyblack	*Baile Bhláca*	
J 6150	"Black's or Blake's townland"	
1. Ballywlake	PCR Eliz. I (Sav. Ards) 175	1559
2. Ballywlake	Fiants Eliz. §2090	1571
3. Ballyblacke	Savage Lands 4	1588
4. Balliblacke	Fiants Eliz. §5264	1588
5. Ballyblacke	Inq. Ult. (Down) §14 Jac. I	1625
6. Ballyblake otherwise Ballyblack	Sav. Ards 373	1637c
7. Ballyblack	Census 91	1659c
8. Ballyblaicke	BSD 86	1661
9. Ballyblack	Wm. Map (OSNB)	1810
10. Ballyblack	High Const. Applot. (OSNB)	1830c
11. Ballyblack	Bnd. Sur. (OSNB)	1830c
12. Ballyblack	Reg. Free. (OSNB)	1833
13. Baile an Bhlácaigh "Black's or Blake's town"	J O'D (OSNB)	1834c
14. ˌbɛliˈblɛk	Local pronunciation	1991
15. ˌbɑliˈblɛk	Local pronunciation	1991

This results from the gaelicization of an earlier Anglo-Norman name, which probably resembled **Blacke(s)ton*. The trouble lies in trying to establish the exact meaning of English surname *Black(e)/Blake*. Reaney (1958:34) shows that Anglo-Norman names in Britain such as *Willelmus Blac, Niger* 1086 did mean "the Black". This is the most likely meaning in our case, but we must also note that when Old English *blaek* "black" (via an inflected form Old Eng. *blaca*) gave Middle English *blāke* a separate Middle English word *blāk(e)*, from Old English *blāc* meaning "bright, shining; pale, wan", would then have been forced out of everyday use, although it may have been fossilized in the personal name *Blake*.

So as some of the forms for *Ballyblack* point to both *-black* and *-blake*, we must bear in mind Reaney's remarks that "the exact meaning of *Blake* is doubtful", as *Blake*, while probably signifying "black", could also mean "the pale one". See also townland of **Ballyblack**, parish of Greyabbey, Upper Ards.

Ballycam	*Baile Cam*	
J 6151	"crooked townland"	
1. (?) Ballyconn	Inq. Earl Ulster (EA) 361 n. g	1333
2. (?) Ballycamdan	Inq. Earldom Ulster 66	1333
3. Ballicam	Savage Lands 4	1588
4. Ballicam	Fiants Eliz. §5264	1588
5. Ballycan	Inq. Ult. (Down) §2 Jac. I	1605
6. Ballecam	Ham. Copy Inq. xxxi; xliv	1623

7. Ballicame	Ham. Copy Inq. xxxv	1623
8. Ballycame	Sav. Ards 368	1628
9. Ballycam	Inq. Ult. (Down) §109 Car. I	1650c
10. Ballycam	Census 91	1659
11. Ballycavall als Ballycam	BSD 85	1661
12. Ballycain	Inq. Ult. (Down) §14 Jac I	1625c
13. Ballycain	Inq. Ult. (Down) §14 Jac I	1625c
14. Ballycam	Inq. Down (Reeves 1) 117	1657
15. Baile Cam "crooked town"	J O'D (OSNB)	1834c
16. ˌbɑliˈkɑm	Local pronunciation	1991

Orpen (*JRSAI* xlvi (1914) 66 n.4) suggests that the form *Ballycamdan* from the Inquisition of the Earldom of Ulster in 1333 (form 2 above) may be "Ballycam(?), a td. in the parish of Ballyphilip". Reeves (*EA* 361, n. g) transcribes this name from the document as *Ballyconn* (form 1) and identifies it with Ballycam. Either of these 1333 forms is difficult to reconcile with the form of the name from the 16th century onwards (forms 3–14). *Ballycain* (forms 12, 13) look like faulty transcriptions of *Ballycam*. On the whole O'Donovan's suggestion *Baile Cam* "crooked town" seems a reasonable one.

Ballygarvigan
J 6353

Baile Uí Gharbhagáin
"townland of *Ó Garbhagáin* (?)"

1. (?) Ballyharvan	PCR Eliz. I (Sav. Ards) 175	1559
2. Ballygarvocan	Fiants Eliz. §2090	1571
3. (?) Balligarviger	Fiants Eliz. §5264	1588
4. Ballegorwocan	Inq. Ult. (Down) §9 Jac.I	1620
5. (?) Ballygarnecone	Inq. Ult. (Down) §14 Jac.I	1624
6. (?) Ballygarnegan	Inq. Ult. (Down) §14 Jac.I	1624
7. Ballegirnegane .. Ballegarnegane	Inq. Ult. (Down) §10 Car.I	1627
8. Ballogarvigan	Sav. Ards 368	1628
9. Ballygarvigan	Sav. Ards 373	1637c
10. Ballygarvegan	Will (Sav. Ards) 247	1640
11. Ballygarvegan	Inq. Ult. (Down) §102 Car.I	1641
12. Ballygarvagan	Census 91	1659
13. Ballygarvegane	BSD 86	1661
14. Ballygarvegan	Forfeit. Estates 384b §16	1702
15. Ballygarvigan	Wm. Map (OSNB)	1810
16. Ballygarvigan	High Const. Applot. (OSNB)	1830c
17. Ballygarvigan	Bnd. Sur. (OSNB)	1830c
18. Baile Uí Gharbhagáin "O'Garvigan's town"	J O'D (OSNB)	1834c
19. ˌbaliˈgɑrvigən	Local pronunciation	1991

O'Donovan suggests "O'Garvigan's Town" (no. 18). No surname of that type is listed by Woulfe (1932), and no record of the personal name *Garb(h)agán* is found in the early Irish genealogies *CGH* or *CSH*. By the same token no noun *garbhagán* appears in the main dictionaries. If *Ballyharvan* (form 1) refers to this townland we may be dealing with an original *Garbhán*, which subsequently became *Garbhagán*. The personal name *Garbhán* (probably "little rough one") was extremely common in early Irish (e.g. *CGH* Index 658–9) and it is possible that a surname *Ó Garbháin* developed to *Ó Garbhagáin*, under the influence of names such as *Ó Flannagáin* "Flanagan", *Ó Branagáin* "Branagan" etc. (cf. **Ballybranigan**, Ballytrustan parish). If this explanation were acceptable we would envisage a Gaelic form *Baile Uí Gharbhagáin*. Indeed the townland **Ballygarvan**, in the northerly Ards parish of Inishargy, suggests that there may have been a Gaelic surname *Ó Garbhagáin* or *Ó Garbháin* in the Ards at one time.

On the other hand *garbhagán* could represent a physical element. It might, for example, refer to "rough land", a view which would seem to be supported by the following description from Lewis (*Lewis' Top. Dict.* i: 161) who states:

> The land [in Ballyphilip parish] is fertile, and, with the exception of about 30 acres of bog, called Ballgaroegan Moss, which supplies the inhabitants with fuel, is in a good state of cultivation.

All things considered, it is difficult to propose a meaning with any degree of certainty for either **Ballygarvigan** (in this parish) or **Ballygarvan** (in Inishargy parish), although the variation in the early spellings of these two names suggests a common origin.

Ballyrusley	*Baile an Ruiséalaigh*	
J 6251	"Russell's townland"	
1. Tolnerussely	Fiants Eliz. §2090	1571
2. Ballyrussell	Fiants Eliz. §5264	1588
3. Ballyrussel	Savage Lands 4	1588
4. Tullenerusheallye	Inq. Ult. (Down) §9 Jac.I	1620
5. Ballirusselie al. Tullenerusselie	Inq. Ult. (Down) §9 Jac.I	1620
6. Ballenrusselly	Inq. Ult. (Down) §9 Jac.I	1620
7. Ballerussely	Inq. Ult. (Down) §9 Jac.I	1620
8. Tollenrushelly	Inq. Ult. (Down) §14 Jac.I	1624
9. Tullrushelly	Inq. Ult. (Down) §14 Jac.I	1624
10. Balletollenrussely	Inq. Ult. (Down) §10 Car.I	1627
11. Ballytollenerussally	Sav. Ards 368	1628
12. Ballytollynerussally	Sav. Ards 373	1637c
13. Ballyrusselly	Will (Sav. Ards) 247	1640
14. Ballevusselly	Inq. Ult. (Down) §102 Car.I	1641
15. Ballyrusselly	Inq. Ult. (Down) §102 Car.I	1641
16. Balletusselly	Inq. Ult. (Down) §104 Car.I	1644
17. Ballyruslelly	Census 91	1659
18. Ballygrosselly	BSD 86	1661
19. Ballyrussally	Forfeit. Estates 384b §16	1702
20. Ballyrusselly	Wm. Map (OSNB)	1810
21. Ballyrusley	High Const. Applot. (OSNB)	1830c
22. Ballyrussaley	Bnd. Sur. (OSNB)	1830c
23. Baile an Ruiséalaigh "Russell's town"	J O'D (OSNB)	1834c
24. ˌbɑli'rǫ̈sli	Local pronunciation	1991

The Gaelic form of this name *Baile an Ruiséalaigh* contains a specific form of the surname *Ruiséil*. In Irish surnames a man called *Ó Ceallaigh* "Kelly" can be referred to specifically as

An Ceallach (literally "The Kelly"), and in the name *Ballyrusley* we are dealing with *An Ruiséalach*, which is a specific form of a Gaelic surname resembling *Ruiséil*. The form *Ruiséil* is, as Woulfe (1923:665) points out, a Gaelic adaptation of Anglo-Norman *Russel* i.e. "red-haired" which is a diminutive of *rous* "red", Old French *rousēl*. The name Russel(l) was widely used in Norman England (see Reaney 1958: 279), and several families of that name were among the early Anglo-Norman settlers in Ireland in a number of areas, including Co. Down, where a branch of that family accompanied de Courcy to Ulster.

Russells are known in the barony of Lecale, Co. Down, e.g. the townland of **Russells Quarter** (the parish of Down). We also have records of them in connection with lands in the Ards. Reeves (*EA* 25, n. v, citing *Cal. Canc. Hib.* vol. 1, p. 144) mentions that "the King [Edward III] committed to Richard Russell the custody of the lands of *Thrustayntone*" (1397 AD). This Richard may well be the Russell who gave his name to *Ballyrusly*. In any case, we have evidence of this family surviving in the Ards down to the 17th century with references such as "Ros' Russell" *Inq. Ult.* §9 Jac. I (1620 AD), or "George Russell" mentioned in *Inq. Ult.* §14 Jac. I (1624), and in *CPR Jas I* 86a (1606).

Quite a few of the earliest forms for the name (nos. 1, 4–5 and 8–12) suggest that *Tulaigh an Ruiséalaigh* "the hillock of *An Ruiséalach*" was an earlier form of the name. For a similar replacement of *tulach* "hillock" by *baile* "townland" see **Ballyskeagh** (parish of Newtownards).

Craigaroddan	*Creag an Rodáin*	
J 6250	"rock of the red area"	
1. Creggrodan, Tullencrevy al'	Inq. Ult. (Down) §10 Jac.I	1627
2. Creggroddan	Sav. Ards 368	1628
3. Creggroddan, Tollenocreeny otherwise	Sav. Ards 368	1628
4. Criggroddan, Tolloneereeir otherwise	Sav. Ards 373	1637c
5. Craigirodan	Census 92	1659
6. Cregruodane	BSD 86	1661
7. Craigaroddan	Wm. Map (OSNB)	1810
8. Craigarodden	Bnd. Sur. (OSNB)	1830c
9. Craigroden	High Const. Applot. (OSNB)	1830c
10. Craigaroddin	Reg. Free. (OSNB)	1832
11. Carraig a Rudáin "Reddan's rock"	J O'D (OSNB)	1834c
12. ˌkrɛgəˈrɔdən	Local pronunciation	1991
13. ˌkriəgɪˈrɔdən	Local pronunciation	1991

There seems to be little evidence in the Ards for the family name Reddan suggested by O'Donovan (form 11), although Woulfe (1923: 633) cites a Gaelic surname *Ó Rodáin* "descendant of Rodán". Woulfe describes this as "an old surname in Donegal, Monaghan and Clare" and interprets *Rodán* as meaning "the strong one", i.e. a diminutive of *rod* "strong". Woulfe further lists anglicized forms such as *(O') Rodane, (O') Rudden, ... Reddan,* etc. It seems likely that the *-roddan* part of *Craigaroddan* refers to a physical feature. If it contains the Irish term *rodán* it may refer to the rock itself or to the reddish colour of the area surrounding. For this latter interpretation we may note that elsewhere in the Upper Ards, near Kirkistown, we have reference to "a long red bogg" in the 17th century (*Descr. Ards* 41).

Derry	*Doire*	
J 6053	"oak-wood"	
1. Daire	Fél. Óeng. May 29 p. 136 n	800c
2. Darii	Mart. Tal. May 29 p. 46 n	800c
3. Doire	Mart. Don. May 29 p. 140 n	1630c
4. Dere, Ecclesia de	Eccles. Tax. 22	1306c
5. Dyrry	Fiants Eliz. §2090	1571
6. Dirrei	S-E Ulster Map	1580c
7. Ballidirrye	Fiants Eliz. §5264	1588
8. Dirrei	Mercator's Ulst.	1595
9. le Derry	Inq. Ult. (Down) §2 Jac. I	1605
10. Derry, the townland and half of	CPR Jas. I 72b	1605
11. Derrie Movilla, Capella de	Terrier (Reeves) 61	1615c
12. Dirrie	Inq. Ult. (Down) §9 Jac. I	1620
13. Dery	Ulster Visit. (Reeves) 57	1622
14. Ballyderry	Ham. Copy Inq. xxxi	1623
15. the Grange or Rectory of Derry	Ham. Copy Inq. xxxi; xliv	1623
16. Derry	Inq. Ult. (Down) §14 Jac. I	1625
17. Ballederry	Inq. Ult. (Down) §10 Car. I	1627
18. Ballederrie	Inq. Ult. (Down) §10 Car. I	1627
20. Balledorry	Sav. Ards 368	1628
21. Ballederry	Sav. Ards 373	1637c
22. Ballyderry	Sav. Ards 368	1628
23. Ballyderry	Sav. Ards 373	1637c
24. the rectory of Derry	Inq. Ult. (Down) §109 Car. I	1650c
25. Ballyderry	Inq. Ult. (Down) §109 Car. I	1650c
26. Baldory	Inq. Down (Reeves 1) 117	1657
27. Derry	Census 91	1659c
28. Derry	BSD 85	1661
29. Rector' de Derry als Ballygalgott	Trien. Visit. (Bramhall) 8	1661
30. Derrie	Sub. Roll Dn 282	1663
31. Derrey	Map, Petty's Sur. (OSNB)	1683
32. Derry	Wm. Map (OSNB)	1810
33. Derry	High Const. Applot. (OSNB)	1830c
34. Derry	Bnd. Sur. (OSNB)	1830c
35. Doire "an oak-wood"	J O'D (OSNB)	1834c
36. 'dɛrı	Local pronunciation	1991

The meaning of the name of this townland is straightforward enough. The reason for its inclusion in early Irish martyrologies is that it contains the remains of two early churches, described in *ASCD* pp.290–1. They appear to be associated with *Cumman*, a female saint who is mentioned in the following stanza for May 29th in the early 9th-century *Martyrology of Oengus*:

Mórślúag Pollionis
ron-snádat dond rindnim
la Cummain co nglanbail
ingen Allén inmain

"May Pollio's great host
convoy us to the starry heaven
with Cummain the pure and good
daughter of loveable Allén!" (*Fél. Óeng.* May 29 p. 126).

In the glossed manuscript notes accompanying this stanza (*Fél. Óeng.* p. 136) we read *Cumain .i. bannóeb 7 a n-Aird Ulad ata* "Cumain, i.e. a female saint, and in Ard Uladh she is". Therefore Stokes' identification (*Mart. Gorm.* index p. 306) of *Doire* as modern Derry City is mistaken, but a full treatment of the exact form of this Ards place-name *Doire* in the various martyrologies need not be undertaken here.

The fact that Saint Cumman had a church in the Ards is hardly surprising as the genealogies claim that she was descended from Echu Gunnat, i.e. the same Echu Gunnat from whom we get the tribe *Uí Echach na hArda*, discussed above in the barony name **Ards**. One genealogy (*CSH* §196 p. 33) states that *Aillén*, the father of Cumman, was seven generations removed from Echu Gunnat. According to these genealogies Cumman's grandmother was *Derinnill Chetharchíchech*, the mother of St *Domangart*, a saint who lived in the generation after St Patrick's arrival and who gave his name to **Slieve Donard** in the Mournes. Therefore, if we can accept this genealogical evidence, Cumman lived a few generations after St Patrick.

Granagh — *An Greanach*
J 6148 — "the gravelly place"

1.	Grenach, villa de	Charts St. Mary's Abbey i 4	1300c
2.	Ballyngrenagh	PCR Eliz. I (Sav. Ards) 175	1559
3.	Ballynegrenagh	Fiants Eliz. §2090	1571
4.	Grennagh	Inq. Ult. (Down) §2 Jac. I	1605
5.	Grannagh	Ham. Copy Inq. xxxv	1623
6.	Grannagh	Inq. Ult. (Down) §14 Jac. I	1625
7.	Granagh	Inq. Ult. (Down) §14 Jac. I	1625
8.	Granagh	Sav. Ards 369	1628
9.	Grenagh	Inq. Ult. (Down) §20 Car. I	1631
10.	Granagh	Sav. Ards 373	1637c
11.	Granagh	Census 92	1659c
12.	Greenagh	BSD 86	1661
13.	Granagh	Sub. Roll Down 282	1663
14.	Granagh	Wm. Map (OSNB)	1810
15.	Granagh	High Const. Applot. (OSNB)	1830c
16.	Granagh	Bnd. Sur. (OSNB)	1830c
17.	Greannach "gravelly"	J O'D (OSNB)	1834c
18.	'granɑ	Local pronunciation	1991
19.	'grɑnəx	Local pronunciation	1991

The location of this townland by the shore would support O'Donovan's suggestion of "gravelly (place)" (no. 17). The word should be spelt *greanach*, i.e. with single *-n-* as *greannach* with double *-nn-* is a separate Irish word which means "hairy, furry, bushy" (= *DIL grendach*). On O'Donovan's occasional confusion of *-n-* and *-nn-* in Irish see Hughes (1989(c):125).

Knockinelder — *Cnoc an Iolair*
J 6351 — "hill of the eagle"

1. Knockavillar	PCR Eliz. I (Sav. Ards) 175	1559
2. Knocknyller	Fiants Eliz. §2090	1571
3. Ballyknockmiller	Savage Lands 4	1588
4. Ballyknockmeller	Fiants Eliz. §5264	1588
5. Carneknockneller	Inq. Ult. (Down) §14 Jac. I	1625
6. Knockeneller	Inq. Ult. (Down) §10 Car. I	1627
7. Cnocmeller	Inq. Ult. (Down) §38 Car. I	1633
8. Knockmiller	Sav. Ards 373	1637c
9. Knockmiller	Will (Sav. Ards) 247	1640
10. Knocknellet	Rental Portaferry, 5	1641
11. Knocknelder	Hib. Reg. Ards	1657c
12. Knockdrelder al. Knockmiller	BSD 84	1661
13. Kill:nelder	Map, Petty's Sur. (OSNB)	1683
14. Knockinelder	Wm. Map (OSNB)	1810
15. Knockanelder	High Const. Applot. (OSNB)	1830c
16. Knockinelder	Bnd. Sur. (OSNB)	1830c
17. Knockanelder	Reg. Free. (OSNB)	1832
18. Cnoc an Oll duir "hill of the great oak"	J O'D (OSNB)	1834c
19. Cnock-an-iolair – the hill of the eagle	O'Laverty i 393	1878
20. nɔkə'nɛldər	Local pronunciation	1991
21. nɔkn̥'ɛldər	Local pronunciation	1991

In the *OSNB* O'Donovan proposed a meaning *Cnoc an Oll-duir* "hill of the great oak" (17) and then went on to add: "Some think that this is a hybrid compound of *knock*, a hill, and English *elder*, a tree but this is scarcely true". While O'Donovan was right to dismiss the local theory that the name *Knockinelder* was a hybrid name composed of Irish *cnoc* "hill" and English *elder* "elder tree", his own suggestion *Cnoc an Oll-duir* is untenable because the grammar is clearly incorrect (Hughes 1991:127). Quite a lot of the earlier written forms (nos. 2 and 5–6) seem to bear out O'Laverty's suggestion (no. 19) of an original Gaelic form resembling *Cnoc an Iolair* "hill of the eagle".

O'Laverty (*loc. cit.* 393–4) discusses the possibility of a church in this townland, referring to an ancient cemetery on the farm of a Mr. James Curran, but his speculation (pp. 394–5) that the church is connected with Saint Cowey (*Cú Mhaighe*, see **Lough Cowey**) is in need of verification.

Tullyboard — *Tulaigh Boird*
J 6049 — "hillock of the flat top or table" (?)

1. Ballytolleborde	Savage Lands 4	1588
2. Ballytolleborde	Fiants Eliz. §5264	1588
3. Ballytolleborred	Inq. Ult. (Down) §2 Jac.I	1605
4. Tulliburred	Inq. Ult. (Down) §9 Jac.I	1620
5. Ballytullyboord	Ham. Copy Inq. xxxv	1623
6. Ballytulleboord	Ham. Copy Inq. xlvi	1623
7. Tolleberid	Inq. Ult. (Down) §14 Jac.I	1624

8. Tullebard	Inq. Ult. (Down) §14 Jac.I	1624
9. Balletolleboord	Inq. Ult. (Down) §10 Car.I	1627
10. Balletallebord	Inq. Ult. (Down) §10 Car.I	1627
11. Ballotollobrood	Sav. Ards 368	1628
12. Ballytollaboord	Sav. Ards 368	1628
13. Ballytollebrood	Sav. Ards 373	1637c
14. Tollebeerd	Census 91	1659
15. Tullibard	BSD 86	1661
16. Ballyboored	Sub. Roll Down 16	1663
17. Tullyboard	Wm. Map (OSNB)	1810
18. Tullyboard	High Const. Applot. (OSNB)	1830c
19. Tullyboard	Bnd. Sur. (OSNB)	1830c
20. Tulaigh Búird "hill of the flat top or table"	J O'D (OSNB)	1834c
21. ˌtǫli'bo:rd	Local pronunciation	1991

This name poses a difficulty in that four of the earlier spellings (3, 4, 7 & 16) seem to show a disyllabic *-borred, boored*, or the like. The majority of later forms appear to support a suggestion along the lines of *Tulaigh Boird* "hill of the flat top or table", as suggested by O'Donovan (20). There is also the possibility that this townland contains an Anglo-Norman name as a second element. It is difficult, however, to opt for any surname in particular although possiblities may be sought in Reaney (1958:) who cites Anglo-Norman surnames such as *Board/Boord* (37) *Burge/Burdge* (53) and *Burret*, with a variant *Burred* (54). For *Tully-* followed by an Anglo-Norman name note some of the early spellings in *Tollenrus(h)elly* for the townland of **Ballyrussely** in this parish. See also **Ballywierd** (parish of Ballytrustan).

Tullymally — *Tulaigh Uí Mhaolaodha* (?)
J 6152 — "Malley's hillock"

1. Tullomayle	PCR Eliz. I (Sav. Ards) 175	1559
2. Tullymayley	Inq. Ult. (Down) §5 Jac. I	1617
3. Tollomalle	CPR Jas I 340b	1617
4. Tollyvally	Hib. Reg. Ards	1657c
5. Tollemally	Census 91	1659c
6. Tullyvally al. Tullinall	BSD 84	1661
7. (?) Ballymayly	Inq. Ult. (Down) §19 Car. II	1662
8. (?) Ballynaghy al' Ballymayly	Inq. Ult. (Down) §19 Car II	1662
9. (?) Ballynaghy al' Ballymayly	Inq. Ult. (Down) §19 Car II	1662
10. Tullymally	Sub. Roll Dn 282	1663
11. Tollyvally	Map, Petty's Sur. (OSNB)	1683
12. Tullymally	Wm. Map (OSNB)	1810
13. Tullmally	High Const. Applot. (OSNB)	1830c
14. Tullymally	Bnd. Sur. (OSNB)	1830c
15. Tullymally	Reg. Free. (OSNB)	1832
16. Tulaigh Ui Mheallaigh "O'Mealley's hill"	J O'D (OSNB)	1834c
17. Tulaigh Ui Mhaille "O'Malley's hill"	J O'D (OSNB)	1834c
18. ˌtǫlɩ'mɑ(:)lɩ	Local pronunciation	1991

The first element of this name is fairly straightforward, Irish *tulaigh*, an oblique form of *tulach* "hillock". The second element poses considerable difficulty. *Tulaigh Máille* "hillock of the link" may be suggested due to the shape of the two adjoining hillocks in the townland which appear to be linked, although it has to be stressed that this is a tentative suggestion. O'Donovan suggested two separate family names (nos. 16 & 17). Woulfe (1923: 604) gives a Gaelic surname *Ó Maolaodha*, i.e. "the descendant of *Maolaodha* (the servant of St Aedh)". He further points out that this is a name of a family of the *Cinél Aonghusa* who were a sept of the *Cinél Eoghain* in Ulster, and that "In the North it seems to have been generally anglicized by assimilation to Malley".

Tullynacrew — *Tulaigh na Craoibhe*
J 6250 — "hillock of the tree"

1. Tollnecrewe	Fiants Eliz. §2090	1571
2. Ballitollomcrewe	Fiants Eliz. §5264	1588
3. Ballytollonecrewe	Savage Lands 3	1588
4. Crewe, 1/2 a townland	Inq. Ult. (Down) §5 Jac.I	1617
5. Tollenecrine	Inq. Ult. (Down) §9 Jac.I	1620
6. Balletollenecrewe	Inq. Ult. (Down) §9 Jac.I	1620
7. Tollenecreen	Inq. Ult. (Down) §14 Jac I	1625c
8. Tollenecreen	Inq. Ult. (Down) §14 Jac I	1625c
9. Tullencrevy al. Creggrodan	Inq. Ult. (Down) §10 Car.I	1627
10. Tollenocreeny otherwise Creggroddan	Sav. Ards 368	1628
11. Tullenecrevy	Rental Portaferry	1641
12. Tobernecreevy	Sub. Roll Dn 16	1663
13. Tullynacrew	Wm. Map (OSNB)	1810
14. Tullynacrewe	High Const. Applot. (OSNB)	1830c
15. Tullinacrew	Bnd. Sur. (OSNB)	1830c
16. Tullinacrew	Reg. Free (OSNB)	1832
17. Tulaigh na Craoibhe "hill of the bush or branch or widespreading tree"	J O'D (OSNB)	1834c
18. ˌtọlənəˈkru:	Local pronunciation	1991
19. ˌtọliˈkrʌ:	Local pronunciation	1991

This appears to be a fairly straightforward name, containing a form of Irish *craobh* "tree". It may contain a genitive singular *Tulaigh na Craoibhe* "hillock of the tree", or genitive plural *Tulaigh na gCraobh* "hillock of the trees". It may have referred to a well known landmark or assembly place.

OTHER NAMES

Islandacorr — *Oileán Corr*
J 5948 — "round island"

1. Islandcorr	Sav. Ards 373	1637c
2. ˌai̥lnəˈkɔr	Local pronunciation	1991

The 17th-century form *Islandcorr* (1) strongly suggests an original Irish form *Oileán Corr*. The difficulty, however, lies in ascertaining the exact meaning of the Irish word *Corr*. Several possibilities present themselves: *Oileán Corr* "island of (the) herons"; or "island of the young gannets" (Dinneen *corr* "young of gannet"). In this case, however, we may also consider the island as having been named from its shape, because from the mainland it stands out as a perfectly round-shaped hill. This points to *Oileán Corr* "round or hump-shaped island". The additional vowel in the present-day form may possibly be explained by metathesis.

Knockinelder Bay A hybrid form
J 6351

"The Bay is small and open to the N. East ... with rocks on the East and South East" J O'Donovan (*OSNB*). For an interpretation of the first element see **Knockinelder** townland above.

Mount Ross (House) An English/Scots form
J 6252

Local pronunciation ['mɔnt 'rɔs]. *Ross* was taken by Anderson (1979:18) to refer to a surname and seven families of that name are included in her study of the modern surnames of the Little Ards (Anderson 1980:2). If we go back to the 17th century we find several references to a Robert Ross gent. in possession of 9 townlands (*Census* 91), and in the *Sub. Rolls Down* there is listed a "Robert Ross of Newcastle"- i.e. a little to the N.W. of Mount Ross. In *Raven's Map Clandeboye*, p. 19 he is referred to as "Robert Ross Lord of ye Ards".

The house was described in the *OSNB c.* 1834 as: "A two storey house, the plantations near the house together with the trees in the hedge rows give the townland a wooded appearance". In *Sav. Ards* 263, n. 2 we read: "The House of Mount Ross, now in the possession of farmers, stands in a rather imposing, and lofty situation some distance from Balyygalget – a solidly built white house with two wings".

Peep o' day An English/Scots form
J 6051

Local pronunciation [pi:p ə 'de:]. This minor name may refer to the Peep o' Day Boys, for which see the following account by Knox:

> About 1793, two other illegal societies, also having adherents in the county, sprang into existence. One of them was termed 'Peep of Day Boys, Protestant Boys, or Wreckers', and their enmity was directed against the Roman Catholics, many of whom they are said to have driven into Connaught. (*Knox Hist.* 25).

Knox (*ibid.* 352) reports: "In 1783 a battle was fought here [i.e. Lisnagead td., Aghaderg par., Co. Down] between the 'Hearts of Steel' and 'Peep-of-day-Boys' when several of the former were killed". Some locals claim that the *Peep o' day* in the Ards has nothing to do with the Peep o' Day Boys. They say it is so called because this is the place on which the sun shines first in the mornings.

Portaferry See parish of Ballytrustan

Rowting Wheel A Scots form

1. ye rowting weele	Descr. Ards 34	1683
2. called by Scotch the Rowling Weel	OSM vii 9	1832c

3. the Routing Wheels	Sav. Ulst. 370	1906
4. [ðə 'rɔutən 'whi:lz]	Local pronunciation	1992
5. [ðə 'rɔundən 'whi:lz]	Local pronunciation	1992

This whirlpool is located in the mouth of the narrow entrance to Strangford, near to the town of Portaferry, off Islandacorr. In *Descr. Ards 1683* 34 we read:

> near ye Ardes syd vnder an hill (by ye Irish called banckmore) there is a whirle poole or Eddy of ye returning tide called by ye Scotts ye rowting weele from ye loud sound it some tymes makes neer to which if smale boats come (except about full sea when ye water is smelt) it is sayd they will be suckt in & swallowed vp, and that a great vessel with a topp saile gale doth pass throw it hardly without being layd about: yett in this last Century wee have nott heard of one boat or person lost by it ... There is an eddy Tide at the Entrance, occasioned by a Rock".

The form *Rowting Wheel* is derived from the Scots verb *rowt* "to shout, bawl, make a great noise". In Scots *rowt* developed a figurative use when applied to wind and water to mean "roar loudly. Hence *rowtin(g)*", according to *Scot. Nat. Dict.* (p. 498 s.v. *rowt* 5). Thus *Rowting Wheel* can be translated "bellowing whirlpool".

It would appear that *Rowting Wheel* also became interpreted as *Rowling*, i.e. "rolling", *Wheel*, but only presuming *Rowling* in the following passage, written by G. Scott in the late 1830s, is not a misprint:

> About 1 mile and a quarter south of the town of Portaferry there is in this river a whirlpool off of Rankmore [*recte* Bankmore] Head, supposed to be caused by Rocks or the incoming or returning tide. It is called by Scotch the Rowling Weel from the sound it makes at times in calm weather. There are times when it would be dangerous for small boats to pass. Scarcely ever an accident occurs as the sailors well know the place".
>
> *OSM* vii 9.

The form *Rowting Wheel* still survives to this day, judging by form no. 4, although the variant local pronunciation (no. 5) suggests a reinterpretation of *Rowting Wheel* as *Rounding Wheel.*

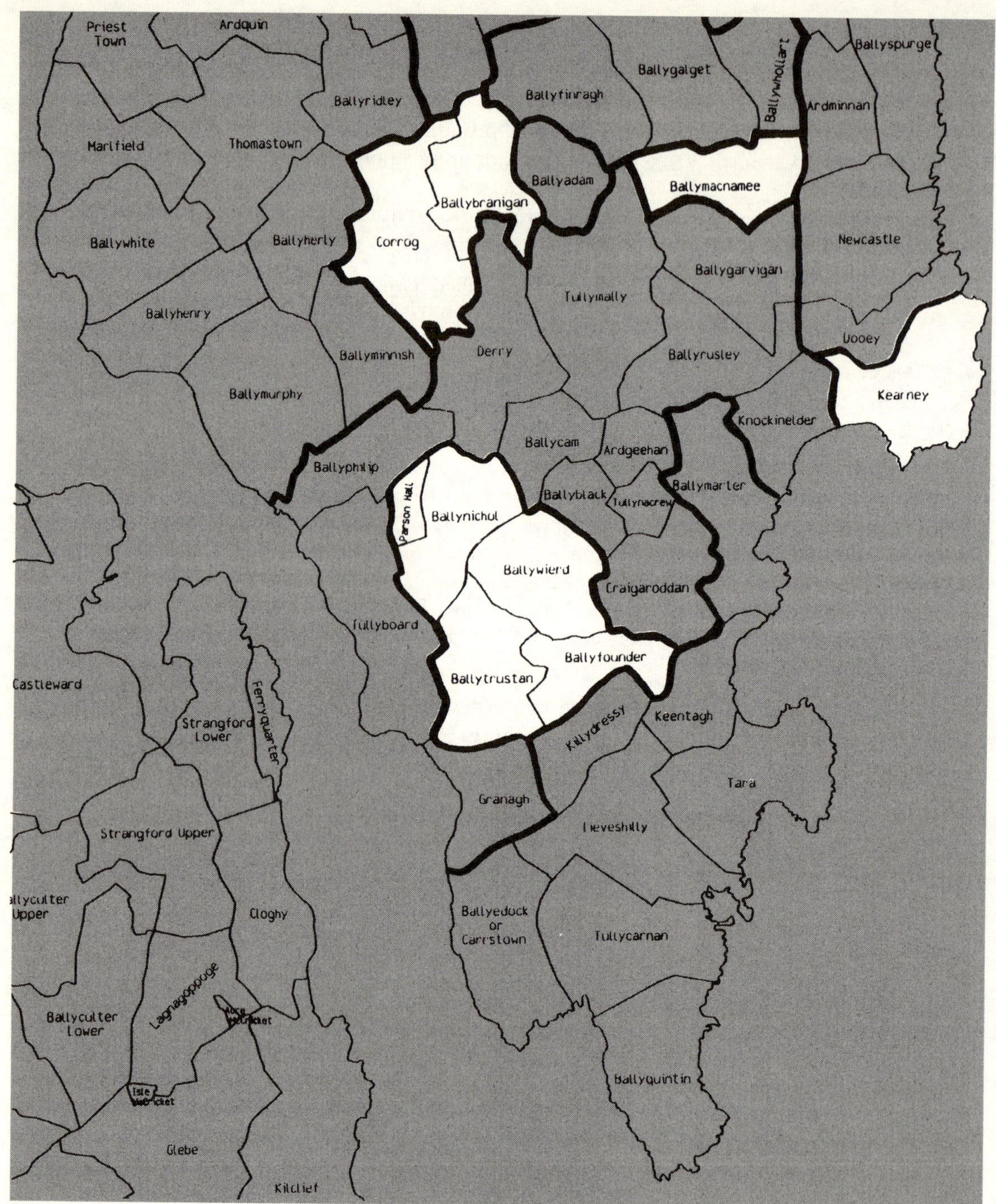

Parish of Ballytrustan

Barony of Ards Upper (4 parts)

Townlands
Ballybranigan
Ballyfounder
Ballymacnamee
Ballytrustan
Ballywierd
Corrog
Kearney
Parson Hall
Tullynichol

PARISH OF BALLYTRUSTAN

This civil parish forms part of the Union of Ballyphilip, Ballytrustan and Slanes, a union discussed under the Parish of Ballyphilip. *Knox Hist.* 468 discusses "the small parish of Ballytrustan" consisting of four detached portions, and comments: "The ruins of the church are in the old churchyard, which is still used as a burying ground by the Roman Catholic population". O'Laverty also gives an account of this parish and its old church (O'Laverty i 395), and his views on the origin of the name *Ballytrustan* are dealt with below under *Parish Name.* Further brief discussions on the parish include Reeves *EA* 25 n. u, *Lewis Top. Dict.* i 168, and *OSM* vii 7, 15.

PARISH NAME

Ballytrustan J 6049	*Baile Thrustáin* "Thurstan's townland"	
1. Thurstayniston, Ecclesia de	Eccles. Tax. 24	1306c
2. Thursantown	Inq. Ed. III (EA) 24 n. u	1343
3. Thrustayntone	Cal. Canc. Hib. (EA) i 144	1397
4. ecclesia de Trossnan al. Ballytroscon	Inq. Ult. (Down) §2 Jac. I	1605
5. vil. de Ballytrossan	Inq. Ult. (Down) §2 Jac. I	1605
6. vil. de Ballitrasenan	Inq. Ult. (Down) §2 Jac. I	1605
7. Ballitrosnan	CPR Jas I 78a	1606
8. Troston	Jas I to Down Cath. 178	1609
9. Trestran, Ecclesia de	Terrier (Reeves) 61	1615c
10. Trustan, Ecclesia de	Terrier (O'Laverty) 328	1615c
11. Troston	Ulster Visit. (Reeves) 25	1622
12. Balletrosnon	Ham. Copy Inq. xlvi	1623
13. Ballytrossnon al. Ballytrustan	Ham. Copy Inq. xxxv	1623
14. Balletrosnon	Ham. Copy Inq. xxxvi	1623
15. Balletrustan, in little Ardes	Inq. Down (Reeves 1) 131	1657
16. Ballytrustan	Census 92	1659c
17. Ballitrustan Parish al. Castleboy	BSD 86	1661
18. Ballytrustane	BSD 86	1661
19. Truston	Trien. Visit. (Bramhall) 9	1661
20. Balletrustan	Trien. Visit. (Margetson) 20	1664
21. Ballitrustan	Trien. Visit. (Boyle) 42	1679
22. B:trustan	Descr. Ards 36	1683
23. Ballytruston	Wm. Map (OSNB)	1810
24. Ballytrustan	Educ. Rept. (OSNB)	1826
25. Ballytrustin	High Const. Applot. (OSNB)	1830c
26. Ballytrustin	Bnd. Sur. (OSNB)	1830c
27. Ballytrustan	Reg. Free. (OSNB)	1832
28. Baile an Trostain "town of the pilgrim's staff"	J O'D (OSNB)	1834c
29. ˌbɑliˈtrɔ̤stn	Local pronunciation	1991

Reeves (*EA* 25, n. u) discusses this name stating that the form *Thursantown* and similar spellings of it found in Anglo-Norman documentation "seem to be varieties of *baile*, or its English form *town*, and *trostan* 'a staff'". On the basis of the anglicized spelling "Bally-trosnan" Reeves cites O'Reilly's Irish dictionary *Trosnan* "a crutch". Dinneen and *DIL* have a word *trostán* which Dinneen translates "a pole or staff, a prop, a crutch, a pilgrim's staff ... *fear an trostáin*, the pilgrim; al. *trosnán*". The theory of *Baile an Trostáin* "town of the pilgrim's staff" would seem to have found its way into Reeves via O'Donovan (form no. 28), and from Reeves into the work of O'Laverty. O'Laverty (i:395) even goes as far as to speculate that *Ballytrustan* "was so named from the staff used by pilgrims journeying to the Holy Sepulchre, for the rectory of the church belonged to the military order of St. John of Jerusalem, whose duty it was to protect pilgrims on their way to the Holy Land". While it is true that the ancient church at Ballytrustan was listed as *Hospitallers* (and thus exempt from a levy) in the Taxation of Pope Nicholas IV (*EA* 25), any assumption of a connection between this place and pilgrims' staffs appears unlikely. The name *Thurstaynistone* contains an Anglo-Norman name (in the same way as neighbouring **Ballyphilip** goes back to an earlier *Feliptone*). Anderson (1979:18) suspects the *-trustan* part of *Ballytrustan* to be a family name, although she cites no evidence. However, Reaney (1958:320) lists 30 examples of *Thurstan*, *Thurstans*, *Thurston* etc., as a surname in England, attested as early as 1066. This surname is interpreted by Reaney as being related to Old Norse *Thorsteinn*, Old Danish *Thorsten* "Thor's stone", which occurred as Old English *Thurstān*. The attestation of an individual named "R. Thurstan" from a document relating to Dublin in 1302 AD (*CDI 1302–7* p. 9) clearly shows that the Anglo-Norman surname found its way to Ireland and thus makes an Anglo-Norman origin more likely for Ballytrustan than the Gaelic origin suggested by O'Donovan, Reeves and O'Laverty. One detail remaining is the fact that we get the form *Ballytrustan*, as opposed to an expected *Ballyturstan*. This metathesis of *-turst-* to *-trust-* in the Gaelic reflex of the Anglo-Norman name *Thurstan* may be viewed as one occurring internally in Gaelic. However, it is probably best viewed as one coming about in the English form of the name before it was gaelicized, as Reaney (320) gives *Thruston* as a by-form of *Thurston*, and for the Ards we may note the spelling *Thrustayntone* from 1397 (no. 3).

TOWNLAND NAMES

Ballybranigan — *Baile Uí Bhranagáin*
J 6053 — "Ó Branagáin's townland"

1. Ballybranigan	Fiants Eliz. §5264	1588
2. Ballybranigan	Savage Lands 4	1588
3. Ballybrannagan	Inq. Ult. (Down) §2 Jac. I	1605
4. Ballybranigan	Ham. Copy Inq. xxxv	1623
5. Ballybranegane	Inq. Ult. (Down) §14 Jac. I	1625
6. Ballyvranegane	Inq. Ult. (Down) §14 Jac. I	1625
7. Ballyoranagan	Inq. Ult. (Down) §10 Car. I	1627
8. Ballyoranagan	Sav. Ards 369	1628
9. Ballyoranigan	Sav. Ards 369	1628
10. Ballevrannegan	Inq. Ult. (Down) §27 Car. I	1631
11. Ballyvranigan	Will (Sav. Ards) 247	1640
12. Ballyvranegan	Inq. Ult. (Down) §100 Car. I	1641
13. Ballyvranagan	Rental Portaferry 5	1641

14. Ballyvranegan	Census 92	1659c
15. Ballyvrannigan	BSD 86	1661
16. Ballyvranigan	Inq. Ult. (Down) §14 Car. II	1662
17. Ballybraniken	Sav. Ards 204	1723
18. Ballybrannigan	Wm. Map (OSNB)	1810
19. Ballybrannigan	High Const. Applot. (OSNB)	1830c
20. Ballybranagan	Bnd. Sur. (OSNB)	1830c
21. Ballybrannigan	Reg. Free. (OSNB)	1832
22. Baile Uí Bhranagáin "O'Brannagan's town"	J O'D (OSNB)	1834c
23. ˌbɑliˈbrɑnigən	Local pronunciation	1991

The Gaelic surname *Ó Branagáin*, anglicized (O')Branigan, Brangan etc., means "descendant of *Branagán*". *Branagán* is a personal name meaning "little raven" and is a derivative of *bran* "crow, raven" + diminutive suffix *-agán*. MacLysaght (1964:31–1) describes the bearers of this Irish surname as "A sept of the Cenél Eoghain, now found mainly as in map [i.e. Armagh-Monaghan]". The origins of the Ards family is in need of clarification, although we may note the townland of **Tullybranigan** (parish of Kilcoo, Co. Down) which also appears to contain this surname.

Ballyfounder
J 6149

Baile Phoinnir
"Poyner's townland"

1. Punyertoun	Inq. Earldom Ulster iii 65	1333
2. Balyfannor	PCR Eliz. I (Sav. Ards) 175	1559
3. Ballyfoynneragh	Fiants Eliz. §1659	1570
4. Ballyfynnor	Fiants Eliz. §2090	1571
5. (?) Ballysoner	Fiants Eliz. §5264	1588
6. Ballifouner	Inq. Ult. (Down) §2 Jac. I	1605
7. (?) Ballefouer	Inq. Ult. (Down) §9 Jac. I	1620
8. Ballefover	Inq. Ult. (Down) §9 Jac. I	1620
9. Ballefenore	Ham. Copy Inq. xlvi	1623
10. Ballefenor	Ham. Copy Inq. xxxv	1623
11. Ballyfouer	Inq. Ult. (Down) §14 Jac. I	1625
12. Ballefowner	Inq. Ult. (Down) §10 Car. I	1627
13. Ballofowner	Sav. Ards 368	1628
14. Ballofoner	Sav. Ards 373	1637c
15. Ballefoner	Census 92	1659c
16. Ballyfoner	BSD 86	1661
17. Ballyfoner	Sub. Roll Down 282	1663
18. Ballyphoner	Wm. Map (OSNB)	1810
19. Ballyfoner	High Const. Applot. (OSNB)	1830c
20. Ballyfounder	Bnd. Sur. (OSNB)	1830c
21. Ballyfonner	Reg. Free. (OSNB)	1832
22. Ballyphonder	Mr. Nugent, Portaferry (OSNB)	1834c
23. Baile Phonnraigh "Fonner's or Bonner's town"	J O'D (OSNB)	1834c

24. Baile na Ponaire "town of the beans"	J O'D (OSNB)	1834c
25. Ballyfoundra	Sav. Ards ix	1888
26. ˌbɑliˈfɔndər	Local pronunciation	1991

This is yet another clear example of an Anglo-Norman name, in this case *Punyertoun* (form 1), undergoing gaelicization. We have definite instances of an Anglo-Norman family of the name *Le Pugneor* in Ulster, as in the following excerpt (from *CDI* vol. 1, no. 700):

> Before 1216 King John granted some lands in Ulster to 'Sir William le Pugneor, the King's Knight'.

More specifically to the Ards we see that in 1225 Henry III granted "to Brian de Scalvariis the two carucates of land in L'Ard [i.e. the Ards] which Robert le Puinnur held (*ibid.* no. 1287)". (Orpen *JRSAI* xliv (1914) 65, n. 1.)

Reaney (1958:258 s.v. *Poyner, Poynor, Punyer*) has examples of this surname in England, such as *Geoffrey le Poinnur* (*Poignur*) 1220 and other 13th-century forms *le Poinur, le Pungneur* (*Puinur*), *Poyner,* etc. These he derives from Old French *poigneur* "fighter" and compares the surname *Champion.*

Ballymacnamee
J 6353

Baile Mhic Con Mí
"*Mac Con Mí*'s townland"

1. (?) Ballyvickneny	Inq. Ult. (Down) §5 Jac. I	1617
2. Ballyvickinny	CPR Jas I 340b	1617
3. Bally McNemee	Census 91	1659c
4. Ballymaneemee	BSD 84	1661
5. Ballyvickneny	Inq. Ult. (Down) §19 Car II	1662
6. Bally mc. ollmee	Map, Petty's Sur. (OSNB)	1683
7. Ballymacnamee	Wm. Map (OSNB)	1810
8. Ballymacnamee	Educ. Rept. (OSNB)	1830c
9. Ballymacnamee	High Const. Applot. (OSNB)	1830c
10. Ballymacnamee	Reg. Free. (OSNB)	1830c
11. Ballymacnamee	Bnd. Sur. (OSNB)	1830c
12. Baile Mhic na Midhe "Mac Namee's town"	J O'D (OSNB)	1834c
13. ˌbɑlimɛknəˈmi:	Local pronunciation	1991

The Irish surname *Mac Con Mí,* earlier spelt as *Mac Con Midhe* (lit. "son of the hound of Meath"), is described as a common surname in Ulster by Woulfe (1923:341), who gives the anglicized forms as: "MacConamy, MacNamee, Conmee, Mee". This latter surname appears to be represented by the 1659 form of the name *Bally McNemee* (no. 3), *Ballymaneemee* (no. 4) plus the 19th-century forms of the name (nos. 7–11). Many members of the Mac Con Mí family were professional poets in medieval Ireland and a member of that family may have received land here in his function as *file*, or *bard*. The forms *Ballyvickneny* (nos. 1 and 5) might suggest that another name is involved. Woulfe (1923:312) discusses an Irish surname *Mac an Éanaigh* which was anglicized as MacAne(a)ny, MacEneany, MacNeny etc., but these latter early spellings of the name could well be merely the result of erroneous transcription.

Ballynichol — *Baile Niocail*
J 6050 — "Nichol's townland"

1. Nicholtown	Inq. Earldom Ulster xliv 64	1333
2. Nicholstoun	Inq. Earl Ulster (EA) 361	1333
3. Ballynyckoll	Fiants Eliz. §2090	1571
4. Ballynyckoll	Fiants Eliz. §2090	1571
5. Ballynicholl	Fiants Eliz. §5264	1588
6. Ballinvcholl	Inq. Ult. (Down) §2 Jac.I	1605
7. Ballvnckoll	Inq. Ult. (Down) §2 Jac.I	1605
8. Ballynicholas al. Tullycaman	Ham. Copy Inq. xxxv	1623
9. Ballenicoll al. Tullecarnan al. Loughduffe	Ham. Copy Inq. xliv	1623
10. Nicholston	Inq. Ult. (Down) §14 Jac.I	1624
11. Ballincoll	Inq. Ult. (Down) §14 Jac.I	1624
12. Ballynikoll	Inq. Ult. (Down) §10 Car.I	1627
13. Ballynycoll	Sav. Ards 368	1628
14. Ballicott otherwise Ballynicott	Sav. Ards 373	1637c
15. Ballynicoll	Census 92	1659
16. Ballynicoll	BSD 86	1661
17. Baile Niocóil "Nicholas's town"	J O'D (OSNB)	1834c
18. ˌbɑliˈnĭkəl	Local pronunciation	1991

The 14th-century forms clearly show that Anglo-Norman *Nichol(s)toun* was the earlier form of this place-name with a subsequent gaelicization *Baile Niocail.* Reaney (1958:229–30) gives an indication of how popular the name *Nicholas* was in Anglo-Norman England. In Ireland we may cite mention of a John Fitz-Nicholas of Slane (*Cal. Canc. Hib.* vol. i p. 28 1320 AD, cited in *EA* 23, n. r). The Latin personal name *Nicolaus* was a borrowing from Greek signifying "victory people" but, as Reaney states, the vernacular form was *Nicol. Nicol* is the form we are dealing with in the townland name in this parish and in the townland of **Ballynichol** (parish of Comber, Co. Down).

Ballywierd — *Baile Bhuraid*
J 6150 — "Burred's townland"

1. Ballywored	PCR Eliz. I (Sav. Ards) 175	1559
2. Ballyworred	Fiants Eliz. §2090	1571
3. Ballyworred	Fiants Eliz. §2090	1571
4. Ballyburde	Fiants Eliz. §5264	1588
5. Ballyburde	Fiants Eliz. §2090	1588
6. Balliward	Inq. Ult. (Down) §5 Jac. I	1617
7. Ballewarrid	Inq. Ult. (Down) §9 Jac. I	1620
8. Ballewarde	Inq. Ult. (Down) §9 Jac. I	1620
9. Ballewarrod otherwise Tallenegore	Sav. Ards 368	1628
10. Ballewored otherwise Tollenegore	Sav. Ards 373	1637c
11. Ballyward	Census 92	1659c
12. (?) Ballyward	Inq. Ult. (Down) §19 Car. II	1662
13. Ballywierd	Wm. Map (OSNB)	1810

14. Ballywierd	High Const. Applot. (OSNB)	1830c
15. Ballywierd	Bnd. Sur. (OSNB)	1830c
16. Ballywierd td., "Wierd's town"	J O'D (OSNB)	1834c
17. ˌbɑliˈwi:rd	Local pronunciation	1991

Our earliest written attestations of this name from the 16th century, *Ballyworred/Ballyburde* (nos. 1–5), indicate a gaelicized form. However, the nature of the contiguous townlands **Ballynichol, Ballyblack, Ballytrustan** and **Ballyfounder**, which have all been shown to have originated as Anglo-Norman forms, leads one to suspect an Anglo-Norman origin for this name. Reaney (1958:54) lists a surname *Burrett* (also spelt in his citations as *Bur(r)ed*) which can go back either to (a) Old English *Burgraēd* "fortress council" or (b) a compound of Old French *bourre* "rough hair, flock of wool" + Old English *hēafod* "head", a nickname for one with rough, shaggy hair. Whatever the etymology of the Anglo-Norman surname *Burret/Burred*, its presence in gaelicized Ballywierd seems to be supported by the early Ballyburde forms (nos. 4–5 in particular, as well as forms 1, and 2–3; see also discussion on **Tullyboard**, parish of Ballyphilip). The 17th-century forms spelt *Ballyward(e)* (nos. 6, 8, 11–2) appear to be due to some form of association with the family of the name *Ward*, and this name occurs in Savage Estate Rolls for 1775–6 according to Anderson (1979:21). The vowel [i:] in the modern forms spelt *Ballywierd* may, perhaps, reflect an Irish *Buiread* alongside *Burad*.

Forms 9 and 10 indicate that this townland was also known as "Tollnegore", which suggests an alias Irish form *Tulaigh na nGabhar* "hillock of the goats".

Corrog | *Corróg*
J 6052 | "little round hill"

1. Corrock	Fiants Eliz. §2090	1571
2. Ballycorrigge	Savage Lands 4	1588
3. Ballicorrogge	Fiants Eliz. §5264	1588
4. Ballicorrock	Inq. Ult. (Down) §2 Jac. I	1605
5. Ballycorog	Ulst. Roll Gaol Deliv. 262	1613
6. Corruck	Inq. Ult. (Down) §9 Jac. I	1620
7. Ballicarrock al. Corrock	Inq. Ult. (Down) §9 Jac. I	1620
8. Ric. Savadge de Corroge	Inq. Ult. (Down) §9 Jac. I	1620
9. le Corroge	Inq. Ult. (Down) §9 Jac. I	1620
10. Derrycorrogg	Inq. Ult. (Down) §14 Jac. I	1625
11. Corrogg	Inq. Ult. (Down) §14 Jac. I	1625
12. Ballecorrogge	Inq. Ult. (Down) §10 Car. I	1627
13. Ballycarrock	Inq. Ult. (Down) §10 Car. I	1627
14. Ballocarrocke othorwise Ballocorroge	Sav. Ards 368	1628
15. Ballycoroge	Sav. Ards 368	1628
16. Ballycoroke otherwise Ballycoroge	Sav. Ards 373	1637c
17. Ballyorock	Sav. Ards 373	1637c
18. Corrog	Census 92	1659c
19. Carrocke	BSD 86	1661
20. Corrogs	Wm. Map (OSNB)	1810
21. Corrag	High Const. Applot. (OSNB)	1830c

22. Correg	Bnd. Sur. (OSNB)	1830c
23. Corrig td., *Carraig* "a rock" Corrog	J O'D (OSNB)	1834c
24. ˈkɔrig	Local pronunciation	1991

The written forms of this name clearly suggest an Irish original *Corróg*, but the meaning is less certain. It may be *corróg* "a corner, an angle, a little pit" (Dinneen); on the other hand it is possibly *corróg*, a diminutive of *corr* "a round hill".

Kearney
J 6551

Cearnach (?)
"area of the angular rocks"

1. (?) Ballycaryne	Compotus Dun. 168	1305
2. (?) Karmarry	Inq. Earldom Ulster iii 65	1333
3. Ballycarnny	Inq. Ult. (Down) §2 Jac. I	1605
4. Ballecarne	Ham. Copy Inq. xlvi	1623
5. Kerney	Inq. Ult. (Down) §10 Car. I	1627
6. Karny	Inq. Ult. (Down) §10 Car. I	1627
7. Karney	Sav. Ards 369	1628
8. Kearney	Inq. Ult. (Down) §27 Car. I	1631
9. Carny	Inq. Ult. (Down) §38 Car. I	1633
10. Karney	Sav. Ards 373	1637c
11. Carny	Inq. Ult. (Down) §102 Car. I	1641
12. Kearny, Dwaltagh Smith de	Inq. Ult. (Down) §102 Car II	1641
13. Kearny	Hib. Reg. Ards	1657c
14. Karny	Census 92	1659c
15. Kearny	BSD 86	1661
16. Kearny	Map, Petty's Sur. (OSNB)	1683
17. Kerney	Wm. Map (OSNB)	1810
18. Kerney	High Const. Applot. (OSNB)	1830c
19. Kearney	Bnd. Sur. (OSNB)	1830c
20. Carnach "full of heaps or cairns"	J O'D (OSNB)	1834c
21. ˈkɛrni	Local pronunciation	1991

In *Inq. Ult.* (§2 Jac. I 1605 AD) mention is made of the McKearneys (and the Magees from Portavogie): "lez **McKearnyes**, lez Magies de Portabogagh". On the other side of Strangford Lough there is also mention of "McKearneys of Duffrin", *CPR Jas I* 511a. Anderson (1980:2) lists ten families of Kearney (Carnie) in the Little Ards, and O'Laverty (i 385) records:

> The 'McKearney's' (the name is now Kearney) were a powerful sept in the Ards, – probably of Kinel-Owen origin, for Kearney is still a name of frequent occurrence in Derry and Tyrone; at all events they were not much loved by the English".

This surname may be preserved in the name **Carney Hill** (parish of Donaghadee). Woulfe (1923:331) assigns "*Mac Ceithearnaigh* 'son of Ceithearnach'" to Roscommon and he further notes that *Ó Ceithearnaigh* seems to be the only form of the name which has survived. It is pointed out, however, by Woulfe (460–1) that the anglicized forms *(O')Kearney, Carney,* etc., can represent the Gaelic surnames *Ó Ceithearnaigh* (i.e. descendant of *Ceithearnach* "foot soldier") or *Ó Cearnaigh* (i.e descendant of *Cearnach* "victorious"). A branch of this latter family attained senior ecclesiastical office as erenaghs of the diocese of Derry and these may be the "McKearneys" spoken of by O'Laverty. A "Mattach Dungan Omungan O Kerny" is mentioned in a source for Co. Down dating to *circa* 1260 AD (*Exch. Accounts Ulst.* p. 157) and the editor's note that "This name [O Kerny] is doubtful, and does not resemble any of the prevalent ones in Antrim or Down" may now need to be reviewed. The confusion in Irish surnames of *Ó* "grandson of" and *Mac* "son of" is a common feature for phonetic reasons, particularly in names beginning with *C-* or *G-*, thus the 17th-century "**McKearnyes** ... de Portabogagh" (cited above) could well be earlier "O'Kearneys". The dropping of the element *Baile* before a family name in a place-name is admittedly unusual, although in *GÉ* 104 the modern anglicized name *Carney* (Co. Sligo) has been derived from Irish *Fearann Uí Chearnaigh* (i.e. "the territory of *Ó Cearnaigh*"). Nevertheless there are difficulties in deriving this place from the McKearney, or O'Kearney family.

O'Donovan may well be right in his suggestion (form 20) that the townland name *Kearney* goes back to *Carnach* "full of heaps". If, however, one is to take the place-name *Kearney* as deriving from a physical feature, one may also consider *Cearnach* "angular shaped" as a meaning for the name, a possible reference to the shape of the rocks on the shore in the east of this townland which is bordered by the Irish Sea. Indeed, for the bay here, which is decribed as a "small bay formed by rocks", see **Kearney Point** (below). *DIL* lists an adjective *cernach* "angular, having corners" and Dinneen has *ceárnach* "square, pointed, having corners". This latter meaning is the one most favoured but with no great degree of confidence.

Parson Hall — An English form
J 6050

1.	3 quarter' de Parsonhall	Inq. Ult. (Down) §14 Jac. I	1625
2.	3 quarter' de Parsonhall	Inq. Ult. (Down) §10 Car. I	1627
3.	Parsonhall	Sav. Ards 368	1628
4.	Parson Hall	Sav. Ards 373	1637c
5.	P'sons Hall	Sub. Roll Down 282	1663
6.	Parson	High Const. Applot. (OSNB)	1830c
7.	Parson	Bnd. Sur. (OSNB)	1830c
8.	'pɑrsən 'hɔ:l	Local pronunciation	1991

Parson Hall is described by O'Donovan as a farm house in *OSNB*, although the 17th-century forms (1 & 2) show that the name was firmly established as a townland at that time. O'Laverty (i 397–8) gives details of Parson Hall's status as, possibly, the glebe of Ballyphilip, which would explain the ecclesiastical nature of the townland name.

OTHER NAMES

Bankmore Hill — *An Banc Mór* "the large bank or hill"
J 6049

1.	Banckmore, out of	CPR Jas I 247a	1613
2.	quarter de Banckmore	Inq. Ult. (Down) §14 Jac. I	1625
3.	the quarter in great Ardes called the Banckmore	Inq. Ult. (Down) §15 Jac. I	1625c

4. Banckmore	Sav. Ards 368	1628
5. Bankmore	Sav. Ards 373	1637c
6. an hill (by ye Irish called banckmore)	Descr. Ards 34	1683
7. Bank Hill	J O'D (OSNB)	1834c
8. baŋk'mo:r	Local pronunciation	1991

This name strongly suggests an Irish original *An Banc Mór* "the great bank". It was noted as *Bank Hill* in the *OSNB* where it is described as "a small round hill 118 feet above sea level. There is a ruined house on it". *Knox Hist.* 467 mentions "one of the large raths so common in the district", while Harris (*Harris Hist.* 137) has: "in good shelter near *Bankmore* (which is a sand Bank a Mile S. of Portaferry on the *Ardes* side, and about two miles N. of the Bar". In *OSM* vii 8 it is stated that "Bankmore is recognised by Mr Nugent as a townland".

Kearney Point — A hybrid form
J 6451

No evidence has been found for an Irish form for this headland and its current name is a combination of the townland name **Kearney** (see above) and English *point.* Kearney Bay described in *OSNB* "A small bay formed by rocks ... on the North and South, and open to winds from the NE and South".

Portaferry — *Port an Pheire*
J 6051 — "port of the ferry"

1. Port na Peireadh	LCABuidhe 160 l. 193	1617c
2. Balliporteferrye	Fiants Eliz. §5264	1588
3. Prtferri	Dartmouth Map 5	1590
4. Port nefery	Jobson's Ulster (TCD)	1590
5. Portferry	Fiants Eliz. §5703	1591
6. Portferrie	Bartlett Map (TCD)	1601
7. Portferre	Boazio's Map (NG)	1609
8. Portneferry	Speed's Antrim & Down	1610
9. Pertneferry	Speed's Ulster	1610
10. Portferry (×2)	Ulst. Roll Gaol Deliv. 262	1613
11. Portaferry	Inq. Ult. (Down) §5 Jac. I	1617
12. Porteferrye	Inq. Ult. (Down) §9 Jac. I	1620
13. Portferry	Inq. Ult. (Down) §9 Jac. I	1620
14. Portfeare	Ulster Visit. (Reeves) 25	1622
15. Portferi	Inq. Ult. (Down) §12 Jac. I	1623
16. Portferry	Inq. Ult. (Down) §14 Jac. I	1624
17. Portferry	Inq. Ult. (Down) §10 Car. I	1627
18. Portferrye	Inq. Ult. (Down) §10 Car. I	1627
19. Portferye	Inq. Ult. (Down) §10 Car. I	1627
20. Portforrie	Sav. Ards 368	1628
21. Portforry otherwise Ballymurphye	Sav. Ards 368	1628
22. Portferry	Sav. Ards 369	1628
23. Portferry otherwise Ballymurphy	Sav. Ards 373	1637c
24. Porteferrie	Inq. Ult. (Down) §20 Car. I	1631

25. Porteferry	Inq. Ult. (Down) §37 Car. I	1633
26. Portferry	Inq. Ult. (Down) §48 Car. I	1634
27. Portaferry	Inq. Ult. (Down) §82 Car. I	1637
28. Portaferry	Will (Sav. Ards) 247	1640
29. Portferry	Inq. Ult. (Down) §102 Car. I	1641
30. Porteferry	Inq. Ult. (Down) §109 Car. I	1650c
31. Porteferry	Census 91	1659c
32. Portferry	Trien. Visit. (Bramhall) 8	1661
33. Portaferry	BSD 86	1661
34. Portaferry	Sub. Roll Down 282	1663
35. Portferry	Map, Petty's Sur. (OSNB)	1683
36. Port Ferry	Lamb Maps	1690c
37. Portaferry	J O'D (OSNB)	1834c
38. Port an Pheire(adh)	Dinneen 837	1927
39. Port an Pheire	AGBP 118	1969
40. ˌpɔrtiˈfɛrı	Local pronunciation	1991

Mac Reachtain (1951:9) took *Peireadh* as an Old Irish word meaning "rapid, treacherous whirlwinds" (*iomghaothanna tobanna, fealltacha*) but as Knox (*Knox Hist.* 467) states: "Portaferry obviously derives its name from its position on the Ferry, which forms the main line of communication between the baronies of Ards and Lecale", a meaning echoed in *Sav. Ards* 122. One of the earliest, but not strictly accurate, attempts at suggesting a meaning for this name was made in 1744 by Harris (*Harris Hist.* 45, n. c):

> "*Portaferry* may be compounded of an obsolete *Irish* and an *English* Word, *Porth* signifying severe or terrible, *i.e.* the terrible Ferry, a Name well adapted to it. But we should choose to make it intirely *English*, i.e. the Port of the Ferry; and the rather as the *English* settled so early in this tract, and built the castle here, under the Protection of which the Town had its beginning".

It is true that the Savages have long been established in this area and that their initial settlement dates back to the Anglo-Norman period and survived until the reign of Elizabeth I and beyond, e.g.: "The chiefe of these Savages was styled in graunts from Elizabeth lord of ye little Ardes, his castle is that of Portiferry aforesaid" *Descr. Ards 1683* 35. However, the structure of the name Portaferry would refute Harris' view of making it "intirely English", as in an Irish bardic poem dated to 1617 we have *Port na Peireadh,* which shows that the place-name existed as an Irish-language name. It should be noted here, however, that a feminine form of the genitive *Port na Peireadh* may not be reflective of ordinary usage, as a feminine form was required by the poet in this particular instance in order to preserve the metrical requirement of perfect alliteration (or *fíoruaim*) between ***Port*** and ***Peireadh***, whereas the presumably more normal masculine form (i.e. *Port an Pheiridh*) would have given *Ph-* (= *F-*) which would not have produced alliteration and thus blemished the metre of the line. Nevertheless, the anglicized forms of the name suggest a masculine form of the word was the more usual in everyday speech. Dinneen has *Port an Pheire,* as does *AGBP,* although the variant genitive given by Dinneen as *Peiridh* would also have given *Port an Pheiridh,* which accords well with the anglicized forms of the name.

Descriptions of the town are many, one of the earliest being: "Portiferry there is a good Creek or bay for barks where they ly at Anchor in five fadomes at ye lowest Ebb". *Descr. Ards 1683* 34. In the mid 18th century *Harris Hist.* 45–6 records:

> It is a market Town, but irregularly built, and few other than thatched Houses in it. Heretofore a pretty brisk Trade was carried on in this Place, and between 30 and 40 ships belonged to its Port; but now there are scarce two; many having been unfortunately lost; which, with the Influence of *Belfast* and *Newry* have upon the Commerce of the Place, has much diminished the Trade of it, which now chiefly consists in the Exportation of Corn and Kelp from the *Ardes* and *Lecale* to *Dublin* and foreign Parts, and the Importation of such Commodities as are in Demand in the Neighbourhood. The Castle of *Portaferry* was the ancient seat of the Savages, and is now inhabited by *Andrew Savage*.

On the history of the town see further: Atkinson (1832:i 202–3, 211 for Portaferry House, and 302 for the Castle); *Youngs Tour in Ireland* vol. i, 50, 136–7, vol. ii 93. *Knox Hist.* 31, 231, 467; *Lewis Top. Dict.* ii 463–4 and *OSM* vii 12–14. On the archaeology of Portaferry see *ASCD* 476.

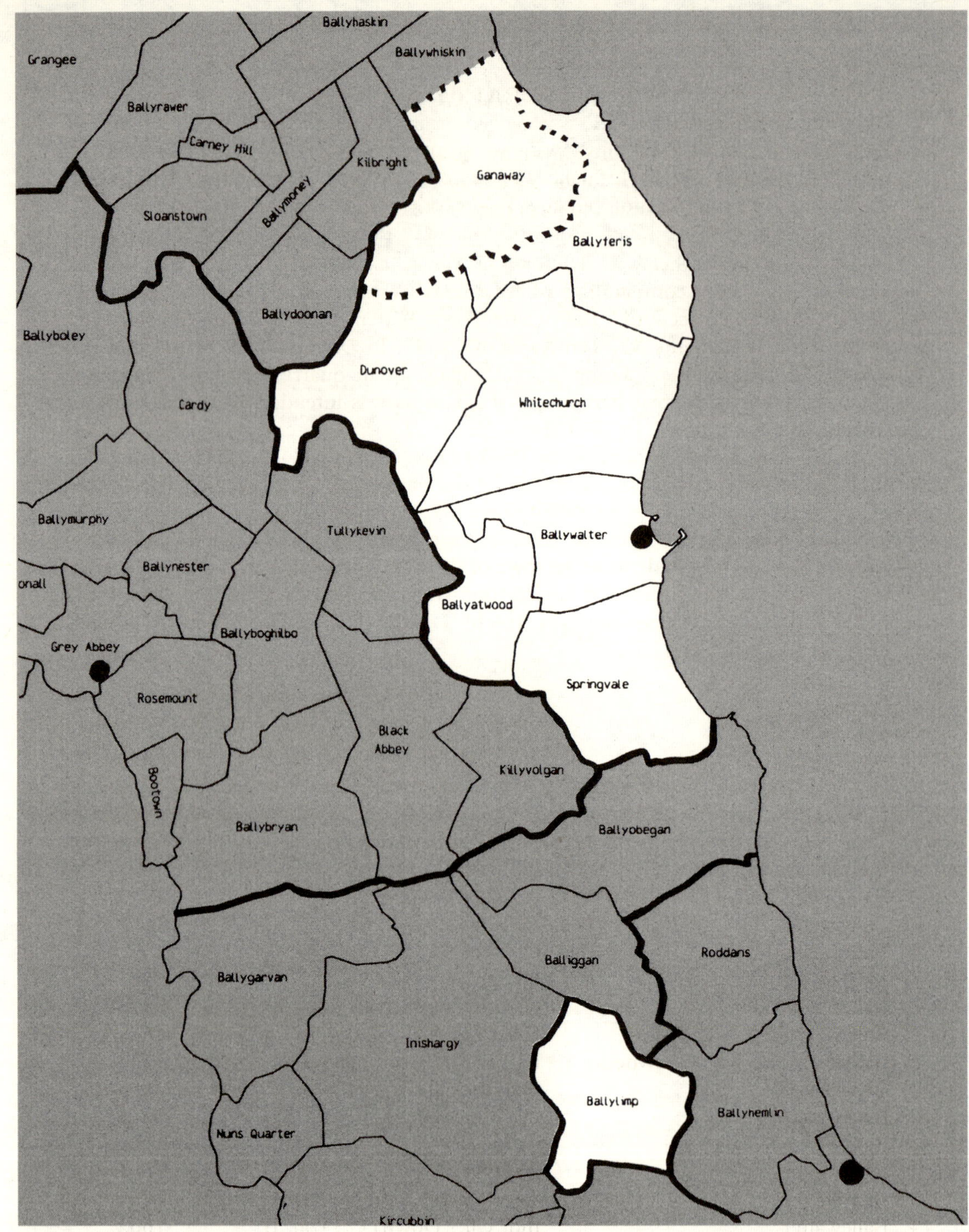

Parish of Ballywalter

Barony of Ards Upper

Townlands	Ballywalter	Whitechurch
Ballyatwood	Dunover	
Ballyferis	Ganaway (shared with Donaghadee)	*Town*
Ballylimp (detached)	Springvale	Ballywalter

PARISH OF BALLYWALTER

The civil parish of Ballywalter is also known by the alias of **Whitechurch**, a name discussed below. Ballywalter is described by Lewis (*Lewis' Top. Dict.* i 169) as a vicarage in the diocese of Down and in the *OSNB* it is said to form part of the "Union of Ballywalter, Inishargy, St. Andrews alias Ballyhalbert".

As regards settlement here, in the *Book of Survey and Distribution* of 1661 we read "Ballywalter & ye village consisting of 24 tenements", and in *Ham. Copy. Inq.* 108 (1681 AD) there is a summary account: "Ballywalter Town, Water Mill and Wind Mill. The Eight Acre Park. Three tenements &c. Ten Acres of Land". In *Descr. Ards* p. 37 the parish of Ballywalter is described as containing "a smale village a slate quarry a creek for smale boats & a place verry fitt for a great harbour, ... if a Key as was intended by y[e] said Earle [of Clanbrazill] were built there". In 1744 Harris (*Harris Hist.* 68) writes: "*Ballywalter*, a Village noted only for a good Slate Quarry, and a Presbyterian Meeting-House is about half a Mile North of *Spring-Vale*". Atkinson (1823:i, 231) describes it as "a pretty little village" while *Knox Hist.* 460 records "The Parish of Ballywalter, Baile Bhaitéir, Walter's Town, sometimes called Whitechurch, Ecclesia Alba, or Templefinn, contains a population of 735 persons to which we should add the residents in the town of Ballwalter, making a total of 1,437". There are also 19th-century descriptions of varying length in *OSM* vii 16–8; *OSNB*, c. 1834; Ewart (1866: 39) and in Lewis (*Lewis' Top. Dict.* 169 b). For the ruins of the (probably) 13th-century church see *ASCD* 300–1.

PARISH NAME

Ballywalter J 6368	*Baile Bháltair* "Walter's townland"	
1. Ballywalter	Inq. Ult. (Down) §2 Jac. I	1605
2. Ballivalter	Inq. Ult. (Down) §2 Jac. I	1605
3. Ballywalter	CPR Jas I 73a	1605
4. Balliwalter	CPR Jas I 326a	1617
5. the baie of Ballewalter	Ham. Copy Inq. lii	1623
6. Ballewalter	Ham. Copy Inq. xlvi	1623
7. Ballywalter al. Ballywaltra	Ham. Copy Inq. xxxi	1623
8. Ballywalter al. Walterstowne	Inq. Ult. (Down) §80 Car. I	1637
9. Ballywalter	Wars Co. Down, 79	1641
10. Ballewalter	Inq. Ult. (Down) §104 Car. I	1645
11. Ballywalter Village	Census 92	1659c
12. Ballewalter & ye village	BSD 89	1661
13. Ballywalter	Trien. Visit. (Bramhall) 9	1661
14. Ballewalter	Inq. Ult. (Down) §23 Car. II	1662
15. Ballywalter	Sub. Roll Down 283	1663
16. Balliwalter als Whitechurch	Trien. Visit. (Boyle) 44	1679
17. Ballywalter	Ham. Copy Rental 108	1681
18. Ballywalter	Wm. Map (OSNB)	1810
19. Ballywalter	High Const. Applot. (OSNB)	1830c
20. Ballywalter	Tythes Applot. (OSNB)	1830c
21. Ballywalter	Bnd. Sur. (OSNB)	1830c

22. Baile Bhaitéir "Walter's town"	J O'D (OSNB)	1834c
23. ˌbali 'wɑltər	Local pronunciation	1991

Walter was a common personal name among the Anglo-Normans, as witnessed by the mention of a "Waltero Purcel" in *Cartae Dunensis* 419 §2 (*c.* 1177). The taxation of Pope Nicholas IV refers to *Rector ville Walteri de Logan*, i.e. "the rector of Walter-de-Logan's town", and Reeves (*EA* 67, n. m) successfully identifies this as modern *Ballywalter* (par. Ballylinny), a grange near Doagh in Co. Antrim.

In the case of *Ballywalter* in the Ards, the alias form *Ballywalter al. Walterstowne* of 1637 (form 8 above) indicates an Anglo-Norman origin, **Walter(s)ton*, which has been then gaelicized between the Anglo-Norman invasion and the Plantation period. For a similar development in this parish, see Anglo-Norman *Pereston* (1333 AD) > modern **Ballyferris** above. One is not in a position at present to identify the Walter of *Ballywalter*.

TOWNLAND NAMES

Ballyatwood — *Baile Acairt*
J 6068 — "Aquart's townland"

1. Ballyaquart	CPR Jas I 326a	1617
2. Balle-Atwart	Ham. Copy Inq. xlii	1623
3. Balleatwart	Ham. Copy Inq. xxxiv; xlvi	1623
4. Balleattward	Inq. Ult. (Down) §104 Car. I	1645
5. Balleattwarte	Inq. Ult. (Down) §104 Car. I	1645
6. Ballyackwart	Census 92	1659c
7. Balleackwars	BSD 89	1661
8. Ballyatwood	Ham. Copy Rental 108	1681
9. Ballyatwood	Wm. Map (OSNB)	1810
10. Ballyatwood	High Const. Applot. (OSNB)	1830c
11. Ballyatwood	Tythes Applot. (OSNB)	1830c
12. Ballyatwood	Bnd. Sur. (OSNB)	1830c
13. Atwood's town	J O'D (OSNB)	1834c
14. ˌbɑli 'ɑtwud	Local pronunciation	1991

Reaney (1958:14) has the surname *At(t)wood* which he etymologizes as "dweller by the wood" (i.e. at the wood), and he cites a "Thomas *Attewode* 1243". The surname *At(t)wood* might appear to lie behind this townland name were it not for the fact that the 17th-century forms (1–7) suggest a different interpretation entirely. Since *-atwood* only appears for the first time in 1681 (form 8) we must view "Atwood's town" as replacing an earlier name. The early spellings of the name up to 1661 vary between *-aquart* and *-atwart* and appear to represent a gaelicized form of an Anglo-Norman reflex of the Old French *Aquart*. Reaney (1958:1) lists "*Achard, Ackert, Ashard, Hatchard*: Acardus de Lincolnia c. 1150 .... O(ld) Fr(ench) *Achart, Aquart* probably from O(ld) G(erman) *Agihard, Akihart*". As regards habitation here, note "*Bally-Atwood*, the House and Improvement of *Hans Hamil* Esq." (*Harris Hist.* 68, more or less repeated in *Knox Hist.* 460).

Ballyferris	*Baile Phéarais*	
J 6271	"Peres's townland"	
1. Perestoun	Inq. Earldom Ulster iii 65	1333
2. Prerestoun	Inq. Earl Ulster (EA) 361	1333
3. Ballifearush	Inq. Ult. (Down) §2 Jac. I	1605
4. Ballifearis	Inq. Ult. (Down) §2 Jac. I	1605
5. Ballifarush	CPR Jas I 73a	1605
6. Balleferish	Ham. Copy Inq. xlii	1623
7. Ballyferish	Ham. Copy Inq. xxxii	1623
8. Ballefirish	Ham. Copy Inq. xxxiv	1623
9. Balleferish	Inq. Ult. (Down) §104 Car. I	1645
10. Ballyferis	Census 92	1659c
11. Balleferrish 3 quarters	BSD 91	1661
12. Ballyfairis	Ham. Copy Rental 108	1681
13. Ballyferis	Wm. Map (OSNB)	1810
14. Ballyferris	Bnd. Sur. (OSNB)	1830c
15. Baile Phiarais "Pierce's town"	J O'D (OSNB)	1834c
16. ˌbɑliˈfɛrəs	Local pronunciation	1991

Reeves (*EA* 361 n. g) cites *Prerestoun* from an Inquisition of the Earl of Ulster in 1333 AD (form 2 above) which, as Orpen points out, occurs as *Prerestoun* in the Summary but *Perestoun* elsewhere in the Inquisition (*JRSAI* xliv, 1914, 565 n. 3). Orpen, quite rightly, equates this Anglo-Norman *Perestoun* with modern *Ballyferris*. This is yet another Anglo-Norman name, in this case *Perestoun* "town of Peres", which has been gaelicized as *Baile Phéarais*. Reaney (1958:251) discusses the surname *Pierce*, derived from Old French *Piers*, a nominative case of *Pierre* "Peter", which has 16 variant spellings including *Peres*. The name *Peres* could be gaelicized as *Péaras* or *Piaras*, but the evidence here suggests *Péaras*.It is also interesting to note the continued use of this personal name in the Ards among old Norman families in the post Anglo-Norman period cf. "Garot bane Fitz Symons fitz *Peirse* of Little Ards". *Fiants Eliz.* §6711 (1602 AD).

Ballylimp	Of uncertain origin	
J 6264		
1. Ballilimpe	CPR Jas I 39a	1604
2. Ballilimpe	Inq. Ult. (Down) §2 Jac. I	1605
3. (?) Ballylunph	Inq. Ult. (Down) §2 Jac. I	1605
4. Ballilimp	Inq. Ult. (Down) §2 Jac. I	1605
5. Ballilimpe	CPR Jas I 73a	1605
6. Balle-Sumpt	Ham. Copy Inq. xlii	1623
7. Ballelimpt	Ham. Copy Inq. xlvi	1623
8. Balle-Lumpt	Ham. Copy Inq. xxxiv	1623
9. Ballelimpt	Inq. Ult. (Down) §104 Jac. I	1644
10. Ballelumpt	Inq. Ult. (Down) §104 Jac. I	1644
11. Ballylimp	Census 92	1659c
12. Ballelimpe	BSD 89	1661
13. Ballylimpt	Ham. Copy Rental 108	1681
14. Ballylimp	Wm. Map (OSNB) No. 44	1810

15. Ballylimp	High Const. Applot. (OSNB)	1830c
16. Ballylimp	Tythes Applot. (OSNB)	1830c
17. Ballylimp	Bnd. Sur. (OSNB)	1830c
18. Baile Leamh "town of the elms"	J O'D (OSNB)	1834c
19. ˌbɑliˈlïmp	Local pronunciation	1991

Although we have a fairly large number of historical spellings for this townland none of them goes back beyond the 17th century. The anglicized forms in *-limp(e)* do not readily suggest a Gaelic original and, although one suspects an Anglo-Norman original, no form springs immediately to mind. Further research and earlier forms will be required to unlock the etymology of this name.

Dunover — *Dún Uabhair*
J 6070 — "fort of loftiness/pride" (?)

1. Donnour	Inq. Earldom Ulster iv 140	1333
2. Doonovery	Inq. Ult. (Down) §2 Jac. I	1605
3. Ballindoonover	Grant Jas I (OSNB)	1605
4. Ballinedoonever	CPR Jas I 73a	1605
5. Dinover, Edward Maxwell of	CPR Jas I 326a	1617
6. Balledownover	Ham. Copy Inq. xxxii; xxxiv	1623
7. Balledownan al. Balledownour	Inq. Ult. (Down) §104 Car. I	1645
8. Balledonouer	Inq. Ult. (Down) §104 Car. I	1645
9. Dunover	Census 92	1659c
10. Dunnover ½ towne	BSD 91	1661
11. Balledownever	Inq. Ult. (Down) §23 Car. II	1662
12. Dunover	Ham. Copy Rental 108	1681
13. Dunover	Wm. Map (OSNB)	1810
14. Dunnover	High Const. Applot. (OSNB)	1830c
15. Dunover	Tythes Applot. (OSNB)	1830c
16. Dunover	Bnd. Sur. (OSNB)	1830c
17. Dunovar	OSM vii 18	1834c
18. Dún Uabhair "fort of the pride"	J O'D (OSNB)	1834c
19. ˌdo̜nˈo̜vər	Local pronunciation	1991

There are three names of the type *Dún Uabhair* cited in *Onom. Goed.* 389. *Joyce* (ii 441–2) discusses some other examples, (a) Castleore "the castle of pride" (Co. Sligo) known as *Caislen an Uabhair* in *AFM* 1389 AD (vi p. 715, n. o) and (b) Lissanover (Cos Galway and Cavan) which he considers to be derived from *Lios an Uabhair* "the fort of pride". *Joyce* (ii 441) suggests several possibilities for the use of "pride" in Irish place-names:

> whether the places got such names from their commanding position, like Benburb, or from some great and strong fortress, or from belonging to a powerful family, or from some other circumstance, it is now I fear beyond our power to discover.

It might be reasonable to envisage the commanding position of these places as responsible for the element "pride, loftiness" in their names.

The remains of the old fort in Dunover townland, where pottery fragments of the later 13th or early 14th century were found, is described in *ASCD* 194. Nearer our own day,

Atkinson (1823:i, 231–2) describes the state of land in Dunover in the early 19th century. Although a brief description of Dunover House is given in *OSNB*, the microfilm has proven virtually illegible.

Ganaway	*An Ghaineamhaigh*	
J 6172	"the sandy area"	
1. Gannagh	Inq. Earl Ulster (EA) 361	1333
2. Ballinaganny	Inq. Ult. (Down) §2 Jac. I	1605
3. Ballyganevine	Grant Jas I (OSNB)	1605
4. Balleganevine	CPR Jas I 73a	1605
5. Gannemy	CPR Jas I 78a	1606
6. Ballygannogh	CPR Jas I 326a	1617
7. the Baie of Canvie	Ham. Copy Inq. lii	1623
8. Balleganvie	Ham. Copy Inq. xlii	1623
9. Balleneganoy	Ham. Copy Inq. xxxii	1623
10. Balleganny	Inq. Ult. (Down) §104 Car. I	1645
11. Ballyganwy	Inq. Ult. (Down) §104 Car. I	1645
12. Ganivy	Census 92	1659c
13. Balleganwy ½ towne	BSD 87	1661
14. le Gamvie	Inq. Ult. (Down) §23 Car. II	1662
15. Balleganwy	Inq. Ult. (Down) §23 Car. II	1662
16. (?) Glanowry	Sub. Roll Down 283	1663
17. Ganway	Ham. Copy Rental 108	1681
18. Ballingamoye	Montgomery MSS 52 24	1696
19. Gemaway or Gannaway	Montgomery MSS 52 24	1717
20. Ganaway	Wm. Map (OSNB)	1810
21. Ganaway	High Const. Applot. (OSNB)	1830c
22. Ganaway	Tythes Applot. (OSNB)	1830c
23. Ganaway	Bnd. Sur. (OSNB)	1830c
24. Grandshaw	OSM vii 18	1834c
25. Gainimheach "sandy"	J O'D (OSNB)	1834c
26. 'gɑnəwe	Local pronunciation	1991

This townland straddles the parishes of Ballywalter and Donaghadee and is classified as belonging to each of these two civil parishes. The anglicized forms resembling *Gan(a)way*, *-ganvie* and the like, presumably represent *Gaineamhaigh*, an oblique case of a nominative *Gaineamhach* "sandy place". An older nominative is reflected in *Gannagh* 1333 (1) and presumably in *Ballygannogh* (6). The townland undoubtedly owes its name to the sandy area along the shore.

Springvale	An English form	
J 6268		
1. Springvale	Wm. Map (OSNB)	1810
2. Springvale	High Const. Applot. (OSNB)	1830c
3. Springvale	Bnd. Sur. (OSNB)	1830c
4. Springvale	Tythes Applot. (OSNB)	1830c
5. Spring Vale	OSM vii 18	1834c
6. 'sbriŋ'viəl	Local pronunciation	1991

Springvale appears to have become a townland in the post-17th-century period. In the *OSNB* of 1834 mention is made of a *Springvale House*, described as being half a mile south of Ballywalter. The house name was changed from *Springvale House* to *Ballywalter Park* between 1834 and the last quarter of the 19th century, as Alexander Knox, writing in 1875, describes this house:

> Ballywalter Park, called Springvale, when in the possession of the Matthews family, from whom it passed by purchase to Mr Andrew Mulholland the father of the present proprietor ... Ballywalter Park is a handsome mansion, and the demesne is well furnished with fine trees, especially the evergreen oaks, one of which is said to be the oldest in Ireland. The farm buildings are on the most approved models, and the stock of cattle of the best descriptions. (*Knox Hist.* 460)

See also *OSM* vii 16.

Whitechurch	*Teampall Fionn*	
J 6270	"white church"	
1. Alba Ecclesia	Eccles. Tax. 26	1306c
2. White-Kirk	Reg. Octavian (EA) 26 n. w	1437
3. Whytekirk	Reg. Prene (EA) 26 n. w	1442
4. Albe Ecclesie in Ardo	Reg. Mey 327	1456
5. Templefinn al. Whitechurch	Inq. Ult. (Down) §2 Jac. I	1605
6. Whitechurch	CPR Jas I 72b	1605
7. Whitekirke, the parish of	CPR Jas I 78a	1606
8. Ecclesia Albe	Jas I to Down Cath. 179	1609
9. Templefin	Terrier (Reeves) 57	1615c
10. Templefin al. Whitechurch	Ham. Copy Inq. xlii; xlvi	1623
11. Rectory of Whitechurch al. Templeffin	Ham. Copy Inq. xlvi	1623
12. Templeffin al. Whitechurch	Ham. Copy Inq. xxiv	1623
13. White Church	Ham. Copy Inq. xxxii	1623
14. Balle-Templefin al. Whitechurch	Ham. Copy Inq. xxxii	1623
15. parish of Whitechurch	Ham. Copy Inq. xxxii; xlvi	1623
16. Whytchurch	Inq. Ult. (Down) §104 Car. I	1645
17. Templefin al. Whytchurch	Inq. Ult. (Down) §104 Car. I	1645
18. Whytchurch al. Templefin	Inq. Ult. (Down) §104 Car. I	1645
19. Whitt Church known by the name Ball[ewa]lter	Inq. Down (Reeves 1) 125	1657
20. Whyte church	Census 92	1659c
21. White Church	BSD 89	1661
22. Whitechurch als Ballywalter	Trien. Visit. (Bramhall) 9	1661
23. Whittchurch	Inq. Ult. (Down) §23 Car. II	1662
24. Whittchurch al. Templefin	Inq. Ult. (Down) §23 Car. II	1662
25. Templefin al. Whittchurch	Inq. Ult. (Down) §23 Car. II	1662
26. Whyte-Church	Sub. Roll Down 283	1663
27. White Church	Ham. Copy Rental 108	1681
28. Whitechurch	Wm. Map (OSNB)	1810
29. White Church	High Const. Applot. (OSNB)	1830c
30. Whitechurch	Tythes Applot. (OSNB)	1830c

31. Whitechurch	Bnd. Sur. (OSNB)	1830c
32. 'whait'tʃo̤rtʃ	Local pronunciation	1991

This name offers a fine insight into how place-names with an easily understood form are translated into various languages with Latin *Alba Ecclesia*, Irish *Teampall Fionn* and English *Whitekirk/Whitechurch* all reflecting the notion "white church". It is also interesting to note that, while *kirk* "church" in Ulster is very often a sign of a later Scots import in the post 17th century, forms 2 & 3 above show that *kirk* in place-names may nevertheless predate this period, as it was evidently also used by the earlier Anglo-Norman settlers. Reeves (*EA* 26, n. w) describes how Whitechurch came to be known as the parish of Ballywalter owing to the growth of the village of Ballywalter. However, the ruins of the old church are in the townland of Whitechurch.

OTHER NAMES

Bairdstown — A Scots/English form
J 6170

The local pronunciation is ['bɛrdz 'tɔun]. According to the notes in the *OSNB*, compiled in May 1833, *Bairdstown Village* consisted of "8 or 10 farm houses and cottages". As can be seen from Black (1946:42–3) *Baird* was common as a family name in Scotland and it probably represents the first element of this place-name. For Bairds represented on a map of Ards family names see *Surnames Dn 1858* facing p. 77.

Ballywalter Park — See **Springvale** above.

The Burn Houses — A Scots/English form
J 6464

In *OSNB* (May 1833) the first element in *Burn Houses Village* is explained as "Burn from *burn* 'a rivulet'".

Craigbrain — *Creag Bhréan* (?) "stinking rock".
J 6371

It has not been possible to discover any written evidence for this name, but the first element appears to be Irish *creag* "rock, crag"; the second might be *bréan* "stinking".

Green Knoll — A Scots/English form
J 6369

Knoll, according to *Scot. Nat. Dict.*, signifies "a large piece or lump" and the place is thus named from its shape.

The Haw — A Scots/English form
J 6264

Haw, according to *Scots Nat. Dict.*, is used "as in English for the hawthorn".

Long Rock — An English form
J 6370

The local pronunciation is [ðə 'lɔŋ 'rɔk]. This name is at least two centuries old, as can be seen from the following account from 1744:

At *Bally-feris*, near a league from *Mill-Isles* the Coast bellys out to the East, and at the End of it a Reef of Rocks stretches a good way into the Sea, called the *Long Rock*, often fatal to Sailors. (*Harris Hist.* 135)

Skullmartin	*Sceir Mhártain*	
J 6468	"Martin's skerry or reef"	
1. Skirmash	Nowel's Ire. (1)	1570
2. Skyr martyn	Mercator's Ire.	1595
3. Skyr Martyn	Mercator's Ulst.	1595
4. Skyr Martin	Speed's Antrim & Down	1610
5. Skyr Martin	Speed's Ulster	1610
6. Scalmartin	Harris Hist. 135	1744
7. ðə 'skọ̈l 'mɑrtən	Local pronunciation	1992

The 16th- and 17th-century forms of the name (forms 1–5) seem to indicate Irish **sceir** "a skerry, a reef", a borrowing into Irish from Norse. This Norse term has also found its way into Scottish Gaelic (e.g. Oftedal 1975:44) and into Welsh place-names (Richards 1983:55ff., and map). The current form *Skullmartin* appears to represent a reinterpretation, by folk etymology or dissimilation, as *Skull* "skull" followed by the personal name *Martin*. This place was apparently a hazard for seafarers, as is indicated by the following account written in 1744: "Scalmartin, the more dangerous, because overflowed every Tide; but it is a Rock so smooth and flat that few suffer by it" (*Harris Hist.* 135). According to Knox (*Knox Hist.* 474) there was a perch erected here, and he also states: "On the Ards coast, a *Pladdy* signifies a flat sunk rock, whilst a rock, always above water, is termed a *Skerry*, and if connected with the land, so as to form a reef, is named a *Skare*, or *Sker*". Knox did not, however, connect *sker* with *Skullmartin* as he was not in possession of earlier forms.

Windmill Hill An English form
J 6269

Local pronunciation ['wïnmɪl 'hɪl]. The tradition of windmills here goes back several centuries. In *Ham. Copy Rental* 108 there is reference to "Ballywalter Town, Water Mill and Windmill", for the year 1681. See also *OSM* vii 17.

PARISH OF CASTLEBOY

The small parish of Castleboy was also known as St. Johnstown/Johnston, owing to its association with the Hospital of St. John of Jerusalem. According to Orpen (*JRSAI* xliv (1914) 59) "the Priory of St John the Baptist in Ards (parish of Castleboy) for knights of the hospital" was founded by Hugh de Lacy in the late 12th century. Lewis, writing in 1837, refers to the parish as "Castlebuoy or St. Johnstowne" (*Lewis' Top. Dict.* i 291). These two alias forms, which are central to both the history and development of the parish, will be considered separately below under *Parish Names*. For a description of the parish in the 1830s see *OSM* vii 26–7.

PARISH NAMES

Castleboy — *An Caisleán Buí*
J 6255 — "the yellow castle"

1.	bhán gCaislén mBuidhe	LCABuidhe 160 l.198	1617c
2.	terram Hospitalariorum in Arte	EA 164	1200c
3.	St Jonestowne	S-E Ulster Map	1580c
4.	manor of Johnestone	Fiants Eliz. §4420	1584
5.	Clst boy	Dartmouth Map 5	1590
6.	Castleboy	Fiants Eliz. §5590	1591
7.	S Iohans towne	Mercator's Ulst.	1595
8.	S Johnstown	Mercator's Ire.	1595
9.	Ca:Bowie	Bartlett Map (TCD)	1601
10.	the preceptorie of the Ardes, with the manor of Johnston	CPR Jas I 10a	1603
11.	Castleboy	Inq. Ult. (Down) §2 Jac.I	1605
12.	vil' de St Johnston al. Castleboy	Inq. Ult. (Down) §2 Jac.I	1605
13.	the manor & preceptory of Ardes and the manor of St Johnstone otherwise Castleboy	CPR Jas I 72b	1605
14.	Ca:Boy	Boazio's Map (NG)	1609
15.	Ca:Boy	Norden's Map	1610c
16.	Ca. Boy	Speed's Antrim & Down	1610
17.	Ca Boy	Speed's Ulster	1610
18.	Castleboy	Terrier (Reeves) 59	1615
19.	Castleboy	Ulster Visit. (Reeves) 57	1622
20.	St Johnstowne al. Castleboie, manor or Preceptorie of	Ham. Copy Inq. xxxv	1623
21.	St Johnston, Manor or Preceptorie of	Ham. Copy Inq. xxxvi;li	1623
22.	St John's-towne	Ham. Copy Inq. xlvi	1623
23.	Castleboy al. Johnstowne	Ham. Copy Inq. xlvi	1623
24.	Castleboy	Inq. Down (Reeves 1) 133	1657
25.	Johnstowne	Hib. Reg. Ards	1657
26.	Castleboy als Ballitrustan Parish	BSD 86	1661
27.	Castleboy	Trien. Visit. (Margetson) 23	1664
28.	a great rvinous pyle called Castleboy	Descr. Ards 36	1683

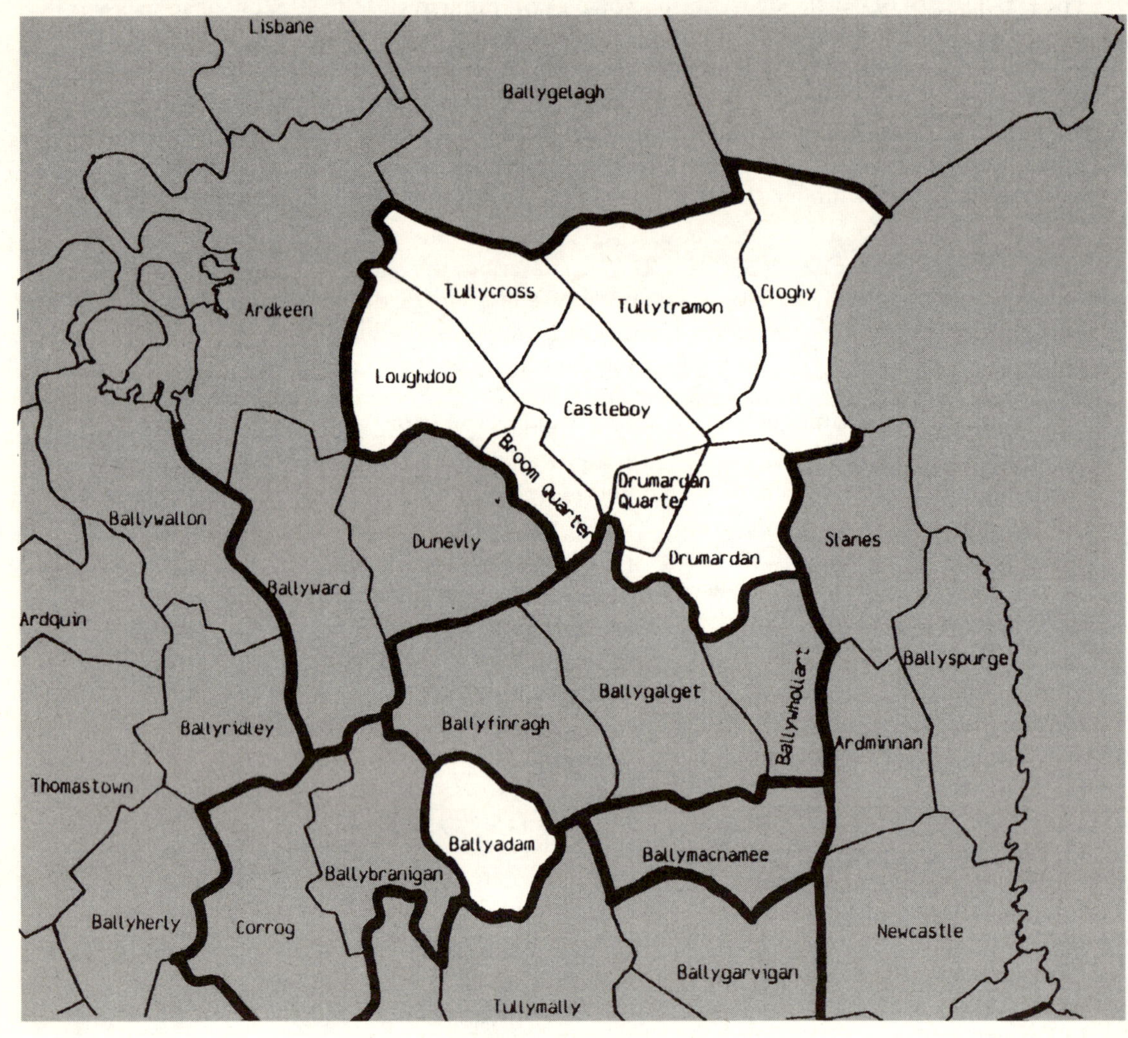

Parish of Castleboy

Barony of Ards Upper

Townlands
Ballyadam (detached)
Broom Quarter
Castleboy
Cloghy
Drumardan
Drumardan Quarter
Loughdoo
Tullycross
Tullytramon

29. Castleboy	Descr. Ards 36	1683
30. Castlebuoy	Sav. Ards 198	1701
31. Castleboy	Wm. Map (OSNB)	1810
32. Castlebuoy	High Const. Applot. (OSNB)	1830c
33. Castlebuoy	Bnd. Sur. (OSNB)	1830c
34. St Johnsone	OSM vii 10	1834c
35. Caistial Buidhe "yellow castle"	J O'D (OSNB)	1834c
36. ˌkɑsəl'bɔi	Local pronunciation	1991

As regards the castle at Castleboy, *ASCD* (230) describes the remains of a tower-house, possibly 15th century. The castle was certainly in use in the early decades of the 17th century, as it is referred to in a Gaelic bardic poem which was composed for Seaán Ó Néill, a member of the Clandeboye O'Neill family from South Antrim, who died in 1617 (form no. 1 above). Ó Donnchadha, in the index to his edition of the poem in question (*LCABuidhe* 306), mentions the fact that a Castleboy is marked on Speed's map, and he tentatively identifies it with Ringboy. We can be sure, however, that it is a reference to Castleboy in the Ards. The castle appears to have been deserted by the late 17th century, judging by the following: "the great ruinous pyle called Castle boy once ye Seate of ye prior of St. John's in ye Ardes which hath a manor Court also" (*Descr. Ards* p. 36).

As is clearly indicated by the list of spellings below, St Johnsto(w)n preceded Castleboy as a name for this place. O'Laverty describes St Johnstown(e) as:

> "the commandery or Preceptory of the Ards belonging to the Knights of the military order of St. John of Jerusalem (now called the Knights of Malta), an order which professed the Rule of St. Augustine, and was instituted to protect the Christians of the Holy Land and pilgrims going to Jerusalem". (*O'Laverty* i 412).

In a roll of *c.* 1200 mention is made of "the hospital land in Ards" (*terram Hospitalariorum in Arte*), and this is identified with Castleboy by Reeves (*EA* 164, n. n). In the index volume to the 16th-century *Fiants Eliz.* p. 771, references are made to hospital possessions of St John of Jerusalem throughout substantial portions of the country. O'Laverty points out that their two Grand Priories in Ireland were in Wexford and Kilmainham and that "The only Commandery or Preceptory, which the order possessed in the diocese of Down and Connor was that of Castleboy, or St John's in the Ards" (*O'Laverty* i 412). It is pointed out by O'Laverty, however, that the order of St John did have other possessions in Ulster: "the rectories of Ballytrustan, Rathmullan, with the chapelry of St. John's Point, Ballyministra, Carncastle, St John's of Carrickfergus, Ballywalter, near Dogh [Co. Antrim], and Ballyrashane, and extensive landed possessions".

The cult of St John was fairly strong among the Anglo-Normans in Down, as may be judged from *Cartae Dun.* 419 §2 where reference is made to "God, the Blessed Virgin, St. John, St Nicholas and St. Clement". In Atkinson (1823:i, 289) we are informed that "At Castle-buy, or John's Town in the Ards, three miles north of Portaferry, a religious institution dedicated to St. John the Baptist, was founded by Hugh de Lacy in the 12th century. Nothing now remains of the building but ruins; the family of Echlin possess several townlands and a manor court, formerly attached to this institution". Knox (*Knox Hist.* 470) dates the foundation of the commandery or preceptory of St John the Baptist of Jerusalem to the year 1189. He further comments that it was kept up until the beginning of the fifteenth century. *Fiants Eliz.* §4420 (1584 AD) records the: "Lease ... to George Alexander, gent.; of the preceptory of Arde, with the manor of Johnestone ...".

In *ASCD* pp. 289 and 301 reference is made to the church; on p. 289 it is listed among "destroyed monuments and lost sites". It was destroyed before 1744, as *Harris Hist.* 67 speaks of "the remains of an old Building called *Castlebuy* or *Johnston*, once a Preceptory of *St. John's of Jerusalem*". *CPR Jas I* 10a (c. 1603) gives some details of the estate of "the late monastery of S^t. John of Jerusalem". See also *Inq. Ult.* §2 Jac. I 1605; *Ham. Copy Inq.* xlvi (which records a weekly market and fair here.); *O'Laverty* i, pp. 411–5; *Sav. Ards* pp. 245–6, n. 2.

TOWNLAND NAMES

Ballyadam — *Baile Adaim*
J 6153 — "Adam's townland"

1.	Ballyadams al. Adamston	Inq. Ult. (Down) §2 Jac.I	1605
2.	Ballyadams al. Adamstowne	Ham. Copy Inq. xxxv	1623
3.	Balladam	Census 91	1659
4.	Ballyardan	BSD 86	1661
5.	Balledam	Wm. Map (OSNB)	1810
6.	Ballyedam	High Const. Applot. (OSNB)	1830c
7.	Ballyedam	Bnd. Sur. (OSNB)	1830c
8.	Ballyedom "Edom's town", *a* is pronounced like *e* ...	J O'D (OSNB)	1843c
9.	bɑ'ledəm	Local pronunciation	1991
10.	bɑli'ɑdəm	Local pronunciation	1991

Judging by the bilingual 17th-century forms resembling "Ballyadams alias Adamstown" (nos 1, 2), and in the light of other local Anglo-Norman place-names in the Ards, since gaelicized, such as *Philipston* > **Ballyphilip**, it would appear that *Ballyadam* was originally coined as *Adamston* in the Anglo-Norman period of the late 12th century. For occurrences of the forename *Adam* in early Anglo-Norman Co. Down, note "Adam de Alneto" *EA* 165; "Adam camerario" *Cartae Dun.* 419 §1; "Adam Janctore" *ibid.* §2; (all *c.* 1180). In *Sav. Ards* 121 there is mention of a witness Adam in a de Courcy charter; this Adam was the chamberlain of William Baron le Savage, and may possibly be the Adam in question in *Ballyadam*.

The townland name is pronounced [bə'ledəm] by the older people (form 9 above). One local informant told me that, at a church service in the area, the priest was interrupted by a member of the congregation who was very annoyed by the priest's pronunciation of the name of this townland as *Ballyadam* [ˌbalɩ 'adəm] rather than [bal'edəm]. It is reported that at this point in the mass the local man leapt to his feet and declared: "It's not *Ballyadam* its *Balledam*!".

Broom Quarter — An English form
J 6155

1.	Broomquarter	Wm. Map (OSNB)	1810
2.	Broomquarter	Bnd. Sur. (OSNB)	1830c
3.	'brïm 'kwartər	Local pronunciation	1991

Reaney (1958:49) lists *Broom(e)*, *Brom* as a family name in England from 1193 onwards where he derived its meaning from someone who dwelt "near a place where broom (Old Eng. *brōm*) grew". However an Anglo-Norman link in this instance is difficult to substantiate. The lack of written forms for this name poses a problem, and it may be that the name is of recent origin. Note also nearby **Broom Hill** [brum 'hïl], possibly named from broom which grew here.

Cloghy	*An Chlochaigh*	
J 6356	"the stony or rocky area"	
1. (?) Clochortan in Ardo	Cartae Dun. §15 425	1280c
2. Clogharne, ½ vil' de	Inq. Ult. (Down) §2 Jac. I	1605
3. Cloghargie	Ham. Copy Inq. xlvi	1623
4. the half town of Cloghie	Ham. Copy Inq. xxxv	1623
5. Cloghy and Tolletramman	Census 91	1659c
6. Cloughy	Sav. Ards 294	1771
7. Cloghy	Wm. Map (OSNB)	1810
8. Cloghey	High Const. Applot. (OSNB)	1830c
9. Cloghey	Bnd. Sur. (OSNB)	1830c
10. Clochach "Stony"	J O'D (OSNB)	1834c
11. An Clochach	Mac Reachtain (1951:8)	1951
12. 'klɔχi	Local pronunciation	1991

The anglicized forms of the name *Cloghy* suggest an original Irish element *Clochaigh*, an oblique case of *Clochach* "stony, rocky area". Some of the early spellings show evidence of a second element following but, as there is no consistency in these, or certainty that they all actually refer to this *Cloghy*, it would be unwise to speculate on the meanings of these qualifiers. The place is described in the *OSNB* as "Cloghy Village, a collection of small houses".

Drumardan	*Droim Ardáin*	
Drumardan Quarter	"ridge of the little height"	
J 6355, 6255		
1. Drumardan	Inq. Ult. (Down) §2 Jac. I	1605
2. Drumarden	Inq. Ult. (Down) §2 Jac. I	1605
3. Dromarden	Ham. Copy Inq. xxxv; xlvi	1623
4. Drumarden	Census 91	1659
5. Dromardan	BSD 86	1661
6. Dromardin	Sav. Ulst. 284	1690c
7. Dromardin	Sav. Ards 197	1702
8. Dromardin	ASE 376a 1	1703
9. Drumarden	Sav. Ards 376	1737
10. Drumardin	High Const. Applot. (OSNB)	1830c
11. Drumardin	Bnd. Sur. (OSNB)	1830c
12. Drummardinquarter	High Const. Applot. (OSNB)	1830c
13. Drumardinquarter	Bnd. Sur. (OSNB)	1830c

14. Druim Ardáin "ridge of the little hill or height"	J O'D (OSNB)	1843c
15. ˌdrĭm'ɑrdən	Local pronunciation	1991

O'Donovan's suggestion *Druim Ardáin* "ridge of the little hill or height" is certainly supported by the earlier spellings of the name.

The lack of earlier spellings for the townland of **Drumardan Quarter** seems to suggest that the modern neighbouring townland of **Drumardan** was formerly larger in extent than it is today and that modern Drumardan Quarter represents a post-17th-century subdivision of Drumardan which went on to develop full townland status.

Loughdoo — *Loch Dubh*
J 6155 — "black lake"

1. Loughduff, vil' de Drometall al'	Inq. Ult. (Down) §2 Jac.I	1605
2. Loughduff, the half town of Dumtayle al'	Ham. Copy Inq. xxxv	1623
3. Loughduffe, Ballenicoll al. Tullecarnan al.	Ham. Copy Inq. xlvi	1623
4. Loughduffe, al. Drumtayle	Ham. Copy Inq. xlvi	1623
5. Loghduff	Census 91	1659
6. Loghduffe	BSD 86	1661
7. Loughduff	Wm. Map (OSNB)	1810
8. Loghdoo	High Const. Applot. (OSNB)	1830c
9. Loghdoo	Bnd. Sur. (OSNB)	1830c
10. Loch Dubh "black lough"	J O'D (OSNB)	1834c
11. lɔx'dû	Local pronunciation	1991
12. lɔx'du	Local pronunciation	1991

This townland takes its name from the lake **Lough Doo** which is situated in it (see below). It is clear from the early 17th-century sources that the townland had a variant, if not earlier, name *Drumtayle*, which may indicate an original *Droim Táil* "ridge of (the) adze", or "ridge of the milk yield".

Tullycross — *Tulaigh na Croise*
J 6165 — "hillock of the cross(roads)"

1. Quarter townland of Tullanacrissi	Will (Sav. Ards) 247	1640
2. Tullycross	High Const. Applot. (OSNB)	1830c
3. Tullycross	Bnd. Sur. (OSNB)	1830c
4. Tulaigh na Croise "cross hill or hill of the cross"	J O'D (OSNB)	1834c
5. ˌtọli'krɔs	Local pronunciation	1991

This name has not been located in early sources with any great frequency and the fact that it is referred to as the "Quarter townland of Tullanacrissi" (form no. 1) seems to suggest that it was formerly a subdivision of a larger townland which then went on to develop full townland status. Presumably the second element *-cross* refers to a crossroads.

Tullytramon — *Tulaigh Tromáin*
J 6256 — "hillock of the elder tree"

1. Tullecreman	Ham. Copy Inq. xlvi	1623
2. (?) Tollytomen	Ham. Copy Inq. xxxv	1623
3. Tullytroman	BSD 86	1661
4. Tollitraman	Sub. Roll Down 282	1663
5. Tullytramon	Wm. Map (OSNB)	1810
6. Tullytramon	Bnd. Sur. (OSNB)	1830c
7. Tulaigh Tramoin "Tramon's hill"	J O'D (OSNB)	1843c
8. ˌtọ̤li 'trɔmən	Local pronunciation	1991

Contrary to O'Donovan's suggestion (no. 7), it would appear that this name goes back to a Gaelic original *Tulaigh Tromáin* "hillock of the elder tree", i.e. *tulaigh*, dative of *tulach* "hillock, mound", plus the gentive of *tromán* rendered by Dinneen as "dwarf elder or bore-tree".

OTHER NAMES

Broom Hill — See **Broom Quarter**
J 6155

Calhame Park — A Scots form
J 6356

Local pronunciation [kɑl'hiəm 'park]. There is not much written evidence available for Calhame in Castleboy parish, but the name is popular in parts of Ulster (especially Donegal) and is derived from a Scots term *Calhame* meaning "cold home(stead)", i.e. *cald* "cold" + *hame* "home(stead)".

Lough Doo — *Loch Dubh*
J 6155 — "black lough"

Local pronunciation [lɔχ 'du]. In the *OSNB* of *c.* 1834 John O'Donovan enters a form "dhu-lough *dubh-loch* 'black lough'" but does not state from where this came. It appears that the name of this lake then went on to become the name of the townland, as has been pointed out under the townland name **Loughdoo** above.

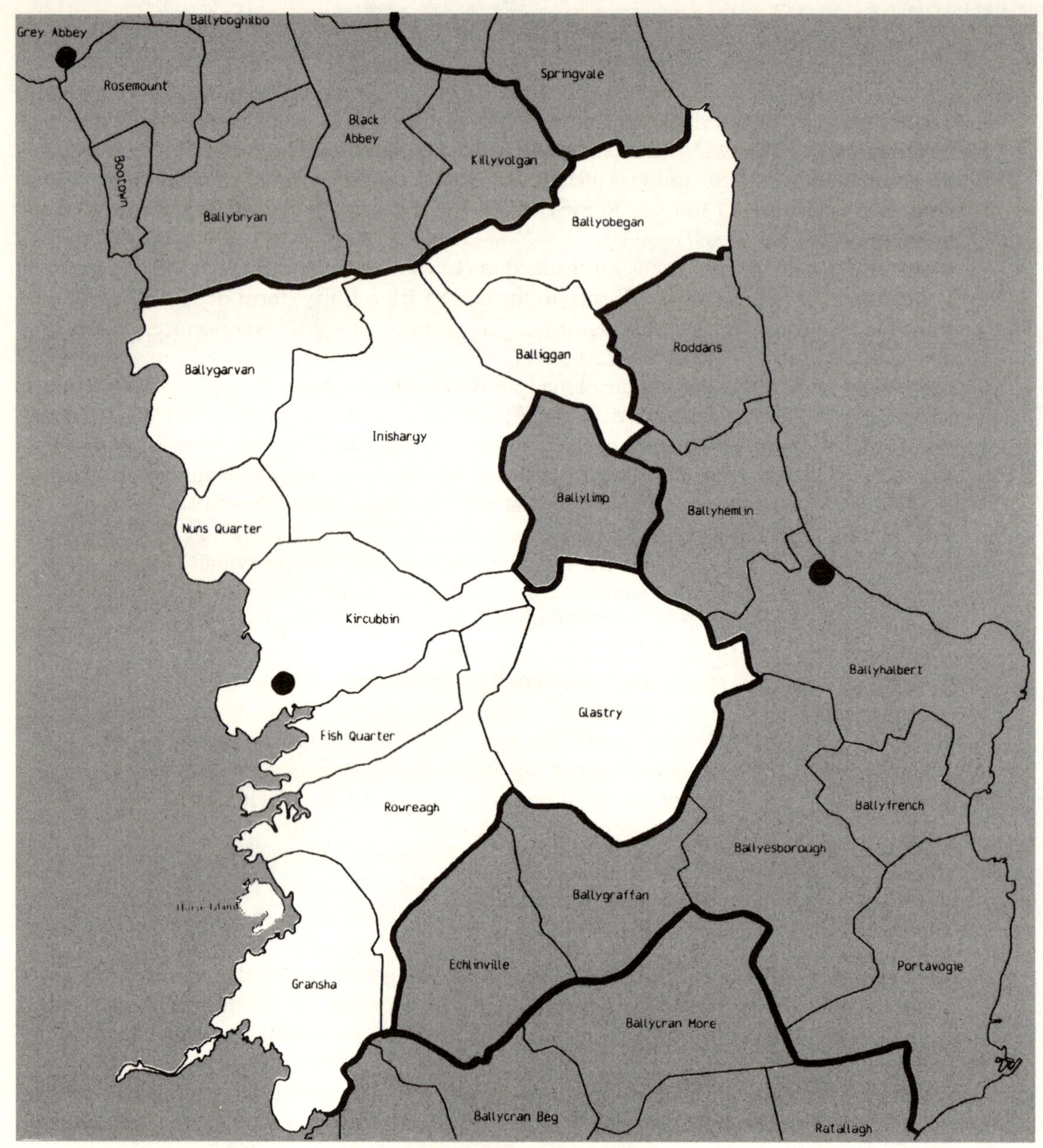

Parish of Inishargy

Barony of Ards Upper

Townlands
Balliggan
Ballygarvan
Ballyobegan
Fish Quarter
Glastry
Gransha
Inishargy
Kircubbin
Nun's Quarter
Rowreagh

Islands
Horse Island
Sheelah's Island

Town
Kircubbin

PARISH OF INISHARGY

Lewis (*Top. Dict.* ii 21) describes the civil parish of "Innishargey" as a vicarage of the diocese of Down and in the *OSNB* the parish is said to belong to the three-parish "Union of Ballywalter, Inishargy and St Andrews alias Ballyhalbert". For an account of the remains of the church mentioned in 1306 see Reeves (*EA* 19 n. h); Bigger-Fennell (1898: 231–2) O'Laverty (i 427–8) and *ASCD* (303).

Flanagan (1973: 65–6) has discussed the settlement of the Gaelic tribe of the *Uí Thuirtre* in this area, and the mention of *lez Turtars* in the early 17th century (form no. 18 below) is a reference to this tribe. In the Anglo-Norman period the Uí Thuirtre were centred in Co. Antrim around the modern baronies of Antrim Lower, Toome Lower, part of Kilconway and Glenarm Lower where they gave their name to a rural deanery there: *Deacantus de Turtrye* "The Deanery of Turtrye", recorded in the *Ecclesiastical Taxation* of 1306 (*EA* 82). Co. Antrim was not the initial homeland of the Uí Thuirtre, however, as in the Early Christian era and the period following they were located in an area west of the Bann and Lough Neagh, principally in Counties Tyrone and Derry (see map in O'Byrne 1973: 120–1). Reeves (*EA* 294) comments on their removal across the Bann: "At an early date ... it would appear that the people of the Hy-Tuirtre removed to the eastern side [of Lough Neagh] and transferred their name to the tract which is comprised in the modern baronies of Upper and Lower Toome". O'Byrne (1973: 124–5) dates this particular Uí Thuirtre expansion from the late 8th century onwards.

The name *Uí Thuirtre* refers to the "descendants of Tort" apparently named after *Fiachra Tort*, a fourth-century king and grandson of *Colla Uais* (d.336), and details relating to Fiachra are to be found in *EA* 297 and O'Laverty (i 427–8). A later sub-branch of the Uí Thuirtre were the *Uí Fhloinn*; indeed in the *Book of Lecan* the genealogy of the Uí Thuirtre was quoted as "The genealogy of the O'Flynns" (i.e. *Genelach Í Floind*, cited in *CGH* p.436 n. a). The surname *Ó Floinn*, meaning "descendant of Flann", refers in this instance to *Flann* son of *Muireadhach*. This Flann was descended from the Uí Thuirtre and came 13 generations after Fiachra Tort. The surname *Ó Floinn* is recorded in Co. Down from as early as the 15th century. In the *Fiants of Elizabeth* §6712, mention is made of an Edm. O Flynn in the Little Ards (1602 AD), and an Inquisition of 1612 (cited by Flanagan 1973: 66) describes this same person as "Edmond O'Flyn de Rowe gent.", i.e. of the modern townlands **Rowreagh** (this parish) and **Rubane** (now **Echlinville** td. in the parish of St. Andrew's or Ballyhalbert). In the unpublished *Exchequer Inquisitions* for Co. Down (1603) "Brian oge O'Flinne de Enischargie" is stated to possess what would amount to the greater part of the modern civil parish of Inishargy: the townlands of Inshargy, Ballygarvan, Kirkubbin, Ballyobegan, Roddans, Ballylimp, Glastry, Fish Quarter plus several other quarters of townlands whose names are now lost. Griffith's Valuation of 1862 shows that the Gaelic surname *Ó Floinn* remained fairly widespread in north Co. Down under its anglicized forms *(O') Flinn, (O')Flynn, Lynn* and *Lynn*, with ten instances of that name in the Ards.

On the recent history of the parish see *OSM* vol. vii, 84–5. *Knox Hist.* 462 mentions that "Inishargy House, near which are the ruins of a church, was the ancient mansion house of the Bailey Family", and for details of how the house was constructed by the Bailey family probably using the stones of an old church see O'Laverty (i 427).

PARISH NAME

Inishargy J 6164	*Inis Mhic Cairrge* (?) "*Mac Cairrge*'s island-hill"	
1. Ynchemackargi, eeclesiam de	Pontif. Hib. i §59	1204

2. Inchemekargi	EA 19n	1213
3. Ynchemkargy, in tenemento de	Cartae Dun. §13 423	1280c
4. Ynchemkargy	EA 19n	1300c
5. Inyscargi, Ecclesia de	Eccles. Tax. 18	1306c
6. (?) Yneston	Inq. Earldom Ulster iii 64	1333
7. (?) Ynestona	Inq. Earl Ulster (EA) 361	1333
8. (?) Agryston	Inq. Earl Ulster (EA) 361	1333
9. Inchemkargy, the tenement of	CPR Ed. III 305	1336
10. Eynes in the Ardes	CPR Hen. IV (EA) 22 n. p	1411
11. Iniskarrek	Reg. Cromer ii §32	1524
12. Enysharghie	S-E Ulster Map	1580c
13. Enys Hargie	Mercator's Ulst.	1595
14. I sharge	Bartlett Maps (Esch. Co. Maps) 1	1603
15. Inishchargy	CPR Jas I 39a	1604
16. Enishchargie	CPR Jas I 39a	1604
17. Inishchargie	CPR Jas I 39a	1604
18. lez Turtars de Iniscargie	Inq. Ult. (Down) §2 Jac. I	1605
19. ecclesia de Iniscargie	Inq. Ult. (Down) §2 Jac. I	1605
20. Enschargie	CPR Jas I 72b	1605
21. Iniscarrge	Jas I to Down Cath. 179	1609
22. Eniser	Speed's Ireland	1610
23. Eniser-	Speed's Antrim & Down	1610
24. Inchargie	Terrier (Reeves) 57	1615c
25. Inischeargie	Ulster Visit. (Reeves) 33	1622
26. Enniscargie al. Neckellen	Ham. Copy Inq. xlii	1623
27. Rectory of Iniscargie	Ham. Copy Inq. xlvi	1623
28. Iniscargie al. Nikillen	Ham. Copy Inq. xlvi	1623
29. Inniscargie	Ham. Copy Inq. xlvi; li	1623
30. Iniscargie	Ham. Copy Inq. xxxii	1623
31. Iniscargie al. M'Killen	Ham. Copy Inq. xxxii	1623
32. Balle-Iniscargie al. Neckgellen	Ham. Copy Inq. xxxiv	1623
33. Iniskargy	Inq. Ult. (Down) §72 Car. I	1636
34. Iniscargie	Inq. Ult. (Down) §104 Car. I	1645
35. Iniscargie al. Nekillen	Inq. Ult. (Down) §104 Car. I	1645
36. Iniscrogie al. Nekillen	Inq. Ult. (Down) §104 Car. I	1645
37. Inishargy	Census 92	1659c
38. Inshargy	BSD 89	1661
39. Inisgargie	Trien. Visit. (Bramhall) 13	1661
40. Inishcargie	Inq. Ult. (Down) §1 Car. II	1662
41. Iniscargy	Inq. Ult. (Down) §23 Car. II	1662
42. Inchcargie	Sub. Roll Down 283	1663
43. Inniscargie	Trien. Visit. (Margetson) 21	1664
44. Inishargie	Ham. Copy Rental 108	1681
45. inshargie, John Beallie of	Sav. Ards 254	1687
46. Inishargy	Wm. Map (OSNB)	1810
47. Inishargy	High Const. Applot. (OSNB)	1830c
48. Inishargy	Tythes Applot. (OSNB)	1830c
49. Innishargy	Bnd. Sur. (OSNB)	1830c
50. Inis Earcaigh "Earcach's Island"	J O'D (OSNB)	1834c

51. Inis-carraige "the island of the rock".	Joyce i 410	1869
52. Inis cairraige "the island of the rock"	UJA iv 231	1898
53. Inis Cargi [i.e. island of the rock]	Onom. Goed. 462	1910
54. ˌïnəʃ'argɩ	Local pronunciation	1991

The first element of this name is almost certainly Irish *Inis* but an interpretation of the second element is fraught with difficulty and uncertainty. O'Donovan's *Inis Earcaigh* "Earcach's Island" (no. 50) is not supported by the forms. Knox (*Hist.* 461) cites O'Donovan's suggestion although he also refers to the meaning suggested by Reeves:

> The original name seems to have been *inis cairraige* 'the island of the rock'. The ruins of the church stand on high ground, surrounded, not by water, but by cultivated fields. It appears, however, that within the last two centuries human industry has converted the morass into arable land, and the island into a hill; for in a roll of the reign of James I [= *CPR* 391a], mention is made of 'an *island* or lough called Inischargy'. (*EA* 19 n. h).

It is true that the Irish word *inis* normally refers to "island" in the conventional sense of a piece of land surrounded by water in the sea or an inland lake. However, *inis* or *island* in place-names can often refer to high land or a small hill surrounded by bog and, despite the fact that Inishargy is inland, one could suggest that *Inis* here might mean "island-hill" or "elevated land surrounded by bog" (Ó Mainnín 1989–90). This latter meaning of *inis*, or *island*, also features in the discussion of the minor name **Islandgorm** (par. St Andrew's alias Ballyhalbert).

If the original name were to consist of Irish *Inis* "island" + *Carraig* "rock" (as implied in nos. 51–3) it would have resembled *Inis Cairrge* "island of (the) rock" (or modern Irish *Inis Carraige*). However, even though an interpretation along the lines of *Inis Cairrge* "island-hill of the rock" seems supported by 17th-century forms (e.g. nos. 18–21, 26–36, etc.) or even earlier *Inishkarrek* 1524 (no. 11), some problems remain with such an interpretation, as an *-m-* appears, and fairly consistently so, in the early spellings of the name (nos. 1–4 & 9). Such early 13th-century spellings of the type *Ynchemackargi* (no. 1) would not support an interpretation *Inis Cairrge* – without some, not wholly convincing, palaeographic re-interpretation, e.g. reading *m* as *ni* to arrive at *Inis na Cairrge* "island of the rock".

Orpen (*JRSAI* xliv (1914) 64 n. 7) suggests that the place-name written in the *Inquisition of the Earldom of Ulster 1333* as *Yneston(a)* (nos. 6 & 7) might refer to modern Inishargy. Similarly, from the same *Inquisition* there is a form *Agryston* (= no. 8 above, transcribed *Agrystone*, Orpen 65). Neither Reeves nor Orpen suggested a location for this place. Any suggestion of a possible link between 13th-century Anglo-Norman names *Yneston(a)*, or even *Argyston(e)*, and modern Inishargy must be abandoned, as forms no. 1–4 seem to provide us with evidence that we are dealing with an original Irish-language name.

The 1204 AD form *Ynchemackargi* (no. 1) would suggest an Irish-language form resembling *Inis Mhic Cairrgi* "the (hill-)island of *Mac Cairrge*" where *Mac Cairrge* (literally "son of stone, or rock") would represent a personal name, rather than a surname of the medieval type. Personal names of this type were common in early Irish, see *CGH* Index pp. 680–4 for examples, although there is no attested example of *Mac Cairrge* in this source. One other possibility might be a personal name *Mac Fairrge*, literally "son of the sea" which would give a genitive *Inis Mhic Fhairrge*. Again no form like *Mac Fairrge* is attested in the Old Irish personal names in *CGH*, although we have two examples of a *Fer Mara*, i.e. "man of (the) sea" (*CGH* Index p.635).

In addition to the substantial interpretative problems posed by the name Inishargy, there is an alias form *Ne(c)kellen*, or the like, in the 17th century (nos. 26, 28, 31–2, 35–6) which is also difficult to interpret, particularly in the absence of any idea of how it was pronounced.

TOWNLAND NAMES

Balliggan — *Baile Uí Uiginn*
J 6165 — "*Ó hUiginn*'s townland"

1. Balliggin	Inq. Ult. (Down) §2 Jac. I	1605
2. Ballegin al. Ballehiggin	Ham. Copy Inq. xlii	1623
3. Ballyhiggin	Ham. Copy Inq. xlv	1623
4. Ballegin al. Ballyhiggen	Ham. Copy Inq. xxxi	1623
5. Ballyggin al.Ballyhigan	Ham. Copy Inq. xxxii	1623
6. Ballegin al. Ballehiggen	Ham. Copy Inq. xxxiv	1623
7. Ballehiggin	Inq. Ult. (Down) §104 Car. I	1645
8. Ballenggin al.Ballehiggin	Inq. Ult. (Down) §104 Car. I	1645
9. Ballyuggin	Census 92	1659c
10. Ballevggin 1/2 towne	BSD 91	1661
11. Ballehigin	Inq. Ult. (Down) §23 Car. I	1662
12. Ballyvigin	Sub. Roll Dn 283	1663
13. Balliggin	Wm. Map (OSNB)	1810
14. Balliggin	High Const. Applot. (OSNB)	1830c
15. Ballygin	Tythes Applot. (OSNB)	1830c
16. Balliggan	Bnd. Sur. (OSNB)	1830c
17. Baile Liagáin "town of the standing stone"	J O'D (OSNB)	1834c
18. ˌbaˈlïgən	Local pronunciation	1991

Baile Uí Uiginn "Ó hUiginn's Town" seems a much more likely Gaelic original for modern Balliggan than O'Donovan's suggested form *Baile Liagáin* "town of the standing stone" (17), particularly in the light of 17th-century forms such as "Ballegin al. Ballyhiggen" (nos. 2–8). The Gaelic surname *Ó hUiginn*, commonly anglicized O'Higgin, Higgins, etc., was the name of a renowned Gaelic family of poets and literary men (Woulfe 1923: 576). Knott (*TD* i p. XX) discusses the origin and background of this family and makes the tentative suggestion that the Irish personal name underlying the surname *Ó hUiginn* is Irish *Uicing*, which is a borrowing from Old Norse *Vikingr* "Viking" and so the surname *Ó hUiginn*, in Knott's view, is "descendant of *Uicing*, i.e. 'the Viking'". This *Ó hUiginn* surname in Balliggan cannot be assumed, however, to indicate any Viking settlement here as it may simply refer to land held by the medieval Irish literary family of *Ó hUiginn*.

Ballygarvan — *Baile Uí Gharbhagáin* (?)
J 5965 — "townland of *Ó Garbhagáin*"

1. Ballegarvagan	CPR Jas I 39a	1604
2. Balligarvagane	Inq. Ult. (Down) §2 Jac. I	1605
3. Balligarvagane	CPR Jas I 73a	1605
4. Balle-Carugan al. Ballecarvegan	Ham. Copy Inq. xlii	1623
5. Ballegarngan	Ham. Copy Inq. xlvi	1623

6. (?) Ballegrangan	Ham. Copy Inq. xxxii	1623
7. Ballegarrugan	Inq. Ult. (Down) §102 Car. I	1644
8. Ballenegargavan	Inq. Ult. (Down) §102 Car. I	1644
9. Ballegarragan	Inq. Ult. (Down) §104 Car. I	1645
10. Ballygargan	Census 92	1659c
11. Ballegarrugan	BSD 89	1661
12. Ballegarrugan	Inq. Ult. (Down) §23 Car. II	1662
13. Ballygarvin	Sub. Roll Down 283	1663
14. Ballygarvan	Ham. Copy Rental 108	1681
15. Ballygarvan	Wm. Map (OSNB)	1810
16. Ballygarvigan	High Const. Applot. (OSNB)	1830c
17. Ballygarvan	Tythes Applot. (OSNB)	1830c
18. Ballygarven	Bnd. Sur. (OSNB)	1830c
19. Baile Garbháin "Garvan's town"	J O'D (OSNB)	1834c
20. ˌbaliˈgɑrvən	Local pronunciation	1991

The written forms of this name suggest *Baile Garbháin*, from earlier *Baile Garbhagáin*, i.e. *garbh* "rough" + suffix *-án* or *-agán*. This might signify rough land, or the like. On the other hand, the name may contain a personal name *Ó Garbhagáin* "descendant of *Garbhagán* (little rough one)". Woulfe (1923: 539) describes a people bearing the surname *Ó Garbháin* as a branch of the southern Uí Néill. The problematic *-garvan* element of this name is discussed in greater detail in the section dealing with the townland of **Ballygarvigan** (par. Ballyphilip).

Ballyobegan — *Baile Oibicín*
J 6266 — "Hopkin's townland"

1. Rune	Pipe Roll John 56	1211c
2. Rone, Ecclesia de	Eccles. Tax. 20	1306c
3. Ballaabakin	CPR Jas I 39a	1604
4. Ballyobbikin	Inq. Ult. (Down) §2 Jac. I	1605
5. Balliobickin	Grant Jas I (OSNB)	1605
6. Balliobickin	CPR Jas I 73a	1605
7. Dromeroan al. Dromefine	CPR Jas I 78a	1606
8. Drumornan	Jas I to Down Cath. 179	1609
9. Ballyobekene	CPR Jas I 326a	1617
10. Balleobkin al. Drumroan	Ham. Copy Inq. xlii	1623
11. Rectorie of Drumroan	Ham. Copy Inq. xlv	1623
12. town of Drumroan	Ham. Copy Inq. xlv; xlvi	1623
13. Balleobikin	Ham. Copy Inq. xlvi	1623
14. grange or rectorie of Ballydrumroan al. Drumfin	Ham. Copy Inq. xxxi	1623
15. Ballydrumroan	Ham. Copy Inq. xxxi	1623
16. Balleobiken	Ham. Copy Inq. xxxiv	1623
17. Drumroan	Inq. Ult. (Down) §104 Car. I	1645
18. Balleobekin	Inq. Ult. (Down) §104 Car. I	1645
19. Balleobekin al. Drumroan	Inq. Ult. (Down) §104 Car. I	1645
20. Drumroan, vil' de	Inq. Ult. (Down) §104 Car. I	1645
21. Ballyobikin	Census 92	1659c

22. Balleobbikin	BSD 91	1661
23. Drumroan	Inq. Ult. (Down) §23 Car. II	1662
24. Balleobeckan	Inq. Ult. (Down) §23 Car. II	1662
25. Ballyobikin	Sub. Roll Dn 283	1663
26. Ballyobikiu	Ham. Copy Rental 108	1681
27. Ballyobegan	Wm. Map (OSNB)	1810
28. Ballyobigan	High Const. Applot. (OSNB)	1830c
29. Ballyobican	Tythes Applot. (OSNB)	1830c
30. Ballyobbegan	Bnd. Sur. (OSNB)	1830c
31. Baile Obigein "Hopkin's town"	J O'D (OSNB)	1834c
32. ˌbaliˈobigən	Local pronunciation	1991

The form Ballyobegan probably results from a gaelicization of an earlier Norman place-name resembling *Hobbekin(s)ton*. MacLysaght (1964: 116) describes *Hopkins* as "a very English name", common in Connacht and Co. Longford, which had been adopted there, in his view, as a form of the gaelicized Norman name *Mac Oibicín*, although in other parts of Ireland he saw the surname Hopkins as of English origin. Leaving aside the surname, we can see that in the case of Co. Down Ballyobegan we are dealing with a Norman personal name *Hobbekin*, *Hobykin*, or the like. The Anglo-Norman personal name *Hobykin* survived in the Upper Ards until the 17th-century period where it is attested in state papers e.g. Hobykin Fitzsymons *Inq. Ult.*, 1631 AD, or Obikine Fitz Symons *Fiants Eliz.* §6711, 1602 AD. Reaney (1958: 169 sv Hopkin(s)) lists forms including *Hobekinus* which he derived from *Hobbe-kin*, or "little Hobbe", where *Hob(be)* (*ibid.* 166) is taken as a variant rhyming pet form of *Rob*, a pet form of *Robert*. Therefore in suggesting an earlier form of this townland as Anglo-Norman *Hobbekin(s)ton*, i.e. "townland of *Hobbekin*", being replaced by a later gaelicized form *Baile Oibicín*, one envisages a development along the lines of the general pattern of Anglo-Norman names in this area.

The written forms of the name listed above suggest that this place has been known by several different names throughout its recorded history. Reeves (*EA* 20, n. l) points out that it occurs as *Ecclesia de Rone* in the Taxation of 1306, to which we can add earlier *Rune* from the Pipe Roll of John for 1212 AD (forms 1–2 above). Reeves' suggestion "Probably *ruadhan* 'redness', in reference to the soil", seems a reasonable enough guess, although in 1212 one might have expected the *-dh-* in Irish *ruadhán* to have been pronounced as a dental fricative and represented as such in Anglo-Norman documents (O'Rahilly 1930: 163 ff.). The exact meaning of *Rune/Rone* (nos. 1 & 2), then, will be a matter for fuller investigation. It seems also to be the second element of the 17th-century spellings *Dromroan* and the like (nos. 7, 10–12, 14–15, etc.). One may even also have evidence for a *Droim Fionn* "white ridge", e.g. Dromeroan al. Dromefine 1605, ... Dromfin" 1623.

There is also a **Ballyobegan House** in this area which is mentioned in Knox (*Knox Hist.* 462) as "Ballyobecan House, belonging to Mr Allen". For an earlier description of "a spacious and rather handsome house" that "presents a bare appearance from the total absence of planting" see *OSM* vii 85.

Fish Quarter — *Ceathrú an Iascaire*

J 6062 — "quarter of the fisherman"

1. the Fishers' quarter	CPR Jas I 39a	1604
2. Ballicarowneescreh	Inq. Ult. (Down) §2 Jac. I	1605
3. Ballicarrownesregh	Inq. Ult. (Down) §2 Jac. I	1605

4. Carrowneescreh	CPR Jas I 73a 1605	
5. Carrowneskra	Ham. Copy Inq. xlvi	1623
6. Carrownesker	Ham. Copy Inq. xxxi	1623
7. Carrownesker	Ham. Copy Inq. xxxii	1623
8. Carrow-Nesteragh	Ham. Copy Inq. xxxiv	1623
9. Carrownesker al. Fisherstowne	Inq. Ult. (Down) §109 Car. I	1650c
10. Fisher Quarter	Census 92	1659c
11. Ffisher Quarter	BSD 89	1661
12. Carrownesca	Inq. Ult. (Down) §23 Car. II	1662
13. Fisher Quarter	Ham. Copy Rental 108	1681
14. Fishquarter	Wm. Map (OSNB)	1810
15. Fishquarter	High Const. Applot. (OSNB)	1830c
16. Fishquarter	Tythes Applot. (OSNB)	1830c
17. Fishquarter	Bnd. Sur. (OSNB)	1830c
18. Fishers Quarter	OSM vii 18	1837
19. 'fɪʃ 'kwartər	Local pronunciation	1991

It is difficult to determine with certainty whether this place-name was coined initially in Irish or English. Indeed the 1650 form *Carrownesker al' Fishertowne* (9) reflects the degree of bilingualism that must have existed in the Ards in the 17th century. *Fisher* was the normal English word for "fisherman" up until the 16th/17th centuries, before the addition of *-man* to *fisher-* in standard English. This addition of *-man* was quite unnecessary as the *-er* of *fisher* was an agent suffix as in *baker*, *thatcher* etc., i.e. a person who fishes, bakes, thatches. In modern Scots the word *fisher* still survives for "fisherman" and, while one might be tempted to see a Scots origin for *fisher* in the 17th-century forms of this name (nos. 1, 9–11 & 13), it must be remembered that the term *fisher* would also have existed in the Anglo-Norman period and, judging by the patterns of other place-names in the Upper Ards, it would seem that an Anglo-Norman origin is possible for *Fisher Quarter* with *Ceathrú an Iascaire* arising as a subsequent Irish translation. For similar names see **Nunsquarter** below, **Ballygelagh** (parish of Ardkeen) and **Whitechurch** (parish of Ballywalter).

Glastry — *An Ghlasrach*
J 6262 — "the green grassy area"

1. Balliglassarie	CPR Jas I 39a	1604
2. Balliglassery	Inq. Ult. (Down) §2 Jac. I	1605
3. Ballynaglassery	Inq. Ult. (Down) §2 Jac. I	1605
4. Ballineglasserie	CPR Jas I 73a	1605
5. Balleneglasserogh	Ham. Copy Inq. xlii	1623
6. Balleglasserogh	Ham. Copy Inq. xlvi	1623
7. Balleglasserogh	Ham. Copy Inq. xxxii; xxxiv	1623
8. Balleglasserogh	Inq. Ult. (Down) §104 Car. I	1645
9. Balleneglasseragh	Inq. Ult. (Down) §104 Car. I	1645
10. Glassery	Census 92	1659c
11. Glasserragh	BSD 89	1661
12. Balleglastragh	Inq. Ult. (Down) §23 Car. II	1662
13. Glaswry	Sub. Roll Down 283	1663
14. Glasseragh	Ham. Copy Rental 108	1681

15. Glastry	Wm. Map (OSNB)	1810
16. Glastry	High Const. Applot. (OSNB)	1830c
17. Glastry	Tythes Applot. (OSNB)	1830c
18. Glastry	Bnd. Sur. (OSNB)	1830c
19. Baile na nGlasraidh "villa herbarum, town of the herbs"	J O'D (OSNB)	1834c
20. 'glastrι	Local pronunciation	1991

The written forms of this name clearly point to an Irish form *An Ghlasrach*, rather than O'Donovan's proposed *Baile na nGlasraidh* (19). O'Donovan's suggestion of *villa herbarum* "town of the herbs" is certainly one possible meaning, although it is difficult to propose an exact meaning for the term *glasrach*. The word is not listed in the main Irish dictionaries but for Scottish Gaelic Dwelly has a noun *glasrach* "Uncultivated land. 2 Green plot". He also has an adjective *glasrach* "Abounding in lea, or unploughed land. 2 Green. 3 Having green groves or meadows. 4 Abounding in pot herbs".

Gransha
J 5960

An Ghráinseach
"the grange, or church granary".

1. Grangia, Ecclesia de	Eccles. Tax. 20	1306c
2. Ballicoolegrange	Inq. Ult. (Down) §2 Jac. I	1605
3. Ballicoollgraunge	CPR Jas I 73a	1605
4. Grange otherwise Collegrange	CPR Jas I 78a	1606
5. Tollunigrange, Capella de	Terrier (Reeves) 59	1615c
6. Tollemgrange	Terrier (O'Laverty) 328	1615c
7. Gransho	CPR Jas I 326a	1617
8. (?) Columgraunge	Ulster Visit. (Reeves) 53	1622
9. Ballegrangeogh al. Coolgrange	Ham. Copy Inq. xlii	1623
10. Coolgrange	Ham. Copy Inq. xlv	1623
11. Coolgrange al. Grange	Ham. Copy Inq. xlv	1623
12. Coolgrange	Ham. Copy Inq. xxx	1623
13. the Rectorie of Coolgrange	Ham. Copy Inq. xxxiii	1623
14. Coolegrange al. Grange	Ham. Copy Inq. xxxiii	1623
15. Grangeogh al. Coolgrange	Ham. Copy Inq. xxxiv	1623
16. Cool-Grange	Ham. Copy Inq. xxxvi	1623
17. Coolgrange al. Grange	Inq. Ult. (Down) §104 Car. I	1645
18. Ballegrangeoh al. Coolegrange	Inq. Ult. (Down) §104 Car. I	1645
19. Granguch	Sav. Ards 191	1648
20. Granshagh	Census 92	1659c
21. Granshagh al. Coolegrange	BSD 89	1661
22. Colegrange	Inq. Ult. (Down) §23 Car. II	1662
23. Coolegrange al. Grange	Inq. Ult. (Down) §23 Car. II	1662
24. Granshogh	Sub. Roll Down 283	1663
25. Granshogh	Ham. Copy Rental 108	1681
26. Grenchoch	Sav. Ards 254	1690c
27. Granshaw	Wm. Map (OSNB)	1810
28. Gransha	High Const. Applot. (OSNB)	1830c

29. Gransha	Tythes Applot. (OSNB)	1830c
30. Gransha	Bnd. Sur. (OSNB)	1830c
31. Gráinseach "a grange"	J O'D (OSNB)	1834c
32. ˈgranʃə	Local pronunciation	1991

The Irish form of the name, *Gráinseach*, is commonly recognized as a borrowing from Norman French *grange* "granary", which in the Anglo-Norman period usually had the meaning of an ecclesiastical or church granary (Flanagan 1981–2(c): 75). The Ards, of course, was particularly noted for its corn production even in the accounts of Elizabethan authors and later. Some of the forms in *Coolegrange* (e.g. nos. 2–4) suggest an alternative Irish form *Cúlghráinseach* "rear or back grange", a form which may have helped distinguish this grange from the many others in the Ards. Forms 5–6 suggest an Irish-language *Tulaigh na Gráinsí* "hillock of the grange".

Kircubbin — Of uncertain origin

J 5962

1. Cubynhillis in tenemento de Ynchemkargy	CPR Ed. III (EA) 19 n. i	1300c
2. Ballecurbubben	CPR Jas I 39a	1604
3. Ballicarcubbin	Inq. Ult. (Down) §2 Jac. I	1605
4. Killcooby	Inq. Ult. (Down) §2 Jac. I	1605
5. Ballicarcubbine	CPR Jas I 73a	1605
6. (?) Kilcooly in the Great Ardes	CPR Jas I 78a	1606
7. Killcubin, Capella de [rectified from Killenbui]	Terrier (Reeves) 59	1615c
8. Kilcubin, Capella de	Terrier (O' Laverty) 328	1615c
9. Killcobin	Ulster Visit. (Reeves) 55	1622
10. Ballekircubin al. Kilcooby	Ham. Copy Inq. xlii	1623
11. Kilcooby al. Kircubin	Ham. Copy Inq. xlv	1623
12. Kilcoby al. Kircubin	Ham. Copy Inq. xxx	1623
13. Rectorie of Kilcooby al. Kircubbin	Ham. Copy Inq. xxxiii	1623
14. Ballekircubin	Ham. Copy Inq. xxxiv	1623
15. Kilcooby	Ham. Copy Inq. xxxvi	1623
16. Kirkubbin	Will (Sav. Ards) 247	1640
17. Kilcouby al. Kircubin	Inq. Ult. (Down) §104 Car. I	1645
18. Ballekircubbin al. Kilcouby	Inq. Ult. (Down) §104 Car. I	1645
19. Kirkcubbine	Census 92	1659c
20. Krikcubbin	BSD 91	1661
21. Killcouby al. Kirkcubin cum decim in vil' de Killcuby al. Kircuby	Inq. Ult. (Down) §23 Car. II	1662
22. Kirkcubbin	Sub. Roll Down 283	1663
23. Kircubbin and Mill	Ham. Copy Rental 108	1681
24. Kirkcubbin	Wm. Map (OSNB)	1810
25. Kircubbin	High Const. Applot. (OSNB)	1830c
26. Kirkcubbin	Tythes Applot. (OSNB)	1830c
27. Kirkcubbin	Bnd. Sur. (OSNB)	1830c

28. Ceathramh Ghobbáin "Gobban's quarter"	J O'D (OSNB)	1834c
29. Cill Chobáin	Post-seanchas 86	1905
30. Cill Ghobáin	AGBP 117	1969
31. Cill Ghobáin	Éire Thuaidh	1986
32. Cill Ghobáin	GÉ 241	1989
33. ˌkər ˈkọbən	Local pronunciation	1991

This name poses considerable difficulty in determining its original form and meaning but, before dealing with these, it is amusing to read that when John O'Donovan read the proposed anglicized spelling *Kirkubbin* which was recommended in the *OSNB*, he then altered this to *Kircubbin* and jokingly entered: "Kirkubbin *Ceathramh Gobbáin* 'Gobban's quarter'. This should be Carcubbin. The presbyterians wish to make everything Kirk. Kircubbin". O'Donovan's own suggestion of *Ceathramh Ghobbáin* "Gobán's Quarter" requires a re-examination for several reasons. Firstly, the 17th-century forms show mixed usage of *Kil-* and *Kir(k)-*, possibly suggesting a variation between *Cill* "church" and *Kirk* "church". Although *kirk* as an ordinary word in the spoken language of latterday Ulster is used to mean "Presbyterian church", the use of *Kirk-* as a place-name element in Ulster certainly cannot always be automatically assumed to be of Scottish Presbyterian origin; we have some evidence of *Kirk* from Anglo-Norman sources in the early medieval period. Indeed in this townland name, it may well be that the 17th-century *Kir(k)-* forms represent an earlier Gaelic word, as *Kirk-* is absent from the earlier 17th-century spellings, such as *Ballecur-* (no. 2) and *Ballicar-* (nos. 3, 5).

O'Donovan's suggestion that the Irish personal name *Gobán* is contained in the second element of Kir*cubbin* has been accepted elsewhere, e.g. *Cill Ghobáin* (nos. 30–32), presumably "church of St Gobán". Hogan (*Onom. Goed.* 194) lists two separate *Cell Gobáin* entries for place-names in Dublin and Kerry, modern Kilgobbin and Kilgoban, in addition to a third *Cell Gobáin* which he identified as Kilgobban near Bandon or Kilgobbin near Mallow. These latter examples, in addition to O'Donovan's suggestion (no. 28), and Laoide's (29), may have influenced *AGBP* to postulate *Cill Ghobáin* (no. 30) for the Co. Down name Kircubbin. It is noteworthy, however, that neither the late nor the earlier written 17th-century forms of the name in *Kil(l)-*, e.g. nos. 7–9, show any trace of a *-g-* which must cast serious doubt on the possibility of a connection with *Gobán*.

Although there is no mention of an existing church site in this area in *ASCD*, Reeves (*EA* 19 n. i) gives details of the remains of a small church which formerly stood in a place called *The Chapel-field*, which was about a furlong east of the village of Kircubbin. Reeves views this now vanished church-site as having been responsible for the village name of Kircubbin, and considers it to be the church named *Ecclesia de Sancti Medumy* (i.e. "the church of St Medumy"), which occurred in the *Ecclesiastical Taxation* of 1306 beside the church of *Inyscargi* (= mod. Inishargy). Reeves was unable to identify this saint with certainty and more research will be required on his background before any definite pronouncement can be made. Reeves (*EA* 19 n. i) further suggests that the form *Cubynhillis* (form no. 1), taken from a grant of *c.* 1300 by William de Maundeville to the prior of St. John the Baptist in Down, is identical with modern Kircubbin. The fact that *Cubynhillis* is described as being in the tenement of Inishargy is certainly a strong indication that it is located in the Kircubbin area, but a meaning for *Cubyn-* is difficult to find. Despite, then, the attestation of early spellings of Kircubbin its etymology and origin still remain, at our current state of research, impenetrable.

As regards the modern village of Kircubbin *ASCD* 417 notes that it was "a very small port established in 1790, with an export trade in kelp". See also *OSM* vii, 84.

Nunsquarter *Ceathrú na gCailleach*
J 5963 "quarter of the nuns"

1.	Ballycarrownecalliogh	Inq. Ult. (Down) §2 Jac. I	1605
2.	Barrecallownecalliogh	CPR Jas I 73a	1605
3.	Carownecalliogh	Ham. Copy Inq. xlii; xlvi	1623
4.	Carrow-Calliogh	Ham. Copy Inq. xxxiv	1623
5.	Carrownecalliagh	Inq. Ult. (Down) §104 Car. I	1645
6.	Nuns quarter	Census 92	1659c
7.	Nunns Quarter	BSD 89	1661
8.	Nunsquarter	Wm. Map (OSNB)	1810
9.	Nunsquarter	High Const. Applot. (OSNB)	1830c
10.	Nunsquarter	Tythes Applot. (OSNB)	1830c
11.	Nunsquarter	Bnd. Sur. (OSNB)	1830c
12.	Nunsquarter	Mr. Allen (OSNB)	1834c
13.	'nọnz 'kwartər	Local pronunciation	1991

It might appear from the current list of early spellings above that an Irish-language form *Ceathrú na gCailleach* "quarter of the nuns" has been translated into English as Nunsquarter. However, given the Anglo-Norman background to this area and the fact that our earliest available spellings only date back as far as the beginning of the 17th century, one cannot be totally certain if *Ceathrú na gCailleach* was the original form of the name or whether it in turn represents a gaelicization of an earlier medieval Anglo-Norman name, cf. **Fish Quarter** above. It is not known what order of nuns occupied this place.

Rowreagh *Rubha Riabhach*
J 5961 "variegated clearing"

1.	Rubha	Mart. Gorm. Jun 24 p122	1170c
2.	Rubha	Mart. Don. Jun 29 p178 n	1630c
3.	le Rowe	Inq. Earldom Ulster iv 140	1333
4.	Ballirowriagh	Inq. Ult. (Down) §2 Jac. I	1605
5.	Ballirowreagh	Grant Jas I (OSNB)	1605
6.	Ballirowriagh	CPR Jas I 73a	1605
7.	Roowe, Manus Offlyn of	Ulst. Roll Gaol Deliv. 262	1613
8.	Rowriagh	Terrier (Reeves) 59	1615c
9.	Ruda	Ulster Visit. (Reeves) 33	1622
10.	Rowreagh	Ham. Copy Inq. xlii; xlv	1623
11.	Balleroreagh	Ham. Copy Inq. xxxi	1623
12.	Ballerowreogh	Ham. Copy Inq. xxxiv	1623
13.	Rowriagh	Inq. Ult. (Down) §20 Car. I	1631
14.	Rawreagh	Inq. Ult. (Down) §104 Car. I	1645
15.	Rowreagh	Census 92	1659c
16.	Rowreagh	BSD 91	1661
17.	Rowreagh	Inq. Ult. (Down) §23 Car. II	1662
18.	Rowreagh	Ham. Copy Rental 108	1681
19.	Rowreagh	Wm. Map (OSNB)	1810
20.	Roureagh	High Const. Applot. (OSNB)	1830c
21.	Ruereagh	Tythes Applot. (OSNB)	1830c

22. Ruereagh	Bnd. Sur. (OSNB)	1830c
23. Rubha Riach "grey land of rue (the herb so called)"	J O'D (OSNB)	1834c
24. ˌru're:	Local pronunciation	1991

In the 17th century there were two separate townlands: *Rowreagh* (in this parish), and a neighbouring townland of *Rubane*. *Rubane* has since become known as Echlinville (see the description of **Echlinville** townland and the name **Rubane** in the section of this book dealing with the parish of St Andrews or Ballyhalbert). It seems likely, however, that both *Rowreagh* and *Rubane* (or *Rowbane*) were subdivisions of a larger unit formerly known simply as *Le Rowe*, in Anglo-Norman documentation (no. 3), or *(An) Rubha* in Irish. The original Irish can be restored most definitely to *Rubha*, as we have reference to a saint named Tiu who dwelt here. In the 12th-century Irish *Martyrology of Gorman* 24 June, p. 122 we read: *Tiu rathmhar Rubha* "gracious Tiu of Rubha". In the glossed notes to this text we are left in no doubt as to the locality of *Rubha* which is described as: *ainm a baile; i n-Aird Ulad ata*, i.e. "the name of his (or her?) place; it is in the Ards of Ulster". In the 17th-century *Martyrology of Donegal* 24 June (p. 178) it is repeated that Tiu is from *Rubha*, and that *Rubha* is the name of a place in the Ards, but we are further informed that Tiu is a female descended from "Eochaidh son of Muiredh, who is of the race of Heremon" (i.e. *Do sliocht Eochadha mic Muiredha ata do shiol Eireamoin di*). In *CSH* (§662.182–7, pp. 100–1), however, there is a list of the saints connected with *Síol Eachach Mic Muiredhaigh* (i.e. "the race of Eochu son of Muireadhach") and in this poem the tribe of the *Dál mBuain* ("Seed of Buan") are connected with the lineage of Eochu mac Muireadhaigh. Earlier on in this same corpus (§154, p. 26) there is a reference to a male saint called *Tiu*:

> *Tiu m. Fínain m. Cassain m. Fergusa m. Niad Cendmóir m. Buain* [*a quo Dál mBuain*].
>
> (Tiu son of Fínan son of Cassan son of Fergus son of Nia Cendmór son of Buan [from whom the *Dál mBuain* are descended]).

Therefore the martyrologies appear to be at odds as to whether Tiu was a male or female saint, but he/she is certainly to be connected with the Ards and the modern townlands of Rowreagh and Rubane. In fact Reeves (*EA* 21, n. m) describes a chapel called "Row alias Grange-row" which stood in a field in modern Echlinville (formerly Rubane or Rowbane) and mentions (*EA* 379, n. y) that no visible trace of the church site remained in the mid–19th century: "The chapel, of which not a vestige remains, formerly stood in the field opposite the entrance to the Echlinville demesne".

Although the church site has now disappeared, and there are but brief passing references to St Tiu in the early Irish material, if we accept the genealogy proposed above, then Tiu's great-great grandfather *Nia Cendmór* was a brother of *Míliuc mac Buain*, a king of Dál nAraide to whom St Patrick was sold as a slave, which at a rough estimate would place St Tiu two to three generations after St Patrick.

Regarding the place-name itself, an element of uncertainty exists about the exact meaning of the Irish word *Rubha*. *Joyce* (ii 323–4) discusses the Irish herb *rubha* "rue" and various place-names which he considers contain the element *rubha* in the meaning "rue-land", among them the Ards names *Rowreagh* and *Rubane* which he takes to represent *Rubha Riabhach* "grey rue-land" and *Rubha Bán* "white rue-land". However in his later discussion of the Cork townland *Ballinrooey* Joyce (iii 65) also continues to consider "rue (herb)" as a possible meaning for *rubha* although he does add that it "sometimes means a point of land".

DIL (s.v. 2 *ruba*) describes *rub(h)a* as a "word of doubtful meaning frequent in place-names", although W. Stokes (*Revue Celtique* xiv 447) identified *rub(h)a* with the modern Scottish Gaelic word *rudha*, defined by Dwelly as "a point of land, promontory". Admittedly the current map does not favour an interpretation of "variegated headland" and "white headland" for *Rubha Riabhach* (Rowreagh) and *Rubha Bán* (modern Echlinville) in the Ards but, when one considers that 17th-century maps show a channel of water dividing the Ards, there may be support for an interpretation of "headland" or "point" for *rubha* in these names. J. O'Donovan (*Mart. Don.* p. 251, n. 1) records that the mouth of the river Maine in Co. Antrim, which is now Shanescastle, was formerly known in Irish as *Rubha Mena* "the point of [the river] Men".

On the other hand, Meyer (1911:126) has a noun *rub(h)a*, which he derives from Irish *ro-ben*, and which he suggests means "brake, clearing". For the latter meaning "clearing" one can compare *DIL* 1 *ruba* "wounding, killing", and envisage a development: "striking with a sword" > "clearing". However, in *DIL ruba* is also listed as "brake", e.g. *rube sciad ocus droigen ocus cróib* "a brake of hawthorn and thorns and branches" (*Trip. Life* Stokes i 78.8). Therefore, while the Irish forms of these names can be reasonably restored to *Rubha Riabhach* and *Rubha Bán*, the meaning of *rubha* is difficult to ascertain with certainty.

Finally, as regards the variation in the spellings of the modern forms of *Rowreagh* and *Rubane*, it is interesting to note that in the *OSNB* there is entered in the margin: "Also Ruereagh as they say", and even the local pronunciation favours a *Rureagh* form.

OTHER NAMES

Black Neb — "black nose"

J 5961

This name is pronounced [(ðə) 'blɛk 'neb] and contains the Scots term *neb* "nose". The rock doubtless owes its name to its shape and *Nat. Scots Dict.* describes the use of *neb* to refer to a piece of land, rock, etc.".

Blackstaff River — *Maide Dubh na hArda* "the black staff of the Ards"

J6159

	Form	Source	Date
1.	the 'blackstaffe' called in Irish Mayddedowneard	Quinn 1933–4:77	1540
2.	Blackstafe	Fiants Eliz. §1530	1570
3.	Blacke Staffe	S-E Ulster Map	1580c
4.	Blakstaffe	Mercator's Ulst.	1595
5.	Blackstuff	Bartlett Maps (Esch. Co. Maps) 1	1603
6.	the river and ford of Blackstaffe	CPR Jas. I 73b	1605
7.	Blackscaff', rivus de	Inq. Ult. §2 Jac. I	1605
8.	Blackstaffe	Norden's Map	1610c
9.	Blackstaffe, the river of	Ham. Copy Inq. xxx	1623
10.	Blackstaffe, neare	Ham. Copy Inq. xxxii, xlv	1623
11.	Blackstaff	Inq. Ult. (Down) §104 Car. I	1644
12.	Blackstaffe	Inq. Ult. (Down) §23 Car. II	1662
13.	Blackstaff River "river of the black stick" "A small slow stream"	J O'D (OSNB)	1830c

Form no. 1 above is extracted from the following citation: "the 'blackstaffe' called in Irish Mayddedowneard where the Scots now inhabit twelve towns by force of arms" (Commission of 1540 cited in Quinn 1933–4:77). This solitary spelling *Mayddedowneard* is extremely valuable in enabling us to project an underlying Irish-language form of *Maide Dubh na hArda* "the black staff of the Ards". Flanagan (1978(c): 25) discusses the term *Blackstaff* in river names, where the *-staff* usually refers to beams of oak that were formerly stretched from stone to stone making it possible to walk across. The *Blackstick* in Co. Louth goes back to an earlier Irish *An Maide Dubh*, according to *L. Log. Lú* 29. It seems likely, therefore, that the Blackstaff in the Ards received its name from the black staffs, or beams of oak, that were placed across it to act as a form of primitive crossing point or bridge.

Bloody Burn Bay | A Scots/English form
J 5864

1. Bloody Burn Bay, i.e. the bloody *stream*	J O'D (OSNB)	1834c
2. 'blọdɩ 'bọrn 'be:	Local pronunciation	1991

The element *Bloody* in this name may refer to a massacre here although there are two local oral versions of the circumstances. One local informant remarked: "There was a battle fought there", while others believe that some nuns were massacred here and that their blood ran down the *Bloody Burn*.

Bullock Pladdies | An English form?
J 5664

On the term *pladdy* "sunken rock" in Strangford Lough, see **McCammon Pladdy**.

Dougherty Rock South | An English form
Dougherty Rock West
J 5763

Five families of Dogherty are listed in modern Upper Ards by Anderson (1980:2), and in *Inq. Ult.* §9 Jac. I (1620 AD) mention is made of "Murtagh, Donell and Arte O'Dougherty" in the townland of Tara (par. Witter) in the Upper Ards.

Downey's Pladdy | An English form ?
J 5665

This name is yet another example of the the use of *pladdy* in Strangford Lough to refer to "a sunken rock" – see **McCammon Pladdy** below.

Dullisk Rock | A hybrid form ?
J 5762

The *dullisk* part of this name refers to a kind of edible sea-weed, although it is difficult to determine if this is an English/Scots name or if an underlying Irish form *duileasc* "dulse" has been transliterated into English.

Long Skart Rock | A Scots form
J 5662

The *Skart* portion of this name represents the word *scart* which is listed in the *Scots Nat. Dict.* as "cormorant". *Scart* is also listed as "cormorant and shag" in Co. Donegal by Traynor

(1953:242). *Long Skart Rock*, then, means "long rock of the cormorants" as opposed to **Round Skart Rock** below.

McCammon Pladdy A hybrid form ?
J 5763

Local pronunciation [mə'kɑmənz ˌplɑdɪ]. The name MacCammon was attested in the parish of Donaghmore, Co. Down where Harris (*Harris Hist.* 253) recorded that a "Jane Johnson, alias the Widow McCamon lived to the ripe old age of 105". Woulfe (1923:307) has *Mac Ámoinn*, MacCammon MacKemman, Hammond, etc. which he derives from "son of Amundr, a Norse personal name". See also **McCammon's Rocks** on the coast of Portavogie (parish of Ballyhalbert).

Quin/Freeman (1947: 88) state that "A *pladdy* is a shoal and the word is used in Strangford Lough, where drumlins are seen in various stages of submergence and some are completely below the waters". The word was given the meaning "sunken rock" in Wrights *English dialect dictionary* vol. 4 p. 534 but the only reference this source had for the use of the term in the English language was the following, taken from a Co. Down ballad *A sunset off Killyleagh* which appeared in a collection published by Savage-Armstrong 1901, p. 176:

> "Round many a **pladdie**, many an island green with
> the glancing shower,
> How fleetly up the Lough we'd sped"

Knox (*Knox Hist.* 474) states: "On the Ards coast, a Pladdy signifies a flat sunk rock, whilst a rock, always above water, is termed a 'Skerry', and if connected with the land, so as to form a reef, is named a 'Skare', or 'Sker'". However, Knox does not state his source for this. Quin and Freeman (88) propose an Irish etymology for this word, although McKeown (1933: 41) considers *Pladdy* "the usual local term for a sunken rock" and compares it with Norse *Flatēy* "flat island". See also **Pladdy Lug** (par. Witter).

Nunsquarter House See **Nunsquarter**

The Ragheries *An Dá Reachraidh*
J 5665 "the two *reachraidhs*"

1. The Two Raghara's	OS 6-inch Map, Down sheet 11	1834
2. The Ragheries	OS 6-inch Map, Down sheet 11	1856
3. The Ragheries	OS 6-inch Map, Down sheet 11	1933
4. ðə 'rɑxərɪz	Local pronunciation	1991

There are several islands off the coast of Ireland which contain the element *reachra*, these are: *Rathlin Island* (Co. Antrim), *Lambay Island* (Co. Dublin, which was known in the Old Irish period as *Rechru*) and Raghlybirne or Rathlin O'Byrne (Co. Donegal). Hogan (*Onom. Goed.* 579) cites references to these three islands from Irish sources and it appears that the original form was *rechra* or *rechru*. The Co. Antrim island is now anglicized *Rathlin* but it was also known by the islanders as *Rachery*, e.g. "Rathlin, or Rachery, as it is commonly pronounced" (Murphy 1987: vi). This form *Rachery*, for Rathlin Island (Co. Antrim), goes back to a Gaelic form *Reachraidh*, pronounced [rɑxəri, rɑheri] by some of the Gaelic-speaking islanders (Holmer 1942: 225). There has been no treatment yet of the etymology of early Irish *rechru* as a place-name element in the three islands mentioned above (although see *Dinnseanchas* vol. 2, no. 1 (1966) 22–5 for the Antrim Rathlin) but it would appear that the

Irish element *reachraidh*, a later reflex of *rechru*, was also used in Strangford Lough, as we find it in the *The Two Ragheries* in this parish and also as an alias form for the townland of **Ballyhaft** (Newtownards parish), e.g. *Ballyheste al. Raghorie* (1627), *Ballyhaft als Raghery* (1675). In the case of Strangford Lough, *reachraidh* seems to refer to a partly submerged reef or promontory. In support of this latter meaning there is also a long finger-shaped *Rathlin Island* which juts out into Lough Neagh (parish of Montiaghs, Co. Armagh). According to the 19th-century Ordnance Survey Memoirs for Co. Armagh the Lough Neagh "island of Rathlin or Raughlin ... is separated [from the mainland] by a bank of sand in summer and water in winter" (*OSM* i 91).

Round Skart Rock — A Scots form
J 5662

This name contains the word *scart* "a cormorant" and means "round rock of the cormorants" as opposed to **Long Skart Rock** above.

Selk Rock — A Scots form
J 5665

This is a Scots name meaning "seal rock". There are three such islands in Strangford Lough, see **Selk Island** (par. Ardquin).

Sheelah's Island — A hybrid form?
J 5764

The element *Sheelagh* in Strangford Lough appears to refer to a rock or a reef below the surface of the water, but the language of origin is difficult to ascertain; see also **Long Sheelagh** (*Other Names*, parish of Ardkeen). There is a record of kelp-gathering on Sheelagh's Island in the mid-19th century according to *OSNB*.

Skartock Rock — A Scots form
J5663

The element *Skartock* in this name is presumably a diminutive of *scart* "cormorant" and refers to some species of this bird.

Tubber na Carrig — *Tobar na Carraige*
J 6063 — "well of the rock"

We have no early historical spellings for this name but its present anglicized form *Tubber na Carrig* and the local pronunciation [ˌto̞bərnə ˈkɑrig] strongly suggest an original Irish *Tobar na Carraige* "well of the rock". According to Knox (*Knox Hist.* 462) "Tubbernacarrig was the residence of the late Colonel Ward".

Whitebank Pladdy — An English form?
J 5762

The term *pladdy* "submerged rock" is discussed above under **Mc Cammon Pladdy**.

PARISH OF ST ANDREWS ALIAS BALLYHALBERT

In the *OSNB* the Parish of St Andrews alias Ballyhalbert is dealt with under the three-parish "Union of Ballywalter, Inishargy and St Andrews alias Ballyhalbert". In addition to the alias "Ballywalter", St Andrews was also known as the Black Abbey and its history is discussed below under the heading **St Andrews** (or **Black Abbey**). The name **Ballyhalbert** is discussed below directly after **St Andrew's** under a separate heading.

PARISH NAMES

St Andrews	*Cill Aindreasa*	
	"Church of (St) Andrew"	
(also known as **Black Abbey**)	*An Mhainistir Dhubh*	
J 6066	"the black abbey"	
1. priore de S. Andrea in Arte	EA 192	1190c
2. prioiri et monachis de sancti Andree de Arce	Pontif. Hib. i 126	1204
3. priori et monachis sancti Andree de Arce	Pontif. Hib. i §59	1204
4. St. Andrew in the Ards	Reg. Sweeteman §88, 244	1356
5. the Black Abbey	CSP Ire 1601–3, Addend 672	1497
6. Black abbaye	Mercator's Ulst.	1595
7. Black ab	Mercator's Ire.	1595
8. Mo:[nastery] Black	Bartlett Map (TCD)	1601
9. Black abbie	Bartlett Map (Esch. Co. Maps) 1	1603
10. the three townlands called Black Abbey, Ballynemanough and Ballecarrock ...	CPR Jas. I 72b	1606c
11. Sancti Andreae, Prebenda de	EA 179	1609
12. Blacke Abbey	Norden's Map	1610c
13. Black Abb	Speed's Antrim & Down	1610
14. Black-Abbey	CPR Jas I 122a	1610c
15. Blackabbey	CPR Jas I 326a	1618c
16. Black-abbey	CPR Jas I 520a	1621
17. Black Abbey	CPR Jas I 546a	1622
18. Ballemonestraduffe alias Ballyliserlane	Ham. Copy Inq. xliv	1623
19. Ballekilvolgan al Ballyknocke and Ballemanagh	Ham. Copy Inq. xliv	1623
20. Ballemonestraduffe al. Ballylisbrane	Ham. Copy Inq. xxxii	1623
21. Black-Abbey	Inq. Ult. (Down) §75 Car. I	1636
22. Blackabbay	Census 93	1659c
23. Blackabby al. Ballemannagh	BSD 87	1661
24. Killandress	Trien. Visit. (Bramhall) 9	1661
25. black Abby	Desc. Ards 38	1683
26. the Black-abbie	Inq. Ult. (Down) §23 Car. II	1662
27. sənt 'ɑndərz	Local pronunciation	1991

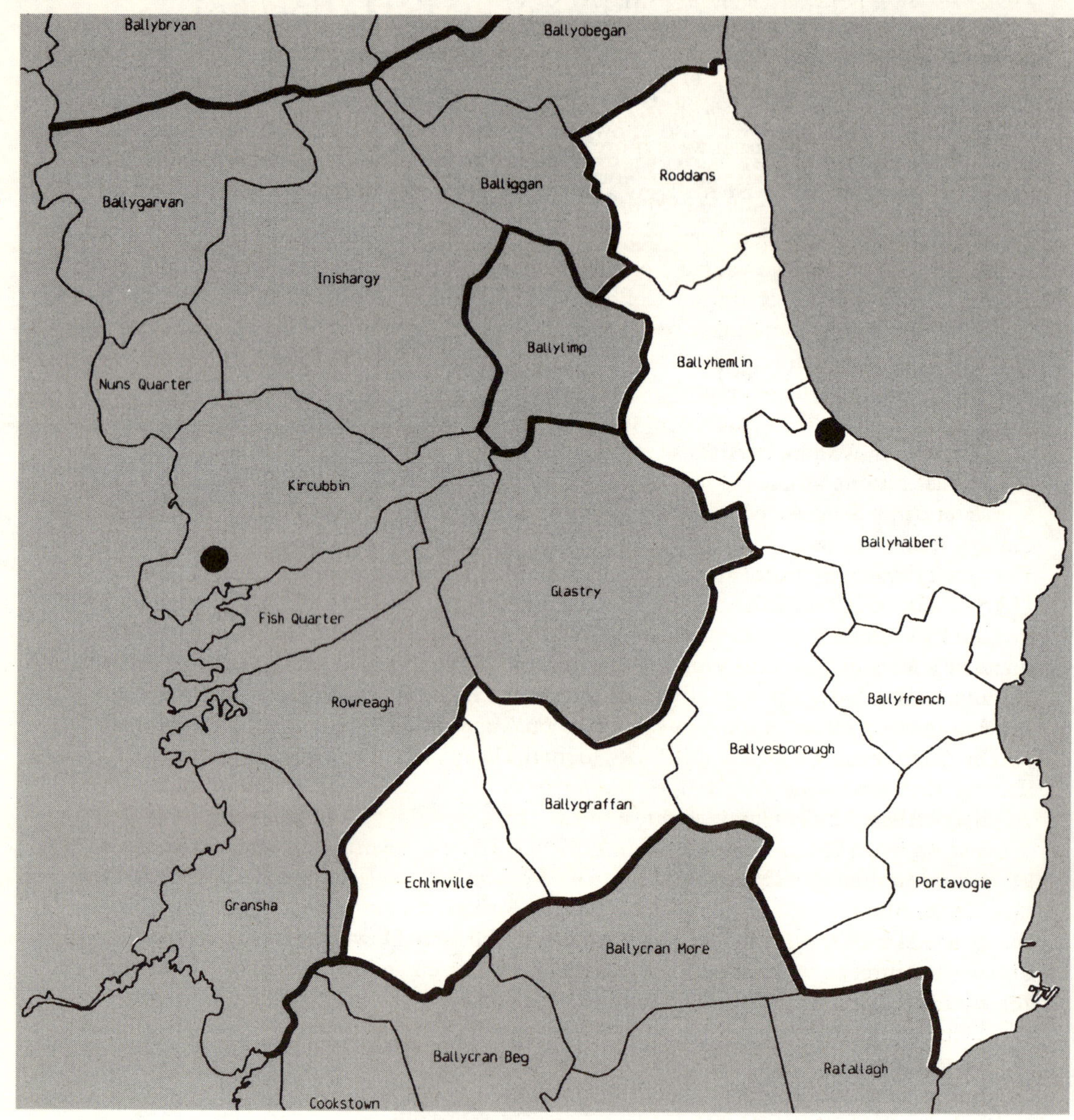

Parish of St Andrews alias Parish of Ballyhalbert

Barony of Ards Upper

Townlands			*Islands*	*Towns*
Ballyesborough	Ballygraffan	Echlinville	Burial Island	Ballyhalbert
Ballyfrench	Ballyhalbert	Portavogie	Green Island	
	Ballyhemlin	Roddans		

The Latin form *prioiri et monachis de sancti Andree de Arce* (form 2) refers to "the prior and monks of Saint Andrew's of the Ards". Although the modern townland of Black Abbey is in the parish of Greyabbey, the abbey itself was formerly known as the Priory of St Andrews, hence the modern parish name *St Andrews alias Ballyhalbert*. Form no. 24 suggests that Saint Andrews was gaelicized as *Cill Aindreasa*, although the majority of written forms indicate that the monastery and parish were more commonly known as Black Abbey, gaelicized *An Mhainistir Dhubh*, in the post-Anglo-Norman period.

The foundation of the abbey resulted from a grant by John de Courcy *c.* 1183–4 and its initial monks were supplied from the Benedictine Abbey of Stogursey in Somerset. Kerr (1989: 45) has provided a valuable précis of events relating to the early years of this establishment. Following the Norman Conquest of England in 1066 and the substantial land grants by William the Conquerer to his Norman knights, a number of Norman priories were founded in England, among them a priory in Somerset which was founded by monks from the Abbey of Lonlay in Normandy. The foundation of the Somerset priory resulted from a grant of the church of St Andrew in the Somerset borough of Stokes, a grant made by the then proprietor William de Falaise in the early 12th century. This borough, known as the Honour of Stokes, then passed by marriage to William de Curci (hence the modern Somerset name Stogursey *Stoke Curci*). John de Courcy, a descendant of William de Falaise, embarked on his extensive conquest of east Ulster in 1177 and in the year 1183, or 1184, he granted ten "carucates of land with all their appurtances in the country of Lart [i.e. L'Art or The Ards]" to St Andrew's priory in Stogursey in England which was, after all, John de Courcy's family seat. This grant of land in the Ards by de Courcy enabled the establishment of a Benedictine priory in the area which was founded in 1204 as the priory of St Andrew of the Ards, although it was better known as the Black Abbey or the Black Priory. Later anglicized forms of the name, such as *Ballemonestraduffe* (nos. 18 & 20), show that it had evidently been gaelicized *(An) M(h)ainistir Dhubh*, i.e. "the black abbey", while forms such as *Ballynemanough* (no. 10), or *Blackabby al. Ballemannagh* (no. 23) indicate a Gaelic *Baile na Manach* "townland of the monks". In a document compiled by Lord Deputy Wentworth in 1637 (and cited in Kerr 1989: 47) there is mention of "the three townlands of *Ballesmonastraduff*, *Ballekilvilgan* and *Ballenamanagh*", suggesting that both "the townland of the black monastery" and "the townland of the monks" formed part of the general priory site, a view confirmed by "the site, &c. of the late abbey or monastery called Blackabbey – the three townlands called Black Abbey, Ballynemanough and Ballecarrock with all their tithes" (*CPR Jas I* 72b, *circa* 1606).

The history of the priory between its foundation and the early 17th century is one of considerable intrigue with claims laid upon it by various ecclesiastical and secular groups. Following the grant of ten carucates of land in the Ards by John de Courcy to the Priory of St Andrews of Stogursey in 1183–4, the Priory of St Andrews, or Black Abbey, in the Ards was founded some twenty years later, a date confirmed by Pope Innocent III on 26 May 1204, (*Pontif. Hib.* vol. 1, pp. 58–9). Kerr (1989: 45) expresses surprise that both de Courcy's charter and a Papal confirmation of 11 June 1204 were addressed to the English church in Stogursey rather than to the church of Lonlay in Normandy which was, after all, Stogursey's mother house. This may imply that Stogursey went ahead with the establishment of Black Abbey in the Ards without consulting the mother house in Normandy. In 1218, however, Hugh de Lacy made Black Abbey a cell of Lonlay which may suggest that Lonlay asserted its rights for, in the period which followed, Black Abbey is no longer mentioned in connection with Stogursey but as "a parcel of the Abbey of Lonlay".

Following the loss of Normandy by King John to the King of France in 1204, Norman ecclesiastical houses in Britain and Ireland became regarded as alien priories. During the course of the 13th century Edward I, and succeeding English monarchs, confiscated the possession of these "alien" houses and rents owed to them when England was at war with France. During the recurrent wars with France at this time many of the alien priories were leased out to the highest bidders. Richard Fitzralph, the then Archbishop of Armagh, offered to buy Black Abbey from Lonlay for the sum of £200, a sum agreed to by Lonlay and the Pope in 1360 but not assented to by the King until 1365. While it appeared that the Black Abbey had lost its status as an alien priory, Lonlay and the Crown were later to renege on their agreement and on the death of Primate Sweteman, Archbishop of Armagh, in 1380 Richard II granted Black Abbey to a monk from Lonlay for a set rent. This was confirmed by the English king in 1391, but Armagh Primate John Colton was obviously pressing Armagh's claim at this time and proved successful, as the monk Thomas and the Abbot of Lonlay both failed to turn up when summoned to appear before the chancery in Ireland, whereupon the king ordered Edmund Savage, Steward of the Liberty of Ulster, to give "John [Colton], now Archbishop of Armagh, ... livery of the Black Priory of St. Andrew in the Arte of Ulster". In 1395, while the Black Abbey was being held by Primate Colton, it was still regarded as an alien priory and was only held by Colton because of the war with France and on account of his payment of rent. With the accession of Henry IV in 1400 a fine roll committed St Andrew's to John Engulard, monk of the monastery of St Mary of Lonlay, and the Bishop of Down & Connor, ignoring the Armagh claims, installed Engulard as prior of Black Abbey. In 1414, however, Henry V finally yielded to parliamentary pressure to have all alien abbeys dissolved.

Although there are brief references to St Andrew's in relation to the Irish primates during the 15th century, its days were numbered and in a papal letter of 19th December 1474 the abbey is described as being long without a convent of monks. The primatial rights suffered further in the 16th century when the Clandeboye O'Neills seized the abbey and its possessions following the dissolution of the monasteries. In 1569, the lands of Shane O'Neill and those of his followers were seized by Elizabeth I, and James I later confirmed the abbey in his possession following inquisitions he set up in 1603. The Abbey then passed to the Hamilton and Montgomery families but by the time of the Ulster Visitation in 1622 the Armagh claims were being revoiced:

> Witheld by Sir Hugh Montgomery Kt. and Sir James Hamilton Kt. ye Black Priory of St. Andrew in the Ards, sometyme the lands of Prior Aliens and bought by one of my predecessors for the mayntenance of his successors table from the Abbot and Convent of Clonley [=Lonlay] in Normandy by license of King Edward the third with allowance of the pope of some 200[l] ster paid by my predecessor in Paules Church in London wch Pryory doth consist of three towne lands and five impropriations. (cited Kerr 1989: 47)

Lord Deputy Wentworth was called in to settle the claims in 1633, and his findings were that the said Lords Viscount of the Ardes and Clandeboye should surrender their title and claims to the three townlands of the Black priory, cited above, and the appropriate rectories of Balliharbert [Ballyhalbert], Inischargie White Church [Ballywalter] and Donoghadie, as these belonged to the Irish Primate, but Wentworth recommended that these should be leased by Armagh to Montgomery and Hamilton at a rent of £40.00 per annum. Later on in the 17th century the following account, by William Montgomery, in addition to providing the reason for the *Black* in Black Abbey, clearly shows that the Abbey was in disarray:

> About a mile thence is a smale ruined Abby with some lands adioyning called Black Abby from Fryars of that Colloured habit belonging to ye Lord Primat in Right of his see of Ardmagh. (*Descr. Ards* 38)

In *An archaeological survey of County Down* the Black Abbey is listed under "Destroyed monuments and lost sites" (*ASCD* 289). In 1847, however, Reeves (*EA* 18 n. f) desribes how the last remains of the building of the site, marked on the first edition of the OS six-inch map, "have lately been cleared away".

For various accounts of the Black Abbey see: Kerr (1989); Atkinson (1823:i 289); *EA* 18 n. f, 382–3; O'Laverty (i 429–32, ii 336); *Knox Hist.* 462; Orpen *JRSAI* xliv (1914) 51, 58–9.

Ballyhalbert	*Baile Thalbóid*	
J 6463	"Talbot's townland"	
1. Talbetona, Ecclesia de	Eccles. Tax. 20	1306c
2. Talbotyston	Inq. Earldom Ulster iv 140	1333
3. Talbots corte	S-E Ulster Map	1580c
4. Talbots court	Mercator's Ire.	1595
5. Talbot's cort	Mercator's Ulst.	1595
6. Ballytalbott	Inq. Ult. (Down) §2 Jac. I	1605
7. Ballytalbott al. Talbotston	Inq. Ult. (Down) §2 Jac. I	1605
8. Talbott's Town	CPR Jas I 72b	1605
9. Ballitalbot	CPR Jas I 73a	1605
10. Talbotstown, the parish of	CPR Jas I 78a	1606
11. Talpestone (×2)	Jas. I to Down Cath. 179	1609
12. Talbot	Speed's Ireland	1610
13. Talbot	Speed's Antrim & Down	1610
14. Talbot	Speed's Ulster	1610
15. Prebend de Talbeston [also Tolbaston]	Terrier (Reeves) 93	1615c
16. Talbertstone, Ecclesia de	Terrier (Reeves) 59	1615c
17. Ballihalbert	CPR Jas I 326a	1617
18. Talpesson	Ulster Visit. (Reeves) 33	1622
19. Church of Ballehalbert al. Talbotstowne	Ham. Copy Inq. xlvi	1623
20. the Parish of Talbotstown	Ham. Copy Inq. xlvi	1623
21. Rectory of Ballehalbert	Ham. Copy Inq. xlvi	1623
22. Balle-Halbert	Ham. Copy Inq. xxxii	1623
23. Ballyhalbert	Ham. Copy Inq. xxxii	1623
24. parish of Talbotstown	Ham. Copy Inq. xxxiii	1623
25. Ballehalbert	Ham. Copy Inq. xxxiv; xlii	1623
26. Talbotstowne	Inq. Ult. (Down) §104 Car. I	1645
27. Ballehalbert	Inq. Ult. (Down) §104 Car. I	1645
28. Ballehalbert al. Talbotstowne	Inq. Ult. (Down) §104 Car. I	1645
29. Ballyhalbert, in great Ardes	Inq. Down (Reeves 1) 131	1657
30. Ballyhalbert	Census 92	1659c
31. Ballehalbert	Census 92	1659c
32. Ballyhilbert	Census 92	1659c
33. Ballehalbert	BSD 91	1661
34. Talpetstowne	Trien. Visit. (Bramhall) 9	1661
35. Ballyhalbert	Trien. Visit. (Bramhall) 9	1661
36. Talbottstowne	Inq. Ult. (Down) §23 Car. II	1662
37. Balleherbert	Inq. Ult. (Down) §23 Car. II	1662
38. Balleholbert	Inq. Ult. (Down) §23 Car. II	1662

39. Ballyhalbert	Sub. Roll Down 283	1663
40. Ballyhalbert als Halbertstowne	Trien. Visit. (Margetson) 21	1664
41. Ballyhalbert als Whitechurch & Inniscargie	Trien. Visit. (Margetson) 21	1664
42. Ballihalbert	Trien. Visit. (Boyle) 44	1679
43. Ballyhalbert	Ham. Copy Rental 108	1681
44. B:halbert	Descr. Ards 37	1683
45. Ballyhalbert	Wm. Map (OSNB)	1810
46. Ballyhalbert	High Const. Applot. (OSNB)	1830c
47. Ballyhalbert	Tythes Applot. (OSNB)	1830c
48. Ballyhalbert	Bnd. Sur. (OSNB)	1830c
49. Halbert's town	J O'D (OSNB)	1834c
50. The signification of Ballyhalbert is Halbert's Town	Knox Hist. 463	1875
51. ˌbaliˈhɑlbərt	Local pronunciation	1991

Reeves (*EA* 20 n. k) provides much valuable information concerning this place whose name, as he correctly points out, "is derived from the family of Talbot, which settled in the counties of Down and Antrim soon after the [Anglo-Norman] invasion. In the Inquisition held in 1333 on the death of William de Burgo, mention is made of certain lands held by "Johannes Talbot in Talbotyston'". The full reference to John Talbot runs: "1 knight's fee which John Talbot holds in Talbotyston in fee" (*Inq. Earldom Ulster* iv 140, 1333 AD). Frequent mention is made of John (and Richard) Talbot in documentation of the Anglo-Norman period, e.g. Johanne Talbot/Ricardo Talebot (*Cartae Dun.* 424 §14, 419 §2, late 12th century); John/Richard Talebot (*CPR Ed. III* pp. 305/6, 1336 AD). Reeves further mentions the Talbot family elsewhere (*Colton Vis.* 14, n. e) stating that "they came from Herefordshire and settled in this country in the reign of Henry II". He goes on to note that the main settlements of the family were in Malahide and Belgard, near Dublin, in addition to Co. Down and S. Antrim. Indeed in Co. Wicklow the modern barony of *Talbotstown* still bears their name and it is interesting to note that the Wicklow name has retained its original Anglo-Norman form while the Co. Down *Talbotston* has since been gaelicized as Ballyhalbert. As regards the demise of the Talbot family in this area *Sav. Ards* 304 cites from Spenser's *View of the State of Ireland* (written c. 1596) "Bruce rooted out the noble families of the Audlies, Talbotts ..."

Various references to the church, standing stone, and mound at Ballyhalbert are contained in *ASCD* 466, and on p. 1, n. 5 we are informed of evidence of human remains dating to *c.* 6,000 BC. In more recent centuries, details of a mill in Ballyhalbert in 1681 are to be found in *Ham. Copy Rental* 108. Brief desriptions of the modern town and parish are to be had in *Harris Hist.* 68; *Lewis' Top. Dict.* 136; *OSM* vii 5–6, and in *Knox Hist* 462–3 where we read: "The village of Ballyhalbert is a littel port on the eastern coast of the Ards, on the road from Portaferry to Donaghadee, opposite to which lies the Burial island the most easterly point in Ireland. The village of Ballyhalbert contains a population of 454 persons, which added to 1872 in the rural districts, brings up the number to 2326".

TOWNLAND NAMES

Ballyesborough Of uncertain origin
J 6361

1. (?) Ballyaspagh	Inq. Ult. (Down) §2 Jac. I	1605

2. Balle-Aspragh	Ham. Copy Inq. xlii	1623
3. Balleuspragh	Ham. Copy Inq. xlvi	1623
4. Balleaspragh	Ham. Copy Inq. xxxii; xxxiv	1623
5. Balleasperagh	Inq. Ult. (Down) §104 Jac. I	1644
6. (?) Balleasragy	Inq. Ult. (Down) §104 Jac. I	1644
7. Ballyesbrough	Census 92	1659c
8. Balleasperragh	BSD 89	1661
9. Bally-Esterewgh	Sub. Roll Down 283	1663
10. Ballyesbrough	Ham. Copy Rental 108	1681
11. Ballyesborough	Wm. Map (OSNB)	1810
12. Ballyesbro	High Const. Applot (OSNB)	1830c
13. Ballyesborough	Tythes Applot. (OSNB)	1830c
14. Ballyesborough	Bnd. Sur. (OSNB)	1830c
15. Ballyesbrough "Esborough's town"	J O'D (OSNB)	1834c
16. ˌbaliˈɛsbərə	Local pronunciation	1991
17. ˌbɑli ˈiəzbo̤rə	Local pronunciation	1991

This name appears to be a gaelicized form of an earlier Anglo-Norman name, although there is difficulty in restoring the original. O'Donovan's suggestion, no. 15, may well be correct although further information is required to elucidate this name.

Ballyfrench *Baile Freanais*

J 6561 "Frenes' townland"

1. Ballifranish	Inq. Ult. (Down) §2 Jac. I	1605
2. Ballifranish	CPR Jas I 73a	1605
3. Balleffringe al. Megallogh	Ham. Copy Inq. xlii	1623
4. Balleneffringe al. Negallogh	Ham. Copy Inq. xlvi	1623
5. Ballyfringe al. Ballenegallogh	Ham. Copy Inq. xxxii	1623
6. Balleffringe al. Ballenegallogh	Ham. Copy Inq. xxxiv	1623
7. Ballenefringe al. Negalloy	Inq. Ult. (Down) §104 Car. I	1645
8. Ballenefringe al. Negallogh	Inq. Ult. (Down) §104 Car. I	1645
9. Ballyfrenge	Census 92	1659c
10. Ballefrennise ½ towne	BSD 89	1661
11. Ballenefringe al. Negallogh	Inq. Ult. (Down) §23 Car. II	1662
12. Ballyfrench	Sub. Roll Down 283	1663
13. Ballyfringe	Ham. Copy Rental 108	1681
14. Ballyfrench	Wm. Map (OSNB)	1810
15. Ballyfrench	High Const. Applot. (OSNB)	1830c
16. Ballyfrench	Tythes Applot. (OSNB)	1830c
17. Ballyfrench	Bnd. Sur. (OSNB)	1830c
18. Ballyfrench "French's town"	J O'D (OSNB)	1834c
19. ˌbɑli ˈfrɛntʃ	Local pronunciation	1991

This name is yet another example of a gaelicized Anglo-Norman name. We can compare similar examples of this Anglo-Norman name in other parts of Ireland where the gaelicization witnessed in the Ards has not taken place. The modern townland of *Fryanstown* (Co. Wicklow), for example, occurs in the Ecclesiastical Taxation of 1306 as *Vill' de Freynes* (*CDI 1302–7* p. 238); or *Freynstoun* (par. Castletown, Co. Meath) which occurs in *Reg. Sweteman*

§157 as *Fringestown*. One could postulate a form similar to *(de) Freneston* "town of (de) Frenes" as the original form of our modern Ballyfrench; indeed compare *Frenestoun* 1333 AD for **Ballyfrenis** (par. Donaghadee). For evidence of this family in Anglo-Norman Ireland note "John de Freines" (*CDI 1302–7* p. 28), or "Henry de Frenes" listed in the Dublin area (*Pipe Roll xxix Ed. I* (1301 AD), details of which are to be found in appendix to *38 Rept. DKPRI* (1905) p. 58).

Woulfe (1923:258) gives details of the Norman surname *de Freynes* which was variously written as Freins, Frensh etc. and gaelicized *de Fréins*, and on p. 83 he also lists *Frinse* as an Irish form of French. Woulfe (258) interprets *de Freynes* as a derivative of Latin *de Fraxinis* "of the ash trees", and Reaney (1958: 126) offers the equally, if not more, plausible suggestion that the surname *French* represents Old Eng. *frencisc* > Mid. Eng. *frennsce / frenche* "French". The early forms of the Ards place-name *Ballyfranish* (nos. 1–2, along with no. 10) point to an Irish form *Freanas* (genitive *Freanais*).

Ballygraffan	*Baile Grafáin* (?)	
J 6261	meaning uncertain	
1. Ballygraffan	Fiants Eliz. §2090	1571
2. Ballygraffane	Inq. Ult. (Down) §2 Jac. I	1605
3. Balligraffane	CPR Jas I 73a	1605
4. Ballygraffan	Terrier (Reeves) 59	1615c
5. Ballygraffan	Ham. Copy Inq. xxxii	1623
6. Ballegraffan	Ham. Copy Inq. xxxiv; xlii; xlvi	1623
7. Ballegraffan	Inq. Ult. (Down) §104 Car. I	1645
8. Ballygraffan	Census 92	1659c
9. Ballegraffane	BSD 89	1661
10. Ballygraffin	Ham. Copy Rental 108	1681
11. Ballygraffan	Wm. Map (OSNB)	1810
12. Ballygraffin	High Const. Applot. (OSNB)	1830c
13. Ballygraffin	Tythes Applot. (OSNB)	1830c
14. Ballygraffen	Bnd. Sur. (OSNB)	1830c
15. Baile Uí Chreámhthainn "O'Graffin's town"	J O'D (OSNB)	1834c
16. ˌbali ˈgrɛfən	Local pronunciation	1991

The suggestion *Baile Uí Chreámhthainn* proposed by John O'Donovan does not appear convincing. On the other hand it is difficult to suggest an original form of this name as several, fairly inconclusive, possibilities present themselves for anglicized *-graffan*. If we look for an Irish origin we may consider the plant name *grafán* (= Dwelly's *grabhan*) which is translated in Dinneen as "horehound, *g. bán* 'white horehound'". We might then postulate *Baile Grafáin* "townland of the horehound", where the spellings in *-ane* might support an Irish *-án*. One strongly suspects, however, an Anglo-Norman origin for the two County Down *Ballygraffan*s, one in this parish and the other in Kilmood parish, as they both occur in areas where other Anglo-Norman names are attested in neighbouring townlands. The difficulty lies, however, in finding a suitable Anglo-Norman name. Reaney (1958:146) lists *Griffin, Griffen* as a surname common in Britain. This name evidently found its way into Ireland as suggested by the fact that *Ballygriffin* occurs as a townland name in several more southerly counties of Ireland. However, any connection between the Anglo-Norman name *Griffin* would require the postulation of an unattested Ulster gaelicized form resembling *Greafán* to give Co. Down *Ballygraffan(e)*. Reaney (143) lists another Anglo-Norman name *Graf*, derived from *graf*, the Norman term for a public scribe, but no diminutive form is given.

Ballyhemlin	*Baile Haimlin*	
J 6364	"Hamlin's townland"	
1. Ballihemeline	CPR Jas I 73a	1605
2. Ballyhemeline	Inq. Ult. (Down) §2 Jac. I	1605
3. Ballyhumlyn	Inq. Ult. (Down) §2 Jac. I	1605
4. Ballehamlin	Ham. Copy Inq. xxxii	1623
5. Balle-Hamlin	Ham. Copy Inq. xxxiv	1623
6. Ballehamlin	Ham. Copy Inq. xlii; xlvi	1623
7. Ballehamlin	Inq. Ult. (Down) §104 Jac. I	1644
8. Ballehamlin	Inq. Ult. (Down) §104 Jac. I	1644
9. Ballyhamline	Census 92	1659
10. Ballehamline	BSD 89	1661
11. Ballyhember (?)	Sub. Roll Down 17	1663
12. Ballyhamlin Half	Ham. Copy Rental 108	1681
13. Ballyhemlin	Wm. Map (OSNB)	1810
14. Ballyhemlin	High Const. Applot. (OSNB)	1830c
15. Ballyhemlin	Bnd. Sur. (OSNB)	1830c
16. Ballyhemlin "Hamlin's town"	J O'D (OSNB)	1834c
17. ˌbali ˈhɛmlən	Local pronunciation	1991
18. ˌbali ˈhiəmlən	Local pronunciation	1991

The 17th-century forms (nos. 1–12) clearly suggest that modern Ballyhemlin represents a gaelicization of an earlier Anglo-Norman place-name **Ham(e)lin(s)ton*. Reaney (1958:152) lists a family name *Hamlin*, *Hamlen*, *Hamblin* etc. in Britain, e.g. Robertus filius Hamelin 1130 AD, and then goes on to describe the medieval name *Hamelin* as a diminutive of Old German *Haimo*. Earlier Reaney (xxiv) describes the suffix *-elin* as a double diminutive containing the particles *el* and *in*. *Ballyhemlin* townland seems to provide us, then, with evidence for the presence of this *Ham(e)lin* family among the Anglo-Norman settlers in the Ards.

Black Abbey — See **St Andrews**

Echlinville	A Scots/English form	
J 6161		
1. Echlinville	Sav. Ards 376	1737
2. Echlinville	Wm. Map (OSNB)	1810
3. Echlinville	High Const. Applot. (OSNB)	1830c
4. Echlinville	Bnd. Sur. (OSNB)	1830c
5. Echlinville, Echlin is a family name	J O'D (OSNB)	1834c
6. ˈɛklənˈvɪl	Local pronunciation	1991

This townland derives its name from the Echlin family who, in turn, derive their name from a territory in Scotland: "The Echlins are of Scotch lineage, being descendants of the ancient family of the Echlins of Pettadro, in the shire of Linlithgow, heirs of Philip le Brun, who obtained the heritage of the estate ... of Echlin" (*Knox Hist.* 466). In the early 17th century Dr Robert Echlin, "a Scotchman by birth", was appointed as bishop of Down and Connor: "King's Letter for a grant to Rob. Echlin of the bishoprick of Down and Connor, vacant by the death of James Dundas" *CPR Jas I* 249b (*c.*1612). This Bishop Robert Echlin settled at a residence in the south of the Ards known as the Abbacy. The *Echlinville* here in Ballyhalbert parish is named after descendants of Robert. Robert's son, John, is mentioned in Inquisitions around 1635 (*Inq. Ult.* §§53, 60 Car. I) and it is known that some members of the family settled at Johnstown, now known as the modern Upper Ards townland and parish of **Castleboy**, e.g. "David Echlin of Johnstown" (*Sub. Roll Down* 17). In *UJA* x (1904) 89 there is mention of Lieutenant Echlin who purchased an estate in Co. Down from the Trustees of Forfeited Estates in 1703, in trust for Patrick son of Valentine Russell. *OSM* vii 84 names a "John Echlin Esquire" as one of the two magistrates for this parish in the 1830s. *Knox Hist.* 466 points out that Bishop Robert Echlin was succeeded by a direct line of three Johns, but that in Knox's own day, 1875, "the present representative of the family is the Rev. John Robert Echlin, now resident in England". For sources on this family see *Harris Hist.* 44; Atkinson (1823 i:210); *EA* 379; *Knox Hist.* 59–60, 407, 462; *Sav. Ards* 182–3; *ASCD* 382–5; and Anderson (1978: 18–9). See also the place-names **Abbacy**, **Bishops Mills** and **Demesne** (parish of Ardquin) and **Echlin Grove** (parish of Bangor).

Reeves (*EA* 379, n. y) and Harris (*Harris Hist.* 44) identify the modern townland of *Echlinville* as the former townland of *Rowbane/Rubane*, a name discussed under **Rubane** (below) and under the neighbouring townland of **Rowreagh** (situated in the parish of Inishargy). The Echlin who gave his name to *Echlinville* may well have been the James Echlin who built *Rubane House* in this townland around the second quarter of the 18th century.

Portavogie — *Port an Bhogaigh*
J 6659 — "place of the bog"

1.	lez Magies de Portabogagh	Inq. Ult. (Down) §2 Jac. I	1605
2.	Ballimulloghmore	CPR Jas I 73a	1605
3.	Portaboggagh, the bog of	CPR Jas I 73b	1605
4.	Balleportevogie al. Mullogmore	Ham. Copy Inq. xlii	1623
5.	Portabogagh	Ham. Copy Inq. xxx	1623
6.	Portovogie	Ham. Copy Inq. xxxii	1623
7.	Balleportevogie al. Mulloghmore	Ham. Copy Inq. xxxiv; xlvi	1623
8.	Balleportivogie al. Mullaghmore	Inq. Ult. (Down) §104 Car. I	1645
9.	Portevoggy	Census 92	1659c
10.	Portevogey	BSD 89	1661
11.	Balleportavogie al. Mullaghmore	Inq. Ult. (Down) §23 Car. II	1662
12.	Portavogy	Ham. Copy Rental 108	1681
13.	Portavogie	Wm. Map (OSNB)	1810
14.	Portavogie	High Const. Applot. (OSNB)	1830c
15.	Portavogie	Tythes Applot. (OSNB)	1830c
16.	Portavogie	Bnd. Sur. (OSNB)	1830c
17.	Port a Bhogaigh "bank of the bog"	J O'D (OSNB)	1834c
18.	ˌpọrti ˈvogi	Local pronunciation	1991

John O'Donovan's suggestion (no. 17) of an Irish form *Port an Bhogaigh* is doubtless correct. Many 17th-century documents refer to the presence of a bog here: "the bog of Portaboggagh" *CPR Jas I* 73b; "ye great bogg" *Descr. Ards 1682* 42 etc. We can also note the modern road name *Bog Road*, but apparently the extensive bog spoken of in the 17th century has been exhausted in recent centuries as, in the following early 19th-century account, for the adjoining parish of Inishargy, it is stated "The bogs are not of very good extent" *OSM* vii 84.

As to an interpretation of Ir. *port* as "bank", it may mean either "port" or "place, spot, locality" (*DIL*), or even *port móna* "turf-bank" (*Ó Dónaill*). *Port an Bhogaigh*, then, could mean "port of the bog", or merely "bank/place of the bog". The 17th-century forms resembling *Mullaghmore* (forms 4, 7–8 & 11) indicate *Port an Bhogaigh* was also known by another Irish name *Mullach Mór* "large hill or summit".

Roddans — Of uncertain origin

J 6365

1. Ballerodine	CPR Jas I 39a	1604
2. Ballyrodiny	Inq. Ult. (Down) §2 Jac. I	1605
3. Ballirodiny	CPR Jas I 73a	1605
4. Ballyrodeny	Grant Jas I (OSNB)	1608
5. Rodony, Michael Cragg of	Ulst. Roll Gaol Deliv. 262	1613
6. Rodine	Ulst. Roll Gaol Deliv. 263	1613
7. Rodin	Ulst. Roll Gaol Deliv. 263	1613
8. the Redene	CPR Jas I 326a	1617
9. Ballekodony	Ham. Copy Inq. xlii	1623
10. Ballerodony	Ham. Copy Inq. xlvi	1623
11. Balle-Rodine	Ham. Copy Inq. xxxii	1623
12. Ballerodony	Inq. Ult. (Down) §104 Car. I	1645
13. Roddins	Census 92	1659c
14. Roddinny	BSD 89	1661
15. Roddins	Ham. Copy Rental 108	1681
16. Roddens	Wm. Map (OSNB)	1810
17. Rodens	High Const. Applot. (OSNB)	1830c
18. Roddens	Tythes Applot. (OSNB)	1830c
19. Roddens	Bnd. Sur. (OSNB)	1830c
20. Baile Uí Ródain "Roddan's or Reddins town"	J O'D (OSNB)	1834c
21. ˈrɔdənz	Local pronunciation	1991
22. ðə ˈrɔdənz	Local pronunciation	1991

O'Donovan's suggestion, *Baile Uí Ródain* "Roddan's or Reddins town", might seem likely if one were to consider modern *Rodanstown* (a parish and townland) in Co. Meath. However, if one considers other Ards examples such as Anglo-Norman *Talbot(s)ton* and *Philipton* giving modern **Ballyhalbert** and **Ballyphilip**, then one has the problem of explaining how an Anglo-Norman **Rodan(s)ton* should undergo gaelicization to *Ballyrodine/Ballyrodiny* and then drop the initial element *Bally-*.

If one searches for an Irish original, it is significant that Hogan (*Onom. Goed.* p. 589) has a citation *Mochummae Rotáin* "Mo Chummae of Rotán" which he links with Rodanstown (Co. Meath), but an alternative location must surely be sought. Any attempt to identify the site of *Rodán*, from where St Mochummae hailed, is thwarted by the fact that there are numerous saints of this name, as may be seen from the long list of saints named *Mochummae* (contained in *CSH* §707.647–68 p. 149). In any case, the early spellings of the Ards name *Roddans* would not support an original element *Rodán*. *DIL* has *rota* "bog-water, bog stuff>

bog, marsh", a form which would be spelt *roda* in the modern language. When one considers "a long red bog" near to Portavogie in *Descr. Ards* 41, then one might propose *Rodanaigh*, an oblique case of *Rodanach* "boggy area" as a possibility (i.e. *rod* + suffix *-anach*, or even a compound of *rod(a)* plus *eanach* "bog"). Alternatively, the proximity of Roddans to the coast may allow the consideration of the word *rod* listed by Dinneen as "a variety of seaweed thrown up on the sand" (which corresponds to Dwelly's *ròd* "quantity of seaweed thrown up on the shore"). Thus forms such as *Ballyrodiny* (nos. 2–5, 9–10, 12 and 14) might suggest *Baile Rodanaí* "townland of the seaweed". However, it must be borne in mind that these latter suggestions are tentative in the extreme.

Rhoddan's House, which takes its name from this townland, is described by Knox (*Knox Hist.* 462) as "the property of Mr. Blakiston-Houston".

Rubane (former townland) *Rubha Bán*
J 6161 "white clearing"

1. Rowbane	Terrier (Reeves) 59	1615c
2. Row	Ulster Visit. (Reeves) 55	1622
3. Rowbane	Ham. Copy Inq. xlii; xlv	1623
4. Ballerobane	Ham. Copy Inq. xxxi	1623
5. the Grange or Rectorie of Rowbane	Ham. Copy Inq. xxxi; xliv	1623
6. Balle-Robane	Ham. Copy Inq. xxxiv	1623
7. Rawbane	Inq. Ult. (Down) §104 Car. I	1645
8. Rowbane	Inq. Ult. (Down) §104 Car. I	1645
9. Rowbane	Census 92	1659c
10. Rowbane	BSD 91	1661
11. Rowbane	Inq. Ult. (Down) §23 Car. II	1662
12. Rowbane	Sub. Roll Down 283	1663
13. Rowbane	Ham. Copy Rental 108	1681
14. ru 'bɑ:n	Local pronunciation	1991

This former townland name has been replaced by Echlinville – see **Echlinville** (this parish) and **Rowreagh** (parish of Inishargy). The older name still survives, however, as a village name and in the name *Rubane House* – "A house built perhaps in the second quarter of the 18th century by James Echlin but possibly of the later 17th century, existed until *c.* 1850, when replaced by the present building"- see *ASCD* 382–5 for extensive details. Although *Rubane House* was known as *Echlinville*, *Knox Hist.* 462 informs us that, when it came into the possession of Mr James Cleland, who carried out extensive repairs and improvements during the course of the 19th century, the "original name of Rheubane or Rowbane" was restored to the mansion. The chapel of an Irish saint, St Tiu, formerly stood in this townland; see Reeves *EA* (379 n. y) and the fuller discussion on the name *Rubha* and St Tiu in the section dealing with **Rowreagh** (parish of Inishargy).

OTHER NAMES

Burial Island *Na Broighill* (?)
J 6663 "the cormorants"

1. Briels	Nowel's Ire. (2)	1570c
2. Briall	Bartlett Maps (Esch. Co. Maps) 1	1603
3. The Bryalle	Mercator's Ulst.	1595

4. The Bryalle	Speed's Ireland	1610
5. The Bryalle	Speed's Antrim & Down	1610
6. The Bryalle	Speed's Ulster	1610
7. The Bryalls	Hib. Del. Down	1672c
8. The Bryalls	Lamb Maps Co. Down	1690c
9. Burial Island	Wm. Map (OSNB)	1810
10. Burial Island, why so called is not known	J O'D (OSNB)	1834c
11. 'bəriəl 'ailn	Local pronunciation	1991

The 19th-century forms of this name point to a seemingly obvious etymology "the island where burials took place", but a marginal entry concerning the name of this island in the *OSNB* states "why so called is not known" (10). However, 19th-century *Burial* seems to have arisen as a result of folk etymology in English, possibly as early as the late 17th century, cf. "a lesser patch of Rocky Land named buriall" *Descr. Ards 1683*. The early spellings (forms 1–8) seem to point to the Irish word *broigheall*, which Dinneen renders as "a cormorant". For Scottish Gaelic Dwelly has *broigheal* "cormorant, sea-raven". The association with the Irish word *broigheall* may be due to the fact that cormorants rest here or from the resemblance of the shape of the island to cormorants.

A reasonably detailed account of the island in 1744 is provided by Harris (*Harris Hist.* 135):

> at the Point of the said Elbow lies a small Island called the *Brialls* and *Bureal Island*, and by some *Berry-Island* from which at low Water a Bank stretches to the main Land; by means whereof Cattle wade over and graze on the Island; which feeds a sum and a half. It abounds with vast quantities of Fish and fowl of several sorts, which breed on top of the island, being a high Rock containing not much more than an Acre of Grass; and the place is remarked for being the farthest Eastern Land in any of *Ireland*.

See also **Green Island**.

Burr Point — *Bior*
J 6663 — "point"

1. Brial Island	Harris Hist. 135	1744
2. 'bọr 'pɔint	Local pronunciation	1992

Earlier written forms of this name are difficult to locate, but Harris' reference to it as *Brial Point* (no. 1) suggests that the point took its name, in his day at any rate, from the nearby **Burial Island**, then known as *Brial(l) Island*. If the island was then *Brial Island* which subsequently gave *Burial Island*, then it is difficult to envisage how *Brial Point* should give *Burr Point*. So it would appear that *Burr* is a distinct name and probably represents Irish *bior* "point", an element also contained in the minor name **Ringburr** (parish of Ardquin).

Butter Lough Rock — An English form

1. Butter Lough Rock	OSNB 35	1834c
2. 'bọtər lɔx 'rɔk	Local pronunciation	1992

Fort Hill — An English form

A minor name listed in *OSNB* p. 37, near Ballygraffan townland. On the remains of the fort here, see *ASCD* p. 466.

Green Island An English form
J 6558

1. Greenisle	Ham. Copy Rental 108	1681
2. green Isle	Descr. Ards 36	1683
3. Green Island	Wm. Map (OSNB)	1810
4. Green Island	J O'D (OSNB)	1834c
5. 'gri:n 'ailən	Local pronunciation	1991

The earliest available references are as follows:

Next lyes a smale Island called green Isle & a lesser patch of Rocky Land called buriall; which are y[e] most Easterly parts of Ireland being a place where vessels often ly at Anchor expecting the desired wind to runn their begunn course. (*Descr. Ards* 36)

Green Island ... which contains two Acres, always green, and to which at low Water a man may walk dry. Hence a kind of Harbour never frequented but by ships in great distress, by reson of a dangerous Entry, having on the S. the fatal N. rocks. (*Harris Hist.* 135–6)

It is true that this island does have a green grassy appearance and hence its name.

Islandgorm *Oileán Gormáin* (?)
J 6459 "island-hill of (the) cornflower"

1. Islandgorman	CPR Jas. I 73b	1605
2. ˌailən 'gɔrm	Local pronunciation	1992

The modern anglicized form of the name seems to represent an original Irish *Oileán Gorm* "blue island". This place is inland but the use of the term *island*, or Irish *oileán*, to refer to an inland feature has been shown, on occasions, to refer to "a hillock surrounded by a bog" Ó Mainnín (1989–90). The following passage from *CPR Jas I* 73b clearly shows that the *Island-* here refers to a hill in the midst of a bog: "the island or hill called Islandgorman in the Great Ardes". Other possible derivations suggested by the 1605 form (no. 1) are: *Oileán Gormáin* "(the) island of (the) cornflower", or *Oileán Uí Ghormáin* "(O)'Gorman's island".

John's Port An English form
J 6661

"A small bay ... in the Rocks having a sandy bottom affording shelter 2 fishing boats". *OSNB* 46.

McCammon Rocks A hybrid form
J 6660

Local pronunciation [me'kɔmənz ˌrɔks]. For this surname in Co. Down in the 18th century cf. "*Jane Johnson* alias the Widow *McCamon* of the Parish of *Donaghmore*", *Harris Hist.* 253. As regards a meaning for this surname Woulfe (1923:307) suggests "*Mac Ámoinn* ... MacCammon, MacCammond, MacKemman, Hammond, (Hammondson)"; "son of Amundr" (a Norse personal name); a person of Norse origin". There is also a **McCammon Pladdy** in Strangford Lough; see parish of Inishargy.

Moore Farm An English form
J 6562

Seven families of Moore are listed for the Upper Ards by Anderson (1980:2), and this name probably refers to a farm held by Moore.

Roddans House See **Roddans**
J 6365

Rubane House See **Rubane** above.
J 6160

Selk Rock "seal island"
J 6660

For Scots *selk* meaning "seal" see **Selk Rock** (par. Ardquin).

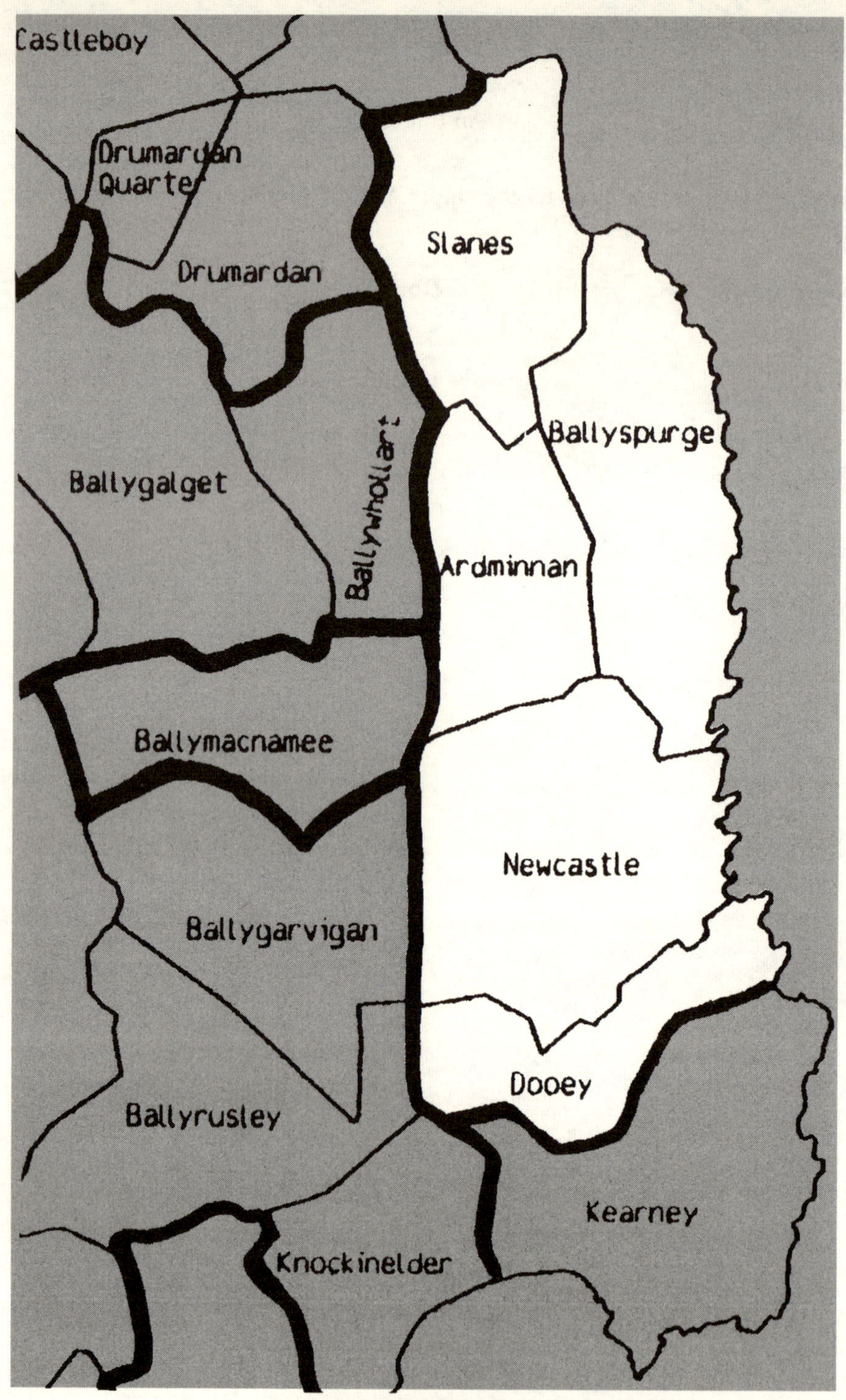

Parish of Slanes

Barony of Ards Upper

Townlands	Ballyspurge	Newcastle
Ardminnan	Dooey	Slanes

PARISH OF SLANES

This small civil parish, formerly a rectory in the diocese, forms part of the Union of Ballyphilip, Ballytrustan and Slanes, a union discussed under the Parish of Ballyphilip. On the archaeology of Slanes see *ASCD* 309, and on recent history see *Lewis' Top. Dict.* ii 562; *OSM* vii 121; and *Knox Hist.* 572.

PARISH NAME

Slanes	*Sláine*	
J 6354	"health-bestowing well (?)"	
1. Ardmacossce, Ecclesia de	Eccles. Tax. 22	1306c
2. Ardmacaisse	Cal. Canc. Hib. (EA) 28	1320
3. ArdmcKasse	Cal. Canc. Hib. (EA) 124	1386
4. Ardmocasse	Cal. Canc. Hib. (EA) 126	1386
5. Ardmacasch	Colton Vis. 13	1397
6. Ardmocasse	Reg. Cromer ii §31	1524
7. Slaine	S-E Ulster Map	1580c
8. Slain	Mercator's Ulst.	1595
9. Slane	Jas. I to Down Cath. 178	1609
10. Slane	Jas. I to Down Cath. 178	1609
11. Slaine	Speed's Antrim & Down	1610
12. Slayne	Speed's Ulster	1610
13. Slane, Ecclesia de	Terrier (Reeves) 59	1615c
14. Slane	Ulster Visit. (Reeves) 25	1622
15. Slanes, four small Townes of the Granges &	Inq. Down (Reeves 1) 119	1657
16. Slane Parish	Hib. Reg. Ards	1657c
17. Slanes	Census 91	1659c
18. Slanes	BSD 84	1661
19. Slane	Trien. Visit. (Bramhall) 9	1661
20. Slanes	Sub. Roll Down 283	1663
21. Slane	Trien. Visit. (Margetson) 20	1664
22. Slanes	Descr. Ards 36	1683
23. Slane	Harris Hist. 167	1744
24. Slanes	Wm. Map (OSNB)	1810
25. Slans	Tythes Applot. (OSNB)	1830c
26. Slans	Bnd. Sur. (OSNB)	1830c
27. Sleamháin "elms"	J O'D (OSNB)	1834c
28. slɑ:nz	Local pronunciation	1991

The suggested origin *Sleamháin* "elms" (form 27) has little support from the historical spellings of the name (from form no. 7 onwards). Reeves (*EA* 23, n. r) lists forms resembling *Ardmacossce* from the taxation of 1306 and subsequent documentation until 1524, concluding that *Ardmacaisse* (or variant) was the name of the parish whereas *Slane* was the name of some sub-denomination in it, but that Slanes then was applied to the townland in which the churchyard was. Reeves continues: "The word 'Slane' comes from Irish *slán*, which Colgan interprets by '*sanus*'; and was formerly applied to holy wells, on account of their supposed sanative virtues". *Slanes* was taken as referring to a well here by Mac Reachtain (1951: 8). See also O'Laverty (i 415–7).

The earlier name *Ardmacossce* seems to suggest a Gaelic original *Ard Mhic Coise* "height of Mac Coise", and Woulfe (1923: 334–5) cites a *"Mac Coise*, anglicized M'Cashie ... MacCosh, Quish, Cush, Legge, Foote", which he translates "son of the courier, footman" and which he records in both Ireland and Scotland.

TOWNLAND NAMES

Ardminnan — *Ard Meannán*
J 6354 — "height of the kid goats".

1. Loghduff and Ardmennan	Census 91	1659
2. Ardmeanan	BSD 84	1661
3. Ardmenan	Inq. Ult. (Down) §12 Car. II	1662
4. Ardminin	Wm. Map (OSNB)	1810
5. Ardminnan	Bnd. Sur. (OSNB)	1830c
6. Ardmenan	High Const. Applot. (OSNB)	1830c
7. Ardminnin	Reg. Free. (OSNB)	1832
8. Ard Mionain "hill of the kid"	J O'D (OSNB)	1834c
9. ˌardˈmïnən	Local pronunciation	1991

Joyce (iii 44) suggests "Ardminnan in Down and Sligo; height of the *mionan* or kid". This latter suggestion is possibly based on O'Donovan (no. 8) and it is a meaning certainly well supported by the historical spellings. One might also note that the Irish word *meannán* also had the meaning "fawn, young deer" (Hughes 1989).

Ballyspurge — *Baile Spoird* (?)
J 6454 — "Sporde's townland"

1. Spordes castel	Mercator's Ulst.	1595
2. Ballespord	CPR Jas. I 455a	1618
3. Ballysport	Inq. Ult. (Down) §14 Jac. I	1622
4. Ballinsport	Inq. Ult. (Down) §2 Car. I	1625
5. Ballynsport	Inq. Ult. (Down) §4 Car. I	1625
6. Ballinespoort	Inq. Ult. (Down) §10 Car. I	1627
7. Ballynesport	Inq. Ult. (Down) §10 Car. I	1627
8. Ballisport	Inq. Ult. (Down) §10 Car. I	1627
9. Ballysport	Inq. Ult. (Down) §10 Car. I	1627
10. Ballyspurt	Inq. Ult. (Down) §10 Car. I	1627
11. Ballyspurdge	Inq. Ult. (Down) §82 Car. I	1637
12. Ballyspurge	Will (Sav. Ards) 247	1640
13. Ballespart al. Drom-Arthure	Inq. Ult. (Down) §98 Car. I	1641
14. Ballespurt	Inq. Ult. (Down) §98 Car. I	1641
15. Ballynsporte vocat' Knockeveile	Inq. Ult. (Down) §102 Car. I	1641
16. Ballinsport	Inq. Ult. (Down) §102 Car. I	1641
17. Ballyspuige and Lismore	Census 91	1659
18. Ballyspruge ½	BSD 84	1661
19. The other ½ of Ballyspruge	BSD 84	1661
20. Ballyspurge	Inq. Ult. (Down) §14 Car. II	1662

21. Ballyspurge	Sav. Ards 204	1723
22. Ballyspurge	Wm. Map (OSNB)	1810
23. Ballyspurge	Bnd. Sur. (OSNB)	1830c
24. Ballyspurge	Reg. Free. (OSNB)	1832
25. Baile Spuirsigh "Spourge's town"	J O'D (OSNB)	1834c
26. ˌbɑliˈsbo̤rdʒ	Local pronunciation	1991

Were it not for the form *Spordes Castle* 1595 (1), one might have supposed an original Gaelic form resembling *Baile an Spóirt* "town of the sport", but in the light of the 1595 spelling, and the Anglo-Norman origin of substantial numbers of the other place-names in this part of the Ards, the *-sport* or *-spord* part of this place-name may well represent an Anglo-Norman personal name. Evidence for an Anglo-Norman (sur)name such as *Spord(e)*, or possibly even *Asporde, Esporde*, is not cited in Reaney (1958) and we are, at present, unable to locate it in Irish sources. O'Laverty mentions *Swords* among the families coming over in the early Anglo-Norman period but any suggested link between *Sword* and *Sporde* demands a phonetic change [s(w)] > [sp] and, as there is mention in Co. Down of "Robert Crolly al' Sowrdes late of Ballydonnell in Lecahill [i.e. the barony of Lecale]" in *Inq. Ult.* §15 Car. I (c. 1622), this change seems unlikely.

The form *Drom-Arthure* which occurs as a 17th-century variant of the name (form 13) reflects an anglicized form of a Gaelic *Droim Artúir* "Arthur's ridge". This seems most likely to be a reference to Arthur Smyth: "Arthur' Smyth de Ballyspart al' Drom-Arthure in Co' Downe" *Inq. Ult.* §98 Car. I, 1641 AD. See also "Art Smith of Ballespord" in *CPR Jas I* 455a, 1618 AD.

Dooey
J 6352

Dumhaigh
"sandbank"

1. Ballydowe	PCR Eliz. I (Sav. Ards) 175	1559
2. Dowy	Census 91	1659c
3. Dooey	Wm. Map (OSNB)	1810
4. Dowey	High Const. Applot. (OSNB)	1830c
5. Dowey	Bnd. Sur. (OSNB)	1830c
6. Dowey td. Dubh-áth "black ford"	J O'D (OSNB)	1834c
7. dui	Local pronunciation	1991

Given the fact that this townland borders the sea on its eastern edge *Dumhaigh*, an oblique case of older nominative *Dumhach* "sandbank", seems more plausible than O'Donovan's suggestion *Dubh-áth* "black ford".

Newcastle
J 6353

An Caisleán Nua
"the new castle"

1. Fan gCaislén Nua	LCABuidhe 160 l. 197	1617c
2. New C st	Nowel's Ire. (1)	1570
3. Newcastle	Jobson's Ulster (TCD)	1590
4. New Cas	Mercator's Ire.	1595
5. New castel	Mercator's Ulst.	1595
6. Newe ca	Bartlett Map (TCD)	1601

7. Newcastle	Bartlett Maps (Esch. Co. Maps) 1	1603
8. Newcastle	Boazio's Map (NG)	1609
9. Newcastle	Norden's Map	1610c
10. New cast	Mercator's/Hole's Ire.	1610
11. Newcastle	Speed's Ireland	1610
12. New Castle	Speed's Antrim & Down	1610
13. New castle	Speed's Ulster	1610
14. Newcastle	Hib. Reg. Ards	1657c
15. Newcastle	Sub. Roll Down 283	1663
16. New Castle	Hib. Del. Down	1672c
17. New Castle	Descr. Ards 36	1683
18. New Castle	Lamb Maps Co. Down	1690c
19. New-castle, otherwise Clogh McGorteen	O'Laverty i, Portaf. 72	1716
20. New-Castle	Harris Hist. 67	1744
21. Newcastle	J O'D (OSNB)	1834c
22. nju'kɛsl̥	Local pronunciation	1991

According to Anderson (1980:5) "Denis Smith ... is recorded as having been resident at New Castle in the Ards in 1568". This Denis Smith, a nephew of Sir Thomas Smith who led an unsuccessful colonization of the Ards, came here to shelter with the Savages after the collapse of the Smith settlement at "Newcastle Comber" (i.e. Comber, Co. Down), according to Quinn (1945: 549), and, following the death of Thomas Smith, "took command of the surviving colonists" (*ibid.* 558). *ASCD* 262 notes the occurrence of a castle on Lord Burghley's map of Ulster of c. 1580, but points out the difficulty in tracing the remains and exact location of the former castle. In a bardic poem composed on the death of one of the Clandeboye O'Neills, *Seaán (mac Briain mheic Fheidhlimthe) Ó Néill*, d.1617, mention is made of a visit to this place by Seaán Ó Néill; but the castle appears to have been deserted by the end of the seventeenth century, judging from the following: "Neer it is a ruinous pile called New Castle which with divers town Lands adjoyning belong to James Hamilton Esquire". (*Descr. Ards* 36). For the castle here, see also *Sav. Ulst.* 359.

The modern village of Newcastle was described in the *OSNB* (1834) as: "A small village – the houses are of one story and .... Much Poverty".

OTHER NAMES

North Rocks
J 6756

An English form

1. North rock	Nowel's Ire. (1)	1570c
2. North Rocks	Nowel's Ire. (2)	1570c
3. North Rock	Dartmouth Map 6	1590
4. North rock	Mercator's Ulst.	1595
5. North Rock	Bartlett Map (TCD)	1601
6. N [Rock]	Bartlett Maps (Esch. Co. Maps) 1	1603
7. North Rock	Boazio's Map (NG)	1609
8. North Rock	Speed's Ireland	1610
9. North Rock	Speed's Antrim & Down	1610
10. North Rock	Speed's Ulster	1610

11. ye North & South Rocks	Descr. Ards 36	1683
12. the North Rock	Knox Hist. 474	1875
13. 'nɔrθ 'rɔk(s)	Local pronunciations	1991

The North and South Rocks have been noted for their treacherous nature among mariners, as shown by the following: "ye North & South Rocks aforesaid [p. 6] noted in all Maps for y[e] Misfortunes that Shipps (Especially foraigners) haue had on them in stormy Dark weather soe that it were to be wished a light house were maintained there". (*Descr. Ards* 36). See also *Sav. Ards* 199: "the fatal N. Rocks, which are a long Range stretching N.N.E. at least a League, and of which many lie sunk at high Water; so that it is hazardous to venture between them and the main Land. On these Rocks 18 Sailors were lost about 30 Years ago, and all buried together in one Grave in the Neighbouring Churchyard of *Slane*".

According to *Harris Hist.* 136 "The North Rocks are otherwise called *St. Patrick's* Rocks from a seat of Stone among them called *St. Patrick's Chair*, from which the rocks have taken this second Name". However, St Patrick's Rocks, which are also mentioned in sixteenth- and seventeenth-century sources, are off the coast of Lecale.

Knox Hist. 474 mentions a stone beacon "erected on the North Rock". (See also the account on **South Rock**).

South Rock — An English form

J 6753

1. South rock	Nowel's Ire. (1)	1570
2. South Rock	Nowel's Ire. (2)	1576
3. South Rock	Dartmouth Map 6	1590
4. South rock	Mercator's Ulst.	1595
5. South Rock	Bartlett Map (TCD)	1601
6. South Rock	Bartlett Maps (Esch. Co. Maps) 1	1603
7. South Rock	Boazio's Map (NG)	1609
8. South Rock	Speed's Antrim & Down	1610
9. South Rock	Speed's Ulster	1610
10. ye South Rock	Descr. Ards 36	1683
11. 'sɔuθ 'rɔk	Local pronunciation	1991

The following mid-18th-century account warns of the dangers of the South Rock:

> From the North to the South Rock is about two Thirds of a league, between which is clean good Ground, and safe sailing in a Water from six to eight Fathom. But beware of the South Rock, on which many brave Ships have perished; for it is overflowed by every Tide, and no Crew can save their lives, (as it stands a full Mile from the Shore,) if the Wind blows high. (*Harris Hist.* 136).

Knox Hist. 471 describes the erection of a lighthouse here to help ships avoid this area:

> The South Rock, on which stands the Kilwarlin Lighthouse, so called in honour of the second Marquis of Downshire, through whose influence it was erected, is off the coast of this parish. The building is of a conical form having a base of thirty feet diameter, on which is raised twenty feet of solid stone-work, built hollow, so as to afford residence for a family. The entire height is sixty-six feet of stone-work, and six feet of a lantern. It was first lighted in 1797. The light is from oil lamps and reflectors, elevated sixty-five

> feet above the level of the sea, at half tide. To distinguish this light from the Copeland, which bears from it nearly north and south, distant six and-a-half leagues, it is necessary to observe, that it revolves on a perpendicular axis, and that it is seen in full force, from every part of the visible horizon, once in every minute. A large bell is tolled, day and night, during the continuance of thick or foggy weather.

Anderson (1982: 4) remarked that: "The Roddy family came to the Upper Ards last century as lightshipmen when a lightship replaced the South Rock lighthouse".
See further *Lewis' Top. Dict.* ii 562.

White House An English form
J 6455

Local pronunciation ['wait 'həus]. *ASCD* 256–7 contains a description of this house, possibly built by a Patrick Savage in the 1640s, and on p. 127 of the same work it is described as of particular interest as a defended farmhouse of the mid-17th century with built in pistol-loops". G.F. Francis-Savage states that Patrick Savage of Ballyspurge (d.1649)

> seems to have built the strongly fortified house at Knockmoyle, close to the sea near Slanes, the ruins of which have long gone by the name 'The White House', and, which, according to tradition, was in later times used as a kind of summer seaside resort by the SAVAGES OF BALLYGALGET. (*Sav. Ulst.* 288, see also 336)

The Knockmoyle upon which the house is reported to have been built would go back to an Irish form *An Cnoc Maol* "the bald hill".

Anderson (1979: 18) records a branch of the Carr family living here in the course of the 18th and 19th centuries, the same family from which **Carrstown** (a townland in Witter parish) receives its name. As to the occupation of the house, it is reported in the 1830s: "In Ballyspurge is the ruins of a house called Whitehouse which, from its style and architecture, is probably not of very ancient date" *OSM* vii 121.

PARISH OF WITTER

Witter is described as a civil parish in *OSNB* (c. 1834) but *Lewis' Top. Dict.* i 53 records that "Ardkeen and the northern part of Witter were constituted a distinct rectory in the patronage of the Bishop in 1834". The result of this merger is the virtual loss of the name Witter. Indeed the "local pronunciation" below is obtained from a written form as a familiarity with this name is not particularly widespread among most of today's locals. It is not listed among the parishes of the *Census 1871* or *Top. Index 1961* and the townlands of Witter are included as part of Ballyphilip parish.

PARISH NAME

Witter	*Uachtar* "the upper part"	
1. in Óchtar Uillne	Descendants Ir 46	1200c
2. grangia de Thewer	Charts St. Mary's Abbey 4	1300c
3. Grange in Ardee, rectory of	Fiants Eliz. §1659	1570
4. the Grange in Ardee	Fiants Eliz. §5767	1592
5. church or rectory of Grangeower in the Little Ardes	CPR Jas I 78a	1605
6. Grangeoughter, ecclesia de	Inq. Ult. (Down) §2 Jac.I	1605
7. Vochter	Terrier (Reeves) 81	1615
8. Grange-Owter, the Rectorie of	Ham. Copy Inq. xxxv; li	1623
9. Grange-Owter, the Vicarage or church of	Ham. Copy Inq. xxxv; li	1623
10. Grange-Owter, Rectorie of	Ham. Copy Inq. xxxvi	1623
11. Grangecotter	Inq. Ult. (Down) §104 Car. I	1644
12. Grangowter	Inq. Ult. (Down) §104 Car. I	1644
13. Woughter or Granges, also Ballegallgatt	Inq. Down (Reeves 1) 129	1657
14. Utter	Hib. Reg. Ards	1657c
15. Woltar	Census 91	1659
16. Wogher	Trien. Visit. (Bramhall) 9	1661
17. Vtter	BSD 84	1661
18. Grangeouter	Trien. Visit. (Margetson) 20	1664
19. Utter	Hib. Del.	1672c
20. Woughter	Descr. Ards 36	1683
21. Utter	Lamb Maps Co. Down	1690c
22. Witter	Wm. Map (OSNB)	1810
23. Witter	Bnd Sur (OSNB)	1830c
24. Íochtar, i.e. the lower part or extremity	J O'D (OSNB)	1834c
25. *Gráinseach Uachtair* "grange of the upper part"	EA 25 n. v	1847
26. "the upper or farther grange"	O'Laverty i 390	1878
27. 'whïtər	Local pronunciation	1991
28. 'wïtər	Local pronunciation	1991

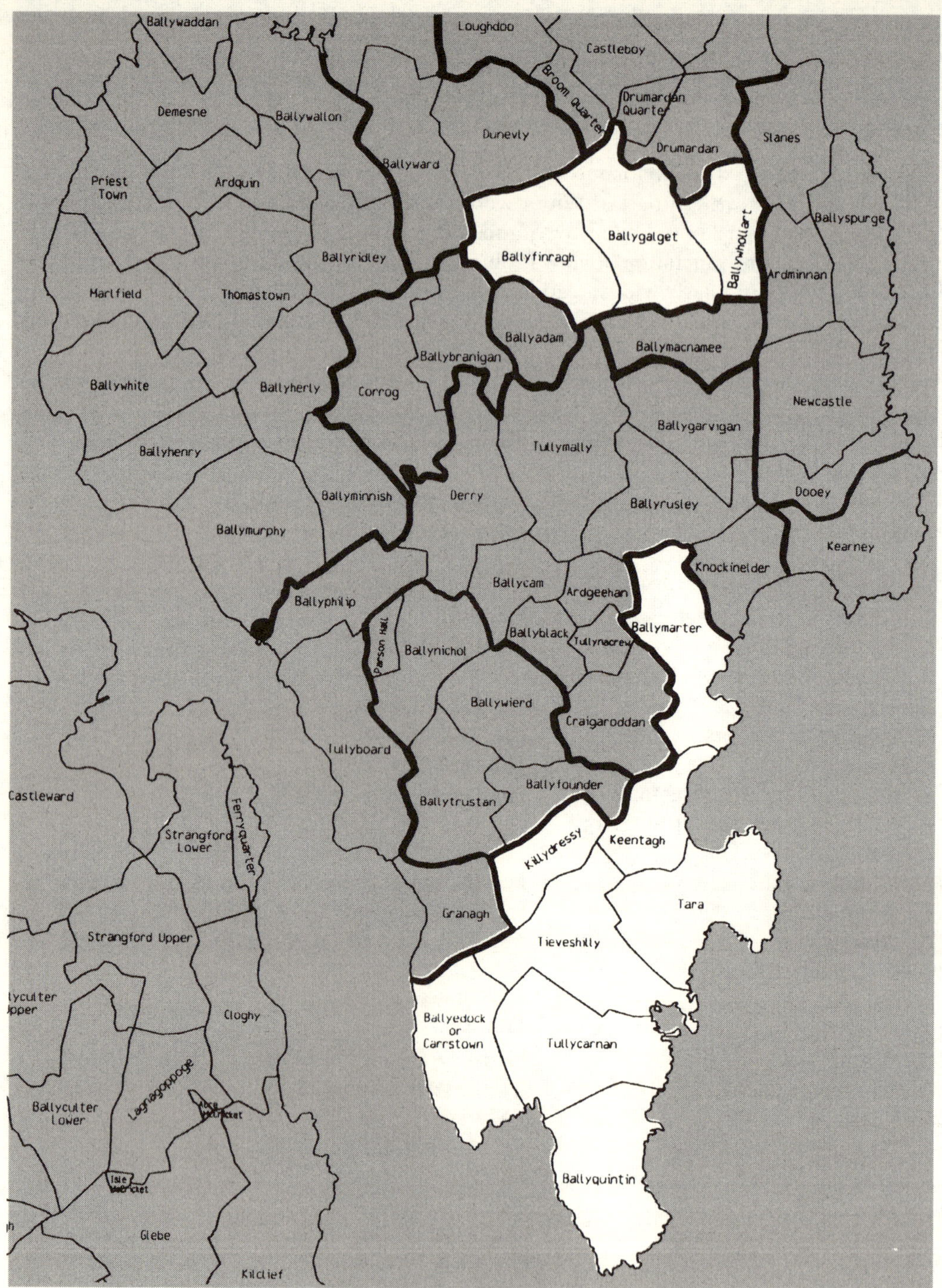

Parish of Witter

Barony of Ards Upper (2 parts)

Townlands
Ballyedock or Carrstown
Ballyfinragh
Ballygalget
Ballymarter
Ballyquintin
Ballywhollart
Keentagh
Killydressy
Tara
Tieveshilly
Tullycarnan

O'Donovan's suggestion, in the *OSNB*, that Witter derived from an original Irish *Íochtar* "lowest extremity, part" cannot be sustained, as the 17th-century forms clearly indicate an earlier *Gráinseach Uachtair*. Reeves *EA* (25 n. v) states: "The modern name [Witter] is a corruption of Irish *uachtair* 'of the upper part'; and is an abbreviation of the compound 'Grange-oughter', by which the parish was generally called". It may even have been O'Donovan who suggested the more correct *Uachtair* "of the upper part" to Reeves when *EA* was in preparation.

Reeves (*EA* 25 n. v) identified the *Capella de Tener*, which occurs in the 1306 papal taxation, with modern Witter, although he did not expand on the reasons for this identification. As has been pointed out above, however, (s.v. **Tara** in this parish) *Tener* was doubtless a scribal error for *Tever*, or the like. The reference to *grangia de Thewer* (c. 1300) not only confirms that *Capella de Tener* should probably have read *Capella de Tever* but also shows that the element *gráinseach* "grange, monastic farm" replaced *capella*. Nevertheless, given that some of the 16th- and 17th-century spellings for the modern townland of *Tara* in this parish resemble *Ballyntauragh*, clearly showing that there was a Gaelic form *Baile na Teamhrach*, we might well wonder why a Gaelic form *Gráinseach na Teamhrach* has not been attested, especially in the light of Latin *grangia de Thewer* (c. 1300). Since an Irish form *Gráinseach na Teamhrach* did not apparently occur, it is obvious that a qualifier of sorts was needed for the element *gráinseach* and the solution lay in a form *Gráinseach Uachtair*.

The reason for the qualifying element in *Gráinseach Uachtair*, i.e. "grange of *Uachtar*" appears to lie in the fact that it was desirable to distinguish the grange at Witter from the many other granges in the corn-wealthy Ards peninsula, e.g. **Gransha** (a townland in the parish of Inishargy), which was known in the taxation of 1306 as *Capella de Grangia* (*EA* 20) and which was also distinguished as *Cúl-Ghráinseach* "back-grange" (details under **Gransha** in Inishargy). While the *Cúl-*, or "back-" element in the Inishargy parish *Cúl-Ghráinseach* refers to the position of the grange, the *Uachtair* part of *Gráinseach Uachtair* does not refer to an "upper grange", but rather to the "grange of (the area known as) *Uachtar*".

The name *Uachtar*, meaning "upper or higher region" was in existence long before there was an Anglo-Norman grange in this area, and it goes back to an Old Irish form *Óchtar* (no. 1). The "upper" meaning for *Uachtar* may possibly refer to the "upper part of the Ards", or even to the relatively high land in the Witter area. In early Irish genealogical material we have references to an *Óchtar* (form 1 above) which occurs as *Óchtar Uillne*, "the height of the elbow". This *Óchtar*, or *Uachtar*, is certainly to be identified as modern Witter, as its occupier is described (*Descendants of Ír* 46) as having been "in the Ards in the time of Conchobar mac Nessa" (*isin Aird i n-aimsir Chonchoba[i]r maic Nessa*), a pre-historic king of the first century AD.

TOWNLAND NAMES

Ballyedock J 6147	*Baile Iodoc* "Idock's townland"	
1. Ballydoke	Fiants Eliz. §2090	1571
2. Gerald bane Fitz Symon of (?) Idockstown	Fiants Eliz. §3401	1578
3. BallIdogge	Fiants Eliz. §5264	1588
4. Balleedog	Ulst. Roll Gaol Deliv. 261	1613c
5. Balledooke	Inq. Ult. (Down) §9 Jac. I	1620
6. (?) Balle-Hocke	Ham. Copy Inq. xxxv	1623
7. Balledogg	Inq. Ult. (Down) §14 Jac. I	1625

8. Ballyidog	Inq. Ult. (Down) §73 Car. I	1636
9. Ballyedocke	Sav. Ards 373	1637c
10. Ballidock	Wars Co. Down, 76	1641
11. Balleedock	Inq. Ult. (Down) §104 Car. I	1645
12. Ballyidock	Census 91	1659c
13. Ballydock	BSD 84	1661
14. Ballydocke	Sub. Roll Dn 282	1663
15. Carrstown	Wm. Map (OSNB)	1810
16. Ballyedock or Carrstown	High Const. Applot. (OSNB)	1830
17. Carrstown	Bnd. Sur. (OSNB)	1830c
18. Ballyedock	Mr. Nugent, Portaferry (OSNB)	1834c
19. Edock's town or Carrstown	J O'D (OSNB)	1834c
20. ˌbɑliˈdɔːk	Local pronunciation	1991

This townland is officially known as *Ballyedock or Carrstown. Ballyedock* is the earlier name of the townland and *Carrstown* arose from the *Carr* family who held land here (details provided under **Carrstown** below). It would appear from the form *Idockstown* 1578 (no. 2) that this townland and the similarly named *Ballyedock Upper* and *Lower* in the parish of Dunsfort, Co. Down, derive from an Anglo-Norman source. One could, then, imagine an original Anglo-Norman *Idockstown* later gaelicized *Baile Iodoc* (whence *Ballyidock*), along the lines of other similar townland names in the Ards, such as *Galgyl(s)ton* > **Ballygalget**. The etymology of the name *Idock/Edock* is uncertain but it may be the Norman name *Id(e)* or *Ed(de)* plus the diminutive suffix *-ock*.

Ballyfinragh
J 6154

Baile Fionnúrach
"townland of the white plain/field (?)"

1. Ballyfonoragh	Fiants Eliz. §2090	1571
2. Ballyforneraghe	Savage Lands 4	1588
3. Ballyfoineraghe	Fiants Eliz. §5264	1588
4. Ballyfoneragh	Ham. Copy Inq. xlvi	1623
5. Ballefenoragh	Ham. Copy Inq. xxxv	1623
6. Ballwhineragh	Ham. Copy Inq. xxxv	1623
7. Ballefuneragh	Inq. Ult. (Down) §14 Jac. I	1625
8. Ballyfinneragh	Inq. Ult. (Down) §14 Jac. I	1625
9. (?) Ballyfamdragh	Inq. Ult. (Down) §10 Car. I	1627
10. Ballfondragh otherwise Ballyfoneragh	Sav. Ards 369	1628
11. (?) Ballyheneragh	Sav. Ards 373	1637c
12. Ballyfunaragh	Will (Sav. Ards) 247	1640
13. Ballyfinneraghe	Inq. Ult. (Down) §100 Car. I	1641
14. Ballefunerergh	Rental Portaferry 5	1641
15. (?) Ballewhitneragh	Inq. Ult. (Down) §104 Car. I	1645
16. Ballefeneragh	Census 92	1659c
17. Ballyfuntebagh & Carrowcomallatt	BSD 84	1661
18. Ballyfuneragh	Sav. Ulst. 285	1703
19. Ballyfinragh	Wm. Map (OSNB)	1810
20. Ballyfinragh	Bnd. Sur. (OSNB)	1830c

21. Ballyfineragh	High Const. Applot. (OSNB)	1830c
22. Baile fionnratha "town of the white fort"	J O'D (OSNB)	1834c
23. Baile-fionn-ratha "the town of the white rath or fort"	Joyce iii 85	1913
24. ˌbɑliˈfɪnərọx	Local pronunciation	1991

The form *Fionnráth*, "white fort" proposed by O'Donovan (no. 22) and Joyce (no. 23) seems to be based on the 19th-century spellings of the name. However, the earlier spellings strongly suggest an Irish-language *Baile Fionnúrach* (Classical Irish *Baile Fionnabhrach*). *Onom. Goed.* (419–20) lists over 20 instances of this element *Findabair*, or *Fionnúir* as it would be spelt in modern Irish. One of these places named *Findabair* is explained by Jocelyn, in his 12th-century life of St. Patrick, as meaning *Campus Albus* (i.e. "white plain"). *Findabair* may have still been used as an ordinary noun, rather than a fossilized place-name element, in Jocelyn's day but its passage from use in the modern spoken language has necessitated various suggested meanings from scholars in more modern times. O'Curry (1861: iii 16) proposed "white-brow" from *fionn* "white" + *abra* "brow", although *Joyce* (ii: 267) objected to O'Curry's theory on grammatical grounds. Joyce himself did not come to any firm conclusion about the etymology of *fionnabhair*, although he proposed "whitish spot" as a meaning. O'Rahilly (1933: 210) proposed an etymology **Vindo-dubris* "white waters". As there are over twenty townlands in Ireland whose modern forms suggest that they contain the element *Fionnabhair*, the word, as a place-name element, merits a further investigation. *Knox Hist.* 470–1 cites a form "Ballyfuneragh als Ballwhymmeragh" from the reign of Edward VI (1547–53), and gives "a curious glimpse of the ancient monastic life, in the Commandery".

Ballygalget
J 6254

Baile Galgail
"Galgyl's townland"

1. Sithe, Ecclesia de	Eccles. Tax. 22	1306c
2. Sythe	Inq. Earl Ulster (EA) 361	1333
3. Ballygalget	PCR Eliz. I (Sav. Ards)	1559
4. Ballygalged, Capella de	Terrier (Reeves) 59	1615c
5. Ballygalgett	Inq. Ult. (Down) §5 Jac. I	1617
6. Ballygalgett	Inq. Ult. (Down) §6 Jac. I	1617
7. Ballygalbat(?)	Ulster Visit. (Reeves) 57	1622
8. Rectorie of Ballegalgat	Ham. Copy Inq. li	1623
9. Ballegalgat al. Ballegnegh	Ham. Copy Inq. xxxv	1623
10. Ballegalgat	Ham. Copy Inq. xxxv	1623
11. Ballygalgat	Ham. Copy Inq. xxxvi	1623
12. Ballygolgett	Inq. Ult. (Down) §14 Jac. I	1625
13. Ballygallgett	Inq. Ult. (Down) §10 Car. I	1627
14. Ballygallgate	Inq. Ult. (Down) §20 Car. I	1631
15. Ballygalgett	Inq. Ult. (Down) §27 Car. I	1631
16. Ballygallgatt	Inq. Ult. (Down) §66 Car. I	1636
17. Ballygalgott	Will (Sav. Ards) 246	1640
18. Ballygallgatt	Inq. Ult. (Down) §100 Car. I	1641
19. Ballygallgett	Inq. Ult. (Down) §102 Car. I	1641

20. Ballegalgett	Inq. Ult. (Down) §104 Car. I	1645
21. Ballgalgat	Inq. Ult. (Down) §108 Car. I	1650c
22. Ballygalgott	Will (Sav. Ards) 193	1655
23. Ballegallgatt	Inq. Down (Reeves 1) 129	1657
24. Balegalgat	Census 92	1659c
25. Grange of Balligallgott	BSD 84	1661
26. Ballygalgott	BSD 84	1661
27. Ballygalgott	Trien. Visit. (Bramhall) 8	1661
28. Ballygallgatt	Inq. Ult. (Down) §16 Car. II	1662
29. Ballygalgat	Sub. Roll Dn 282	1663
30. Ballgollgot	Lamb Maps Co. Down	1690c
31. Ballygalgit	Sav. Ards 198	1701
32. Ballygalget	Sav. Ards 204	1723
33. B.gelget	Sav. Ards 376	1737
34. Ballygilget	Wm. Map (OSNB)	1810
35. Ballygalgot	High Const. Applot. (OSNB)	1830
36. Ballygalget	Bnd. Sur. (OSNB)	1830c
37. Baile galgat "town of the hero or champion"	J O'D (OSNB)	1834c
38. ˌbaliˈgalgɛt (One speaker claimed that his grandmother pronounced this as ˌbɑli gilˈgal).	Local pronunciation	1991

The suggestion that this townland means the "town of the hero or champion" (no. 37) seems to be based solely on the 19th-century spellings but the earlier forms of the name do not support that theory. *Ecclesia de Sithe* is mentioned in the taxation of Pope Nicholas IV, *c.* 1306, and the name *Sith/Syth*, or variant, survived in sources as late as the 17th century. Reeves (*EA* 22 n. q) derives *Sithe* from Irish *Síth* "taken in the sense of 'a hill'". A successful explanation for the replacement of the name *Syth* by *Ballygalget*, due to the occupation of *Le Sythe* by an Anglo-Norman tenant named Nicholas Galgyl, is offered by Reeves (*EA* 22–3, n. q):

> It was found by Inquisition in 1334, that certain lands `in *le Syth*', in the county of Newtown of Blaethwic [= modern Newtonards], were held under William de Burgo by 'Nicholas Galgyl'; and these lands are elsewhere called, probably from him, 'Ballygalgell' – *Cal. Canc. Hib.* i p. 144. Which latter name has been changed to 'Ballygalget'.

One can imagine, then, an original Anglo-Norman **Galgyl(s)ton* being gaelicized as *Ballygalgell* > modern *Ballygalget*. The following, cited by Orpen (*Inq. Earl Ulst.* p. 65), relates to the Nicholas Galgyl from whom this townland gets its name:

> 1 pair of Silver Spurs or 3*d* rent for lands in Balytoun which Nicholas Galghyl holds in fee. 1 Otterskin or 1*d* from lands and tenements in le Syth which the same Nicholas holds in fee.

Ballymarter	*Baile Mhartair*	
J 6350	"Marter's/Martel's townland"	
1. Balywarter	PCR Eliz. I (Sav. Ards) 175	1559
2. Ballywartor	Fiants Eliz. §2090	1571

3. Ballymarter	Fiants Eliz. §5264	1588
4. (?) Tollemart	Ham. Copy Inq. xxxv	1623
5. Ballyverter	Inq. Ult. (Down) §14 Jac. I	1624
6. Ballymartre	Inq. Ult. (Down) §3 Car. I	1625
7. Ballymarter	Inq. Ult. (Down) §10 Car. I	1627
8. Ballymarter, vocat' Carrowboy	Inq. Ult. (Down) §10 Car. I	1627
9. Ballimarter	Inq. Ult. (Down) §10 Car. I	1627
10. 1/2 vil' & ter de Quintonbay al' Ballymartire	Inq. Ult. (Down) §38 Car. I	1633
11. Carraboy al. Ballymarter	Inq. Ult. (Down) §82 Car. I	1637
12. Carrowboy al. Ballymartir	Inq. Ult. (Down) §82 Car. I	1637
13. Balymartyr	Will (Sav. Ards) 247	1640
14. Tullemarter	Inq. Ult. (Down) §104 Car.I	1644
15. (?) Ballymartin	Hib. Reg. Ards	1657c
16. Ballymartire	Census 92	1659
17. The qr of Ballymartine	BSD 84	1661
18. Ballymartin	BSD 84	1661
19. Ballymarter	Wm. Map (OSNB)	1810
20. Ballymarter	Bnd. Sur. (OSNB)	1830c
21. Baile martra "town of the massacare"	J O'D (OSNB)	1834c
22. ˌbɑliˈmɑrtər	Local pronunciation	1991

O'Laverty (i: 394–5) interprets the *-marter* element of the name as the Irish term *martra* "saint's relics", and considers it as a possible reference to the remains of St Cowey, or *Cú Mhaighe*, an Upper Ards saint discussed under the names **Ballyquintin** and **Templecowey** in this parish. The word *martra* is solidly attested in Early Irish sources (see, for example, *Reeves Ad.* 314, n. m and p. 452, and *DIL* s.v. *martrae*) but O'Laverty's suggestion of a connection between the naming of Ballymarter and St. Cowey is a fairly speculative one. Ballymarter may, however, be of Anglo-Norman origin. The *Martels* are listed among the Anglo-Norman families who accompanied de Courcy to Ulster in the late 12th century, see *Sav. Ards* 121, Stevenson (1920: 17). The *-marter* portion of this name, then, may well represent an assimilated form of the Anglo-Norman surname *Martel* which, according to Reaney (1958:215), could either be a hypocoristic form of *Martin*, or a nickname derived from Old French *martel* "hammer". However, rather than view *Ballymarter* as stemming from an Anglo-Norman **Martelton* which we may connect with the *Martel* family, there is also an Anglo-Norman surname *Marter* which Reaney (s.v.) interprets as a nickname from Old Fr. *martre* "weasel".

Ballyquintin — Of uncertain origin

J 6245

1. Ballynacontowne	PCR Eliz. I (Sav. Ards) 175	1559
2. Ballyncontome	Fiants Eliz. §2090	1571
3. Ballyconton	Fiants Eliz. §5264	1588
4. (?) Ballytollynecanton	Savage Lands 4	1588
5. Ballytollynecarton	Fiants Eliz. §5264	1588
6. Candan Point	Mercator's Ulst.	1595

7. Candan poynnt	Speed's Ulster	1610
8. Ballineconton	Inq. Ult. (Down) §9 Jac. I	1620
9. Ballenecontain	Inq. Ult. (Down) §9 Jac. I	1620
10. Ballyconton	Inq. Ult. (Down) §14 Jac. I	1625
11. Balleconton	Inq. Ult. (Down) §10 Car. I	1627
12. Ballyconton	Sav. Ards 368	1628
13. Ballycontow	Sav. Ards 373	1637c
14. Ballequinteene	Inq. Ult. (Down) §104 Car. I	1645
15. Ballyquintine	Census 91	1659c
16. Ballyquinten	BSD 84	1661
17. Ballyquintane	Sub. Roll Down 282	1663
18. Ballyquintin	Wm. Map (OSNB)	1810
19. Ballyquintin	Bnd. Sur. (OSNB)	1830c
20. Ballyquinton	Reg. Free. (OSNB)	1832
21. Ballyquintin	Mr. Nugent, Portaferry (OSNB)	1834c
22. Baile Conmhaighe "Quintin's town"	J O'D (OSNB)	1834c
23. *Baile Chuintín	Éire Thuaidh	1988
24. ˌbɑliˈkwïntən	Local pronunciation	1991
25. ˌbaliˈkwïntn	Local pronunciation	1991

It is evident from the *OSNB* form (no. 22) that O'Donovan sees the *-quintin* part of this name as referring to an Irish name *Cú Mhaighe*, "hound of (the) plain". Reeves (*EA* 25, n. v) dicusses the local tradition of a St Quintin, whom he associates with Irish *Cú Mhaighe*, and points out that locals associated this Quintin with the Upper Ards place-names Ballyquintin, Quintin Bay, Lough Cowey and Templecowey. Reeves' views on this were reproduced in *Joyce* (ii 153–4) but details relating to St Cú Mhaighe are difficult to obtain. *AU* (Mac Airt) 1102 AD records: "*Cú Mhaighi H. Cairill airchinnech Duin mortus est* Cú Maigi ua Cairill, superior of Dún [i.e. Downpatrick] died", and although this Cú Mhaighe (d.1102) probably lived much later than our assumed St *Cú Mhaighe*, the 1102 name may have been in honour of an earlier St *Cú Mhaighe*. O'Brien's index (*CGH* Index p.575) shows the name *Cú Mhaighe* was fairly common as a secular name in early Irish sources and, while one can fairly safely propose an ecclesiastical association between Cú Mhaighe and the local names **Templecowey** and **Cowey's** (or **Cooey's**) **Well**, in this parish, and **Lough Cowey** in Ardkeen, we are faced with the difficulty of having *-cowey* in these latter three instances yet *-quintin* in the townland of *Ballyquintin*.

The issue of *-cowey* versus *-quintin* needs, then, to be addressed. O'Donovan and Reeves have both commented on how the Irish name *Cú Mhaighe* was anglicized as *Quintin*. This anglicization, if it actually took place, is likely to have been in the post-Anglo-Norman period. Reaney (1958: 264–5) lists a British surname *Quinton* from 1176 AD onwards and suggests that the Norman surname in Britain may have been from "Saint-Quentin (La Manche) or, possibly, Saint-Quentin-en-Tourmont (Somme)' and that both of these derive from a Latin name *Quintinus* "fifth", "popular in France from the cult of St. Quentin of Amiens [a third century martyr] and brought to England by the Normans". On the name *Quintin* in Ireland one may note the references to the 16th-century bishops Quintin O'Higgin, Clonmacnoise, and Quintin O'Quigley, Dromore d.1538, (details of whom are to be found in *Mediev. Prov. Arm.* 284, 285). In 1311 AD there is mention of a Richard Quyntyn resident in Co. Kildare (*Pipe Roll* VI Ed. III). Therefore, considering *Templecowey*,

Loughcowey on the one hand, and *Ballyquintin* on the other, and bearing in mind the Anglo-Norman source for *Quintin* as a name in Ireland, it is possibile that rather than being associated with a saint Cú Mhaighe, the townland of *Ballyquintin* may in fact owe its origins to an Anglo-Norman *Quintonton*, along the lines of other place-names in the Ards, such as *Felipton* > **Ballyphilip**, *Galgyllton* > *Ballygalgell* > **Ballgalget**, etc.

This latter Anglo-Norman solution would seem quite plausible were it not for the fact that most of our earliest available anglicized spellings of the Gaelic forms of the name (nos. 1–2, 4–5 & 8–9) indicate the presence of the Gaelic definite article *na*. In cases where we have a definite article before surnames in Irish we usually find a form ending in *-ach*, e.g. *Ó Dochartaigh* "O'Doherty" becomes *An Dochartach*. In the nearby parish of Ballyphilip there is a townland **Ballyrusley** which can be traced back to *Baile an Ruiséalaigh*, in which the Norman name *(de) Ruiséil* "Russel" became specific *An Ruiséalach* i.e. "the Russel". If, then, a form resembling *Ballineconton* (1620 AD) represents a gaelicized form of an Anglo-Norman **Quintonton* one may have expected some reflex of *-aigh* (gen. sg. of the suffix *-ach*) but, as this does not appear, the name is of the type *Baile* + definite article *na* + noun.

Form no. 22 is derived from the bilingual map *Éire Thuaidh/Ireland North*, where Ballyquintin Point is rendered *Pointe Bhaile Chuintín*. This form, however, must now be reviewed in the light of the earlier spellings.

One possibility suggested by *Ballenecontowne* (no. 1) and similar forms (nos. 3, 8, 10–12) is an original Irish *Baile na Contóna* "townland (resembling the shape) of the dog's bottom". This may be suggested from the shape of the townland which forms the tip of the Ards peninsula. A compound of two nouns such as *con-tóin* is not unusual in Irish place-names; other examples are *muc-ais*, literally "pig-back", and *each-dhroim*, "horse-back" which are found in the names Muckish and Aughrim.

Ballywhollart	*Baile Choiléir*	
J 6354	"Collyer's or Colier's townland"	
1. Ballycoller	PCR Eliz. I (Sav. Ards) 175	1559
2. Balleculler	CPR Jas I 340b	1617
3. Ballyculler	Inq. Ult. (Down) §5 Jac. I	1617
4. Ballewhillerat	Ham. Copy Inq. xxxv	1623
5. Ballewhilterate or Balleciller	Ham. Copy Inq. lvii	1644
6. Ballyculler	Census 92	1659
7. (?) Ballycullagh als Ballycollen	BSD 84	1661
8. Ballycollyer	Inq. Ult. (Down) §19 Car. II	1662
9. Ballywhollert	Sav. Ards 376	1737
10. Ballywhollart	Wm. Map (OSNB)	1810
11. Ballywhollart	Bnd. Sur. (OSNB)	1830c
12. Ballywhilert	High Const. Applot. (OSNB)	1830c
13. Baile an h-ab[h]all-ghoirt "town of the orchard"	J O'D (OSNB)	1834c
14. ˌbaliˈwhïlərd	Local pronunciation	1991
15. ˌbɑliˈwhɑlərt	Local pronunciation	1991

The earlier forms of the name show variation but *Ballyculler/-coller* seems to be the most settled rendering. O'Donovan's suggestion (no. 13), based on the 19th-century spellings, is unlikely. If, as one suspects, *Ballywhollart* is a gaelicized Anglo-Norman name, it may originally have been **Collar(s)ton*. Reaney (1958: 74) discusses a surname *Collard*, which he derives from *Col*, a pet form of *Nicholas*, with French suffix *ard*. However, a more likely Anglo-Norman original would seem to be Reaney's form *Collar / Coller* (p. 74), variants of *Collier* (derived from Old Eng. *col* "coal") and signifying "maker or seller of charcoal". Indeed the form *Ballycollyer* 1662 would seem to favour this interpretation. As regards the presence of final *-t* in modern *Ballywhollart* we may note the form *Colliard* listed by Reaney (p. 74) as a variant form of *Collier*. On the other hand, this *-t* might be due to a development in the gaelicized form of the name, as the modern townland of **Ballystockart** (par. Comber, Co. Down) was spelt *Ballystoker* from 1623–1650c, yet *Ballystockart* in 1659.

Carrstown | A Scots/English form
J 6146

1. Carrstown	Wm. Map (OSNB)	1810
2. Ballyedock or Carrstown	High Const. Applot. (OSNB)	1830
3. Carrstown	Bnd. Sur. (OSNB)	1830c
4. Ballyedock	Mr. Nugent, Portaferry (OSNB)	1834c
5. 'kɑrztɔun	Local pronunciation	1991
6. 'kɛrztɔun	Local pronunciation	1991

This townland has the dual name of *Ballyedock or Carrstown* (see also **Ballyedock** above). Anderson (1979:18) describes how a family of the name *Carr* was granted a lease of Ballyedock and "Since then the townland has been known by two alternative names:- Carrstown and Ballydock". Evidence of the Carr family in the Ards goes back to the early 17th century. In *Inq. Ult.* §10 Car. I (1627 AD) mention is made of a "Hen[ry]' Carr de Ards" who held land in "Ballydock" and who was related to a "Joh' Carr". In *Wars Co. Down* 76 mention is made of George and "David Carr of S[ct] John's Point". Anderson (*loc. cit.*) records that one of the family resided at the White House (Ballyspurge td., Slanes parish) where the name survived in the district in the 1830s, and further makes the point that: "Carr is a variant of the name Kerr. The Kerrs were a Scottish border clan, descended from a Norman family who settled there in the 12th century. Although most of the Scottish settlers came to Ulster in the 17th century, the Carrs were here almost half a century earlier". On the origin of the surname *Carr*, see further Reaney (1958: 61) and Black (1946: 137).

Keentagh | *Caointeach* (?)
J 6249 | "fair house"

1. (?) Ballynekyntyny	Fiants Eliz. §2090	1571
2. Kyntagh, John or Gilduff Fitz Symon of	Fiants Eliz. §3401	1578
3. (?) Kentonges	Inq. Ult. (Down) §9 Jac. I	1620
4. Kintagh	Inq. Ult. (Down) §9 Jac. I	1620
5. Quintagh, the half towne of	Ham. Copy Inq. xxxv	1623
6. Kintagh	Inq. Ult. (Down) §14 Jac. I	1624
7. Kintagh	Sav. Ards 373	1637c
8. Quintagh	Inq. Ult. (Down) §104 Car. I	1644
9. Kintagh and Carrowdressagh	Census 91	1659
10. Kintagh	BSD 84	1661
11. Keentagh	Wm. Map (OSNB)	1810
12. Keentagh	Bnd. Sur (OSNB)	1830c
13. Kintagh	High Const. Applot. (OSNB)	1830c

14. Keentagh	Mr. Nugent, Portaferry (OSNB)	1834c
15. Cinteach, Mr Lavery of	OSNB	1834c
16. Cinn Teach "head or hill of the houses"	J O'D (OSNB)	1834c
17. 'kɪntʃöx	Local pronunciation	1991
18. 'kɪntəx	Local pronunciation	1991
19. 'ki:ntʃɑ	Local pronunciation	1991

Joyce (ii 318–9) discusses *caonach* "moss" and other derivative forms in names such as Keenaghan and Keenoge, but there is no mention of a derivative *caointeach* "mossy (area)". Another suggestion might be *Caointeach* "fair house", from *caoin* "fair" + *teach* "house", but the name *Keentagh* poses interpretative difficulties.

Killydressy — *Ceathrú Dhreasach*
J 6148 — "brambly quarter"

1. Carrowdrissagh	Inq. Ult. (Down) §20 Car. I	1631
2. Carrowdressagh	Sav. Ards 373	1637c
3. Carrowdressagh	Inq. Ult. (Down) §104 Car. I	1644
4. Carrowdressagh	Census 91	1659
5. Killydressy	Wm. Map (OSNB)	1810
6. Killydressy	Bnd. Sur. (OSNB)	1830c
7. Killydressy	High Const. Applot. (OSNB)	1830c
8. Killydressy	Reg. Free. (OSNB)	1832
9. Killydrissy	Mr. Nugent, Portaferry (OSNB)	1834c
10. Coille driseach "wood of brambles"	J O'D (OSNB)	1834c
11. ˌkɪlə'dresɪ	Local pronunciation	1991

The *Killy-* portion of this name, which doubtless prompted the *OSNB* suggestion *Coille Driseach* "wood of brambles", appears to have replaced an earlier *Carrowdressagh* (nos. 1–4) which strongly suggests an original *Ceathrú Dhreasach* "brambly quarter".

Tara — *An Teamhair*
J 6348 — "the eminent, or dark hill (?)"

1. Temair na hArdda	LL v l. 35088	1170c
2. Temuir Arda .i. Ard Ulad	Mesca Ulad 129	1450c
3. Thewer, grangia de	Charts St. Mary's Abbey i 4	1300c
4. Tener, Capella de	Eccles. Tax 24	1306c
5. Teure, the tenement of	Great Rolls Pipe 45 Rept. DKPRI	1328c
6. Teuyr, the tenement of	Great Rolls Pipe 53 Rept. DKPRI	1341c
7. Ballentonragh	PCR Eliz. I (Sav. Ards) 175	1559
8. Ballyntawragh	Fiants Eliz. §2090	1571
9. Ballytawraghe	Fiants Eliz. §5264	1588
10. Tarragh als Bull	Mercator's Ulst.	1595
11. Ballinetamragh	Inq. Ult. (Down) §9 Jac. I	1620
12. Ballenetawragh al. Balletouragh	Inq. Ult. (Down) §9 Jac. I	1620
13. Tawragh	Inq. Ult. (Down) §9 Jac. I	1620

14. Teragh	Inq. Ult. (Down) §9 Jac. I	1620
15. Tussellhauragh	Ham. Copy Inq. xxxv	1623
16. Ballyntawragh	Inq. Ult. (Down) §14 Jac. I	1625
17. Ballytawragh	Inq. Ult. (Down) §14 Jac. I	1625
18. Ballenetauragh	Inq. Ult. (Down) §10 Car. I	1627
19. (?) Torreyonyle al. Toradonill	Inq. Ult. (Down) §10 Car. I	1627
20. Ballenetauragh	Sav. Ards 373	1637c
21. Balletaura	Inq. Ult. (Down) §104 Car. I	1645
22. Taragh	Census 91	1659c
23. Turragh	BSD 84	1661
24. Tara	Wm. Map (OSNB)	1810
25. Tarra	High Const. Applot. (OSNB)	1830c
26. Tarrah	Bnd. Sur. (OSNB)	1830c
27. Tarah	Mr. Nugent, Portaferry (OSNB)	1834c
28. Teamhair "a pleasant hill"	J O'D (OSNB)	1834c
29. 'tɑrə	Local pronunciation	1991

The unidentified *Capella de Tener* in the taxation of Pope Nicholas IV 1306, which Reeves (*EA* 24, n. v) locates at Witter, doubtless refers to the modern name *Tara*; *Tener* may be a scribal error for *Tever*, or the like, as borne out by *grangia de Thewer* in *c.* 1300 AD. The 16/17th-century forms resembling *Ballyntawragh* reflect an Irish-language form *Baile na Teamhrach* but, judging by the available attestations of the name, the prefixing of *Baile* appears to have occurred at some point between the mid-14th and late 16th century. We are fortunate in having a reference to Tara in the Ards in the tale *Mesca Ulad* "The Intoxication of the Ulstermen". This tale forms a part of the corpus of stories loosely referred to as the Ulster Cycle, a corpus which revolves around the *Ulaid*, or Ulstermen, ruled by King Conchobor at *Emain Macha*, modern Navan Fort, Co. Armagh. The centre piece of the corpus of tales making up the Ulster Cycle is the epic *Táin Bó Cuailnge*, or "Cattle Raid of Cooley", and the exploits of the boy-warrior Cú Chulainn. Our earliest written versions of these stories survive in the 12th-century *Book of Leinster*, but they were composed several centuries earlier (*c.* 8th century), and their setting concerns life in pre-Christian Ireland. The tale *Mesca Ulad* concerns a frenzied expedition by various Ulster heroes into Munster where they burned the residence of *Cú Ruí mac Dáire*, king of west Munster, at *Teamhair Luachra* (in modern Co. Kerry). On pp. 36–7 of the text and translation, provided by Hennessy (1889), we read of the approach to *Cú Ruí*'s residence of one *Blad Briuga mac Fiachna a Temair na hArda* "Blad Briuga, son of Fiachna, from Temair of the Ard", who was surrounded by nine charioteers. Hennessy (1889: v, n. II) tentatively suggested that "*Temair-na-hArda*" was "now probably Tara, barony of Upper Ards, Co. Down", a view repeated, equally tentatively, by Hogan (*Onom. Goed.* 630), but the identity of the residence of *Blad Briuga* (i.e. "Blad the Hospitaller") as Tara in the Ards was put beyond all reasonable doubt by J. C. Watson (*M. Ulad* p. 129) who cited from the relevant portion of a 15th-century version of this tale preserved in a Scottish manuscript, which described the place in question as *Temuir Arda .i. Ard Ulad*, which we can translate as: "Temuir of the Ards, i.e. the Ards of Ulster" (form no. 2 above).

Having established, then, the origin of Tara as *(An) Teamhair*, there is the problem of the etymology of this term. *DIL* (s.v. *temair*) has details of the etymology offered in the *Metrical Dindsenchus* where *Temair* (Tara, Co. Meath) is etymologized as *te múr*, i.e. "rampart (*múr*) of *Tea* daughter of Lugaid", but this can be safely dismissed. In *Cormac's Glossary* (10th-century), and in *LL* (12th century) the opinion is expressed that the Irish word "*temair* means any high place, eminence, hill from which a view can be had and that it is borrowed from a Greek word *temoro*". (The entry reads *a verbo Greco temoro .i. conspicio. uair is temair ainm do cech inad asind soirb fegad radairc* in *LL* 159[a]9). The Greek origin is rejected by the modern scholar Vendryes (*LÉIA* s.v. *temair*), although the noun *teamhair* was clearly understood by Irish scribes and glossators in the medieval period to mean a conspicuous or eminent height, a view subsequently shared by O'Donovan, Hennessy (1889: v), Joyce (i 294–6), in addition to the editors of *DIL* (s.v. *temair*). However, Wagner (1979: 26), in his discussion of the identification of the Earth-goddess with sacred hills and the dual function of life and death, took *Teamair* to mean "the dark one", stating: "It is almost certain that the root **tem-* (cf. Old Irish *temel* "darkness") from which we can derive *Temair*, is also contained in the name of the river *Themes* [modern *Thames*, London] (*Tamessa* in Roman times; cf. Sanskrit *tamasa-* "dark-coloured")". On the etymological level *Temair* would appear to derive from a root *tem-* "dark", possibly a reference to the inner hill, although Harris (*Harris Hist.* 131) describes Tara in the Ards as "an inconsiderable place". However, it seems that the term *teamhair* came to be understood as "eminent height" in ordinary spoken Irish from as early as the Old Irish period, although it has since disappeared from the everyday vocabulary of modern Irish.

The ring-fort in this townland is briefly described in *ASCD* 173, while the archaeological remains of the church here appear only to have been noted by Reeves (*EA* 25 n. v). On the change of this church from *Capella de Tever* to the modern parish name *Witter*, see the entry on **Witter** above.

Tieveshilly J 6247	*Taobh Sailí* "hillside of the willowy area"	
1. Tewesities	PCR Eliz. I (Sav. Ards) 175	1559
2. Tewesilie	Fiants Eliz. §2090	1571
3. Ballytussillye	Fiants Eliz. §5264	1588
4. Towshillie	Inq. Ult. (Down) §9 Jac. I	1620
5. Towshillie al. Ballitonshillie	Inq. Ult. (Down) §9 Jac. I	1620
6. Balletywshilly	Inq. Ult. (Down) §9 Jac. I	1620
7. Tewsilly	Inq. Ult. (Down) §14 Jac. I	1625
8. Tewshallee al. Ballytewsheliee	Inq. Ult. (Down) §14 Jac. I	1625
9. Tewshillie	Inq. Ult. (Down) §10 Car. I	1627
10. Ballotewshilly	Sav. Ards 373	1637c
11. Towsilly	Census 91	1659c
12. Tussilly	BSD 84	1661
13. Tressilly	Sub. Roll Down 282	1663
14. Tieveshilly	Wm. Map (OSNB)	1810
15. Tooshilly	High Const. Applot. (OSNB)	1830c
16. Tieveshilly	Bnd. Sur. (OSNB)	1830c
17. Tieveshilly	Mr. Nugent, Portaferry (OSNB)	1834c
18. Taobh Silidh "hillside of the trickling, dropping"	J O'D (OSNB)	1834c
19. ˌti:v'ʃɩlɩ	Local pronunciation	1991
20. ˌtʎ'ʃili	Local pronunciation	1991

O'Donovan's suggestion of *Taobh Silidh* "hillside of the trickling, dropping" (18) seems plausible enough, although an association with willows is suggested by the anglicized forms in *-s(h)illy*, *-shallee* etc. from the 16/17th centuries. The more usual Irish form for "willow" is *saileach*, i.e. with broad *s*-, which may be reflected by forms in *-silly*. The forms in *-shilly* reflect a rarely attested slender *s*-, but we may note that, for Scottish Gaelic, Dwelly has *Seileach* "Willow – salix 2. Willow copse. 3 Place where willows grow", and it would appear that a form of this nature lies behind the name *Tieveshilly*.

Tullycarnan J 6147	*Tulaigh Charnáin* "hillock of the cairn, or heap of stones"	
1. Tullagharnan	PCR Eliz. I (Sav. Ards) 175	1559
2. Tullagharnan	Fiants Eliz. §2090	1571
3. Tollicaron al. Tollyharnan	Inq. Ult. (Down) §9 Jac. I	1620
4. Tollehernan al. Balletollehernan	Inq. Ult. (Down) §9 Jac. I	1620
5. (?)Carnane	Inq. Ult. (Down) §9 Jac. I	1620
6. Tulliherin	Inq. Ult. (Down) §9 Jac I	1620
7. Ballytullycarnan al. Listyagnew	Ham. Copy Inq. xlii	1623
8. Ballenicoll al. Tullecarnan al. Loughduffe	Ham. Copy Inq. xlvi	1623
9. (?) Tullycaman	Ham. Copy Inq. xxxv	1623
10. Tullycarnon	Inq. Ult. (Down) §14 Jac. I	1625
11. Tollcharnan	Inq. Ult. (Down) §14 Jac. I	1625
12. Tollekarnan al. Ballytollekearnan	Inq. Ult. (Down) §10 Car. I	1627
13. Tollekernan	Inq. Ult. (Down) §26 Car. I	1631
14. Tullycarnan	Inq. Ult. (Down) §37 Car. I	1633
15. Tullecarnan al. Ballytullecarnan	Inq. Ult. (Down) §48 Car. I	1634
16. Ballytollecarnan otherwise Tollecarnan	Sav. Ards 373	1637c
17. Tullycarnan	Wars Co. Down 76	1641
18. Balletullecarnan	Inq. Ult. (Down) §104 Car. I	1645
19. Balletullecarnan al. Listiagnewe	Inq. Ult. (Down) §104 Car. I	1645
20. Tollecarnan	Census 91	1659c
21. Tollycarnane	BSD 84	1661
22. Tullycarnon	Wm. Map (OSNB)	1810
23. Tullycarnan	Bnd. Sur. (OSNB)	1830c
24. Tullycarnan	High Const. Applot. (OSNB)	1830c
25. Tullycarnan	Reg. Free. (OSNB)	1832
26. Tullycarnan	Mr. Nugent, Portaferry (OSNB)	1834c
27. Tulaigh an Charnáin "hill of the heap"	J O'D (OSNB)	1834c
28. ˌto̤liˈkɑrnən	Local pronunciation	1991

This name appears to be made up of *tulach* "hillock" and *carnán* "mound", although a personal name *Earnán* may also be a slim possibility for the second element. Some of the alias forms such as *Ballytullycarnan alias Listyagnew*, suggest that this place was also known as *Lios Tí Uí Ghnímh*, i.e. "fort/enclosure of the house of Ó Gnímh", a Gaelic bardic family now more commonly known by the anglicized form Agnew. Indeed in *CPR* 326a (c. 1618) we have mention of two people of this surname in the Ards, most notably "Andrew Agnewe of Carnie [= mod. td. Kearney, Ballyphilip parish]".

OTHER NAMES

Angus Rock J 6145	*Creag Aonghasa* "Angus' rock"	
1. Angwys rocke	S-E Ulster Map	1580c
2. Angwys rok	Mercator's Ulst.	1595
3. Cragancows	Bartlett Map (Esch. Co. Maps) 1	1603
4. Anguis Rock	Speed's Ireland	1610
5. Angwis Rock	Speed's Antrim & Down	1610
6. Angwis rock	Speed's Ulster	1610
7. Angus	Map, Petty's Sur. (OSNB)	1683
8. Angus Rock	OSNB	1834c
9. rɔk 'aŋəs	Local pronunciation	1991
10. 'rɔkən 'gu:s	Local pronunciation	1991

The name has been subject to quite a few interpretations, such as that by Harris (*Harris Hist.* 137): "on the West side near *Killard* Point is another dangerous rock called *Anguish Rock* which, however, appears above Water". Reeves (*UJA* 2 (1854) 53) remarks: "South of the ferry about midway across, is *Angus Rock*, which Harris calls *Anguish Rocks*, but which the vulgar use of the neighbourhood has converted into the ludicrous combination of the *Rocking-Goose*! (Rock Angus)". This form is still current judging by form 10 above.

Knox (*Knox Hist.* 472–3) gives the following description of the rock: "A light-house was petitioned for, in 1846, and built on Rock Angus, being completed in 1853, but, strange to say, it has never as yet been lighted, although in readiness to receive the necessary apparatus. It merely stands in position, on a rock, at the entrance of Lough Strangford, as a beacon, and so far it is useful, being forty feet in height .... Midway between Killard and Ballyquintin, is the reef called Rock Angus, on the inner or northern part of which stands the lighthouse tower .... There is a passage between Rock Angus and Killard Point, with thirteen feet of water, but it is intricate from the number of sunken rocks, and should not be attempted by strangers".

CSP Ire. 1601–2 317–8 mentions an island at the entrance to *Lough Cone* which, if fortified, could prevent any vessel from entering into the inner lake. This may well refer to Rock Angus.

Ballyfinragh Lough J 6145	A hybrid form

This lake which borders the townlands of Balyfinragh and Ballygalget in this parish, and Dunevely in Ardkeen parish, was formerly known as Ballygalget Lough, e.g. *B.gelget Lough* (*Sav. Ards* 376) 1737. See **Ballyfinragh** above.

Bar Hall **Bar Hall Bay** J 6246, J 6146	A Scots/English form	
1. Barr Hall	Sav. Ards 330	1759
2. 'bar 'hɔ:l	Local pronunciation	1991

Bar here refers to the family name *Barr*. Locally the names are spelt *Barr Hall* on signposts. We have details of "John Barr of Balleedog" who was one of the jurors at an Inquisition taken at Down before Judge Christopher Sibthorp in Feb. 1613 AD (*Ulst. Roll Gaol Deliv.* 261).

The hall in question is not described in *ASCD* but it is referred to in *Sav. Ards*: "A small house known as 'Bar Hall' still stands at the head of Bar Hall Bay, the most southern of the inlets of the Ards".

Bells Quarter — An English form
J 6247

Local pronunciation ['belz 'kwartər]. Probably so-called from the surname *Bell.* Anderson (1980:2) lists 10 families of Bells in the Little Ards.

Croft — An English form
J 6144

In the *OSNB* a minor name *Croft* is listed, near to Ballyedock, two miles SSE of Portaferry, which O'Donovan derived from *Crochta* "a croft, close or garden". This may of course be English/Scots *Croft.*

Garter Rock — An English form
J6144

The local pronunciation is [ðə 'gɑrtər rɔk]. Possibly named from a mark on the rock. "Garter Rock which dries at half-ebb and is marked by a perch twenty feet high" *Knox Hist* 474.

Knockdoo — See **Rock Savage** below
J6254

Millin Bay — A hybrid form
J 6349

1. Cuttingbay & Quintenbay	Inq. Ult. (Down) §10 Car. I	1627
2. Cuttinbay	Inq. Ult. (Down) §102 Car. I	1641
3. 'mïl̥n 'be:	Local pronunciation	1991
4. 'nɔrθ 'be:	Local pronunciation	1991

Millin Bay appears to take its name from nearby **Millin Hill**. It would appear from forms 1 and 2 that it was formerly known as *Cuttingbay*. Locally it is sometimes referred to as *The North Bay* (no. 4) or even *The North Bay of Tara.*

Millin Hill — *An Mhuinchille* (?) "the sleeve"
J 6348

1. Le Monechillis	Charts St. Mary's Abbey i 4	1300c
2. Munkhill in the tenement of Teuere near the sea	Great Rolls Pipe 45 Rept. DKPRI	1328c
3. Monkilles in Ulster County	Great Rolls Pipe 53 Rept. DKPRI	1341c
4. Monkilles in the tenement of Teuyr	Great Rolls Pipe 53 Rept. DKPRI	1341c
5. (?) The monyl	Mercator's Ulst.	1595
6. Ballemullin	Inq. Ult. (Down) §10 Car. I	1627
7. Ballemollen	Inq. Ult. (Down) §26 Car. I	1631
8. Millín "a small knoll"	J O'D (OSNB)	1834c
9. 'mïl̥n 'hɪl	Local pronunciation	1991

Anderson (1979:18) takes Millin Bay to be derived from a surname, although this assumption is based "merely from a glance at the O.S. map". Elsewhere, Anderson (1980:6), describes the Scottish surname of MacMillan stating that the name came to Ulster "mainly with settler families during the Plantation". She also points out, however, that the Irish name McMullan was in the Ards in the pre-Plantation period, e.g. Aidan McMullan who signed his name in Irish on a document for Patrick, Lord Savage, in 1590. Nevertheless, one cannot be certain that *Millin* in this name represents a surname. O'Donovan's suggestion *Millín* "a small knoll" (no. 6) seems plausible although, if the 17th-century forms *Ballemullin/Ballemollen* (nos. 6 & 7) refer to this place, a problem of interpretation arises. These latter forms, nos. 6 & 7, might suggest *Baile Muilinn*, or *Baile an Mhuilinn* "townland of the mill", but the meaning of the name *Millin Hill* is difficult to determine with any degree of certainty.

In the medieval period this hill was known by the Anglo-Normans as *Munkill*, *Le Monechilles* etc. (nos. 1–4) which may suggest a "monk-hill" or perhaps an original Irish *An Mhuinchille* "the sleeve". This latter suggestion would certainly apply to the short-sleeved shape of the peninisula on which Millin Hill stands. For the element *muinchille* "sleeve" as a place-name element we may note the Co. Cavan place-name Cootehill, which is known in Irish as *Muinchille* (*GÉ* 207). Returning to Millin Hill, if form no. 5 is a genuine form, this place may even also have been known as *An Muinéal* "the neck".

Nuns Bridge — An English form

J 6255

1. Nun's bridge	Sav. Ulst. 350	1790
2. Nunsbridge	Sav. Ulst. 352	1790
3. Nunsbridge	Sav. Ards 294	1809
4. Nunsbridge	OSNB	1834c
5. 'nọnz 'brïdʒ	Local pronunciation	1991

According to *Sav. Ards* (265, n. 2) "The Property and House of Nunsbridge took their name from the bridge called 'Nun's Bridge'" but "... Why the bridge was called 'Nun's' Bridge is not known". According to Knox (*Knox Hist.* 470) the house was still occupied in the 1870s: "In the townland of Ballygalget, anciently Ballygalga, there is a very old mansion house, called Nunsbridge, which is still occupied as a place of residence". (*Knox Hist.* 470).

Pladdy Lug — A hybrid form?

J 6145

The local pronunciation is ['plɑdi 'lọg]. *Pladdy* is a term given to a partly submerged drumlin-shaped small island, fairly common in Strangford Lough. The etymology and language origin of the term is problematic but the first element may be Norse *Flatēy* "flat island", see **McCammon Pladdy** (par. Inishargy) for discussion. The second element may be the English word *lug* "ear" or a representation of Irish *lag* "hollow".

Knox Hist. 474 contains the following:

> A stone beacon has been recently erected on Pladdy Lug, by the Commissioners of Irish Lights, to replace a wooden perch which was often swept away, The height of the stonework is thirty-three feet, surmounted by a diamond-shaped iron framed top, nine feet high in height, the total elevation being forty-two feet.

Quintin Bay A hybrid form
J 6350

1.	Quintenbay	Inq. Ult. (Down) §10 Car. I	1627
2.	Quintonbay	Inq. Ult. (Down) §27 Car. I	1631
3.	Quintonbay	Inq. Ult. (Down) §38 Car. I	1633
4.	Ballymartin otherwise Quintonbay	Sav. Ards 373	1637c
5.	Quintin Bay	Will (Sav. Ards) 247	1640
6.	Quintin Bay	Rental Portaferry, 5	1641
7.	Quintinbay	Descr. Ards 36	1683
8.	Quintin Bay	Sav. Ards 199	1701
9.	ˈkwəntn̩ ˈbeː	Local pronunciation	1991

This may also have been called *Tara Bay* if Harris is correct: "Near four Miles S.W. of the South Rock is *Quintin Bay*, called also the Bay of *Tara* from an inconsiderable place" (*Harris Hist.* 136, 241). However, this may refer to **Millin Bay** above. A meaning for *Quintin* is difficult to ascertain. See **Ballyquintin** above.

Quintin Castle A hybrid form
J 6350

ASCD (246) refers to "Smith's Castle" appearing on a map dated *c.* 1580. Anderson (1980:5) notes that Sir James Montgomery purchased Quintin Castle from Dualtagh Smith around 1635. In *Descr. Ards (1683)* we read:

> Quintinbay Castle with an house adioyning thervnto in good repair with a stone walled Court or Bawn & Flankers all *which* (except y[e] pyle) Sir James Montgomery, Knight (who purchased y[e] same & lands therevnto belonging from Smith a depender of y[e] late chiefe Savage) and his sonn and heir William built and repaired[:] it commands y[e] bay which can receave a bark of fifty tunns burthen.

ASCD adds that William Montgomery sold it to George Ross about 1700, but that it had fallen into disrepair by the mid-19th century. In the *OSNB* of 1834 the castle is described as being "in ruins", although in 1875 Knox (*Knox Hist.* 469) comments: "It was one of the old square keeps, but it was rebuilt and modernised by the late Mr, Calvert, into whose possession it had come". We may also consult Byres (1982). See **Ballyquintin** above.

Quintin Village A hybrid form
J 6350

"A small village containing about 10 houses". (*OSNB* 1834c). On the meaning of *Quintin* see **Ballyquintin** above.

Rock Savage (also **Knockdoo**) *Cnoc Dubh*
J 6254 "black hill"

The local pronunciation is [ˌnɔkˈdu]. Reeves (*EA* 22, n. q) talks of the ruins of a church at "Knockdoo, otherwise Rock-Savage". The "Rock-Savage" is doubtless in imitation of "Rock Savage" a seat of the English Savages, cf. "SIR WILLIAM LE SAVAGE, KNT., [born *c.* 1150] afterwards a Baron of Ulster, was, as we have seen, a scion of the house of

SAVAGE of SCARCLIFFE, STAINSBURY, and CLIFTON (ROCK SAVAGE) ..." (*Sav. Ards* 119); see also p. 258.

Rock Savage House was located in the townland of Ballygalget and *Sav. Ards* 268 contains a description of how Major John Boscawen Savage (1760–1843), who had spent most of his life in the English military, inherited Rock Savage House in the 48th year of his age and how he sold the house for a ridiculously low sum, with the property being dismantled shortly afterwards. Elsewhere, G.F. Savage Armstrong states that Philip Savage (b. 1691) "gave to his house the name of 'Rock Savage'", going on to add that the mansion "was prettily situated on the side of Knockdhu Hill" (*Sav. Ulst.* 289). See also *Sav. Ards* 197.

South Bay
J6347

See **Millin Bay** and **Quintin Bay** above.

St Cooey's Wells
J 6347

A hybrid form

These wells are found at *Templecooey*, or *Templecowey* (see **Templecowey Point** below). *O'Laverty* (i 390–1) describes them as follows:

> Along the eastern boundary of the little disused cemetery are three holy wells; that to the north east is called the Drinking Well, that to the south east is called the Washing Well, and the middle is called the Eye Well.

The tradition of taking water from these St Cooey's Wells for drinking and washing one's eyes is still practised to this day. One local informant told me that both Protestants and Catholics used to go there for water.

Templecowey Point
J 6347

Teampall Chú Mhaighe
"Cú Mhaighe's church"

1. Tamplekawy	Fiants Eliz. §1659	1570
2. (?) St Keuens	S-E Ulster Map	1580c
3. Teamplekenny	Fiants Eliz. §5767	1592
4. (?) Ballcowee	BSD 85	1661
5. (?) Bally Temple	BSD 85	1661
6. Teampull Conmhaighe "Cooey's or Quintin's church"	J O'D (OSNB)	1834c
7. ˌtɛmpl ˈkui	Local pronunciation	1991
8. ˌtɛmpl ˈkaui	Local pronunciation	1991

The early spellings listed above show considerable variation in form. No. 2 occurred on the map of S-E Ulster near to modern **St Cooey's Wells** which are located at the church site here. The modern form of the name – *Templecowey*, as it is on the map, or *Temple Cooey* as it is spelt locally – suggests a more recent genitive *Teampall Chú Mhaighe* rather than a more archaic *Teampall Con Maighe*, hinted at by O'Donovan (form no. 6). Reeves (*EA* 25, n. v) discusses the traditions of a St *Cú Mhaighe* (i.e. "hound of the plain"). Reeves states that *Cú Mhaighe* was later anglicized *Quintin* although there are problems associated with this theory, as may be seen from the discussion of **Ballyquintin** in this parish.

At the current site there is a marble slab, erected in 1977, which is inscribed as follows:

TEMPLE COOEY
Founded in the 7th century by St Cooey from
Knockinelder. He died in 731 Abbot of Movilla Ards.
The Church was pillaged at times by Norse Pirates.
Rebuilt in the 12th century it served the district
in the persecution and attracted pilgrims up to
1912 and 1928 to the holy wells and penance stone.
Local gifts of land and labour in 1977 preserve
Temple Cooey

The reference to an Irish St Cooey, Abbot of Movilla cannot be found in the Irish Annals and the historical details furnished on this inscription are in need of review. *O'Laverty* (i 390–1) discusses several local traditions about St *Cú Mhaighe*, such as holy wells (see **St Cooey's Wells** above), but admits that historical details about St Cooey are not forthcoming:

> At the distance of about twenty perches from the church there is shown on the margin of a bay a flat rock in which pebbles are embedded. Prostrated on this rock, St. Cowey performed, it is said, his penitential exercises; the pebbles and some indentations in the rock, according to popular belief, mark where he placed his hands, his knees, his feet, while certain other indentations mark the spot where fell the tears which he shed. The traditions of the Lower Ards have preserved the memory of this holy man, about whom our ancient manuscripts have not recorded anything.

The Tongue An English form
J 6346

Probably so-named from its shape. For a discussion of the element "tongue" in place-names see **Kiltonga** (parish of Newtownards).

PARISH OF BANGOR

The parish of Bangor is located in the north-east of Co. Down and lies in two baronies, the greater area being situated in the most northern part of the barony of the Lower Ards, with a much smaller portion in the north-east of Lower Castlereagh. Of the thirty townlands in the parish only seven and a half are in Castlereagh Lower. The Copeland Islands are also included in this parish which comprises 17,027 acres, and 2 perches. It is bounded on the north by Belfast Lough, on the east by the parish of Donaghadee; to the south lies the parish of Newtownards, and the parish of Holywood borders it on the west. It is interesting to note that among the possessions of the monastery of Bangor outside the parish were lands centred around Glenmaye in the Isle of Man (Broderick 1981–2: 24).

According to the *Annals of Ulster* (*AU*) the monastery of Bangor was founded by St *Comgall* in 555 or 559. Bangor also has an association with St Columbanus, a pupil of Comgall, who founded the famous monastery of Bobbio in Italy. The monastery at Bangor was in its heyday in the 7th and 8th centuries but its coastal position made it an easy and frequent target for Viking raids. A particularly vicious attack took place here in 810 AD when the shrine of Comgall was pillaged and many of the clergy slain. It seems to have fallen into decline in the 10th century but was restored by St Malachy during the ecclesiastical reforms in the first quarter of the 12th century. Because of its importance in ecclesiastical terms the name Bangor is well documented in native Irish sources such as the annals and martyrologies. It also appears in the Old Irish text *Táin Bó Fraích* (*TBF*), *The Metrical Dindshenchas* (*Met. Dinds.*) and the works of the 17th-century historian, Geoffrey Keating (*Céitinn*).

As well as occurring in Irish-language sources Bangor is frequently mentioned in English language and Latin sources, both ecclesiastical and secular. In the *Ecclesiastical Taxation* 1302–6 (*Eccles. Tax.*), the church of *Bangowre* is valued at 28 marks and is cited under the rural deanery of *Blaethwyc* (see p. 213 below). The earliest records show that Bangor was generally regarded as belonging to the civil territory of the Ards. The *Book of Armagh* states the monastery of Bangor was situated in the region known as *Altitudo Ultorum*, "the height of the Ulstermen" (*EA* 13 n.p). For the re-interpretation of Ards meaning "high ground" see the introduction to the barony of the Ards.

Among the documents cited in an inquisition taken at Downpatrick on 13 October 1623 (*Ham. Copy Inq. 1623*) is an indenture dating to 5 October 1571 between Elizabeth I, Sir Thomas Smith and his son Thomas. This is interesting in that it shows that the Crown had set its sights on North Down and the Ards a quarter of a century or so before the arrival of Hamilton and Montgomery, the two principal Scottish settlers in the area in the first part of the 17th century, and before the Plantation of Ulster itself. Under the terms of this indenture the Smiths were to be granted as much land in certain parts of Ulster as they were able to conquer. Had they been successful, they would have profited greatly as the grant covered not only North Down and the Ards but extensive lands in South Antrim as well. The younger Smith was to be in charge of the military side of the affair. He landed in the Ards in 1572 but was killed by Irishmen in his own command in 1573. His father died in 1575 leaving the terms of the patent unfulfilled and, although Sir Thomas' nephew, William Smith, attempted to benefit from the grant towards the end of the first decade of the 17th century, it had by that time expired. Even though William's cause was a lost one, he persisted in making his claim to lands in the area by virtue of the 1571 indenture to his uncle and cousin. Although his challenge posed no real threat, Hamilton and Montgomery had to oppose him on this matter as late as 1623. In a grant dated to the end of the 16th century it appears that a Welshman, *Rice Ap Hugh*, was granted a lease which included the "... possesions of the

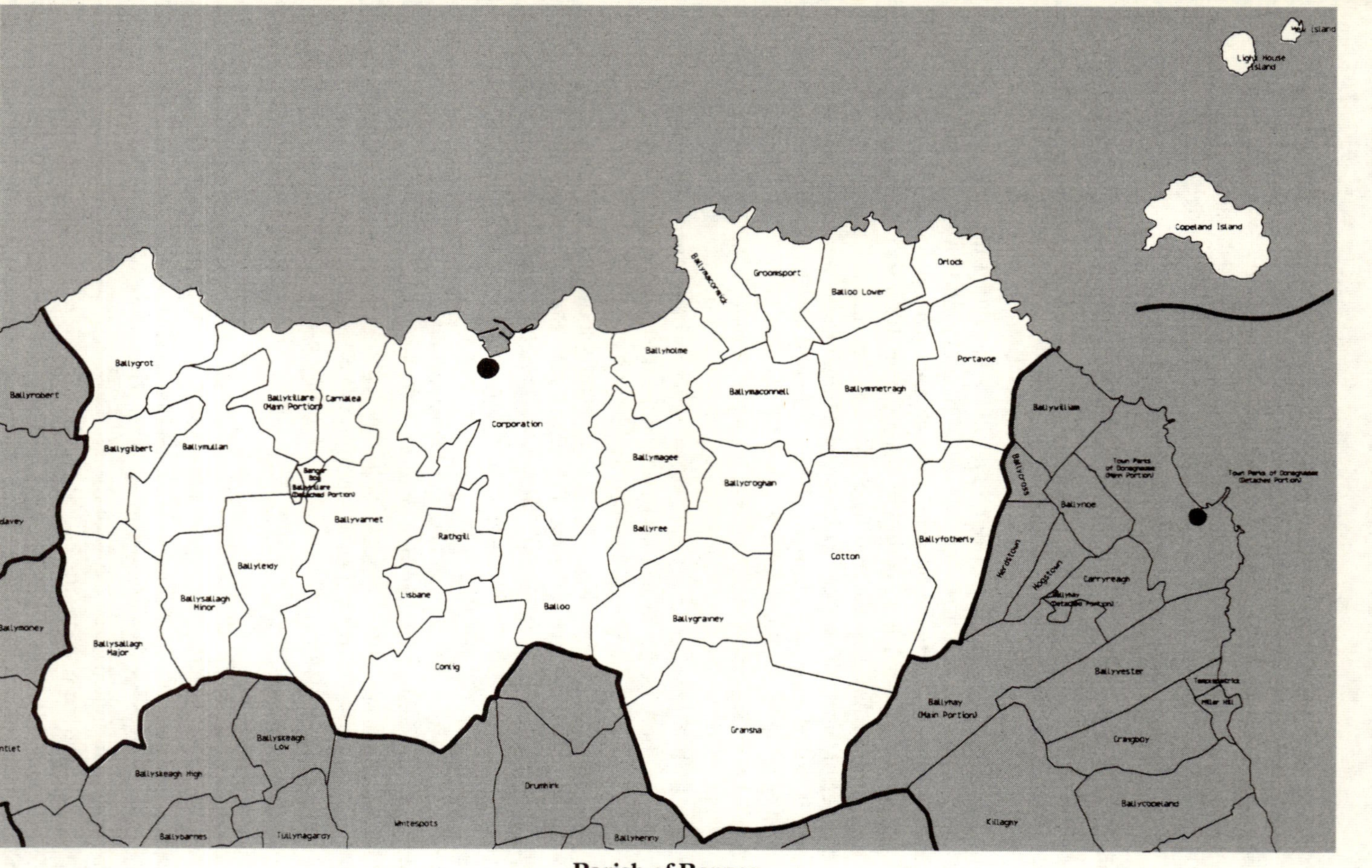

Parish of Bangor

Barony of Ards Lower (some townlands in Barony of Castlereagh Lower)

Townlands
Balloo
Balloo, Lower
Ballycroghan
Ballyfotherly
Ballygilbert
(Castlereagh Lower)
Ballygrainey
Ballygrot
(Castlereagh Lower)
Ballyholme
Ballykillare
(Castlereagh Lower)
Ballyleidy
(Castlereagh Lower)
Ballymaconnell
Ballymacormick
Ballymagee
Ballyminetragh
Ballymullan
(Castlereagh Lower)
Ballyree
Ballysallagh Major
(Castlereagh Lower)
Ballysallagh Minor
(Castlereagh Lower)
Ballyvarnet
Bangor Bog (part in
Castlereagh Lower)
Carnalea
Conlig
Corporation
Cotton
Gransha
Groomsport
Lisbane
Orlock
Portavoe
Rathgill

Islands
Copeland Island
Lighthouse Island
Mew Island
Towns: Bangor
Crawfordsburn
(Castlereagh Lower)
Groomsport

monastery of Bangar in Cloneboye" (*Fiants Eliz.* §4788 1585 A.D.) In 1604 we find that the monastery of Bangor along with its "...lands, tithes, and hereditaments..." were included in a grant to John Thomas Hibbotts and John Kinge of Dublin (*CPR Jas. I* 38a/b).

The principal Irish landowner in North Down at the start of the 17th century was Con O'Neill. As a result of some of his followers attacking a group of English soldiers Con was imprisoned in Carrickfergus castle. Hugh Montgomery of Braidstone in Ayrshire got to hear of Con's predicament and sought to gain from it by making a deal with him. In return for arranging Con's escape, passage to Scotland, and seeking his pardon from the king, with whom he had good relations, Hugh was to obtain half of Con's lands in North Down. However, before Montgomery was able to complete his side of the bargain a third party, namely James Hamilton, a Scot living in Ireland, intervened on Con's behalf in return for a portion of his lands.

On 6 December 1605 (*CPR Jas. I 84a*) the king made a grant to Thomas Ireland, a London merchant, which included substantial tracts of land in the Ards. This grant conflicted with the aforementioned grant made to Hibbots and Kinge (*CPR Jas. I* 38a-b). On 26 February 1606 Thomas Ireland assigned his rights by this grant to Hamilton. In October of the same year Hugh Montgomery purchased Movilla, Newtown (Newtownards) and Grey Abbey from Hamilton. As a result of Hamilton's role in the O'Neill affair and the tripartite agreement between Hamilton, Montgomery and Con O'Neill, he obtained a third of Con's territory, a third was later granted to Hugh Montgomery, and Con himself retained only a third of his original lands. The area Con O'Neill retained was centred round his estate at Castlereagh. James Hamilton built a house for himself in Bangor using some of the rubble from the old monastery; Montgomery first resided at *Newton* and subsequently built himself a residence in Grey Abbey which he called Rosemount. The Great Ards was apportioned to the two Scots so that the Crown might have a foothold on the east coast of Ulster where forces might be landed to control any attempt by the native Irish to usurp the newly-founded settlements.

A long and drawn out wrangle over land was to emerge between Hamilton and Montgomery and on its settlement Hamilton came out the better of the two. Montgomery continued to buy lands as well as timber and mining rights from Con O'Neill. He also covered expenses and waived debts of Con's amounting to over £2000 and, given his earlier deals with Con, it is unlikely that he did so without the precondition of gaining more of his lands. However Sir James Fullerton managed to produce documents which stated that, if O'Neill wished at any stage to sell more of his lands, he could sell only to Hamilton or, at least, not without his permission. The Earl of Abercorn, a cousin of Hamilton, was asked to settle the matter and, not surprisingly, he ruled largely in favour of his kinsman. It was decided that Hamilton and Montgomery should share the territories acquired by Montgomery from O'Neill, and Hamilton was to regrant the abbey lands allocated to Montgomery in 1605. The dispute between Hamilton and Montgomery was not finally resolved until 1626. A detailed account of the whole affair is given in M. Perceval-Maxwell (1973: 234–51).

In 1605, the site etc. of the monastery of Bangor, and its associated townlands were among the lands granted to James Hamilton by the king (*CPR Jas. I* 72b). This document shows similarities to an inquisition taken at Ballymaghan on 5 November 1603 (*Ex. Inq. 1 Jac. I*) in that the townlands occur in much the same order but the spelling of the townlands is not always the same. The townlands of the parish of Bangor are recorded in another inquisition taken at Ardquin on 4 July 1605 where they are described as having been in the possession of William O'Dornan, abbot of the monastery of Bangor, at the time of the dissolution of the monasteries in the middle of the 16th century (*Inq. Ult.* §2 Jac. I). This document bears similarities to a grant made to James Hamilton in 1605 (*CPR Jas. I* 72b). The townlands appear in roughly the same order in the two documents but there are differences in spelling. A patent dated to 14 March 1620 (*Ham. Patent* 1620) also shows similarities to the previous two documents in its citation of the townlands in Bangor parish, although again there are some differences in spelling. The same can also be said of a patent dated to 20 April 1630 (*Ham. Patent* 1630) which is a grant from Charles I to James Hamilton. A further list of the lands of the late monastery of Bangor is included in the inquisition taken at Downpatrick in 1623 (*Ham. Copy Inq.* 1623) which has already been alluded to in relation to the 1571 indenture to the Smiths. A more complete text of the 1623 inquisition than that found in *The Hamilton Manuscripts* (*Hamilton MSS.*) is housed in PRONI and this has been discussed at length by D.A. Chart (1941). A version of the same inquisition is to be found in a document dated to 1627 (*CPR Chas. I* 226–233). An inquisition taken at Killyleagh on 14 January 1644 (*Inq. Ult.* §104 Car. I) and another taken at Downpatrick on 9 April 1662 (*Inq. Ult.* §23 Car. II 1662) cite some of the lands in James Hamilton's possession, including the parish of Bangor, and again the order in which the townlands appear is similar to that of the 17th-century grants quoted above. These documents were drawn up after James' death. Other copies of them appear in *The Hamilton Manuscripts* (*Ham. Copy Inq.* 1644; *Ham. Copy Inq.* 1662) but there are differences in spelling and the text of the 1662 inquisition which appears in *Hamilton MSS* is more detailed.

An interesting source for the area has been the maps of James Hamilton's lands which were made by Thomas Raven in 1625–6 (*Raven Map Clandeboye*). The maps were commissioned not for any aesthetic value but for commercial reasons. It was important for landlords to know how many acres they had so as to maximize the potential profit from their estates and an estate survey was usually the best method of ascertaining this. One of the most notable aspects of the maps is the attention given to the boundaries of the holdings of the various tenants. Again this would be important if, for example, a dispute arose between neighbouring tenants concerning the limits of their holdings. Another notable feature of the maps is the detail given to towns such as Bangor and Holywood. As the towns held a large number of tenants, it was desirable to have them mapped carefully. Bangor is depicted as having approximately 70 English-style houses, as well as numerous rough-looking huts which probably predate the post-Plantation expansion.

In the *Census* of c. 1659 (93) Bangor is cited in the section dealing with the barony of the Ards. As the number of people in each townland is recorded in the document, we can establish that the total number of residents in the parish at this time was 595. However, "census" is something of a misnomer for this source, as it includes only those who were of a certain financial status liable to pay tax. The *Census* differentiates between Irish and English/Scottish tenants. However, as this distinction was not made on the ground but in Dublin, the figures for these two categories may not necessarily reflect the true ratio. As it stands, from a total of 595 enumerated in the parish, it appears 417 were English or Scottish. The extremely high proportion of English and Scottish planters in the parish, if accurate, is not typical of the Barony of the Ards as a whole for, out of a total of 2,431 inhabitants, the *Census* enumerates 984 as being Irish. The document also lists "tituladoes", i.e. people who held title to certain townlands. We find Robert and James Ross associated with Portavo, the Copeland Islands and Ballyfotherly; the name of George Ross, perhaps a relation of Robert and James, is listed beside Balloo; the name of William Barclay appears beside the other Balloo, i.e. *Balloo juxta Bangor* "Balloo near Bangor" as it appears in 17th-century documents; we find "Robert Cunynghame" in Ballysallagh Minor; William Crawford's name appears beside Ballymullan, and Robert Hamilton is associated with Ballygrot and the now obsolete townland of Ballyskelly. The *Subsidy Roll* of 1663 (*Sub. Roll Down*) also gives a list of those who held lands in the area, and in addition to some of the people mentioned in the *Census* of 1659 we find, among others, "James m'Dowell" of Ballymaconnell, "James o'Mulcrieve" of Ballygrainey and "John Carothers" of Groomsport.

Irish-language sources for the parish are rare apart from early references in the annals and martyrologies to Bangor itself and the territorial name Clandeboy. One source worth mentioning is a funeral oration delivered at the grave-side of Eoghan Ó Néill in 1744 (*O'Neill Fun. Oration*), which contains a small number of place-names in North Down including three from this parish *viz.* Bangor, Groomsport and Conlig. When John O'Donovan was working under the auspices of the Ordnance Survey in this area in 1834 it appears he was unable to find Irish-speaking informants in much of North Down to help him to ascertain the origin and meaning of the place-names. Writing of the parishes of Holywood and Dundonald in the *Ordnance Survey Letters* (*OSL* 6) he complains that the inhabitants were ignorant of the place-names in their area and he also felt that even their pronunciation of the names was of little use to him as it was so corrupt. Although O'Donovan makes no specific reference to Bangor in the published letters, it is likely that what he said of the inhabitants of Holywood and Dundonald regarding local knowledge of place-names could equally be applied to the people of Bangor he met during his visit. From the name-book for Bangor it is clear that the Bangor informants he did meet were all English speakers. Compared with other parishes in the south of the county for example, he made relatively little use of local informants. Among those referred to in the Bangor name-book are Colonel Ward, an unnamed farmer in the townland of Cotton, and D. Banes, chief officer of the coast guard who supplied a form for Cross Isle, one of the Copeland Islands.

A study of the documents mentioned above shows that three townland names formerly current in the parish, and five minor names within the old townland of Bangor, have fallen out of use since the 17th century. The townland names which are now defunct are *Ballyclamper*, *Carrowreagh* and *Ballyskelly*. The first two appear to have been situated in different areas of the modern townland of Ballyminetragh; *Ballyskelly* was a townland to the south of the current townland of Ballygrot and a vestige of it is to be found in the name Skelly's Hill (see **Ballyminetragh** and **Skelly's Hill** below). *Raven Map Clandeboye* contains a record of the "five" quarters of the townland Bangor. The names of the quarters appear along with a description of their position in the townland, and although part of the names has been lost due to wear of the document, it has been possible to identify three of the five quarter divisions from other sources, including *Ex. Inq. 1 Jac. I*, *CPR Jas. I*, *CPR Chas. I*, *Inq. Ult.*, *Ham. Patent 1620*, *Ham. Copy Inq. 1623*, and *Ham. Patent 1630*. The Gaelic originals of the three divisions which are identifiable from historical spellings appear to be *Ceathrú na Siúr* "the nuns' quarter"; *Ceathrú na Sruthán* "the quarter of the (small) streams"; and *Ceathrú Chnocán Dubh* "the quarter of the black hillocks".

As regards the composition of the names in the parish, it is worth noting that *baile* appears as the first element in 19 of the 30 townlands. Of these *baile*-names, native surnames appear as the second element of two of them *viz* **Ballymaconnell** and **Ballymacormick**; the Anglo-Norman name *Gilbert* forms the second element in **Ballygilbert**, while the second element in **Ballyholme** may either reflect Norse influence or it may be an English surname. As the parish has a considerable length of coastline, it is no surprise to find two townlands containing the element *port* "a port", **Portavoe** and **Groomsport**. The elements *lios* and *ráth* can both be translated "fort", and are found in two townland names in the parish, **Rathgill/Rathgael** and **Lisbane**. As the late Deirdre Flanagan has pointed out, *lios* is commonly used in the north and west of Ireland for fort, whereas *ráth* is more frequent in the east and south-east (Flanagan 1980–1(a)). Compared with the neighbouring parish of

Donaghadee, the Norman element in the place-names of Bangor is slight. **Ballygilbert** has already been mentioned in this respect and the only other instances of Norman influence on the toponymy appear to be the townland name **Gransha** which derives from Irish *Gráinseach* (a borrowing from French *grange*), and the name of the **Copeland Islands** which may have been derived from the Norman family of de Coupland.

PARISH NAME

Bangor J 5082	*Beannchar* meaning uncertain	
1. Beannchair, natiuitas Comgaill	AU (Mac Airt) 62	516
2. Bendchair, eaccluis	AFM i 188	552
3. Bennchuir, eclesia	AU (Mac Airt) 78	555
4. Bendchair, iascaire Comhgaill	AFM i 202	559
5. Benncair, eclesia	AU (Mac Airt) 80	559
6. Bendchair, S. Comhgall	AFM i 224	600
7. Bendchair Uladh, abb	AFM i 224	600
8. Bennchair, Quies Comghaill	AU (Mac Airt) 100	602
9. Bennchoir, abbatis	AU (Mac Airt) 104	610
10. Bennchair Uladh, ecclas	AFM i 236 *et passim*	611
11. Benncoir, abbas	AU (Mac Airt) 106	613
12. Benncoir, combustio	AU (Mac Airt) 108	616
13. Benchuir bona regula	Antiph. Bangor i 30r	650c
14. mBendchair Uladh, hi	AFM i 278	666
15. Benncuir, abbas	AU (Mac Airt) 180	728
16. mBennchoir, for altóir	AFM i 340	739
17. Bennchuir, abb	AFM i 342	742
18. Bendchuir, abb	AFM i 410	800
19. Bendchor	Triads of Ireland 2	800c
20. Bendchuir	Triads of Ireland 4	800c
21. Bennchur, oc	TBF 16	800c
22. mBennchoir, Trácht	TBF 16	800c
23. Bennchor, o	AU (Mac Airt) 280 *et passim*	824
24. Bennchair, ab[ad]	Mart. Tal. Feb 28 19	830c
25. Bennchair, ab[ad]	Mart. Tal. April 8 31	830c
26. Bendchair, ab[ad]	Mart. Tal. June 12 49 *et passim*	830c
27. Bennchoir, hi féil Silláin	Fél. Óeng. Feb 28 63	830c
28. Bennchuir, Cenn-faelad abb	Fél. Óeng. April 8 105	830c
29. Bennchuir, Comgall buadach	Fél. Óeng. May 10 123	830c
30. Bennchuir, comarbai búain	Fél. Óeng. Dec 15 251	830c
31. Beannchair, abb	AFM i 534	884
32. Bennchur, co	San. Corm. (YBL)	1000c
33. mBennchar, a	AU (Mac Airt) 502	1065
34. Bennchair, co amsir Comgaill	LU l. 3093	1100c
35. Beannchor Ulad	Met. Dinds. iv 224	1100c
36. Bennchair, Comgall	CSH 97. 16 *et passim*	1125c
37. Bennchuir, Mochoemoc	CSH 707.740 150	1125c
38. Bendchur, Mobae ó	CSH 707.803 151	1125c

39.	Bennchoir, Comgall	CSH 712.11 161	1125c
40.	Bennchuir (gen.)	Fél. Óeng. May 10 p130n	1400c
41.	Bennchur	Fél. Óeng. May 10 p130n	1400c
42.	Bennchor	Fél. Óeng. March 30 p102n	1453
43.	Bennchuir, abb	Mart. Don. May 10 p122 *et passim*	1630c
44.	Bennchair, abb	Mart. Don. April 8 p98 *et passim*	1630c
45.	Bennchair Uladh, abb	Mart. Don. Feb 28 p58	1630c
46.	Bendchair, abb	Mart. Don. Aug 1 p208	1630c
47.	Beannchuir, Reghuil	Mart. Don. June 11 p166	1630c
48.	Beannchair	Céitinn iii 138	1633c
49.	Beannchair, Magh	Céitinn iii 138	1633c
50.	mBeannchuir, fa iath mbraonsholus	LCABuidhe 106	1680c
51.	Bheannchuir, ó bhaidhbh	LCABuidhe 107	1680c
52.	Beannchuir, eó	LCABuidhe 260	1680c
53.	Benchor	MacCana's Itinerary 55	1700c
54.	Beanchor	O'Neill Fun. Oration 267	1744
55.	Benchorensis	Antiph. Bangor 36v	650c
56.	Bangowre	Eccles. Tax. 12	1306c
57.	Beandehar	Annates Ulst. 295	1429
58.	Bangor, Mon. de	Annates Ulst. 117 app.	1454
59.	Beannchor	Annates Ulst. 110	1470
60.	Bengor	Annates Ulst. 113	1500
61.	Bangor	Annates Ulst. 114	1510
62.	Bangar	Goghe's Map	1567
63.	Bangor Ca[...]	Early Chart B'fast Lough	1570c
64.	Bangar	Nowel's Ire. (1)	1570c
65.	Bang[a?r]	Ortelius Map	1572
66.	Banger Abbay	S-E Ulster Map	1580c
67.	Bangar	Fiants Eliz. §4788	1585
68.	Bangan	Hondius' Map	1591
69.	Bangor ab	Mercator's Ire.	1595
70.	Bangor abb	Mercator's Ulst.	1595
71.	Banchorie	CSP Ire. 676	1598
72.	Bancor	Bartlett Maps (Esch. Co. Maps) i	1603
73.	Bangor al Banger	Ex. Inq. 1 Jac. I	1603
74.	Bangor al val Angloru	Inq. Ult. (Down) §2 Jac. I	1605
75.	Bangor	Inq. Ult. (Down) §2 Jac. I	1605
76.	Bangor otherwise Banger	CPR Jas. I 72b	1605
77.	M[c] Banger	Speed's Ulster	1610
78.	M[c] Banger	Speed's Antrim & Down	1610
79.	M. Banger	Speed's Ireland	1610
80.	Bancher monasterium	Mercator's/Hole's Ire.	1610
81.	Bancor	Norden's Map	1610c
82.	Bangor	Terrier (Reeves) 49	1615c
83.	Bangor	Terrier (O'Laverty) 326	1615c
84.	Bangor	Ham. Patent xx	1620
85.	Bangor	Ulster Visit. (Reeves) 47	1622

86.	Bangor	Raven Map Clandeboye 11	1625c
87.	Bangor	CPR Chas. I 225	1627
88.	Bangor	Ham. Patent x	1630
89.	Bangor	Inq. Down (Reeves1) 137	1657
90.	Bangor	Trien. Visit. (Bramhall) 13	1661
91.	Bangor	Trien. Visit. (Margetson) 22	1664
92.	Bangor	Trien. Visit. (Boyle) 44	1679
93.	Bangor	Collins B'fast Lough	1693
94.	Bangor	Wm. Map (OSNB) No. 54	1810
95.	Bangor	Bnd. Sur. (OSNB) No. 54	1830c
96.	Beannchair "little peaks, cows horns"	J O'D (OSNB) No. 54	1834c
97.	Beannchar Árd Uladh	Post-Sheanchas 33	1905
98.	Beannchar	AGBP 144	1969
99.	Beannchar	Éire Thuaidh	1988
100.	Beannchar	GÉ 118	1989
101.	'baŋgər	Local pronunciation	1991

Although there is no shortage of stories explaining how Bangor was named, there is no certainty as to which of them, if any, is correct. A number of Irish-language sources offer origin legends and meanings for the name *Bennchor*, later *Beannchar*. The Old Irish text *Táin Bó Fraích* (*TBF* 15–6) contains an explanation of *Trácht mBennchoir* "Bangor strand". The Connaught warrior *Fróech* and the Ulster warrior *Conall Cernach* were returning to Ireland from the Alps with Fróech's cattle when Conall's servant, *Bicne mac Láegaire*, died at the place which then came to be known as *Inber mBicne*, today Bangor Bay. When they came to shore, the cattle shed their horns, thus giving rise to the name *Trácht mBennchoir*, "the strand of the horn-casting". Here *Bennchor* is taken to derive from *benn* "horn" + *cor* "casting". In a poem in *Met. Dinds.* (iv 224) which echoes the above incident from *TBF*, *Beannchor Ulad* is explained as "the horn-casting of the Ulstermen". Another explanation of how *Bennchor* was named is given in *Fél. Óeng.* (10 May 130). It is obviously based on the *TBF* episode already mentioned but in this case Conall Cernach, on hearing of the death of the Ulster champion *Cú Chulainn*, put the horns of the cattle in the ground. Here, *Bennchor* is taken as a compound of *benn* "horn" + *cor*, in the sense "putting". An etymology of the name *Bennchor* is offered in the genealogy of the *Osraige* in The Book of Leinster (*CGH* 101). According to this account the name *Beannchar* came about as a result of a cattle tribute imposed by *Bressal Brecc*. In this case *Bennchor* literally meant "horn contract" i.e. "cattle contract".

The 17th-century historian Geoffrey Keating (*Céitinn* iii 138) gives an explanation of the name *Beannchar* along the same lines as, and probably influenced by, the *TBF* account of the name already referred to. It is noteworthy that reference is made here to the Leinster king Breasal Breac, who also featured in the rather obscure explanation of the name *Bennchor* in the genealogy of the Osraige. It is strange that the nom. sing. form here is *Beannchair*, as this is the normal gen. sing. of the name. Perhaps it has been influenced by forms in the annals and martyrologies where the gen. form tends to prevail due to entries such as *abb Bennchuir* "abbot of Bangor" etc. Alternatively, it may be simply a mistake on the part of the editor.

> *Agus is uime ghairthear Beannchair don áit sin, Breasal Breac rí Laighean do chuaidh le líon sluath do chreachadh Alban, go dtug iomad buair is bótháinte leis in Éirinn, agus iar dteacht i dtír dó féin is dá shluath do rinneadh forlongphoirt leo san áit dá ngairthear Beannchair*

anois, is marbhthar iomad do na buaibh leo mar fheolmhach, go ráinig iomad d'adharcaibh na mbó nó da (sic) mbeannaibh feadh an mhachaire, go ráinig Magh Beannchair d'ainm ar an áit de sin. Agus aimsear imchian dá éis sin an tan do thógaibh an t-abb naomhtha Comhghall mainistear san áit chéadna, tug fá deara a slonnadh ón áit ionar tógbhadh í, gonadh uime sin ráidhtear mainistear Bheannchair ria.

"And the reason why this place is called *Beannchair* is this. *Breasal Breac*, king of Leinster, went with a full host to plunder Scotland, and brought a great deal of cattle and herds with him to Ireland, and when he and his host came to land they made a camp in the place which is now called *Beannchair*, and they killed many of the cows for meat, and many of the cows' horns....came to be (left) throughout the plain, and the name of *Magh Beannchair* came to be given to the place. And a long time after that when the holy abbot *Comhghall* built a monastery in the same place, he had it named from the place in which it was built, and so it is called the monastery of Bangor."

According to Reeves, Ware and Colgan took Bangor to mean "white choir"; Colgan glosses Irish *Ban-chora* with Latin *pulcher chorus vel albus chorus* "beautiful or white choir" (*EA* 199). It is worth mentioning that the word *choir* was originally applied to the part of the church which housed the band of singers who performed during services. Reeves also quotes an extract from Jocelin's *Life of St Patrick* according to which the saint had a vision near the site where the monastery came to be built (*EA ibid.*). Looking down on the glen filled with heavenly light, he and his company saw a host of heavenly soldiers and heard the singing of the celestial choir. It is thought that this tradition gave rise to the Latin name *Vallis Angelorum* "vale of angels", which is sometimes found applied to Bangor, even as late as the 17th century (74).

More recent scholars have not been convinced by these explanations of *Bennchor*, *Beannchar*. The most likely theory, though it is by no means certain, is that of Joyce who says that *Beannchar* contains the word *beann* "horn" which "signifies horns, or pointed hills or rocks, and sometimes simply peaked hill" (*Joyce* i 385). Joyce seems to be suggesting a compound *beannach* + *ar*, where the first element consists of *beann* + adjectival suffix *-ach*, followed by the suffix *-ar*. This would result in a form *Beannachar*, which would become *Beannchar* by syncope. Joyce also mentions Bannagher in Co. Offaly, which he claims was named from the sharp rocks in the adjacent River Shannon. It is also possible that Bangor, Co. Down, was named from sharp rocks around the shore.

There are a number of townlands in various parts of Ireland which have been anglicized Banagher and derive from an original *Beannchar*: examples include Banagher, parish of Fiddown, Co. Kilkenny, Loch Banagher, parish of Killymard, Co. Donegal, and **Drumbanagher**, parish of Killevy, Co. Armagh. It seems strange, however, that *Beannchar* in North Down should be anglicized as *Bangor*. Perhaps it was influenced by the name Bangor which is commonly used as the name of ecclesiastical sites in Wales. The two names may share some common attributes. In a forthcoming article in *Ainm* v, Bedwyr Lewis Jones draws some interesting parallels between the name Bangor in Wales, and Bangor in Co. Down. Alfred Neobard Palmer has suggested that Bangor in Wales normally meant "high choir" (Palmer 1990); however, he also states (*ibid.*) that *bangor* is found in the Welsh laws meaning "wattling". Ifor Williams derives Welsh Bangor from *ban* "a band used to strengthen something" + *côr* "a plaiting" (Williams 1990). Melville Richards takes Welsh Bangor to mean "a cross-bar in a wattled fence", which referred to either the wattled construction of the monastic cell, or to a fence surrounding it (Richards 1970). This suggests another possible derivation for Irish *Beannchar*. One meaning for the first element *benn* is "prong" (*DIL* s.v.); the second element could be *cor* "act of putting, placing; setting up". If this etymology is accepted, it could be argued that *beannchar* refers to a type of fence constructed with prongs surrounding the monastic site, and that it subsequently came to mean the area within the enclosure.

TOWNLAND NAMES

Balloo — *Baile Aodha*
J 5079 — "Hugh's townland"

1. Balow juxta Bangor	Inq. Ult. (Down) §104 Car. I	1645
2. Ballow next Bangor	Census 93	1659c
3. Ballow juxta Bangor 3 quarters	BSD 90	1661
4. Ballow ppe Bangor	Inq. Ult. (Down) §23 Car. II	1662
5. bɑ'lu:	Local pronunciation	1991

See **Balloo Lower**.

Balloo Lower — *Baile Aodha*
J 5482 — "Hugh's townland"

1. Ballow	Ex. Inq. 1 Jac. I	1603
2. Ballowe	CPR Jas. I 38a	1604
3. Ballow	Inq. Ult. (Down) §2 Jac. I	1605
4. Ballow	CPR Jas. I 72b	1605
5. Ballowe	Ham. Patent xx	1620
6. Ballowe-juxta mare	Ham. Copy Inq. xxx	1623
7. Balowe	Raven Map Clandeboye 17	1625c
8. Ballowe	Raven Map Clandeboye 11	1625c
9. Balow	Raven Map Clandeboye 18	1625c
10. Ballow	Raven Map Clandeboye 20	1625
11. Ballow	Ham. Patent x	1630
12. Balow	Inq. Ult. (Down) §104 Car. I	1645
13. Ballow	Census 93	1659c
14. Ballow, juxta Mare, the two parts of	BSD 90	1661
15. Ballow ppe mare	Inq. Ult. (Down) §23 Car.II	1662
16. Ballow	Wm. Map (OSNB) No. 54	1810
17. Ballow	Bnd. Sur. (OSNB) No. 54	1830
18. Baile Logha "Luoy's town"	J O'D (OSNB) No. 54	1834c
19. Bail'-Lugha, the town of Lugh/Lewy	Joyce iii 101	1913
20. bɑ'lu:	Local pronunciation	1991

The name Balloo is applied to two separate townlands in this parish, **Balloo** and Balloo Lower. It should be pointed out that this is not an example of a townland having been divided. In such cases the two townlands are generally contiguous such as **Ballysallagh Major** and **Ballysallagh Minor**, also in this parish. From the map it is clear that the two townlands called Balloo in the parish of Bangor are separated by quite a distance. Balloo

Lower is in the north-eastern corner of the parish and borders the sea; the other Balloo occupies a central position in the parish to the south of the town of Bangor.

The order in which forms 1–5 and 11–13 appear in their respective documents establishes that they refer to what is today designated Balloo Lower. Balloo Lower appears in some documents with the qualifier *juxta mare* "beside the sea", to distinguish it from the other Balloo, which in turn appears with the qualifier, *juxta Bangor* "beside Bangor".

Ballycroghan — *Baile Cruacháin*
J 5380 — "townland of the (small) stack/hill"

1.	Balecrohan	Ex. Inq. 1 Jac. I	1603
2.	Ballecrohane	CPR Jas. I 38a	1604
3.	Ballicrioghan	Inq. Ult. (Down) §2 Jac. I	1605
4.	Ballecrohan	CPR Jas. I 72b	1605
5.	Ballicroghan	Ham. Patent xx	1620
6.	Ballycroghen	Ham. Copy Inq. xxx	1623
7.	Ba: Crohan	Raven Map Clandeboye 15	1625c
8.	Ballecroghan	Ham. Patent xi	1630
9.	Ballecroghan	Inq. Ult. (Down) §104 Car. I	1645
10.	Ballycroghan	Census 94	1659c
11.	Ballecroghane	BSD 90	1661
12.	Ballycroghan	Inq. Ult. (Down) §23 Car. II	1662
13.	Ballycroghan	Wm. Map (OSNB) No. 54	1810
14.	Baile Cruacháin "town of the round hill"	J O'D (OSNB) No. 54	1834c
15.	ˌbɑliˈkrɔxən	Local pronunciation	1991

O'Donovan seems to have been correct in identifying the second element of this place-name as the gen. sing. of the word *cruachán* which is defined in *DIL* as "small rick, hill" and in *Ó Dónaill* as "a (small) stack". It occurs in a number of place-names in Ireland including the Irish form for Crookhaven, Co. Cork, namely *An Cruachán*, and in the name Croghan, Co. Offaly.

Ballyfotherly — *Baile Phúdarlaigh*
J 5579 — "Powderly's townland"

1.	Ballefredor	Ex. Inq. 1 Jac. I	1603
2.	Ballyfredon al Balliphooderlie	Inq. Ult. (Down) §2 Jac. I	1605
3.	Ballifredor al Ballipheoderly	Ham. Patent xx	1620
4.	Ballyffoderlie al Ballypheoderlie	Ham. Copy Inq. xxx	1623
5.	Ba: fuderle	Raven Map Clandeboye 18, 25	1625c
6.	Ba: Fuderlee	Raven Map Clandeboye 20	1625c
7.	Ba: Fvderle	Raven Map Clandeboye 19	1625c
8.	Ballyfoderlies or Ballepheoderlie	Ham. Patent x	1630
9.	Ballefodderlie al Ballepheoderlie	Inq. Ult. (Down) §104 Car. I	1645
10.	Ballyfutherly	Census 93	1659c
11.	Ballefodderly	BSD 89	1661
12.	Ballyfoddyglan al Ballyfadderly	Inq. Ult. (Down) §23 Car. II	1662
13.	Ballyfotherly	Wm. Map (OSNB) No. 54	1810

14. Ballyfotherly	Bnd. Sur. (OSNB) No. 54	1830c
15. Baile Uí Fotharlaigh "O'Fotherly's town"	J O'D (OSNB) No. 54	1834
16. ˌbɑliˈfɔðərli	Local pronunciation	1991

The second element of this name is somewhat problematic but it may be an attempt to represent the uncommon surname Powderly. Unfortunately little is known of this name at present. Woulfe (1923: 147) gives a Gaelic form of it, *Púdarlaigh*. MacLysaght (1985: 247) suggests that Powderly is derived from Powderlough in Co. Meath. He also states that the majority of the references he has to it are from Cos. Meath and Louth and that none of them predate 1750.

Ballygilbert
J 4580

Baile Ghilbeirt
"Gilbert's townland"

1. Ba: Gilbarte	Raven Map Clandeboye 4	1625c
2. Ba: Gilbarte	Raven Map Clandeboye 6	1625c
3. Ba: Gilbart	Raven Map Clandeboye 2	1625c
4. Ballegilbert	Inq. Ult. (Down) §104 Car. I	1645
5. Ballygilbert	Census 94	1659c
6. Ballegillbert	BSD 124	1661
7. Ballygilbert	Ham. Copy Rental 110	1681
8. Ballygilbert	Wm. Map (OSNB) No. 54	1810
9. Ballygilbert	Bnd. Sur. (OSNB) No. 54	1830c
10. Ballygilbert	Grand Jury Pres. (OSNB) No. 54	1834c
11. Baile Ghilbert "Gilbert's town"	J O'D (OSNB) No. 54	1834c
12. ˌbaliˈgilbərt	Local pronunciation	1991

The second element is clearly the name Gilbert which was common among the Anglo-Normans. According to Rainey (1958: 134) this name is of Germanic origin. He cites two Old German forms, *Gisilbert*, *Gislebert*, meaning "pledge- or hostage-bright". There is another **Ballygilbert** in the parish of Bright in the barony of Lecale, Co. Down.

Ballygrainey
J 5278

Baile na Gréine
"sunny townland" lit. "townland of the sun"

1. Balleocrane	Ex. Inq. 1 Jac. I	1603
2. Ballyreeny al Ballyocrane	Ham. Copy Inq. xxxi	1623
3. Balliorane al Ballinegrene	Ham. Patent xx	1630
4. Ballereeny or Balliocrane	Ham. Patent xi	1630
5. Ballenegreme al Balleocrane	Inq. Ult. (Down) §104 Car. I	1645
6. Ballygreny	Census 94	1659c
7. Ballegrenny	BSD 124	1661
8. Ballygrany	Wm. Map (OSNB) No. 54	1810
9. Ballygrainey	Bnd. Sur. (OSNB) No. 54	1830
10. Ballyrainey	Grand Jury Pres. (OSNB)	
11. Baile Gráine "Gracey's town"	J O'D (OSNB) No. 54	1834c
12. Baile na Gréine	AGBP 113	1969

13. Baile na Gréine	GÉ 23	1989
14. ˌbali'gre:ni	Local pronunciation	1991

Forms 1, 2b, 3a and 4b all contain an internal *o* which could indicate that the second element is a surname. However, it is likely that forms 2b, 3a and 4b emanate from form 1 which is cited from a document containing a number of unreliable spellings (*Ex. Inq. 1 Jac. I*).

Forms 3b and 5a show vestiges of the gen. sing. fem. form of the definite article which is no longer present in the modern anglicized form of this name. The gen. sing. of *grian* "sun" is used as an element in a number of place-names: Tuamgraney, in Co. Clare derives from *Tuaim Gréine*, (*GÉ* 169), and note the townland of Ballynagrena in Co. Louth which derives from the same Irish original as Ballygrainey in the parish of Bangor (*L. Log. Lú* 8).

Ballygrot
J 4582

Baile na gCrot
"townland of the small eminences"

1. Ballirotte	Ex. Inq. 1 Jac. I	1603
2. Ballecrotte	CPR Jas. I 38a	1604
3. Ballicrott	Inq. Ult. (Down) §2 Jac. I	1605
4. Ballecrotte	CPR Jas. I 72b	1605
5. Ballecrott	Ham. Patent xx	1620
6. Bally-Crott	Ham. Copy Inq. xxxi	1623
7. Balle Grott	Raven Map Clandeboye 3, 4	1625c
8. Ballecrott	Ham. Patent xi	1630
9. (?)Ballerott	Inq. Ult. (Down) §104 Car. I	1645
10 . Ballecrott	Inq. Ult. (Down) §104 Car. I	1645
11. Ballygrott	Census 94	1659c
12. Ballegrot + Ballyskelly	BSD 124	1661
13 Ballycrott	Inq. Ult. (Down) §23 Car. II	1662
14. Ballygrott	Ham. Copy Rental 110	1681
15. Ballygrotte	Wm. Map (OSNB) No. 54	1810
16. Ballygrot	Bnd. Sur. (OSNB) No. 54	1830
17. Baile gCrot "town of the hillocks or tummocks"	J O'D (OSNB) No. 54	1834c
18. ˌbali'grɔt	Local pronunciation	1991

It seems that the final element of this place-name is *crot* "small eminence". Forms 1–6 would suggest an original *Baile Crot*, but forms 7, 11, 12a, 14–16 where the second element begins with a *g*, may derive from *Baile na gCrot*, with subsequent loss of the gen. pl. form of the article. Alternatively, they may emanate from an acc. sing. form of the name, *Baile (g)Crot*.

Ballyholme
J 5382

Baile Hóm
meaning uncertain

1. Ballehum	Ex. Inq. 1 Jac. I	1603
2. Ballehunne	CPR Jas. I 38a	1604
3. Ballihum al Ballihummogh	Inq. Ult. (Down) §2 Jac. I	1605
4. Ballihome al Balliniminagh	Ham. Patent xx	1620
5. Ballyholme	Ham. Copy Inq. lii	1623
6. Ballyholmie	Ham. Copy Inq.xxx	1623

7. B[a: H]olmie	Raven Map Clandeboye 11	1625c
8. Balle Holme	Raven Map Clandeboye 14	1625c
9. Balleholmie	Raven Map Clandeboye 11	1625c
10. Ballyholviev or Ballehomie	Ham. Patent xi	1630
11. Ballehelme al Ballehomie	Inq. Ult. (Down) §104 Car. I	1645
12. Ballyholme	Census 94	1659c
13. Ballehollin	BSD 90	1661
14. Ballyholin	Wm. Map (OSNB) No. 54	1810
15. Ballyholm	Bnd. Sur. (OSNB) No. 54	1830c
16. Baile Holme "Holme's Town"	J O'D (OSNB) No. 54	1834c
17. Baile Hóm	AGBP 113	1969
18. Baile Hóm	GÉ 19	1989
19. ˌbaliˈho:m	Local pronunciation	1991

This name is troublesome in that it is difficult to decipher the second element from the historical forms. Among the meanings given under "holm" in the *Shorter OED* is "a piece of flat low-lying ground by a river"; the definition in *Concise Scots Dict.* of "holm" is in agreement with this. In an unpublished lecture, the late Deirdre Flanagan suggested that the second element of Ballyholme might be the Old Norse word *holmr* "river meadow", which was borrowed into English as "holm". It is significant that one of the few noteworthy Viking burial sites in Ireland has been found near the shore at Ballyholme, and indeed other artifacts attributed to the Vikings have also been found in the area (*ASCD* 102, 140).

There is also a possibility that the second element of Ballyholme is a surname.The name Holm(es) derives from Old Norse *holmr*. The surname is understood to have arisen from someone who lived in a "residence near a flat piece of land in a fen or by a piece of land partly surrounded by streams" (Reaney 1958: 168). Furthermore Reaney explains that Middle English *holm* can also derive from Old English *hole(g)n* > Middle English *holin, holm* "holly, holm-oak". In this case the meaning would be "dweller by a holm-oak".

Ballykillare — *Baile Cille Láir*

J 4781 — "townland of the central church

1. Ballen, Cellor	Ex. Inq. 1 Jac. I	1603
2. Ballen-Cellor	CPR Jas. I 38a	1605
3. Ballen-Celloe al Ballikillar	Inq. Ult. (Down) §2 Jac I	1605
4. Ballencellor	CPR Jas. I 72b	1605
5. Ballincelloer al Ballikillar	Ham. Patent xx	1620
6. Bally-Killare al Ballincellor	Ham. Copy Inq. xxxi	1623
7. Ballekillare or Ballincellor	Ham. Patent xi	1630
8. Ballekillare al Ballecollor	Inq. Ult. (Down) §104 Car I	1644
9. Killaire & Carnelea	Census 94	1659c
10. Ballykillare al. Ballycoller	Inq. Ult. (Down) §23 Car. II	1662
11. Part Killare	Ham. Copy Rental 110	1681
12. Ballykillare	Wm. Map (OSNB) No. 54	1810
13. Ballykillare	Bnd. Sur. (OSNB) No. 54	1830c
14. Ballykillare	Treas. Warrant (OSNB) No. 54	1830c
15. Baile an Choiléir "town of the quarry"	J O'D (OSNB) No. 54	1834c

16. "townland of the western church"	O'Laverty ii 130	1880
17. ˌbalikəˈleːr	Local pronunciation	1991

The main part of this townland is on the North Down coast; the detached portion encroaches on the village of Crawfordsburn from the west. The forms seem to suggest two possible Irish origins for this name: *Baile Cille Láir* "townland of the central church", and *Baile an Cheallóra* "townland of the cellarer". However, for the latter to be feasible the stress in the current form would have to be on *kil*. On the strength of the local pronunciation, *Baile Cille Láir* seems to be the more likely of the two.

Ballyleidy — *Baile Uí Lidí*
J 4779 — "Ó Lidí's townland"

1. Ba: Leede	Raven Map Clandeboye 9	1625c
2. Ba: Leade	Raven Map Clandeboye 10	1625c
3. Balleliddie	Ham. Patent xi	1630
4. Balledie	Inq. Ult. (Down) §104 Car I	1644
5. Ballylidie	Census 94	1659c
6. Ballelidie	BSD 127	1661
7. Ballylidie	Inq. Ult. (Down) §23 Car II	1662
8. Ballyleidy	Wm. Map (OSNB) No. 54	1810
9. Ballyleidy	Bnd. Sur. (OSNB) No. 54	1830c
10. Baile Lideadha "Liddy's town"	J O'D (OSNB) No. 54	1834c
11. Baile-Ui-Lideadha "the town of O"Leidy/Liddy"	Joyce iii 101	1913
12. ˌbaliˈleːdi	Local pronunciation	1991

Despite having numerous forms from the 17th century, it is difficult to ascertain the original Irish form of this name. O'Donovan suggested that the second element was the surname *Ó Lideadha* (later *Ó Lidí*). According to MacLysaght, the bearers of this surname held considerable sway in Thomond. He also informs us that the surname is found in Co. Cavan where it is generally anglicized Leddy (MacLysaght 1985: 195). This is noteworthy since it shows that the name was not unknown in Ulster. Unfortunately, the first *i* is short in this surname, but it is possible that the vowel sound changed under the influence of the English word "lady".

Ballymaconnell — *Baile Mhic Dhónaill*
J 5381 — "McConnell's townland"

1. Ballemaconmell	Ex. Inq. 1 Jac. I	1603
2. Ballem^{c}connell	CPR Jas. I 38a	1605
3. Ballem^{c}connell	CPR Jas. I 72b	1605
4. Ballimackonnill	Inq. Ult. (Down) §2 Jac I	1605
5. Ballimaconnell	CPR Jas. I 326a	1618
6. Ballymaconnell al Bally-M'Conyle	Ham. Copy Inq. xxx	1623
7. Ba: mac Connell	Raven Map Clandeboye 14, 15	1625c
8. Balle M'Connell or Balle M'Koneile	Ham. Patent xi	1630
9. Ballemaconell al. Ballemackonill	Inq. Ult. (Down) §104 Car I	1644

10. Bally McConnell	Census 93	1659c
11. Ballym^{cc}connell	BSD 91	1661
12. Ballym'Connell	Sub. Roll Down 281	1663
13. Ballymaconnell	Ham. Copy Rental 110	1681
14. Ballymaconnell	Wm. Map (OSNB) No. 54	1810
15. Ballymaconnell	Bnd. Sur. (OSNB) No. 54	1830c
16. Baile Mic Conaill "Mac Connell's town"	J O'D (OSNB) No. 54	1834c
17. ˌbaliməˈko.nəl	Local pronunciation	1991

As MacLysaght (1985: 54) points out, the surname Mac Connell is very common in Antrim, Down and Tyrone. It can usually be traced back to Irish *Mac Dhónaill* earlier *Mac Dhomhnaill*. Initial *dh* is pronounced [ɣ] but in the anglicization process, since the sound [ɣ] does not occur in English, the *c* of *mac* prevailed and this resulted in the anglicized form Mac Connell. A number of other *mac*-surnames contain an initial aspirated *d* and these too give rise to anglicized forms beginning with *c*. For example, *Mac Dhonnchaidh*, which is anglicized Mc Conaghy, Mc Conkey etc, and *Mac Dhaibhéid*, from which emanate Mc Cavitt, Mc Kevitt etc.

Ballymacormick *Baile Mhic Cormaic*
J 5283 "Mc Cormick's townland"

1. Ballecormack	Ex. Inq. 1 Jac. I	1603
2. Ballycormack al Ballmacormuck	Inq. Ult. (Down) §2 Jac. I	1605
3. Ballycormach	CPR Jas. I 72b	1605
4. Ballycormach(?)	CPR Jas. I 72b	1606
5. Ballicormagh al Ballimaccormick	Ham. Patent xx	1620
6. Bally-Mc Cormick al Ballymacormugh	Ham. Copy Inq. xxx	1623
7. Balle ma Cormack	Raven Map Clandeboye 15	1625c
8. Balle Ma Cormock	Raven Map Clandeboye 16	1625c
9. Ballemacormick or Ballemacosmaghs	Ham. Patent xi	1630
10. Ballenacormuck al Ballemacormagh	Inq. Ult. (Down) §104 Car. I	1645
11. Bally Mc Cormick	Census 93	1659c
12. Ballemc cormicke, 2 parts	BSD 90	1661
13. Ballymaccormick al Ballymaccormagh	Inq. Ult. (Down) §23 Car. II	1662
14. Ballymacormick	Ham. Copy Rental 110	1681
15. Ballycormick	Wm. Map (OSNB) No. 54	1810
16. Ballycormack	Downshire Direct. 318	1823
17. Ballymacormick	Bnd. Sur. (OSNB) No. 54	1830c
18. Ballycormack	Grand Jury Pres. (OSNB)	
19. Baile Mic Cormaic "Mac Cormack's town"	J O'D (OSNB) No. 54	1834c
20. ˌbaliməˈkɔrmik	Local pronunciation	1991

It is no surprise to find the surname Mac Cormick as the second element of this place-name, as it is one of the fifty most common surnames in Ulster (Bell 1988: 145). Forms 15, 16, and 18 have lost the *mac* of the surname but the earlier forms illustrate its presence quite clearly.

Ballymagee *Baile Mhig Aodha*
J 5280 "Magee's towland"

1.	Ballenoghur	Ex. Inq. 1 Jac. I	1603
2.	Ballinenoghue al. Ballmaguigh	Inq. Ult. (Down) §2 Jac I	1605
3.	Ballenoghue	CPR Jas. I 38a	1605
4.	Ballnoghue	CPR Jas. I 72b	1605
5.	Ballinenoghwe al Ballinaghie al Ballimagwigh	Ham. Patent xx	1620
6.	Bally-Naghie al Bally-Nenoghne al Ballymenaghne	Ham. Copy Inq. xxx	1623
7.	Ba Naghue	Raven Map Clandeboye 11	1625c
8.	Ballenaghue	Raven Map Clandeboye 11	1625c
9.	Ba: Ma[c] Gee	Raven Map Clandeboye 13	1625c
10.	Balle mac[c] Gee Hill	Raven Map Clandeboye 14	1625c
11.	Ballynaghie or Ballenenoghnie or Ballemenaghne	Ham. Patent xi	1630
12.	Bally Neghee	Census 94	1659c
13.	Ballynogher	BSD 90	1661
14.	Ballinagud al. Balynathud al. Ballynahugh	Inq. Ult. (Down) §23 Car II	1662
15.	Ballenayue al. Ballenehue al. Balleneaghugh	Inq. Ult. (Down) §104 Car. I	1664
16.	Ballynegee	Ham. Copy Rental 110	1681
17.	Ballymagee	Wm. Map (OSNB) No. 54	1810
18.	Ballymagee	Bnd. Sur. (OSNB) No. 54	1830c
19.	Baile Mic Aodha "Magee's town"	J O'D (OSNB) No. 54	1834c
20.	ˌbaliməˈgi:	Local pronunciation	1991

Some of the forms (2b, 5c, 9 etc.) clearly indicate that the second element derives from the Irish surname *Mag Aodha*, frequently anglicized as Magee; forms such as 14c and 15c are also of note as they contain an anglicization of the second element of the surname *Mag Aodha*. It is significant that this surname is not uncommon in the Ards; note the reference to "Cormock Mc Ghee" of the Upper Ards in an early 17th-century grant (*CPR* Jas. I 72b 1605).

A number of the historical spellings suggest that this townland name emanates from an original *Baile na Gaoithe*, "townland of the wind", i.e. "windy townland". However, it is difficult to explain why such a transparent name would have been reinterpreted; it is likely that the forms which seem to indicate the presence of the gen. sing. fem form of the article originated in a scribal mistranscription of an *n* for an *m*.

Ballyminetragh *Baile Meannán Íochtarach*
J5481 "townland of the kid-goats, lower"

1.	Ballememan	Ex. Inq. 1 Jac. I	1603
2.	Ballememan	CPR Jas. I 38a	1604

3. Ballememan	CPR Jas. I 72b	1605
4. (?)Ballimenan al Ballinenowghtragh	Inq. Ult. (Down) §2 Jac. I	1605
5. Ballmyn-Itragh	Ham. Copy Inq. xxx	1623
6. Balle Menaght	Raven Map Clandeboye 17	1625c
7. Ba: Menat etragh	Raven Map Clandeboye 20	1625c
8. Ballemynitragh, Ballemynultragh	Ham. Patent x	1630
9. (?)Ballynaghie or Balleneoghnie or Ballemenaghne	Ham. Patent xi	1630
10. Ballemenen-itragh	Inq. Ult. (Down) §104 Car. I	1645
11. Ballemannanjtragh	BSD 90	1661
12. Ballymenen-itragh	Inq. Ult. (Down) §23 Car. II	1662
13. Ballymenatragh	Ham. Copy Rental 110	1681
14. Ballymenenitragh	Wm. Map (OSNB) No. 54	1810
15. Ballymenenitragh	Wm. Map (OSNB) No. 54	1810
16. Ballyminetra	Bnd. Sur. (OSNB) No. 54	1830c
17. Baile Min Iochtrach "smooth lower town"	J O'D (OSNB) No. 54	1834c
18. ˌbaliˈmintra	Local pronunciation	1991
19. ˌbalimiˈni:trə	Local pronunciation	1991

Forms 5, 8, 13 and 16, seem to indicate that the second element derives from *meann*, "kid" rather than *meannán* which is a diminutive of *meann* (for *meannán* also meaning "fawn" see Hughes 1989a: 179–86). Alternatively these forms may be explained by haplology, for it is understandable that a syllable, in this instance the suffix *-án* of *meannán*, might be lost from such a lengthy grouping as *Baile Meannán Íochtarach*.

The final *t* of forms 6 and 7 probably represents the *t* of *íochtarach*. Forms 9a and 9b appear to refer to the nearby townland of Ballymagee, but 9c could be a corrupt spelling of this townland.

The current anglicized form is interesting in that it preserves the suffix *íochtarach* "lower". As one might expect, some of the forms (i.e. 4b, 8b) show that the antonym *uachtarach* "upper", was also applied to *Baile Meannán*. For whatever reason, however, *Baile Meannán Uachtarach* is now obsolete whereas *Baile Meannán Íochtarach* has survived down to the present day in the anglicized form Ballyminetragh.

In the *OSNB* for Bangor John O'Donovan writes, "Ballyminetragh is sometimes called Ballyclamper". Sandra Millsop (1991: 38) has located the "lost" townland of Ballyclamper in the south-west of Ballyminetragh. Ballyclamper is also referred to in an advertisement in the *Belfast Newsletter*, 19 June 1752. Sandra Millsop has identified another lost townland, namely, Carryreagh, to the north-west of Ballyminetragh. In view of its location, is it possible that this Carryreagh was the name of the townland which was superseded by the now obsolete townland of *Baile Meannán Uachtarach* "townland of the kid-goats, upper"?

Ballymullan — *Baile Maoláin*

J 4680 — "townland of the low rounded hill"

1. Ballemulle	Ex. Inq. 1 Jac. I	1603
2. Ballemulle	CPR Jas. I 38a	1604
3. Ballimulle al Ballimullen	Inq. Ult. (Down) §2 Jac. I	1605

4.	Ballemulle	CPR Jas. I 72b	1605
5.	Ballymullen al Ballymulla	Ham. Copy Inq. xxxi	1623
6.	Ballimullen	Ham. Patent xx	1630
7.	Ballemullan or Ballemulla	Ham. Patent xi	1630
8.	Ballemullen al Ballemulle	Inq. Ult. (Down) §104 Car. I	1645
9.	Ballemullen	Census 94	1659c
10.	Ballemullen	BSD 127	1661
11.	Ballemullen al Ballemule	Inq. Ult. (Down) §23 Car. II	1662
12.	Ballymullan	Bnd. Sur. (OSNB) No. 54	1830c
13.	Ballymullan	Wm. Map (OSNB) No. 54	1830c
14.	Baile an Mhulláin "town of the little hill or summit"	J O'D (OSNB) No. 54	1834c
15.	ˌbaliˈmo̤lən	Local pronunciation	1991

Forms 3b, 5a, 6, 7a, 8a etc. indicate that the second element could be gen. sing. of *maolán* "low rounded hill". The forms ending in a vowel, 1–3a, 4, 5b, 7b, etc. may have come about as a result of a contraction for an *n* in an early manuscript being omitted by a scribe, and this error was in turn copied by other scribes.

Other possible Gaelic origins for this place-name are *Baile an Mhuilinn* "townland of the mill", and *Baile Uí Mhaoláin* "Mullan's townland".

Ballyree — *Baile an Fhraoigh*
J 5280 — "townland of the heather"

1.	Ballonere	Ex. Inq. 1 Jac. I	1603
2.	Ballonere	CPR Jas. I 38a	1604
3.	Ballonere or Ballinrie	CPR Jas. I 72b	1605
4.	Ballinere al. Ballinroigh	Inq. Ult. (Down) §2 Jac I	1605
5.	Ballonery al Ballinroigh	Ham. Patent xx	1620
6.	Ballionery al Bally-Nyrie al Ballinroigh	Ham. Copy Inq. xxx	1623
7.	Balleonerie or Ballenriogh or Ballenyrie	Ham. Patent xi	1630
8.	Balleonerie al. Ballenreagh al. Ballenrie	Inq. Ult. (Down) §104 Car I	1644
9.	Ballerie	Census 94	1659c
10.	Ballerin	BSD 90	1661
11.	Ballyrea	Ham. Copy Rental 110	1681
12.	Ballyree	Wm. Map (OSNB) No. 54	1810
13.	Ballyree	Bnd. Sur. (OSNB) No. 54	1830c
14.	Ballyray	Grand Jury Pres. (OSNB) No. 54	1830c
15.	Baile an Rígh "Kingstown, town of the king"	J O'D (OSNB) No. 54	1834c
16.	ˌbɑliˈri:	Local pronunciation	1991

Although there is no trace of the Irish article in the present-day form of this name, the *n* in forms 1–8 indicates that it was part of the original Irish form. As initial *fh-* is silent in Irish, it is understandable that the *fh-* of *fhraoigh* (gen. sing. of *fraoch* "heather") is not represented in the historical anglicized forms. The word *fraoch* can also mean "heath, moor" (*Ó Dónaill* s.v.).

Ballysallagh Major Minor J 4678	*Baile Salach* "dirty townland"	
1. Balesallogh	Ex. Inq. 1 Jac. I	1603
2. Ballesallogh	CPR Jas. I 38a	1604
3. Ballisallagh	Inq. Ult. (Down) §2 Jac. I	1605
4. Ballesallagh	CPR Jas. I 72b	1605
5. Ballysallogh	Ham. Copy Inq. xxxi	1623
6. Ba: Sallagh	Raven Map Clandeboye 2, 6, 8	1625
7. Ballysallagh	Ham. Patent xx	1630
8. Ballesallagh	Ham. Patent xi	1630
9. Ballysallagh minor	Census 94	1659c
10. Ballysallagh Major	Census 94	1659c
11. Balleselloghnunor	BSD 124	1661
12. Ballesellagh Major	BSD 127	1661
13. Ballėsallagh	Inq. Ult. (Down) §23 Car. II	1662
14. Ballysallogh major	Ham. Copy Rental 110	1681
15. Ballysallogh Major	Wm. Map (OSNB) No. 54	1810
16. Ballysalla	Downshire Direct. 316	1823
17. Ballysallagh Major	Bnd. Sur. (OSNB) No. 54	1830
18. Ballysallogh	Treas. Warrant (OSNB) No. 54	1830c
19. Baile Salach "dirty town"	J O'D (OSNB) No. 54	1834c
20. Baile Salach	GÉ 26	1989
21. ˌbɑliˈsɑlə	Local pronunciation	1991

Forms 9–12, 14, 15, and 17 with the suffixes major/minor, indicate that this townland had been sub-divided as early as the beginning of the second half of the 17th century. This name may seem somewhat peculiar but it is not unknown elsewhere in Ireland; there are two examples of it in Co. Waterford and two in Co. Limerick (*L. Log. P. Láirge* 11; *L. Log. Luimnigh* 16).

Ballyvarnet J 4978	*Baile Bhearnan* "townland of (the) gap"	
1. Ballenbarnen	Ex. Inq. 1 Jac. I	1603
2. Ballenbarnen	CPR Jas. I 38a	1605
3. Ballenebarnen	CPR Jas. I 72b	1605
4. Ballinebarnans, le 2	Inq. Ult. (Down) §2 Jac I	1605
5. (?)Ballebarne or Ballenebernen	Ham. Patent xi	1630
6. Ballevernon or Ballevernocke	Ham. Patent xi 1630	
7. Ballebarnes al. Ballebrenan	Inq. Ult. (Down) §104 Car I	1644
8. Ballyvernon	Civ. Surv. x 68	1655c
9. Ballevernane	BSD 90	1661
10. Ballyvernan al. Ballyvernocke	Inq. Ult. (Down) §23 Car II	1662

11. Ballyvernan	Sub. Roll Down 281	1663
12. Ballyvernon	Ham. Copy Rental 110	1681
13. Ballyvarnet	Wm. Map (OSNB) No. 54	1810
14. Ballyvernon	Downshire Direct. 316	1823
15. Ballyvarnet	Bnd. Sur. (OSNB) No. 54	1830c
16. Ballyvarnett	Grand Jury Pres. (OSNB) No. 54	1830c
17. Baile Bhearnáin "town of the little gap..."	J O'D (OSNB) No. 54	1834c
18. ˌbɑliˈvɑrnət	Local pronunciation	1991

The 17th-century forms show that the present form derives from Irish *Baile Bhearnan* "townland of the gap", the final *n* having been dissimilated to *t*. In standard Modern Irish the normal gen. sing. of *bearna* "a gap" undergoes no change from the nom. sing. However, a variant gen. sing. form is *bearnan*, which shows that *bearna* was also treated as an *n*-stem. Forms 1–4 and 5b show that, at one time, the gen. sing. fem. form of the article *na*, was a part of this name. These forms represent an Irish original *Baile na Bearnan* "townland of the gap".

Forms 6, 8–16 in which the second element begins with a *v* reflect aspiration of the initial *b* of *bearnan* as a result of the name being in the dative case. It is quite common for the dative form of a place-name to supersede the nominative as the name would be more frequently used in the dative than in the nominative. The modern anglicized form reflects this phenomenon.

Bangor Bog — An English form
J 4780

1. Great Moss of Bangor, The	Raven Map Clandeboy 5	1625
2. Com[m]on Moss of Bangor, The	Raven Map Clandeboy 7 *et passim*	1625
3. Bangor Bog	OSNB	1834c

This small townland seems to be of comparatively recent origin but the bog itself appears to be marked on *Raven Map Clandeboy*.

Carnalea — *Carnán Lao* "the small mound of the calf"
J 4881

1. Ballencarndeogh	Ex. Inq. 1 Jac. I	1603
2. Balleneardogh	CPR Jas. I 38a	1604
3. Ballencarnedeogh al Ballincornonleigh	Inq. Ult. (Down) §2 Jac. I	1605
4. Ballencarnedeigh	CPR Jas. I 72b	1605
5. The Rockie Hill al The Rock of Carnanleagh	Ham. Copy Inq. xxx	1623
6. The rocky hill alias the rock of Carmanleagh	CPR Chas. I 227	1627
7. Ballycornedeogh al Ballincarnamleigh	Ham. Patent xx	1630
8. Ballinecamanleagh or Ballecamanedeagh	Ham. Patent xi	1630
9. Ballecarnanleagy al Ballecarnedeagh	Inq. Ult. (Down) §104 Car. I	1645

10. Carnelea	Census 94	1659c
11. Carnelea + Killarie	BSD 129	1661
12. Ballecarnaneleagh al Ballenecarnedeagh	Inq. Ult. (Down) §23 Car. II	1662
13. Carnalea	Wm. Map (OSNB) No. 54	1810
14. Carnalea	Bnd. Sur. (OSNB) No. 54	1830c
15. Carn Liath "grey carn or heap"	J O'D (OSNB) No. 54	1834c
16. Carn Liath "grey carn"	Joyce iii 167	1913
17. ˌkɑrnəˈli:	Local pronunciation	1991

Forms 3b, 5b, 6b, 7b, 9a and 12a indicate that the first element is *carnán* "small heap, mound" and not *carn* "heap, pile" which might seem likely from the current anglicized form. In *Ham. Copy Inq. 1623* we find reference to "The Rockie Hill alias the Rock of Carnanleagh". Is it possible that this "rockie hill" is the location of the *carnán* which features in the first element of this name?

Conlig — *An Choinleac*
J 5077 — "the hound-stone"

1. Coinnleice, feall na	O'Neill Fun. Oration 267	1744
2. Conlack	Raven Map Clandeboye 9	1625c
3. Conlegg	Civ. Surv. x 68	1655c
4. Couleck	Census 94	1659c
5. Conlige, half of	Ham. Copy Rental 110	1681
6. Conlig	Wm. Map (OSNB) No. 54	1810
7. Conlig	Bnd. Sur (OSNB) No. 54	1830c
8. Con-liag "stone of the hounds"	J O'D (OSNB) No. 54	1834c
9. An Choinleic	AGPB 115	1969
10. An Choinleic	Éire Thuaidh	1988
11. An Choinleic	GÉ	1989
12. kɔnˈlig	Local pronunciation	1991

Although there are only a few anglicized forms of this name, we are fortunate in having an authoritative Irish-language form for this place from the middle of the 18th century (form 1). As place-names which are a compound of two nouns are unlikely to have been coined after the 6th century (Mac Giolla Easpaig 1981), the name *Coinleac* clearly belongs to an early stratum of nomenclature. This name is not very common but there is another Conlig, a minor name, in the parish of Knockbreda, Co Down (J 3867).

Corporation — An English form
J 5081

1. Bangor Corporac[i]on	Census 93	1659c
2. Corporac[i]on of Bangor, the	BSD 90	1661
3. Corporation of Bangor	OSNB No. 54	1834c

According to *OSM* (vii 19) the townland of Bangor Corporation contained twenty-five acres of rocky ground and three acres of mill-dam.

Cotton	An English form	
J 5479		
1. Cotton	Wm. Map (OSNB) No. 54	1810
2. Cott-town	Downshire Direct. 320	1823
3. Cottown	Bnd. Sur. (OSNB) No. 54	1830c
4. Town of the Cots or little boats	J O'D (OSNB) No. 54	1834c
5. ðə 'kɔtn	Local pronunciation	1991

The place-name Cotton is common throughout England where it derives from the dat. pl. of Old English *cot* "cottage, dwelling". It is possible that Cotton in North Down is a transferred name brought to Ireland by English or Scottish settlers. The surname Cotton arose from association with the habitational name (Hanks & Hodges 1988: 125). MacLysaght (1985: 60) points out that the surname has been associated with Dublin and South-East Leinster since the 17th century. It is interesting that the definite article in English is currently used with this name.

Gransha	*Baile na Gráinsí*	
J 4583	"townland of the grange"	
1. Balliorrane al Ballinegrench	Inq. Ult. (Down) §2 Jac. I	1605
2. Ballynegrangeogh	Ham. Copy Inq. xxxi	1623
3. Ballenegrangeogh	Ham. Patent xi	1630
4. Balleneyrange	Inq. Ult. (Down) §104 Car. I	1645
5. Granshagh	Census 94	1659c
6. Granshagh	BSD 90	1661
7. Granshough	Ham. Copy Rental 110	1681
8. Granshaw	Wm. Map (OSNB) No. 54	1810
9. Granshaw	Bnd. Sur. (OSNB) No. 54	1830c
10. Granshaw	Grand Jury Pres. (OSNB) No. 54	1830c
11. Gráinseach "a grange"	J O'D (OSNB) No. 54	1834c
12. 'granʃə	Local pronunciation	1991

The element *gráinseach* "a grange", (from French *grange*) is quite a common element in Irish place-names (see Flanagan, D. 1981–2(c): 75). It reflects Anglo-Norman influence and, therefore, it is not surprising to find a number of names containing this element in the Ards (see **Ballygrangee** in the parish of Grey Abbey, **Gransha** in the parish of Inishargy, and **Grangee** in the parish of Donaghadee). Gransha also appears as a townland in a number of other counties including Derry, Fermanagh, Monaghan, and Kerry. Forms 1b–4 show that at one time an Irish form, *Baile na Gráinsí*, was in use, and this is also true of **Grangee** in Donaghadee. The form without *baile*, *viz. An Ghráinseach*, did not come into prominence until the second half of the 17th century.

Groomsport	*Port an Ghiolla Ghruama*	
J 5383	"the port of the gloomy fellow/attendant"	
1. Purt-a-ghiolla-ghruama	O'Neill Fun. Oration 269	1744
2. Mollerytoun	Inq. Earldom Ulster iii 66	1333
3. Ballevullecragh	Ex. Inq. 1 Jac. I	1603
4. Ballevullecragh	CPR Jas. I 38a	1604

5. Gilgroomes	Ham. Patent xxii	1620
6. Ballivulleragh al Ballimulleragh	Ham. Patent xx	1620
7. Ballymulleragh al Gilgrooms-Port	Ham. Copy Inq. xxx	1623
8. Gromes Port	Raven Map Clandeboye 15	1625c
9. Grooms, Porte	Raven Map Clandeboye 16	1625c
10. Gromes Porte	Raven Map Clandeboye 20	1625c
11. Ballimulleragh or Gilgroumsport	Ham. Patent x	1630
12. Portgillegroome	Inq. Ult. (Down) §41 Car. I	1633
13. Ballemulleragh al Gillgroomsporte	Inq. Ult. (Down) §104 Car. I	1645
14. Groomsport	Civ. Surv. x 68	1655c
15. Groomsport	Census 94	1659c
16. Ballemulleragh al Gurmesporte	BSD 91	1661
17. Ballymulleragh al Gillgroomsporte	Inq. Ult. (Down) §23 Car. II	1662
18. Grahams Port	Descr. Ards 38	1683
19. Groomsport	Wm. Map (OSNB) No. 54	1810
20. Groomsport	Bnd. Sur. (OSNB) No. 54	1830c
21. Groomsport	Grand Jury Pres. (OSNB) No. 54	1830c
22. Graham's Port	Knox Hist. 548	1875
23. Grimsport	Knox Hist. 548	1875
24. Port a' Ghiolla Gruamdha "Gilgroom's port"	J O'D (OSNB) No. 54	1834c
25. Port an Ghiolla Ghruama	Post-Sheanchas 75	1905
26. Baile Maoilmhuire	Post-Sheanchas 75	1905
27. Port an Ghiolla Ghruama	AGBP 116	1969
28. Port an Ghiolla Ghruama	Éire Thuaidh	1988
29. Port an Ghiolla Ghruama	GÉ 146	1989
30. ˌgru:mzˈpo:rt	Local pronunciation	1991

The 19th-century historian Alexander Knox (*Knox Hist.* 548) claimed that Groomsport was of Scandinavian origin but on the evidence of the historical forms there is no justification for this view. Nevertheless, it is interesting to note that toponymy was of sufficient interest to the public in the closing decades of the 19th century to merit a place in a history of Co. Down.

The anglicized form *Groomsport* is based on a semi-translation of the Irish name for this place, *Port an Ghiolla Ghruama* "the port of the gloomy fellow/attendant". We know this place had another name, *Ballivulleragh*, *Ballimulleragh,* etc. which is attested as an alias in 17th-century documents. Furthermore it is listed in the early 14th-century document *Inq. Earldom Ulster* as *Mollerytoun*, the first element being a surname followed by the English element *tūn* "town". This Norman form of the name was gaelicized, as is clear from forms 3, 4, 6, 7a, 11a, 13a, 16, and 17, all of which have *baile* as a first element. Forms 3, 4, and 6a are interesting, as the *v* would indicate that the preceding masc. noun *baile* has caused aspiration of the initial *m* of the following proper noun, a phenomenon which first appears in Early Modern Irish.

There is no record of a surname Mollery, but it is possible that the surname in question is Mallory, which derives from Old French, *maloret* "the unfortunate, the unlucky" (Reaney 1958: 213). Given this meaning, it seems possible that *giolla gruama* in the Irish form of this name is a calque on the Anglo-Norman surname Mallory. Form 26 appears to be a calque on the alias form.

Lisbane — *An Lios Bán*
J 4978 — "the white fort

	Form	Source	Date
1.	Ballesbane	Ex. Inq. 1 Jac. I	1603
2.	Ballesebane	CPR Jas. I 38a	1604
3.	Ballinlissebane	Inq. Ult. (Down) §2 Jac. I	1605
4.	Ballesebane	CPR Jas. I 72b	1605
5.	Ballinlissebane	Ham. Patent xx	1620
6.	Ballylisbane al Ballinlisselane	Ham. Copy Inq. xxxi	1623
7.	Ballelisbane or Ballinlisselane	Ham. Patent xi	1630
8.	Ballelisbane al Ballelissebane	Inq. Ult. (Down) §104 Car. I	1645
9.	Lisbane	Census 94	1659c
10.	Lissbanne	BSD 91	1661
11.	Ballelisbane al Ballylisebane	Inq. Ult. (Down) §23 Car. II	1662
12.	Lisbane	Bnd. Sur. (OSNB) No. 54	1830
13.	Lios Ban	J O'D (OSNB) No. 54	1834c
14.	lis'bɑ:n	Local pronunciation	1991

The first *n* in forms 3, 5, 6b, and 7b indicates the presence of the gen. sing. masc. of the definite article. Forms containing the article seem to have existed side by side with forms without it (see forms 6, 7); by the second half of the 17th century, however, it would seem that the article fell out of use as an integral part of this name.

The first element is *lios* "a fort" and it is significant that there are two enclosures in this townland, one of which seems to be known locally as Thora's Fort (*NIMSR* sheet 2 §§23, 24).

Orlock — *Orlóg*
J 5583 — meaning uncertain

	Form	Source	Date
1.	Horloghe	Early Chart B'fast Lough	1570
2.	Horologhe	Mercator's Ulst.	1595c
3.	Carrowerlogie	Inq. Ult. (Down) §2 Jac. I	1605
4.	Caroworlog	Ham. Copy Inq. xxx	1623
5.	Orlogh	Raven Map Clandeboye 17	1625c
6.	Carroworlag	Ham. Patent x	1630
7.	Carroworloye	Inq. Ult. (Down) §104 Car. I	1644
8.	Orlog	Census 93	1659c
9.	Orloge Quarter	BSD 90	1661
10.	Carrowerloge	Inq. Ult. (Down) §23 Car. II	1662
11.	Orlog	Wm. Map (OSNB) No. 54	1810
12.	Orloch	Bnd. Sur. (OSNB) No. 54	1830c
13.	Orlock	OSNB No. 54	1834c
14.	Orlag "golden hollow"	J O'D (OSNB) No. 54	1834c
15.	'ɔrlɔk	Local pronunciation	1991

Forms 3, 4, 6, 7, and 10 clearly show that *ceathrú* "quarter" was sometimes used as the first element in this townland name. The element *ceathrú* "quarter" may signify a quarter of a townland but it can also refer to a *Baile Biataigh* "land of the food-provider", anglicized "ballybetagh", in which case it refers to a unit containing three or four townlands. The data indicate an Irish original *Orlóg* but no such word is attested in the dictionaries.

Orlock must have been a significant point on the coast for sailors, as it appears on the first known chart of Belfast Lough which dates to 1570, and it also appears on early 17th-century maps.

Portavo	*Port an Bhotha*	
J 5682	"the port of the (monastic) cell	
1. Balleportano	Ex. Inq. 1 Jac. I	1603
2. Balleportavo	CPR Jas. I 38a	1604
3. Balliportano al Balliportabo	Inq. Ult. (Down) §2 Jac. I	1605
4. Ballineportavo	CPR Jas. I 72b	1605
5. Balliportavo al Balliportabo	Ham. Patent xx	1620
6. Bally-Portavo al Ballyportabo	Ham. Copy Inq. xxx	1623
7. Portavow	Raven Map Clandeboye 17	1625c
8. Portauow	Raven Map Clandeboye 20	1625c
9. Balleportavo or Balleportabo	Ham. Patent x	1630
10. Portavo	Inq. Ult. (Down) §104 Car. I	1645
11. Portevoe 3 quarters of	BSD 91	1661
12. Portavo	Inq. Ult. (Down) §23 Car. II	1662
13. Portavo	Ham. Copy Rental 110	1681
14. Portavo	Descr. Ards 38	1683
15. Portte[r]oe	Collins B'fast Lough	1693
16. Portavo	Wm. Map (OSNB) No. 54	1810
17. Portavoe	Bnd. Sur. (OSNB) No. 54	1830c
18. Portavoe	Grand Jury Pres. (OSNB) No. 54	1830c
19. Port a Bho "the cow's port or bank"	J O'D (OSNB) No. 54	1834c
20. ˌportəˈvo:	Local pronunciation	1991

The second element appears to be the word *both* "booth, hut" which is used in a number of place-names including **Boho**, Co. Fermanagh which derives from *Botha* (lit. booths); *Boith Mhéabha* "Méabh's booth" is the Irish form of **Bovevagh**, Co. Derry (where *boith* is an oblique form of *both*). Although generally feminine in Irish, there are examples of *both* being masculine in Scottish Gaelic (*Dwelly* s.v.) and it would appear to be masculine in this place-name. It is interesting to note that *both* was also applied to cells, oratories, etc. (*DIL* s.v.).

Rathgill	*Ráth Giall*	
J 4879	"fort of (the) hostages"	
1. (?)Ráth nGuala do loscadh la Fiachna mac Baotain	AFM i 242	618
2. (?)Rath nGuala, ro gab tene	AFM i 242	618
3. (?)Ratho Guali, expugnatio	AU (Mac Airt) 112	623
4. (?)Raith nGuaili, ro gab tene	AU (Mac Airt) 112	623
5. Carroghe Rawgele	Ex. Inq. 1 Jac. I	1603
6. Carrogh-Raloghele	CPR Jas. I 38a	1604
7. Rawgele al Ballifraghoguile	Inq. Ult. (Down) §2 Jac. I	1605
8. Rawgeile	CPR Jas. I 72b	1605
9. Rawgeile al Ballyfragheguile	Ham. Patent xx	1620

10. Ballekawgeile or Ballefraghoguile	Ham. Patent xi	1630
11. Ballerangeile al Ballefyanghognile	Inq. Ult. (Down) §104 Car. I	1645
12. Rafegill	Civ. Surv. x 68	1655c
13. Rafgill	Census 94	1659c
14. Rafgill 3 quarters	BSD 90	1661
15. Rathgill	Wm. Map (OSNB) No. 54	1810
16. Rathgill	Bnd. Sur. (OSNB) No. 54	1830c
17. Rathgill	Grand Jury Pres. (OSNB) No. 54	1830c
18. Rath Gaill "fort of the foreigner"	J O'D (OSNB) No. 54	1834c
19. Rath Guala	J O'D (OSNB) No. 54	1834c
20 Rath-Guala	O'Laverty ii 131	1880
21. rɑθ'giəl	Local pronunciation	1991
22. rɑθ'gil	Local pronunciation	1991

Forms 5 and 6 clearly show that the element *ceathrú* "quarter", was applied to this place-name at least as early as the beginning of the 17th century (see **Orlock** above for the meaning of *ceathrú* as a place-name element). The first element of the modern anglicized form is definitely *ráth* "a fort". *O'Laverty* (ii 130) informs us that the rath at Rathgill extended over two acres and that its site was occupied by Rathgael House, which itself was demolished in 1960.

The Irish language forms for Rathgael (1–4) are problematic in that there is no certainty that they refer to modern Rathgill. O'Donovan suggests (*AFM* i 242 n.r) that Rathgill is to be identifed with *Ráth Guala* which was burned by the Ulster king *Fiachnae mac Báetáin* (+ 626) in 618. While there is no conclusive evidence for this theory, it is a possibility. This event is also recounted in *AU* under the year 623:

Ro gabh tene Raith nGuaili,
taiscid biucatan uaidhi!
is dian ad-randat ind uilc
tenid i rraith Aeda Builc

"Fire has seized Ráth Guala
Save ye a little from it!
Swiftly do the evil men kindle
a fire in the fort of Áed Builc."

It has been suggested that the title of a lost tale concerning Fiachnae, *Sluagad Fiachna maic Baítáin co Dún nGuaire i Saxanaib* "the hosting of Fiachnae mac Baítáin to Dún Guaire in England", indicates that the *AFM* and *AU* entries for 618 and 623 concerning *Ráth Guala* are in fact references to Fiachnae's exploits in Dún Guaire in Britain (Byrne 1973: 112). The latter has been identified as Bamburgh in North-East England (Byrne *ibid.*). However, there is little similarity between the names *Dún Guaire* and *Ráth (n)Guala* and there is certainly no conclusive proof that they refer to the same place. It should also be borne in mind that it would not be at all surprising if Fiachnae mac Baítáin had been involved in an attack on a fort in North Down in the first quarter of the 7th century, so there is a possibility that the annals are referring to a fort which once existed in the present day townland of Rathgill.

O'Laverty (ii 130–1) believed that the *Colmán mac hui-Gále* mentioned in *Fél. Óeng.* (230) was a descendant of *Guala*, from whom Rathgill was named. However it is difficult to substantiate this as the said entry from *Fél. Óeng.* states merely that the *Gáilinne*, to which Colmán belonged, were a tribe in Ulster. O'Laverty's claim that they were located in the Bangor area seems to be speculative and is an attempt to connect Guala with Rathgill. The only association Colmán may have had with Bangor is that there is a possiblity that he was the Colmán who was abbot of Comgall's monastery of Camus near Coleraine. However, even this is by no means certain; *Fél. Óeng.* states that he may have been the Colmán who was abbot of another church in Co. Down, namely *Lann Mocholmóc*, which Reeves (*EA* 110 n.l) and O'Laverty (*ibid.*) have identified as **Magheralin** in Co. Down. It is not at all certain, however, that *Lann Mocholmóc* refers to Magheralin and the matter requires further investigation.

The nasalization of the second element of form 1 may be explained by analogy with form 2, which is accusative and closely follows it in the same source. There is to date no firm evidence of *ráth* "fort" being neuter. The place-name *Áth mBude* (*TBC Rec. I* l. 1506) is another example where a calcified accusative form showing nasalization of the second element has replaced the nominative. Forms 7b, 9b, 10b and 11b are curious, largely because of the *f* immediately following the element "balli-" etc. It may be tentatively suggested that this *f* was a misreading by a copyist of a capital *c*, i.e. the initial of *carroghe* which occurs in forms 5 and 6, used as an abbreviation. The form may have been something like *Balli Craghoguile*, and with the *c* being mistaken for an *f* this would result in a form such as *Ballifraghoguile*.

The second element appears to be gen. pl. of *giall* "hostage". Forms 5–7a, 8, 9a and 10a, where the final syllable ends in *-ge(i)le*, and forms 7b, 9b, 10b ending in *-guile* could be argued to be a representation of [g´iəl] i.e. *giall*. The latter forms may reflect the sound [gi:l] which may have been how [g´iəl] was pronounced by speakers of English. This sound may also be intended in the 17th-century forms ending in *-gill* (12–14). The most common local pronunciation of the second element of this name (21) is a reasonable approximation of the pronunciation of our suggested Irish form. In *Top. Index 1961* this townland is cited as Rathgill, which is the form O'Donovan suggested on the strength of the forms from *Wm. Map*, *Bnd. Sur.* and *Grand Jury Pres.* These spellings, which also occur in documents from the 17th century, seem to have prompted O'Donovan to suggest an alternative Irish form to *Ráth Guala*, namely *Ráth Gaill*, "fort of the foreigner". The spelling *Rathgael* is still in frequent use, even on DOE road signs, no doubt due to the influence of Rathgael House.

Rathgael

See **Rathgill**

OTHER NAMES

Bangor Bay — *Inbhear Bige*
"estuary of the river *Beag*"

1. Inber mBicne	TBF 16	800c
2. Inber Bice, trácht	San. Corm. (YBL) 28	1000c
3. Bice, ostivum fiuvi nomine	Life of St. Comgall 1 (O'Laverty i 36)	1000c
4. Inber mBicne	Met. Dinds. iv 224	1100c
5. Inbir Bice, Colmán	CSH 707.212 143	1125c
6. Inver Beg	Life of St. Comgall 2 (O'Laverty i 36)	n.d.

The Old Irish text *Táin Bó Fraích* (16) contains a passage which attempts to explain how the bay at Bangor got the name of *Inber mBicne* "*Bicne's* rivermouth". The passage in question has been set in context in the discussion of **Bangor**, so perhaps it will suffice to say here that, according to this source, the place we now know as Bangor Bay was called *Inber mBicne* because it was there that *Conall Cernach*'s servant *Bicne mac Láegaire* died.

In the 10th-century text *Sanas Cormaic* (*San. Corm. YBL* 28), the strand of Bangor is called *trācht Inbir Bice*. *Inber Bice*, we are informed, was named from *Bice*, a favourite dog of the merchant *Brecān*, that was drowned along with its master in the sea between Ireland and Rathlin. Their fate was not known until the poet *Lugaid Dall* came to Bangor. When his followers were going up the strand at *Inber Bece* they found a skull which they brought to *Lugaid* to identify.

In *Met. Dinds.* (iv 224) we find an account of how the name *Inber mBicne*, "*Bicne's* river-mouth, estuary" was applied to what is today Bangor Bay. This poem has been clearly influenced by the passage already referred to in *TBF*. A more plausible explanation is contained in form 3 which may be translated, "the mouth of the river called *Bice*". This clearly indicates that the second element is a river-name and this is how O'Laverty (ii 36) interprets it, "the place where the River Beg – the Little (river) – falls into the sea". There are several instances of *inber* (later *inbhear*) followed by a river-name in the onomasticon, for example *Inber mBóinne* refers to the mouth of the Boyne at Drogheda, and *Inber Sláine* is an old name for the estuary of the river Slaney which flows into Wexford harbour. In the light of this evidence, it appears that O'Laverty's interpretation is likely. Our postulated Irish form for what is today known as Bangor Bay is based on the premise that a river known as **An B(h)eag* "the little (river)" entered the sea at that place. We have been unable to locate a river flowing into Bangor Bay but that is not to say there was not one in the locality in the past.

Clandeboy — *Clann Aodha Buí*
"family of *Aodh Buí*, or yellow-haired Hugh"

1.	Cloinn Aedha buidhe, le	ALC i 596	1319
2.	Cla[i]nn-Aedha-buidhe, le	AU ii 434	1319
3.	Clainni Aeda Buide,...nert	A. Conn. 254	1319
4.	Clainn Aeda Buide, le	A. Conn. 254	1319
5.	Clann Aeda buide	AFM iii 586	1345
6.	Chloind Aedha buidhe, do	ALC ii 11	1354
7.	Chloind Aedha Buidhe, do	A. Conn 310	1354
8.	ccloinn Aodha bhuide, i	AFM iv 854 *et passim*	1422
9.	Cloinne Aedha buide, argain	AFM iv 934 *et passim*	1444
10.	Clainni Aeda Buide, tigerna	A. Conn. 544	1468
11.	Clann-Aedha-buide	AU iii 228	1470
12.	Clainn Oeda Buide, etir...	A. Conn. 570	1474
13.	Clainn-Aedha-buidhe, le	AU iii 276	1481
14.	Claind-Aedha-buidhe, a	AU iii 374	1493
15.	Clann Aodha buide	AFM v 1282	1505
16.	Cloind-Aodha-buidhe	AU iii 518	1515
17.	Clainn Aodho Buide, a	A. Conn. 628	1515
18.	gclainn Aodha buidhe, a	ALC ii 222	1515
19.	Cloinn-Aodha-buidhe, do	AU iii	1517
20.	Cloinn-Aodha-buidhi, ar	AU iii 590	1533
21.	Chlainni Aodho Buidhe, righ	A. Conn. 682	1533
22.	Clann Aedha buidhe	ALC ii 306	1537
23.	Chloinn Aodha buidhe, ar	AFM v 1512	1548
23.	Cloinn Aodha buidhe, for	AFM v 1536	1554
24.	Cloinne Aodha Buidhe, hi	AFM v 1538 *et passim*	1555
25.	Clainn Aodha buidhi, ar	ALC ii 462	1584

No.	Form	Source	Date
26.	Clainne Aodha buidhe, tigerna	ALC ii 508	1590
27.	Clann Aodh Buidhe	Cín Lae Ó M. 6 *et passim*	1645c
28.	Clann Aodh Buidh, muinter Uachtar	Cín Lae Ó M. 14	1645c
29.	Clann Aodha Buidhi, huachtar	Cín Lae Ó M. 24	1645c
30.	gClann Aodh Buidhi, i	Cín Lae Ó M. 44	1645c
31.	Chlanna Aodha Buidhe, a onchoin	LCABuidhe 281	1680c
32.	gclann Aodh-buidhe, a	O'Neill Fun. Oration 267	1744
33.	Clandebvy	Goghe's Map	1567
34.	Clanboye	Fiants Eliz. §1066	1567
35.	Clanyboy	Fiants Eliz. §1330	1568c
36.	Clonebuy	Fiants Eliz. §1659	1570
37.	Clandeboy	Fiants Eliz. §2104 *et passim*	1572
38.	Glandeboy	Fiants Eliz. §2349	1573
39.	Claneboy	Fiants Eliz. §2979	1576
40.	Clan de Boy	S-E Ulster Map	1580c
41.	Clandeboie	Fiants Eliz. §3977	1582
42.	Cloneboye	Fiants Eliz. §4788	1585
43.	Clandeboy, Lower	Fiants Eliz. §4767 *et passim*	1585
44.	Clandeboye, lower	Fiants Eliz. §5239	1589
45.	Clandeboy, Upper	Fiants Eliz. §5443	1590
46.	Clandhuboy	Fiants Eliz. §5620	1591
47.	Cloneboy	Fiants Eliz. §5767	1592
48.	Clandeboys, both the	Fiants Eliz. §6127 *et passim*	1597
49.	Clandeboyes, both	Fiants Eliz. §6235 *et passim*	1598
50.	Sovth Clandeboie	Bartlett Map (Esch. Co. Maps) i	1603
51.	Clan de Boy	Bartlett Map (Esch. Co. Maps) ii	1603
52.	Claneboy	Inq. Ult. (Down) §2 Jac. I *pass*	1605
53.	Clandeboy, le upper	Inq. Ult. (Down) §2 Jac. I	1605
54.	Upper-Clandeboy	Inq. Ult. (Down) §2 Jac. I	1605
55.	Clandeboy, lower	Inq. Ult. (Down) §2 Jac. I *pass.*	1605
56.	Clandeboys, upper	CPR Jas. I 55b	1605
57.	Clandeboy upper	CPR Jas. I 78a	1605
58.	South Glan de Boy	Speed's Ulster	1610
59.	South Glan de Boy	Speed's Antrim & Down	1610
60.	Clandeboyes, higher	CPR Jas. I 312b	1617
61.	Clandeboys, the upper	Inq Ult. (Down) §8 Jac. I	1618
62.	Clandeboy, le inferiori	Inq. Ult. (Antrim) §7 Jac. I	1621
63.	Claneboy, in inferior pte de	Inq. Ult. (Antrim) §7 Jac. I	1621
64.	Clandeboy, le lower	Inq. Ult. (Antrim) §7 Jac. I	1621
65.	Clandeboys, lower	CPR Jas. I 487a	1621
66.	Claneboys	Inq. Ult. (Down) §1 Car. I	1625
67.	Claneboys, ad rivos sup-ioris	Inq. Ult. (Antrim) §2 Car. I	1625
68.	Claneboyes, upper	Inq. Ult. (Down) §75 Car. I	1636
69.	Claneboye	Inq. Ult. (Down) §104 Car. I	1645
70.	Clann Aodha Buidhe	Post-Sheanchas 47	1905
71.	Clann Aodha Buí	GÉ 202	1988
72.	ˈklɑndiˌbɔi	Local pronunciation	1991

Clandeboy is an anglicization of Irish *Clann Aodha Buí* (earlier *Clann Aodha Buidhe*) "family of *Aodh Buidhe*, or yellow-haired *Aodh*". (The *d* in the anglicized form of Clandeboy is due to an early spelling of *clann*, i.e. *cland*.) The Clann Aodha Buidhe were a branch of the Northern Uí Néill and descended from *Aodh Buidhe Ó Néill* who died in 1283. Aodh Buidhe's grandson, *Éinrí*, was known as *Tighearna Cloinne Aodha Buidhe* (Lord of Clandeboy) and it was in his time that the name Clann Aodha Buidhe gained widespread currency. Following Éinrí, the next chieftain of the sept was *Muircheartach Ceannfhada* (also known as *Ó Néill Buidhe*) who died in 1395. Muircheartach's son, *Brian Ballach*, is referred to in the Annals as *Mac Uí Néill Buidhe*, and it was in his time that the Clandeboy O'Neills played a crucial role in the history of Ulster.

In the middle of the 14th century the *Clann Aodha Buidhe* moved east of the Bann from their original homeplace and won territories for themselves in south Antrim and north Down. This expansive area was split into two parts in the 17th century. The northern section was divided into four baronies Toome, Antrim, Masserene, and Belfast; their lands in Co. Down were divided into three baronies Castlereagh, Dufferin, and the Lower Ards. In the early 17th century their estates in North Down were gradually broken up as a result of the acquisitions of the Hills and Montgomerys. For further discussion on this, see D.A. Chart (1942: 119–51), and the introduction to the parish of Bangor (141, 143).

Many people today associate the name Clandeboy with the Clandeboy estate situated in the parish of Bangor. This has no real historical significance, however, as Frederick Hamilton-Temple-Blackwood (Lord Dufferin) changed the name of the estate to Clandeboy from Ballyleidy, the old townland name. It appears that he changed the name to Clandeboy in the last century because of the former status of that name. As well as calling his estate and house Clandeboy, he also built a tree-lined lane to Helen's Bay which he called Clandeboy Avenue (see also the note on **Helen's Bay** below).

Copeland Island J 5983	*Oileán Chóplainn* "Copeland's island"	
1. Kaupmanneyjar	Hákonar Saga Gamla 194	1230
2. Copland ylles	Goghe's Map	1567
3. Conplande Island	Early Chart B'fast Lough	1570
4. Copmans Iles	Nowel's Ire. (1)	1570
5. Helaine Harr[o]n[e]	Early Chart B'fast Lough	1570c
6. Coplands Iles	S-E Ulster Map	1580c
7. Copland [isl?]es	Jobson's Ulster (TCD)	1590c
8. Copland yles	Hondius' Map	1591
9. Helayne harrons	Mercator's Ulster	1595c
10. Copland iles	Mercator's Ulster	1595c
11. Copland ylles	Goghe's Map	1597
12. Topeman Iles	CSP Ire. 676	1598
13. Copman Iles	Boazio's Map (BM)	1599
14. Copl' Iland	Ex. Inq. 1 Jac. I	1603
15. Copland islands	CPR Jas. I 72b	1605
16. Hellayne Harons	Speed's Antrim & Down	1610
17. Hellayne Harrons	Speed's Ulster	1610
18. Copland Iles	Speed's Ulster	1610
19. Hellayne Harrons	Speed's Antrim & Down	1610

20. Copland Isles	Speed's Antrim & Down	1610
21. Copland Iles	Speed's Ireland	1610
22. Copland Islands	Ham. Patent xx	1620
23. Copland Isles	CPR Chas. I 228	1627
24. Copeland Islands	Ham. Patent xi	1630
25. Copeland-isles	Inq. Ult. (Down) §104 Car. I	1645
26. Coplan Iles	Census 93	1659c
27. Copeland Isles	BSD 89	1661
28. Copeland-islands	Inq. Ult. (Down) §23 Car. II	1662
29. Copland Isles, ye	Descr. Ards 38	1683
30. Copland Isle	Collins B'fast Lough	1693
31. Big-Island	Harris. Hist. 130	1774
32. Copeland Island	Wm. Map (OSNB) No. 54	1810
33. Copeland Island	Bnd. Sur. (OSNB) No. 54	1830c
34. Oileán Chóplainn	Éire Thuaidh	1988
35. Oileán Chóplainn	GÉ 207	1989
36. 'ko:plənd 'əilənd	Local pronunciation	1991

If form 5 does refer to the islands, it would seem to be an attempt to represent *Oileáin Árann*, and it could well be that this was the original Gaelic name for the islands. *Árainn* is used as the group-name for the Aran islands in Galway Bay, and for Aranmore island off the Donegal coast. *Árainn* is also to be found in other place-names in Ireland, e.g. *Tiobraid Árann*, Tipperary. *Árainn* is an old dative sg. form of *ára*, "kidney". In place-names, however, it generally means "(kidney-shaped) ridge".

Form 1, *Kaupmanneyjar* 1230 A.D., is of interest as it occurs in Sturla Thordarson's *Hákonar Saga Gamla*, "The Saga of Hákon the Old" (iii 194). *Kaupmann* is Norse for "merchant", and *ey* is Norse for "island". This has led to the suggestion that the Copeland Islands were at one time used as a Viking merchant store.

The text reads in translation:

> Then they sailed north to Kintyre and lay there for a while and made many forays...Then they sailed over to the Kaupmanneyjar and lay there for a long time that winter. Then they sailed south to Man...

If the account of the journey from Kintyre to the *Kaupmanneyjar*, and from there south to Man is accurate, it seems likely that *Kaupmanneyjar* refers to what we now call the Copeland Islands. McKeown (1929: 107) believes that Copeland is a development from Copman which he derives from *Kaupmann*. It is interesting to note that the form *Copman* appears in late 16th- and early 17th-century maps, as does *Copeland*.

It seems more probable, however, that the name Copeland Islands stems from the de Coupland family who arrived in the Ards in Norman times (*O'Laverty* ii 35; *Sav. Ards* 121). They also left their mark on the opposite coastline in the townland of Ballycopeland in the parish of Donaghadee, and there is a Copeland Water near Carrickfergus, Co. Antrim. It is interesting to note that Willelmo and Henrico de Couplan are mentioned in late 12th-century charters (*Cartae Dun.* §§4, 5, 7, 420–1, 1183 AD).

According to *OSM* (vii 22), the islands known collectively as the Copeland Islands were the property of David Ker of Portavoe House. Up until the last century the islands were much used by smugglers who imported tobacco and spirits to the Co. Down coastline.

Crawfordsburn A Scots form
J 4781

1. Crawford's-Burn	Harris. Hist. 69	1744
2. Crawford's-bourn	Downshire Direct. 320	1823
3. Crawfordsburn	OSNB No. 54	1834c
4. Baile Uí Mhaoláin	Post-Sheanchas 54	1905
5. Sruth Chráfard	AGBP	1969
6. Sruth Chráfard	GÉ 162	1989
7. 'krɔ.fərdzbərn	Local pronunciation	1991

The surname Crawford derives from the barony name of Crawford in Lanarkshire (Black 1946: 182–3). According to Hill, the Crawfords who settled in North Down at this time were more than likely part of the Kilbirne branch of the family from Ayrshire (*Montgomery MSS* 138 n.54). It is noteworthy that there is a place near Greenock in Ayrshire known as Crawfordsburn. Hill also states (*ibid.*) that a certain John Crawford attended the funeral of the first Viscount Mountgomery at Newtown (i.e. Newtownards) in 1636 AD. *O'Laverty* (ii 130) states that the Crawfords arrived at the place we now call Crawfordsburn as tenants of James Hamilton, the chief land owner in the Bangor area, in the reign of James I. It is interesting that the name of Andrew Crawford appears on an early 17th-century map (*Raven Map Clandeboye* 8). There is, however, no reference to Crawfordsburn in this source, which would seem to indicate that the name had not been coined until later in 17th century.

Form 4 is merely a postulated Gaelic form of the townland name in which Crawfordsburn is situated. Forms 5 and 6 are literal translations of the name into Irish. *O'Laverty* (ii 130) states that the village of Crawfordsburn is situated in the townland of Ballykillare; however, it appears to be in the neighbouring townland of Ballymullan.

Echlin Grove An English form
J 5178

The surname Echlin is derived from the lands of Echline in the parish of Dalmeny in West Lothian (Black 1946: 236). For further information on this surname see **Abbacy, Bishop's Mills,** and **Demesne** in the parish of Ardquin, and **Echlinville** in the parish of St Andrews alias Ballyhalbert.

Glenganagh Origin uncertain
J 5282

1. Glenghanna	Knox Hist. 545	1875

The only reference we have to this name is in *Knox Hist.* where we are informed that it had been the residence of the late Baroness Dufferin, and that at the time of writing (1875) was the residence of Andrew Cowan, who had previously lived in the Hillsborough area.

Grey Point *Rinn Riabhach*
J 4583 "grey point, headland"

1. Ronriagh	Early Chart B'fast Lough	1570c
2. Roneraiaghe	Mercator's Ulster	1595
3. Gray P^{t}	Collins B'fast Lough	1693

4. Grey Point	J O'D OSNB No. 54	1834c
5. Grey Point	Knox Hist.	1875

Forms 1 and 2 indicate that the current form of this name is a literal translation of an Irish original *Rinn Riabhach* "grey point". Harris points out (*Harris Hist.* 69) that Grey Point forms a safe harbour and its potential as a natural haven was undoubtedly recognized by seafarers long before Harris' time. Given its prominent coastal position, it is only to be expected that this name would appear on maritime maps. Forms 1 and 2 with an *o* in the first syllable probably reflect the modification of the *i* of *rinn* resulting from the broadening of *-nn* before the following *r*.

Helen's Bay — An English form
J 4482

1. Cuan Bhaile na gCrot	Post-Sheanchas 76	1905
2. Cuan Héilin	AGBP 116	1969
3. Cuan Héilin	GÉ 83	1989
4. 'hɛlnz'be:	Local pronunciation	1991

The name, Helen's Bay, is unlikely to have been coined before the 1860s. Born in Italy in 1826, Frederick Hamilton-Temple-Blackwood became the fifth Lord Dufferin at the age of 15 on the death of his father in 1841. During his varied public career he came to be Governor General of Canada, Viceroy of India, and ambassador to Russia, France and Italy. His mother was Helen Selina Sheridan, a grand-daughter of the noted playwright Richard Brinsley Sheridan. Frederick named Helen's Bay and Helen's Tower after his mother.

Form 1 is based on the townland name in which Helen's Bay is situated, namely Ballygrot; forms 2 and 3 are literal translations of Helen's Bay into Irish.

Kearney's Hill — An English form
J 5582

For a note on the family name Kearney, Carney (<*Mac Cearnaigh*) see **Carneyhill** in the parish of Donaghadee.

Light House Island — An English form
J 5985

1. Crosse Ile	S-E Ulster Map	1580c
2. Crosse ile	Mercator's Ireland	1595
3. (?)Laune	Mercator's Ulster	1595c
4. Crosse ile	Mercator's Ulster	1595c
5. Crosse Ile	Boazio's Map (BM)	1599
6. Crosse Ile	Speed's Ulster	1610
7. (?)Laune	Speed's Ulster	1610
8. Crosse Ile	Speed's Antrim & Down	1610
9. (?)Laane	Speed's Antrim & Down	1610
10. (?)Laune	Speed's Ireland	1610
11. Crosse	Collins B'fast Lough	1693
12. Cross-Island	Harris Hist. 130	1744
13. Light House Island, the	Harris Hist. 130	1744

14. Light House Island	Wm. Map (OSNB) No. 54	1810
15. Light House Island	Bnd. Sur. (OSNB) No. 54	1830c
16. Cross Island	OSNB No. 54	1834c
17. 'ləithəus 'əilnd	Local pronunciation	1991
18. 'bïrd 'əilnd	Local pronunciation	1991

The current name of the island came about as a result of the light-house which was built c. 1820. Before its erection fires were lit through the night on the same spot as a warning to passing ships (*OSM* vii 21). We know from late 16th- and early 17th-century maps that it was previously called Cross Island, and Harris (*Harris Hist.* 132) also refers to this older name:

> The Cross Island lies East of the Big Island, and is near a Mile in compass by Water, though it contains only thirty Acres, or thereabouts of arable Land. On it stands a Light-House (called therefore by some the Light House Island).

Early maps show another name by which the islands might have been known i.e. *Lann* "church". The island's ecclesiastical associations obviously gave rise to the name Cross Island and the name *Lann* "church" must reflect the presence of an early ecclesiastical site.

Mew Island — An English form
J 6086

1. Mew	Collins B'fast Lough	1693
2. Mew-Island	Harris. Hist. 130	1774
3. Mew Island	Wm. Map (OSNB) No. 54	1810
4. Mew Island	Bnd. Sur. (OSNB) No. 54	1830c
5. Mew Island	OSNB Inf. No. 54	1834c
6. Oileán na bhFaoileann	Éire Thuaidh	1988
7. ðə 'mɔ:'əil	Local pronunciation	1991
8. ðə 'mɔ:	Local prounuciation	1991

The 18th-century historian Harris (*Harris Hist.* 134) seems to have a plausible explanation of how this place was named:

> The *Mew-Island*, so called from the Abundance of Sea-Mews or Gulls frequenting it, is a little flat Island not far distant from the Cross Island.

McKeown (1929: 108) has made an alternative suggestion based on the local pronunciation of the name which he gives as "Maw". We have also recorded this pronunciation during field-work in the Donaghadee area in 1991 (8). McKeown (*ibid.*) believes that the name derives from *magh* "a plain", and by way of corroborative evidence, states that the island is one vast flat rock no more than forty feet above sea level. The historical evidence, however, does not support this theory. Form 6, is a translation meaning "the island of the seagulls".

Port Dandy — An English form
J 5883

Port Dandy is situated on the western shore of Copeland Island. The form of the name, apparent noun followed by a genitive, might suggest a Gaelic origin but Harris claims that this place was named after a local resident (*Harris Hist.* 132). For another example of the practice of reversing the normal word order of names coined in English see **Rosemount**, Grey Abbey parish.

Skelly's Hill An English form
J 4682

1.	Balleschalle	Ex. Inq. 1 Jac. I	1603
2.	Balleshalle	CPR Jas. I 38a	1604
3.	Balleskalle	CPR Jas. 72b	1605
4.	Ballyscally	Ham. Patent xx	1620
5.	Bally-Skelly al Bally-Skally	Ham. Copy Inq. xxxi	1623
6.	Ballyskellce al Ballyskady	Inq. Ult. (Down) §104 Car. I	1644
7.	Ballyskelly	Census 94	1659c
8.	Ballyskelly al Ballyskally	Inq. Ult. (Down) §23 Car. II	1662
9.	Ballyskelly	Ham. Copy Rental 110	1689
10.	ˌskɛliz ˈhil	Local pronunciation	1991

The above forms refer to the the now obsolete townland of Ballyskelly which was formerly the name of the townland in which Skelly's Hill is situated. Skelly's Hill contains the same surname that forms the second element of Ballyskelly.

MacLysaght (1985: 273) informs us that Skelly is an Oriel form of the surname Scally. The latter was common in Cos. Roscommon and Westmeath, and its Gaelic form *Mac Scalaí* may be derived from the attributive element of the surname *Ó Scolaí*, *scolaí* meaning "schoolman, scholar". Unfortunately we have no evidence of which language Skelly's Hill was originally coined in; it may be a translation of a Gaelic original, or it may have been named by English speakers.

Slaty Port An English form
J 5985

Slaty Port is to be found on the south-west shore of Light-House Island. The 17th-century historian Walter Harris states that this place got its name from a nearby slate quarry (*Harris Hist.* 132).

PARISH OF DONAGHADEE

The parish of Donaghadee is in the north-east of Co. Down in the barony of Lower Ards. It is bounded on the east and north-east by the Irish sea, the parish of Ballywalter lies to the south, and to the west lie the parishes of Bangor, Newtownards and Grey Abbey. The entire parish contains 9,593 acres.

The rectory of Donaghadee was held by the monastery of St Andrews in the Ards (i.e. Black Abbey). The earliest reference we have to Donaghadee is in an early 13th-century document (*Pontif. Hib.* i §59 AD 1204). This document confirms certain possessions belonging to Black Abbey and two names from the parish are included in it, Donaghadee and Kilbright. The next reference to Donaghadee we find is in the *Ecclesiastical Taxation* of 1302–6 (*Eccles. Tax.*) where the church is valued at ten marks. A number of other townland names in the parish are also mentioned in this document: the churches at Ballyhay and Ballyrolly were valued at four and six marks respectively. An inquisition relating to the lands of William de Burgh, Earl of Ulster, taken in 1333 (*Inq. Earldom Ulster*) refers to three townlands in this parish, namely, Hogstown, Ballyfrenis and Ganaway.

In the early 17th century Donaghadee came into the hands of James Hamilton and was later granted to Sir Hugh Montgomery, the principal land-owner of much of the territory in the neighbouring parishes of Newtownards and Grey Abbey. In 1605 James Hamilton was granted the "tithes of the towns and parishes" of lands in the Ards, among them Donaghadee (*CPR Jas. I* 72b). Other townlands in the parish granted to him on 5 November of the same year are mentioned in an extensive grant in the same document (*CPR Jas. I* 73a). This latter grant shows strong similarities to the townlands listed in the inquisition taken at Ardquin in 1605 (*Inq. Ult.* §2 Jac. I 1605). The townlands occur in much the same order in both documents but there are some minor differences in spelling. The inquisition refers to 10 of the townlands belonging to the church of Donaghadee. An inquisition taken at Downpatrick in 1623 (*Ham. Copy Inq.* 1623) also cites townlands in the parish, as does a copy of this document which dates to 1627 (*CPR Chas. I* 227). The Downpatrick inquisition includes the 1618 grant by which James Hamilton distributed extensive lands in the Ards to Hugh Montgomery, as directed by the Earl of Abercorn. This included townlands lying within the parish of Donaghadee. A list of the lands which had belonged to Sir Hugh Montgomery, including townlands in this parish, is contained in an inquisition taken at Downpatrick in 1636 (*Inq. Ult.* §75 Car. I). Another inquisition dated to c. 1650 (*Inq. Ult.* §109 Car. 1) also contains a similar list of the possessions of Hugh Montgomery, and this includes townlands in Donaghadee.

According to the *Census* of c.1659 the population of the parish at that time was 385; 168 of these were described as being of English or Scottish descent, the remainder Irish. Eoin Mac Néill, however, has suggested that these figures and classifications are not trustworthy (*Census* xiii n.13). The "tituladoes" include John Cunynghame who appears beside Drumfad, and Roger Crymble, Robert Brearely and Henry Cresans whose names are among those listed beside Donaghadee village. The *Subsidy Roll for the County of Down* (*Sub. Roll Down.* 281 AD 1663) records some of the townlands and we find several of the "tituladoes" from the Census mentioned here also, e.g. Patrick Montgomery of Craigboy and William Browne of Donaghadee.

The second element of a number of townlands in the parish are Anglo-Norman surnames. O'Donovan was aware of this when he was trying to ascertain the origin of such names as Ballyvester, Ballywhiskin, etc., and it is interesting to note that he did not supply a postulated Irish form for names of this type. The Irish form for Donaghadee which O'Donovan collected from John Mc Greevy from Saul, namely, *Domhnach Díogbhalach*, "the injurious

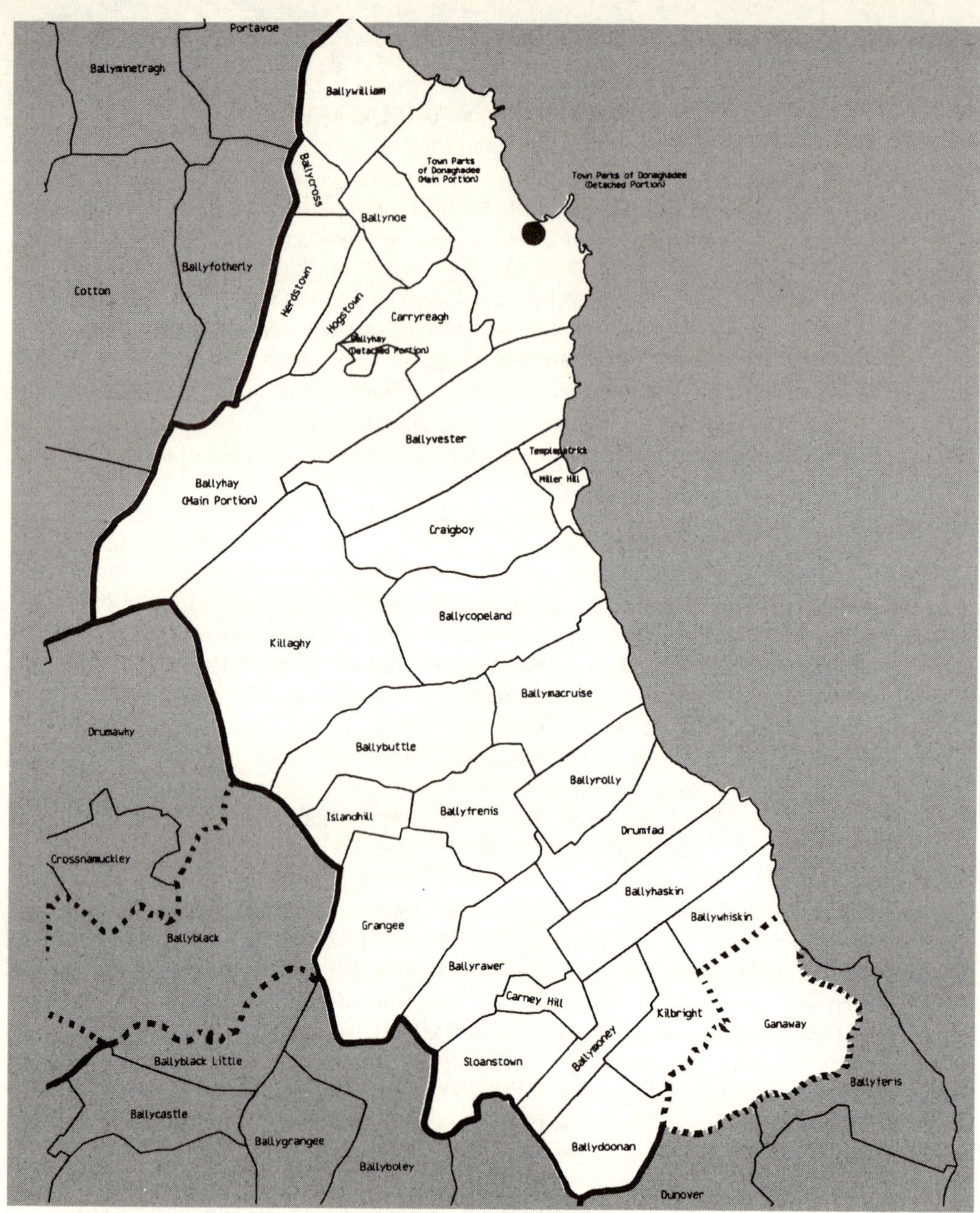

Parish of Donaghadee

Barony of Ards Lower

Townlands
Ballybuttle
Ballycopeland
Ballycross
Ballydoonan
Ballyfrenis
Ballyhaskin
Ballyhay
Ballymacruise
Ballymoney
Ballynoe
Ballyrawer
Ballyrolly
Ballyvester
Ballywhiskin
Ballywilliam
Carneyhill
Carryreagh
Craigboy
Drumfad
Ganaway (shared with Ballywalter)
Grangee
Herdstown
Hogstown
Islandhill
Kilbright
Killaghy
Millerhill
Sloanstown
Templepatrick
Townparks of Donaghadee

Towns
Carrowdore
Donaghadee
Millisle

or hurtful Sunday", is of note in that it shows that the origin and meaning of the name was obscure to the last generation of Irish speakers in the county in the 1830s.

The town of Donaghadee took shape in the early years of the 17th century under the direction of Hugh Montgomery. The impressive motte close to the shoreline overlooking the harbour, however, indicates that there was a settlement there in much earlier times. Montgomery rebuilt the harbour in 1626 and also improved the harbour at Portpatrick in Scotland, with the result that Portpatrick-Donaghadee became the favoured route between Galloway and Ireland. Even before the harbour at Donaghadee was improved many Scots landed their cattle there when transferring from their Scottish estates to their newly-acquired lands in Ireland.

PARISH NAME

Donaghadee — *Domhnach Daoi* (?)
J 5980 — "*Daoi's* church"

1. Donanachti, ecclesiam de	Pontif. Hib. i §59	1204
2. Dofnachti, Ecclesia de	Eccles. Tax. 16	1306c
3. Donaghdyth	Reg. Cromer viii 339 §32	1524
4. Ba: Done	Bartlett Maps (Esch. Co. Maps) i	1603
5. Damaugh Dee	Ex. Inq. 1 Jac. I	1603
6. Ballidonoghdee	Inq. Ult. (Down) §2 Jac. I	1605
7. Dony	Speed's Ulster	1610
8. Dony	Speed's Antrim & Down	1610
9. Donaghadee	Terrier (Reeves) 57	1615c
10. Donaghadee	Terrier (O'Laverty) 327	1615c
11. Donoghdie	CPR Jas. I 326a	1617
12. Donoghdee	Ulster Visit. (Reeves) 35	1622
13. Donoghdie	Ham. Copy Inq. xliv	1623
14. Donaghodie	Ham. Copy Inq. xxxiv	1623
15. Donaghadee	CPR Chas. I 66	1625
16. Donadee	CPR Chas. I 230	1627
17. Donaghdee	CPR Chas. I 230	1627
18. Donoghdee	Inq. Ult. (Down) §41 Car. I	1633
19. Donoghdee	Inq. Ult. (Down) §75 Car. I	1636
20. Donaghdy	Inq. Ult. (Down) §75 Car. I	1636
21. Donaghdee	Inq. Ult. (Down) §105 Car. I	1645c
22. Donaghdee al Downadee	Inq. Ult. (Down) §109 Car. I	1650c
23. Donoghadee	Inq. Down (Reeves1) 137	1657
24. Donnadee	Census 93	1659c
25. Donnaghadee, ye Parishes of Newtowne &	BSD 88	1661
26. Donnaghadee al Balleno	BSD 88	1661
27. Donnacaha dee	Trien. Visit. (Bramhall) 13	1661
28. Donaghdee	Sub. Roll Down 281	1663
29. Donnaghadee	Trien. Visit. (Margetson) 22	1664
30. Donachadee	Trien. Visit. (Boyle) 44	1679
31. Donaghadee	Collins B'fast Lough	1693
32. Donaghadee	Reg. Deeds abstracts ii §26	1739

33. Donaghadee	Wm. Map (OSNB) E 167, E 24	1810
34. Donaghadee	Bnd. Sur. (OSNB)	1830c
35. Domhnach a Díth "church of the destruction"	J O'D (OSNB) E 167, E 24	1834c
36. Domhnach Díoghbhalach "the injurious or hurtful Sunday"	John Mc Greevy, Saul (OSNB) E 167, E 24	1834c
37. Domhnach Dith "the church of loss"	EA 17 n. b	1847
38. Domhnach Diagh	Post-Sheanchas 58	1905
39. Domhnach Daoi	AGBP 115	1969
40. Domhnach Daoi	Éire Thuaidh	1988
41. Domhnach Daoi	GÉ 89	1989
42. ˌdɔnəxəˈdi:	Local pronunciation	1991

Donaghadee is problematic in that it is difficult to establish what the second element is. The first element is undoubtedly *domhnach* "church" and, while many *domhnach*-names are traditionally associated with St Patrick, others may have been coined independently of the Patrician mission. There can be no doubt, however, that place-names containing the element *domhnach* can be dated to the Early Christian period, for the word *domhnach* fell out of natural linguistic use by the end of the 7th century (Flanagan, D. 1981–2(c): 70).

There have been several theories put forward over the years as to what the second element of Donaghadee might be. Reeves thought that the spelling of the name in forms 2 and 3, might suggest an original *Domhnach Díth* "church of loss" (*EA* 17 n. b). The somewhat curious suggestion that Donaghadee derives from *Doun da ghee* "the mount or burial place of the two warriors or heroes", is undoubtedly a spurious folk etymology (*Montgomery MSS* 122). Since the first element is *domhnach*, it seems likely that the second element might be the name of a saint. As there is no evidence to date of an Irish saint whose name would suit the historical forms, is it possible that the name in question might be that of a British saint? Hogan (*Onom. Goed.* 560) suggests that *Oirer Caoin* is an early name for Donaghadee but this is probably Ardkeen (see **Ardkeen**).

TOWNLAND NAMES

Ballybuttle
J 5774

Baile Bhuitléara
"Butler's townland"

1. Ballybutler	Inq. Ult. (Down) §75 Car. I	1636
2. Ballybutler	Inq. Ult. (Down) §109 Car. I	1650c
3. Ballybutler	Montgomery MSS 54 n.34	1650c
4. Ballybutle	Census 93	1659c
5. Ballebuttle	BSD 88	1661
6. Ballybuttle	Sub. Roll Down. 281	1663
7. Ballybuttle	Wm. Map (OSNB) E 167, E 24	1810
8. Ballybuttle	Bnd. Sur. (OSNB) E 167, E 24	1830c
9. Ballybuttle	High Const. Applot. (OSNB) E 167, E 24	1833

10. Buttle is an English family name	J O'D (OSNB) E 167, E 24	1834c
11. ˌbaliˈbo̤tl	Local pronunciation	1991
12. ˌbaliˈbo̤ʔl	Local pronunciation	1991

The second element of this name seems to be derived from the Anglo-Norman surname Butler. Reaney (1958: 55), lists a number of variant forms of this name including *Buteiller* 1055 AD, *le Butiller* 1174–84 AD, and *le Boteller* 1260 AD. In Old French, *bouteillier* was applied to the servant in charge of the wine cellar, who was also usually the head servant. Reaney (*ibid.*) also informs us that some of the early attestations of the word indicate that the term could also be applied to an officer of high rank responsible for the supply and importation of wine.

Ballycopeland
J 5876

Baile Chóplainn
"Copeland's townland"

1. Ballicoppland	CPR Jas. I 73a	1605
2. Ballicopland	CPR Jas. I 326a	1617
3. Ballecopland	Ham. Copy Inq. xlii	1623
4. Balle Copland	Ham. Copy Inq. xliv	1623
5. Ballycopland	Ham. Copy Inq. xxxiv	1623
6. Ballecopland	CPR Chas. I 230	1627
7. Ballycopland	Inq. Ult. (Down) §75 Car. I	1636
8. Ballycoplan	Inq. Ult. (Down) §109 Car. I	1650c
9. Ballycoplan	Census 93	1659c
10. Ballecopeland	BSD 88	1661
11. Ballycopeland	Wm. Map (OSNB) E 167, E 24	1810
12. Ballycopeland	Bnd. Sur (OSNB) E 167, E 24	1830c
13. "Copeland's town"	J O'D (OSNB) E 167, E 24	1834c
14. ˌbɑliˈkoːplənd	Local pronunciation	1991

O'Donovan correctly identified the second element of this name as the surname Copeland which derives from the Norman surname *de Coupland*. This family also appears to have given its name to the **Copeland Islands** in the neighbouring parish of Bangor. There is also a **Copeland Water** near Carrickfergus, Co Antrim.

Ballycross
J 5680

Baile na Croise
"townland of the cross"

1. Ballinecross	Inq. Ult. (Down) §2 Jac. I	1605
2. Ballinacross	Inq. Ult. (Down) §2 Jac. I	1605
3. Ballinecrosse	CPR Jas. I 73a	1605
4. Ballimacrosse	CPR Jas. I 326a	1617
5. Ballenecrosse	Ham. Copy Inq. xlii	1623
6. Ballenecrosse	Ham. Copy Inq. xxxiv	1623
7. Ballenecrosse	CPR Chas. I 230	1627
8. Ballenecross	CPR Chas. I 230	1627
9. Byllynacrosse	Inq. Ult. (Down) §75 Car. I	1636
10. Ballynecross	Inq. Ult. (Down) §109 Car. I	1650c

11. Ballynecrosse	Montgomery MSS 54 n.34	1650c
12. Ballenocross	Census 93	1659c
13. Ballenecrosse	BSD 88	1661
14. Ballycross	Wm. Map (OSNB) E 167, E 24	1810
15. Ballycross	Bnd. Sur. (OSNB) E 167, E 24	1830c
16. Baile Croise "cross town, town of the cross	J O'D (OSNB) E 167, E 24	1834c
17. Baile-Croise "the town of the cross"	Joyce iii 78	1913
18. ˌbaliˈkrɔs	Local pronunciation	1991

As an element in place-names Irish *cros* usually means either a cross in the ecclesiastical sense or a cross-roads; in the absense of any ecclesiastical association with Ballycross, it is probably safe to translate *cros* as cross-roads. As it is difficult to know whether or not the final *e* of forms 3–7 etc. was pronounced, it could be argued that the final element of this name is gen. pl. of *cros* as opposed to gen. sing. as we have suggested. However, as it is unlikely that the townland contained more than one cross-roads, it is probably best to interpret the final element as a gen. sing.

The 17th-century spellings reveal the presence of the gen. sing. fem. form of the definite article, i.e. *na*, which is not apparent in the modern form or in the forms from the *OSNB*. It is not uncommon to find place-names the modern anglicized forms of which show no trace of the article despite it having been an integral part of the name in former times (see also **Ballydoonan**).

Ballydoonan
J 5971

Baile na nDúnán
"townland of the little forts"

1. Ballinedoonan	Inq. Ult. (Down) §2 Jac. I	1605
2. Ballinedoonan	CPR Jas. I 73a	1605
3. Donan	CPR Jas. I 326a	1617
4. Ballydonane	CPR Jas. I 326a	1617
5. Ballydonnan	Inq. Ult. (Down) §109 Car. I	1650c
6. Ballydownan	Montgomery MSS 54 n.34	1650c
7. Ballydonnan	Census 93	1659c
8. Balledonnane	BSD 87	1661
9. Ballydoonan	Wm. Map (OSNB) E 167, E 24	1810
10. Ballydownan	Bnd. Sur. (OSNB) E 167, E 24	1830c
11. Ballydownan	High Const. Applot. (OSNB) E 167, E 24	1833
12. Baile Uí Dhunáin "O'Dunan's town"	J O'D (OSNB) E 167, E 24	1834c
13. Baile-Ui-Dhúnain "O'Doonan's town"	Joyce iii 81	1913
14. ˌbaliˈdu:nən	Local pronunciation	1991

Forms 1 and 2 contain vestiges of the gen. pl. of the definite article (i.e. *na*) which are not found in the later forms. This contradicts O'Donovan's theory that the second element is a surname. The second element is gen. pl. of *dúnán*, (diminutive of, *dún*), "small fort".

Ballyfrenis	*Baile Freanais*	
J 5874	"Frenis's townland"	
1. Frenestoun	Inq. Earldom Ulster iii 65	1333
2. Ballifranish	Inq. Ult. (Down) §2 Jac. I	1605
3. Ballyfrenzies	CPR Jas. I 326a	1617
4. Ballyfrainys	Ham. Copy Inq. xxxiii	1623
5. Ballyfrenish	Inq. Ult. (Down) §75 Car. I	1636
6. Ballyfrenish	Inq. Ult. (Down) §109 Car. I	1650c
7. Ballyfrenish	Montgomery MSS 54 n.34	1650c
8. Ballyfrenis	Census 93	1659c
9. Ballefrennish	BSD 88	1661
10. Ballyfrenis	Wm. Map (OSNB) E 167, E 24	1810
11. Balyfrenis	Bnd. Sur. (OSNB) E 167, E 24	1830c
12. "Freynis Town"	J O'D (OSNB) E 167, E 24	1834c
13. ˌbɑliˈfre:nəs	Local pronunciation	1991

The second element seems to be a surname and, given the strong influence of the Anglo-Normans in this part of North Down, it could well be a corruption of the surname *French*, which comes from Old English *frencisc* > Mid. Eng. *frennsce, frenche*. Reaney (1958: 126) cites two variants of this surname: *le Frensch*, and *le Frenche*. MacLysaght (1957: 152) states that there was another form, *de Freynes* and this seems to have been the form O'Donovan had in mind. MacLysaght (*ibid.*) also claims that this surname was brought from France to England by one *Theophilus de French*, who was among William the Conquerer's retinue. It is interesting that there is another townland of the same origin now known as **Ballyfrench** in the parish of St Andrews alias Ballyhalbert.

Ballyhaskin	**Baile Hascain** (?)	
J 6073	"Hoskin's townland"	
1. Ballyhosker	Census 93	1659c
2. Ballyhaskin	Wm. Map (OSNB) E 167, E 24	1810
3. Ballyhoskin	Bnd. Sur. (OSNB) E 167, E 24	1830c
4. "Town of the sheskin or marsh"	Joyce iii 92	1913
5. Baile Sheasgainn "town of the quagmire"	J O'D (OSNB) E 167, E 24	1834c
6. ˌbaliˈhaskən	Local pronunciation	1991

Despite O'Donovan's suggestion, it seems likely that the second element of this townland name is a surname. Although the Irish surname *Ó hUiscín*, (anglicized Hoskins, Heskin, etc.) may be a possibility, it is unlikely that an Irish form such as *Baile Uí Uiscín* would be anglicized as Ballyhaskin; there is an additional problem in that this surname is found mainly in Connacht (Woulfe 1923: 577). The second element could also conceivably derive from an English surname, Askin, which is sometimes used as a synonym of Heskin (MacLysaght 1985: 8).

Ballyhay	*Baile Hae*	
J 5677	"Hay's townland"	
1. Haytone	Great Rolls Pipe 32	1275c
2. Villa Haye	Cartae Dun. §12 423	1280c

3. Hayton, Ecclesie del	Cartae Dun. §12 423	1280c
4. Haytona, Ecclesia de	Eccles. Tax. 14	1306c
5. Haytoun (manor of)	Great Rolls Pipe xxxix 52	1314c
6. Haye, the town of	CPR Ed. iii 305	1336
7. Haytown, the church of St. Mary	CPR Ed. iii 305	1336
8. Haytoū, 4 mes' & 4 caruc; in	CPR (Tresham) i 242	1427
9. Ballihay	Inq. Ult. (Down) §2 Jac. I	1605
10. Ballihaies, the	CPR Jas. I 78a	1606
11. Ballyhaies	Terrier (Reeves) 57	1615c
12. Ballyhaies	Terrier (O'Laverty) 327	1615c
13. Ballyhay	CPR Jas. I 326a	1617
14. Ballheyes	Ulster Visit. (Reeves) 53	1622
15. Ballyhayes, the two	Montgomery MSS 54 n.34	1650c
16. Ballehay & Ballevester	BSD 88	1661
17. Ballyhay	Wm. Map (OSNB) E 167, E 24	1810
18. Ballyhay	High Const. Applot. (OSNB) E 167, E 24	1833c
19. Baile Ui Aodha "Hughes's town"	J O'D (OSNB) E 167, E 24	1834c
20. "the town of the cave"	O'Laverty ii 28	1880
21. ˌbaliˈhe:	Local pronunciation	1991

This townland contains the surname Hay which originally meant "dweller by the enclosure" or "forest fenced off for hunting..." (Reaney 1958: 157–8). The forms from the Anglo-Norman period (1–8) clearly show the presence of the suffix *-to(w)n*. The later forms, with *bally* as the first element indicate that the Anglo-Norman form, *Hayton*, became gaelicized. We know from a document dated to 1606 (*CPR Jas. 1* 78a) that this townland had probably been divided some time before the start of the 17th century: "The Ballihaies, 2 townlands in the parish of Donoghdee, in the Great Ardes." *O'Laverty* (ii 28) claims that there was a cave under a rath in this townland and his translation of the original Irish name for Ballyhay is "the town of the cave" (22). This would suggest an original *Baile na hUaimhe* but such an etymology is extremely unlikely.

There appears to be no information regarding the exact date of the demise of the church at Ballyhay which is referred to in some of the early forms. However, there was certainly no trace of it in 1622 as an ecclesiastical document from that year reports that no church was known to exist there (*Ulster Visit. (Reeves)* 53).

Ballymacruise — *Baile Mhic Naosa*
J 5975 — "*Mac Naosa's* townland"

1. Bally Mc Shrew	Census 93	1659c
2. Ballemc chrew	BSD 88	1661
3. Ballymacrews	Wm. Map (OSNB) E 167, E 24	1810
4. Ballymacruise	Bnd. Sur. (OSNB) E 167, E 24	1830c
5. Ballymacruse	High Const. Applot. (OSNB) E 167, E 24	1833c
6. Macruise's town	J O'D (OSNB) E 167, E 24	1834c
7. Baile Mhic Crúis	Post-sheanchas 96	1905
8. ˌbɑlimәˈkru:z	Local pronunciation	1991

The second element is obviously a surname and may be traced back to an Irish form *Mhic Naosa*, where *Naosa* is a contraction of *Aonghasa*. *Mac Naosa* is usually anglicized *Mac Neice* or *Mac Creesh*. The *r* in *Macruise* arises from the well-known phenomenon of *cn* (in this case the *c* of *Mac* and *n* of *Naosa*) giving a pronunciation [kr] in the Irish spoken in the northern half of Ireland (O'Rahilly 1932: 22–4).

Form 7 from *Post-sheanchas* is given as a suggested Irish form for Millisle; when dealing with English names the compiler of this work generally gives a suggested Irish form for the townlands in which they are situated.

Ballymoney	*Baile na Móna*	
J 5971	"townland of the moor"	
1. Ballinemoyne	Inq. Ult. (Down) §2 Jac 1	1605
2. Ballinimoyne	CPR Jas. I 73a	1605
3. Ballenemonie	Ham. Copy Inq. xxxiv	1623
4. Ballenemony	Ham. Copy Inq. xlii	1623
5. Ballemoyne	Ham. Copy Inq. xliv	1623
6. Ballenemoyne	CPR Chas. I 230	1627
7. Balynemoney	Inq. Ult. (Down) §75 Car 1	1636
8. Ballynemony al. Mooretown	Inq. Ult. (Down) §109 Car I	1641
9. Ballymoney	Census 93	1659c
10. Ballemoney	BSD 88	1661
11. Ballymoney	Wm. Map (OSNB) E 167, E 24	1810
12. Ballymoney	Bnd. Sur. (OSNB) E 167, E 24	1830c
13. Baile Muine "town of the brake, shrubbery"	J O'D (OSNB) E 167, E 24	1834c
14. ˌbaliˈmo̤ni	Local pronunciation	1991

The place-name Ballymoney is found in many counties throughout Ireland including Galway, Wicklow, Sligo and Antrim and sometimes represents an original Irish *Baile (na) Muine*, "townland of the thicket. The *oy* in the final element in forms 1, 2, 5, and 6 seems to represent a long *o* vowel, and this indicates an original Irish form *Baile na Móna*. It is noteworthy that there was a quantity of bog in the neighbouring townland of Sloanstown in the early 1830s (*OSM* vii 45). Form 8 is interesting in that the alias form, *Mooretown*, could well be a translation of the Irish form of this name.

Ballynoe	*Baile Nua*	
J 5780	"new town"	
1. Ballynowe	CPR Jas I 73a	1605
2. Newton of Donoghdie	CPR Jas. I 326a	1617
3. Ballenona	Ham. Copy Inq. xliv	1623
4. Ballenowa	CPR Chas. I 230	1627
5. Ballynova	Inq. Ult. (Down) §75 Car. 1	1636
6. Ballynova	Inq. Ult. (Down) §109 Car. 1	1641
7. Balleno	Census 93	1659c
8. Balleno al Donnaghadee	BSD 88	1661
9. Ballynoe	Wm. Map (OSNB) E 167, E 24	1810

10. Ballynoe	Bnd. Sur. (OSNB) E 167, E 24	1830
11. Baile Nua "new town"	J O'D (OSNB) E 167, E 24	1834c
12. ˌbaliˈno:	Local pronunciation	1991

The reference to the "Newton of Donoghdie" in form 2 above suggests that the name *Baile Nua* "new town" was given to this place because it was a new settlement built beside the well-established town of Donaghadee. Ballynoe borders the town of Donaghadee on the west, and form 8 actually gives it as an alias form for Donaghadee. This phenomenon of naming an adjacent townland as an alias form is quite common in historical documentation. Field-work in the Donaghadee area in the summer of 1991 revealed that few people outside this townland had heard of it, doubtless because it is becoming absorbed into modern Donaghadee.

Ballyrawer
J 5872

Baile Ramhar
"fat/thick townland"

1. (?)Ballirowe	Inq. Ult. (Down) §2 Jac. I	1605
2. Balliroe	CPR Jas. I 73a	1605
3. Ballirowe	Inq. Ult. (Down) §2 Jac I	1605
4. Ballirowe	CPR Jas. I 73a	1605
5. Ballyraer	Census 93	1659c
6. Ballyraer	Wm. Map (OSNB) E 167, E 24	1810
7. Ballyraer	Downshire Direct. 316	1823
8. Ballyrawer	Bnd. Sur. (OSNB) E 167, E 24	1830
9. Ballyrare	High Const. Applot. (OSNB) E 167, E 24	1833
10. Baile Ramhar "fat or rich town"	J O'D (OSNB) E 167, E 24	1834c
11. ˌbaliˈrɔ:r	Local pronunciation	1991

The adjective *ramhar* "fat, thick" is used in the formation of place-names all over Ireland. *Joyce* (i 395–6) gives numerous examples including Carrigrour, Co. Cork, and Reenrour, Co. Kerry. He also mentions that in the north, the *m* of *ramhar* is sometimes delenited in place-names, for example **Killyramer**, Co. Antrim, and **Kinramer** on Rathlin Island. In Ballyrawer the lenited consonant was retained, as is clear from the historical forms. It is slightly worrying that forms 1–4 do not contain the final *r* which appears in the later forms. Nevertheless, the sources concerned are related and perhaps the form without the final *r* has been copied from an earlier incorrect spelling.

Ballyrolly
J 5873

Baile Rolaí
"Rolly's townland"

1. Ralfetona, Ecclesia de	Eccles. Tax. 18	1306c
2. Balliroly	Inq. Ult. (Down) §2 Jac. I	1605
3. Ballyerollie	Terrier (Reeves) 57	1615c
4. Ballyrollie	Terrier (O' Laverty) 327	1615c
5. Ballyrolly	CPR Jas. I 326a	1617
6. Ballyrolly, the bay of	Ham. Copy Inq. li	1623
7. Ballyrolly	Ham. Copy Inq. xxxiii	1623

8. Balle-Rolloy	Ham. Copy Inq. xxxiv	1623
9. Ballyrolly	Inq. Ult. (Down) §75 Car. I	1636
10. Ballyrolly	Inq. Ult. (Down) §109 Car. I	1650c
11. Ballyrolly	Montgomery MSS 54 n.34	1650c
12. Bellie Rollie	Montgomery MSS 135 n.41	1652
13. Ballyrolly	Census 93	1659c
14. Ballerolley	BSD 88	1661
15. (?)Ballyelly	Sub. Roll Down 281	1663
16. Ballyrolly	Wm. Map (OSNB) E 167, E 24	1810
17. Ballyrolly	Bnd. Sur. (OSNB) E 167, E 24	1830c
18. Rawley's Town	J O'D (OSNB) E 167, E 24	1834c
19. ˌbɑliˈrɔli	Local pronunciation	1991

The earliest attested form is important as it shows that this name was of Norman origin containing the personal name *Ralfe*, followed by an inflected form of *tūn* "town", meaning "Ralfe's town". Black (1946: xliv) informs us that the name Ralph, although introduced to these islands by the Normans, is of Germanic origin. Woulfe (1923: 196) states that Ralph was one of the most common names among the Normans who came to Ireland but that its popularity was short-lived. It is normally gaelicized *Radhulbh* (later *Ráulph*) but this townland name seems to contain a by-form, possibly hypocoristic.

The presence of *baile* shows the name was subsequently gaelicized. There is another townland of this name in the parish of Down, Co. Down, which may derive from the same Irish original as this name.

Ballyvester
J 5777

Baile Bheastair
"Wester's townland"

1. Balliwester	Inq. Ult. (Down) §2 Jac. I	1605
2. Ballewaster	Ham. Copy Inq. xlii	1623
3. Ballevaster	Ham. Copy Inq. xxxiv	1623
4. Ballevaster	CPR Chas. I 230	1627
5. Ballyvaster	Inq. Ult. (Down) §75 Car. I	1636
6. Ballyvestor	Inq. Ult. (Down) §109 Car. I	1650c
7. Ballyvaster	Montgomery MSS 54 n.34	1650c
8. Ballyvester	Census 93	1659c
9. Ballevester & Ballehay	BSD 88	1661
10. Ballyvester	Reg. Deeds abstracts ii §26	1739
11. Ballyvester	Wm. Map (OSNB) E 167, E 24	1810
12. Ballyvester	Bnd. Sur. (OSNB) E 167, E 24	1830c
13. Ballyvester	High Const. Applot. (OSNB) E 167, E 24	1833
14. Vester's Town	J O'D (OSNB) E 167	1834c
15. ˌbaliˈvestər	Local pronunciation	1991

The second element seems be the relatively rare surname Wester which derives from Old English *wester* "the westerner" (Reaney 1958: 347).

Ballywhiskin	*Baile Uí Uiscín* (?)	
J 6073	"Whiskin's townland"	
1. Ballywhiskan	Reg. Deeds abstracts i §30	1707
2. Whiskin	Wm. Map (OSNB) E 167, E 24	1810
3. Ballywhiskin	Bnd. Sur. (OSNB) E 167, E 24	1830c
4. Ballywhiskin	High Const. Applot. (OSNB) E 167, E 24	1833
5. Whiskin is an English surname	J O'D (OSNB) E 167, E 24	1834c
6. ˌbaliˈwiskən	Local pronunciation	1991

The second element is somewhat elusive. It could be a corruption of either an English surname, as O'Donovan suggested, or an Anglo-Norman one, but Whiskin, as it stands, does not appear to have existed as a surname. One possibility is that the second element could be an anglicized form of the Gaelic surname *Ó hUiscín*; the problem with this suggestion is that *Ó hUiscín* is attested only as a Galway surname (Woulfe 1923: 577).

Ballywilliam	*Baile Mhic Uilliam*	
J 5781	"McWilliam's townland"	
1. Ballimacwilliam	Inq. Ult. (Down) §2 Jac. I	1605
2. Balle-McWilliam	Ham. Copy Inq. xxxiv	1623
3. Ballemcwilliam	CPR Chas I 230	1627
4. Ballymacwilliam	Inq. Ult. (Down) §75 Car. I	1636
5. Ballymacwilliam	Inq. Ult. (Down) §109 Car. I	1650c
6. Ballywilliam	Inq. Ult. (Down) §109 Car. I	1650c
7. Ballymacwilliam	Montgomery MSS 54 n.34	1650c
8. Ballywilliam	Census 93	1659c
9. Ballewilliam	BSD 88	1661
10. Ballywillan	Sub. Roll Down 281	1663
11. Ballywilliam	Wm. Map (OSNB) E 167, E 24	1810
12. Ballywilliam	Bnd. Sur. (OSNB) E 167, E 24	1830c
13. William's Town	J O'D (OSNB) E 167, E 24	1834c
14. ˌbaliˈwiljəm	Local pronunciation	1991

Since *m(a)c* occurs in forms 1–5, 7, it is clear that the second element is the surname *Mac Uilliam*, as opposed to the forename *Uilliam*, as one might be led to believe from the current form of the name. The English name William is a borrowing of Old German *Willihelm*, *Willelm* which has been the source of a great many surnames throughout Europe. *Mac Uilliam* is anglicized Mc William(s), Williamson, Wilson, etc.

Carneyhill	Of uncertain origin	
J 5972		
1. Carnyhill	Census 93	1659c
2. Carneyhill	Wm. Map (OSNB) E 167, E 24	1810
3. Carneyhill	Bnd. Sur. (OSNB) E 167, E 24	1830c
4. Carneyhill	High Const. Applot. (OSNB) E 167, E 24	1833
5. Carney's Hill	J O'D (OSNB) E 167, E 24	1834c
6. ˌkɑrniˈhil	Local pronunciation	1991

Despite its apparent transparency, this name may not derive from the surname Carney + hill, as the forms suggest. It is possible that it derives from an Irish original *Carnaigh Choill* "stony place of the hazel", where *carnaigh* is dat. sing. of *carnach*. In Scottish Gaelic *càrnach* can mean "stony ground" (*Dwelly* s.v.). For a discussion of this possible derivation see **Carney Hill** in the parish of Drumgooland, Co. Down.

However, in the absence of further historical forms the evidence for such a derivation is not conclusive, and it must be borne in mind that the surname Kearney was common in the Ards in the 17th century. We know that this family was resident in the Upper Ards in the early 17th century as *lez Mc Kearneys* are cited in an inquisition taken at Ardquin in 1605 (*Inq. Ult.* §2 Jac. I). There is also a minor name in the parish of Bangor known as **Kearney's Hill**. If Carneyhill had been named by English speakers, we might expect a form such as *Carney's Hill.* However, it is noteworthy that in this parish there is another townland, **Millerhill**, which shows obvious similarities with Carneyhill and which is also mentioned in the *Census* of c.1659. In view of this, it is more probable that the name Carneyhill was coined by English speakers than that it derived from *Carnaigh Choill.*

Carrowdore — *Ceathrú Dobhair*
J 5772 — "water quarter"

1. Kerrowe Dorne	CPR Chas. I 228	1627
2. Corrondorne	Inq. Ult. (Down) §75 Car. I	1636
3. Carrowdorne	Inq. Ult. (Down) §109 Car. 1	1650c
4. Carrowdore	Montgomery MSS 54 n.34	1650c
5. Carradoran	Reg. Deeds abstracts i §30	1707
6. Carrodore	Downshire Direct. 319	1823
7. Carrowdore	OSNB E 167, E 24	1834c
8. Ceathramha Doir "Dore's Quarter"	J O'D (OSNB) E 167, E 24	1834c
9. Ceathramha Dobhair	Post-Sheanchas 43	1905
10. Dore's Quarter	Joyce iii 185	1913
11. Ceathrú Dobhair	AGBP 114	1969
12. Ceathrú Dobhair	Éire Thuaidh	1988
13. Ceathrú Dobhair	GÉ 198	1989
14. 'kɑrədor	Local pronunciation	1991

The element *ceathrú* "quarter" is not uncommon in the place-names of the Lower Ards, though it has sometimes been dropped as a first element as, for example, in the early forms for **Crossnamuckley** in the neighbouring parish of Newtownards. The second element of Carrowdore i.e. *dobhar* "water" is no longer used in Modern Irish dialects except in calcified compounds such as *dobharchú* "otter" (lit. "water-hound"). However, it is preserved in place-names; for example, Gweedore, Co. Donegal is an anglicization of *Gaoth Dobhair* "water inlet".

Carryreagh — *An Cheathrú Riabhach*
J 5778 — "the grey quarter"

1. Ballinecarrowreogh	Inq. Ult. (Down) §2 Jac 1	1605
2. Ballinecarrowreogh	CPR Jas. I 73b	1605
3. Balle-Carowreogh	Ham. Copy Inq. xliv	1623

4. Ballekerrowreagh al Ballencreaghie	CPR Chas. I 230	1627
5. Ballycarrowreagh al Ballenecreagh	Inq. Ult. (Down) §75 Car 1	1636
6. Carrowreagh	Census 93	1659c
7. Ballecarrowreagh	BSD 88	1661
8. Canneyreagh	High Const. Applot. (OSNB) E 167, E 24	1833
9. Cannyreagh	OSNB E 167, E 24	1834c
10. Ceathramha Riach "grey quarter"	J O'D (OSNB) E 167, E 24	1834c
11. ˈkɑniˈre:	Local pronunciation	1991
12. ˈkarəˈre:	Local pronunciation	1991

Forms 1 and 2 indicate that *baile* was formerly the first element in this place-name, followed by the gen. sing. fem. of the article. Traces of the article are also evident in forms 4b and 5b. Forms 8 and 9, which were collected in the area in the 1830s by the Ordnance Survey, tally with one of our recorded local pronunciations (form 11) where the *rr* of *carry* (*ceathrú*), has become *nn* due to dissimilation.

Craigboy — *An Chré Bhuí*

J 5876 — "the yellow clay"

1. Ballinecreaghy	CPR Jas. I 73b	1605
2. Ballencreboy alias Ballymcabry	CPR Chas. I 230	1627
3. Ballynecreaboy al. Ballymaccabry	Inq. Ult. (Down) §75 Car. 1	1636
4. Ballycreboy	Inq. Ult. (Down) §75 Car. I	1636
5. Ballycreboy	Census 93	1659c
6. Creboy	Descr. Ards 38	1683
7. Cragbuy	Montgomery MSS 420 n.93	1717
8. Craigboy	Reg. Deeds abstracts ii §636	1776
9. Craigboy	Wm. Map (OSNB) E 167, E 24	1810
10. Craigboy	Bnd. Sur. (OSNB) E 167, E 24	1830
11. Creg Buidhe "yellow rock"	J O'D (OSNB) E 167, E 24	1834c
12. ˈkre:gˈbɔi	Local pronunciation	1991

Forms 2a, 3a, 4–6 would suggest that the first element was originally *cré*, "clay", as opposed to *creig* "crag, rock", which is indicated by forms 7–10. Since Irish would not have been particularly strong in the Donaghadee area in this period, it is perhaps more likely that this change in the first element occurred among English speakers. Speakers of English would probably have been quite familiar, and therefore more comfortable, with an anglicized form of *creig*, which occurs more frequently as a place-name element than *cré*.

Drumfad — *Droim Fada*

J 5973 — "long ridge"

1. Drumfad	Census 93	1659c
2. Balledrumfade	BSD 87	1661
3. Drumfad	Wm. Map (OSNB) E 167, E 24	1810
4. Drumfad	Bnd. Sur. (OSNB) E 167, E 24	1830c

5. Druim Fada "long ridge"	J O'D (OSNB) E 167, E 24	1834c
6. ˌdrəmˈfa:d	Local pronunciation	1991

This is one of the few instances of *droim* "ridge" being used as a first element in the place-names of the Lower Ards. Drumfad also appears as a townland name in Donegal, Tyrone and Sligo.

Ganaway — See parish of St Andrews alias Ballyhalbert

Grangee — *Baile na Gráinsí*
J 5773 — "townland of the grange"

1. Ballinegrangee	Inq. Ult. (Down) §2 Jac. I	1605
2. Ballenegrange	Ham. Copy Inq. xlii	1623
3. Ballenegrange	Ham. Copy Inq. xxxiv	1623
4. Ballygrange	Inq. Ult. (Down) §75 Car. I	1636
5. (?)Ballygrangeenare	Inq. Ult. (Down) §109 Car. I	1650c
6. Ballygrange	Montgomery MSS 54 n.34	1650c
7. Granshagh	Census 93	1659c
8. Grangee	Wm. Map (OSNB) E 167, E 24	1810
9. Grangee	Bnd. Sur. (OSNB) E 167, E 24	1830
10. Grainseach Aedha "Hugh's grange"	J O'D (OSNB) E 167, E 24	1834c
11. ˌgrɑnˈdʒi	Local pronunciation	1991

The historical forms show that this name has undergone a number of changes since the 17th century. The first three forms attest the presence of *baile* + the gen. sing. of the article and indicate an Irish original *Baile na Gráinsí* "townland of the grange". Form 7, however, appears to reflect merely a nominative *Gráinseach* "grange" and the *OSNB* forms seem to derive from a dative form *Gráinsigh*. The local pronunciation is somewhat surprising but may have undergone a shift in stress and probably prompted O'Donovan's suggested Irish form.

Herdstown — *Baile Heird* (?)
J 5679 — "Herd's townland"

1. Herdstown	Wm. Map (OSNB) E 167, E 24	1810
2. Herdstown	Bnd. Sur. (OSNB) E 167, E 24	1830c
3. Herdstown	High Const. Applot. (OSNB) E 167, E 24	1833
4. Heard is a family name	J O'D (OSNB) E 167, E 24	1834c
5. ˈherdztəun	Local pronunciation	1991

The first element is the English surname Herd which derives from Old English *hierde* "herdsman" (Reaney 1958: 162). This name may appear to be of a similar construction to nearby Hogstown but it is not nearly as old. The earliest form for Hogstown dates from the 14th century and shows that it derives from the surname Hog followed by English "town". Many names of this type were subsequently gaelicized, for example the name **Ballyrolly**, also in this parish, was known in the Anglo-Norman period as *Ralfetona*. One might expect 17th-century forms for Herdstown to have followed this pattern, but the absence of forms such as *Ballyherd* may suggest that Herdstown is a relatively late name coined, perhaps in the 18th century, by English speakers along the same lines as **Cronstown** and **Gregstown** in the neighbouring parish of Newtownards.

Hogstown	An English form	
J 5779		
1. Hogetown	Inq. Earldom Ulster iii 64	1333
2. Hogstown	Wm. Map (OSNB) E 167, E 24	1810
3. Hogstown	Bnd. Sur. (OSNB) E 167, E 24	1830c
4. Hogstown	High Const. Applot. (OSNB) E 167, E 24	1833
5. ˈhɔgztəun	Local pronunciation	1991

Form 1 follows a structure common to a number of names in the Ards *viz.* Anglo-Norman surname/personal name + English *tūn* "town". The English surname Hogg/Hogge derives from Old English *hogg* "pig"; however Hog and Hogge are also alternative forms of the English surname Hodge(s), a pet form of Roger, so it is difficult to state with any certainty which of these two surnames is the first element in this place-name (Reaney 1958: 166–7). It is curious, however, that we find *Hogetown* in a document from the 14th century and yet it does not seem to appear in the 17th-century sources which contain references to the other townlands in the area. The discussion on **Herdstown** refers to the gaelicization of names of this type, which would lead one to expect forms such as *Ballyhog* for this name. Given the fact that there are no examples of such a form, and that the current form differs from the 14th century spelling in all but the possessive *s*, it is likely that this name was never gaelicized.

Island Hill	An English form	
J 5774		
1. Iland Hill	Census 93	1659c
2. Islandhill	Bnd. Sur. (OSNB) E 167, E 24	1830c
3. Island Hill	Tythes Applot. (OSNB) E 167, E24	1830c
4. Islandhill	High Const. Applot. (OSNB) E 167, E 24	1833
5. ˌailənd ˈhil	Local pronunciation	1991

The form of this name and paucity of early spellings suggest that it was coined by English speakers (for a discussion of the element *island* in Ulster place-names see Ó Mainnín 1989–90). There is an area of high ground in the vicinity (on which a rath is situated) which is probably the "island" the townland is named from.

Kilbright	*Cill Bhreachtáin* (?) "church of the variegated place"	
J 6072		
1. Kilbracti, ecclesiam de	Pontif. Hib. i §59	1204
2. Ballikillbratten	Inq. Ult. (Down) §2 Jac. I	1605
3. Kilbratan	Ham. Copy Inq. xlvi	1623
4. Kilbrate	Ham. Patent xii	1630

5.	Ballykilbraten	Ham. Patent xiii	1630
6.	Ballekilbraten	Ham. Patent xiii	1630
7.	Ballykilbrackton	Inq. Ult. (Down) §75 Car. I	1636
8.	Ballekilbratten	Inq. Ult. (Down) §104 Car. I	1645
9.	Ballekillrattan	Inq. Ult. (Down) §104 Car. I	1645
10.	Ballykilbracton	Montgomery MSS 54 n.34	1650c
11.	Kilbright	Census 93	1659c
12.	Ballekillbright	BSD 88	1661
13.	Kilbreght	ASCD 324	1723
14.	Kilbright	Wm. Map (OSNB) E 167, E 24	1810
15.	Kilbright	Bnd. Sur. (OSNB) E 167, E 24	1830c
16.	Kilbright	High Const. Applot. (OSNB) E 167, E 24	1833
17.	Cill Bhríghde "Bridget's church"	J O'D (OSNB) E 167, E 24	1834c
18.	kil'brait	Local pronunciation	1991

Since form 1 clearly indicates the presence of a church in this townland, the first element is likely to be *cill* "a church", rather than *coill* "a wood". The second element seems to be a diminutive form, *brechtán* "variegated place" (later *breachtán*) which derives from *brecht* (Old Irish *mrecht*) "variegated, diversified". Forms such as 2, 3, 5–10 reflect the presence of the diminutive suffix *-án* in the final syllable which appears in words such as *sruthán* "a small stream", and *ardán* "a small height".

Bright, a parish and townland name in the barony of Lecale, also comes from a by-form of this word *mrecht*, later *brecht*, and appears in *The Tripartite Life of St Patrick* (*Trip. Life* i 38) as *Mrechtan*. It is interesting to note that this form also seems to contain the diminutive suffix *-án*.

Killaghy
J 5676

Cill Achaidh
"the church of the field"

1.	Ballikillaghie	Inq. Ult. (Co. Down) §2 Jac. I	1605
2.	Bally-killaghie	Ham. Copy Inq. xxxiv	1623
3.	Ballekillaghee	CPR Chas. I 230	1627
4.	Ballykillaghy	Inq. Ult. (Down) §75 Car. I	1636
5.	Ballykillaghy	Inq. Ult. (Down) §109 Car. I	1650c
6.	Ballykillaghy	Montgomery MSS 54 n.34	1650c
7.	Killaghy	Census 93	1659c
8.	Ballekillaghy	BSD 88	1661
9.	Killaghey	Wm. Map (OSNB) E 167, E 24	1810
10.	Killaughy	Tythes Applot. (OSNB) E 167, E 24	1830c
11.	Killaughey	High Const. Applot. (OSNB) E 167, E 24	1833
12.	Coill Eachdha "Eochy's wood"	J O'D (OSNB) E 167, E 24	1834c
13.	ˌki'lɔxi	Local pronunciation	1991
14.	'klɔxi	Local pronunciation	1991
15.	ˌkil'ɑxi	Local pronunciation	1991

O'Laverty (ii 27–8) states that a part of a field in this townland was thought to have been a graveyard. He also claims that a mud-walled building near the boundary between Ballybuttle and Killaghy was used for ecclesiastical purposes. This structure was removed in the last quarter of the 18th century. O'Laverty believed that Killaghy, before it became a separate townland, was initially a portion of the townland of Ballyhay and that the Church of St Mary was situated in it (see **Ballyhay**). In view of the ecclesiastical evidence, the first element is more likely to be *cill* "a church" than *coill* a wood".

Millisle J 5975	*Baile an Mhuilinn* (?) "townland of the mill"	
1. (?)Ballinwillin	Inq. Ult. (Down) §2 Jac. I	1605
2. (?)Ballywillen al Ballymullen, the river and bay of	Ham. Copy Inq. lii	1623
3. (?)Ballewillen, the bay of	Ham. Copy Inq. li	1623
4. Mill Isle	OSNB E 167, E 24	1834c
5. Baile Mhic Crúis	Post-Sheanchas 97	1905
6. Oileán an Mhuilinn	AGBP 118	1969
7. Oileán an Mhuilinn	GÉ 142	1989
8. məˈləil	Local pronunciation	1991

The earliest version of the name which resembles the current form is taken from the *OSNB* c. 1834. In the *OSNB* for Donaghadee O'Donovan writes, "Mille Isle supposed from Milles Isles, thousand islands, the shore being rocky, and a great number of them appear above water when the tide is at ebb."

However, forms 1–3 indicate an Irish original *Baile an Mhuilinn* "the townland of the mill" which may well have been an earlier name for Millisle. Unfortunately there is no conclusive evidence that these forms refer to Millisle. *Oileán an Mhuilinn*, "island of the mill" (forms 6, 7) is simply a translation of "mill isle". Form 5 is a postulated Irish form of the townland in which the village of Millisle is situated, namely, Ballymacruise.

Millerhill J 5977	An English form	
1. Miller Hill	Bnd. Sur. (OSNB) E 167, E 24	1830c
2. Millar Hill	Tythes Applot. (OSNB) E 167, E 24	1830c
3. ˌmələr ˈhil	Local pronunciation	1991

We have found no documentary evidence of this place-name prior to the *OSNB* for Donaghadee. It would seem likely, therefore, that this is a relatively late name coined by English speakers which replaced an earlier name. It should be borne in mind, however, that Miller Hill may be a translation of an earlier Irish name, especially if the forms for Millisle (also in this parish) which seem to represent *Baile an Mhuilinn*, "town of the mill" are authentic. If this is the case, it is strange that there is no trace of a compatible anglicized Gaelic form for Millerhill in the historical sources.

Sloanstown J 5871	An English form	
1. Slewanstowne	Census 93	1659c
2. Sloanstown	Wm. Map (OSNB) E 167, E 24	1810

3. Sloanstown	Bnd. Sur. (OSNB) E 167, E 24	1830c
4. Sloanstown	High Const. Applot. (OSNB) E 167, E 24	1833
5. 'slo:nztəun	Local pronunciation	1991

The East Ulster surname Sloan is common in Co. Down and the Sloans have left a lasting record of their presence in this townland name. The name *Slowan* is cited as one of the most common Irish surnames in the *Census* of c.1659 for the Newry and Mourne area (*Census* 83). Woulfe (1923: 647) informs us that the Sloans of Antrim and Down are of Scottish origin. We have found no forms for Sloanstown earlier than c. 1659 and, while it may well be the case that there was an Irish form for this place-name such as *Baile Uí Shluáin*, we have no evidence of it.

Templepatrick — *Teampall Phádraig*
J 5877 — "Patricks's church"

1. Temple-Patrick	Inq. Ult. (Down) §2 Jac. I	1605
2. Templepatrick	Terrier (Reeves) 57	1615c
3. Templepatrick	Wm. Map (OSNB) E 167, E 24	1810
4. Templepatrick	Bnd. Sur. (OSNB) E 167, E 24	1830c
5. Teampul Phátraic "Patrick's church"	J O'D (OSNB) E 167, E 24	1834c
6. ˌtɛmpəl'patrik	Local pronunciation	1991

According to tradition, St. Patrick landed here after a journey from Scotland and left the imprint of his hand and foot on a rock near the shore. A well in the vicinity has been credited with healing qualities (*O'Laverty* ii 34–5; *Harris Hist.* 68; *Descr. Ards* 38; *Knox Hist.* 485).

Townparks of Donaghadee — An English form
J 5980

1. Town and Parks of Donaghadee	OSNB E 167, E24	1834c

OTHER NAMES

Foreland Point — An English form
J 5881

It is often difficult to find references to minor names such as this, but Knox (*Knox Hist.* 487) mentions this one briefly in relation to seafaring matters:

> About a mile north of Donaghadee is Foreland Point, from which extends a ledge of rocks to the eastward, with an iron perch in it. Deputy Rock, on which is a red buoy, lies half way between Donaghadee and Copeland, and has about eight feet of water at low tide. The proper course through the sound is between the Foreland and the East Deputy buoys.

Kennedy's Hill	An English form
J 5572	

The Gaelic surname *Ó Cinnéide* derives from *ceann* "head", and *éidigh* "ugly" (MacLysaght 1985: 176). We know that there were Kennedys in this area in the first half of the 17th century; note a certain H. Kennedy of Greengraves in the parish of Newtownards who attended the funeral of the first Viscount Montgomery in 1636 (*Montgomery MSS* 131 n.10). Kennedy is among the fifty most common surnames in Ulster (Bell 1988: 110); for information on the Kennedys in Scotland see Black (1946: 392–3). This surname appears in a number of place-names in Ireland, including Newtownmountkennedy, Co. Wicklow; Ballykennedy, Co. Waterford; and Garrykennedy, Co. Tipperary. This hill was probably named after a local tenant or landowner.

Mill Burn	*Abhainn an Mhuilinn* (?)
J 5775	"the river of the mill"

1. (?)Owen Mullen	Ham. Copy Inq. lii	1623

It is possible that the above form, which appears to represent an Irish original *Abhainn an Mhuilinn*, is a reference to Mill Burn.

St Patrick's Well	An English form
J 5977	

See **Templepatrick** above.

PARISH OF GREY ABBEY

Grey Abbey, a parish of 7,689 acres, is bounded on the west by Strangford Lough, the parish of Newtownards lies to the north, the parishes of Donaghadee and Ballywalter are to the east, and the parish of Inishargy lies to the south. Fourteen islands in Strangford Lough are also included in the parish.

The earliest reference to the monastery we now call Grey Abbey comes from *Grace's Annals* (*EA* 92 n.c) 1193 AD, where it is referred to both as *Jugum Dei* "yoke of God" and *Monasterlech*, the latter being an attempt to represent Irish *Mainistir Liath* "grey abbey". The founder of the monastery was Affreca, daughter of Godred King of Man and wife of John de Courcy and this is documented in an early 13th-century Latin source compiled in the Isle of Man (*Chron. Man* §60 71):

> *Iohannes quidem de Cursi habuit filiam Godredi nomine Affrecam in matrimonium quae fundavit abbatium Sanctae Mariae de Jugo Dei, quae ibidem sepulta est.*
>
> "That John de Courcy had in marriage the daughter of Godred, in name Affreca, who founded the Abbey of St. Mary of *Jugum Dei*, who is buried in the same place."

We find reference to the monastery of *Jugum Dei* in *The Chronicle of Mailros* (*Chron. Mailros*) under the years 1222 and 1237 (*EA* 92 n. c). According to the *Ecclesiastical Taxation of Ireland 1302–6* (*Eccles. Tax.*) the temporalities of the abbot of *Jugum Dei* came to a total of £35. 6s. 8d. Two townlands from the parish, Ballymurphy and Ballycastle, are found in an important 14th-century Anglo-Norman document (*Inq. Earldom Ulster*), although the form for Ballymurphy may refer to the townland of that name in the parish of Ardquin.

At the time of the dissolution of the monasteries in the mid-16th century the abbey was in possession of 16 townlands in the surrounding area and of the rectories of two parishes (*EA ibid.*). These townlands are cited in an inquisition taken in Downpatrick in 1636 (*Inq. Ult.* §75 Car I). In 1604 John Kinge and John Thomas Hibbots were granted the site, ambit and precinct of Grey Abbey (*CPR Jas. I* 38b). A large area of land, including territories in the Ards, was granted to Thomas Ireland in 1605 but he assigned his rights by this grant to James Hamilton. Grey Abbey was among the lands Hamilton sold to Montgomery in 1605 (*CPR Jas. I* 72b) but a dispute over land emerged between them which the Earl of Abercorn was called in to settle. He decreed that Hamilton was to regrant to Montgomery the same abbey lands which he had sold him in 1605. Thus Hamilton granted Grey Abbey along with Black Abbey, Movilla and Newtown to Hugh Montgomery in a deed dated 1618 (Chart, D.A. 1942: 141). An inquisition taken at Ardquin in 1605 (*Inq. Ult.* §2 Jac. 1) cites the seven "adjoining" townlands of Grey Abbey in much the same order as the grant in *CPR Jas. I* 72b but there are some spelling differences. An inquisition taken at Ballymaghan in 1603 (*Ex. Inq. 1 Jac. I*) follows the same order as the Ardquin inquisition but there are spelling differences.

According to the *Census* of c. 1659 there was a total of 117 people resident in the parish at that time. However, this information must be tempered with the fact that it is unlikely that the figures given are representative of the total population. The list of "tituladoes" in the parish of Grey Abbey includes William Montgomery, George Austine, whose name appears beside Ballymurphy, and John Peacock who is mentioned beside Tullykevin. *The Book of Survey & Distribution* (*BSD*) of 1661 AD and *Subsidy Roll for the county of Down* (*Sub. Roll Down*) of 1663 AD, cite a number of townlands in the parish. Documents concerning the sale of the Rosemount estate in 1703 and 1717, which are cited in *The Montgomery Manuscripts* (*Montgomery MSS* 419–20 n.93), also contain a number of forms for place-names in the Grey Abbey area.

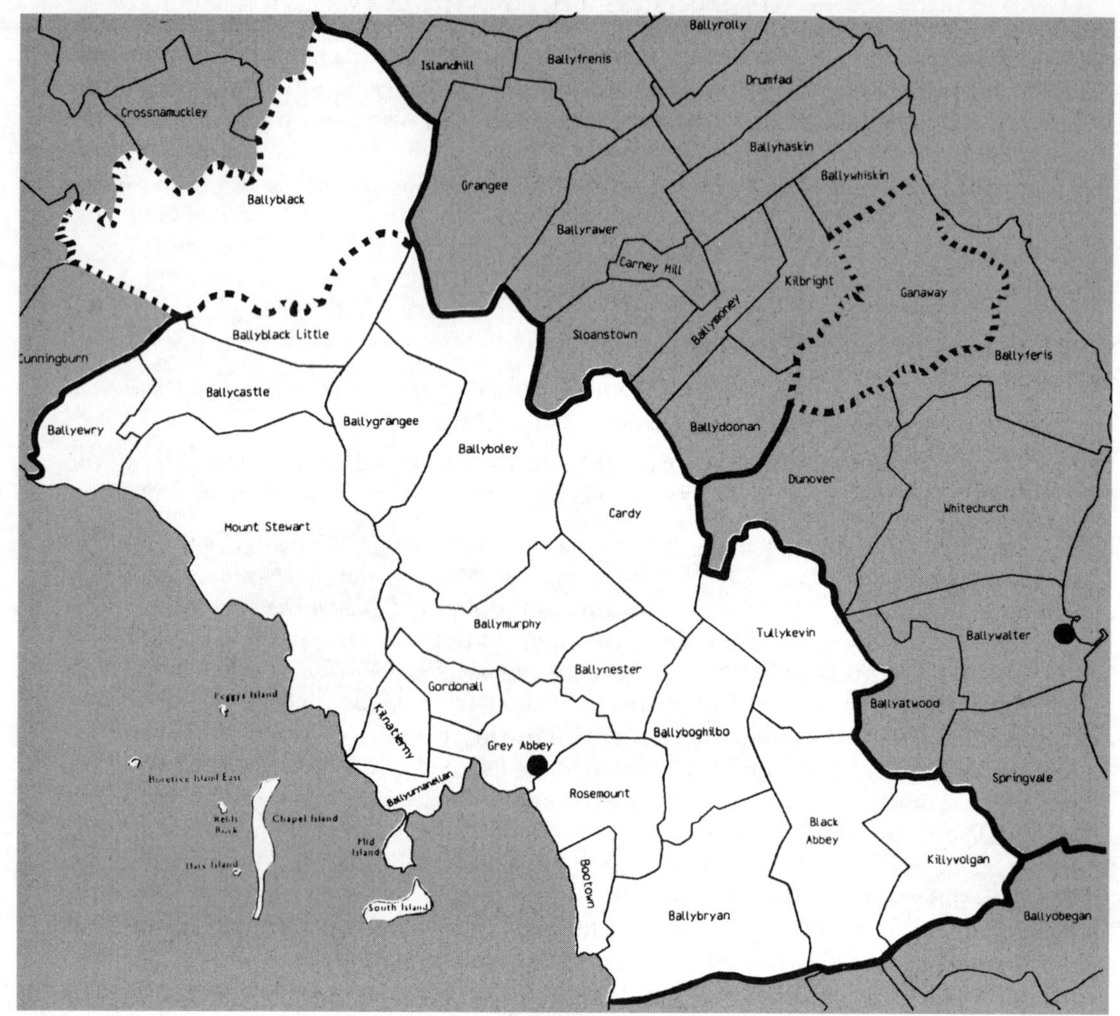

Parish of Grey Abbey

Barony of Ards Lower

Townlands

Ballyblack (shared with Newtownards)
Ballyblack, Little
Ballyboghilbo
Ballyboley
Ballybryan
Ballycastle
Ballyewry
Ballygrangee
Ballymurphy
Ballynester
Ballyurnanellan
Black Abbey
Bootown
Cardy
Gordonall
Grey Abbey
Killyvolgan
Kilnatierny
Mount Stewart
Rosemount
Tullykevin

Islands

Boretree Island, East
Chapel Island
Mid Island
South Island

Town: Grey Abbey

Given its high frequency in the barony of the Lower Ards as a whole, it is no surprise to find that *baile* "townland" is the first element of 11 of the 21 townlands in Grey Abbey. In the *OSNB* for Grey Abbey O'Donovan informs us that he had difficulty in recording the names of the islands from the locals and, as was the case in the Ards in general, he did not meet with any local native Irish speakers.

PARISH NAME

Grey Abbey J 5768	*An Mhainistir Liath* "the grey abbey"	
1. Mainistir Liath	MacCana's Itinerary 55	1700c
2. de Jugo Dei, Whit Abbey al	Grace's Annals (EA) 92 n.c	1193
3. de Iugo Dei, abbatiam Sanctae Mariae	Chron. Man §60 71	1204
4. de Iugo Dei, abbas	Chron. Mailros (EA) 92 n.c	1222
5. Jugo Dei, Temperalia Abbatis de	Eccles. Tax. 92	1306c
6. Jugo Dei, Greyabbey, Mon. de	Annates Ulst. 117 app	1491
7. Yuo Dei	Annates Ulst. 113	1505
8. Graye abbaye	S-E Ulster Map	1580c
9. Hore Abbey al Leighe al Jugo Dei	Fiants Eliz. §4788	1585
10. Hore Abbey al Leighe al Jugo Dei	Fiants Eliz. §4788	1585
11. Gray	Hondius' Map	1591
12. Graye ab	Mercator's Ire.	1595
13. Graye abb	Mercator's Ulst.	1595
14. M° Graie abby	Boazio's Map (BM)	1599
15. de Leigh, monasterium al Jugo Dei al Grey Abbay	Ex. 1 Inq. Jac. I	1603
16. Gray-Abbey otherwise Monesterlee	CPR Jas. I 12b	1603
17. Hoare-Abbey otherwise Leigh or Jugo Dei in Arde	CPR Jas. I 14a	1603
18. Mo Graia	Bartlett Maps (Esch. Co. Maps) i	1603
19. Cistercen de Leigh al Jugodei al Gray-abby	Inq. Ult. (Down) §2 Jac. I	1605
20. Gray Abb	Speed's Ulster	1610
21. Gray Abb	Speed's Antrim & Down	1610
22. Gray ab	Speed's Ireland	1610
23. Mo. Graye	Norden's Map	1610c
24. Grey Abbey	CPR Chas. I 65	1625
25. Gray Abbey	CPR Chas. I 225	1627
26. Gray-Abbey	Inq. Ult. (Down) §75 Car. I	1636
27. Gray-Abbey	Inq. Ult. (Down) §104 Car. I	1645
28. Gray-abbay	Inq. Ult. (Down) §109 Car. I	1650c
29. Gray Abbey	Inq. Down (Reeves1) 133	1657
30. Gray Abbay	Census 92	1659c
31. Gray Abby	Trien. Visit. (Bramhall) 1	1661
32. de Leigh, Abbie al Jugo-Dei al Gray-Abby al Hore-Abby	Inq. Ult. (Down) §1 Car. II	1662

33. de Leigh abbia al Jugo-Dei al Gray abby al Hoar-abby	Inq. Ult. (Down) §1 Car. II	1662
34. Greyabby	Trien. Visit. (Margetson) 22	1664
35. Gray Abbey	Trien. Visit. (Boyle) 44	1679
36. Monestrelea	Descr. Ards 38	1683
37. Grey Abbey	MacCana's Itinerary 55	1700c
38. Greyabbey	Montgomery MSS 419 n. 93	1703
39. Abbey of Leigh al Jugo Dei al Grayabbie al Hoare Abbey	Montgomery MSS 420 n. 93	1717
40. Grey Abbey	Wm. Map (OSNB) No. 92	1810
41. An Mhainistir Liath	Post-Sheanchas 75	1905
42. An Mhainistir Liath	AGBP 116	1969
43. An Mhainistir Liath	Éire Thuaidh	1988
44. An Mhainistir Liath	GÉ 135	1989
45. ˌgreːˈɑbi	Local pronunciation	1991

The ruins of the monastery of Grey Abbey are to be found in the eastern part of the village of Grey Abbey. Founded in 1193 by Affreca, wife of John de Courcy and daughter of Godred, king of Man, it was a Cistercian monastery and was colonized by monks from Holm Cultram in Cumberland. It was dissolved c. 1541–3. The monastery was formerly known in Latin as *Abbatia de Jugo Dei* "abbey of the yoke of God" and, in Irish, as *An Mhainistir Liath* "the grey abbey" (*ASCD* 275–9).

TOWNLAND NAMES

Ballyblack
Ballyblack Little
J 5573, 5571

Baile Bhleaic
"Black's townland"

1. (?)Ballivlack	Inq. Ult. (Down) §2 Jac. I	1605
2. Ballipisragh	Inq. Ult. (Down) §2 Jac. I	1605
3. Ballyvlacke	CPR Jas. I 73a	1605
4. Balleblack al Ballinepistraghe	CPR Chas. I 228	1627
5. Balleblacks al Ballynepistragh	Inq. Ult. (Down) §75 Car. I	1636
6. Ballyblacks al Ballynepistragh	Inq. Ult. (Down) §109 Car. I	1650c
7. Ballybrack	Hib. Reg. Ards	1657c
8. Ballyblack	Census 93, 94	1659c
9. Ballyblacke al. Ballybracke	BSD 83	1661
10. Balleblacke Towne	BSD 87	1661
11. Ballyblakes al Ballynepistragh	Inq. Ult. (Down) §1 Car. II	1662
12. Ballyblakes	Inq. Ult. (Down) §1 Car. II	1662
13. Ballyblachs al. Ballintragh	Inq. Ult. (Down) §1 Car II	1662
14. Ballyblack	Montgomery MSS 419 n. 93	1703
15. Ballyblack	Montgomery MSS 420 n. 93	1717
16. Ballyblack	Wm. Map (OSNB) E 32	1810
17. Ballyblack	Bnd. Sur. (OSNB) E 32	1830c
18. "Black's town"	J O'D (OSNB) E 32	1834c
19. ˌbɑliˈblɛk	Local pronunciation	1991

This townland is divided between the parishes of Newtownards and Grey Abbey. In the *OSNB* for Newtownards O'Donovan expresses the opinion that this place was called Ballyblack due to its proximity to Black Abbey. It seems more likely, however, that the second element is the surname Black which is, perhaps surprisingly, difficult to etymologize. It may be derived from Old English *blaec* "black"; however, the inflected form *blaca* became *blake* in Middle English and was confused with Middle English *blake* "bright, shining; pale" (Reaney 1958: 34).

Form 1 is interesting since the *v* suggests that the initial of *Black* was aspirated, as would be expected in this type of genitive construction in Irish. The forms indicate that a Gaelic version of the townland name was current in the spoken Irish in this area at the start of the 17th century, and it is for this reason that a gaelicized form of the surname Black has been suggested in the postulated Irish language form.

Ballyboley — *Baile na Buaile*
J 5770 — "townland of the summer pasturage"

1. Ballenboyle	Ex. Inq. 1 Jac. I	1603
2. Ballenboly	CPR Jas. I 38b	1604
3. Ballenbolly	CPR Jas. I 72b	1605
4. Balleneboyle	CPR Chas. I 228	1627
5. Balleneboile	Inq. Ult. (Down) §75 Car. I	1636
6. Ballyneboyle	Inq. Ult. (Down) §109 Car. I	1650c
7. Ballybelly	Hib. Reg. Ards	1657c
8. Ballyboly	Census 92	1659c
9. Ballineboyle	Inq. Ult. (Down) §1 Car. II	1662
10. Ballyboley	Montgomery MSS 419 n. 93	1703
11. Ballyboley	Montgomery MSS 420 n. 93	1717
12. Ballyboley	Wm. Map (OSNB)	1810
13. Ballyboley	Bnd. Sur. (OSNB) No. 9	1830c
14. Baile na Buaile "town of the byre"	J O'D (OSNB) No. 92	1834c
15. ˌbɑliˈboːli	Local pronunciation	1991

The gen. sing. fem. form of the definite article is apparent in forms 4–6 and 9, and the *n* of forms 1–3 may also indicate this. Forms 7 and 8, however, indicate that it was beginning to be omitted from the name in the middle of the 17th century. Its absence from forms 10 and 11 seems to show that it had been lost from the name from the start of the 18th century. The final element of this name is *buaile*, which means "milking place in summer pasturage". This word has given us the Hiberno-English term "booleying" which refers to the practice of moving cattle to mountain pastures in summer (*Joyce* i 239–40).

Ballyboghilbo — *Baile Buachalla Bó*
J 5968 — "the townland of the cowherd"

1. Bogleboe	Montgomery MSS 420 n. 93	1717
2. Ballyboghillboo	Wm. Map (OSNB) No. 92	1810
3. Ballybogilboo	Bnd. Sur. (OSNB) No. 92	1830c
4. Ballyboghillbow	High Const. Applot. (OSNB) No. 92	1833
5. Baile Buachail Bo "Herdstown"	J O'D (OSNB) No. 92	1834c

6. Baile-buachalla-bo "the town of the cowboy"	Joyce iii 71	1913
7. ˌbɑliˌbo̤gəl'bo:	Local pronunciation	1991
8. ˌbɔkəl'bo:	Local pronunciation	1991

There is a townland in Co. Limerick known as Boughilbo, from Irish *Buachaill Bó* "herd-boy". It has been tentatively suggested that this name derives from a boundary marker (Ó Maolfabhail 1990: 76). It is noteworthy that form 1 and one of the local pronunciations show affinity with Boughilbo, Co. Limerick, in that the element *baile* has been dropped from these forms. The current gen. sing. of *buachaill* is used in the suggested Gaelic form but there is justification for a form *Baile Buachaill Bó* since *buachaill* is a variant gen. sing. (*DIL* s.v. *búachaill*).

Blackabbey — *An Mhainistir Dhubh*
J 6066 — "the black abbey"

A townland belonging both to Grey Abbey and St Andrews alias Ballyhalbert. See parish of **St Andrews alias Ballyhalbert**.

Ballybryan — *Baile Bhriain*
J 5866 — "Brian's townland"

1. Ballybrenny	Ex. Inq. 1 Jac. I	1603
2. Ballybrene	Ham. Copy Inq. xxxi	1623
3. (?)Ballebrone	Inq. Ult. (Down) §75 Car. I	1636
4. Ballybryan	Census 93	1659c
5. Ballybrene al Ballybryan	Inq. Ult. (Down) §1 Car. II	1662
6. Ballybune al Ballybrian	Montgomery MSS 420 n. 93	1717
7. Ballybrene al Ballybrian	Montgomery MSS 420 n. 93	1717
8. Ballybrean	Wm. Map (OSNB) No. 92	1810
9. Ballybryan	Bnd. Sur. (OSNB) No. 92	1810
10. Ballybrian	High Const. Applot. (OSNB) No. 92	1830c
11. Baile Bruighne "town of the fairy palace"	J O'D (OSNB) No. 92	1834c
12. ˌbɑli'briən	Local pronunciation	1991
13. ˌbɑli'braiən	Local pronunciation	1991

While it is most likely that the second element is the personal name Brian, there is also a possibility that it is the adjective *bréan* "foul, putrid". It is significant that one of the two local pronunciations (form 12) would support this origin. Forms 1, 2, 5a, and 7a could well represent an original *Baile Bréine* "townland of (the) stench" and, as part of the townland borders the shore of Strangford Lough, it is possible that it was given this name from a bad smell which may have been prominent at low tide. Against that, however, forms 5b, 6b, 7b, 9 and 10 all point towards *Baile Bhriain*.

Ballycastle — *Baile an Chaisleáin*
J 5571 — "townland of the castle"

1. Castletoun	Inq. Earldom Ulster iii 65	1333
2. Ballicaslane	Ex. Inq. 1 Jac. I	1603

3. Ballecaslane	CPR Jas. I 39a	1604
4. Ballecaslane or Ballecusbane	CPR Jas. I 72b	1605
5. Ballycaslen	Ham. Copy Inq. xxxi	1623
6. Ballycastle	Inq. Ult. (Down) §75 Car. I	1636
7. Ballycastlen al Templecrone	Inq. Ult. (Down) §75 Car. I	1636
8. Ballycastle	Census 93	1659c
9. Ballecastle	Inq. Ult. (Down) §75 Car. I	1662
10. Ballycaslen als Castletowne als Ballyheighly	Montgomery MSS 268 n. 35	1675
11. Ballycastle	Wm. Map (OSNB) No. 92	1810
12. Ballycastle	Bnd. Sur. (OSNB) No. 92	1830c
13. Castletown or Ballycastle	Knox. Hist. 482	1875
14. Baile an Chaisleáin "town of the castle"	J O'D (OSNB) No. 92	1834c
15. ˌbali'kasl	Local pronunciation	1991

Form 1 is patently the Anglo-Norman formation of noun or name followed by *tūn*. Later forms such as *Ballycaslane* (2–4), *Ballycastle* (6, 8, 9 etc.) indicate that the Anglo-Norman form was gaelicized. It is interesting to note that the name *Castletown* was still occasionally applied to this townland as late as the last quarter of the 19th century (10b, 13a).

Ballyewry — *Baile Iúraí*
J 5371 — "townland of the place of yew trees"

1. Ballyhewry	Inq. Ult. (Down) §2 Jac. I	1605
2. Balliurah	Inq. Ult. (Down) §2 Jac. I	1605
3. Ballynerrew	Inq. Ult. (Down) §72 Car. I	1636
4. Ballyewry	Wm. Map (OSNB) No. 92	1810
5. Ballyewry	Bnd. Sur. (OSNB) No. 92	1830c
6. Baile Iubhraighe "town of the yew"	J O'D (OSNB) No. 92	1834c
7. Baile-Iubhraigh "the town of the yew-trees"	Joyce iii 84	1913
8. ˌbali'ju:ri	Local pronunciation	1991

The second element of this name would appear to be the gen. sing. of the word *iúrach* "vessel made of yew-wood", etc. In place-names this word also had the meaning "a place of yew trees" and according to *DIL*, the word *ibrach* (later *iúrach*) can also mean "a house of yew wood", although this meaning seems restricted to *Colmán*'s cell.

The element *iúrach* preceded by the article has given rise to the modern anglicized form of **Newry,** Co. Down. Newrath and Newragh in Co. Louth derive from Irish *An Iúrach* (*L. Log. Lú.* 16). See **Ballyurnanillan** in this parish for another possible instance of this element.

Ballygrangee — *Baile na Gráinsí*
J 5670 — "townland of the grange"

1. Ballygrangeeh	Inq. Ult. (Down) §2 Jac. I	1605
2. Ballynegrange	Ham. Copy Inq. xxxi	1623
3. Ballygrangy	Inq. Ult. (Down) §75 Car. I	1636
4. Ballygrange	Inq. Ult. (Down) §109 Car. I	1650c

5.	Ballygrangee al Kilmanagh	Inq. Ult. (Down) §109 Car. I	1650c
6.	Ballygrange	Hib. Reg. Ards	1657c
7.	Ballygrangee	Census 92	1659c
8.	Ballingrangeoh al Killmanagh	Inq. Ult. (Down) §1 Car. II	1662
9.	Ballygrange	Montgomery MSS 419 n. 93	1703
10.	Ballygrange	Montgomery MSS 420 n. 93	1717
11.	Ballygrangee	Wm. Map (OSNB) No. 92	1810
12.	Ballygrangee	Bnd. Sur. (OSNB) No. 92	1830c
13.	Baile Gráinsighe Gaoithe "town of the windy grange"	J O'D (OSNB) No. 92	1834c
14.	ˌbaliˈgrɛndʒi	Local pronunciation	1991
15.	ˌbɑliˌgrɑnˈdʒi	Local pronunciation	1991

Forms 2 and possibly 8a indicate the presence of the gen. sing. fem. form of the article. There is a townland in the neighbouring parish of Donaghadee known as **Grangee** and it is interesting that its historical forms also point to an original *Baile na Gráinsí*. The stress in form 15, which was the pronunciation of a woman aged c. 30, was probably influenced by the current written form.

The alias *Kil(l)managh* suggests an original *Cill Manach* "(the) church of (the) monks".

Ballymurphy — *Baile Uí Mhurchú*
J 5769 — "Murphy's townland"

1.	(?)Balymorky	Inq. Earldom Ulst. iii 65	1333
2.	Ballymencok	Ham. Copy Inq. xxxi	1623
3.	Ballemurcocke	Inq. Ult. (Down) §75 Car. I	1636
4.	Ballymorcock	Hib. Reg. Ards	1657c
5.	Ballymurcock	Census 92	1659c
6.	Ballymurcocke	Inq. Ult. (Down) §1 Car. II	1662
7.	Ballymurphy al Ballymurcock	Montgomery MSS 420 n. 93	1717
8.	Ballymurphy	Wm. Map (OSNB) No. 92	1810
9.	Ballymurphy	Bnd. Sur. (OSNB) No. 92	1830c
10.	Baile Ui Mhurchadha	J O'D (OSNB) No. 92	1834c
11.	ˌbaliˈmərfi	Local pronunciation	1991

There is an element of doubt as to whether form 1 refers to this townland or to **Ballymurphy** in the parish of Ardquin.

The forms ending in *-(c)k(e)* seem to indicate that the *-dh-* in *Ó Murchadha*, which is an earlier form of *Ó Murchú*, was pronounced in the 17th century as a voiced velar fricative [ɣ].

Murphy is one of the commonest surnames in Ireland and Ballymurphy occurs as a townland name in Cos. Antrim, Carlow, Clare, Galway, Limerick, Mayo, Meath, Tyrone and Cork. For a note on the surname Murphy, see **Ballymurphy** in the parish of Ardquin.

Ballynester — *Baile an Aistire*
J 5868 — "the townland of the doorkeeper"

1.	Ballynestore	Ham. Copy Inq. xxxi	1623
2.	Ballenestore	Inq. Ult. (Down) §75 Car. I	1636
3.	Ballynester	Inq. Ult. (Down) §109 Car. I	1650c

4. Ballenestore	Inq. Ult. (Down) §1 Car. II	1662
5. (?)Ballyvestore	Inq. Ult. (Down) §1 Car. II	1662
6. Ballymistore	Montgomery MSS 420 n. 93	1717
7. Balynester	Wm. Map (OSNB) No. 92	1810
8. Ballynester	Bnd. Sur. (OSNB) No. 92	1830c
9. Nestor's Town	J O'D (OSNB) No. 92	1834c
10. ˌbɑliˈnəstər	Local pronunciation	1991

This name seems to consist of *baile* "townland" + definite article (i.e. *an*) + noun. On the basis of this, three possible Irish language forms come to mind, *Baile an Aistire* "townland of the doorkeeper", *Baile an Adhastair* "townland of the halter" and possibly even *Baile an Dísirt* "townland of the hermitage". The element *díseart* "hermitage", frequently found in place-names, is sometimes anglicized *ister*, *ester* (*Joyce* i 325) and it could be argued that it is the origin of the second element of this name. The form given for the parish name **Kilbroney**, Co Down, in the *Ecclesiastical Taxation* of 1302-06 is *Nister* (*Eccles. Tax.* 115) which is obviously similar to the second element of the forms for Ballynester cited above. However, the forms seem best suited to the first of these suggestions. The word *aistire* has ecclesiastical connotations; this was the term applied to the doorkeeper of a monastery who was also responsible for ringing the bell (*DIL* s.v.).

Ballyurnanellan
J 5667

Baile Iúir an Oileáin
"the townland of the yew of the island"

1. Ballenallane	Ex. 1 Inq. Jac. I	1603
2. Ballywanell al Ballynellan	Ham. Copy Inq. xxxi	1623
3. Ballevrannell als Ballenellen	CPR Chas. I 228	1627
4. Ballevranellan al. Ballenellan	Inq. Ult. (Down) §75 Car 1	1636
5. Ballyvnanellan al. Ballyneneta	Inq. Ult. (Down) §1 Car 11	1662
6. Balloranellan	Inq. Ult. (Down) §1 Car 11	1662
7. Ballyvnanellan al Ballyneneta	Inq. Ult. (Down) §1 Car 11	1662
8. Balloranellan	Inq. Ult. (Down) §1 Car 11	1662
9. Ballyurnanellon	Wm. Map (OSNB) No. 92	1810
10. Ballyurnanillan	OSNB No. 92	1830c
11. Baile Ur na nOilen "town of the brink of the islands"	J O'D (OSNB) No. 92	1834c
12. ˌbɑlijuriˈnïlən	Local pronunciation	1991

Forms 1, 2b, 3b, and 4b are interesting in that these alias forms seem to suggest that a shorter form of the name was in use in the 17th century, *Baile an Oileáin* "the townland of the island".

O'Donovan's suggestion that the second element in forms 3a, 4a, 5a, 6–10 is the word *ur* "edge, brink" is attractive considering the position of this townland on the shore of Strangford Lough with a view of Chapel Island and Mid Island. The local pronunciation, however, would suggest that the second element is *iúr*, "yew tree", and possibly later, an inflected form of *iúrach* "place of yew trees" under the influence of **Ballyewry**, also in this parish. O'Donovan's postulated form indicates that he thought that the gen. pl. of the article was an element of this name and he appears to have drawn this conclusion from forms 9 and 10. The majority of the historical forms, however, seem to have the gen. sing. form of the article. The first *n* in forms 5a and 7a may be a scribal error for *r*, a feature which is quite common in documents from this period.

Bootown An English form
J 5866

1.	Buetown	Montgomery MSS 420 n. 93	1717
2.	Butown	Montgomery MSS 420 n. 93	1717
3.	Bootown	Wm. Map (OSNB) No. 92	1810
4.	Bootown	Bnd. Sur. (OSNB) No. 92	1830c
5.	Booth-Town	J O'D (OSNB) No. 92	1834c
6.	bu:tn	Local pronunciation	1991

We are fortunate in having more historical forms for this townland name than for other relatively late names in the area, such as **Gregstown** and **Cronstown** in the neighbouring parish of Newtownards. Bootown may be a combination of the surname Booth followed by the element town. The English surname Booth, an occupational name for a cowman or herdsman, derives from a word meaning "cow-house, herdsman's hut" (Reaney 1958: 39). There is another townland called **Bootown** in the parish of Newtownards.

Cardy *An Cheardaidh*
J 5870 "the forge"

1.	Cardie, the	Ham. Copy Inq. xxxi	1623
2.	Cardee, the	CPR Chas. I 228	1627
3.	Cardy, the	CPR Chas. I 226	1627
4.	Le Cardy	Inq. Ult. (Down) §75 Car. I	1636
5.	Cardie, the	Inq. Ult. (Down) §109 Car. I	1650c
6.	Cardree	Hib. Reg. Ards	1657c
7.	Le Cardy al Cardy, the quarter land called	Montgomery MSS 419 n. 93	1703
8.	Cardy	Wm. Map (OSNB) No. 92	1810
9.	Cardy	Bnd. Sur. (OSNB) No. 92	1830c
10.	Cardaidhe "cards"	J O'D (OSNB) No. 92	1834c
11.	'kɑrdi:	Local pronunciation	1991

Despite having a number of historical forms for this place-name, its origin is by no means certain. It would appear to be a form of the word *ceárta* (< *ceardcha*) "a forge, workshop". By analogy with forms such as *teanga* "tongue", gen. *teangtha*; *leaba*, "bed" gen. *leabtha* which developed new nominative forms *teangaidh* and *leabaidh*, from a genitive form *ceardcha* a new nominative was created, *ceardaidh*. Alternatively it might be a dat. sing. form of a nom. sing. fem. *ceardach*; note *cèardach*, a nom. sing. fem. form which has been attested in Scottish Gaelic (*Dwelly* s.v.). As the definite article appears in no less than six of the historical forms we have included it in the suggested Irish language form. The French definite article *le* occurs in forms 4 and 7 and has probably been copied from earlier Anglo-Norman documents.

Gordonall
J 5768

Of uncertain origin

1.	Gordonall	Bnd. Sur. (OSNB) No. 92	1830c
2.	Gordonall	High Const. Applot. (OSNB) No. 92	1830c
3.	Garrdha Domhnaill "Donnell's garden"	J O'D (OSNB) No. 92	1834c
4.	Gordonall	Treas. Warrant (OSNB) No. 92	1830c
5.	gɔrd'nɔ:l	Local pronunciation	1991

The absence of historical forms prior to the first half of the 19th century makes it difficult to postulate the origin of this name and it may well be that it was coined by English speakers. O'Donovan's suggestion necessitates the stress to be on the initial syllable of his proposed second element, but this does not accord well with the current local pronunciation which shows elision of this syllable. A form such as *Gort Donn an Fháil* "the brown field of the fence" could be defended but with no great conviction.

Grey Abbey
J 5768

See parish name.

Killyvolgan
J 6167

Coillidh Bholgáin
"central wood"

1.	Kilbolgan, 1 q[r] in	CPR Jas. I 78a	1606
2.	Ballekilvolgan al Ballyknocke	Ham. Copy Inq. xliv	1623
3.	Ballykillvolgan al Ballykeroge	Inq. Ult. (Down) §75 Car. I	1636
4.	Kilvolgan	Inq. Ult. (Down) §104 Car. I	1645
5.	Killivolgan	Census 93	1659c
6.	Killivalgan	BSD 87	1662
7.	Killyvolgan	Wm. Map (OSNB) No. 92	1810
8.	Killyvalgan	Bnd. Sur. (OSNB) No. 92	1830
9.	Killyvalgan	Treas. Warrant (OSNB) No. 92	1830c
10.	Coill Uí Bholgáin "O'Bolgan's wood"	J O'D (OSNB) No. 92	1834c
11.	ˌkiliˈvo̤lgən	Local pronunciation	1991

The word *bolgán* is normally translated "bag; belly", but it also has the meaning "central". It may be significant that this townland is roughly centrally positioned in this part of the Ards peninsula between Strangford Lough on the west, and the Irish Sea on the east. *Coillidh* is an old dative of *coill* "wood", and this calcified form is often preserved in place-names. Other examples include *Coillidh Chanannáin*, the Irish name of **Middletown** in Co. Armagh, *Coillidh Brón* anglicized Killybrone in Co. Monaghan and *Coillidh*, now **Quilly** in Co. Down.

Kilnatierny
J 5668

Coillín an Tiarna
"the lord's little wood"

1.	Callinaterny	Census 93	1659c
2.	Ballekillmaterny	BSD 87	1661

3. Killenterny al Carrownester al Fishertowne	Montgomery MSS 268 n. 35	1675
4. Kilnatierny	Wm. Map (OSNB) No. 92	1810
5. Kilnatierny	Bnd. Sur. (OSNB) No. 92	1830c
6. Killenaterny	High Const. Applot. (OSNB) No. 92	1830c
7. Coill na dTighearnaigh "wood of the lords"	J O'D (OSNB) No. 92	1834c
8. Cill Naoimh Tighearnaigh "St Tierny's church"	J O'D (OSNB) No. 92	1834c
9. ˌkilnəˈterni	Local pronunciation	1991

Despite the apparent transparency of the modern anglicized form this name poses considerable difficulties, partly due, perhaps, to the absence of forms prior to c. 1659. Forms 1 and 6 seem to suggest *Coillín an Tiarna* as does form 2 if *m* is read as *in*; forms 4 and 5 could also represent this, allowing for loss of the final vowel of *coillín* by reduction. An alternative suggestion, since the suffix *-ín* is rare in Ulster Irish, might be *Coillidh an Tiarna* "the lord's wood" (see **Killyvolgan** below) but the former proposal seems to suit the historical forms better.

The two aliases in form 3 refer to **Fishquarter** in the adjacent parish of Inishargy; *Carrownester* is an anglicization of the Irish name for Fishquarter, namely, *Ceathrú an Iascaire* "the quarter of the fisherman" (the *t* of *Carrownester* is undoubtedly an error for *c*).

Mount Stewart An English form

J 5570

1. Templecrone	Inq. Ult. §75 Car. I	1636
2. Templechrone al Ballenhall al Oulestowne	Inq. Ult. §109 Car. I	1650c
3. Templecrone	Census 93	1659c
4. Mount Stewart	Wm. Map (OSNB) No. 92	1810
5. Mount Stewart	Bnd. Sur. (OSNB) No. 92	1830c
6. Mount Stewart	Tythes Applot. (OSNB) No. 92	1830c
7. ˈməunˈʃtju:rt	Local pronunciation	1991

According to Reeves (*EA* 19 n.g) the church site situated in what we know today as Mount Stewart Demesne was known as *Templecrone*. This seems to have been used as a townland name, as we find it mentioned in some 17th-century documents alongside other townlands from this parish. The name *Templecrone* was superseded by Mount Stewart which was applied to the house built there in the late 18th century. According to *ASCD* (374) a road book published in 1786 refers to the construction by the Rt. Hon. Robert Stewart of "a magnificent seat", namely Mount Stewart. The present house was built c. 1840–50 (*ASCD ibid*).

Rosemount An English form

J 5867

1. Mountross	Mountgomery MSS 1 n. 3	1634
2. Rosemount	Inq. Ult. (Down) §109 Car. I	1650c

3. Rosemount	Inq. Ult. (Down) §1 Car. II	1662
4. Rosemount	Descr. Ards 37	1683
5. Rosemount, manor of	Montgomery MSS 419 n. 93	1703
6. Rosemount	Wm. Map (OSNB) No. 92	1810
7. Rosemount	Bnd. Sur. (OSNB) No. 92	1830c
8. Rosemount	Tythes Applot. (OSNB) No. 92	1830c
9. ˈroːzmənt	Local pronunciation	1991

This is the name Sir James Montgomery gave to a defended house he built in 1634 to the south of the present Grey Abbey village. Apparently *Rosemount* was a popular name for houses in Ireland and Scotland at this time. Form 1 is taken from the *Funeral Entry* of Catherine, first wife of James Montgomery. It is unlikely that it was ever in common use and its elements appear to have been deliberately reversed to give it an air of sophistication.

Montgomery received a grant from the crown on 19th March 1638 of all the lands he then had in his possession in the parish of Grey Abbey and the house-name Rosemount came to be applied to the manor. The original building was burnt down in 1695 and another house was constructed on or near the same site some time before 1744. After the erection of this second house it seems that the name *Grayabbey House* came to be used alongside *Rosemount* (*Montgomery MSS* 1–2 n. 3; *Knox Hist.* 482; *ASCD* 263, 405–8).

Tullykevin — *Tulaigh Chaoimhín*
J 5969 — "Kevin's hillock"

1. Tulloghkeivin	CPR Jas. I 78a	1606
2. Carrowtullikevin or Tundon	Ham. Copy Inq. xxxi	1623
3. Tullycavan	OSNB No. 92	1625
4. Kearrontullekeavin al Tuardon	CPR Chas. I 228	1627
5. Corrantullekeavin al Turrardon	Inq. Ult. (Down) §75 Car. I	1636
6. Tullekeavin	Inq. Ult. (Down) §75 Car. I	1636
7. Tullycavan	Hib. Reg. Ards	1657c
8. Tullecavone	Census 93	1659c
9. Carrowtullikeaven al Tuardon	Inq. Ult. (Down) §1 Car II	1662
10. Tullykeavan al Carrow Tullykeavan	Montgomery MSS 420 n. 93	1717
11. Tullykevin	Wm. Map (OSNB) No. 92	1810
12. Tullykevin	Bnd. Sur. (OSNB) No. 92	1830c
13. Tullycavey	High Const. Applot. (OSNB) No. 92	1830c
14. Tulaigh Caoimhghin	J O'D (OSNB) No. 92	1834c
15. ˌtọlịˈkɛvən	Local pronunciation	1991

Forms 2a, 4a, 5a, 9a, 10b clearly indicate that the element *ceathrú* "quarter" was formerly part of this name. The full reference for form 1 from *CPR* is, "1 q[r] in Tulloghkeivin in the Great Ardes". This seems to indicate that *ceathrú* in this instance refers to a quarter of the townland.

Forms 3, 7, and 8 would appear to suggest that the second element is *cabhán* "a hollow"; but the remainder of the 17th-century spellings indicate a sound which rhymes with "leaving", as does the personal name *Caoimhín*, normally anglicized as Kevin. The forms ending in *-cavan* etc. may have been intended to reflect this anglicized form.

OTHER NAMES

Boretree Island East
Boretree Island West
J 5467

An English form

1. Island Bourtree	Montgomery MSS. 420 n. 93	1717
2. Bourtree-Isle	Harris Hist. 154	1744
3. West Boretree Island	Wm. Map (OSNB) No. 92	1810
4. West Bortree Island	Treas. Warrant (OSNB) No. 92	1830c

In a note on this place in the *OSNB* John O'Donovan states that this island was named from "from [a] Bore Tree (elder tree) which grows on one of the Bore Tree rocks." This explanation is in agreement with form 2 collected by Harris some ninety years before O'Donovan's visit.

Boretree Rock North
Boretree Rock South
Boretree Rock West
J 5468, 5367

An English form

1. North Boretree Island	Wm. Map (OSNB) No. 92	1810

As there is apparently no evidence of the name Boretree Island North, it seems that the above form relates to Boretree Rock, North.

Chanderies
J 5567

A Scots (?) form

1. Chanderies	OSNB Inf. No. 92	1834c

Traynor (1953:49) gives *Chander,-y* as an alternative form of an adjective, *Channery* which is glossed, "of land: having many small...stones; gravelly". It is possible that this adjective is used as a plural substantive in this place-name with the meaning "gravelly places".

Chapel Island
J 5567

An English form

1. Church Island	Hib. Reg. Ards	1657c
2. Island Chapel	Montgomery MSS. 420 n. 93	1717
3. Chapel Island	Wm. Map (OSNB) No. 92	1810
4. Chapel Island	Bnd. Sur. (OSNB) No. 92	1830
5. Chapel Island	Treas. Warrant (OSNB) No. 92	1830c

There is a ruined church on this island which has obviously given it its present name (*ASCD* 296).

Gabbock Island
J 5665

A hybrid form

1. Island Gobback	Montgomery MSS. 420 n. 93	1717
2. Gabbock Island	Wm. Map (OSNB) No. 92	1810

3. Gabbock Island Treas.	Warrant (OSNB) No. 92	1830c
4. Giobóg "a shred"	J O'D (OSNB) No. 92	1834c

The word *gabbock*, as well as meaning "mouthful, morsel", can also mean "a kind of fish" (*Scot. Nat. Dict.* v 221). Traynor (1953: 112) defines *gabbuck* as "the common dog-fish" (note Irish *gobóg* "dog-fish", *Dinneen* 588). Since Gabbock is here applied to an island, the latter meaning is probably more appropriate.

Hare Island An English form
J 5567

1. Hare Island	OSNB	1834c

Mid Island An English form
J 5667

1. Island Middle	Montgomery MSS. 420 n. 93	1717
2. Mid Island	Wm. Map (OSNB) No. 92	1810
3. Mid Island	Treas. Warrant (OSNB) No. 92	1830c

Patterson's Hill An English form
J 5668

Patterson is among the twenty most common surnames in Scotland. Of Lowland origin, it became widespread in Ulster and ranks among the five most common surnames in Co. Down (Bell 1988: 212–3).

Peggy's Island An English form
J 5568

1. Peggy's Island	Wm. Map (OSNB) No. 92	1810
2. Peggy's Island	Treas. Warrant (OSNB) No. 92	1830c

Pig Island An English form
J 5470

1. Pig Island	Wm. Map (OSNB) No. 92	1810
2. Pig Island	Treas. Warrant (OSNB) No. 92	1830c

South Island An English form
J5666

1. Island South	Montgomery MSS. 420 n. 93	1717
2. South Island	Wm. Map (OSNB) No. 92	1810
3. South Island	Bnd. Sur. (OSNB) No. 92	1830c
4. South Island	Treas. Warrant (OSNB) No. 92	1830c

Turley Rock An English form
J 5468

In the *OSNB* John O'Donovan suggests that Turley might be a name, presumably a surname, though he does not specify. MacLysaght (1964: 198) states that the name Turley, deriving from Gaelic *Mac Toird[h]ealbhaigh*, later *Mac Toirealaigh*, is common in Cos Down and Armagh. We learn from the *OSNB* (under the heading "Authority") that O'Donovan recorded the name of the rock from people employed in making kelp on the islands.

Whaup Rock A Scots/English form
J 5467

1.	Whaup Rock	OSNB Inf. No. 92	1834c

The *OSNB* entry for this name states that a whaup is a kind of gull. More scientific authorities define whaup as curlew (*Scot. Nat. Dict.* x 126; Traynor 1953: 326)

PARISH OF NEWTOWNARDS

The parish of Newtownards is situated at the head of Strangford Lough in the north-east of Co. Down with the lough shore forming part of the southern boundary of the parish. The parish of Dundonald lies to the west of Newtownards, Comber borders it on the south-west, and to the north lie the parishes of Bangor and Holywood. Donaghadee parish lies to the east and Grey Abbey is found on the south-east. The parish has a total of 33 townlands 17 of which lie in the barony of Ards Lower and the remaining 16 in Castlereagh Lower. The parish comprises 14,803 acres.

In the 13th century the Earldom of Ulster was divided into counties, one of these being the *Comitatus Nove Villa de Blawico*, or "the county of the New Town of Blathewic", the *New Town* being the predecessor of modern Newtownards. The present-day baronies of Lower Castlereagh, the Ards, and part of Dufferin were included in the old territorial division of Blathewyc. This is derived from Old Irish *Uí Blathmaic* i.e. the descendants of *Blathmac* ("famous son"). Reeves cites an extract from *Mac Firbhisigh's* genealogies on the *Dál Fiatach* which indicates that the eponym of the Uí Blathmaic was Blathmac, son of the Ulster over-king *Áed Róin mac Bécce Bairrche* who died in 735 (Byrne 1973: 285): *Blathmac d[a]no mac Aodha Roin ottaid ui Blathmeic* "Blathmac, moreover, son of Aodh Rón, from whom are the Uí Blathmeic" (*EA* 360).

The church of *Neuton[e]* is cited in the *Ecclesiastical Taxation* of 1302–6 (*Eccles. Tax.*) under the deanery of *Blaethwyco* and is valued at 14 marks (*EA* 12). We know that there were a number of ecclesiastical sites in the parish, Movilla and Newtown being the more prestigious, but there were also sites at Kiltonga, Craigantlet, and Ballyskeagh. Curiously, Movilla is not cited in this document but there is an an entry for a church known as *Monketone* which is difficult to identify with any of the aforementioned sites (*EA* 14). The church of *Monketone* is valued at only 2 marks in *Eccles. Tax.*, so it is unlikely that *Monketone*, apparently one of the minor ecclesiastical sites in the area, refers to the important ecclesiastical site at Movilla.

The establishment of the Dominican Priory to the south-east of Newtownards is credited to the Savage family of the Ards and dated to c. 1244 (see H.C. Lawlor 1940: 85 cited in *ASCD* 284; *Harris Hist.* 56). This date, if accurate, would contradict O'Laverty's opinion (*O'Laverty* ii 1) that the monastery was built by de Burgo, as he did not receive control of the earldom until 1264. It was burnt in 1572 by Sir Brian Mac Felim O'Neill along with the other principal monasteries in the area including Bangor, Movilla, Holywood and Grey Abbey so that it might not be used by the English. On the secular front, we know that a monthly county court was held at the *New Town* in the first third of the 14th century (*Inq. Earldom Ulster* iii 66). At the start of the 17th century, however, Sir Hugh Montgomery found the area largely desolate and the town was developed under his auspices (*Montgomery MSS* 58-9). He obtained lands in the area in 1605, and in 1609 Newtownards was described by the Plantation Commissioners as having "a hundred houses or thereabouts, all peopled by Scots" (Camblin 1951: 30).

Newton was among the lands granted in 1604 (*CPR Jas. I* 38a/b) to John Kinge and John Thomas Hibbots, both from Dublin, and was also included among the lands in a grant from the king to James Hamilton in 1605 (*CPR Jas. I* 72b). The inquisition taken at Ardquin in 1605 (*Inq. Ult.* §2 Jac. I) cites the seven townlands belonging to the monastery of Movilla in much the same order as that which appears in the 1605 grant to James Hamilton (*CPR Jas. I* 72b), and the inquisition taken at Ballymaghan in 1603 (*Ex. Inq. 1 Jac. I*). However, some of the names have become illegible in the original copy of the Ardquin inquisition of 1605 and it should be noted that there are some spelling differences between these documents.

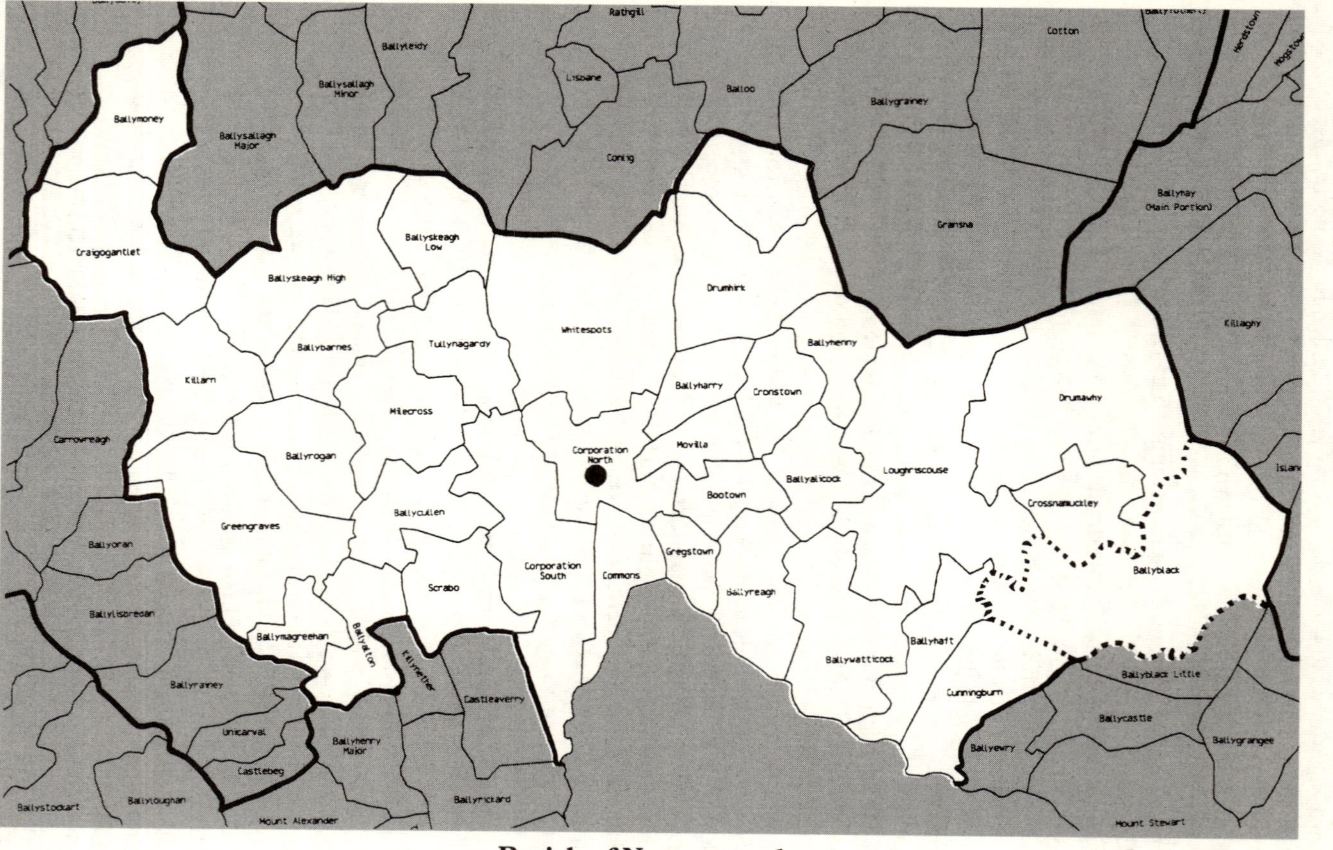

Parish of Newtownards

Barony of Ards Lower (Some townlands in Barony of Castlereagh Lower)

Townlands
Ballyalicock
Ballyalton (Castlereagh Lower)
Ballybarnes (Castlereagh Lower)
Ballyblack (shared with Greyabbey)
Ballycullen (Castlereagh Lower)
Ballyhaft
Ballyharry
Ballyhenny
Ballymagreehan (Castlereagh Lower)
Ballymoney (Castlereagh Lower)
Ballyreagh
Ballyrogan (Castlereagh Lower)
Ballyskeagh, High (Castlereagh Lower)
Ballyskeagh, Low (Castlereagh Lower)
Ballywatticock
Bootown
Commons (Castlereagh Lower)
Corporation, North
Corporation, South (Castlereagh Lower)
Craigogantlet (Castlereagh Lower)
Cronstown
Crossnamuckley
Cunningburn
Drumawhy
Drumhirk
Greengraves (Castlereagh Lower)
Gregstown
Killarn (Castlereagh Lower)
Loughriscouse
Milecross (Castlereagh Lower)
Movilla
Scrabo (Castlereagh Lower)
Tullynagardy (Castlereagh Lower)
Whitespots

Towns
Newtownards (part in Castlereagh Lower)

The Ardquin inquisition also contains references to the churches of Kiltonga and Craigantlet which do not appear in the 1605 grant to James Hamilton (*CPR Jas. I* 72b).

Townlands in the parish of Newtownards are cited in an inquisition taken in Downpatrick on 13 October 1623 (*Ham. Copy Inq.* 1623) and in what appears to be a copy of this inquisition dated to 1627 (*CPR Chas I* 227). The Downpatrick inquisition of 1623 also includes the grant of 1618 from Hamilton to Montgomery which was part of the Earl of Abercorn's settlement of the controversy between the two. The monasteries of Newtown and Movilla were among the abbey lands allocated to Montgomery by the terms of this grant (for further information on the 1623 inquisition see the introduction to the parish of Bangor). An inquisition taken at *Newton* c. 1650 (*Inq. Ult.* §109 Car I) contains a list of the lands which had belonged to Hugh Montgomery. The townlands do not occur in the same order as either the 1605 grant to James Hamilton (*CPR Jas. I* 72b) or the inquisition taken at Ardquin in 1605 (*Inq. Ult.* §2 Jac 1), nor does the spelling of the inquisition taken at *Newton* c. 1650 bear much resemblance to that of the other two.

The *Census* of c. 1659 records a total of 332 inhabitants in the parish at that time, of whom 207 were English and Scottish, and the remaining 125 native Irish. As has been explained in the Bangor parish introduction these figures need to be treated with caution. The list of "tituladoes" includes Hugh Montgomery, John Shaw whose name appears beside the townland of *Ballywitticock*, and the name of Hugh McGill alongside Ballyhenny. The *Book of Survey and Distribution* (*BSD*) for Co. Down has a list of the townlands of Newtownards drawn up in 1661, as does the *Subsidy Roll for the county of Down, AD 1663* (*Sub. Roll Down*). Of the six townlands listed under Newtownards in this latter document only four actually belong to the parish, although four townlands belonging to Newtownards are to be found listed under the neighbouring parish of Comber in the same document. This may indicate that the parish boundary has undergone some change but it should be stated that the *Census* of c. 1659 does not always appear to be accurate.

The Montgomery Manuscripts (*Montgomery MSS*) have been a useful source not only from the point of view of historical background but also as a repository of historical forms for the place-names of the area. Captain Robert Colville acquired the manor of *Newtown* on 12 November 1675 and a list of the townlands he received as a result are found in *Montgomery MSS* 267 n. 35. The order of the townlands is similar to the inquisition taken at *Newton* c. 1650 (*Inq. Ult.* §109 Car. I) but there are differences in spelling.

Of the 33 townlands in the parish, *baile* "town, townland" is the most common first element, appearing in 15 place-names in composition with native and Anglo-Norman surnames (e.g. **Ballymagreehan** and **Ballywatticock**) as well as in formations with nouns (e.g. **Ballybarnes**). Two interesting names worthy of a mention are **Greengraves** and **Whitespots**, as their current anglicized guise differs somewhat from their original Irish forms, *Baile Chloch Tógála* "townland of the dolmen" and *Ceathrú Chamchoise* "crooked-leg quarter". As was usually the case in the Ards, O'Donovan failed to meet a native Irish-speaking informant in the parish of Newtownards to assist him in ascertaining the origin of the place-names. We know from the *OSNB* for Newtownards that he collected some anglicized forms from a Rev. Mc Cullough, including Greengraves and Ballycullen.

PARISH NAME

Newtownards J 5074	*Baile Nua na hArda* "new town of the promontory"	
1. an Bhaile nuadh, láimh leis	O'Neill Fun. Oration 267	1744
2. Villanovano seù Newtonensi, de	De Burgo's Hib. Dom. 20	1244

3.	Villam Novam al Newtonam, apud	De Burgo's Hib. Dom. 20	1244
4.	Neuton[e], Ecclesia de	Eccles. Tax. 12	1306c
5.	New Town	Inq. Earldom Ulster iii 65	1333
6.	New Town of Blathewyc	Inq. Earldom. Ulster iii 65	1333
7.	Villanove	Annates Ulst. 113	1505
8.	Newe	Nowel's Ire. (1)	1570c
9.	Newtown	Ortelius Map	1573
10.	Neuwe towne abbaye	S-E Ulster Map	1580c
11.	Newton ab	Mercator's Ire.	1595
12.	Newtoun abb	Mercator's Ulster	1595c
13.	Newtown mo.	Bartlett Maps (Esch. Co. Maps) i	1603
14.	Newton	Ex. Inq. 1 Jac. I	1603
15.	Newton	CPR Jas. I 39a	1604
16.	Newtowne	CPR Jas. I 72b	1605
17.	Newton	CPR Jas. I 72b	1605
18.	Lisnevan juxta Newton	Inq. Ult. (Down) §2 Jac. I	1605
19.	Newtown Abb	Speed's Ulster	1610
20.	Newtown Abb	Speed's Antrim & Down	1610
21.	Newton	CPR Jas. I 254b	1614?
22.	Villa Nova	Terrier (Reeves) 53	1615c
23.	Villa Nova	Terrier (O' Laverty) 326	1615c
24.	Newton	CPR Jas. I 339a	1617
25.	Newtowne	CPR Jas. I 326a	1617
26.	Newtown	Ulster Visit. (Reeves) 51	1622
27.	Newton	Ham. Copy Inq. xliv	1623
28.	Newtown	Ham. Copy Inq. xxxi	1623
29.	Newton	Ham. Copy Inq. xxxi	1623
30.	Ballenova	Ham. Copy Inq. xxxiv	1623
31.	Newtone	CPR Chas. I 65	1625
32.	Newton	CPR Chas. I 131	1626
33.	Newton	CPR Chas. I 225, 230	1627
34.	Lisneavan	CPR Chas. I 229	1627
35.	Ballelisneavan al Ballenoe	CPR Chas. I 230	1627
36.	Newtown	Inq. Ult. (Down) §75 Car. I	1636
37.	Newtowne	Inq. Ult. (Down) §75 Car. I	1636
38.	Ballylisnevan al Ballynoe al Newtowne	Inq. Ult. (Down) §109 Car. I	1650c
39.	Ballynova	Inq. Ult. (Down) §109 Car. I	1650c
40.	Newton	Inq. Down (Reeves1) 135	1657
41.	Newtowne	Census 94	1659c
42.	Ballenova al. Newtowne	BSD 87	1661
43.	Newtowne & Ballynaskea	Trien. Visit. (Bramhall) 11	1661
44.	Newtowne	Trien. Visit. (Margetson) 22	1664
45.	Newtowne	Trien. Visit. (Boyle) 44	1679
46.	Ballyno	Descr. Ards 39	1683
47.	Newtown	Reg. Deeds abstracts i §30	1707
48.	Newtown	Montgomery MSS 420 n.93	1717
49.	Newtown	Wm. Map (OSNB) E 32	1810
50.	Newtownards	Bnd. Sur. (OSNB) No. 16	1830c

51. Baile Árd Uladh	Post-Sheanchas 102	1905
52. Baile Nua na nÁrd	Post-Sheanchas 102	1905
53. Baile Nua na hArda	AGBP 118	1969
54. Baile Nua na hArda	Éire Thuaidh	1988
55. Baile Nua na hArda	GÉ 25	1989
56. ˌnjətnˈɑrdʒ	Local pronunciation	1991
57. ˌnjətnˈardz	Local pronunciation	1991

The *New Town of Blathewyc* occupied the site at the head of Strangford Lough on which the town of Newtownards came to be built. In Latin, Newtownards was known as *Villa Nova* "new town"; in Irish it was called *Baile Nua*, which is a calque on the earlier Anglo-Norman name. Form 49 is interesting in that it shows that *Newtown* was still in use in the first decade of the 19th century, and it is likely that it continued to be used later than this. The form *Newtownards* does not appear to have been used before the first quarter of the 19th century. The second element of form 51 and the final element of form 52 appear to be gen. pl. of *ard* "height", but this interpretation of "-ards" in the anglicized form *Newtownards* is not compatible with the evidence. Our postulated Irish form, *Baile Nua na hArda* translates literally "new town of the promontory", where *arda* is a variant of the gen. sing. of *aird* "promontory" (see pp 3–4 above).

Regarding the alias *(Bally)lisnevan* which occurs in forms 18, 34, 35a, and 38a, Reeves cites an extract from *Mac Firbhisigh*'s tract on the genealogy of the *Dál Fiatach* (*EA* 361) which seems to relate the origin of this name with the *Uí Nemand*:

> *Coicc aicme umorro o Blathmac mac Aodha Roin .i. Clann Laitheasa, Clann Domhnaill, acus Ui Naemhain, Clann Cuileannain, acus Ui Craoibhe.*
>
> (Five tribes moreover descended from Blathmac son of Aodh Rón, namely, Clann Laitheasa, Clann Domhnaill and Uí Naemhain, Clann Cuileannain, and Uí Craoibhe.)

We know from the Laud genealogies that the eponym of the Uí Nemhand was *Nem*, one of the twelve sons of *Forg mac Dalláin* of the Dál Fiatach: *Nem, a quo hUí Nemand la Cremthaind*, "Nem from whom (are descended) the Uí Nemand beside(?) Cremthaind" (*ZCP* viii, 1912, 328).

TOWNLAND NAMES

Ballyalicock — *Baile Ealacoc*
J 5274 — "Allicock's townland"

1. Ballyacgo	Ex. Inq. 1 Jac. I	1603
2. Bally-Allicocke al Drumchyne al Ballyalgo	Ham. Copy Inq. xliv	1623
3. Ballyallicocke al Drumchynne al Ballyalgo	Ham. Copy Inq. xxxi	1623
4. Bally-Allicocke al Drumchyne al Ballalgo	CPR Chas. I 229	1627
5. Ballyallecock al Drumchin al Ballalgo al Drumnehenny	Inq. Ult. (Down) §109 Car. I	1650c
6. Ballyallycock al Drumchin al Balaloo al Drumhenry	Montgomery MSS 267 n.35	1675

7.	Balleallecock	BSD 87	1661
8.	Ballyallicock	Wm. Map (OSNB) E 32	1810
9.	Ballyallicock	Bnd. Sur. (OSNB) E 32	1830c
10.	Baile Ui Ealgaigh "O'Halgy's town"	J O'D (OSNB) E 32	1834c
11.	ˌbɑliˈeːləkɔk	Local pronunciation	1991
12.	ˌbɑliˈɑləkɔk	Local pronunciation	1991

The second element of this place-name is a variant of the Anglo-Norman surname Alcock which Reaney (1958: 3) describes as a "pet-form of some short name in *Al-*". The suffix *-cock* is attested from the end of the 12th century and becomes very common in the middle of the 13th century (Reaney *ibid.* xxxv).

It is somewhat surprising that O'Donovan's suggested Irish form (10) indicates that he thought that the second element was a Gaelic surname. His translation of Ballywatticock (also in this parish) as "Watticock's town", suggests that he recognized the second element of that name as an English surname, so it is curious that he did not identify the second element of Ballyallicock as such. Perhaps O'Donovan's *Baile Uí Ealgaigh* is based on the alias form *Ball(y)algo* which occurs, or is intended, in forms 1–6 (taking the *c* of form 1 as a misreading for an *l* and the first *o* of 6c as a *g*).

Ballyalton
J 4673

Baile Altáin
"townland of (the) streamlet/ravine/hillock"

1.	(?)Ballanlialton	CPR Jas. I 73a	1605
2.	(?)Ballytullyalton	Inq. Ult (Down) §2 Jac. 1	1605
3.	Ballyalton	CPR Jas. I 254b	1613
4.	Ballymalton	Inq. Ult. (Down) §109 Car. I	1650c
5.	Ballymolton als Ballyalton	Montgomery MSS 268 n.35	1675
6.	Ballyalton	Montgomery MSS 268 n.37	1679
7.	Ballyalton	Wm. Map (OSNB) E 32	1810
8.	Ballyalton	Bnd. Sur. (OSNB) E 32	1830c
9.	Baile Ui Altáin "O'Halton's town"	J O'D (OSNB) E 32	1834c
10.	ˌbɑliˈɑltən	Local pronunciation	1991

Forms 4 and 5a contain an *m* which may be a scribal error for *n* and may represent the *n* of the definite article in Irish. There is also a possibility that the first *n* in form 1 reflects the presence of the article. This form, however, looks like a corrupt transcription of a form such as *Ballitullialton* and, since the current anglicized form of the name corresponds to the oldest form (3) which has no trace of the article, preference is given to an Irish original without the article. The word *altán* can mean one of three things: a streamlet; a ravine; a hillock. Exactly which meaning is intended here is difficult to say.

In an unpublished lecture the late Deirdre Flanagan derived the second element of **Ballyalton** in the parish of Saul, Co. Down from the Anglo-Norman personal name *Alton* which gave rise to the surname Dalton. This derivation, however, is not compatible with the historical forms for Ballyalton in Newtownards.

Ballybarnes J 4675	*Baile na Bearnaise* "townland of the gap"	
1. Barnes	Ex Inq. 1 Jac. I	1603
2. Barnes	CPR Jas. I 39a	1604
3. Bernes or Barnes	CPR Jas. I 72b	1605
4. Ballinebarnes al Ballibarnes	Ham. Patent xx	1620
5. Ballenebearnes al Barnes	Ham. Copy Inq. xliv	1623
6. Ballynebearnes al Barnes	Inq. Ult. (Down) §75 Car. I	1636
7. Ballybairnes	Census 94	1659c
8. Ballebairnesse	BSD 121	1661
9. Ballynabarnes als Barnes	Montgomery MSS 268 n.35	1675
10. Ballybarnes	Wm. Map (OSNB) E 32	1810
11. Ballybarnes	Bnd. Sur. (OSNB) E 32	1830c
12. Ballybarns	OSNB E 32	1834c
13. Baile Bearnais "town of the gap"	J O'D (OSNB) E 32	1834c
14. Baile-bearnais "town of the ... gap"	Joyce iii 70	1913
15. ˌbɑliˈbɑrnz	Local pronunciation	1991

Although there is no trace of the gen. sing. fem. article in the current form, it is clearly identifiable in forms 4a, 5a, 6a and 9a. The second element contains the word *bearnas*, a form of *bearna* "a gap". For other place-name elements which contain this *-as* termination, see *Joyce* (ii 12–13) and Ó Máille (1989–90: 125–143). Ó Máille cites this townland in his examples (*ibid.* 128). Forms 1–3 seem to suggest that *Bearnas*, without the prefix *baile*, was formerly an accepted form of this place-name. Although *bearnas* is masculine in Donegal Irish, it was obviously feminine in the variety of Irish spoken in some parts of East Ulster as is evident from the historical forms for Ballybarnes above and the townland of **Ballynabarnish** in the parish of Templepatrick, Co. Antrim.

Ballyblack J 5573	*Baile Bhleaic* "Black's townland"

A townland belonging both to Newtownards and Grey Abbey parishes. See pp 200–1.

Ballycullen J 4774	*Baile Mhic Coilín* "Quillan's townland"	
1. Ballequillan	Census 95	1659c
2. Ballyquillane	BSD 121	1661
3. Ballycullen als Ballykillconan als Kilcoman als Scrabo als Wilson's land	Montgomery MSS 268 n. 35	1675
4. Ballycallen	Wm. Map (OSNB) E 32	1810
5. Ballycullen	Bnd. Sur. (OSNB) E 32	1830c
6. Baile Ui Cuilinn/Coilen "Cullin's town"	J O'D (OSNB) E 32	1834c
7. ˌbaliˈko̤ln	Local pronunciation	1991

The surname *Mac Coilín* was common in Donegal, Antrim and Down at the close of the 16th century (Woulfe 1923: 334). Its anglicized forms include MacCullion, MacCullen, MacQuillin and Quillan. It is not uncommon for Irish surnames with *Mac* or *Ó* followed by a broad *C* to have an initial *q* in their anglicized forms: *Ó Caollaí, Ó Cuileannáin, Mac Coinn, Mac Coise* give Queally, Quinlan, McQuinn, Quinlan. The second element in forms 1 and 2 above seem to represent Quillan. Forms 3a, 5, and possibly 4, could represent *Baile Cuilinn*, "townland of the holly"; the second element of these forms may also derive from the obsolete word *cuilleann* "slope" (Ó Máille 1960) but the overriding evidence favours a surname.

The "lost" townland of Killcoman appears to have been situated in Ballycullen and Scrabo (see **Scrabo** below).

Ballyhaft — *Baile Hoiste*
J 5372 — "Hodge's townland"

1.	(?)Ballenhaulta	Ex. Inq. 1 Jac. I	1603
2.	(?)Ballenhaulta or Ballyhasta	CPR Jas. I 72b	1605
3.	(?)Ballyhest al Raghone al Ballinhalta	Ham. Copy Inq. xxxi	1623
4.	(?)Balleheste al Raghorie al Ballinhaulta	CPR Chas. I 229	1627
5.	(?)Ballyhest al Raghorie	Inq. Ult. (Down) §109 Car. I	1650c
6.	(?)Ballyhest al Raghory al Ballinhaulta	Inq. Ult. (Down) §109 Car. I	1650c
7.	(?)Ballehest	BSD 87	1661
8.	Ballyhefte	Sub. Roll Down. 281	1663
9.	Ballyheft als Raghary als Ballinhaulter	Montgomery MSS 267 n.35	1675
10.	Ballyhaft	Wm. Map (OSNB) E 32	1810
11.	Ballyhaft	Bnd. Sur. (OSNB) E 32	1830c
12.	Ballyhest	OSNB E 32	1830c
13.	Baile Hoiste "Hest's town"	J O'D (OSNB) E 32	1834c
14.	ˌbɑliˈhaːft	Local pronunciation	1991

It is noteworthy that the forms show that there may have been some confusion, where this name is concerned, between "long *s*", which resembles an *f* without its cross, *ſ*, and *f*. In Early Modern English orthography, ordinary *s* occurred normally at the end of a word (though there are exceptions) and long *s* occurred anywhere else (Barber 1976: 15). The majority of the early forms above end in *-est(e)*, which suggests that final *-st* was what was intended by the early scribes and that later the long *s* was misinterpreted as an *f*.

Among the historical forms O'Donovan had at his disposal for this townland was *Ballyhest* (form 12) which he claimed was cited in "all the grants to the Montgomerys"; he appears to have based his postulated Irish form on this evidence. *Hoiste* is a gaelicization of the English surname Hodge (Woulfe 1923: 298) and it is possible that *-hasta*, *-hest(e)* in forms 2b, 3a, 4a, etc. are attempts to represent Irish *Hoiste* in English orthography.

The alias form *Raghorie* etc. which appears in forms 3b, 4b, 5b, 6b, and 9b, derives from Irish *reachraidh*, and seems to apply to a number of large stones, including Butterlump

Stone, just off the shore in Strangford Lough. In this area it appears to mean "rocky reef" (for a discussion of the element *reachraidh*, see **The Raghories**, parish of Inishargy).

Ballyharry	*Baile Haraí*	
J 5075	"Harry's town"	
1. Balleharry	Ex. Inq. 1 Jac. I	1603
2. Ballenharry	CPR Jas. I 72b	1605
3. Ballyhenrie	CPR Jas. I 255a	1613
4. Ballyhary	Ham. Copy Inq. xxxi	1623
5. Ballyharrye	CPR Chas. I 229	1627
6. Ballehenrye al Drumharvy	CPR Chas. I 229	1627
7. Ballyhary	Inq. Ult. (Down) §109 Car. I	1650c
8. Ballyharry	Inq. Ult. (Down) §109 Car. I	1650c
9. (?)Ballyhenry al Ballydrumharid	Inq. Ult. (Down) §109 Car. I	1650c
10. Ballyhary	Census 94	1659c
11. Ballyharry	Wm. Map (OSNB) E 32	1810
12. Ballyhery	Bnd. Sur. (OSNB) E 32	1830c
13. Baile Harry "Henry's town"	J O'D (OSNB) E 32	1834c
14. ˌbaliˈhari	Local pronunciation	1991

The second element of this place-name appears to be simply Harry, either as a personal name or a surname. Harry is the English form of the Old French name *Henri* and, after the Norman conquest, the personal name Harry became extremely common in England (Reaney 1958: 155, 161). Note also O'Donovan's postulated Irish form and translation (13). There is a **Ballyhenry** in the parish of Ardquin.

Forms 3, 6a and 9a are interesting as they contain a form of Henry. The *n* in form 2 is problematic as it could indicate a form of the definite article in Irish but, since there is no trace of it in any other forms, we are probably safe in dismissing it as a scribal error.

Ballyhenny	*Baile Uí Shionnaigh*	
J 5175	"O'Sheny's townland"	
1. (?)Drumhenny	Ex. Inq. 1 Jac. I	1603
2. Balleheine	Ham. Copy Inq. xliv	1623
3. Ballyhonney	Census 94	1659c
4. (?)Balledrumhenny	BSD 87	1661
5. (?)Ballyhaine	Montgomery MSS 268 n. 35	1675
6. Ballyhenny	Montgomery MSS 420 n. 93	1717
7. Ballyhenny	Wm. Map (OSNB) E 32	1810
8. Ballyhinny	Bnd. Sur. (OSNB) E 32	1830c
9. Baile Uí Eanaigh "O'Heny's town"	J O'D (OSNB) E 32	1834c
10. ˌbɑliˈhəni	Local pronunciation	1991

O'Donovan's suggestion is dubious in that *Ó hÉanaigh*, usually anglicized Heaney, has a long *e*-vowel, which is not compatible with either the historical forms or the current local pronunciation.

The second element appears to be a Gaelic surname beginning with either *s* or *t* as, following *Uí*, an aspirated *s* or *t* is generally pronounced [h] in Irish. The most likely possibility is *Ó Sionnaigh*, which is often translated as Fox, and is anglicized O'Sheny, O'Sunny. Unfortunately no indication has so far come to light of its occurrence in East Ulster.

If forms 1 and 4 refer to this place, it seems that the element *droim* "ridge" was sporadically used as a component of this name.

Ballymagreehan — *Baile Mhig Riabhacháin*
J 4572 — "*Mag Riabhacháin*'s townland"

	Form	Source	Date
1.	Ballimagreevaghan	CPR Jas. I 73a	1605
2.	Balle-M'Greiveigan	Ham. Copy Inq. xliii	1623
3.	Ballemagreevegan als Balleygyn	CPR Chas. I 229	1627
4.	Ballemakeaghan	CPR Chas. I 230	1627
5.	Ballymacgrevogan	Inq. Ult. (Down) §75 Car I	1636
6.	Ballymagrevagan al Ballymagrevaghan	Inq. Ult. (Down) §109 Car. I	1650c
7.	Ballymagrevagan al Ballygin	Inq. Ult. (Down) §109 Car. I	1650c
8.	Ballymagwoghan	Census 95	1659c
9.	Ballemagreuagan al Logherevony	BSD 121	1661
10.	Ballymaghreragan als Ballymagrevaghan	Montgomery MSS 268 n.35	1675
11.	Ballymagreehan	Wm. Map (OSNB) E 32	1810
12.	Ballymagrehan	Bnd. Sur. (OSNB) E 32	1830c
13.	Baile mac Criocháin "Mag Grehan's town"	J O'D (OSNB) E 32	1834c
14.	ˌbɑlimə'gri:kən	Local pronunciation	1991

The forms indicate that the second element is undoubtedly a Gaelic surname. O'Donovan was certainly correct in identifying the second element as such but his suggestion does not satisfy the early forms of the name, as it does not take into account the *v* in the majority of the historical forms (1–3a, 5, etc.) which seem to indicate *Baile Mhig Riabhacháin*. Such a surname has not been attested but our forms indicate that it existed in this area.

There is another **Ballymagreehan** in the parish of Drumgooland, Co. Down but it does not have the same origin as this name.

Ballymoney — *Baile na Móna*
J 4478 — "townland of the moor"

	Form	Source	Date
1.	Ballenownecarrogh	Ex. Inq. 1 Jac. I	1603
2.	Ballemowne	CPR Jas. I 38a	1604
3.	Ballinemony	CPR Jas. I 73a	1605
4.	Ballynemony	Ham. Copy Inq. xxxi	1623
5.	Ballenemoynie	Ham. Copy Inq. xxxiv	1623
6.	Ballymoney	Census 94	1659c
7.	Ballynemoney	Montgomery MSS 267 n.35	1675
8.	Ballymoney	Wm. Map (OSNB) E 32	1810
9.	Ballymoney	Bnd. Sur. (OSNB) E 32	1830c

10. Baile na Móna "town of the bog"	J O'D (OSNB) E 32	1834c
11. ˌbɑləˈmo̤ni	Local pronunciation	1991

The gen. sing. fem. form of the definite article, i.e. *na*, appears to be present in forms 3–5, and 7, although no trace of it survives in the current anglicized form. The *w* of forms 1 and 2, and the *y* of form 5, may be an indication that the preceding vowel was long. For this reason an original *Baile na Móna* "townland of the moor" has been suggested as opposed to *Baile na Muine* "townland of the thicket".

The final element of form 1, *carrogh*, does not belong to this townland, but was at one time the first element of the townland of Rathgill in the parish of Bangor which follows Ballymoney in this inquisition. A scribal error has resulted in it being attached to the end of this townland, instead of the beginning of Rathgael which follows it in this source. See **Rathgill** in the parish of Bangor.

Ballyreagh
J 5172

Baile an Reithe (?)
"townland of the ram"

1. Ballenrya	Ex. Inq. 1 Jac. I	1603
2. Ballenria	CPR Jas. I 72b	1605
3. Ballinieagh al Movilla	Ham. Copy Inq. xliv	1623
4. Ballinreagh al Movilla	Ham. Copy Inq. xxxi	1623
5. Ballinreaghe al Movilla	CPR Chas. I 228–9	1627
6. Ballencreagh al Ballinry	Inq. Ult. (Down) §109 Car. I	1650c
7. Ballinreagh al Ballinry al Movilla	Inq. Ult. (Down) §109 Car. I	1650c
8. Ballerea	Census 94	1659c
9. Ballerae al. Ballinry	BSD 87	1661
10. Ballinreagh als Movilla als Bowtowne als Ballypreo	Montgomery MSS 267 n.35	1675
11. Ballyrea	Wm. Map (OSNB) E 32	1810
12. Ballyrea	Bnd. Sur. (OSNB) E 32	1830c
13. Baile Riach "grey town"	J O'D (OSNB) E 32	1834c
14. ˌbɑliˈre:	Local pronunciation	1991

The final element of this name is difficult to establish. The presence of *n* in forms 1–8 seems to indicate a structure *baile* + article + gen. sing. of noun. One possibility might be *Baile an Fhraoigh* "townland of the heather", but this appears to be the origin of **Ballyree** in the neighbouring parish of Bangor and there is little similarity between the forms for it and the forms for Ballyreagh. It could be argued that the second element is gen. sing. of *reithe* "a ram" as intervocalic *-th-* was frequently lost in East Ulster Irish and this may account for the current local pronunciation. This phenomenon is attested in other Ulster place-names: the Co. Monaghan town Ballybay, pronounced [ˌbaliˈbe:], derives from Irish *Béal Átha Beithe* and Glenveigh, Co. Donegal, pronounced [ˌglenˈve:], is an anglicization of Irish *Gleann Bheithe.*

Movilla appears as an alias for Ballyreagh in forms 3–5, 7, and 10. Although these two townlands are separated by Bootown, it is likely that they were contiguous in the 17th century. In historical documentation, neighbouring townlands frequently appear as alias forms for each other. Bootown, appears to be of English origin and, therefore, not as long established as the other two townlands. Our earliest reference to it is in a document from the last quarter of the 17th century (10c). It probably comprises territory which was formerly included in the townlands of Movilla and Ballyreagh.

Ballyrogan	*Baile Uí Ruagáin*	
J 4674	"O'Rogan's townland"	
1. Ballirogan	CPR Jas. I 73a	1605
2. Ballirogane	CPR Jas. I 326a	1617
3. Ballerogan	Ham. Copy Inq. xliii	1623
4. Ballerogan	Ham. Copy Inq. xliv	1623
5. Ballerogan	Ham. Copy Inq. xxxi	1623
6. Ballerogan	CPR Chas. I 229	1627
7. Balleroga	Inq. Ult. (Down) §75 Car. I	1636
8. Ballyrogan	Inq. Ult. (Down) §109 Car. I	1650c
9. Ballyvogan	Census 94	1659c
10. Ballyrogganloughmaroony	Montgomery MSS 268 n.35	1675
11. Ballyrogan	Wm. Map (OSNB) E 32	1810
12. Ballyrogan	Bnd. Sur. (OSNB) E 32	1830c
13. Baile Ui Rógáin "O'Rogan's town"	J O'D (OSNB) E 32	1834c
14. ˌbɑliˈrogən	Local pronunciation	1991

The second element of this townland is the surname *Ó Ruagáin*, *Ruagán* meaning "little red-haired one". According to Woulfe (1923: 635), this is an Oriel name whose bearers were one time rulers of *Uí Eathach* which was coterminous with the present-day barony of Armagh. O'Rogan was one of the most common surnames in the Co. Down baronies of Kinelarty and Dufferin in the second half of the 17th century (*Census* 86). The suffix *-loughmaroony*, which appears in form 10, no doubt refers to a lough which was once in the area; however, there is no longer any trace of it. **Ballyrogan** is also a townland name in the parishes of Kilkeel, Co. Down, and Errigal, Co. Derry.

Ballyskeagh High	*Baile na Sceiche*	
Ballyskeagh Low	"townland of the hawthorn"	
J 4676, 4674		
1. Tullacheskeyche	Exch. Accounts Ulst. 158	1260c
2. Thalascheagh, Capella de	Eccles. Tax. 14	1306c
3. Ballineskeaghes, the two	CPR Jas. I 73a	1605
4. Ballynaskeynan	Ulster Visit. (Reeves) 35	1622
5. Ballenaskey	Ulster Visit. (Reeves) 51	1622
6. Ballyskeagh	Census 94	1659c
7. Ballynaskea & Newtowne	Trien. Visit. (Bramhall) 11	1661
8. Ballynaskeagh	Trien. Visit. (Margetson) 23	1664
9. Ballyskeaghs, the two	Montgomery MSS 268 n.35	1675
10. Ballyskeaugh	Wm. Map (OSNB) E 32	1810
11. Ballyskeagh-beg	Wm. Map (OSNB) E 32	1810
12. Ballyskeagh Low	Bnd. Sur. (OSNB) E 32	1830c
13. Ballyskeagh High	Bnd. Sur. (OSNB) E 32	1830c
14. Baile na Sceach "town of the briars, thorns"	J O'D (OSNB) E 32	1834c
15. Baile-sceach "townland of the ...thorn bushes"	Joyce iii 119	1913
16. ˌbaliˈske:	Local pronunciation	1991

The forms *Tullacheskeyche* c. 1260 and *Tulascheagh* c. 1306, indicate that at an early period, the first element of this name was *tulach* "hillock", and a likely postulated Irish original for these forms is *Tulach Sceiche*. From some of the later forms (3, 6, 8, etc.) it could be argued that a gen. pl. form of *sceach* may have been used as the final element as opposed to a gen. sing. form as seems evident from forms 1, 5 and possibly 7a. This, however, is by no means conclusive as forms such as 3, 6, 8 etc. could also represent a gen. sing. form if *-skeagh* is to be pronounced [ʃke:] as seems likely. Although there is no trace of the article in the current anglicized form it is present in forms 3–5, 7a and 8.

In *Exch. Accounts Ulst.* c. 1260, we find the following extract (in translation from the Latin) which relates to this place:

> Robert Logan renders an account of 120 marks for 5 carucates of land which were of William de Gyseburn in Tullachskeyche within the cantred of Blathewyk in Ulster, by the pledge of Nicholas de Dunhened and of others

We know that a chapel existed here from at least as early as the beginning of the 14th century (*EA* 14) and it is interesting to note that *O'Laverty* (ii 131) informs us that in his time a field in this townland was known as *The Chapel Field*. This townland is divided into two parts, known today as Ballyskeagh High and Ballyskeagh Low, and this division clearly dates to at least the beginning of the 17th century (3, 9).

Ballywatticock — *Baile Uaiteacoc*
J 5172 — "Watticock's town"

1.	Ballewattecock	Ham. Copy Inq. xliv	1623
2.	Ballywatticock	Ham. Copy Inq. xxxi	1623
3.	Ballewitticock	CPR Jas. I 585a	1625
4.	Ballowatecoke	CPR Chas. I 229	1627
5.	Ballywattycock	Inq. Ult. (Down) §109 Car. I	1650c
6.	Ballywattecock	Inq. Ult. (Down) §109 Car. I	1650c
7.	Ballewitticock	Census 94	1659c
8.	Ballewittcock	BSD 87	1661
9.	Ballywatticock	Montgomery MSS 268 n.35	1675
10.	Ballywittecock	Wm. Map (OSNB) E 32	1810
11.	Ballywitticock	Bnd. Sur. (OSNB) E 32	1830c
12.	"Watticock's town"	J O'D (OSNB) E 32	1834c
13.	ˌbɑliˈwitəkɔk	Local pronunciation	1991
14.	ˌbɑliˈwïdikɔk	Local pronunciation	1991

The second element of this place-name is almost certainly an English surname which may well contain the diminutive suffix *-cock* (see note on *Ballyallicock* in this parish). However, it is difficult to establish the name of which Watticock is a diminutive. Whittock and Whitewick are possibilities; see Reaney (1958: 351, 352). The former is a diminutive of Old English *hwit*, "white"; the latter, which derives from Whitwick in Leicestershire, is pronounced *Whittick*, and if the suffix *-cock* were added to this, it would quite likely result in a pronunciation approaching *Watticock*.

Another possibility is the surname Walthew (Reaney 1958: 342). Among the variant forms Reaney lists under this name is *Waddy* (1312 AD). Again, if the suffix *-cock* were added to this form it would strongly resemble Watticock.

Bootown J 5074 — An English form

1.	Bowtowne als Ballinreagh als Moville als Ballypreo	Montgomery MSS 267 n. 35	1675
2.	Bowtown	Wm. Map (OSNB) E 32	1810
3.	Bowtown	Downshire Direct. 319	1823
4.	Bowtown	Bnd. Sur. (OSNB) E 32	1830c
5.	bu:tn	Local pronunciation	1991

The origin of the name Bootown is discussed under **Bootown**, parish of Grey Abbey. For a note relating to the area covered by Bootown, parish of Newtownards, see **Ballyreagh** above. **Bootown** also appears as a townland name in the parishes of Ballymoney and Dunluce Co. Antrim. There is a minor name in the parish of Comber known as **The Booten** (J 4770) which may well have the same origin as Bootown.

Commons J 4973 — An English form

1.	Common	Bnd. Sur. (OSNB) E 32	1830c
2.	Commons	J O'D (OSNB) E 32	1834c

The name suggests that this townland was formerly common land.

Corporation North
Corporation South
J 4974, 4872 — An English form

1.	Newtowne Corporac[i]o[n]n	Census 94	1659c
2.	Corporation	Bnd. Sur. (OSNB) E 32	1830c
3.	Corporation	OSNB E 32	1834c

Craigantlet J 4377 — See **Craigogantlet**.

Craigogantlet J 4377 — *Carraig Ó gCaoindealbháin* "*Ó Caoindealbháin*s' rock"

1.	Ballicarigogandolane	Inq. Ult. (Down) §2 Jac. I	1605
2.	Carrickogandolan	Inq. Ult. (Down) §2 Jac. I	1605
3.	Ballicarrigoganedelane	CPR Jas. I 73a	1605
4.	Carrigownantalan, Capella de	Terrier (O' Laverty) 326	1615c
5.	Carrigomantalan	Terrier (Reeves) 51	1615c
6.	Carivguntela	Ulster Visit. (Reeves) 49	1622
7.	Carrickgagantelon	Ham. Copy Inq. xliv	1623
8.	Ballecarigogautelen	Ham. Copy Inq. xxxiv	1623
9.	Cregegantlet	Raven Map Clandeboy 28	1625
10.	Carrigogantelan	CPR Chas. I 229	1627
11.	Ballycorrigogantilan	Inq. Ult. (Down) §75 Car. I	1636
12.	Carregogaltelan	Inq. Ult. (Down) §109 Car. I	1650c
13.	Ballycarregogancelan	Inq. Ult. (Down) §109 Car. I	1650c

14. Carrickgantelan	Census 94	1659c
15. Carrigogantelan als Cregogantlett	Montgomery MSS 268 n.35	1675
16. Craigogantlet	Wm. Map (OSNB) E 32	1810
17. Craigagantlet	Bnd. Sur. (OSNB) E 32	1830c
18. Creag Ua gCaindealbhan "O'Ganndolan's town"	J O'D (OSNB) E 32	1834c
19. ˌkre.ˈgɑntlət	Local pronunciation	1991

The majority of the forms (1–5, 7, 8, etc.) contain an *o* (an *a* in forms 7 and 17) which suggests that the final element emanates from *Ó gCaoindealbháin* "of the descendants of *Caoindealbhán*", the initial *c* of *Caoindealbhán* being eclipsed due to the preceding genitive plural, *Ó*, earlier, *Ua* "descendant, grandson". Woulfe (1923: 451) states that the bearers of the surname *Ó Caoindealbháin* were chiefs of *Cinél Laoghaire* near Trim. He claims that they descend from *Caoindealbhán* who died in 925 AD, a descendant of *Laoghaire*, son of *Niall* of the Nine Hostages. The surname is usually anglicized (O) Kennellan, Quinlan, etc.

The final *t* in a number of the forms, which first appears in 1625 (9), may be a result of either assimilation or dissimilation: assimilation which results in the final *t* being similar to the *t* in the previous syllable (present in forms 4–11, 13–16) or dissimilation which results in the final *n* being changed to *t* to make it different from the *n* in the previous syllable (which appears in almost all the written forms). The second *c* in form 13 is probably a scribal error for *t*.

The majority of the forms show that the first element was originally *carraig* "rock", as opposed to *creig* "crag, rocky eminence"; the first instance of *creig* does not appear until 1675 (14). The form cited in *Top. Index 1961* is Craigogantlet which preserves the *Ó* of the surname which forms the second element of the place-name. The form Craigantlet, however, is in common use.

Cronstown
J 5175

An English form

1. Cronstown	Wm. Map (OSNB) E 32	1810
2. Cronstown	Bnd. Sur. (OSNB) E 32	1830c
3. ˌkrɔnzteun	Local pronunciation	1991

This name does not appear in those 17th-century documents which refer to other townlands in this parish. It appears to have been coined some time after the 17th century and is of English origin (see **Gregstown** also in this parish). The surname Crone is derived from Irish *crón* "swarthy" (MacLysaght 1991: 66); it is also attested in Scotland (Black 1946: 187).

Crossnamuckley
J 5473

Cros na Muclaí
"the cross of the piggery"

1. Ballicrossnemucklogh	Inq. Ult. (Down) §2 Jac. I	1605
2. Carow-Crossenemucklie	Ham. Copy Inq. xliv	1623
3. Correncrosie, Mucklie	Inq. Ult. (Down) §75 Car. I	1636
4. Carrowcrosnemuckley	Inq. Ult. (Down) §109 Car. I	1650c
5. Ballydrumchaie al Crosslemucke	BSD 87	1661

6. Carrowcrossnemuckley als Drumchey als Drumnewhay	Montgomery MSS 268 n.35	1675
7. Crossnemuckley	Wm. Map (OSNB) E 32	1810
8. Crossnamuckley	Bnd. Sur. (OSNB) E 32	1830c
9. Cros na Muclaighe "cross of the piggery"	J O'D (OSNB) E 32	1834c
10. ˌkrɔsnəˈmo̤kli	Local pronunciation	1991

Forms 2–4 and 6 show that the word *ceathrú* "quarter" was at one time the first element in this townland name (see **Orlock**, parish of Bangor, for the meaning of *ceathrú* as a place-name element). According to *Joyce* (i 478–9), the word *muclach* "place where pigs are kept, piggery", is frequently used as an element in place-names throughout Ireland, and is found in counties Galway, Leitrim, Fermanagh, Sligo, Tyrone and Kildare. In the absence of any ecclestiastical association with this townland, it would appear that the element *cros* referred here to a crossroads.

Form 3 is interesting in that the comma shows the scribe thought that *Correncrosie* and *Mucklie* were two different names (see **Rathgill** in the parish of Bangor for a similar error).

Cunningburn — A Scots/English form

J 5370

1. Cuningburne	CPR Jas. I 326a	1617
2. Cunneburne	Ham. Copy Inq. li	1623
3. Ballehawly al. Cunyngburne	BSD 87	1661
4. Coninburn	Sub. Roll Dn. 281	1663
5. Cunningburnes, the two town Parks, lands of,	Montgomery MSS 268 n.35	1675
6. Kinningbourne	Reid's Presb. Hist. 282	1690c
7. Cunningburn	Wm. Map (OSNB) E 32	1810
8. Cunningburn	Bnd. Sur. (OSNB) E 32	1830c
9. ˈko̤niŋbərn	Local pronunciation	1991

This name appears to have been coined in the variety of English spoken by Scottish and English settlers at an early stage in the plantation of North Down. It is likely that it was named after the nearby stream known as Cunning Burn. According to MacLysaght (1985: 70, 140) Cunning is an Ulster variant of the English surname Gunning which derives from Old German *Gund(e)win* "battle-friend" (Reaney 1958: 148)

Drumawhy — *Droim Chuaiche* "ridge of (the) cuckoo"

J 5475

1. Balle-Drumchey	Ham. Copy Inq. xlii	1623
2. Balledrumchaye	CPR Chas. I 230	1627
3. Balledrumcheriff	Ham. Patent xiii	1630
4. Drumchay	Census 94	1659c
5. Drumahays	Sub. Roll Down 281	1663

6. Drumchey als Drumnewhay als Carrowcrossnemuckley	Montgomery MSS 268 n.35	1675
7. Drumawhy	Wm. Map (OSNB) E 32	1810
8. Drumawhy	Bnd. Sur. (OSNB) E 32	1830c
9. Drumacohey	OSNB E 32	1834c
10. Druim na Cuaiche "ridge of the cuckoo"	J O'D (OSNB) E 32	1834c
11. Druim Áithe "ridge of the kiln"	J O'D (OSNB) E 32	1834c
12. ˌdrọməˈhwe:	Local pronunciation	1991

Forms 1, 2, 4, and 6a all seem to represent *Droim Chuaiche* "ridge of the cuckoo". Form 6b may be an attempt to represent *Droim na Cuaiche*. Forms 7–9 have an additional syllable which may be epenthetic, as opposed to being representative of the gen. sing. fem. form of the definite article. Another possibility for the second element, albeit less likely, is *cuach* meaning "bowl", which may refer to the shape of the ridge.

Drumhirk
J 5177

Droim Thoirc
"ridge of (the) boar"

1. Ballegromherd	Ex. Inq. 1 Jac. I	1603
2. Ballegromeherke	CPR Jas. I 72b	1605
3. Ballydrumhurke al Ballegreinhirk	Ham. Copy Inq. xliv	1623
4. Ballydrumhurke al Ballygunnhirk	Ham. Copy Inq. xxxi	1623
5. Ballydrumhurcke al Ballygromhircke	CPR Chas. I 229	1627
6. Ballydrumhurke al Gromhirke	Inq. Ult. (Down) §109 Car. I	1650c
7. Ballydrumhurke al Dromhirke	Inq. Ult. (Down) §109 Car. I	1650c
8. Drumhirk	Census 94	1659c
9. Ballydrumhirk	BSD 87	1661
10. Ballydrumhircke als Gramhirk als Drumhirk	Montgomery MSS 267 n.35	1675
11. Drumhirk	Wm. Map (OSNB) E 32	1810
12. Drumhirk	Bnd. Sur. (OSNB) E 32	1830c
13. Druim Thuirc "ridge of the hog"	J O'D (OSNB) E 32	1834c
14. drọmˈhərk	Local pronunciation	1991

On examining the historical forms two possible Irish originals come to mind: *Droim Thoirc* "ridge of the boar" and *Droim an Choirce* "ridge of the oats". Perhaps the former is the more likely of the two for if the current anglicized form derived from *Droim Choirce*, one might reasonably expect to find some historical spellings with the final element beginning with *k*.

Greengraves
J 4573

Baile Chloch Tógála
"townland of (the) dolmen"

1. Ballymoghloe al Greenegranes	Inq. Ult. (Down) §109 Car. I	1650c
2. Ballycloghcogall al Greenegraves	Inq. Ult. (Down) §109 Car. I	1650c
3. Ballegreengranes	BSD 121	1661

4. Ballycloghtogall als Greengraves	Montgomery MSS 268 n.35	1675
5. Greengraves al Ballycloghtogall	Deeds and Wills (DF)	1720
6. Cloch Togbhail "raised stone"	J O'D (OSNB) E 32	1834c
7. "town of the lifted stone	O'Laverty ii 134	1880
8. 'gri:ngrɛvz	Local pronunciation	1991
9. gri:n'gre:vz	Local pronunciation	1991

The alias form of this name, *Ballycloghtogall*, derives from Irish *Baile Chloch Tógála*, "townland of (the) dolmen". Irish *cloch tógála* literally means "building stone", but *Dinneen* (s.v. *tógáil*) defines it as "dolmen". *Joyce* (i 342) refers to the application of *cloch tógála* in place-names, which appears to be confined to Ulster. He cites (*ibid.*) three townlands which derive from *cloch t(h)ógála*: **Cloghogle**, in the parish of Donaghedy, Co. Tyrone; another **Cloghogle** in the parish of Ardstraw, Co. Tyrone: and **Cloghtogle** in the parish of Enniskillen, Co. Fermanagh. The Hiberno-English word "cloghogle" also means dolmen and it appears as a heading in *OSM* (v 12) under which follow descriptions of a number of dolmens. It is interesting to note that an anglicized alias form of *Baile Chloch Tógála* was still being applied to the townland now known as Greengraves in the first decade of the 18th century (5). The name *Baile Chloch Tógála* is very apt for this townland as there is an impressive dolmen in it known locally as the *Kempe Stones*. The word *kempe* survives in ballads and place-names and means "champion, warrior" (*Scot. Nat. Dict.* s.v.). *O'Laverty* (ii 134) has an interesting description of the dolmen that shows he was aware both of the Irish name of the townland and the local name for the monument (the dolmen is also described in *ASCD* 80).

John O'Donovan rarely had access to 17th-century documentation for the majority of the place-names he was working on in Co. Down but it is apparent from the *OSNB* for Newtownards that he had obtained forms from a patent, described as "12 Car 1", which refers to this place as *Ballycloghtogall al "Greengraves"*. Having access to the form *Ballycloghtogall*, O'Donovan's postulated Irish language form for Greengraves was *Cloch Togbhail*. In the light of other 17th-century forms at our disposal it is clear that his deduction was correct, although it is strange that he did not use the gen. sing. form of *tógbháil* (later *tógáil*), namely, *tógbhála* (later *tógála*).

We have no concrete evidence of the origin of Greengraves, the current name of this townland, but it may be a corruption of *Gráinne's* Grave(s) as the term *Leaba Dhiarmada agus Ghráinne* "Dermot and Gráinne's bed" is frequently applied to dolmens in Irish in many parts of the country. This term came into existence as a result of the influence of the Early Modern Irish tale *Tóruigheacht Dhiarmada agus Ghráinne* "the pursuit of Diarmaid and Gráinne" (*Joyce* i 341–2). It is not uncommon for a particular dolmen to be referred to in English as a "Giant's Grave", so perhaps the name Greengraves came into being as a result of the fusion of this phenomenon and the effects of the tradition of *Tóruigheacht Dhiarmada agus Ghráinne* on the onomasticon.

Gregstown — An English form

J 5073

1. Gregstown	Bnd. Sur. (OSNB) E 32	1830c
2. Greg is a family name	J O'D (OSNB) E 32	1830c
3. 'gregztəun	Local pronunciation	1991

The absence of forms earlier than the 19th-century suggests that this is a relatively recent name similar to **Cronstown** (see p. 227 above); it is composed of what appears to be either a personal name or a surname followed by the element "town". Reaney (1958: 145) cites Greg as a surname and states that it is a short form of Gregory.

Killarn	*Cill Earnáin*	
J 4475	"Earnán's church"	
1. Ballikelarmid	CPR Jas. I 73a	1605
2. Ballikillarnud	Inq. Ult. (Down) 2 Jac. I	1605
3. Killarncid	Terrier (Reeves) 51	1615c
4. Killernoed, Capella de	Ulster Visit. (Reeves) 49	1622
5. Killeman	Ham. Copy Inq. xxxi	1623
6. Killemed	Ham. Copy Inq. xliv	1623
7. Kilkernan	CPR Chas. I 229	1627
8. Killerned	Inq. Ult. (Down) §75 Car. I	1636
9. Ballykillarnid	Inq. Ult. (Down) §109 Car. I	1650c
10. Ballykillariod	Inq. Ult. (Down) §109 Car. I	1650c
11. Killerny	Census 94	1659c
12. Ballykilcarine als Killarne	Montgomery MSS 268 n.35	1675
13. Killarn	Wm. Map (OSNB) E 32	1810
14. Killarn	Bnd. Sur. (OSNB) E 32	1830c
15. Cill Athairne "Athairne's church"	J O'D (OSNB) E 32	1834c
16. ki'lɑ:rn	Local pronunciation	1991

An examination of the historical forms for this name reveals that it is quite complex.This is because a number of 17th-century attestations seem to have an additional syllable which has been lost from the current anglicized form. The derivation of the first element, however, does not pose a serious problem. The fact that this name is cited in ecclesiastical documents such as *Terrier (Reeves)* and the *Ulster Visit. (Reeves)* indicates that the first element is more likely to be *cill* "church" than *coill* "wood". It is noteworthy that a field in this townland was known as *The Chapel Field* as late as the closing decades of the 19th century (*O'Laverty* ii 141).

Allowing for certain changes which affected the name, the second element can be argued to have emanated from the gen. sing. of the Irish personal name *Earnán*. The forms ending in *-d* (1–4, 6, 8–10), could have derived from *Cill Earnáin* by dissimilation. The form *Killarn* is likely to be a reduction from *Cill Earnáin* due to haplology just as the Scottish place-name *Oirear Gael* "coast of the Irish" has been anglicized in the reduced form of Argyll (see further **Ardkeen**). O'Laverty seems to have been puzzled by the 17th-century forms for Killarn which ended in *d*, as he suggests that they might have referred, not to Killarn, but to **Killynether** in the neighbouring parish of Comber (*O'Laverty ibid.* 142). He bases this theory on an entry in the Ulster Visitation of 1622 which he cites as follows (*ibid.* 142):

> *Cappella de Killernord* impropriate to ye priory of Down, and belongs to ye Countess of Kildare. Noe curate, nor able to mainteyne one, the people repayre to Comber and partly to Downe Donald, ye next churches.

It should be noted that 17th-century sources such as *Census* (87, 94) and the *BSD* (120, 121) contain distinct forms for both Killarn and Killynether under their respective parishes.

Kiltonga *Cill Teanga*
J 4774 "church of (the) tongue of land"

1.	Beltuga	Ex. Inq. 1 Jac. I	1603
2.	Killtuga	Inq. Ult. (Down) §2 Jac. I	1605
3.	Kiltaga	CPR Jas. I 72b	1605
4.	Kiltuga	Ham. Copy Inq. xxxi	1623
5.	Kiltego	Ham. Copy Inq. xliv	1623
6.	Killengar	CPR Chas. I 229	1627
7.	Killorga	Inq. Ult. (Down) §75 Car. I	1636
8.	Kiltonga	Inq. Ult. (Down) §109 Car. I	1650c
9.	Kiltonga	Descr. Ards 40	1683
10.	ˌkil'tɔŋgə	Local pronunciation	1991

In place-names the word *teanga* generally has the meaning "a tongue of land". *Joyce* (ii 404) refers to this application and cites several townlands which contain the element *teanga* including **Bryantang**, Co. Antrim, Tangaveane, Co. Donegal, and Tangincartoor, Co. Mayo. Note also the minor name **The Tongue** in the parish of Witter. The forms without *n* (1–5) may be the result of a manuscript contraction not being expanded.

O'Laverty (ii 141) suggests that Kiltonga is an attempt to represent Killysugan, the name of an old graveyard in the townland of Milecross also in this parish. It is difficult to justify this theory, however, as none of the historical forms for Kiltonga bear any resemblance to Killysugan. According to two inquisitions, one taken at Ardquin in 1605, the other in Newtownards c. 1650, the townlands of Ballyrogan and Killarn were attached to the chapel of Kiltonga (*Inq. Ult.* §2 Jac. 1, §§75, 109 Car. 1). A late 17th-century description of the Ards refers to the ecclesiastical site at Kiltonga as being in ruins (*Descr. Ards* 40).

Loughriscouse *Luachras Cua*
J 5274 "rushy place of (the) hollow"

1.	Ballyloghniscowe	Ham. Copy Inq. xliv	1623
2.	Ballyloghiescowe	Ham. Copy Inq. xxxi	1623
3.	Ballyloughreskowe	CPR Chas. I 229	1627
4.	Ballyloghriskowe	Inq. Ult. (Down) §75 Car I	1636
5.	Ballyloghrescow	Inq. Ult. (Down) §109 Car. I	1650c
6.	Loghrescow	Census 94	1659c
7.	Ballyloughrescoy als Loughrescow als the three Loughrescowes	Montgomery MSS 268 n.35	1675
8.	Lougheries-scouse	Wm. Map (OSNB) E 32	1810
9.	Loughriescouse	Bnd. Sur. (OSNB) E 32	1830c
10.	Loughryscouse	OSNB E 32	1834c
11.	Luachrais Cuas "rushy-land of the cave"	J O'D (OSNB) E 32	1834c
12.	'lɔxriz	Local pronunciation	1991

Forms 1–7b show no trace of an *s* in the final syllable and this, coupled with the fact that the first instance of an *s* (7c) is an obvious English plural ending, indicates that the *s* in the final syllable has no historical basis in the original Irish-language form.

The first element is *luachras* which consists, according to Ó Máille (1990: 136), of *luachair*, "rushes" + the suffix *-as*; *luachras* can be translated "place of rushes" and this appears to be the derivation of Luachras, Co. Donegal. Forms 1–6 and 7b above might suggest that the second element derives from *cunga* "narrow neck of land", with the vocalization of *ng* resulting in a pronunciation approaching [kũ:]. This trait is in keeping with other areas where East Ulster Irish was spoken and is attested in place-names; for example, **Aghaloo**, Co.Tyrone derives from Irish *Achadh Longa* "field of (the) house" (de hÓir 1964a: 10; note also Flanagan 1981–2a: 22). The previous name, **Kiltonga**, however, suggests that the vocalization of *ng* was not a feature of this area. It seems more likely, therefore, that the second element of Loughriscouse derives from Irish *cua*, an obsolete word meaning "hollow, cavity, (empty) expanse" (*DIL* s.v.).

Milecross — An English form
J 4775

1. Ballyhawlie	CPR Chas. I 229	1627
2. Milecross al Tomegardy	Census 94	1659c
3. Ballyhawly, quarter of als Milecross	Montgomery MSS 268 n.35	1675
4. Milecross	Wm. Map (OSNB) E 32	1810
5. Milecross	Bnd. Sur. (OSNB) E 32	1830c
6. ˈməilˈkrɔs	Local pronunciation	1991

Forms 1 and 3a are probably anglicizations of an Irish name for this place which was supplanted by *Milecross*, but it is difficult to say what Irish form these anglicized spellings represent. The alias form 2b, *Tomegardy*, may be a misspelling for the neighbouring townland of Tullynagardy.

Movilla — *Maigh Bhile*
J 5074 — "plain of (the) ancient tree"

1. Moige Bile, quies Finniae	AIF 76	580
2. Maighe bile, epscop	AFM i 230 *et pass.*	602
3. Moige Bili, mors...Sillain	AIF 86	621
4. Maighi Bili, mors Cronain	AU (Mac Airt) i 126 *et pass.*	650
5. Mhaighe bile, hUidhreini	AFM i 296	691
6. Maige Bile, quies... Udrine epscoip	AIF 100	693
7. Maigi Bile, abbas	AU (Mac Airt) i 188 *et pass.*	736
8. Mag Bile	AIF 124	824
9. Maige Bile, prinnceps	AU (Mac Airt) i 280 *et pass.*	825
10. Maige Bili, abb	Mart. Tal. Jan. 2 p4	830c
11. Maigi Bile, abb	Mart. Tal. Feb. 3 p14	830c
12. Maighe Bile, episcopi	Mart. Tal. Feb. 11 p16	830c
13. Maigi Bili, abbatis	Mart. Tal. Apr. 29 p37 *et pass.*	830c
14. Maige Bile, episcopus	Mart. Tal. May 3 p39	830c
15. Maigi, Findbair	Mart. Tal. Sep. 10 70	830c
16. Muighe bile, ab	Fél. Óeng. Feb. 3 p68 *et pass.*	830c
17. Maige Bili, Findbarr	Fél. Óeng. Sep. 10 p193	830c

18. Muighi bili, Finnen	Fél. Óeng. Sep. 10 p204	830c
19. Maigi bile, Findian	Fél. Óeng. Sep. 10 p204	830c
20. Maige bile, Finnian	Fél. Óeng. Sep. 10 p204 *et pass.*	830c
21. Bili, ecclesiam	Trip. Life (Stokes) ii 310	900c
22. Muigi Bile, comarba Finnen	AU (Mac Airt) i 438 *et pass.*	1007
23. Maige Bile, Finnian	CSH 136.1, 23	1125c
24. mMaig Bile, i	CSH 136.2, 23	1125c
25. Muigi Bili, Finden	CSH 423, 64	1125c
26. Maighe Bile bain, Finden	CSH 662.140, 96	1125c
27. Maige Bili, Finnen	CSH 703.18, 132	1125c
28. Maigi Bile, Finnian	CSH 712.5, 160	1125c
29. Maigi Bili, iar cúl Ḟinniain	CSH 729.1 185	1125c
30. Maighe bile, abb	Mart. Gorm. Jan. 2 p6n *et pass.*	1170c
31. Maighi Bili, epscop	Mart. Gorm. Apr. 29 p86n	1170c
32. Maighi Bile, epscop	Mart. Gorm. May 3 p88n	1170c
33. Maigi bili, ab	Mart. Don. Jul. 16 p19	1630c
34. Maighe bile, epscop	Mart. Don. Sep. 10 p242 *et pass.*	1630c
35. Muighe bile, epscop	Mart. Don. May 3 p118 *et pass.*	1630c
36. Mhuighe bile, ab	Mart. Don. May 31 p140	1630c
37. Magh-bile	MacCana's Itinerary 55	1700c
38. Campi Bili, episcopus	AU (Mac Airt) i 100 *et pass.*	603
39. Maynbil, abbey of	Great Rolls Pipe 33	1275c
40. Moville, Mon. de	Annates Ulst. 116 app.	1420
41. Moyvilli	Annates Ulst. 113	1505
42. Monvil	Bartlett Maps (Esch. Co. Maps) i	1603
43. Mavilla	Ex. Inq. 1 Jac. I	1603
44. Ballemavill	Ex. Inq. 1 Jac. I	1603
45. Ballymaville	CPR Jas. I 72b	1605
46. Mavilla	CPR Jas. I 72b	1605
47. Monuell abb	Speed's Ulster	1610
48. Movill	Terrier (Reeves) 45	1615c
49. Movilla	Terrier (Reeves) 45	1615c
50. Movilla	Terrier (O' Laverty) 326	1615c
51. Movilla	CPR Jas. I 546a	1621
52. Moyvill	Ulster Visit. (Reeves) 51	1622
53. Movilla	Ham. Copy Inq. xliv	1623
54. Ballinieagh al Movilla	Ham. Copy Inq. xliv	1623
55. Movilla	Ham. Copy Inq. xxxi	1623
56. Ballinreagh al Movilla	Ham. Copy Inq. xxxi	1623
57. Movilla	Ham. Copy Inq. xxxii	1623
58. Movilla	CPR Chas. I 131	1626
59. Ballinreaghe al Movilla	CPR Chas. I 228	1627
60. Moville	CPR Chas. I 225	1627
61. Movilla	CPR Chas. I 228	1627
62. Movilla al Ballinry al Ballencreagh	Inq. Ult. (Down) §109 Car. I	1650c
63. Movilla al Ballinreagh al Ballinry	Inq. Ult. (Down) §109 Car. I	1650c
64. Movilla al. Ballehary	BSD 87	1661
65. Mowhill	Sub. Roll Down 281	1663

66. Movilla	Wm. Map (OSNB) E 32	1810
67. Movilla	Bnd. Sur. (OSNB) E 32	1830c
68. Magh Bile "plain of the old tree"	J O'D (OSNB) E 32	1834c
69. ˌmo'vilə	Local pronunciation	1991

The first element, *maigh*, is the dat. sing. of Old Irish *mag* "a plain" and this oblique form is used in the majority of Irish language forms listed above. The second element is *bile* "ancient and venerated tree"; in pagan times the *bile* frequently had religious significance (*DIL* s.v. ; *Joyce* i 499–501). The name *Mag Bile*, as it is was known in Old Irish, "plain of (the) ancient tree", suggests that the monastery there was deliberately built on a site close to a *bile* (the practice of founding ecclesiastical sites near sacred trees is discussed in Lucas 1963: 30–4).

The monastery at *Mag Bile*, became the chief church of the *Ulaid* and was on the borders of their own *túath* (Kenny 1929: 390–1). It was founded c. 540 by St *Finian*, whose death is recorded in *AU* under the year 579 AD. It is possible that this Finian was the *Episcopus Finnio*, *Episcopus Vinnianus* etc., mentioned in *Adamnán*'s 7th-century life of St Columba. According to *AU* Moville was plundered by the Norsemen in 824 AD. We know from an inquisition taken at Ardquin in 1605, that the monastery of Moville possessed a number of the townlands within the civil parish of Newtownards, not to mention other lands both in the Ards and further afield (*Inq. Ult.* §2 Jac. I). For the incidence of *Ballyreagh* as an alias (forms 54, 56, 59, etc.) see **Ballyreagh** above.

Scrabo	*Screabach*	
J 4772	"thinly covered rock; light, stony ground"	
1. Sgrabaigh, i Sioghbhrugh	Neilson's Intro. 74	1808
2. Scraboc	Great Rolls Pipe xxxvi 32	1275c
3. Strabok, 1 caru' in le hill de	CPR (Tresham) i 242	1427c
4. Scrabocke	S-E Ulster Map	1580c
5. Scrabocke	Mercator's Ulster	1595c
6. Knock Scraboh	Speed's Ulster	1610
7. Knock Scraboh	Speed's Antrim & Down	1610
8. Straboe, the hill of	CPR Jas. I 255a	1613
9. Scrabo	Ham. Copy Inq. xliii	1623
10. Scrabo	Census 95	1659c
11. Ballykillconan als Killcoman als Ballycullen als Scrabo Hills als Wilson's Land	Montgomery MSS 268 n.35	1675
12. Scrabo	Descr. Ards 41	1683
13. Scraba	Harris Hist. 70	1774
14. Scrabo	Wm. Map (OSNB) E 32	1810
15. Scrabo	Bnd. Sur (OSNB)E 32	1830c
16. Scraith Bo "sward of the cow"	J O'D (OSNB) E 32	1834c
17. Screabach	AGBP 119	1969
18. Screabach	GÉ 270	1989
19. 'skrɑbo	Local pronunciation	1991

Given its striking and prominent position overlooking Strangford Lough, it is only to be expected that reference to the hill from which this townland is named should be found in a number of interesting sources, including *Great Rolls Pipe*, *Speed's Ulster* and *Neilson's Intro.*

Neilson, probably on the basis of local tradition, indicates that Scrabo was regarded as being a fairy hill and that its guardian was one *Mac an Eantoin* (*Neilson's Intro.* 74, 88).

O'Laverty (ii 10) may have been the first to discover the "lost" townland of Killcoman. On the evidence of the 1675 AD forms (11) "Ballykillconan, als Kilcoman, als Ballycullen, als Scrabo Hills, als Wilson's Land", he was of the opinion that an area of land in the townlands of Scrabo and Ballycullen formerly delineated the townland of Killcoman.

The 19th-century historian Knox (*Knox Hist.* 557) has this to say about Scrabo:

> The highest ground in this district, except the adjoining hill of Karnav Gar (i.e. Goat's mount) is Scrabo Hill, the "Knock Scraboh" of Speed's Map, on which several very valuable freestone quarries have been opened. On its summit there is a handsome turreted memorial, visible to a great distance, erected from a design by Sir Charles Lanyon, in honour of the third Marquis of Londonderry.

A hill-fort is situated on the top of this prominent hill and traces of a number of hut-groups can be seen below the summit (*ASCD* 147, 179).

Tullynagardy	*Tulaigh na gCeardaithe*	
J 4775	"hillock of the artisans/ artificers"	
1. Carrowntullehagard	Inq. Ult. (Down) §75 Car. I	1636
2. Tomegardy al Milecross	Census 94	1659c
3. Carrowtullehaggard als Tullenegardy	Montgomery MSS 268 n.35	1675
4. Ballynegardis	Bnd. Sur. (OSNB) E 32	1830c
5. Tulaigh na Gárda "hill of the guard"	J O'D (OSNB) E 32	1830c
6. ˌtọlənəˈkɑrdi	Local pronunciation	1991

In forms 1 and 3a it is interesting to note that *ceathrú*, "quarter" was formerly the first element of this name (see **Orlock**, parish of Bangor, for the meaning of *ceathrú* as a place-name element). Forms 1 and 3a above indicate that an early form of the name was *Tulaigh na gCeard*, "hill of the artisans, artificers", where *ceard* is another form of *ceardaí*.

Whitespots	*Ceathrú Chamchoise*	
J 4976	"crooked-leg quarter"	
1. Carowcamcoyse	Ham. Copy Inq. xliv	1623
2. Carrowchamchoise	Inq. Ult. (Down) 75 Car. I	1636
3. Carrowchamcoise	Inq. Ult. (Down) 109 Car. I	1650c
4. Carrowcamcoise als Couacks als Whitespots	Montgomery MSS 268 n.35	1675
5. Whitespots	Wm. Map (OSNB) E 32	1810
6. Whitespots	Bnd. Sur. (OSNB) E 32	1830c
7. ˈhwəitspɔts	Local pronunciation	1991

We have been unable to find any information about how this place was named in English, but it is likely that it refers to some significant physical feature in the landscape. As the historical forms indicate, however, there was an interesting older name i.e. *Ceathrú Chamchoise* "lit. crooked-leg quarter". **Altacamcossy**, in the parish of Lower Bodoney, Co. Tyrone, seems to share the same second element as the original Irish name of this place.

OTHER NAMES

Cairngaver J 4576	*Carn Gabhair* "(the) goat's cairn"	
1. Karn-Gavr	Harris Hist. 70	1774
2. Cairngaver	Wm. Map (OSNB) E 32	1810
3. Carngaver	Bnd. Sur. (OSNB) E 32	1830c
4. Karnav Gar	Knox Hist.	1875
5. Carn Gabhair "carn of the goat"	J O'D (OSNB) E 32	1834c

This is the highest hill in the parish. The 17th-century historian Walter Harris derives it from "Goats-Mount" (*Harris Hist.* 70).

Cunning Burn — See **Cunningburn**.

APPENDIX A

ASPECTS OF IRISH GRAMMAR RELEVANT TO PLACE-NAMES

The following types of place-names can be identified:

1. Those which consist of a noun only:

   Sabhall "a barn" (Saul, Dn)
   Tuaim "a tumulus" (Toome, Ant.)

There is no indefinite article in Irish, that is, there is no word for *a*, e.g. *Sabhall* means "barn" or "a barn".

English nouns generally have only two forms, singular and plural, and the plural is normally formed by adding *s*, e.g. *wall, walls; road, roads*. Occasionally a different ending is added – *ox, oxen* – and occasionally the word is changed internally – *man, men*; sometimes there is both addition and internal change – *brother, brethren*. Irish nouns have not only distinctive forms for the plural but also for the genitive singular and sometimes for the dative and vocative as well. These distinctive forms are made by addition, by internal change and sometimes by both. Five principal types of noun change are identified in Irish and nouns are therefore divided into five major groups known as *declensions*. Examples of change will be seen later.

2. Singular article + masculine noun:

   An Clár "the plain" (Clare, Arm.)
   An Gleann "the valley" (Glen, Der.)

The only article in Irish is the definite article, that is, the word corresponding to *the* in English.

The singular article *an* "the" prefixes *t* to masculine nouns beginning with a vowel in certain cases. The nouns *éadan* "front, forehead" and *iúr* "yew tree", for example, appear in the place-names:

   An tÉadan "the face (of a hill)" (Eden, Ant.)
   An tIúr "the yew tree" (Newry, Dn)

3. Singular article + feminine noun:

   An Chloch "the stone" (Clough, Dn)
   An Bhreacach "the speckled place" (Brockagh, Der.)

The article *an* aspirates the first consonant of a following feminine noun.

Aspiration is indicated by putting *h* after the consonant (*cloch* "a stone"; *an chloch* "the stone") and the sound of that consonant is modified, just as in English the sound of *p*, as in the word *praise*, is changed when *h* is added, as in the word *phrase*. Only *b, c, d, f, g, m, p, s*, and *t* are aspirated. The other consonants, and vowels, are not aspirated.

The singular article *an* does not affect feminine nouns beginning with a vowel, e.g.

   An Eaglais "the church" (Eglish, Tyr.)

4. Masculine noun + adjective:

   Domhnach Mór "great church" (Donaghmore, Tyr.)
   Lios Liath "grey ring fort" (Lislea, Arm.)

In Irish the adjective normally follows the noun (but see §8).

5. Feminine noun + adjective:

Bearn Mhín "smooth gap" (Barnmeen, Dn)
Doire Fhada "long oak-wood" (Derryadd, Arm.)

The first consonant of the adjective is aspirated after a feminine noun.

6. Singular article + masculine noun + adjective:

An Caisleán Riabhach "the brindled castle" (Castlereagh, Dn)
An Baile Meánach "the middle town" (Ballymena, Ant.)

7. Singular article + feminine noun + adjective:

An Charraig Mhór "the large rock" (Carrickmore, Tyr.)
An Chloch Fhionn "the white stone" (Cloghfin, Tyr.)

Note that the first consonant of the feminine noun is aspirated after the definite article as in §3 above and that the adjective is aspirated after the feminine noun as in §5 above.

8 Adjective + noun:

fionnshliabh "white mountain" (Finlieve, Dn)
Seanchill "old church" (Shankill, Ant.)

Sometimes an adjective precedes a noun. In such cases the two words are generally written as one and the second noun is usually aspirated. In compounds aspiration sometimes does not occur when *d, t* or *s* is preceded by *d, n, t, l* or *s*.

9. Article + adjective + noun:

An Seanmhullach "the old summit" (Castledawson, Der.)
An Ghlasdromainn "the green ridge" (Glasdrumman, Dn)

Dromainn is a feminine noun and the initial consonant of the compound is aspirated in accordance with §3 above.

10. Masculine noun + genitive singular of noun:

Srath Gabhláin "(the) river valley of (the) fork" (Stragolan, Fer.)
Port Rois "(the) harbour of (the) headland" (Portrush, Ant.)

These two examples contain the genitive singular forms of the nouns *gabhlán* and *ros*. Many nouns form the genitive singular by inserting *i* before the final consonant.

11. Feminine noun + genitive singular of noun:

Maigh Bhile "(the) plain of (the) sacred tree" (Movilla, Dn)
Cill Shléibhe "(the) church of (the) mountain" (Killevy, Arm.)

Note that in these examples the qualifying genitive is aspirated after the feminine noun. However the forms *maigh* and *cill* are also both old datives, and in the older language aspiration followed any dative singular noun.

Two other types of genitive are illustrated here: many nouns which end in a vowel, like *bile*, do not change at all, whereas others, like *sliabh*, form their genitive by adding *e* (and sometimes an internal change is necessary).

12. Noun + *an* + genitive singular:

> Léim an Mhadaidh "(the) leap of the dog" (Limavady, Der.)
> Baile an tSéipéil "(the) town of the chapel" (Chapeltown, Dn)

The noun *an madadh* "the dog" has a genitive *an mhadaidh* "of the dog". Note that, as well as the end of the noun changing as in §10 above, the genitive is aspirated after *an*.

Instead of aspirating *s* the article *an* prefixes *t* to it: *an sac* "the sack", *an tsaic* "of the sack"; *an séipéal* "the chapel", *an tséipéil* "of the chapel".

13. Noun + *na* + genitive singular:

> Muileann na Cloiche "(the) mill of the stone/the stone mill" (Clogh Mills, Ant.)
> Coill na Baice "(the) wood of the river bend" (Cullybacky, Ant.)

The genitive singular feminine article is *na*. It does not aspirate the following noun: *an chloch* "the stone", *na cloiche* "of the stone".

It prefixes *h*, however, to words beginning with a vowel e.g.

> Baile na hInse "(the) town of the water-meadow" (Ballynahinch, Dn)

The genitive in all these examples is formed by adding *e* to the nominative singular and making a slight internal adjustment.

14. Plural noun:

> Botha "huts" (Boho, Fer.)

The plural form of a substantial group of nouns in Irish is formed by adding *-a*. In the examples in §15 below an internal adjustment has also to be made.

15. *Na* + plural noun:

> Na Creaga "the rocks" (Craigs, Ant.)
> Na Cealla "the churches" (Kells, Ant.)

Na is also the plural article. *Creaga* and *cealla* are the plural forms of the nouns *creig* "rock" and *cill* "church".

16. Noun + genitive plural:

> Droim Bearach "(the) ridge of (the) heifers" (Dromara, Dn)
> Port Muc "(the) harbour of (the) pigs" (Portmuck, Ant.)

As in the case of *bearach* "a heifer" and *muc* "a pig" the genitive plural form is the same as the nominative singular.

17. Noun + *na* + genitive plural:

> Lios na gCearrbhach "(the) fort/enclosure of the gamblers" (Lisburn, Dn)
> Lios na nDaróg "(the) fort/enclosure of the little oaks" (Lisnarick, Fer.)

After *na* the first letter of the following genitive plural is eclipsed. Eclipsis involves adding to the beginning of a word a consonant which obliterates the sound of the original consonant, e.g.

bó "a cow", pronounced like English "bow"
(*na*) *mbó* "(of the) cows", pronounced like "mow"

The following are the changes which take place:

Written letter	Is eclipsed by
b	m
c	g
d	n
f	bh
g	ng
p	b
t	d
vowel	n

The other consonants are not eclipsed, e.g.

Áth na Long "(the) ford of the ships" (Annalong, Dn)

18. Noun + genitive of personal name:

Dún Muirígh "Muiríoch's fort" (Dunmurry, Ant.)
Boith Mhéabha "Maeve's hut" (Bovevagh, Der.)

In the older language the genitive of a personal name was not aspirated after a masculine noun but it was after a feminine noun. In the above examples *dún* is masculine and *boith* is feminine. In current Irish aspiration of the personal name is also usual after a masculine noun and this is reflected in many place-names in areas where Irish survived until quite recently, e.g.

Ard Mhacha, interpreted as "the height of Macha" (Armagh, Arm.)

19. Noun + genitive singular of *Ó* surname:

Baile Uí Dhonnaíle "Donnelly's townland" (Castlecaulfield, Tyr.)
Coill Uí Chiaragáin "Kerrigan's wood" (Killykergan, Der.)

Surnames in *Ó*, e.g. Ó Dochartaigh "(O') Doherty", Ó Flannagáin "Flannagan", etc. form their genitive by changing *Ó* to *Uí* and aspirating the second element – UÍ Dhochartaigh, Uí Fhlannagáin.

20. Noun + genitive singular of *Mac* surname:

Lios Mhic Dhuibhleacháin "Mac Duibhleacháin's town"
(Lisnagelvin, Der.)
Baile Mhic Gabhann "Mac Gabhann's town (angl. McGowan, Smith, etc.)
(Ballygowan, Dn)

Surnames in *Mac*, e.g. Mac Dónaill "McDonnell", Mac Muiris "Morrison, fitzmaurice", etc. form their genitive by changing *Mac* to *Mhic* and aspirating the second element (except those beginning with *C* or *G*).

23. Noun + genitive plural of *Ó* surname:

    Doire Ó gConaíle "the oak-wood of the Ó Conaíle family (angl. Connelly)" (Derrygonnelly, Fer.)

In the genitive plural of Ó surnames the second element is eclipsed.

25. Neuter noun + genitive or adjective:

    Sliabh gCuillinn "mountain of (the) steep slope" (Slieve Gullion, Arm.)
    Loch gCaol "(the) narrow lake" (Loughguile, Ant.)

The neuter gender no longer exists in Irish but traces of it are found in place-names. The initials of nouns and adjectives were eclipsed after neuter nouns.

APPENDIX B

LAND UNITS

TERRITORIAL DIVISIONS IN IRELAND

The old administrative system, used in the arrangement of these books, consisted of land units in descending order of size: province, county, barony, parish and townland. Theoretically at least the units fit inside each other, townlands into parishes, parishes into baronies, baronies into counties. This system began piecemeal, with the names of the provinces dating back to prehistoric times, while the institution of counties and baronies dates from the 13th to the 17th century, though the names used are often the names of earlier tribal groups or settlements. Parishes originate not as a secular land-unit, but as part of the territorial organization of the Christian Church. There they form the smallest unit in the system which, in descending order of size, goes from provinces to dioceses to deaneries to parishes. Some Irish parishes derive from churches founded by St Patrick and early saints, and appear as parish units in Anglo-Norman church records: parish units are thus older than counties and baronies. Townlands make their first appearance as small land units listed in Anglo-Norman records. However the evidence suggests that land units of this type (which had various local names) are of pre-Norman native origin.

The 17th-century historian Geoffrey Keating outlined a native land-holding system based on the *tríocha céad* or "thirty hundreds", each divided in Ulster into about 28 *baile biadhtaigh* "lands of a food-provider" or "ballybetaghs", and about 463 *seisrigh* "six-horse plough-teams" or "seisreachs" (*Céitinn* iv 112f.). The term *tríocha céad*, which seems to relate to the size of the army an area could muster, is not prominent in English accounts, though there is a barony called Trough (*Tríocha*) in Co. Monaghan. The ballybetagh (land of a farmer legally obliged to feed his lord and retinue while travelling through the area) is mentioned in Plantation documents for west Ulster, and there is some evidence, from townlands grouped in multiples of three and four, that it existed in Armagh, Antrim and Down (McErlean 1983, 318).

Boundaries of large areas, such as provinces and dioceses, are often denoted in early Irish sources by means of two or four extreme points (Hogan 1910, 279–280; *Céitinn* iii 302). There was also a detailed native tradition of boundary description, listing landmarks such as streams, hills, trees and bogs. This can be demonstrated as early as the 8th century in Tírechán's record of a land grant to St Patrick (*Trip. Life (Stokes)* ii 338–9),[1] and as late as the 17th century, when native experts guided those surveying and mapping Ireland for the English administration. The boundary marks on the ground were carefully maintained, as illustrated in the *Perambulation of Iveagh* in 1618 (*Inq. Ult.* xliii), according to which the guide broke the plough of a man found ploughing up a boundary. However very often Irish texts, for example the "Book of Rights" (*Lebor na Cert*), the "topographical" poems by Seaán Mór Ó Dubhagáin and Giolla-na-naomh Ó hUidhrín (*Top. Poems*), and "The rights of O'Neill" (*Ceart Uí Néill*), refer to territories by the names of the peoples inhabiting them. This custom has been preserved to the present in some place-names, particularly those of provinces and baronies.

SECULAR ADMINISTRATIVE DIVISIONS

Townlands

Twelfth-century charters provide the earliest documentary evidence for the existence in Ireland of small land units, although we do not know what these units were called. Keating's smallest unit, the *seisreach*, a division of the ballybetagh, is given as 120 acres (the word *acra* is apparently borrowed from English). The size of the *seisreach* seems to have been approximately that of a modern townland, but the word does not occur much outside Keating's *schema*. Many other terms appear in the sources: *ceathrú* "quarter" (often a quarter of a ballybetagh), *baile bó* "land providing one cow as rent" (usually a twelfth of a ballybetagh), *seiseach* "sixth" and *trian* "third" (apparently divisions of a ballyboe). In most of Ulster the ballyboe and its subdivisions are the precursors of the modern townlands, and were referred to in Latin sources as *villa* or *carucata*, and in English as "town" or "ploughland" (the term used for similar units in 11th-century England in the Domesday Book). The Irish term *baile* (see below) seems to have been treated as equivalent to English "town", which had originally meant "settlement (and lands appertaining)"; and the compound term "townland" seems to have been adopted to make the intended meaning clear. It was used in 19th-century Ireland as a blanket term for various local words. In the area of Fermanagh and Monaghan the term for the local unit was "tate". In an English document of 1591 it is stated that the tate was 60 acres in size and that there were sixteen tates in the ballybetagh (*Fiants Eliz.* §5674). Tate appears in place-names in composition with Gaelic elements, but was regarded by Reeves (1861, 484) as a pre-1600 English borrowing into Irish.

There is no evidence for the use of the word *baile* in the formation of place- names before the middle of the 12th century. The earliest examples are found in a charter dating to c. 1150 in the Book of Kells which relates to lands belonging to the monastery of Kells. At this period *baile* seems to mean "a piece of land" and is not restricted to its present-day meaning "hamlet, group of houses", much less "town, village". After the coming of the Normans, *baile* appears more frequently in place-names, until it finally becomes the most prevalent type of townland name. By the 14th century, *baile* had acquired its present-day meaning of "town", probably in reference to small medieval towns, or settlements that had arisen in the vicinity of castles. Price suggests that the proliferation of the use of the word in place-names was a result of the arrival of settlers and their use of the word "town" (*tūn*) in giving names to their lands (Price 1963, 124). When the Irish revival took place in the 14th century many English-language names were translated into Irish and "town" was generally replaced by *baile*. The proportion of *baile* names is greatest in those parts of Ireland which had been overrun by the Anglo-Normans but subsequently gaelicized, and is lowest in the counties of mid-Ulster in which there was little or no English settlement (*ibid.* 125).

Despite attempts at schematization none of the units which predated the modern townlands was of uniform size, and it is clear from the native sources that evaluation was based on an area of good land together with a variable amount of uncultivated land. Thus townlands on bad land are usually larger than those on good land. The average size of a townland in Ireland as a whole is 325 acres, and 357 acres in the six counties of Northern Ireland, though these averages include huge townlands like Slievedoo (4551 acres, Co. Tyrone) and tiny townlands like Acre McCricket (4 acres, Co. Down). There is also considerable local variation: townlands in Co. Down average 457 acres (based on the ballyboe), compared to 184 acres (based on the tate) in Fermanagh (Reeves 1861, 490).

Parishes

Early accounts of the lives of saints such as Patrick and Columcille refer to many church foundations. It seems that land was often given for early churches beside routeways, or on the boundaries of tribal territories. Some of the same church names appear as the names of medieval parishes in the papal taxation of 1302-06 (*Eccles. Tax.*). Some parish names include ecclesiastical elements such as *ceall*, *domhnach*, *lann*, all meaning "church", *díseart* "hermitage" and *tearmann* "sanctuary", but others are secular in origin. Parish bounds are not given in the papal taxation, but parishes vary considerably in size, probably depending on the wealth or influence of the local church. The medieval ecclesiastical parishes seem to have come into existence after the reform of the native Irish church in the course of the 12th century; in Anglo-Norman areas such as Skreen in Co. Meath the parochial system had already been adopted by the early 13th century (Otway-Ruthven 1964, 111–22). After the Reformation the medieval parish boundaries were continued by the established Church of Ireland, and used by the government as the bounds of civil parishes, a secular land unit forming the major division of a barony. (The boundaries of modern Roman Catholic parishes have often been drawn afresh, to suit the population of worshippers).

As well as the area inhabited by local worshippers, lands belonging to a medieval church often became part of its parish. These were usually close by, but it is quite common, even in the early 19th century when some rationalization had occurred, for parishes to include detached lands at some distance from the main body (Power 1947, 222–3). Kilclief in the barony of Lecale, Co. Down, for example, has five separate detached townlands, while Ballytrustan in the Upper Ards and Trory in Co. Fermanagh are divided into several parts. While an average parish might contain 30 townlands, parishes vary in the number of townlands they contained; for example, Ballykinler in Co. Down contained only 3 townlands, while Aghalurcher contained 237 townlands (including several islands) in Co. Fermanagh plus 17 townlands in Co. Tyrone. Although most of its townlands are fairly small, Aghalurcher is still much larger than Ballykinler. There were usually several parishes within a barony (on average 5 or 6, but, for example, only 2 in the barony of Dufferin, Co. Down, and 18 in the barony of Loughinsholin, Co. Derry). Occasional parishes constituted an entire barony, as did Kilkeel, for example, which is coterminous with the barony of Mourne. However parish units also frequently extended across rivers, which were often used as obvious natural boundaries for counties and baronies: Newry across the Newry River, Clonfeacle over the Blackwater, Artrea over the Ballinderry River, Blaris over the Lagan. This means that civil parishes may be in more than one barony, and sometimes in more than one county.

Baronies

The process of bringing Irish tribal kingdoms into the feudal system as "baronies" under chieftains owing allegiance to the English crown began during the medieval period, although the system was not extended throughout Ulster until the early 17th century. Many of the baronies established in the later administrative system have population names: Oneilland, Irish *Uí Nialláin* "descendants of Niallán" (Arm.); Keenaght, Irish *Cianachta* "descendants of Cian" (Der.); Clankelly, Irish *Clann Cheallaigh* "Ceallach's children" (Fer.). Others have the names of historically important castles or towns: Dungannon (O'Neills, Tyr.), Dunluce (MacDonnells, Antr.), Castlereagh (Clandeboy O'Neills, Down). The barony of Loughinsholin (Der.) is named after an island fortification or crannog, *Loch Inse Uí Fhloinn* "the lake of O'Flynn's island", although by the 17th century the island was inhabited by the O'Hagans, and the O'Flynn area of influence had moved east of the Bann.

The barony system was revised and co-ordinated at the same time as the counties, so that later baronies always fit inside the county bounds. Both counties and baronies appear on maps from 1590 on. These later baronies may contain more than one older district, and other district or population names used in the 16th and 17th centuries, such as *Clancan* and *Clanbrasil* in Armagh, *Slutkellies* in Down, and *Munterbirn* and *Munterevlin* in Tyrone, gradually fell out of use. Baronies were not of uniform size, though in many cases large baronies have been subdivided to make the size more regular. The barony of Dungannon in Co. Tyrone has three sections (Lower, Middle and Upper) while Iveagh in Co. Down has been divided into four (Lower, Lower Half; Lower, Upper Half; Upper, Lower Half; Upper,

Upper Half). The number of baronies in a county in Ulster varies between five in Co. Monaghan and fifteen in Co. Antrim. Armagh, Fermanagh and Tyrone have eight.

Counties

Over the centuries following the Anglo-Norman invasion the English government created a new administrative system in Ireland, adapting the native divisions of provinces, tribal districts (as baronies), parishes and townlands, and dividing each province of Ireland into counties. The counties were equivalent to the shire in England, where a sheriff exercized jurisdiction on behalf of the King. To begin with the county system applied to only those areas where English rule was strong, but was eventually extended, through the reigns of Elizabeth and James I, to cover the whole of the country. Although a commission to shire Ulster was set up in 1585 (*Fiants Eliz.* §4763), the situation in 1604 was expressed, rather hopefully, in a document in the state papers:

> "each province, except Ulster and other uncivil parts of the realm, is subdued into counties, and each county into baronies and hundreds, and every barony into parishes, consisting of manors, towns and villages after the manner of England."
> (*CSP Ire.* 1603–6, 231).

Most of the counties created in the north were given the names of important towns: Antrim, Armagh, Coleraine (later Londonderry), Down, Donegal, Monaghan and Cavan. Fermanagh and Tyrone, however, have population names. *Fir Manach* "the men of the *Manaig*" (probably the *Menapii* of Ptolemy's *Geography*) had been important in the area before the Maguires. *Tír Eoghain* "Eoghan's land" derives its name from the *Cenél nEógain* branch of the *Uí Néill*, who had expanded southwards from *Inis Eógain* (Inishowen) during the centuries and whose dominant position continued right up until the Plantation. Counties were generally formed out of an amalgam of smaller territorial units, some of which were preserved as baronies within each county.[2] The bounds of these older units were often of long standing, and usually followed obvious physical features, like the lower Bann, the Blackwater, and the Newry River.

Down and Antrim, as part of the feudal Earldom of Ulster (see below) had been treated as counties since the 13th or 14th century (Falkiner 1903, 189; *Inq. Earldom Ulster* ii 141, iii 60). However other districts within the earldom could also be called counties, and up to the mid-16th-century the whole area was sometimes called the "county of Ulster" (*Cal. Carew MSS* 1515–74, 223–4). The settling of Down and Antrim with their modern bounds began in 1570–1 (*Fiants Eliz.* §1530, §1736). Coleraine had also been the centre of an Anglo-Norman county (*Inq. Earldom Ulster* iv 127). Jobson's map of 1590 shows *Antrym, Armagh, Colrane, Downe, Manahan, Farmanaugh, Terconnel,* and *Upper and Nether Terone* as the names of counties. However, Ulster west of the Bann was still referred to as "four seigniories" (Armagh? plus *Terreconnell, Tyren, Formannoche*) in 1603 (*Cal. Carew MSS* 1601–3, 446–454), although Tyrone had been divided into baronies from 1591 (*Colton Vis.* 125–130). Armagh was settled into baronies in 1605 (*CSP Ire.* 1603–6, 318). The "nine counties of Ulster" were first listed in 1608: *Dunegal or Tirconnel, Tirone, Colraine, Antrim, Downe, Ardmagh, Cavan, Monoghan,* and *Fermanagh* (*CSP Ire.* 1606-8, 401), and these counties are shown on Hole's adaptation of Mercator's map of Ireland for Camden's atlas *Britannia* (1610). The county of Coleraine was renamed as a result of the plantation grant to the London companies. Under the terms of the formal grant of the area in 1613, the barony of Loughinsholin, which had hitherto been part of Tyrone, was amalgamated with the old county of Coleraine, and Londonderry was made the new county name (Moody 1939, 122–3).

Provinces

Gaelic Ireland, in prehistory and in early historic times, was made up of many small native kingdoms (called *tuatha*), but a sense of the underlying unity of the island is evident from the name of the earliest division in Ireland, that represented by the four modern provinces of Connaught, Leinster, Munster and Ulster. In Irish each is called *cúige* (older *cóiced*) "a fifth", followed by a district or population name. *Cúige Chonnacht* means "the fifth of the Connaughtmen" *Cúige Laighean* "the fifth of the Leinstermen", *Cúige Mumhan* "the fifth of Munster", *Cúige Uladh* "the fifth of the Ulstermen". The connection between population and place-names is evident at this very early stage. The ancient fifth "fifth" making up the whole was that of Meath, in Irish *Midhe* "middle". The division into these five provinces was taken over when Henry II of England invaded Ireland: Leinster, (North and South) Munster, Connaught, Ulster and Meath *quasi in medio regni positum* (as if placed in the middle of the kingdom), but the number was reduced by the 17th century to the modern four (*CSP Ire.* 1603-6 §402, 231), by incorporating Meath in Leinster.

The Province of Ulster

As mentioned above, the province of Ulster took its name from the tribal name *Ulaid* "Ulstermen" (Flanagan 1978d). The earliest record of the tribal name is the form quoted by the 2nd-century Greek geographer Ptolemy, as *Uoluntii* (O'Rahilly 1946, 7). The precise origin of the English form of the name is obscure, though it has been suggested that it derives from something like *Ulaðstir*, an unusual combination of the original Irish name plus the Norse possessive suffix *-s* and the Irish word *tír* "land" (Sommerfelt 1958, 223–227). Ptolemy mentions various other tribes in the north of Ireland, but it appears that the *Ulaid* were the dominant group.

The ancient province of the Ulstermen, according to the native boundary description, stretched south to a line running between the courses of the rivers *Drobaís* (Drowse, on the border between Donegal and Leitrim) and *Bóann* (Boyne, Co. Meath). The "fifth" of the legendary king of the Ulaid, Conchobar (*Cóiced Conchobair*) thus included modern Co. Louth (Hogan 1910, 279b). It became contracted in historical times, as a result of the expansion of the *Uí Néill* "descendants of Niall", who drove the rulers of the Ulaid from the provincial capital at *Emain Macha* (Navan fort near Armagh) across the Bann into modern Antrim and Down.[3] From the 5th century the area stretching south from Derry and Tyrone to Monaghan and most of Louth belonged to a confederation of tribes called the *Airgialla*, who have been described "as a satellite state of the Uí Néill" (Byrne 1973, 73). Three groups of Uí Néill established themselves in the west, *Cenél Conaill* "Conall's kin" in south Donegal, *Cenél nÉndae* in the area around Raphoe, and *Cenél nEógain* in Inishowen (*Inis Eógain* "Eógan's island"). On the north coast, east of the river Foyle, the *Cianachta* maintained a separate identity, despite continuing pressure from *Cenél nEógain*.

East of the Bann the *Dál Fiatach* (the historic Ulaid) shared the kingship of the reduced Ulster with *Dál nAraide* and *Uí Echach Coba*, both originally *Cruthin* tribes.[4] In the 12th century the Anglo-Norman conquest of Antrim and Down resulted in the creation of a feudal lordship of the area under the English crown called the Earldom of Ulster. During the same period the kings of Cenél nEógain had extended their influence eastward, and after the extinction of the Dál Fiatach kingship in the 13th century they assumed the title of *rí Ulad* "king of the Ulaid" to forward their claim to be kings of the whole of the North. It is this greater Ulster which was the basis for the modern province, although there was some doubt at the beginning of the 17th century as to whether or not this included Co. Louth. By the time of the Plantation in 1609 Ulster had been stabilized as nine counties and Louth had been incorporated into the neighbouring province of Leinster.

ECCLESIASTICAL ADMINISTRATIVE DIVISIONS

Dioceses

Under the Roman Empire Christianity developed an administrative structure of dioceses led by bishops based in the local towns. In early Christian Ireland a bishop was provided for each *tuath*, but since the main centres of population were the monasteries established by the church, the bishop often became part of the monastic community, with less power than the abbot. The invasion of the Anglo-Normans in the 12th century encouraged the re-organization and reform of the native church along continental lines, and by the beginning of the 14th century the territories and boundaries for Irish bishops and dioceses had been settled. Most dioceses are named after important church or monastic foundations: Armagh, Clogher, Connor, Derry, Down, Dromore, Kilmore and Raphoe in the North. The ancient secular province of Ulster was included in the ecclesiastical province of Armagh, which became the chief church in Ireland. The bounds of individual dioceses within the province reflect older tribal areas, for example Derry reflects the development of *Cenél nEógain*, Dromore *Uí Echach Coba*. In the 8th century *Dál Fiatach*, who had settled in east Down, pushed northward into the land of *Dál nAraide*, and the bounds of the diocese of Down reflect their expansion as far north as the river *Ollarba* (the Larne Water). The diocesan bounds differ from those of similarly-named later counties because by the time the county boundaries were settled in the 17th century the leaders of many of the larger native territories had been overthrown. County boundaries were generally not based on large native kingdoms but were put together from an amalgam of smaller districts.

Deaneries

The medieval church divided dioceses into rural deaneries, the names of which often derive from old population names. *Blaethwyc* (modern Newtownards) in the diocese of Down, for example, derives from *Uí Blathmaic* "the descendants of Blathmac", whereas *Turtrye*, in the diocese of Connor, derives from *Uí Thuirtre* "the descendants of (Fiachra) Tort". The deaneries of Tullyhogue (Irish *Tulach Óc*) in the diocese of Armagh and *Maulyne* (Irish *Mag Line*) in Connor are named after royal sites. *Mag Line* was the seat of the *Dál nAraide* and *Tulach Óc* was probably the original seat of the Uí Thuirtre, whose area of influence had by this time moved east across the Bann, as the deanery name reveals. The deanery of Inishowen reflects the earlier homeland of the Cenél nEógain. Deanery names are often a useful source of information on important tribal groups of medieval times. Some of these same population names were used later as the names of baronies, while in other cases the earlier population group had lost its influence and the area had become known by another name.

TRIBAL AND FAMILY NAMES

Many personal or population names of various forms have been used as place- names or parts of place-names in Ireland, from provinces, counties, deaneries and baronies to townlands. As with different types of land divisions, different types of family names have come into being at various times.

The names of early Irish tribal groupings were sometimes simple plurals, for example *Ulaid*, *Cruthin*, and sometimes the personal name of an ancestor or some other element in composition with various suffixes: *Connachta*, *Dartraige*, *Latharna*. Other types prefixed *uí* "grandsons", *cenél* "kin", *clann* "children", *dál* "share of", *moccu* "descendants", *síol* "seed", *sliocht* "line" to the name of the ancestor, for example *Dál nAraide* "share of (fiacha) Araide", and *Uí Néill* "grandsons of Niall", who are supposedly descended from the 5th-century *Niall Noígiallach* "Niall of the Nine Hostages".

In early Ireland individuals were often identified by patronymics formed by using *mac* "son of" or *ó* (earlier *ua*) "grandson" plus the name of the father or grandfather, rather than giving by the name of the larger group to which the individual belonged. Thus the most straightforward interpretation of *Eoghan mac Néill* is "Eoghan son of Niall", *Eoghan ó Néill* "Eoghan grandson of Niall". Sometimes the same formation can occur with female names. However, in the course of the 10th and 11th centuries patronymics began to be used as surnames. In Modern Irish orthography surnames are distinguished from simple patronymics by using capital *M* or *Ó*: *Eoghan Ó Néill* "Eoghan O'Neill", *Eoghan Mac Néill* "Eoghan MacNeill". However, in early documents, in either Irish or English, it is often difficult to distinguish between surnames and patronymics. This is particularly true of sources such as the *Fiants* where a name such as Donagh M'Donagh may represent the patronymic Donagh, son of Donagh, or the surname Donagh MacDonagh.

As families expanded it was common for different branches to develop their own particular surnames. Some of these have survived to the present, while others, which may have been important enough in their time to be incorporated in place-names, have either died out or been assimilated by similar, more vigorous surnames. In cases such as this the place-name itself may be the only evidence for the former existence of a particular surname in the locality.

Kay Muhr

(1) See also *Geinealach Chorca Laidhe* (O'Donovan 1849, 48–56); *Críchad an Caoilli* (Power 1932, 43–47).
(2) See *Fiants Eliz.* §1736 (1570) for Co. Down; *Colton Vis.* 125–30 (1591) for Cos Derry and Tyrone.
(3) North-east Derry and Louth were also held by the Ulaid, but their influence had been reduced to Down, Antrim and north Louth by the 7th century (Flanagan 1978d, 41).
(4) The *Cruthin* were a population group widespread in the north of Ireland. The name is of the same origin as "Briton".

ABBREVIATIONS

acc. Accusative
adj. Adjective
al. Alias
angl. Anglicized
Ant. Co. Antrim
Arm. Co. Armagh
art. cit. In the article cited
BM British Museum
c. About
cf. Compare
Co(s). County (-ies)
col. Column
coll. Collective
d. Died
dat. Dative
Der. Co. Derry
Dn Co. Down
eag. Eagarthóir/Curtha in eagar ag
ed. Edited by
edn Edition
Eng. English
et pass. And elsewhere
et var. And variations (thereon)
f. Following page
fem. Feminine
Fer. Co. Fermanagh
ff. Folios/Following pages
fol. Folio
gen. Genitive
HMSO Her Majesty's Stationery Office
ibid. In the same place
IE Indo-European
iml. Imleabhar
IPA International Phonetic Alphabet
l(l). Line(s)
lit. Literally
loc. Locative
loc. cit. In the place cited
Lr. Lower
masc. Masculine
Mid. Eng. Middle English
Mid. Ir. Middle Irish
Mod. Eng. Modern English
Mod. Ir. Modern Irish
MS. Manuscript
MSS Manuscripts
n. (Foot)note
neut. Neuter
NLI National Library of Ireland, Dublin
no. Number
nom. Nominative
O.Ir. Old Irish
op. cit. In the work cited
OSI Ordnance Survey, Dublin
OSNI Ordnance Survey, Belfast
p(p). Page(s)
par. Parish
pass. Here and there
pl. Plural
PRO Public Record Office, London
PROI Public Record Office, Dublin
PRONI Public Record Office, Belfast
pt. Part
RIA Royal Irish Academy, Dublin
s. Shilling
sa. Under the year
sect. Section
ser. Series
sing. Singular
SS Saints
St Saint
sv(v). Under the word(s)
TCD Trinity College, Dublin
trans. Translated by
Tyr. Co. Tyrone
uimh. Uimhir
Up. Upper
viz. Namely
voc. Vocative
vol(s). Volume(s)

PRIMARY BIBLIOGRAPHY

A. Conn. — *Annála Connacht: the annals of Connacht (AD 1224–1544)*, ed. A. Martin Freeman (Dublin 1944).

Aeidhe ma chroidhe — "[*Aeidhe ma chroidhe, ceann Bhriain*:], poem on the Battle of Dun by Gilla-Brighde Mac Conmhidhe", ed. John O'Donovan, *Miscellany of the Celtic Society* (Dublin 1849) 146–83.

AFM — *Annála Ríoghachta Éireann: annals of the kingdom of Ireland by the Four Masters from the earliest period to the year 1616*, ed. John O'Donovan, 7 vols (Dublin 1848–51; reprint Dublin 1856 and 1990).

AGBP — *Ainmneacha Gaeilge na mbailte poist*, Oifig an tSoláthair (Baile Átha Cliath 1969).

AIF — *The Annals of Innisfallen*, ed. Seán Mac Airt (Dublin 1951).

Ainm — *Ainm: bulletin of the Ulster Place-name Society* (Belfast 1986–).

ALC — *The annals of Loch Cé: a chronicle of Irish affairs from AD 1014 to AD 1590*, ed. William Hennessy, 2 vols (London 1871; reprint Dublin 1939).

Anal. Hib. — *Analecta Hibernica* (Dublin 1930–69; Shannon 1970–).

Annates Ulst. — *De annatis Hiberniae: a calendar of the first-fruits' fees levied on papal appointments to benefices in Ireland, AD 1400–1535*, vol. i (Ulster), ed. Michael A. Costello and Ambrose Coleman (Dundalk 1909; reissue Maynooth 1912).

Antiph. Bangor — *The Antiphonary of Bangor*, 2 parts, ed. F.E. Warren (London 1893–95).

Archiv. Hib. — *Archivium Hibernicum; or, Irish historical records*, ser. 1, vols i-vii (Maynooth 1912–21); ser. 2, vol. viii– (1941–).

ASCD — *An archaeological survey of County Down*, Archaeological Survey of Northern Ireland (Belfast 1966).

ASE — "Abstracts of grants of lands and other hereditaments under the acts of settlement and explanation, AD 1666–84", compiled by John Lodge and published in the appendix to the *15th Annual report from the commissioners... respecting the public records of Ireland* (1825), 45–340.

AU — *Annála Uladh: annals of Ulster; otherwise Annála Senait, annals of Senait: a chronicle of Irish affairs, 431–1131, 1155–1541*, ed. William Hennessy and Bartholomew MacCarthy, 4 vols (Dublin 1887–1901).

AU (Mac Airt) — *The annals of Ulster* (vol. i to 1131 AD), ed. Seán Mac Airt & Gearóid Mac Niocaill (Dublin 1983).

Bartlett Map (TCD)	*The descriptione of a parte of Ulster containing the p[ar]ticuler places of the Righte Ho. the Lo. Montjoie now Lo. Deputie of Irelande his jorneies & services in the North part of that kingdome, from his entrie therinto until this present August 1601*, by Richard Barthelett (Bartlett), TCD MS 2379 (formerly 21 U 19). Reproduced in reduced form as frontspiece in *Dúiche Néill* vol. 1, no. 2 (1987).
Bartlett Maps (Esch. Co. Maps)	Three maps by Richard Bartlett published together with the *Esch. Co. Maps*: (i) *A Generalle Description of Ulster*; (ii) South-east Ulster; (iii) North-west Ulster, (PRO London MPF 35–37; copies in PRONI T1652/1–3). These maps have been dated to 1603 by G.A. Hayes-McCoy, *Ulster and Other Irish Maps, c. 1600*, p. 2, n. 13 (Dublin 1964).
Béaloid.	*Béaloideas: the journal of the Folklore of Ireland Society* (Dublin 1927–).
Bnd. Sur. (OSNB)	*Boundary Survey sketch maps c. 1830*, cited in *OSNB, passim.*
Boazio's Map (BM)	*Gennerall discription or Chart of Irelande*, AD 1599, by Baptista Boazio. Three impressions are known, one in the British Museum, one in TCD, and a third in private hands.
Boazio's Map (NG)	Reprint of *Boazio's Map (BM)* published in Ortelius' *Theatrum Orbis Terranum* from 1606 on. Copy from Neptune Gallery, Dublin, reprinted with *AFM* 1990.
Brit. Mus. MS (EA)	British Museum MS. 4793, cited in *EA* 16n.
BSD	*Book of survey & distribution, AD 1661: Armagh, Down & Antrim* (Quit Rent Office copy), PRONI T370/A.
BUPNS	*Bulletin of the Ulster Place-name Society*, ser. 1, vols i-v (Belfast 1952–7); ser. 2, vols 1–4 (1978–82).
Cáin Adomnáin	"The guarantor list of *Cáin Adomnáin*, ed. M. Ní Dhonnchadha, *Peritia* 1 (1981), 178–215.
Cal. Canc. Hib. (EA)	*Calendarium Rot. Cancellar. Hib.*, cited in *EA, passim*. Probably the same as *CPR (Tresham)*.
Cal. Carew MSS	*Calendar of the Carew manuscripts preserved in the Archiepiscopal Library at Lambeth*, ed. J.S. Brewer and W. Bullen, 6 vols (London 1867–73).
Cartae Dun.	"Cartae Dunenses XII-XIII céad", eag. Gearóid Mac Niocaill, *S. Ard Mh.* vol. 5, no. 2 (1970), 418–28.
CDI	*Calendar of documents relating to Ireland, 1171-1307*, ed. H.S. Sweetman and G.F. Handcock, 5 vols (London 1875–86).
Ceart Uí Néill	*Ceart Uí Néill*, ed. Myles Dillon, *Stud. Celt.* 1 (1966), 1–18. Trans. Éamonn Ó Doibhlin, "*Ceart Uí Néill*, a discussion and translation of the document", *S. Ard Mh.* vol. 5, no. 2 (1970), 324–58.

Céitinn — *Foras Feasa ar Éirinn: the history of Ireland by Seathrún Céitinn (Geoffrey Keating)*, ed. Rev. Patrick S. Dinneen, 4 vols, Irish Texts Society (London 1902–14).

Celtica — *Celtica*, Dublin Institute for Advanced Studies (Dublin 1946–).

Census — *A census of Ireland, circa 1659, with supplementary material from the poll money ordinances (1660–1)*, ed. Séamus Pender (Dublin 1939).

Census 1851 — *Census of Ireland, 1851. General alphabetical index to the townlands and towns, parishes and baronies of Ireland...* (Dublin 1861).

Census 1871 — *Census of Ireland, 1871. Alphabetical index to the townlands and towns of Ireland...* (Dublin 1877).

CGH — *Corpus genealogiarum Hiberniae*, vol. 1, ed. M.A. O'Brien (Dublin 1962).

Charts Nendrum — Nendrum charters, ed. William Reeves, *EA* 190–4.

Charts St. Mary's Abbey — *Chartularies of St. Mary's Abbey, Dublin: with the register of its house at Dunbrody and annals of Ireland*, 2 vols, ed. John T. Gilbert (London 1884).

Chron. Mailros (EA) — *The chronicle of Mailros*, cited in *EA* 92.

Chron. Mann — *Chronicle of the kings of Mann and the Isles* part 1, ed. George Broderick & Brian Stowell (Edinburgh 1973).

Cín Lae Ó M. — *Cín lae Ó Mealláin*, ed. Tadhg Ó Donnchadha (alias Torna), *Anal. Hib.* 3 (1931), 1–61.

Civ. Surv. — *The civil survey, AD 1654–6*, ed. Robert C. Simington, 10 vols, Irish Manuscripts Commission (Dublin 1931–61).

Close Roll Hen. III (EA) — Close Rolls of the reign of Henry III, cited in *EA, passim.*

CMR(2) — *The banquet of Dún na nGedh and the battle of Magh Rath, an ancient historical tale,* ed. John O'Donovan, Irish Archaeological Society (Dublin 1842).

Collect. Hib. — *Collectanea Hibernica: sources for Irish history* (Shannon 1958–).

Collins B'fast Lough — "Reduced facsimile of first published chart of Belfast Lough", by Captain Greenville Collins, AD 1693, reproduced in Owen 1917, 12.

Colton Vis. — *Acts of Archbishop Colton in his metropolitical visitation of the diocese of Derry, AD 1397*, ed. William Reeves (Dublin 1850).

Compotus Dun. — *Compotus Dunensis*, being an account of the receipts from the see lands of Down between March 4 and July 1, 1305, rendered into the exchequer by the escheator, Walterus de la Hay, ed. William Reeves, *EA* 167–8.

Concise Scots Dict. — *The concise Scots dictionary*, ed. Mairi Robinson (Aberdeen 1985).

Confirm. Lands Nendrum (EA) Confirmation by John of Salernum, papal legate, of lands granted to the monastery of Nendrum by John de Courcy and others in 1203. Cited in *EA* 193–4.

CPR (de hÓir) *Calendar of Patent and Close Rolls,* cited in de hÓir 1965.

CPR Chas. I *Calendar of patent and close rolls of chancery in Ireland, Charles I, years 1–8,* ed. James Morrin (Dublin 1864).

CPR Ed. III *Calendar of patent rolls of chancery, Edward III, 1327–77,* 16 vols (London 1891–1916).

CPR Ed. VI *Calendar of the patent rolls preserved in the Public Record Office: Edward VI, 1547–53,* 6 vols (London 1924–29).

CPR Hen. IV (EA) *Calendar of patent rolls, Henry IV,* cited in *EA, passim.*

CPR Jas. I *Irish patent rolls of James I: facsimile of the Irish record commissioners' calendar prepared prior to 1830,* with a foreword by M.C. Griffith (Dublin 1966).

CPR (Tresham) *Rotulorum patentium et clausorum cancellariae Hiberniae calendarium,* 2 vols (vol. 2 has no title), ed. Edward Tresham (Dublin 1828–[1830]).

CSH *Corpus genealogiarum sanctorum Hiberniae,* ed. Pádraig Ó Riain (Dublin 1985).

CSP Ire. *Calendar of the state papers relating to Ireland, 1509–1670,* ed. H.C. Hamilton, E.G. Atkinson, R.P. Mahaffy, C.P. Russell and J.P. Prendergast, 24 vols (London 1860–1912).

Cymmrodor *Y Cymmrodor: the magazine of the Honourable Society of Cymmrodorion* 44 vols (London 1877–1935).

Dartmouth Map A maritime chart/map of Ireland dating to 1590 preserved in the National Maritime Museum, Greenwich, Dartmouth Collection nos 5–7.

De Burgo's Hib. Dom. De Burgo's *Hibernia Dominicana.* Cited in *Sav. Ulst., passim.*

Deeds and Wills (DF) Transcripts by Deirdre Flanagan, presently in the Department of Celtic, Queen's University of Belfast, of unidentified deeds and wills in PROI.

Descendants Ir "The history of the descendants of Ir", 2 parts, ed. Margaret Dobbs, *ZCP* xiii (1921), 308–59; xiv (1923), 44–144.

Descr. Ards "William Montgomery and the description of the Ards, 1683", ed. D.B. Quinn, *Ir. Booklore* vol. 2 no. 1 (1972), 29–43.

DF Suggested Irish forms by Deirdre Flanagan extracted from unpublished papers presently in the Department of Celtic, Queen's University Belfast.

DIL	*Dictionary of the Irish language: compact edition* (Dublin 1983).
Dinneen	*Foclóir Gaedhilge agus Béarla: an Irish-English dictionary*, Rev. Patrick S. Dinneen (Dublin 1904; reprint with additions 1927 and 1934).
Dinnsean.	*Dinnseanchas*, 6 vols (Baile Átha Cliath 1964–75).
Dongl. Ann.	*Donegal Annual: journal of the County Donegal Historical Society* (1947–).
Donnellan MSS	Manuscripts in the possession Rev. L. Donnellan, PP Loughgall, Co. Armagh. Cited in *Éigse* i (1939), 38–9.
Dower Charter	"Dower charter of John de Courcy's wife", ed. Jocelyn Otway-Ruthven, *UJA* ser. 3 vol. xii (1949), 77–81.
Downshire Direct.	"Directory to the seats of Downshire, with their respective post towns alphabetically arranged", A. Atkinson, *Ireland exhibited to England, in a political and moral survey of her population*, vol. i, 315–30 (London 1823).
Dúiche Néill	*Dúiche Néill: journal of the O'Neill Country Historical Society* (Benburb 1986–).
Dwelly	*The illustrated Gaelic-English dictionary*, Edward Dwelly (Glasgow 1901–11; reprint 1920 etc.).
EA	*Ecclesiastical antiquities of Down, Connor and Dromore, consisting of a taxation of those dioceses compiled in the year 1306*, ed. William Reeves (Dublin 1847).
Early Chart B'fast Lough	"Reduced facsimile of first known chart of Belfast Lough, about 1570", reproduced in Owen 1917.
Eccles. Tax. (CDI)	"Ecclesiastical taxation of Ireland", ed. H.S. Sweetman & G.F. Handcock, *Calendar of documents relating to Ireland..., 1302-07* (London 1886), 202–323.
Eccles. Tax.	"Ecclesiastical taxation of the dioceses of Down, Connor, and Dromore", ed. William Reeves, *EA* 2–119.
Educ. Rept. (OSNB)	Education report, cited in *OSNB, passim.*
Éigse	*Éigse: a journal of Irish studies* (Dublin 1939–).
Éire Thuaidh	*Éire Thuaidh/Ireland North: a cultural map and gazetteer of Irish place-names*, Ordnance Survey of Northern Ireland (Belfast 1988).
Enc. Brit.	*The new Encyclopaedia Britannica*, 15th edn (Chicago...).
Eng. Hist. Rev.	*The English Historical Review* (London 1886–).
Esch. Co. Map	*Barony maps of the escheated counties in Ireland, AD 1609*, 28 maps, PRO London. Published as *The Irish Historical Atlas*, Sir Henry James, Ordnance Survey (Southampton 1861).

Ét. Celt.	*Études Celtiques* (Paris 1936–).
Exch. Accounts Ulst.	"Ancient exchequer accounts of Ulster", *UJA* ser. 1, vol. iii (1855), 155–62.
Ex. Inq. 1 Jac. I	*Inquisition of the court of exchequer in Ireland taken at Ballymaghan, November 5, 1st year of the reign of James I, AD 1603.* All the original exchequer inquisitions have been lost, but there is a manuscript calendar in PROI and transcripts of some of the Ulster inquisitions in PRONI.
Féil. Torna	*Féilscríbhinn Torna.i. tráchtaisí léanta in onóir don Ollamh Tadhg Ua Donnchadha...*, eag. Séamus Pender (Corcaigh 1947).
Fél. Óeng.	*Félire Óengusso Céli Dé: the martyrology of Oengus the culdee*, ed. Whitley Stokes (London 1905; reprint 1984).
Fiants Eliz.	"Calendar and index to the fiants of the reign of Elizabeth I", appendix to the *11–13th, 15–18th and 21–22nd Reports of the Deputy Keeper of public records in Ireland* (Dublin 1879–81, 1883–86, 1889–90).
Forfeit. Estates	"Abstracts of the conveyances from the trustees of the forfeited estates and interests in Ireland in 1688", appendix to the *15th Annual report from the commissioners... respecting the public records of Ireland* (1825), 348–99.
GÉ	*Gasaitéar na hÉireann/Gazetteer of Ireland: ainmneacha ionad daonra agus gnéithe aiceanta*, Brainse Logainmneacha na Suirbhéireachta Ordanáis (Baile Átha Cliath 1989).
GJ	*Gaelic Journal: Irisleabhar na Gaedhilge*, 19 vols (Dublin 1882–1909).
Goghe's Map	*Hibernia: Insula non procul ab Anglia vulgare Hirlandia vocata, AD 1567*, by John Goghe, PRO London MPF 68. Reproduced in *SP Hen. VIII* vol. ii, pt. 3.
GOI	*A grammar of Old Irish*, Rudolf Thurneysen, trans. D.A. Binchy and Osborn Bergin (Dublin 1946).
Graces's Annals (EA)	*Graces's annals*, cited in *EA, passim.*
Grand Jury Pres. (OSNB)	*Grand jury presentment*, cited in *OSNB, passim.*
Grant Jas. I (OSNB)	Grant from the reign of James I, cited in *OSNB, passim.*
Grant Ralph Bp. Down	Grant by John de Courcy to Ralph, Bishop of Down, AD 1202–3, ed. William Reeves, *EA* 165–7.
Great Rolls Pipe	"Accounts on the great rolls of the pipe of the Irish exchequer, 13 Henry III to 22 Edward III", ed. M.J. McEnery, *35th–54th Reports of the Deputy Keeper of public records in Ireland* (Dublin 1903–27).
Hákonar Saga Gamla	*Hákonar Saga Gama*, ed. Guðni Jónsson, *Konunga sö gur* iii (Reykjavik 1957).

Hamilton MSS — *The Hamilton manuscripts: containing some account of the settlement of the territories of the Upper Clandeboye, Great Ardes and Dufferin, in the County of Down, by Sir James Hamilton, Knight*, ed. T.K. Lowry (Belfast 1867).

Ham. Copy Inq. 1623 — "Copy inquisition, dated 13th October, 1623", ed. T.K. Lowry, *Hamilton MSS*, appendix iv, xxix-lvi.

Ham. Copy Inq. 1644 — "Copy inquisition, dated 14th January, 1664", ed. T.K. Lowry, *Hamilton MSS*, appendix v, lvi-lx.

Ham. Copy Inq. 1662 — "Copy inquisition, dated 9th April, 1662", ed. T.K. Lowry, *Hamilton MSS*, appendix vi, lxi-lxiii.

Ham. Copy Rental — "[Copy of] a rent roll for the year 1681", ed. T.K. Lowry, *Hamilton MSS* 108–11.

Ham. Patent 1620 — "Letters patent to James Hamilton, dated 14th March (19th James I), 1620", ed. T.K. Lowry, *Hamilton MSS*, appendix iii, xix-xxviii.

Ham. Patent 1630 — "Letters patent of 20th April, 1630, from Charles I to James Viscount Claneboy", ed. T.K. Lowry, *Hamilton MSS*, appendix ii, x-xix.

Harris Hist. — *The antient and present state of the county of Down*, Walter Harris (Dublin 1744).

Hermathena — *Hermathena: a Dublin University review* (Dublin 1873–).

Hib. Del. — *Hiberniae Delineatio*: an atlas of Ireland by Sir William Petty comprised of one map of Ireland, 4 maps of provinces and 32 county maps. It was engraved c. 1671–72 and first published in London c. 1685 (Goblet 1932, viii). A facsimile reprint was published in Newcastle-Upon-Tyne in 1968 and a further reprint, with critical introduction by J.H. Andrews, in Shannon, 1970.

Hib. Reg. — *Hibernia Regnum:* a set of 214 barony maps of Ireland dating to the period AD 1655–59. These maps were drawn at the same time as the official parish maps which illustrated the Down Survey of Sir William Petty. The original parish maps have been lost but the *Hibernia Regnum* maps are preserved in the Bibliothèque Nationale, Paris (Goblet 1932, v-x). Photographic facsimiles of these maps were published by the Ordnance Survey, Southampton in 1908.

High Const. Applot. (OSNB) — *High Constable's Applotment*, cited in *OSNB, passim.*

Hist. J. — *The Historical Journal* (Cambridge 1958–).

Hondius Map — *Hyberniae Novissima Descriptio, AD 1591*, drawn by Jodocus Hondius and engraved by Pieter van den Keere, copy published by Linen Hall Library, Belfast, 1983.

Inq. Down (Reeves1) — *An inquisition of Down, AD 1657*, transcribed by William Reeves, PRONI DIO/1/24/8/2.

Inq. Earldom Ulster	"The earldom of Ulster", Goddard H. Orpen, *JRSAI* xliii (1913), 30–46, 133–43; xliv (1914), 51–66; xlv (1915), 123–42.
Inq. Earl Ulster (EA)	"The Inquisition of the Earl of Ulster, AD 1333", ed. William Reeves, *EA* 360–1, n. g.
Inq. Ed. III (EA)	Inquisition(s) of King Edward III, cited by William Reeves, *EA, passim.*
Inq. Ult.	*Inquisitionum in officio rotulorum cancellariae Hiberniae asservatarum repertorium*, vol. ii (Ulster), ed. James Hardiman (Dublin 1829).
Ir. Booklore	*Irish Booklore* (Belfast 1971–80).
Ir. Geog.	*Irish Geography: bulletin of the Geographical Society of Ireland* (Dublin 1944–).
Jas. I to Down Cath.	Grant of James I to the Cathedral of Down, AD 1609, ed. William Reeves, *EA* 177–9.
J Cork HAS	*Journal of the Cork Historical and Archaeological Society* ser. 1, vol. i-iii (Cork 1892–4); ser. 2, vol. i– (Cork 1895–).
JDCHS	*Journal of the Down and Connor Historical Society*, 10 vols (Belfast 1928–39).
J Lisburn HS	*Journal of the Lisburn Historical Society* (Lisburn 1978–)
J Louth AS	*Journal of the County Louth Archaeological Society* (Dundalk 1904–).
Jobson's Ulster (TCD)	A set of three maps of Ulster by Francis Jobson, the first of which dates to AD 1590, TCD MS 1209, 15–17.
J O'D (OSNB)	Irish and anglicized forms of names attributed to John O'Donovan in the *OSNB*.
John Mc Greevy, Saul (OSNB)	Irish forms supplied by John McGreevy of the parish of Saul, *OSNB, passim.*
Joyce	*The origin and history of Irish names of places*, P.W. Joyce, 3 vols (Dublin 1869–1913).
JRSAI	*Journal of the Royal Society of Antiquaries of Ireland* (Dublin 1849–). Also called *Transactions of the Kilkenny Archaeological Society* (vols i-ii, 1849–53); *Proceedings and Transactions of the Kilkenny and South-east Ireland Archaeological Society* (vol. iii, 1854–55); *Journal of the Kilkenny and South-east Ireland Archaeological Society* (new ser., vols i–vi [consecutive ser. vols iv-ix] 1856–67); *Journal of the Historical and Archaeological Association of Ireland* 3rd ser. vol. i [consecutive ser. vol. x], 1868–89); *Journal of the Royal Historical and Archaeological Association of Ireland* (4th ser. vols i-ix [consecutive ser. vols xi-xix] 1870–89); *Journal of*

Proceedings of the Royal Society of Antiquaries of Ireland (5th ser. vol. i [consecutive ser. vol. xxi] 1890–91); 5th ser. vols ii-xx [consecutive ser. vols xxii-xl] (1892–1910); 6th ser. vols i-xx [consecutive ser. vols xli-lx] (1911–30); 7th ser. vols i-xiv [consecutive ser. vols lxi-lxxiv] (1931–44); thereafter numbered only as consecutive series vol. lxxv– (1945–).

J Up. Ards HS — *Journal of the Upper Ards Historical Society* (Portaferry 1977–).

Knox Hist. — *A history of the county of Down from the most remote period to the present day*, Alexander Knox (Dublin 1875; reprint Ballynahinch 1982).

Lamb Maps — *A Geographical Description of ye Kingdom of Ireland Collected from ye actual Survey made by Sir William Petty...Containing one General Mapp of ye whole Kingdom, with four Provincial Mapps, & 32 County Mapps...Engraven & Published for ye benefit of ye Publique* by Francis Lamb (London [c. 1690]).

LASID — *Linguistic atlas and survey of Irish dialects*, Heinrich Wagner and Colm Ó Baoill, 4 vols (Dublin 1958–69).

LCABuidhe — *Leabhar Cloinne Aodha Buidhe*, ed. Tadhg Ó Donnchadha alias Torna (Dublin 1931).

Leabharlann — *An Leabharlann*: journal of *Cumann na Leabharlann* (later, the Library Association of Ireland), vols 1–29 (Dublin 1906–71); new ser., vols 1–11 (1972–82); 2nd new ser., vol. 1– (1984–).

Lebor na Cert — *Lebor na Cert: the Book of Rights*, ed. Myles Dillon, Irish Texts Society xlvi (Dublin 1962).

LÉIA — *Lexique étymologique de l'irlandais ancien*, ed. J. Vendryes, *et al.* (Paris 1960–).

Lewis' Top. Dict. — *A topographical dictionary of Ireland, comprising the several counties, cities, boroughs, corporate, market and post towns, parishes and villages with statistical descriptions*, ed. Samuel Lewis, 2 vols and atlas (London 1837; 2nd edn 1842).

LGD Map — *Local government district series showing townlands and wards within the various districts and showing the layout of the OS 1:10,000 sheets*, Ordnance Survey of Northern Ireland (Belfast 1974).

Life of St. Comgall 1 — *The first Life of St Comgall published by the Bollandists*, cited in *O'Laverty* ii, 36.

Life of St. Comgall 2 — *The second Life of St Comgall published by the Bollandists*, cited in *O'Laverty* ii, 36.

LL	*The Book of Leinster, formerly Lebar na Núachongbála*, ed. R.I. Best, O. Bergin, M.A. O'Brien & A. O'Sullivan, 6 vols (Dublin 1954–83).
L. Log. Lú	*Liostaí logainmneacha: Contae Lú/County Louth*, arna ullmhú ag Brainse Logainmneacha na Suirbhéireachta Ordanáis (Baile Átha Cliath 1991).
L. Log. Luimnigh	*Liostaí logainmneacha: Contae Luimnigh/County Limerick*, arna ullmhú ag Brainse Logainmneacha na Suirbhéireachta Ordanáis (Baile Átha Cliath 1991).
L. Log. P. Láirge	*Liostaí logainmneacha: Contae Phort Láirge/County Waterford*, arna ullmhú ag Brainse Logainmneacha na Suirbhéireachta Ordanáis (Baile Átha Cliath 1991).
Local pronunciation	Local pronunciation recorded by the editors.
Lochlann	*Lochlann: a review of Celtic studies* (Oslo 1958–).
Longman Dict.	*Longman Dictionary of the English language* (Harlow 1984, 2nd edn 1991).
L/P Hen. VIII	*Letters and papers, foreign and domestic, of the reign of Henry VIII, preserved in the Public Record Office, British Museum, and elsewhere in England*, ed. J.S. Brewer, R.H. Brodie and J. Gairdner, 21 vols (London 1862–1910). Addenda published in 2 parts (London 1929–32). Vol. i revised and enlarged by R.H. Brodie (London 1920).
LU	*Lebor na hUidre: Book of the Dun Cow*, ed. R.I. Best and Osborn Bergin (Dublin 1929).
MacCana's Itinerary	"Irish itinerary of Father Edmund MacCana", trans. William Reeves, *UJA* ser. 1, vol. 2 (1854), 44–59. Reeves' dating of the document appears to be inaccurate; we have dated it on internal evidence to c. 1700.
Mac Cumhaigh (b)	*Art Mac Cumhaigh: dánta*, eag. Tomás Ó Fiaich (Baile Átha Cliath 1973).
Mac Domhnaill	*Aodh Mac Domhnaill: dánta*, eag. Colm Beckett (Dún Dealgan 1987).
MacDonnells Antrim	*An historical account of the MacDonnells of Antrim*, Rev. George Hill (Belfast 1873).
Map NMM Dartmouth	A map of the north of Ireland dating to 1590 from the National Maritime, Greenwich, Dartmouth Collection, no. 5.
Map, Petty's Sur. (OSNB)	The Down Survey maps of William Petty, cited in *OSNB*, *passim*.
Mart. Don.	*The martyrology of Donegal: a calendar of the saints of Ireland*, trans. John O'Donovan, ed. James H. Todd and William Reeves (Dublin 1864).

Mart. Gorm. — *Félire Húi Gormáin: the martyrology of Gorman*, ed. Whitley Stokes (London 1895).

Mart. Tal. — *The martyrology of Tallaght*, ed. R.I. Best and H.J. Lawlor (London 1931).

Mediev. Prov. Arm. — *The medieval province of Armagh 1470–1545*, Rev. Aubrey Gwynn (Dundalk 1946).

Mercator's/Hole's Ire. — A map of Ireland, AD 1610, drawn by Gerard Mercator and engraved by William Hole, and published in William Camden's atlas *Britannia, sive florentissimorum regnorum Angliae, Scotiae, Hiberniae, et insularum adiacentium....*

Mercator's Ire. — *Irlandiae Regnum*, by Gerard Mercator, first published in his atlas entitled *Atlas sive Cosmographicae Meditationes de Fabrica Mundi et Fabricati Figura*, AD 1595.

Mercator's Ulst. — *Ultoniae Orientalis Pars* by Gerard Mercator, first published in his *Atlas sive Cosmographicae Meditationis de Fabrica Mundi et Fabricati Figura*, AD 1595.

Mesca Ulad — *Mesca Ulad*, ed. J. Carmichael Watson, Medieval and Modern Irish Series xiii (Dublin 1961).

Met. Dinds. — *The metrical Dindshenchas*, ed. Edward J. Gwynn, 5 vols (Dublin 1903–35).

Mon. Ang. — *Monasticon Anglicanum: a history of the abbies and other monasteries, hospitals and frieries...in England and Wales*, William Dugdale (London 1661). New edn John Caley, Sir Henry Ellis and Bulkeley Bandinel, 6 vols (London 1846).

Mon. Hib. — *Monasticon Hibernicum: or a history of the abbeys, priories and other religious houses in Ireland*, Mervyn Archdall, 3 vols (Dublin 1786). New edn Patrick F. Moran (Dublin 1873–6).

Montgomery MSS — *The Montgomery manuscripts (1603–1706) compiled from family papers by William Montgomery...*, ed. Rev. George Hill (Belfast 1869).

Mr Allen (OSNB) — Mr Allen, a local informant cited in *OSNB, passim.*

Neilson's Intro. — *An introduction to the Irish language*, William Neilson, 3 parts in 1 vol. (Dublin 1808; reprint Belfast 1990).

NISMR — *Northern Ireland sites and monuments record:* stage I published by the Department of the Environment (NI) and the Archaeological Survey (Belfast 1979).

Norden's Map — "The plott of Irelande with the confines", formerly included in *A discription of Ireland*, c. 1610, by John Norden. This map had been preserved in the State Paper Office but is now in PRO London MPF 67. It is reproduced in *SP Hen. VIII* vol. ii, pt. 3.

Norsk. Tids.	*Norsk tidsskrift for sprogvidenskap*, under medvirkning av Olaf Broch..., utgitt av Carl J.S. Marstrander (Oslo 1928–).
Nowel's Ire. (1)	A map of Ireland, c. 1570, attributed to Laurence Nowel, dean of Lichfield (d. 1576). British Museum Cotton MS, Domitian A18, ff. 101–103. Reproduced by the Ordnance Survey, Southampton.
Nowel's Ire. (2)	A map of Ireland c. 1570 attributed to Laurence Nowel, dean of Lichfield (d. 1576). British Museum Cotton MS, Domitian A18, f. 97. Reproduced by the Ordnance Survey, Southampton.
Mr Nugent (OSNB)	Mr A. Nugent of Portaferry, a local informant cited in *OSNB, passim.*
Ó Dónaill	*Foclóir Gaeilge-Béarla*, eag. Niall Ó Dónaill (Baile Átha Cliath 1977).
OED	*Oxford English dictionary*, ed. J.A. Simpson, E.S.C. Weiner (2nd edn Oxford 1989).
O'Laverty	*An historical account of the diocese of Down and Connor ancient and modern*, Rev. James O'Laverty, 5 vols. (Dublin 1878–95).
O'Neill Fun. Oration	"An Irish funeral oration over Owen O'Neill, of the House of Clanaboy", ed. Douglas Hyde, *UJA* ser. 2, vol. iii (1897), 258–71; vol. iv (1898), 50–5.
Onoma	*Onoma: bibliographical and information bulletin*, International Centre of Onomastics (Louvain 1950–).
Onom. Goed.	*Onomasticon Goedelicum locorum et tribuum Hiberniae et Scotiae*, Edmund Hogan (Dublin 1910).
Ortelius Map	*Eryn. Hiberniae, Britannicae Insulae, Nova Descriptio. Irlandt* by Abraham Ortelius. Published in the second edition of his *Theatrum Orbis Terrarum* (Antwerp 1573).
OS 1:10,000	*The Ordnance Survey 1:10,000 series maps*, Ordnance Survey of Northern Ireland (Belfast 1968–).
OS 1:50,000	*The Ordnance Survey 1:50,000 series maps*, also known as *The Discoverer Series*, Ordnance Survey of Northern Ireland (Belfast 1978–88).
OS 6-inch	*The Ordnance Survey six-inch series maps*, first published in the 1830s and 1840s with numerous subsequent editions. It has now been replaced by the OS 1:10,000.
OSL	"Letters [written by John O'Donovan] containing information relative to the [history and] antiquities of the County of Down collected during the progress of the Ordnance Survey in 1834", published as a supplement to *An Leabharlann* iii (Dublin 1909).

OSM	*Ordnance Survey memoirs of Ireland*, ed. Angélique Day and Patrick McWilliams (Belfast 1990–).
OSNB	Name-books compiled during the progress of the Ordnance Survey in 1834–5 and preserved in the Ordnance Survey, Phoenix Park, Dublin.
OSNB Inf.	Informants for the Irish forms of place-names in the *OSNB*.
PBNHPS	*Proceedings and reports of the Belfast Natural History and Philosophical Society*, 74 vols (Belfast 1873–1955).
PCR Eliz. I (Sav. Ards)	Patent and Close Rolls of the reign of Elizabeth I. Cited in *Sav. Ards*.
Peritia	*Peritia: journal of the medieval academy of Ireland* (Cork 1982–).
Pipe Roll John	"The Irish pipe roll of 14 John, 1211–2", ed. Oliver Davies and David B. Quinn, supplement to *UJA* ser. 3, vol. iv (1941).
Pontif. Hib.	*Pontificia Hibernica: medieval papal chancery documents concerning Ireland, 640–1261*, ed. Maurice P. Sheehy, 2 vols (Dublin 1962–5).
Post Chaise Comp. (OSNB)	*Post Chaise Companion*, cited in *OSNB, passim*.
Post-Sheanchas	*Post-Sheanchas i n-a bhfuil cúigí, dúithchí, conntaethe, & bailte puist na hÉireann*, Seosamh Laoide (Baile Átha Cliath 1905).
PRIA	*Proceedings of the Royal Irish Academy* (Dublin 1836–). Published in three sections since 1902 (section C: archaeology, linguistics and literature).
Raven Map Clandeboye	*A Book of Survey of Lands belonging to Ye Right Lord Vict. Claneboy* by Thomas Raven, AD 1625–6, PRONI T870/1
Reeves Ad.	*The life of St. Columba founder of Hy written by Adamnnan*, ed. William Reeves (Dublin 1857).
Reg. Cromer	"Archbishop Cromer's register", ed. L.P. Murray, *J Louth AS* vii (1929–32), 516–24; viii (1933–6), 38–49, 169–88, 257–74, 322–51; ix (1937–40), 36–41, 124–30; x (1941–44), 116–27, completed by Aubrey Gwynn, 165–79.
Reg. Deeds abstracts	*Registry of Deeds, Dublin. Abstracts of wills, 1708–1832*, ed. P. Beryl Eustace and Eilish Ellis, 3 vols (Dublin 1954–84).
Reg. Free. (OSNB)	*Register of Freeholders*, cited in *OSNB, passim*.
Reg. Mey	*Registrum Johannis Mey: the register of John Mey, Archbishop of Armagh 1443–56*, ed. W.G.H. Quigley and E.F.D. Roberts (Belfast 1972).

Reg. Octavian (EA)	*Register of Octavian de Palatio, Primate 1478-1513*, cited in *EA, passim.*
Reg. Prene (EA)	*Register of John Prene, Primate 1439–43*, cited in *EA, passim.*
Reg. Swayne	*The register of John Swayne, Archbishop of Armagh and Primate of Ireland 1418–39*, ed. D.A. Chart (Belfast 1935).
Reg. Sweteman	"A calendar of the Register of Archbishop Sweetman", ed. Rev. H.J. Lawlor, *PRIA* vol. xxix, sect. C (1911), 213–310.
Regal Visit. (Reeves)	*Regal visitation of Down, Connor & Dromore, AD 1633–34*, transcribed by William Reeves, and collated and corrected from originals in the Prerogative Office [now the Record Office] Dublin, PRONI DIO/1/24/2/4.
Reid's Presb. Hist.	Reid's *History of the presbyterian church in Ireland.* Cited in *Hamilton MSS, passim.*
Rental Portaferry, 1641	"Rental regarding the number of tenants in the town of Portaferry, AD 1641", PRONI D552/B/3/2/84–5. For a typescript of these lands see MS catalogue p. 5.
Rept. DKPRI	*Report of the Deputy Keeper of the Public Records of Ireland.*
Rev. Celt.	*Révue Celtique*, 51 vols (Paris 1870–1934).
Rot. Ant. Ecc. Dun.	*Ex rotulis antiquis Ecclesiae Dunensis penes hodiernum Episcopum Dunensem Ia. [recte Hen.] Leslaeum*, cited William Reeves, *EA* 169.
San. Corm. (YBL)	"*Sanas Cormaic*... from the copy in the Yellow Book of Lecan", ed. Kuno Meyer, *Anecdota from Irish Manuscripts* iv (Dublin 1912).
S. Ard Mh.	*Seanchas Ard Mhacha: journal of the Armagh Diocesan Historical Society* (Armagh 1954–).
Sav. Ards	*The ancient and noble family of the Ards ...*, G.F. Armstrong (London 1888).
Sav. Ulst.	*A genealogical history of the Savage family in Ulster being a revision and enlargement of certain chapters of "The Savages of the Ards"*, ed. G.F.S.A. [George Francis Savage-Armstrong] (London 1906).
Savage Lands	"Confirmation of the lands of Patrick Savage, AD 1588", PRONI D552/B/1/1/4. For typescript of these lands see MS catalogue p. 3.
Scot. Nat. Dict.	*Scottish National Dictionary*, ed. William Grant (1929–46) & David D. Murison (1946–76), 10 vols (Edinburgh).
Scot. Stud.	*Scottish Studies*, School of Scottish Studies (Edinburgh 1957–).

S-E Ulster Map — A map of south-east Ulster (from Olderfleet in the north to Dundrum in the south), c. 1580, PRO London MPF 87.

Shaw Mason's Par. Sur. — *A statistical account, or parochial survey of Ireland, drawn up from the communications of the clergy*, William Shaw Mason, vol. i (Dublin 1814).

Shorter OED — *The shorter Oxford English dictionary on historical principles*, prepared by W. Little, H.W. Fowler & J. Coulson; revised and ed. C.T. Onions. 3rd edn revised with addenda (Oxford 1944; reprint 1969 etc.).

Speed's Antrim & Down — A map entitled *Antrym and Downe*, AD 1610, by John Speed. Reproduced in *UJA* ser. 1, vol. i (1853) between pp. 123 and 124.

Speed's Ireland — *The Kingdome of Irland devided into severall Provinces and then againe devided into Counties. Newly described*, AD 1610, by John Speed. Also published in his atlas *The Theatre of the Empire of Great Britain* (Sudbury & Humble 1612).

Speed's Ulster — *The Province Ulster described*, AD 1610, by John Speed. Also published in his atlas *The Theatre of the Empire of Great Britain* (Sudbury & Humble 1612).

SP Hen. VIII — *State papers published under the authority of His Majesty's Commission: King Henry VIII*, 11 vols (London 1830–52).

Stud. Celt. — *Studia Celtica*, published on behalf of the Board of Celtic Studies of the University of Wales (Cardiff 1966–).

Sub. Roll Down — *Subsidy roll for the county of Down, AD 1663*, PRONI T/307.

Surnames Dn — "Surnames in the County of Down", *UJA* ser 1. vol. 6 (1858), 77–90.

Swanzy's Dromore — *Succession lists of the diocese of Dromore*, Henry B. Swanzy, ed. J.B. Leslie (Belfast 1933).

TBC (Rec. I) — *Táin Bó Cúailnge Recension I*, ed. Cecile O'Rahilly (Dublin 1976).

TBF — *Táin Bó Fraích*, ed. Wolfgang Meid, Medieval and Modern Irish Series xxviii (Dublin 1967).

TD — *The bardic poems of Tadhg Dall Ó hUiginn (1550–1591)*, ed. E. Knott, 2 vols, Irish Texts Society (London 1922).

Terrier (O'Laverty) — "Terrier or ledger book of Down and Connor, c. 1615", *O'Laverty* v, 318–334.

Terrier (Reeves) — *Terrier or ledger book of Down and Connor, c. 1615*, transcribed by William Reeves, PRONI DIO/1/24/2/3.

TNCT — *Townland names of County Tyrone*, P. M'Aleer (c. 1920; reprint Portadown & Draperstown 1988).

Tombstone (Sav. Ards) — Tombstones cited in *Sav. Ards, passim.*

Top. Index 1961 — *Census of population 1961: topographical index*, Government of Northern Ireland, General Register Office (Belfast 1962).

Townland Index Map — *Index maps showing townlands and other administrative units and the disposition of six–inch sheets and 1:2,500 plans*, Ordnance Survey of Northern Ireland (Belfast 1970).

Treas. Warrant (OSNB) — *Treasury Warrant*, cited in *OSNB, passim.*

Triads of Ireland — *The Triads of Ireland*, ed. Kuno Meyer, Todd Lecture Series xiii (Dublin 1906).

Tribes Ire. — *The tribes of Ireland,* ed. J. O'Donovan (Dublin 1852).

Trien. Visit. (Boyle) — Boyle's *Triennial visitation of Down, Connor and Dromore, AD 1679*, transcribed by William Reeves, PRONI DIO/1/24/16/1, pp. 34–49.

Trien. Visit. (Bramhall) — Bramhall's *Triennial visitation of Down, Connor and Dromore, AD 1661*, transcribed by William Reeves, PRONI DIO/1/24/16/1, pp. 1–16.

Trien. Visit. (Margetson) — Margetson's *Triennial visitation of Down, Connor and Dromore, AD 1664*, transcribed by William Reeves, PRONI DIO/1/24/16/1, pp. 19–33.

Trip. Life (Stokes) — *The tripartite life of Saint Patrick, with other documents relating to that Saint*, ed. Whitley Stokes, 2 vols (London 1887).

Tythes Applot. (OSNB) — *Tythes Applotment*, cited in *OSNB, passim.*

UJA — *Ulster Journal of Archaeology*, ser. 1, 9 vols (Belfast 1853–62); ser. 2, 17 vols (1894–1911); ser. 3, (1938–).

Ulst. Roll Gaol Deliv. — "Ulster roll of gaol delivery, 1613–18", ed. James F. Ferguson, *UJA* ser. 1, vol. 1 (1853), 260–70; vol. 2 (1854), 25–8.

Ulster Visit. (Reeves) — *The state of the diocese of Down and Connor, 1622, as returned by Bishop Robert Echlin to the royal commissioners*, copied from TCD E.3.6. by William Reeves, PRONI DIO/1/24/1.

Ultach — *An tUltach: iris oifigiúil Chomhaltas Uladh* (1923–).

VSSH (Heist) — *Vitae sanctorum Hiberniae ex codice olim Salamanticensi nunc Bruxellensi*, ed. William W. Heist (Bruxelles 1965).

VSSH (Plummer) — *Vitae sanctorum Hiberniae partim hactenus ineditae ad fidem codicum manuscriptorum...*, ed. Charles Plummer, 2 vols (Oxford 1910).

Wars Co. Down — "The wars of 1641 in County Down: the deposition of High Sheriff Peter Hill (1645)", transcribed and annotated by Thomas Fitzpatrick with additional notes by Rev. Monsignor O'Laverty and Edward Parkinson, *UJA* ser. 2, vol. x (1904), 73–90.

Will (Sav. Ards) — Wills cited in *Sav. Ards, passim.*

Wm. Map (OSNB) — *James Williamson's map of Co. Down*, AD 1810, cited in *OSNB, passim.*

Young's Tour in Ireland — *A tour in Ireland: with general observations on the present state of that kingdom made in the years 1776, 1777, and 1778 ...*, Arthur Young (Dublin 1780).

ZCP — *Zeitschrift fur Celtische Philologie* (1897–).

SECONDARY BIBLIOGRAPHY

Adams, G.B.	1964	"Ulster dialects", *Ulster dialects: an introductory symposium* 1–4 (Ulster Folk and Transport Museum, Holywood).
Anderson, A.	1979	"Surnames of the Ards: part 1", *J Up. Ards HS* iii, 18–21.
	1980	"Surnames of the Ards: part 2", *J Up. Ards HS* iv, 2–7.
	1981	"Surnames of the Ards: part 3", *J Up. Ards HS* v, 2–8.
	1982	"Surnames of the Ards: part 4", *J Up. Ards HS* vi, 2–7.
	1983	"Surnames of the Ards: part 5", *J Up. Ards HS* vii, 2–5.
Andrews, J.H.	1974	"The maps of the escheated counties of Ulster, 1609–10", *PRIA* vol. lxxiv, sect. C, 133–70.
	1975	*A paper landscape; the Ordnance Survey in nineteenth-century Ireland* (Oxford).
	1978	*Irish maps: the Irish heritage series, no. 18* (Dublin).
	1985	*Plantation acres: an historical study of the Irish land surveyor and his maps* (Belfast).
Arthurs, J.B.	1955–6	"The Ulster Place-name Society", *Onoma* vi, 80–2.
Atkinson, A.	1823	*Ireland exhibited to England in a political and moral survey of her population and in a statistical and scenographic tour of certain districts ...*, 2 vols (London).
Barber, Charles	1976	*Early Modern English* (London).
Bell, Robert	1988	*The book of Ulster surnames* (Belfast).
Bigger, F.J. & Fennell W.J.	1898	"Inishargie old church in the Ards, in the County of Down", *UJA* ser. 2, vol. iv, 231–2.
Black, G.F.	1946	*The surnames of Scotland* (New York).
Broderick, G.	1981–2	"The baronial possessions of Bangor and Saul in Man", *BUPNS* ser. 2, vol. iv, 24–6.
Byres, T.	1982	"Quintin Castle", *J Up. Ards HS* vi, 7–9.
Byrne, F.J.	1973	*Irish kings and high-kings* (London).
Canavan, Tony	1991	*Every stoney acre has a name: a celebration of the townland in Ulster,* Federation for Ulster Local Studies (Belfast).
Chart, D.A.	1942	"The break-up of the estate of Con O'Neill, Castlereagh, County Down", *PRIA* vol. xlviii, sect. C, no. 3, 119–51.

Camblin, Gilbert	1951	*The town in Ulster* (London).
de hÓir, Éamonn	1964(a)	"An t-athru *onga* > *ú* i roinnt logainmneacha", *Dinnsean.* iml. i, uimh. 1, 8–11.
	1965	"*Aird* i logainmneacha", *Dinnsean.* iml. i, uimh. 2, 79–86.
Dunlop, Robert	1905	"Sixteenth-century maps of Ireland", *English Historical Review* vol. 20, 309–37.
Ewart, L.M.	1886	*Handbook of the united Diocese of Down and Connor and Dromore...* (Belfast).
Falkiner, C.L.	1903	"The counties of Ireland: an historical sketch of their origin, constitution, and gradual delimitation", *PRIA* vol. xxiv, sect. C, 169–94.
	1904	*Illustrations of Irish history and topography, mainly of the seventeenth century* (London).
Flanagan, D.	1971	"The names of Downpatrick", *Dinnsean.* iml. iv, uimh. 4, 89–112.
	1973	"Three settlement names in County Down: the Turtars of Inishargy; Dunsfort; Tullumgrange", *Dinnsean.* iml. iv, uimh. 3, 65–71.
	1978(c)	"Seventeenth-century salmon fishing in County Down (river-name documentation)", *BUPNS* ser. 2, vol. i, 22–6.
	1978(d)	"Transferred population or sept-names: *Ulaidh* (a quo Ulster)", *BUPNS* ser. 2, vol. i, 40–4.
	1978(e)	"Places and their names: Quoile and British", *BUPNS* ser. 2, vol. i, 44–7; 51–2.
	1979(a)	"Common elements in Irish place-names: *ceall, cill*", *BUPNS* ser. 2, vol. ii, 1–8.
	1979(f)	"Review of *The meaning of Irish place names* by James O'Connell (Belfast 1978)", *BUPNS* ser. 2, vol. 2, 58–60.
	1980–1(a)	"Common elements in Irish place-names: *dún, ráth, lios*", *BUPNS* ser.2, vol. iii, 16–29.
	1980–1(b)	"A reappraisal of *Da* in Irish place-names", *BUPNS* ser. 2, vol. iii, 16–29.
	1981–2(a)	"Places and their names: Raloo and Ballyarnot", *BUPNS* ser. 2, vol. iv, 22–3.
	1981–2(b)	"Some guidelines to the use of Joyce's *Irish names of places*, vol. i", *BUPNS* ser. 2, vol. 4, 61–9.
	1981–2(c)	"A summary guide to the more commonly attested ecclesiastical elements in place-names", *BUPNS* ser. 2, vol. iv, 69–75.
Goblet, Y.M.	1932	*A topographical index of the parishes and townlands of Ireland in Sir William Petty's Mss. barony maps (c. 1655–9)... and Hiberniae Delineatio (c. 1672)* (Dublin).

Hanks, P. & Hodges, F. 1988 *Dictionary of surnames* (Oxford).

Hennessy, R. 1889 *Mesca Ulad, or the intoxication of the Ultonians*, Todd Lecture Series i (Dublin).

Holmer, N.M. 1942 *The Irish language in Rathlin Island, Co. Antrim*, Todd Lecture Series xviii (Dublin).

Hughes, A.J. 1989(a) "Old Irish *mennán, bennán*", *ZCP* 43, 179–86.

1989(c) "Aistriúchán Gaeilge ar chuid d'aiste Locke", *S. Ard Mh.* vol. 13, no. 2, 121–66.

1991 "Irish place-names: some perspectives, pitfalls, procedures and potential", *S. Ard Mh.* vol. 14, no. 2, 116–48.

Kenney, J.F. 1929 *The sources for the early history of Ireland: an introduction and guide* (New York).

Kerr, William 1989 "Black Abbey, the archbishops of Armagh and the church of Derryaghy", *J Lisburn HS* vii, 45–9.

Klein, Ernest 1966–7 *A comprehensive etymological dictionary of the English language*, 2 vols (Amsterdam, London & New York).

Lucas, A.T. 1963 "The sacred trees of Ireland", *J Cork HAS* vol. 68, 16–54.

Mac Aodha, B.S. 1978 "Rian an Bhéarla ar áitainmneacha oirthuaisceart an Dúin", *BUPNS* ser. 2, vol. i, 19–21.

McErlean, Thomas 1983 "The Irish townland system of landscape organisation", *Landscape archaeology in Ireland*, ed. Terence Reeves-Smyth and Fred Hamond, 315–39 (Oxford).

Mac Giolla Easpaig, D. 1981 "Noun and noun compounds in Irish place-names", *Et. Celt.* xviii, 151–63.

1986 "Lough Neagh and Tynagh revisited", *Ainm* i, 14–40.

McKeown L. 1929 "The Maidens and the Copeland Islands", *JDCHS* ii, 105–8.

MacLysaght, Edward 1957 *Irish families: their names, arms and origins* (Dublin).

1964 *A guide to Irish surnames* (Dublin).

1982 *More Irish families: a new revised and enlarged edition of "More Irish families" (1960) incorporating "Supplement to Irish families" (1964), with an essay on Irish chieftainries* (Dublin).

1985 *The surnames of Ireland* (Dublin; 4th edn; 1st edn 1957).

Mac Reachtain, L. 1951 "Fánaíocht in Ultaibh", *Ultach* (Aibreán-Bealtaine), 8–10.

Mallory, J.P. & McNeill, T. E.	1991	*The archaeology of Ulster from colonization to Plantation* (Belfast).
Meyer, K.	1911	*Betha Colmáin maic Luacháin, Life of Colmán son of Luachán*, Todd Lecture Series xvii (Dublin).
Millsopp, Sandra	1991	"A townland study: Bangor, Co. Down", in Canavan 1991, 36–41.
Moody, T.W.	1939	*The Londonderry plantation, 1609–41: the city of London and the plantation in Ulster* (Belfast).
Morgan, Hiram	1985	"The colonial venture of Sir Thomas Smith in Ulster, 1571–1575", *The Historical Journal* vol. 28, pt. 2, 261–78.
Morton, Deirdre	1956–7	"Tuath-divisions in the baronies of Belfast and Masserene", *BUPNS* ser. 1, vol. iv, 38–44; vol. v, 6–12.
Munn, A.M.	1925	Notes on the place names of the parishes and townlands of county Londonderry (reprint, Ballinascreen 1985).
Murphy, M.J.	1987	*Rathlin: island of blood and enchantment* (Dundalk).
Ní Dhonnchadha, M.	1981	"The guarantor list of *Cáin Adomnáin*", *Peritia* i, 178–215.
Nicolaisen, W.F.H	1970	*The names of the towns and cities of Britain* (London & Batsford).
Ó Casaide, Séamus	1929	"The Irish language in Belfast and County Down, 1601–1850", *JDCHS* ii, 4–63.
Ó Corráin, D. & Maguire, F.	1981	*Gaelic personal names* (Dublin).
Ó Cuív, Brian	1975	*The impact of the Scandinavian invasions on the Celtic-speaking peoples c. 800–1100 AD* (Dublin 1975; reprint 1983).
O'Curry, Eugene	1861	*Lectures on the manuscript materials of ancient Irish history* (Dublin 1861).
O'Donovan, John	1842	*The banquet of Dún na nGedh and the battle of Magh Rath, an ancient historical tale*, Irish Archaeological Society (Dublin).
	1847	*Leabhar na g-Ceart or the Book of Rights* (The Celtic Society Dublin).
	1852	*The tribes of Ireland* (Dublin).
Ó Duibhín, Ciarán	1991	*Irish in County Down since 1750* (Cumann Gaelach Leath Chathail).

Ó Foghludha, R. 1935 *Log-ainmneacha .i. dictionary of Irish place-names...* (Dublin).

Oftedal, Magne 1975 "Norse place-names in Celtic Scotland", in Ó Cuív 1975, 43–50.

Ó Maille, T.S. 1960 "*Cuilleann* in áitainmneacha", *Béaloid.* xxviii, 50–64.
1989–90 "Irish place-names in *-as, -es, -is, -os, -us*", *Ainm* iv, 125–43.

Ó Mainnín, M.B. 1989–90 "The element *island* in Ulster place-names", *Ainm* iv, 200–210.

Ó Maolfabhail, Art 1990 *Logainmneacha na hÉireann, iml. i: Contae Luimnigh* (Baile Átha Cliath).

O'Rahilly, T.F. 1930 "Notes on Middle Irish pronunciation" *Hermathena* xx, 159–95.
1932 *Irish dialects past and present* (Dublin 1932; reprint 1976).
1933 "Notes on Irish placenames", *Hermathena* xxiii, 196–220.
1946 *Early Irish history and mythology* (Dublin 1946; reprint 1971).

O'Riordan, M. 1990 *The Gaelic mind and the collapse of the Gaelic world* (Cork).

Otway-Ruthven, A.J. 1964 "Parochial development in the rural deanery of Skreen", *JRSAI* xciv, 111–22.

Owen, D.J. 1917 *A short history of the port of Belfast* (Belfast).

Palmer, A.N. 1890 "Notes on the early history of Bangor Is Y Coed", *Cymmrodor* x, 16–7.

Perceval-Maxwell, M. 1973 *The Scottish migration to Ulster in the reign of James I* (London).

Petty, William 1672 *The political anatomy of Ireland* (1672), reprinted in *Tracts and treatises illustrative of Ireland*, vol. ii, 72–3 (Dublin 1860–1).

Power, Patrick 1907 *The place-names of Decies* (London).
1932 *Críchad an chaoilli: being the topography of ancient Fermoy* (Cork).
1947 "The bounds and extent of Irish parishes", *Féil. Torna*, 218–23.

Price, Liam 1963 "A note on the use of the word *baile* in place-names", *Celtica* vi, 119–126.

Quiggin, E.C. 1906 *A dialect of Donegal, being the speech of Meenawannia in the parish of Glenties* (Cambridge).

Quin, E.G. & Freeman, T.W.	1947	"Some Irish topographical terms", *Irish Geography* vol. i, no. 4, 85–9.
Quinn, D.B.	1933–4	"Anglo-Irish Ulster in the early sixteenth century", *PBNHPS* 56–78.
	1945	"Sir Thomas Smith (1513–77) and the beginnings of English colonial theory", in *Proceedings of the American Philosophical Society* (USA 1876–) vol. 89, 543–60.
Reaney, P.H.	1958	*A dictionary of British surnames* (London).
Reeves, William	1861	"On the townland distribution of Ireland", *PRIA* vii, 473–90.
Reid, Professor	1957	"A note on *cinament*", *BUPNS* ser. 1, vol. v, 12.
Richards, Melville	1970	"Bangor", in Nicolaisen 1970, 46.
	1983	"Norse place-names in Wales", in Ó Cuív 1983, 51–60.
Sommerfelt, Alf	1958	"The English forms of the names of the main provinces of Ireland", *Lochlann* i, 223–7.
Stevenson, John	1920	*Two centuries of life in Down* (Belfast).
Taylor, Isaac	1896	*Names and their histories* (1896), reprinted in the Everyman edition of his *Words and places* (1911), 205.
Traynor, Michael	1953	*The English dialect of Donegal: a glossary* (Dublin).
Wagner, Heinrich	1979	"Origins of pagan Irish religion and the study of names", *BUPNS* ser. 2, vol. ii, 22–40.
Williams, Ifor	1945	*Enwae lloed* (Liverpool).
Woulfe, Patrick	1923	*Sloinnte Gaedheal is Gall: Irish names and surnames; collected and edited with explanatory and historical notes* (Dublin).
Wright, Joseph	1898–1905	*English dialect dictionary*, 6 vols (Oxford).

GLOSSARY OF TECHNICAL TERMS

advowson The right of presenting a clergyman to a vacant benefice.

affricate A plosive pronounced in conjunction with a fricative; e.g. the sounds spelt with *(t)ch* or *-dge* in English.

alveolar Pronounced with the tip of the tongue touching the ridge of hard flesh behind the upper teeth; e.g. *t* in the English word *tea.*

analogy The replacement of a form by another in imitation of words of a similar class; e.g. in imitation of *bake – baked, fake – faked, rake – raked* a child or foreigner might create a form *shaked.*

anglicize Make English in form; e.g. in place-names the Irish word *baile* "homestead, townland" is anglicized *bally.*

annal A record of events in chronological order, according to the date of the year.

annates Later known as First Fruits; a tax paid, initially to the Pope, by a clergyman on appointment to a benefice.

apocope The loss of the end of a word.

aspiration (i) The forcing of air through a narrow passage thereby creating a frictional sound; e.g. *gh* in the word *lough* as pronounced in Ireland and Scotland is an aspirated consonant, (ii) the modification of a consonant sound in this way, indicated in Irish writing by putting *h* after the consonant; e.g. *p* aspirated resembles the *ph* sound at the beginning of *phantom*; also called **lenition**.

assimilation The replacing of a sound in one syllable by another to make it similar to a sound in another syllable; e.g. in some dialects of Irish the *r* in the first syllable of the Latin *sermon-* was changed to *n* in imitation of the *n* in the second syllable, giving a form *seanmóin.*

ballybetagh Irish *baile biataigh* "land of a food-provider", native land unit, the holder of which had a duty to maintain his lord and retinue when travelling in the area (*Colton Vis.* p.130).

ballyboe Irish *baile bó* "land of a cow", a land unit equivalent to a modern townland, possibly so-named as supplying the yearly rent of one cow (*Colton Vis.* p. 130).

barony In Ireland an administrative unit midway in size between a county and a civil parish, originally the landholding of a feudal baron (*EA* p. 62).

benefice An ecclesiastical office to which income is attached.

bilabial Articulated by bringing the two lips together; e.g. the *p* in the English word *pea.*

Brittonic Relating to the branch of Celtic languages which includes Welsh, Cornish and Breton.

calendar A précis of an historical document or documents with its contents arranged according to date.

calque A word or phrase introduced into a language through direct translation of the constituents of a term in another language; e.g. the colloquial *No way* is a calque on German *keineswegs*.

carrow Irish *ceathrú* "a quarter". See **quarter**.

cartography The science of map-making.

cartouche An ornamental frame round the title etc. of a map.

carucate Latin *carucata* "ploughland", a territorial unit, the equivalent of a townland.

Celtic Relating to the (language of the) Irish, Scots, Manx, Welsh, Cornish, Bretons, and Gauls.

centralized Pronounced with the centre of the tongue raised; e.g. the vowel sound at the beginning of *again* or at the end of *the*.

cess Tax.

cinament A territorial unit of lesser size than a tuogh (which see). Three derivations have been suggested: (i) from Irish *cine* "a family", (*cineamhain*?) (*EA* 388); (ii) from French *scindement* "cutting up, division" (Morton 1956–7, 39); (iii) from French *(a)ceignement* "enclosure(?)" (Reid 1957, 12).

civil parish An administrative unit based on the medieval parish.

cluster See **consonant cluster-**

coarb Irish *comharba*, originally the heir of an ecclesiastical office, later a high-ranking hereditary tenant of church land under the bishop. The coarb may be in charge of other ecclesiastical tenants called erenaghs, which see.

compound A word consisting of two or more verbal elements; e.g. *aircraft, housework*.

consonant (i) An element of the alphabet which is not a vowel, e.g. *c, j, x*, etc., (ii) a speech sound in which the passage of air through the mouth or nose is impeded, e.g. at the lips *(b, p, or m)*, at the teeth *(s, z)*, etc.

consonant cluster A group of two or more consonants; e.g. *bl* in *blood, ndl* in *handle, lfths* in *twelfths.*

contraction (i) The shortening of a word or words normally by the omission of one or more sounds, (ii) a contracted word; e.g. *good-bye* is a contraction of *God be with you*; can not is contracted to *can't*.

county Feudal land division, equivalent to an English shire, created by the English administration in Ireland as the major subdivision of an Irish province.

deanery Properly called a rural deanery, an ecclesiastical division of people or land administered by a rural dean.

declension A group of nouns whose case-endings vary according to a fixed pattern. (There are five declensions in modern Irish).

delenition Sounding or writing a consonant as if it were not aspirated; see **aspiration**.

dental A sound pronounced with the tip of the tongue touching the upper teeth; e.g. *th* in the English *thumb*.

devoicing Removing the sound caused by the resonance of vocal cords; see **voiced**.

dialect A variety of a language in a given area with distinctive vocabulary, pronunciation or grammatical forms.

digraph A group of two letters expressing a single sound; e.g. *ea* in English *team* or *ph* in English *photograph*.

diocese The area or population over which a bishop has ecclesiastical authority.

diphthong A union of two vowel sounds pronounced in one syllable; e.g. *oi* in English *boil*. (Note that a diphthong cannot be sung on a single sustained note without changing the position of the mouth).

dissimilation The replacing of a sound in one syllable by another to make it different from a sound in another syllable e.g. Loughbrickland comes from an original Irish form, *Loch Bricrenn*.

eclipsis The replacement in Irish of one sound by another in initial position as the result of the influence of the previous word; e.g. the *c* of Irish *cór* "choir" (pronounced like English *core*) is eclipsed by *g* in the phrase *i gcór* "in a choir" due to the influence of the preposition *i*, and *gcór* is pronounced like English *gore*; also called **nasalization**.

elision The omission of a sound in pronunciation; e.g. the *d* is elided in the word *handkerchief*.

emphasis See **stress**.

epenthetic vowel A vowel sound inserted within a word; e.g. in Ireland an extra vowel is generally inserted between the *l* and *m* of the word *film*.

erenagh Irish *airchinnech* "steward", hereditary officer in charge of church lands, later a tenant to the bishop (*Colton Vis.* pp. 4–5).

escheat Revert to the feudal overlord, in Ireland usually forfeit to the English crown (Moody 1939, 30).

etymology The facts relating to the formation and meaning of a word.

fiant A warrant for the making out of a grant under the royal seal, or (letters) patent.

fricative A speech sound formed by narrowing the passage of air from the mouth so that audible friction is produced; e.g. *gh* in Irish and Scottish *lough*.

Gaelic Relating to the branch of Celtic languages which includes Irish, Scottish Gaelic and Manx.

glebe The house and land (and its revenue) provided for the clergyman of a parish.

glide A sound produced when the organs of speech are moving from the position for one speech sound to the position for another; e.g. in pronouncing the word *deluge* there is a *y*-like glide between the *l* and the *u*.

gloss A word or phrase inserted in a manuscript to explain a part of the text.

Goedelic = **Gaelic** which see.

grange Anglo-Norman term for farm land providing food or revenue for a feudal lord, frequently a monastery.

haplology The omission of a syllable beside another with a similar sound; e.g. *lib(ra)ry, deteri(or)ated.*

hearth money A tax on the number of hearths used by a household.

impropriator The person to whom rectorial tithes of a monastery etc. were granted after the Dissolution.

inflect To vary the form of a word to indicate a different grammatical relationship; e.g. *man* singular, *men* plural.

inquisition A judicial inquiry, here usually into the possessions of an individual at death.

International Phonetic Alphabet The system of phonetic transcription advocated by the International Phonetic Association.

labial = **bilabial** which see.

lenition See **aspiration**.

lexicon The complete word content of a language.

lowering Changing a vowel sound by dropping the tongue slightly in the mouth; e.g. pronouncing *doctor* as *dactor*.

manor Feudal estate (Anglo–Norman and Plantation), smaller than a barony, entitling the landowner to jurisdiction over his tenants at a manor court.

martyrology Irish *féilire*, also translated "calendar", lists names of saints and gives the days on which their feasts are to be celebrated.

mearing A boundary.

metathesis The transposition of sounds in a word; e.g. saying *elascit* instead of *elastic*.

moiety French *moitié*, "the half of", also a part or portion of any size.

morphology The study of the grammatical structure of words.

nasalization See **eclipsis**.

oblique Having a grammatical form other than nominative singular.

onomasticon A list of proper names, usually places.

orthography Normal spelling.

palatal A sound produced with the tongue raised towards the hard palate.

parish A subdivision of a diocese served by a single main church or clergyman.

patent (or letters patent), an official document conferring a right or privilege, frequently here a grant of land.

patronymic A name derived from that of the father.

phonemic Relating to the system of phonetic oppositions in the speech sounds of a language, which make, in English for example, *soap* a different word from *soup*, and *pin* a different word from *bin*.

phonetic Relating to vocal sound.

phonology The study of the sound features of a language.

plosive A sound formed by closing the air passage and then releasing the air flow suddenly, causing an explosive sound; e.g. *p* in English *pipe*.

ploughland Medieval English land unit of about 120 acres, equivalent to a townland.

prebend An endowment, often in land, for the maintenance of a canon or prebendary, a senior churchman who assisted the bishop or had duties in the cathedral.

precinct *Ad hoc* land division (usually a number of townlands) used in Plantation grants.

prefix A verbal element placed at the beginning of a word which modifies the meaning of the word; e.g. *un-* in *unlikely*.

proportion *Ad hoc* land division (usually a number of townlands) used in Plantation grants.

province Irish *cúige* "a fifth": the largest administrative division in Ireland, of which there are now four (Ulster, Leinster, Connacht, Munster) but were once five.

quarter Land unit often a quarter of the ballybetagh, and thus containing three or four townlands, but sometimes referring to a subdivision of a townland. See also **carrow**.

raising Changing a vowel sound by lifting the tongue higher in the mouth; e.g. pronouncing *bag* as *beg*.

realize Pronounce; e.g. *-adh* at the end of verbal nouns in Ulster Irish is realized as English *-oo*.

rectory A parish under the care of a rector supported by its tithes; if the rector cannot reside in the parish he appoints and supports a resident vicar.

reduction (i) Shortening of a vowel sound; e.g. the vowel sound in *board* is reduced in the word *cupboard*, (ii) = **contraction** which see.

register A document providing a chronological record of the transactions of an individual or organization.

rounded Pronounced with pouting lips; e.g. the vowel sounds in *oar* and *ooze*.

seize To put in legal possession of property, especially land.

semantic Relating to the meaning of words.

semivowel A sound such as *y* or *w* at the beginning of words like *yet*, *wet*, etc.

sept Subgroup of people, for instance of a tribe or ruling family.

sessiagh Irish *seiseach* "a sixth", usually referring to a subdivision of a townland or similar unit. Apparently three sessiaghs were equivalent to a ballyboe.

shift of stress The transfer of emphasis from one syllable to another; e.g. *Belfast* was originally stressed on the second syllable *fast* but because of shift of stress many people now pronounce it **Bel***fast*. See **stress**.

stem (dental, o-, etc.) Classification of nouns based on the form of their endings before the Old Irish period.

stress The degree of force with which a syllable is pronounced. For example, the name Antrim is stressed on the first syllable while Tyrone is stressed on the second.

subdenomination A smaller land division, usually a division of a townland.

substantive A noun.

suffix A verbal element placed at the end of a word which modifies the meaning of the word; e.g. *-less* in *senseless*.

syllable A unit of pronunciation containing one vowel sound which may be preceded or followed by a consonant or consonants; e.g. *I, my, hill,* have one syllable; *outside, table, ceiling* have two; *sympathy, understand, telephone* have three, etc.

syncopation The omission of a short unstressed vowel or digraph when a syllable beginning with a vowel is added; e.g. *tiger+ess* becomes *tigress.*

tate A small land unit once used in parts of Ulster, treated as equivalent to a townland, although only half the size.

termon Irish *tearmann*, land belonging to the Church, with privilege of sanctuary (providing safety from arrest for repentant criminals), usually held for the bishop by a coarb as hereditary tenant.

terrier A list of the names of lands held by the Church or other body.

tithes Taxes paid to the Church. Under the native system they were shared between parish clergy and erenagh (as the tenant of the bishop), under the English administration they were payable to the local clergyman of the Established Church.

topography The configuration of a land surface, including its relief and the position of its features.

toponymy Place-names as a subject for study.

townland The common term or English translation for a variety of small local land units; the smallest unit in the 19th-century Irish administrative system.

transcription An indication by written symbols of the precise sound of an utterance.

tuogh Irish *tuath* "tribe, tribal kingdom", a population or territorial unit.

unrounded Articulated with the lips spread or in neutral position; see **rounded**.

velar Articulated with the back of the tongue touching the soft palate; e.g. *c* in *cool.*

vicarage A parish in the charge of a vicar, the deputy either for a rector who received some of the revenue but resided elsewhere, or for a monastery or cathedral or lay impropriator.

visitation An inspection of (church) lands, usually carried out for a bishop (ecclesiastical or episcopal visitation) or for the Crown (regal visitation).

vocalization The changing of a consonant sound into a vowel sound by widening the air passage; akin to the disappearance of *r* in Southern English pronunciation of words like *bird, worm, car.*

voiced Sounded with resonance of the vocal cords. (A test for voicing can be made by closing the ears with the fingers and uttering a consonant sound. e.g. *ssss, zzzz, ffff, vvvv.* If a buzzing or humming sound is heard the consonant is voiced; if not it is voiceless).

voiceless See **voiced**.

INDEX TO IRISH FORMS OF PLACE-NAMES

(with pronunciation guide)

The following guide to the pronunciation of Irish forms suggested in this book is only approximate. Words are to be sounded as though written in English. The following symbols have the value shown:

ă	as in *above, coma*
ā	as in *father, draught*
ċ	as in *lough, Bach*
ch	as in *chip, church*
dge	as in *porridge*
ġ	does not occur in English. To approximate this sound try gargling without water, or consider the following: *lock* is to *lough* as *log* is to *loġ*. If you cannot manage this sound just pronounce it like *g* in *go*.
gh	as in *lough, Bach*; not as in *foghorn*
ı	as in *five, line*
ky	as in *cure, McKeown*
ly	at beginning of words as in *brilliant, million*
ō	as in *boar, sore*
ow	as in *now, plough*

Stress is indicated by writing the vowel in the stressed syllable in bold, e.g., Arm**a**gh, Ballym**e**na, L**u**rgan.

Place-Name	Rough Guide	Page No.
Abhainn an Mhuilinn	ōne ă w**i**llin	196
Aird Uladh	ardge **u**lloo	1
Ard Caocháin	ard k**ee**hine	42
Ard Caoin	ard k**ee**n	9
Ard Choinn	ard ċ**i**n	27
Ard Meannán	ard m**a**nnan	116
Baile Acairt	ballă **a**kirch	68
Baile Adaim	ballă **a**dim	78
Baile Altáin	ballă **a**ltine	218
Baile an Aistire	ballin **a**shchirră	204
Baile an Chaisleáin	ballin ċ**a**shline	202
Baile an Fhraoigh	ballin r**ee**	159
Baile an Mhuilinn	ballin w**i**llin	194
Baile an Reithe	ballin r**e**yhă	223
Baile an Riodalaigh	ballin r**i**ddăly	32
Baile an Ruiséalaigh	ballin r**u**shăly	45
Baile Aodha	ball**oo**	150
Baile Aodha	ball**oo**	150
Baile Bhaird	ballă w**ā**rdge	13
Baile Bhaldúin	ballă w**a**ldoon	34
Baile Bháltair	ballă w**a**lter	67
Baile Bhearnan	ballă v**a**rnăn	160
Baile Bheastair	ballă v**a**ster	187

Place-Name	Rough Guide	Page No.
Baile Bhláca	ballă wl**ā**kă	43
Baile Bhleaic	ballă vl**a**ck	200
Baile Bhodáin	ballă w**u**ddine	33
Baile Bhriain	ballă vr**ee**in	202
Baile Bhuitléara	ballă w**i**tlerră	180
Baile Bhuraid	ballă w**u**rridge	59
Baile Buachalla Bó	ballă booċăllă b**ō**	201
Baile Cam	ballă k**a**m	43
Baile Chloch Tógála	ballă ċlough t**ō**gallă	229
Baile Chócaire	ballă ċ**ō**ckirră	14
Baile Choiléir	ballă ċ**i**ller	129
Baile Chóplainn	ballă ċ**ō**plin	181
Baile Cille Láir	ballă killyă l**ā**r	154
Baile Crannaí Beag	ballă cranny b**e**g	11
Baile Crannaí Mór	ballă cranny m**o**re	12
Baile Cruacháin	ballă cr**oo**ċine	151
Baile Ealacoc	ballă **a**lăcock	217
Baile Faoite	ballă fw**ee**chă	34
Baile Fionnúrach	ballă f**i**nooragh	124
Baile Freanais	ballă fr**a**nish	183
Baile Freanais	ballă fr**a**nish	105
Baile Gaelach	ballă g**ay**lagh	12
Baile Galgail	ballă g**a**lgăl	125
Baile Ghilbeirt	ballă y**i**lbirch	152
Baile Grafáin	ballă gr**a**ffine	106
Baile Hae	ballă h**ay**	183
Baile Haimlin	ballă h**a**mlin	107
Baile Haraí	ballă h**a**rry	221
Baile Hascain	ballă h**a**skin	183
Baile Héinrí	ballă h**ey**nree	29
Baile Heird	ballă h**e**rge	191
Baile Hoiste	ballă h**o**shchă	220
Baile Hóm	ballă h**o**me	153
Baile Iodoc	ball**i**dăck	123
Baile Iúir an Oileáin	ballă oorăn y**i**lline	205
Baile Iúraí	ballă **oo**ree	203
Baile Maoláin	ballă mw**ee**line	158
Baile Meannán Íochtarach	ballă m**a**nnăn **ee**ċtăragh	157
Baile Mhartair	ballă w**a**rtir	126
Baile Mhic Coilín	ballă vick k**i**lleen	219
Baile Mhic Con Mí	ballă vickăn m**ee**	58
Baile Mhic Cormaic	ballă vick c**o**rmick	156
Baile Mhic Dhónaill	ballă vick ġ**ō**nill	155
Baile Mhic Nais	ballă vick n**a**sh	31
Baile Mhic Naosa	ballă vick n**ee**să	184
Baile Mhic Uilliam	ballă vick **i**lliam	188
Baile Mhig Aodha	ballă vig **ee**	157

Place-Name	Rough Guide	Page No.
Baile Mhig Riabhacháin	ballă vig **ree**waghine	222
Baile na Bearnaise	ballă nă **bar**nishă	219
Baile na Buaile	ballă nă b**oo**ilă	201
Baile na Croise	ballă nă cr**o**shă	181
Baile na gCrot	ballă nă gr**o**t	153
Baile na Gráinsí	ballă nă gr**ā**nshee	163
Baile na Gráinsí	ballă nă gr**ā**nshee	191
Baile na Gráinsí	ballă nă gr**ā**nshee	203
Baile na Gréine	ballă nă gr**ey**nă	152
Baile na Móna	ballă nă m**ō**nă	222
Baile na Móna	ballă nă m**ō**nă	185
Baile na nDúnán	ballă nă n**oo**nan	182
Baile na Sceiche	ballă nă shk**ey**hă	224
Baile Niocail	ballă ny**i**ckill	59
Baile Nua	ballă **noo**ă	185
Baile Nua na hArda	ballă nooă nă h**ā**rdă	215
Baile Oibicín	ballă **i**bbikeen	87
Baile Phéarais	ballă f**ai**rish	69
Baile Philib	ballă f**i**llib	41
Baile Phoinnir	ballă f**u**nyir	57
Baile Phúdarlaigh	ballă f**oo**dărly	151
Baile Ramhar	ballă r**ā**wăr	186
Baile Rolaí	ballă r**o**lly	186
Baile Salach	ballă s**a**lagh	160
Baile Shéarla	ballă h**ai**rlă	30
Baile Spoird	ballă sp**u**rge	116
Baile Thalbóid	ballă h**a**lbodge	103
Baile Thrustáin	ballă hr**u**stine	55
Baile Uaiteacoc	ballă **oo**chăcock	225
Baile Uí Bhranagáin	bally wr**a**năgine	56
Baile Uí Gharbhagáin	bally ġ**a**rwăgine	44
Baile Uí Gharbhagáin	bally ġ**a**rwăgine	86
Baile Uí Lidí	bally l**i**dgee	155
Baile Uí Mhurchaidh	bally w**u**rraghy	32
Baile Uí Mhurchú	bally w**u**rraghoo	204
Baile Uí Ruagáin	bally r**oo**ăgine	224
Baile Uí Shionnaigh	bally h**u**nny	221
Baile Uí Uiginn	bally **i**ggin	86
Baile Uí Uiscín	bally **i**shkeen	188
Banc Mór, An	ă bank m**o**re	62
Beannchar	b**a**nnaghăr	146
Bior	b**i**rr	111
Broighill, Na	nă br**ee**ill	110
Caisleán Buí, An	ă kashlan bw**ee**	75
Caisleán Nua, An	ă kashlan n**oo**ă	117
Caointeach	k**ee**nchagh	130
Carn Gabhair	karn g**o**re	237

Place-Name	Rough Guide	Page No.
Carnán Lao	karnan **lee**	161
Carraig Ó gCaoindealbháin	karrick o **gee**njalwine	226
Cearnach	ky**ā**rnagh	61
Ceathrú an Iascaire	karhoon **yee**skirră	88
Ceathrú Chamchoise	karhoo ċ**a**mċushă	236
Ceathrú Chnocán Dubh	karhoo ċrockan d**oo**	145
Ceathrú Dhreasach	karhoo ġr**a**ssagh	131
Ceathrú Dobhair	karhoo d**o**re	189
Ceathrú na gCailleach	karhoo nă g**a**lyagh	93
Ceathrú na Siúr	karhoo nă sh**oo**r	145
Ceathrú na Sruthán	karhoo nă sr**u**han	145
Cheardaigh, An	ă ċy**a**rdy	206
Cheathrú Riabhach, An	ă ċyarhoo r**ee**wagh	189
Chlochaigh, An	ă ċl**ou**ghy	79
Choinleac, An	ă ċ**i**nlyack	162
Chré Bhuí, An	ă ċrey w**ee**	190
Cill Achaidh	kill **a**ghy	193
Cill Aindreasa	kill **a**ndrăsă	99
Cill Bhreachtáin	kill vr**a**ċtine	192
Cill Earnáin	kill **a**rnine	231
Cill Teanga	kill ch**a**ngă	232
Clann Aodha Buí	clan ee bw**ee**	169
Cnoc an Iolair	crock ăn y**i**llir	49
Cnoc Dubh	crock d**oo**	138
Coillidh Bholgáin	kăllyee w**u**llăgine	207
Coillín an Tiarna	kăllyeen ă ch**ee**rnă	207
Corróg	c**o**rrog	60
Creag an Rodáin	crag ă r**u**ddine	46
Creag Aonghasa	crag **ee**nġusă	135
Creag Bhréan	crag vr**ey**n	73
Creag na bhFiach	crag nă v**ee**agh	18
Cros na Muclaí	cross nă m**u**ckly	227
Dá Reachraidh, An	ă d**ā** r**a**ghry	97
Doire	d**i**rră	47
Domhnach Daoi	dōnagh d**ee**	179
Dorn, An	ă d**o**rn	19
Droim Ardáin	drim **ā**rdine	79
Droim Chuaiche	drim ċ**oo**iċyă	228
Droim Fada	drim f**a**ddă	190
Droim Thoirc	drim h**i**rk	229
Dumhaigh	d**oo**ey	117
Dún Eichmhílidh	doon **e**ċveely	14
Dún Uabhair	doon **oo**wir	70
Ghaineamhaigh, An	ă ġ**a**nyăwy	71
Ghlasrach, An	ă ġl**a**sragh	89
Ghráinseach, An	ă ġr**ā**nshagh	90
Greanach, An	ă gr**a**nagh	48

Place-Name	Rough Guide	Page No.
Inbhear Bige	inver bi**gg**ă	168
Inis an Fhéir	inish ăn y**ai**r	20
Inis an Róin	inish ă r**ō**ne	20
Inis Mhic Cairrge	inish vick c**a**rgă	83
Lios Bán	liss b**ā**n	17
Lios Bán, An	ă liss b**ā**n	165
Loch Chú Mhaighe	lough ċoo w**y**ă	37
Loch Cuan	lough c**oo**an	5
Loch Dubh	lough d**oo**	80, 81
Luachras Cua	looċrăs k**oo**ă	232
Maide Dubh na hArda	madjă doo nă h**ā**rdă	95
Maigh Bhile	mwy v**i**llă	233
Mhainistir Dhubh, An	ă wanishtir ġ**oo**	99
Mhainistir Liath, An	ă wanishtir l**ee**ă	199
Mhuinchille, An	ă w**i**nċillyă	136
Mion-ais Bheag	m**i**nnash v**e**g	22
Mion-ais Mhór	m**i**nnash w**o**re	22
Nead Dubh, An	ă nyad d**oo**	22
Oileán an Dromáin	illan ă dr**u**mine	19
Oileán Chóplainn	illan ċ**ō**plin	171
Oileán Corr	illan c**o**rr	51
Oileán Glas, An t	ă tillan gl**a**s	238
Oileán Gorm, An t	ă tillan g**o**rrăm	21
Oileán Gormáin	illan g**o**rrămine	112
Oileán Partán	illan p**a**rtan	22
Oileán Rua, An t	ă tillan r**oo**ă	24
Oileán Scathdeirge	illan sc**a** jerrigă	25
Oileán Trasna	illan tr**a**snă	26
Oileán Uí Bhraoin	illan ee wr**ee**n	21
Oileán Uí Chonghaile	illan ee ċ**o**nillă	18
Orlóg	**o**rlog	165
Port an Bhogaigh	purt ă w**u**ggy	108
Port an Bhotha	purt ă w**o**hă	166
Port an Ghiolla Ghruama	purt ă yillă ġr**oo**ămă	163
Port an Pheire	purt ă f**e**rră	63
Ráth Giall	rag y**ee**ăl	166
Ráth tSaileach	ra t**a**llagh	17
Ré-inis	r**ay**inish	23
Rinn Beara	rin b**a**rră	38
Rinn Bhuí, An	ă rin w**ee**	24
Rinn Riabhach	rin r**ee**wagh	173
Rubha Bán	rooă b**ā**n	110
Rubha Riabhach	rooă r**ee**wagh	93
Sceir Mhártain	shker w**ā**rtin	74
Screabach	shkr**a**bbagh	235
Sláine	sl**ā**nyă	115
Taobh Sailí	teeoo s**a**lly	133

Place-Name	Rough Guide	Page No.
Teamhair, An	ă ch**ow**ir	131
Teampall Chú Mhaighe	chample ċoo w**y**ă	139
Teampall Fionn	chample **fi**n	72
Teampall Phádraig	chample f**ā**drick	195
Tobar na Carraige	tubber nă k**a**rrigă	98
Tulaigh Bhric	tully vr**i**ck	26
Tulaigh Boird	tully b**o**rdge	49
Tulaigh Chaoimhín	tully ċ**ee**veen	209
Tulaigh Charnáin	tully ċ**a**rnine	134
Tulaigh na Craoibhe	tully nă cr**ee**vă	51
Tulaigh na Croise	tully nă cr**o**shă	80
Tulaigh na gCeardaithe	tully nă gy**a**rdy	236
Tulaigh Tromáin	tully tr**u**mmine	81
Tulaigh Uí Mhaolaodha	tully weel**ee**	50
Uachtar	**oo**aghtăr	121

PLACE-NAME INDEX

Sheet numbers are given below for the OS 1:50,000 map only where the name occurs on that map. Not all the townlands discussed in this volume appear on the published 1:50,000 map and no sheet number is given for those names. The sheet numbers for the 1:10,000 series and the earlier 6-inch series, which is still important for historical research, are supplied for townlands, although not for other names. The 6-inch sheet numbers refer to the Co. Down series except where otherwise stated.

Place-Name	1:50,000	1:10,000	6 inch	Page
Abbacy	21			36
Angus Rock	21			135
Ardgeehan		207	32	42
Ardkeen	21	187, 188	25	9
Ardminnan		188, 207	25	116
Ardquin		187	24, 25	27
Ards				1
Bairdstown	15, 21			73
Balliggan	15, 21	169	12, 18	86
Balloo	15	115, 116, 131, 132	2, 6	150
Balloo Lower	15	116	2	150
Ballyadam		207	25	78
Ballyalicock	15	132, 149	6	217
Ballyalton	15, 21	148	5	218
Ballyatwood	15, 21	150	12	68
Ballybarnes	15	131	5	219
Ballyblack (Ballyphilip)	21	207	32	43
Ballyblack (Grey Abbey/ Newtownards)	15, 21	132, 149	6	200
Ballyblack Little	15, 21	132, 149	6	200
Ballyboghilbo		132, 149	12	201
Ballyboley	15, 21	149	6, 11	201
Ballybranigan	21	206, 207	25, 32	56
Ballybryan	15, 21	149, 168	12	202
Ballybuttle	15	132	6, 7	180
Ballycam		207	32	43
Ballycastle	15, 21	149	6, 11	202
Ballycopeland	15	132	6, 7	181
Ballycran Beg	21	187, 188	18, 25	11
Ballycran More	21	169, 188	18, 25	12
Ballycroghan	15	116, 132	2	151
Ballycross	15	116	2	181
Ballycullen	15	131, 148	5	219
Ballydoonan	15, 21	149	12	182
Ballyedock or Carrstown		207, 225, 226	32	123
Ballyesborough	21	169, 188	18	104
Ballyewry	15, 21	149	11	203
Ballyferris	15, 21	150	7, 12	69

Place-Name	1:50,000	1:10,000	6 inch	Page
Ballyfinragh	21	188, 207	25	124
Ballyfinragh Lough				135
Ballyfotherly	15	116, 132	2, 6	151
Ballyfounder	21	207	32	57
Ballyfrench	21	169	18	105
Ballyfrenis	15	132	6, 7	183
Ballygalget	21	188, 207	25	125
Ballygarvan	15, 21	168	12, 18	186
Ballygarvigan		207	25, 32	44
Ballygelagh		188	25	12
Ballygilbert	15	115, 131	1	152
Ballygraffan	21	169, 188	18	106
Ballygrainey	15	132	2, 6	152
Ballygrangee	15, 21	149	6, 11	203
Ballygrot	15	116	1	153
Ballyhaft	15, 21	149	6, 11	220
Ballyhalbert	21	169	18	103
Ballyharry	15	132	6	221
Ballyhaskin		132, 133, 149, 150	7	183
Ballyhay	15	132	2, 6	183
Ballyhemlin		169	18	107
Ballyhenny	15	132	6	221
Ballyhenry	21	206	24, 25, 31, 32	29
Ballyherly	21	206	25, 32	30
Ballyholme	15	116	2	153
Ballykillare		115	1, 2	154
Ballyleidy		115, 131	1, 5	155
Ballylimp	21	169	18	69
Ballymacnamee	21	207	25	58
Ballymaconnell		116	2	155
Ballymacormick	15	116	2	156
Ballymacruise	15	132	7	184
Ballymagee		116, 132	2	157
Ballymagreehan	15, 21	148	5	222
Ballymarter		207	32	126
Ballyminetragh	15	116	2	157
Ballyminnish		206	25, 32	31
Ballymoney	15	131	1, 5	222
Ballymoney		149	7, 12	185
Ballymullan	15	115, 131	1	158
Ballymurphy (Ardquin)	15, 21	149	11, 12	32
Ballymurphy (Grey Abbey)		206	31, 32	204
Ballynester	15, 21	149	11, 12	204
Ballynichol	21	206, 207	32	59
Ballynoe		116, 132	2, 3	185
Ballyobegan	15, 21	150, 169	12	87
Ballyphilip		206	32	41

Place-Name	1:50,000	1:10,000	6 inch	Page
Ballyquintin	21	226	32, 39	127
Ballyrawer	15, 21	132, 149	6, 7	186
Ballyreagh	15, 21	131, 132, 148, 149	6	223
Ballyree		116, 132	2	159
Ballyridley		187, 206	25	32
Ballyrogan	15	131	5	224
Ballyrolly	15, 21	132	7	186
Ballyrusley		207	32	45
Ballysallagh Major		131	1, 5	160
Ballysallagh Minor	15	131	1, 5	160
Ballyskeagh, High		131	5	224
Ballyskeagh, Low		131	5	224
Ballyspurge		188, 207	25	116
Ballytrustan	21	206, 207	32	55
Ballyurnanellan		149	11	205
Ballyvarnet		115, 131	1, 2, 5, 6	160
Ballyvester	15	132	2, 3, 6, 7	187
Ballywaddan		187	24, 25	23
Ballywallon	21	187	25	34
Ballywalter	15, 21	150	12	67
Ballywalter Park		150		73
Ballyward		187, 188, 206, 207	25	13
Ballywatticock	15, 21	149	6, 11	225
Ballywhiskin	15, 21	133, 149, 150	7	188
Ballywhite	21	206	24, 31	34
Ballywierd	21	207	32	59
Ballywhollart			25	129
Ballywilliam	15	116	2, 3	188
Bankmore Hill	21			62
Bangor	15			146
Bangor Bay	15			168
Bangor Bog		115, 131	1	161
Bar Hall	21			135
Bar Hall Bay	21			135
Bells Quarter	21			136
Bird Island	21	188	31	18
Bishops Mill	21			37
Black Abbey	15, 21	149, 150, 168, 169	12	107
Black Neb	21			95
Blackstaff River	21			95
Bloody Burn Bay	21			96
Bootown		131, 132, 149	6	206
Bootown		132, 149	6	226
Boretree Island East	15, 21	149	11	210
Boretree Island West	15, 21	149	11	210
Boretree Rock, North	15, 21	149	11	210
Broom Hill	21			81

Place-Name	1:50,000	1:10,000	6 inch	Page
Broom Quarter	21	188	25	78
Bullock Pladdies	21			96
Burial Island	21	169	18	110
Burn Houses, The	21			73
Burr Point	21			111
Butter Lough Rock	21			111
Cairngaver	15			237
Calf Island	15, 21	168	17	18
Calheme Park	21			81
Cardy	15, 21	149	11, 12	206
Carnalea	15	115	1, 2	161
Carneyhill		149	7	188
Carrowdore	15, 21			189
Carrstown or Ballyedock	21	207, 225, 226	32	130
Carryreagh		132	2, 3, 6	189
Castleboy		188	25	75
Chanderies	15, 21	149	11	210
Chapel Island	15, 21	149, 168	11	210
Clandeboye	15			169
Cloghy	21	188	25	79
Commons		131, 148	6	226
Conlig	15	131	2, 6	162
Conly Island	21	168, 187	17	18
Cookstown	21	187, 188	18, 25	14
Copeland Island	15	116	3	171
Corporation		115, 116, 132	2	162
Corporation, North		131	6	226
Corporation, South		131, 149	5, 6, 11	226
Corrog	21	206, 207	25, 32	60
Cotton	15	116, 132	2, 6	163
Craigaroddan		207	32	46
Craigaveagh Rock	21	168	17	18
Craigboy		132	6, 7	190
Craigbrain	15, 21			73
Craigogantlet (Craigantlet)	15	131	5	226
Crawfordsburn	15	115		173
Croft	21			136
Cronstown	15	132	6	227
Crossnamuckley	15, 21	132, 149	6	227
Cunningburn	15, 21	149	6, 11	228
Deer Park	21			19
Demesne		187	24, 25	35
Derry	21	206, 207	25, 32	47
Donaghadee	15			179
Dooey	21	207	32	117
Dorn, The	21			19
Dougherty Rock, South	21			96

Place-Name	1:50,000	1:10,000	6 inch	Page
Dougherty Rock, West	21			96
Downey's Pladdy	21			96
Drumardan		188	25	79
Drumardan Quarter		188	25	79
Drumawhy	15	132	6	228
Drumfad	15	132, 133, 149	7	190
Drumhirk	15	131, 132	2, 6	229
Drummond Island	21	168, 187	17	19
Dullisk Rock	21			96
Dunevly	21	187, 188	25	14
Dunover	15, 21	149, 150	12	70
Echlin Grove	15			173
Echlinville		169, 188	18	107
Fish Quarter	21	168, 169	18	88
Foreland Point	15			195
Fort Hill	21			111
Gabbock Island	15, 21	168	11	210
Ganaway	15, 21	149, 150	7, 12	71
Garter Rock	21			136
Glastry	21	169	18	89
Glenganagh	15			173
Gordonall	15, 21	149	11	207
Granagh	21	206, 207, 225, 226	32	48
Grangee	15, 21	132, 149	6, 7	191
Gransha (Inishargy)	15	132	2, 6	90
Gransha (Bangor)	21	168, 187	18, 25	163
Green Island	21	188	25	112
Green Knoll	21			73
Greengraves	15, 21	131, 148	5	229
Gregstown	15, 21	132, 149	6	230
Grey Abbey	15, 21	149	11, 12	199
Grey Point	15			173
Groomsport	15	116	2	163
Hare Island	21			211
Haw, The	21			73
Helen's Bay	15			174
Herdstown	15	116, 132	2, 6	191
Hogstown	15	132	2	192
Inishanier Island	21	168	17	20
Inishargy	21	168, 169	12, 18	83
Inisharoan Island	21	168	17	20
Islandabreen	21			21
Islandacorr	21		32	51
Islandgorm (Ardkeen)	21			21
Islandgorm (Ballyhalbert)	21			112
Islandhill	15	132	6	192
John's Port	21			112

Place-Name	1:50,000	1:10,000	6 inch	Page
Kearney	21	207	32	61
Kearney's Hill	15			174
Kearney Point	21			63
Keentagh		207	32	130
Kennedy's Hill	15, 21			196
Kilbright	15, 21	149, 150	7, 12	192
Killaghy	15	132	6	193
Killarn	15	131	5	231
Killydressy		207	32	131
Killyvolgan	15, 21	150, 169	12	207
Kilnatierny		149	11	207
Kiltonga	15			232
Kircubbin	21	168, 169	18	91
Kirkistown	21	188	18, 25	15
Knockdoo	21			136
Knockinelder	21	207	32	49
Knockinelder Bay	21			52
Knowehead	21			21
Light House Island	15	116	3, 3a	174
Limestone Pladdies	21			37
Lisbane (Ardkeen)	21	187, 188	25	17
Lisbane (Bangor)		131	2	165
Long Island	21	187	24	21
Long Rock	15, 21			73
Long Scart Rock	21			96
Long Sheelagh	21			21
Lough Cowey	21			37
Lough Doo	21			81
Loughdoo	21	188	25	80
Loughriscouse	15	132, 149	6	232
Lythe Rock	21	168	17	21
Marlfield	21	197, 206	24	37
McCammon Pladdy	21			97
McCammon Rocks	21			112
Mew Island	15	116	3, 3a	175
Mid Island	15, 21	149, 168		211
Milecross	15	131	5	233
Mill Burn	15			196
Mill Park	21			38
Millerhill		132	7	194
Millin Bay	21			136
Millin Hill	21			136
Millisle	15	132		194
Minnis's Island Great	21	187	17	22
Minnis's Island Little	21	187	17	22
Moore Farm	21			113
Mount Ross	21			52

Place-Name	1:50,000	1:10,000	6 inch	Page
Mount Stewart	15, 21	149	11	208
Movilla	15	132	6	233
Needoo	21			22
Newcastle	21	207	25, 32	117
Newtownards	15	131		215
North Rocks	21			118
Nuns Bridge	21			137
Nunsquarter	21	168	18	93
Nunsquarter House	21			97
Old Man's Head	21			22
Orlock	15	116	2	165
Parson Hall	21	206, 207	25, 32	62
Parton Island	21	187	17	22
Patterson's Hill	15, 21			211
Peeltown	21			23
Peep O' Day	21			52
Peggy's Island	21			211
Phersons Island	21	187	25	23
Pig Island	21			211
Pladdy Lug	21			137
Port Dandy	15			175
Portaferry	21			63
Portaferry House	21			38
Portavoe	15	116	2	166
Portavogie	21	169, 188	18, 25	108
Pound, The	21			38
Priest Town		187, 206	24	35
Quintin Bay	21			138
Quintin Castle	21			138
Quintin Village	21			138
Ragheries, The	15, 21			97
Rainey Island	21	168	17	23
Ratallagh	21	188	18, 25	17
Rathgill (Rathgael)	15	115, 131	2	166
Rig Pladdy	21			24
Ringboy	21			24
Ringboy Point	21			24
Ringburr Point	21			38
Rock Savage	21			138
Roddans	15, 21	169	12, 18	109
Roddans House	21			113
Rosemount	15, 21	149, 168	11, 12	208
Round Island	21	187	24	24
Round Skart Rock	21			98
Rowreagh	21	168, 169, 187, 188	18	93
Rowting Wheel	21			52
Rubane	21			110

Place-Name	1:50,000	1:10,000	6 inch	Page
Rubane House	21			113
Saltwater Bridge	21			25
Scrabo	15, 21	148	5, 6	235
Selk Rock (Ardquin)	21			38
Selk Rock (Inishargy)	15, 21			98
Selk Rock (Ballyhalbert)	21			113
Seneschal's Port	21			25
Sheelah's Island	21	168	17	98
Skartock Rock	21			98
Skelly's Hill	15			176
Sketrick Island	21	168	17	25
Skullmartin	15, 21			74
Slanes	21	188, 207	25	115
Slaty Port	15			176
Sloanstown	15, 21	149	6, 7, 11, 12	194
South Bay	21			139
South Island	15, 21	168	11	211
South Rock	21			119
Springvale		150	12	71
St Andrews				99
St Cowey's Wells	21			139
St Patrick's Well	15			196
Strangford Lough	21			5
Tara	21	207, 226	32	131
Templecowey Point	21			139
Templecraney	21			39
Templepatrick	15	132	7	195
Thomastown	21	187, 206	24, 25	36
Thomastown House	21			39
Tieveshilly	21	207, 226	32	133
Tongue, The	21			140
Town Parks of Donaghadee		116, 132	2, 3	195
Trasnagh Island	21	168	17	26
Tubber Na Carrig	21			98
Tullyboard		206	32	49
Tullybrick	21			26
Tullycarnan	21	226	32	134
Tullycross	21	188	25	80
Tullykevin	15, 21	149, 150	12	209
Tullymally	21	207	25, 32	50
Tullynacrew		207	32	51
Tullynagardy	15	131	5, 6	236
Tullytramon	21	188	25	81
Turley Rock	15, 21			211
Walter Rocks, The	21			39
Whaup Rock	15, 21	149	11	212

Place-Name	1:50,000	1:10,000	6 inch	Page
White House	21			120
Whitebank Pladdy	21			98
Whitechurch	15, 21	150	12	72
Whitespots	15	131	5, 6	236
Windmill Hill	15, 21			74
Witter				121